Opera for Everybody

Susie Gilbert has worked for many years as an archival researcher and editor on numerous books of twentieth-century history, including the official biography of Winston Churchill. She is also the author of *A Tale of Four Houses* (2003), which traces the history of Covent Garden and the Metropolitan Opera since 1945. Susie Gilbert lives in London.

# Opera for Everybody

## *The Story of English National Opera*

SUSIE GILBERT

FABER & FABER

First published in 2009 by Faber and Faber Ltd
Bloomsbury House
74–77 Great Russell Street
London WC1B 3DA

This paperback edition first published in 2017

Typeset by Ian Bahrami
Printed and bound by CPI Group (UK) Ltd, Croydon, CR0 4YY

A CIP record for this book
is available from the British Library

ISBN 978–0–571–22494–4

FSC
www.fsc.org
MIX
Paper from
responsible sources
FSC® C013604

To David and Josh, who, in the spirit of Lilian Baylis, work
on behalf of the vulnerable in society.

# Contents

# Illustrations

# Preface and Acknowledgements

The uniqueness of Sadler's Wells/ENO lies in its collective memory and sense of mission, as defined by its joint founder Lilian Baylis in the late-Victorian era. For over a hundred years the dual aims of the company have been to extend the appreciation of opera to the fullest possible extent and to make the drama equal partner with the music. Both of these objectives were built on the foundation stone of singing in the language of the audience. More than a hundred years after Baylis set out on the task of creating a permanent opera company, her beliefs are no less relevant.

Based on Baylis's foundations, the company remained into the late twentieth century an ensemble of individuals who had consistently worked together – back and front of stage – each generation handing the torch on to the next. The company has inhabited many homes and worked in many locations. It began life in the cramped conditions of the Old Vic before moving on to the intimate though acoustically unforgiving pre-war Sadler's Wells theatre; it played in village halls and regional cinemas during the Second World War, toured and travelled from Bournemouth to Kiev after it, and in 1968 relocated to the generous and infinitely more demanding expanses of the Coliseum. In 2008 it returned for a short season to its birthplace in Southwark. The scope of its work has grown with its locations and ambitions, but the presentation of opera in English as a means of communicating to the audience remains at the core of its mission.

ENO's biography illuminates the story of the development of British cultural life during the last hundred and twenty years. Its output has both reflected and responded to the political and social attitudes of the day. Emerging during the era of the great Christian philanthropists and social workers of the late nineteenth century, the company began to flourish with the growth of a middle class able to enjoy the possibilities of longer periods of leisure. It managed to survive two world wars with great fortitude and creativity and played its part in the post-war development of the welfare state and state-funded arts. The company waxed strong in the period of expansion of universities and cultural life in the 1960s and 1970s. Then, in the Thatcher years, it fought for its place with a doggedness and anger worthy of the time. In the free-market ideology of the new millennium it had to fight for its survival, and today the remnant of the ensemble, bloodied but unbowed, remains constant in its commitment to the collective memory of the company.

ENO has a long and proud history, and its story reveals the continued determination of those involved not to abandon one of the country's unique cultural institutions.

I owe a debt of gratitude to all those who took the time and trouble to talk to me along the way: Tim Albery, Iris Arlen, John Baker, Dame Josephine Barstow, John Berry, Rodric Braithwaite, Henrietta Bredin, Paul Daniel, Sir Colin Davis, Graham Devlin, David Dyer, Sir Mark Elder, Richard Elder, David Elliott, Vernon Ellis, J. Audrey Ellison, Dame Anne Evans, David Fielding, Edward Gardner, Charlotte Higgins, Anne Howard, Nicholas Hytner, Sir Peter Jonas, Richard Jones, Alice King-Farlow, Brian Kinsey, Ralph Koltai, Charles Kraus, Zeb Lalljee, Dennis Marks, Sir Brian McMaster, Rebecca Meitlis, Sir Jonathan Miller, Steve Moffitt, Gerry Morrissey, Maddie Morton, Tony Morton, Ted Murphy, John Nelson, Timothy O'Brien, Nicholas Payne, Andrew Porter, David Pountney, David Ritch, Rupert Rhymes, Martin Smith, Noel Staunton, Lord Stevenson, David Sulkin, Catherine Sutton, Loretta Tomasi, Horace Trubridge, Philip Turner, Sir Brian Unwin and Dave Webster.

Jeremy Caulton spent many long hours advising and scrutinising the text of his period at ENO, and Sir Charles Mackerras gave generously of his time to talk to me during rehearsals for *The Makropoulos Case* in April 2006 and over the ensuing months to answer my many queries. I am indebted to them as well as to one of the great opera impresarios of our time, Lord Harewood, who not only granted me four interviews but tolerated endless emails and queries over the years of my researches.

It was Professor Dent, the great Cambridge musicologist, translator and mentor to Lilian Baylis, who provided the inspiration for the title of this book. Shortly before the end of the Second World War he wrote a history of the three Old Vic/Sadler's Wells companies – drama, opera and ballet – in which he discussed the prospect of a state-subsidised National Theatre and a 'National English Opera'. He called his book *A Theatre for Everybody*.

My sincere thanks to the following archives and archivists for their help: Patricia and Elizabeth Ennion-Smith McGuire at The Archives Centre, King's College, Cambridge; Edward J. Dent's biographer Karen Arrandale for her help and encouragement; Jo Elsworth, Bex Carrington, Anna Fineman and Rachel Hassall at the University of Bristol Theatre Collection; Brian Crimp for permission to use the unpublished Joan Cross material; Bob Tuggle at the Metropolitan Opera in New York; Nick Clark at the Britten-Pears Foundation, Aldeburgh, where the Cross archive is housed; Faber and Faber for extracts from *Letters from a Life: Selected Letters and Diaries of Benjamin Britten*, edited by Donald Mitchell and Philip Reed; Oxford University Press for permission to quote from the *Oxford Dictionary of National Biography*; Ann Morton and the staff of The National Archives in Kew; Suzanne Waters and the staff of the Victoria and Albert Museum Archives, whose Archive of Art and Design in the Word & Image Department houses the Arts Council archive and whose British Architectural Library, Drawings & Archives Collections, now houses the Denys Lasdun archive; the staff of Islington Local History Centre; and to Henry Hardy on behalf of the Isaiah Berlin Literary Trust for quotations from letters written by Isaiah Berlin © The Isaiah Berlin Literary Trust, 2009. Rodric Braithwaite, Lady Lasdun and Sir Brian Unwin kindly allowed me access to their private collections.

John Allison, editor of *Opera*, provided both help with photographs and research and permission to use the formidable resources of his magazine. A host of newspaper critics and proprietors kindly gave permission to quote from reviews and articles in the text. A complete list of publications appears in the Sources section and quotations are individually referenced in the endnotes.

Finally, I am indebted to the board and management of ENO for allowing me to use the archive of the company. Clare Colvin, ENO's archivist, is a deeply knowledgeable servant of ENO and her calm and soothing efficiency provided wonderful support and assistance. With infinite good humour and with great patience she has shared her monk's cell with me both at Hoxton and at Lilian Baylis House.

I am very grateful to my readers: David Cairns, Dr Martin Gilbert, Amanda Holden, Naomi Layish and my great teacher and encourager Dr John Walsh. Lance Blackstone's accounting skills aided greatly my endeavours to unravel the mysteries of arts funding and ENO accounting. Oliver Timms and John Ward read and checked some of the chapters, while Oliver Pearce and Nicola Seed helped organise the vast amount of material. Thanks also to Belinda Matthews, Elizabeth Tyerman, Dave Watkins and Anne Owen at Faber for their care and attention during the last five years, and to Trevor Horwood and Ian Bahrami. My agent Caradoc King has given constant support and encouragement. My son David helped me with the layout for the illustrations and with all computer problems, and my son Joshua read some of the chapters with great insight. I have been constantly heartened and sustained by both of them.

Above all I am indebted to Rodney Milnes, who has not only read every word but has done so more than once. Rupert Christiansen wrote of Rodney when he took over his column in *The Spectator* on 29 September 1990: 'Rodney is without equal – his wit, his wisdom, his erudition, his charm, his jokes and wheezes, there hasn't been anyone to touch him since George Bernard Shaw.' In particular he has been, in Sir John Drummond's memorable words, much 'tainted by experience', and as a critic and the editor of *Opera* he has played his own part in the story of ENO. For these reasons I have taken Rodney as my main guide and adviser on all matters to do with ENO and its music-making. Committed to opera in general and ENO in particular, Rodney believes that the main object of life is to learn something new about the world every day and that ENO has played, and should continue to play, a major role in that process of discovery.

# 1869–1912: Beginnings at the Old Vic

The story of the Sadler's Wells and English National Opera companies began with an enterprise intended to make life better for the poor and destitute of Victorian London. The founding mothers were two extraordinary and indomitable women. Their every waking moment was spent in working towards a better future for the people they saw as their family, friends and community – the working class of Lambeth and the artists and volunteers who were to provide them with entertainment and art. Together they planted the seeds of a great drama and lyric theatre project, and created an audience at a time when there was no audience for such fare and few prospects of there ever being one.

Amongst the impoverished and grim tenements of 1880s south London, Emma Cons and her niece Lilian Baylis were inspired to create and develop an artistic endeavour that was to grow far beyond their imaginings and objectives. From the temperance coffee houses and her new model music hall, Cons laid the groundwork for artistic creativity which, with the spiritual inspiration of Baylis, developed over time into firmly rooted and enduring national theatre, ballet and opera companies.

Emma Cons was born on 4 March 1837. She was an extraordinary woman at a time of remarkable women, who found themselves fighting not only for their own equality but also for the rights and conditions of the poor and destitute. Cons was small and gentle yet fearless, utterly lacking in pomposity or self-importance, who devoted herself to social reform in many different spheres. Her interests and involvements had a range that included housing, campaigning for urban parks and open spaces, setting up crèches and clinics for working-class women, providing cheap food, extending evening-school education and working for women's suffrage and the right of women to serve in local government. She also wished to see public entertainment staged in less bawdy settings than the pubs and music halls in which it was then almost exclusively found.*

There were three powerful strands running through the backgrounds of Cons and Baylis: religion, music and social reform. Music came from the Cons family, who were of German origin and had been music-cabinet- and piano-makers. Lilian Baylis's mother Liebe Cons, Emma's younger sister, was a professional singer.

Emma Cons became involved in social reform as a consequence of her family circumstances, having been forced to make her own way in the world after the death of her father in 1851. Her redoubtable personality and resourcefulness equipped her well for the challenges she encountered. At the time it was hard for women to find independent work, but Emma joined the Ladies' Co-operative Guild, which provided employment for 'ladies with artistic ability'. It was one of twelve self-governing co-operatives promoted in London by Christian Socialists, and the only female one. The co-operatives were based on mild socialism, on the concept 'that the principle of co-operation was "stronger and truer" than the principle of competition'. The principle of co-operation was an essential ingredient in the Cons/Baylis enterprise.†

The Ladies' Co-operative Guild was managed by Caroline Hill, whose daughter Octavia became a close friend of Emma. The young women were Christian Socialists, influenced by the writings of Thomas Hughes, Charles Kingsley and above all John Ruskin. Their faith drove them to engage with the social ills resulting from the untrammelled development of industrial manufacturing capital. Equally influential on their lives was the great Victorian journalist Henry Mayhew, whose writings about the wretched conditions in

---

* Two excellent biographies are indispensable sources for the origins of the Vic-Wells: Richard Findlater's *Lilian Baylis, the Lady of the Old Vic*, published in 1975, and Elizabeth Schafer's *Lilian Baylis: A Biography*, published in 2006. The latter contains much new research from Baylis's own archive, as well as reassessing her in the light of her consciously created public image and role as a woman in a man's world.

† Most leading church reformers of the 1850s were middle-class, with a paternalistic, even condescending attitude to the working class, whom they regarded as unfit for political democracy, and so endorsed co-operation rather than collectivism and state intervention. Hence their advocacy of workers' co-operatives. (For the Christian Socialist movement, see *The Christian Socialist Revival* by Peter d'A. Jones, Princeton: Princeton University Press, 1968.)

which the poor lived in London encouraged Cons to work with local 'ragged children'.

London of the 1860s was a place ripe for evangelical missionaries driven by the imperatives of conscience to tackle the terrible social problems of an industrialising society. Overcrowding and pollution led to disease, pauperism, misery and crime. There was no effective public health service, and local government boards attempted in a piecemeal way to deal with the problems of sanitation and ensure the supply of uncontaminated water. There were frequent outbreaks of cholera and typhus, and instances of starvation. Road improvements from 1850, driving through such slums as St Giles/New Oxford Street, had exacerbated the shortage of accommodation, creating yet more overcrowding and insanitary conditions – twelve to a room was common. By 1889 irregular and seasonal work left 100,000 people in penury.

Charity and moral amelioration, not state intervention, were middle-class responses to the social evils. Activists inspired by Ruskin, William Morris and others took on the role of missionaries in their efforts to tackle the chronic poverty, alcoholism and prostitution. There was a prevailing belief amongst Christian Socialists and philanthropists that 'rational recreation' would provide an effective counterweight to the attractions of drink and gambling, forge more effective behavioural constraints and help build a community of common sentiment and interest between the classes. This was expressed in the form of 'respectable' working men's clubs, which started in the 1860s with temperance and education at their centre, but later also came to embrace activities that could compete with the gin palaces and beer houses of London.

Activists saw housing reform as linked to cultural amelioration, and both as central in the battle against poverty. In the slum tenements conditions were appalling. Octavia Hill described the 'dens of darkness: narrow, filthy, dark places, winding stairs, where light never comes, three, four or five children and their parents living, of course, in one room only: oh but such rooms!'[1] In these overcrowded conditions alcoholism, violence – especially against women – rape and incest were prevalent, with destitute mothers and neglected children seeking escape in drink. There were many abandoned starving children.

In order to buy and clean up slum houses Cons, like Hill, enlisted the help of rich friends and benefactors. Turning her attention to the Lambeth area, she bought a manor house with gardens and set up the South London Dwellings Company to provide 'model dwellings for working folk'.[2] She herself lived in the cottages with friends and helpers, remaining there for thirty years until her death.

Cons, who had originally intended to be an artist rather than a social worker and who had attended the women-only School of Ornamental Art for Females in Gower Street, believed that the concept of 'rational recreation' embraced an aesthetic as well as an educational ideal. Intellectual and artistic pursuits as well as 'beauty and harmony' were essential to maintain the physical improvements of the 'mass of the people' and their surroundings. Cons battled staunchly to win the confidence of her tenants, maintain the improvements against vandals and collect the rent. She did not give up planting trees even when the saplings were destroyed, and never lent money or gave charity. She opened a women's club and a children's playground, working with builders and plumbers, policemen, lawyers, bankers and accountants. Within four years her tenement was transformed.

In 1870 Octavia Hill put the Central London Dwellings Improvement Company, which owned slums in the Drury Lane and Clare Market area, under the management of Cons. This was a dangerous neighbourhood of overcrowded tenements inhabited by market porters, criminals, prostitutes and costermongers who sold their wares from barrows in the streets. Cons fearlessly collected the rent and talked to the women and men about drunkenness. It was from here that she launched her coffee-tavern movement by setting up the Shelton Street tavern.

Cons, who campaigned for women's suffrage and in 1889 became the first woman alderman on the London County Council, was not merely a middle-class philanthropic missionary. She was implacable on the question of temperance as a result of her experience in the tenements, believing that the cycle of poverty and violence, especially against women, was fuelled by alcohol. In her Shelton Street tavern, working men could get cheap refreshments, but drinking and gambling were strictly prohibited. At the tavern, coffee cost 1d, tea and cocoa ½d and a hot beef drink 6d. Businessmen soon saw profits in catering for the working classes, and chains of cheap eating places opened up across London.

The concept of 'rational recreation' as an aesthetic as well as educational ideal soon inspired Cons to bring her other passion into her work. Deeply committed to the notion that art and music should be available to the poor, she soon determined to bring music into the lives of her tenants. In 1870 she took over Barrett's Court, a terrible slum off Wigmore Street, which she also transformed, even at the cost of evicting the most disruptive families. There, she started to provide entertainment, with a brass band giving concerts on Saturday nights. In 1874 – the year of Lilian Baylis's birth – a concert was given at Barrett's Court by Liebe Cons.

In the latter part of the nineteenth century there was, amongst Christian Socialist reformers, a growing belief in the power of entertainment to relieve poverty and encourage 'moral amelioration'. They hoped to counteract the growing attraction of the music halls, where alcohol was an intrinsic part of the entertainment and where many of the acts were considered by them to be lewd and profane.

The lack of respectable entertainment had been exposed in 1861 by Henry Mayhew, the journalist, who had argued in *London Labour and the London Poor* that if costermongers were to be lifted out of 'the moral mire in which they are wallowing, the first step must be to provide them with wholesome amusement'. He was particularly horrified by the popular 'penny gaff' entertainment of the costermongers, which he described as a 'platform to teach moral debauchery', where girls as young as nine 'have learnt to understand the filthiest sayings and laugh at them as loudly as the grown up lads' around them. The singing and dancing, and lusty audience participation – especially in the 'filthy words' that ended the stanzas – had a powerful place in the lives of the costermongers at a time when poverty meant there was no time for childhood and no opportunity for education. The drunkenness and violence that accompanied the 'gaffs', and the resulting terrible abuse of women as well as the perceived need for respectability, gave ample incentive to Cons and others to seek to provide alternative entertainment. One costermonger had told Mayhew: 'Give 'em better singing and better dancing and they'd go, if the price was as cheap as this.'[3]

Cons was determined to provide 'purified entertainment which shall amuse without degrading' at venues where there would be no alcohol. In February 1880 she decided – with the support of her wealthy friends and patrons – to form the Coffee Music Halls Company and open new model music halls. It was a radical move. The Church still often regarded the theatre as sinfully profane and a place of corruption and vice. Only a handful of Christian Socialists, especially the Reverend Stewart Headlam, curate of St John's Drury Lane, believed in the power and beauty of the theatre. In a lecture in October 1877 he encouraged young people to go to the theatre and music halls. For his pains he was denounced and his licence removed, after which he founded the Church and Stage Guild in 1879 to try and educate the Church out of its anti-theatre prejudices. The guild stressed that Christ was present in culture, not least in the theatre, and that the stage was 'a place of education, providing art for the people'.[4]

As theatre made its tentative steps into popular culture, so too did classical music. The philanthropic Samuel Barnett and his wife Henrietta, who devoted their lives in the 1880s to creating cultural institutions, including the Whitechapel Library and Art Gallery in the East End, founded Toynbee Hall, a mission in Stepney. There they lived and worked, leading the way for the development of other such 'settlements' – as they were called. The Barnetts had a more religious mission than that of Emma Cons when they started working men's concerts and church oratorios. 'The religion of amusement has been lost sight of,' Barnett wrote; 'by music one may be helped to find God.'

The Victoria Theatre in Waterloo Road – known since 1833 as the 'Old Vic' – was to be the site for Cons' experiment. At the time it was a house of melodrama and alcohol set in the midst of the Lambeth slums, where Cons saw new black eyes on the women when she collected the rents on Monday mornings after their menfolk had come back drunk from the Vic on Saturday night.[5] Looking back fourteen years later, those involved in the Victoria Hall project recalled how they had come to realise that 'the prevailing relation between recreation and strong drink was causing untold evils, particularly amongst working people, who (from the cramped and crowded conditions of their homes) were more dependent than people of leisure on *public* recreation'. The provision of such recreation, they believed, could not be left 'to commercial speculators'. They also hoped to bridge the 'chasm' between the classes, as the old feudal order gave way to something new.[6]

The Victoria Theatre had undergone many incarnations since its foundation in 1816 as the new Royal Coburg Theatre, in the then sparsely populated Surrey marshes. It had been built with the prospect of attracting audiences both from across the Thames, with the imminent construction of the Waterloo Bridge, and from the expected development of elegant suburbs to the south of it.

It was an intimate theatre built on the horseshoe model, described by Henry Crabb Robinson, a contemporary diarist, as 'a pretty suburban playhouse, not so large but a fit match for the Paris suburban theatres'.[7] As a minor theatre, however, it was barred by the Licensing Act of 1737 from performing Shakespeare or the other classics, which were the prerogative of the two large patent theatres in town: Drury Lane and Covent Garden. The Act required the Lord Chamberlain's approval for any play to be performed. This prevented the theatre becoming a forum for political debate and satire. Soon after the theatre was built the Haymarket, which specialised in Italian opera, had also received a patent.

Although the concept of the original owners had been a theatre set in an area of grand mansions and pleasure gardens, the development of New Cut, linking Waterloo Road and Blackfriars Road, was in fact designated as third-class housing in the builder's lease. The reputation of the theatre fell as the condition of the surrounding area became increasingly run down, with a population dominated by costermongers.

Repeated attempts to give the theatre a fresh start had ended in bankruptcy, including one in 1833, when new management gave the theatre a new name, the Royal Victoria, in the hope of royal patronage. The task of managing the Victoria successfully in both artistic and financial terms proved Herculean and successive managements failed to raise the standard of performance or repertoire. The audience, although enthusiastic and comradely, were impoverished, illiterate and undiscriminating. Despite a change in the Licensing Act of 1843, which finally abolished the privileges of the patent theatres and transferred the minor theatres to the jurisdiction of the Lord Chamberlain, the Victoria continued to struggle to bring in an audience for the classics.

The opening of Waterloo station in 1848 brought a change in population, but the New Cut remained a locality with high levels of poverty and social problems. It was known for its crime and for the gin palaces, drunkenness and prostitution that were dominant features of its street life. According to George Augustus Sala, a leading journalist, it reeked of 'the vilest tobacco, of stale corduroy suits, of oilskin caps, mildewed umbrellas, of decaying vegetables, of escaping gas, of deceased cats, of ancient fish, of dubious mutton pies and of unwashed, sodden, unkempt, reckless humanity'.[8]

A renovation in September 1871 attempted to reincarnate the Victoria as a music hall. But increasing competition from new music halls, touring companies, local theatres and 'penny gaffs' meant that its fortunes continued to decline under successive managements.

Thus it was that the theatre was sublet to the Coffee Music Halls Company at a rent of £950 a year, for a maximum term of seventeen years. Redecorated with the help of Emma Cons' supporters, the theatre reopened on Boxing Day 1880 as the Royal Victoria Coffee and Music Hall, with the intention of providing a full-time music hall with a resident company. There was a programme of 'comic songs, clog-dancing, hornpipes, acrobatic performers, nigger minstrels, performing animals and comic ballets . . . cleansed from objectionable matter'.[9] To such fare was later added temperance meetings. The difference between the Victoria and other music halls was that there were no prostitutes parading and, above all, no alcoholic beverages. Refreshments were available but anyone caught with alcohol was unceremoniously thrown out by stewards dressed in long red overalls.

The problems of running such a theatre fast became apparent. Cons and her inexperienced helpers were endeavouring to succeed where professional managers had failed over the years, and without even the benefit of bar receipts. The theatrical profession watched the management's discomfiture with scorn: 'Coffee and singing don't seem to work well together,' wrote The Age, a theatrical periodical. 'Whether it is the fault of the singing (which is none of the best) or the coffee (which is worse) I can't pretend to say, at any rate I hear the establishment is soon to close down.'[10]

A deficit of £2,800 meant that within eight months the hall was once again faced with closure. Emma Cons did not give up, however, claiming that the local churches and police had already noticed its beneficial effect. She formed a new committee of social reformers and philanthropists and musicians, including the composer Arthur Sullivan, the German impresario Carl Rosa and the composer-conductor Julius Benedict.* Cons was also helped from this time by the deeply religious Lady Frederick Cavendish, wife of the Chief Secretary of Ireland, who was assassinated in Phoenix Park in Dublin in 1882. 'Lady Fred' – second daughter of George William Lyttelton, 4th Baron Lyttelton – was related or connected to many important people, and was willing to bring them into the orbit of the Vic. She remained a friend and supporter of Cons' work at the Hall until her death in 1925.

The theatre reopened in October 1881 under the management of William Poel. The twenty-nine-year-old Poel, who started the Elizabethan Theatre movement in 1894, was interested in the authentic staging of Shakespeare on an open stage with minimal scenery, in reaction to Henry Irving's extravagant productions at the Lyceum. Poel improved the offerings of the theatre and reduced expenses.

It was at this time that Cons introduced classical opera sung in English. That month the Royal Academy of Music sang a concert performance of the first act of Così fan tutte, in English and in costume. Handel's Messiah was also received in an attentive, enthusiastic and orderly fashion. There were tableaux vivants, pantomimes, musical entertainments and ballad concerts. On 5 June 1882 the programme offered 'scenes from the Italian opera, sung in English under the direction of Signor Garcia', and in June 1883 selections in costume from Fidelio. Poel also introduced Shakespeare nights, with scenes from Macbeth and Othello. The writer and novelist Hugh Walpole remembered 'Shakespeare read by ladies and gentlemen dressed in rather mediocre costumes . . . the chilly half empty hall, and the desperate attempts of the readers or the actors whichever they were, to get some liveliness into the proceedings'.[11]

---

* Carl Rosa (1842–89) opened the Carl Rosa Opera Company in September 1875 to test the fortunes of opera in English. Seasons in London and the provinces followed, during which performances of works of Wagner and Verdi were given. German-born Julius Benedict (1804–85), who had been Weber's first composition pupil in Dresden, came in 1836 to London, where he became music director of Drury Lane in 1838, composing three ballad-style operas. His most famous work, The Lily of Killarney, composed in 1862, was a work much performed at the Vic.

There were other activities. Cons introduced scientific lectures on Tuesdays. Also on Tuesdays Lilian Baylis, with the help of volunteers, collected children from the tenements where she lived with Emma Cons to teach them games and songs. Friday nights became temperance nights. There were so many non-theatrical offerings by December 1883 that Poel left after only two years, saying that the Vic was 'aiming too high, was too didactic and was not listening to what the audience wanted'.[12]

By 1884, with the theatre again on the verge of bankruptcy, Cons appealed once more to her wealthy associates. The millionaire textile manufacturer Samuel Morley, though a nonconformist with a puritanical suspicion of entertainment, was impressed by the theatre's impact on local behaviour and joined Cons' committee. He soon discovered that he actually enjoyed the shows and offered £1,000 towards acquiring the lease, in return for Cons agreeing to appoint a committee to run the Vic along his lines, which would involve more temperance meetings and lectures.

The lecture series grew in popularity, attracting good attendances and a wide variety of speakers, and eventually developed into the Morley Memorial College for Working Men and Women after the patron's death in 1886. The college, which opened on 29 September 1889, was separate from the music hall, though based at the same location. It admitted women on equal terms, even on the board, and the students could go to the entertainments. In 1889 the theatre became known as the Royal Victoria Hall, with a new board.

That year Cons was serving on six London County Council committees and eleven subcommittees concerned with working-class housing, asylums, industrial and reformatory schools and theatres. Despite these demands, she also took on the management of the theatre, with Frederick Phillips as her assistant. The theatre's music-hall licence still prohibited the full performance of plays, in which Cons had a limited interest in any case, but in 1884 a chorus was brought from the choir of the Church of the Sacred Heart in Camberwell for the premiere of *Robert Macaire*, a melodrama of fifty years earlier. The show proved so popular that she decided to go on using the choir.

In January 1886, however, a pantomime that broke the terms of the licence incurred the wrath of neighbouring theatre managements, who brought a successful prosecution against Cons. She was fined a nominal half a crown by the magistrate and had to take the show off. As a result of the case, Cons never again attempted to stage a complete play, concentrating on music-hall variety and concert performances of opera. The People's Entertainment shows on Mondays and Saturdays continued to include the music-hall acts, as well as a military band. Cons kept a careful eye on the variety shows to be sure they did not 'fall into vulgarity'.

It was not long before the musical evenings turned into something with more potential. From 1889 Emma Cons began to provide regular fortnightly presentations of opera, sung in English. Since the music-hall licence ruled out a complete performance – Cons explained to her audience that if they took out a dramatic licence they would have to stop smoking in the auditorium, and that she hoped the licensing laws would be changed so they would be 'less hampered by vexatious restrictions' – the operas were reduced to about twenty musical excerpts and the same number of tableaux.[13]

Guest artists stood in front of the curtain to sing the most celebrated songs from popular operas. At the climaxes the curtain rose to reveal a tableau of people semi-costumed – but fully clothed – silently holding poses. Some of the guest singers, however, were well known, including the baritone Charles Santley, for whom Gounod composed the aria 'Even Bravest Hearts' in *Faust*.

In the 1891/2 season Cons offered selections from nine operas for fifteen performances including Verdi's *Il trovatore*, Gounod's *Faust* and Bellini's *La sonnambula*, as well as native favourites *The Bohemian Girl*, William Wallace's *Maritana* and Benedict's *The Lily of Killarney*. *The Bohemian Girl* had been written by Michael William Balfe in 1841. It was his greatest success and the most popular English opera of its time, its tunes whistled in the streets after its first performance. It remained a mainstay for the Old Vic for many years. The English romantic operas of the mid-nineteenth century involved spoken dialogue, airs, duets, ensembles and dances, and included simple and sentimental ballads that were intended to be bought as sheet music and played on barrel organs.

Not only did this tableau style of performance avoid further conflict with the local theatre managers, it also proved to be popular with audiences, appealing more directly to people than did drama. A letter of 28 April 1892 to the Chairman of the Trustees enclosed bills recording healthy audiences for both the ballad concerts and the Saturday-night varieties.

These were the early days of opera for the people. The programme notes for *Il trovatore* apologised for the delays between tableaux when the 'artistes' had to change their costumes. The performers were mostly amateur but included some professionals who gave their services free. Amongst them was Antoinette Sterling, an American Quaker. Sterling was, in the words of Edward J. Dent, the Cambridge musicologist, the classic example of the '"cavernous contralto" . . . obsessed by the conviction that her incomparable voice had been bestowed upon her by God as an instrument for the conversion of sinners'. She insisted that her audience abstain from smoking while she sang.[14] Alfred Dove, who later became principal conductor at the London Coliseum, was the main conductor.

Until this time, Italian opera in the original language had been very much the preserve of the rich in London, in contrast to Europe, where from the late eighteenth century it had been customary to translate operas into the vernacular, and where translation meant a gradual popularisation. In nineteenth-century French- and German-speaking countries, opera in the vernacular was the norm, with composers often involved with the process of translation, including musical modification if it was thought necessary. In England, from the eighteenth century, opera had been a commercial venture, consisting of a regular season in December and January, usually at the Haymarket Theatre. Private patrons, including King George I, were responsible for Handel's great series of operas from 1720 to 1728. The importation and popularity of Italian castratos in the 1700s added to the development of operatic performance in a language not understood by the audience, although bilingual word-books were always available. In the early and mid-nineteenth century, Italian opera seasons took place at Her Majesty's and at Covent Garden, presenting mainly operas in Italian by contemporary Italian composers. Even non-Italian works such as Berlioz's *Benvenuto Cellini* and Balfe's *Bohemian Girl* were translated into Italian in 1853 and 1858 for performance on the London stage.

At the other end of the social scale was Emma Cons' venture. In March 1888, with the help of an appeal presided over by the Duke of Westminster, the Trustees bought the freehold of the Vic for

£16,000. The terms of the order of the new Trust were to define, and later confine, the work of the Vic and Sadler's Wells for many years. The theatre was to provide 'public lectures and other entertainments and exhibitions suitable for the education and instruction of the poorer classes. Admission shall not be gratuitous, but it will be at such prices as will make them available to artisans.' The licence still strictly precluded alcohol, while alternative refreshments were to be provided, with tea and coffee at a penny. Thus began the tradition that was to inspire the work of the Baylis theatre and opera companies for nearly a century.

It was the arrival of Lilian Baylis as manager of the Royal Victoria in 1898 that began the steady transformation of the theatre into a venue for serious drama and opera. She had fallen seriously ill in South Africa, where her family were living, and her exhausted 'Aunt Emmie' decided to bring her back to London to help her.

Independence and a deep love of music ran through Baylis's life and character as strongly as they did through her aunt's. Her mother, Liebe Cons, was a devout Christian as well as a professional musician. Like her sister Emma, Liebe was an independent-minded woman who had managed to maintain her teaching career after her marriage, despite ten pregnancies in fifteen years. Lilian's father, Newton Baylis, was a baritone who sang in church choirs, particularly All Saints, Margaret Street, just off Oxford Street – the centre of the Oxford movement working for the Catholic revival in the Church of England. Together, Liebe and Lilian had started a small vocal, instrumental and operetta group which performed in lunatic asylums (public and private) and at the Vic after temperance demonstrations.

Lilian Baylis had nine brothers and sisters, five of whom survived infancy. She attended a convent school, but only every second week, alternating learning with household chores and compromising her education as a result. Her musical training, however, while incomplete, was rigorous from a young age. She studied the violin at the Royal Academy of Music, where she was taught by John Tiplady Carrodus, who led the Covent Garden orchestra for twenty-five years and imbued her with a lasting love of opera.

Baylis appeared with the family troupe at operatic costume recitals and provided free concerts for the people and Penny

Popular Concerts on piers and in town halls, workhouses, mission halls and prisons. She grew up accustomed to performing under the most demanding and rigorous of circumstances. In 1889 the Baylises formed the Gypsy Revellers concert troupe, which performed Gypsy music at society engagements. Lilian played the fiddle. The Revellers and the concert parties provided Baylis with both performing experience and an extensive repertoire of excerpts from light opera and Gilbert and Sullivan. In 1891 the family troupe was taken by a manager to South Africa, where they travelled and performed, finally settling there.

Baylis inherited both the religious and musical sides of her unusual family in equally strong measure. Her biographer, Elizabeth Schafer, describes the deep spirituality and ecstatic experience that lay behind her mission. She had a belief in miraculous intervention, writing of several religious visions she had experienced at times of great stress. Regular prayer and meditation and periods of retreat helped her survive the turmoil and stresses of theatre management. Baylis's religious conviction and faith imbued her with extraordinary mental strength and determination, without which it is doubtful whether the Vic-Wells project would have survived.

When Baylis was brought back from South Africa in 1897 by Emma Cons she was a plain, stocky, bespectacled young woman who had decided not to take up any of the offers of marriage she encountered there. After the outbreak of the Boer War in December 1899, there was to be no return to South Africa, despite Baylis's intention to rejoin her family. Instead, the Royal Victoria Hall became her whole life as she organised ballad concerts, opera recitals, temperance meetings, scientific lectures and variety bills. Baylis dealt with everything from the theatre's board to negotiations with the police and publicans, as well as cleaning and keeping order. Two years after her return, her name first appeared in the programme as acting manager. She received affection and encouragement from her remarkable aunt, whose own interests and involvements were so varied that Baylis quickly became an indispensable part of the theatre enterprise.

As Baylis took over the management of the Victoria, thirty-nine-year-old Charles Corri became the Vic's first music director, a position he was to hold for thirty years. Descended from an Italian family of dancers, composers and instrumentalists, Corri was himself a cellist who had played with the Carl Rosa company. He was a true professional and skilled at rescoring operas for the eighteen-player orchestra. The soprano Joan Cross later described Corri as an unlikely character, shabby and usually smoking an 'unwholesome pipe', who enjoyed a beer with his cronies after rehearsals. This, she noted, no doubt contributed to his stormy relationship with Baylis.[15] Nonetheless, he and Baylis shared a belief in their crusade to popularise opera in London.

Although the Vic's opera performances continued to be staged as recitals, they were garnering an increasingly loyal public. At this time opera was gaining popularity, both through the countrywide tours of the Carl Rosa Opera Company, formed in 1869, and the Moody-Manners company, formed in 1897 with the aim of producing grand opera in English. From the mid-1870s the operettas of Gilbert and Sullivan were presented by Richard D'Oyly Carte with such success that he was able to build the Savoy Theatre in 1881 and devote it to their work. Attempts to start a national opera company, the Royal English Opera House, by D'Oyly Carte in 1891 were, however, abortive, and 'real' Italian opera continued to be performed only at Covent Garden for short seasons of eight to ten weeks a year, with visiting foreign virtuosi. It was an integral part of the London social season but remained both very grand and very expensive.*

The 1890s was an auspicious decade for a venture such as Baylis's. The gradual improvement of public-welfare services and sanitation combined with increased charitable intervention meant that Londoners were experiencing unprecedented social integration. Above all there was more regular employment and more money to be spent. The last two decades of the nineteenth century saw real wages increase by one third – a development that for the first time enabled all but the very poorest in society to engage in leisure pursuits. The 1890s saw the introduction of the eight-hour day and the birth of the concept of working people as citizens rather than solely providers of labour. Playing and watching sport – especially football – bank holidays, museums, libraries, seaside holidays, cycling,

---

* Classical music was also gaining popularity. In 1895 Henry Wood started his London Promenade concerts, which drew large crowds in the summer.

reading circles and dramatic societies all testified to the growth of leisure and the enjoyments of relaxation.

The churches linked up with successful businessmen and public-spirited landowners to provide civic and cultural projects. The Christian authorities' vision of a need to combat ignorance and 'barbarism' expanded to include a more optimistic concept of a society reintegrated through a shared cultural heritage. Canon Samuel Barnett, the settlement leader, had pointed the way to a society in which 'simpler living and higher thinking would bring rich and poor nearer together'. There would be a shared pride in libraries, art galleries and good music. It was also a golden age for amateur music-making: sheet music and pianos had a vast and growing market.[16] The rapidly expanding public transport system, suburban railways and the London Underground enabled audiences to reach the amenities from far and wide.

In October 1894 the Morley College magazine proudly described the social changes in the locality around the Vic. Fourteen years earlier, when the hall had opened on a temperance basis, its audience had 'sunk into all that is disorderly'. Since then the same audience had furnished only one case of Saturday-night violence for the police courts to deal with. It was, the magazine argued, 'a striking instance of what may be done by breaking the connection between drink and amusement'.[17]

Despite the enormous financial and social challenges she faced, Baylis slowly and painfully managed to increase her audience attendance and to develop her beloved opera programme. She had one advantage over the professional opera companies: since most of her performers were unpaid amateurs she was able to keep ticket prices down.* Standards nonetheless suffered from the lack of resources. Problems were many: the amateur chorus, who had full-time jobs, could not rehearse in the day; there was not enough cash to pay fees for the orchestra at night; and singers wore their own costumes, learnt parts on their own and, with virtually no rehearsal time, stood and sang as best they could. Technical and production standards were primitive.

* In 1901 prices for the Thursday ballad opera concerts and Saturday variety were 2d and 3d in the gallery, 4d in the pit and 9d in the balcony. Stalls seats cost from 1s to 3s (Old Vic Archive, annual report 1901).

Although there were warm family feelings between Cons and Baylis, there were growing ideological tensions to cope with at the Vic. Baylis was keen to widen the provision of music and opera, but Cons insisted on maintaining the educational and temperance work at a time when competition in the entertainment world was increasing. Music halls were gaining respectability in the West End, where Oswald Stoll and Edward Moss developed acts suitable for family audiences in their great new variety palaces with their proscenium arches and fixed seating. The Coliseum, which opened in 1904, was the most extravagant and spectacular of these. New purpose-built theatres were safer and were developing a respectable image and clientele. By the early 1900s about 45,000 people a night were crowding into the thirty-five largest London halls, all of which were paying higher fees to their artists than the Victoria Hall could afford. With its continuing moral censorship and low pay the Vic was unable to attract first-class music-hall acts. Instead, Baylis decided to develop her operatic recitals, which were becoming more popular. In 1904 she introduced Wagner to the Vic with extracts from *Tannhäuser* and, in 1906, *Lohengrin*.

The task was extremely daunting. Not only was Baylis introducing new music, she also had to make a profit, or at the very least not lose too much money. While insisting on maintaining her educational programmes, Cons sought to encourage Baylis in her endeavours. On 4 February 1904 she wrote to say she did not see why Baylis was so 'down' about the balance sheet, as she had taken £1,804 at the doors, which more than covered the artists' fees of £1,756. 'Never say die,' she urged, and added, 'If we do not make money by our work, we do make dear kind friends, who stick to us through every turn of the tide.'[18]

The concerts had a mixed programme. The programme for 22 October 1906 included the overture to *The Mastersingers*, Mendelssohn's Italian Symphony and the overture to Gounod's *Mireille*. Attendances were slowly increasing, however, and, although the concerts remained financially unsuccessful, it was decided to continue the experiment until the end of the 1906 season. When in March 1907 Baylis urged the Executive Committee to discontinue the concerts as they were losing too much money, Cons refused, arguing that they received their modest grant from the City Parochial Fathers in order to 'give good music to the people and raise their tastes for the same'.[19] These ambitious projects were partially subsidised by showing films on Monday nights. All the programmes contained a note from Lilian Baylis: 'All possible care is taken to attract and amuse by genuine talent and humour alone. The managers will however be greatly obliged to members of the audience who will report to them anything in the slightest degree objectionable.'

There were also gradual improvements to conditions and salaries. On 13 September 1906 Baylis offered Mr Rawson 7s 6d if he would come to an extra rehearsal of *Lohengrin*, although for other Saturday rehearsals she could only offer 5s. In 1907 the programme for *Martha* listed Fred Hudson, a bass baritone who sang many roles with the company, as the stage manager.

Audiences continued to grow, both for the opera and the 'animated pictures', which brought in a profit of £242 in 1908.[20] On 29 January 1908 Cons wrote with a great hurrah to Baylis after she produced an excellent balance sheet for these two ventures, encouraging her and telling her that it was the reward for her efforts to keep down expenses. The Thursday programme for April–May 1910 comprised a costume recital of Auber's *Fra Diavolo*, a ballad concert, *Carmen*, *Il trovatore*, another ballad concert and *Faust*.

In March 1910 Baylis organised an evening at the Vic for the Prince and Princess of Wales, which filled the streets with crowds of onlookers and the theatre with nobility. The event cost £5 to stage and made £40. On the whole, however, keeping the books balanced was nearly impossible. Only the films and operas were proving successful – the ballad and symphony concerts, military bands and variety were all losing money. Even the films were losing out to the new cinemas that were springing up all over south London. The stress proved too much for Baylis, who was so overstrained that she suffered a breakdown in 1910. She was granted a long summer holiday and a voyage abroad.

Baylis returned invigorated to find the operas doing so well that hundreds of people were being turned away each evening. A *Tannhäuser* recital was a big hit in November 1910. Overall takings, however, continued to decline, not helped in 1911 by bills of £5,000 for redecoration and £10,000 for alterations that had been ordered by the London County Council. By March of that year the bank balance was so low that Baylis had to borrow £200 from one of the governors in order to meet the expenses. It was decided to launch an appeal.

The Lord Chamberlain again insisted on imposing difficult conditions for a new licence that would permit smoking. These included a stipulation that each performance should contain fewer than six distinct numbers and that the act drop be lowered between each item. The governors decided not to take up the new licence, since it would be more likely to harm than help the opera work. Instead, it was agreed to put on some Shakespeare in costume without scenery and call them recitals. It was felt to be a worthwhile experiment, even if the recitals made a loss.[21]

On 24 July 1912 Emma Cons died. She was seventy-four. Not only did she leave Baylis in charge of the Vic, she also left her the bulk of the money that she had acquired but not spent during her working life – £4,233 before death duties. This meant that Baylis would be free to devote herself to the Vic without worrying about her income.

Beatrice Webb described Cons as 'one of the most saintly as well as one of the most far-sighted of Victorian philanthropists'. She was also courageous in the face of all obstacles, even violence.[22] Furthermore, she had, according to one biographer, nothing of the 'condescending kindliness of the old-style Lady Bountiful or the piety of the more ardent church workers'. She was 'a great do-gooder who rejected the *seigneurial* condescension and sanctimonious severity that made philanthropy seem a dirty word to a later generation; one of the splendid sisterhood of secular nuns who helped to nurse the consciences of the rich and the cancers of the poor'.[23]

By the time Baylis took full control of the Vic, opera audiences regularly reached 2,000 for each performance and the future pattern of its work and the nature of its ideal and purpose was established. The endeavour that had sprung from the Christian Socialist belief in 'rational recreation', the offering of opportunities for a richer and fuller life to all members of society and alcohol-free entertainment, was slowly being transformed, not least by its audience's enthusiasm, into Baylis's beloved 'people's opera house'.

# 2

# 1912–1931: 'The People's Opera House'

In the decade following her aunt's death, Lilian Baylis transformed the Vic into a serious drama and opera house with a growing and loyal audience. She continued to base her work on the community with whom she worked and to whom she was devoted. Although she was devastated by her aunt's death, she found solace in her faith and in the crowds of stage staff, students, friends and locals who followed the horse-drawn hearse down The Cut past the Vic. Many of them attended the cremation at Golders Green.

It was at this time that Father Andrew, a young Anglo-Catholic monk, became an important part of Baylis's life. Father Andrew (born Henry Ernest Hardy, 1869–1946) had founded a neo-monastic group, the Society of the Divine Compassion, in 1894. In the tradition of High Church Anglican socialism, he combined his religious vocation with work in the East End. He was a source of endless encouragement for Baylis, offering her prayer, comfort and calming advice, as well as providing opportunities for her to attend his retreats. Amongst his projects was a home for lepers in East Hanningfield in Essex, where Baylis would often entertain the residents. Father Andrew was also an artist and playwright. As a ritualist, he believed in the use of theatrical techniques in the service of God and was a strong supporter of religious drama. In 1919 the Vic produced his first play, a nativity titled *The Hope of the World*. It was shown on the three following Christmases, after which the directors objected that it was not dramatic enough.

A typical letter from Father Andrew records the warmth of his support. 'Keep a good heart and go on with your fight,' he wrote. 'I think really you are doing one of the finest things I know. Your provision of good fare & your brave assertion that theatre is a noble art brings a clear stream of noble suggestion into London where it is most needed.'[1] In 1918, after Father Andrew praised her Old Vic work from the pulpit, Baylis wrote to Ivy Smithson: 'I love Father

Andrew with all my heart & he is so strong, bursting with life & the joy of living, yet he is so loving and tender and beautiful.'[2] The combination of Baylis's prayers, meditation and visits to retreats, together with the support of Father Andrew, helped her fulfil what was an extraordinarily rigorous and stressful mission.

At last in 1912 a new Act was passed by Parliament that allowed theatre licences to be granted to music halls. In September 1912 the governors agreed to apply for a theatre licence, which would permit the presentation of certain selections from plays and operas, with occasional full performances. In November it was granted. The loss-making ballad and symphony concerts were soon dropped, to be replaced by opera recitals, and full operas on Thursdays and, later, Saturdays. These rapidly gained in popularity. 'On the first Saturday night of the opera,' wrote Baylis in 1936, 'we were crowded out, and this has been the rule ever since.' Alterations to the building, however, were putting a heavy burden on the finances.[3] With only £800 raised by August 1912, the governors feared they would have to close the hall. Appeals for funds were a constant feature of life at the Vic.

Despite the financial pressures, Baylis's nurturing instincts succeeded in fostering an indispensable and dedicated family spirit amongst her audience and company. The 1911/12 annual report quoted a description in *Musical Opinion* of the throngs of people in the theatre. It described a 'thoroughly happy' and absorbed local audience made up largely of small shopkeepers who were not well off, and 'superior working class'. Some veterans who had moved away from the neighbourhood continued to attend regularly, even when this meant walking long distances. The article described a woman with small children, seated on the stairway, with no hope of a seat, 'reconciled to hearing only'. Such people were seeking refuge from their own streets and houses. Up in the balcony were the regulars, including one who 'knew "Maritana" and "Rigoletto" by heart' and whistled 'the song of the Toreador at work'. He tramped in from Haggerston; 'his boots are not sound but he is "orf to the opera". He's only got 3d in his pocket. You can't mend boots for that, but after deducting 1d for a "screw of baccy" you have enough left to carry you to the Vine-yards of Castille.' Of course, there followed an appeal for funds, as 'tuppence a head will not pay for Grand Opera'.

At the end of the 1913 season Rosina Filippi, a retired actress who hoped to create a 'people's theatre', was brought in by Baylis and the governors.* It was hoped to build up an audience as large as the opera had achieved. From April 1914 Filippi started, on a shoe-string, to present two Shakespeare plays a week. Her season was, however, short-lived and ill-attended, and the two powerful women soon parted ways. According to Russell Thorndike, Baylis insisted on putting a slip in the drama programmes advising patrons not to spend their money on the Shakespeare if that meant they could not afford the opera. She was heard to say, 'Shakespeare may be all right in his way, but Opera is right in every way for the success of the Vic.'[4]

The 1913/14 annual report outlined the progress made by the Vic since 1886. Already by the end of January 1914 two performances of the same opera were given to crowded and enthusiastic audiences and the experiment was continued with great success. While interest in the cinema and variety had decreased owing to competition from halls providing alcohol, interest in opera had grown considerably. An article in November 1913 noted: 'In every direction there is a longing to rise out of all that is low and sordid and ugly. Who can tell what it may foreshadow in the future to put the best form of entertainment within reach of those who are already seeking higher things?'[5] The weary, cockney, New Cut folk were attending the Vic, happy and eager, 'listening with rapt attention to Verdi or Bizet or perhaps Wagner, for pennies are saved for many weeks for the inevitable Wagner night and though prices vary from 2d to 1s that is no mean sum to our audiences. It had been achieved by the living loving power of human life, and a knot of faithful friends and workers sharing a common courage and common faith.'

To maintain the momentum, more money was needed. In 1914 there was a major appeal for funds, supported by such luminaries as

* Unlike other liberal advocates of a National Theatre at the time, Filippi found her model not in Germany but in Italy. *The Times* on 23 October 1913 reported her saying that Milan's Società Umanitaria had converted a hall into a 2,300-seat theatre, and produced a programme that helped 'to reduce crime . . . and to serve as a bridge between primary education and the responsible duties of the voter'. Filippi announced she was pursuing the same objectives by producing 'only the best plays by the greatest authors, living and dead, and charging only fourpence for every seat in the house' (Richard Findlater, *Lilian Baylis, the Lady of the Old Vic*, London: Allen Lane, 1975, p. 104).

Thomas Beecham, Henry Wood and Dame Nellie Melba. Melba sent a large cheque for what was becoming known colloquially as the People's Opera House, and the event was followed by a supportive article in the *Daily Telegraph*.

Although Baylis's first love and area of greatest experience was opera, she soon decided to run the Shakespeare plays herself, helped by husband-and-wife team Matheson Lang and Hutin Britton. On 9 September 1914, five weeks after the outbreak of war, an advertisement appeared in the *Era* trade paper appealing for experienced Shakespearean actors.

The problems were overwhelming. The only publicity was the green-sheet programmes that were distributed by hand. There was sawdust on the floor, rats abounded, and none of the dressing rooms had running water. The wardrobe consisted of borrowed or hired costumes and props. The gas lighting sometimes needed reigniting in the middle of a show, but its dim inadequacy at least helped to hide the tatty scenery, which consisted of stage backcloths that served as the cottage, the palace or the wood. New scenery was painted by apprentices or amateurs. There were no rehearsal rooms and no time for rehearsals; singers and actors competed for every inch of space. The audience sat on wooden benches and the gallery seats were bare boards with no backs. Morley College was still housed in the Old Vic and there were students milling around and completely taking over two evenings a week. With no public subsidy and no civic aid the conditions presented a daunting challenge.

Baylis, however, cultivated and maintained the warmth between audience and stage, and created a community atmosphere which distinguished the Vic from its competitors. She made frequent speeches from the stage, organised family get-togethers and parties, and made a rousing oration at the end of each season.

The first combined Shakespeare/opera season took place from October 1914 to April 1915. Sixteen operas and sixteen plays – thirteen by Shakespeare – were staged in under thirty weeks. The operas were *Carmen*, Donizetti's *The Daughter of the Regiment* and *Lucia di Lammermoor*, *Lohengrin*, *Faust*, *La traviata*, *Il trovatore*, *Rigoletto*, *Cavalleria rusticana* and *Pagliacci*, Flotow's *Martha*, *Fra Diavolo*, *The Lily of Killarney*, *Maritana*, *The Bohemian Girl* and *Don Giovanni*, which was new to the Vic. Charles Manners of the

Moody-Manners company provided Baylis with scores and parts.
Findlater quotes an unnamed critic in 1914:

The scenery is crude, the dresses are garish, the limelight is will o' the wisp,
the orchestra has insufficient bass; but the singing is in tune, the dancing
fresh and graceful, the chorus hearty, the audience too intent on the play to
eat chocolate; for the applause all of them are in the firing line and there
are no reserves; and the prices rise from two pence. Here are the essentials
of opera at any rate. It is possible that English Opera might be born south
of the Thames, not far from the scene of Shakespeare's activities.[6]

The opera audience was growing while the drama struggled.
Nevertheless, Baylis wrote in the Shakespeare League journal after
the first season, 'we rejoice more over the presence of one rough lad
who has never heard Shakespeare, than over the attendance of half
a dozen Shakespeare students'. She was, she wrote, 'trying to bring
Shakespeare home to the less educated classes'. It was a huge struggle, involving many sacrifices. When the actress Beatrice Wilson
went to work for Baylis, she was told that her salary would be £2 a
week: 'Can't pay my leading ladies any more. Business isn't good
for Shakespeare, not like my opera. Her face glowed: "You must
hear my opera . . ."'[7]

In June 1915, as the fighting on the Western Front and at
Gallipoli intensified, Baylis sent out an appeal in the name of the
'Royal Victoria Hall, "Old Vic", *The People's Opera, Play and
Lecture House*'. The title, she wrote, appeared Utopian at a time
when thoughts were with 'our dear ones on the battle-field'.
Nonetheless, it was of the utmost importance to 'enable the people
to enjoy the higher pleasures of life'. The Old Vic was a 'perfect
oasis and mind-resting place to many sorely tried people' and a joy
to thousands of young people and their teachers.

The opera indeed helped to pay for Shakespeare, but the whole
enterprise might well have foundered had not Baylis's prayers been
answered, as she put it, by the arrival of the director Ben Greet.
Greet, like Father Andrew a High Anglican, offered his services to
her gratis in 1915. His thirty years' experience in the theatre gave
him a distinct advantage in casting, and his Shakespeare work with
the Woodland Players, who had provided 'instant' travelling
Shakespeare, had made him flexible, unflappable and good at

improvising within modest means. The Vic posed a manageable challenge for Greet, who followed Edward Gordon Craig's theories of production and design, not least because he had no money.* Beyond his ideals and attitude towards production, Greet accepted that the theatre had a social function. A programme note written by him in 1917 described the Old Vic as a 'Family Theatre'. It was, he elaborated, 'jolly for the audience to get to know each other'.[8]

In October 1914 the thirty-two-year-old Sybil Thorndike, who became a lifelong friend of Baylis, joined the Vic on Greet's suggestion. She played many roles in her first season, including Lady Macbeth, while full of anxiety for her husband Lewis and her brother Russell, who were serving in the army. Thorndike recalled Baylis's rough, warm, cockney voice and found her enduringly 'kind and sharp – humorous and scolding – infinitely friendly'. She was also the most original person Thorndike had ever met.[9]

During the second season the critics began to come and a new audience began to filter in for the Shakespeare, as the West End was only providing light wartime fare. Children were coming to matinees organised by the Reverend Stewart Headlam. During one week 4,000 schoolchildren saw *As You Like It*.[†] In 1916 the temperance Friday nights gave way to Shakespeare, and lectures were reduced so that the opera could rehearse. That year Baylis started staging Mendelssohn's *Elijah* in operatic form on Sundays.

Many actors were called up; many did not return. Greet was forced to cast women in male roles. In 1916 the government

---

* Craig, who was born in 1862, has been described by Peter Brook as the crucial influence on modern theatre. He 'aspired to a fusion of poetry, performer, music, light, colour and movement', using space and light as elements of the design and abolishing lighting battens and footlights, which just illuminated the actors' faces. Instead, he used techniques such as concealed lighting bars and colour changes and double gauzes, which were to become, in Richard Eyre's words, the 'syntax' of modern lighting designers. Above all he sought to maximise the power of the text through the actor and to exploit the 'theatreness of theatre' (Richard Eyre, *Changing Stages*, London: Bloomsbury, 2001, p. 33).
† There were performances in other parts of London, including the then mainly Jewish district of Bethnal Green. 'I do like to see the Jews coming,' said Baylis to Thorndike, 'don't you dear? Even though they aren't Christians, it must do them good, but I wish we didn't have to give them *The Merchant of Venice*, the Christians all behave so badly' (Sybil and Russell Thorndike, *Lilian Baylis*, London: Chapman & Hall, 1938, p. 73).

imposed an entertainment tax, from which Baylis tried and failed to gain exemption. 'Members of the audience have written to say they are practically saved from insanity by the healing power of our plays,' she argued.[10] Audiences nevertheless declined as the war took its toll. Air raids from late 1916 to 1918, carried out by the formidable German Gotha bombers, frequently left the auditorium empty, causing heavy financial losses. Through it all, the loyalty of the company kept it going, with Greet's devotion to the cause proving equal to that of Baylis. The Vic usually played right through the bombing.

The financial crises in the war were resolved by grants from the London Parochial Charities, including one of £500 at the end of the 1917/18 season.[11] In 1918 the Carnegie Trust – which had been set up in 1913 by Andrew Carnegie, a philanthropic Scotsman who had made his fortune in the Pittsburgh steelworks – gave £1,000 over two years towards increases in salaries and setting up a wardrobe. But with a repertoire of more than thirty plays and twenty operas, the cost of the wardrobe was estimated at £5,000. It was also necessary to make some changes to the scenery and sets, to replace the 'grimy' and dangerous front curtain and slightly increase the salaries of the leading players. Reserved seats went up to 4s 3d, but the gallery remained 3d.

The Vic's reputation had grown considerably during the war. Queen Mary attended a gala matinee to celebrate the theatre's centenary in October 1918. Princess Marie Louise attended a matinee of *Macbeth* and was asked to become a member of the council, despite Baylis's determination that she was not going to let the Old Vic become 'fashionable'. In this she was successful and the Vic remained true to its egalitarian ideals. Edward J. Dent observed: 'Nobody appeared in evening dress, and, as the difference in price between the stalls and the gallery was very little, the difference in comfort still less, the whole house seemed to acquire a unity of character that was to be observed in the Old Vic and nowhere else.'[12]

In the aftermath of war, the Vic became a hub of activity. Its reputation and community work made it a vibrant cultural centre. From the end of 1919 the Vic published a magazine, started by Elisabeth Corathiel, who was hired in 1915 as a press agent. The *Old Vic Magazine* became an educational tool, including articles about the work being done by directors, writers and performers. It also became a vehicle for the development of Baylis's growing image as theatre manager, and a way of maintaining close links with the audience. It was, the magazine stated, 'some tangible expression of the interest and affection felt by those before the curtain for those behind and vice versa'.[13]

A recurrent theme in the articles the magazine published, as articulated in April 1920, was that the company was 'a great family with a collective soul'. The two strands of the Vic's ideal were formulated at this time. It was 'democratic', and at the same time its watchword was 'art for art's sake'. A Christmas greeting to the magazine in December 1919, from a 'mere man in the stalls', thanked the Vic and its artists for providing a spirit of true fellowship, a '"home from home" for old and young men and women, where a man can bring his family without hesitation or fear'. The 'People's Theatre and Opera House' was accessible even to the poorest.

Above all, Baylis wrote in the magazine in May 1921, it was the teamwork and growing ensemble at the Vic in which she delighted. Edward J. Dent wrote of 'an extraordinary sense of what one can only call family affection and family pride' within the theatre.[14] Another theme of the magazine was the competition with the West End theatres, who stole the Vic's stars and paid them higher salaries but who did not have the distinct personality of the Vic. In April 1920 the magazine urged regular punters to book their seats early before outsiders rolled up and ousted the Vic's own folk. The competition was intended to reinforce the Vic's distinct identity.

Adding to the costs of wartime inflation was the growing professionalism of the company. Producers had begun to ask for three-year contracts and annual salaries of £500. Although the contracts could be argued against as representing too great a commitment, there was no alternative but to agree to higher salaries if the company were to improve standards. In July 1920 it was decided that the increase in production costs necessitated a rise in seat prices, with stalls going up to 3s and the balcony to 1s 6d.

That year Robert Atkins, who had worked for Baylis as an actor and assistant director, was demobbed and came back to work at the Vic. From 1920 to 1923 Atkins was in charge of the Old Vic's performance of the complete First Folio, comprising thirty-six plays. He was extremely flexible and aware of the company's needs, mainly relying on imaginatively lit curtains and a selective use of painted scenery, with a platform extending from the proscenium.

The theatre was beginning at last to gain a following equal to, if not exceeding, that of the opera, and the Old Vic style was becoming recognised. In 1920 a *Daily Telegraph* critic wrote that the Old Vic was doing 'great work and work for which future generations of playgoers will owe them more thanks than they are likely to repay'. It was, he wrote, creating a 'real taste for the comprehension of good drama . . . very few of the best plays ever do soar above the heads of the simple-minded people'.[15]

Baylis never let the drama supporters forget that it was the opera company that enabled the theatre to survive. She wrote in 1921: 'There's nothing like music for the illiterate. It awakes their souls and when they are awake, there is something for the high thoughts and language of Shakespeare to appeal to.'[16] The first performances of *Tristan and Isolde*, adapted by Corri for the Vic's small orchestra at the end of 1920, met with a rapturous response from the audience despite the lack of rehearsal and Corri's own admission of imperfection of execution.[17] 'The gallery and pit were audibly at sea at the beginning,' wrote *The Times* critic, but as the opera progressed, the audience's interest rose to a level equal to their loyalty and 'the great adventure was justified'.[18]

By September 1921 the *Daily Telegraph* was writing that 'to form part of an Old Vic audience is a real tonic. The people really love the theatre for itself: they love the plays, the acting, the players.' The audience made its own stars. One of the opera company's stalwart artists was Sam Harrison, who sold gramophone records in the day and whose short stature, thick northern accent and socialist outlook made him an 'incredibly funny' and distinctive Masetto for Dent. Dent also appreciated his Speaker in the *Magic Flute* and Germont in *La traviata*.[19]

It was a formula that applied equally to the opera and the drama. Joan Cross later recalled that the audience responded with understanding, devotion and loyalty. 'They partook in the real sense of the word,' she wrote, and 'although not averse to offering criticism, they felt part and parcel of the institution; it was their theatre as well as Miss Baylis's'.[20] Geoffrey Whitworth wrote in *John O'London's Weekly* in February 1922 that the Old Vic audience really 'assists as the French say'. Together, audience and performers become a single group and group consciousness 'is one of the most important factors in dramatic representation'. The backbone of the Vic's audience remained the people of the surrounding district, but it had begun to reach out to the suburbs of Hampstead and Hammersmith, and even the 'farthest wilds of Golders Green'. Yet within the theatre the atmosphere remained 'parochial, even domestic'. The tragedy, the commentators said, was that it was unique both in policy and clientele.[21] The close relationship and loyalty between audience and artists was a vital ingredient of Baylis's legacy and never failed so long as it was adhered to.

Although the opera had helped to create the audience for Shakespeare, the Shakespeare productions began to make strides artistically, while the opera only slowly began to adopt new production values. Those participating were mostly still amateur. Harcourt Williams, producer at the Old Vic from 1929 to 1933, described the stage crew as consisting of the 'more pertinacious students from the Royal College and Academy who wanted to learn about opera and could not find anywhere else to do it in London; quiet young men who could speak authoritatively of Dresden and Salzburg; there were milkmen and miners who sang with lovely liquid vowels and lapsed cheerfully into the vernacular when they spoke'.[22] The amateur chorus was still singing for love, lemonade and biscuits, while students acted as telephonists and assisted in other administrative roles.

Baylis found the old conventions of opera – solo singers down at the footlights and the chorus standing still in rows – convenient, for they allowed her to present opera with the minimum of rehearsal. The only way she could pay her performers so little was by demanding as little as possible from them and compromising on artistic standards. Professional operatic direction was in its infancy and even in the 1930s the role of the director was seldom singled out for comment by the critics. The work of Sidney Russell, who was responsible for preparing at least twenty-one operas for the Old Vic, was more akin to that of a stage manager. Soon after the war, however, the company became more ambitious in its endeavours, as Baylis started employing more professional singers, including the light soprano Muriel Gough, who had sung before the war with the Moody-Manners company and at the Weimar Court Opera. With her vocal and personal charm and vivacious acting, Gough soon became a popular favourite with the Vic audiences in such roles as Susanna, the Queen of Night and Zerlina. With her knowledge, personal integrity and experience she also became a trusted adviser to Baylis.[23]

It was through Gough that the baritone and director Clive Carey and his mentor Edward J. Dent came into Baylis's life. In January 1920 Gough recommended that Carey direct and sing in a new *Figaro*, which Dent would translate. Dent was a fellow of King's College Cambridge and, from 1926, Professor of Music at the university. He was a scholar of eighteenth-century Italian opera and a pioneer in preparing singable translations in understandable contemporary English which were not stilted and fitted the music. As well as having a wry sense of humour, Dent had a keen feeling for the needs of the theatre and the voice. He was the teacher and patron of a generation of musicians at Cambridge, in both performance and scholarship. One of those was Carey, who had been a chorister at King's and an organ scholar at Clare College.

In 1911 Dent and Carey, determined to return to the text and eliminate accumulated traditions of performance, had put on a groundbreaking production of *The Magic Flute* in Cambridge, which Dent translated and in which Carey sang Papageno. This production and Dent's translation marked the beginning of the two men's crusade to put intelligible, dramatic productions before the public, thus widening both the appeal and the understanding of the works. Dent's aim was to use words that enabled the singers to pronounce them as naturally as actors could and were simple enough to be intelligible when sung. The words should make the story clear, fit the music and allow audiences to become familiar with the text as well as the music – not always the case with previous translations, many of which were contrived and full of awkward inversions.*

The joint mission of the two men was, and remained, as Carey put it in 1943, 'to make audiences want to hear the words'.[24] This focus on the text meant that the performances would need more

---

* In his book *Going to the Opera* (Puffin, 1955), Lionel Salter gave some striking examples of horribly stilted translation. One was from the standard *Tosca* translation, not by Dent, when Angelotti runs into the church:
　　　'Ah I have baulked them!
　　　Dread imagination makes me quake
　　　With uncalled for perturbation.'

rehearsal. In the *Old Vic Magazine* in October 1921, Dent appealed for the opera to be given as much care in production as the plays were. 'Would you pitchfork a man on to the stage without rehearsal to play Hamlet?' he asked.

Carey agreed to direct *Figaro* on condition that Dent's new translation was used. At first Baylis refused, fearing that it would be too much work for the cast to learn new words and too expensive to copy them into the old books.[25] In the end, however, she employed a new cast and Carey agreed to cut the opera to three hours, which involved losing the Act III sextet. Dent himself ended up copying the parts for the chorus in 'that horrid room', while the chorus rehearsed *Lohengrin*.[26]

The singers, most of whom were new to their roles, agreed that Carey could take far longer than usual over the rehearsals. Carey and Dent, inspired by Mahler's Vienna production, were determined to avoid the Dresden-china prettiness of the German court theatres, and succeeded in conveying something of the 'squalor' of Figaro's bedroom.[27] The production was a critical and popular success, with Dent's translation clearly audible and the laughs erupting mid-ensemble.

Baylis, quick to recognise Carey's skill, asked him to stage *The Magic Flute* in December 1920, again in Dent's translation. Carey used the costumes of his legendary 1911 Cambridge production, and Steuart Wilson repeated his Tamino while Winifred Kennard sang Pamina. According to Dent, she looked nice, was a good musician, and although she had a wobble, it was always 'exactly on the note'.[28] Despite Baylis's earlier suggestion that Wilson sing for no fee and with no rehearsal, the reformers were successful and both of Carey's productions remained a feature of every season up to the outbreak of war in 1939.

The arrival of Dent and Carey brought a European, academic dimension to the Vic. Both men had travelled extensively, Dent having attended opera performances and pursued his research on eighteenth-century Italian opera in Trieste, Florence, Rome and Genoa, as well as in Dresden, Munich and Berlin.

The baritone and director Sumner Austin also joined the company during the 1919/20 season, after his wartime spell in Ruhleben prisoner-of-war camp near Berlin and subsequent touring with the Carl Rosa company. Findlater described him as a 'gentle intelligent artist' with a university background. Between them, Carey, Austin and Dent improved the standard of production and changed the habits of the audience, especially discouraging applause after every number.

Also in the 1919/20 season the thirty-two-year-old conductor Lawrance Collingwood joined the music staff, playing the piano for rehearsals, his salary paid by the Carnegie Trust for the first year. He had trained at the St Petersburg conservatory, and after the war conducted at the Mariinsky theatre. Collingwood, a sensitive, reticent man, at first hated the work, which consisted of 'labouring on an ancient piano through crude versions of standard works with a motley chorus of amateurs who never got enough rehearsals'. He was, however, so infected by Baylis's enthusiasm and so interested in the whole establishment that he stayed on despite the difficulties, accepting a drop in his salary and an increase in his workload.[29]

In November 1921 Carey directed Dent's translation of *Don Giovanni*. Dent and Carey were determined to present the work as a comic opera, not as a romantic tragedy, and reinstated the usually omitted finale of Act II. Robert Atkins, the Vic's theatre director, advised on the set and lighting, suggesting clever arrangements for the curtains and bits of scenery. J. B. Trend, who was working on Spanish music and was later the first Professor of Spanish at Cambridge, gave lessons in how to wear combs and mantillas, and provided Spanish postcards of Goya prints from which period costumes were designed.

Rehearsal time was still severely limited since the orchestral run-through had to be squeezed into one day; the gallant cast, director and even Dent himself were treated to baked potatoes from New Cut for lunch. Furthermore, the absence of trapdoors meant Giovanni had to be escorted off to hell by sinister black figures, 'vaguely suggesting the Inquisition'. The production was nonetheless a further advance. The pace insisted upon by Dent and Carey, which precluded applause between scenes, was approved of by Atkins. Dent proudly recollected that German critics would admit to him that the freshness of the Vic's Mozart productions and the absence of traditional stage business made them see the works anew.[30]

By 1921 the critics were beginning to see the Old Vic as the most important theatre for drama in London. That year the company received an official invitation to perform in Brussels. The improvements were also helping the box office. Between May 1921 and May 1922 the credit balance increased by £2,800. In June 1922 the governors suggested that an endowment fund be set up to improve the salaries of the company and staff.[31] They voted Atkins an additional £200 per annum in recognition of his work. Baylis agreed that with the improved financial situation she would continue to arrange more rehearsal time for the opera. The governors also agreed that an opera producer should be employed especially to help train the younger members of the company.[32]

In order to try to create the endowment fund and meet the growing financial demands, the Vic Association was formed in 1923 with an annual subscription of £10. Blocks of seats would be reserved for members, who would also have a private room set aside for them. That year the annual costume ball was inaugurated.

Atkins and Baylis endured a stormy relationship. He detested the atmosphere of good works, the dowdiness and stinginess; he resented her 'meddling in his productions, when she knew next to nothing about Shakespeare'. He was also 'heavy-drinking, hard-swearing and womanising'.[33] Yet the partnership somehow managed to survive five years, despite a serious car accident in October 1923 which left Baylis in need of rest and convalescence and did nothing to ease the tensions.

The reputation of Baylis and her theatre was becoming national as well as local. She started to broadcast on the BBC, and continued to use her end-of-season speeches as a means both of fundraising and of maintaining the family spirit of her audience. Her reputation as 'The Manager' was built up in the Vic magazine as well as in national publications. Her biographer Elizabeth Schafer shows how Baylis developed what might today be described as something of a personality cult, with her carefully presented image as a woman who was determined, religious, obstinate, humorous, parsimonious, outspoken and eccentric. Stories of her activities at the Vic – from her beloved and omnipresent pet dogs, to her cooking on her gas ring by the stage to feed her hungry artists, to her stage interventions – abounded. Above all, the Vic magazine celebrated her role as a woman in a man's world. She was a plain woman who wore thick glasses and simple clothes that did nothing to disguise her dumpy figure. She was also painfully conscious of the slight paralysis in the corner of her mouth. Her appearance was described as a cross between schoolmarm and charwoman. Her face became increasingly well known, especially from postcards of her sitting at her desk, 'pen poised and at the ready, looking kindly but efficient'.[34]

On 6 May 1924 Baylis received an honorary Master of Arts from Oxford University. It was the first such honour for the stage, and only one woman, Queen Mary, had ever been similarly favoured. In 1929 Baylis was made a Companion of Honour, a particularly high award for civic achievement. As distinctions were showered upon her, she began to appear in full regalia in photographs and postcards. She also supported the publication of books about the Vic, to which appeals for funds were unashamedly attached.

Those funds were always desperately needed. Even the fabric of the theatre demanded constant attention. In March 1921 the London County Council had insisted that the Vic must undergo substantial reconstruction for reasons of health and convenience, at a cost of about £30,000. As this sum was impossible to raise, the Vic was on the verge of closure until the theatrical manager George Dance donated the whole amount. A month later it was decided to ask Morley College to leave, in order to make more room to expand the work and rehearsal space of the company, especially for the opera. Rehousing the college would cost another £20,000, which consumed much of Dance's donation.

After further public appeals for funds the building works were begun and the college's eviction was completed for the 1924/5 season. There were now purpose-built dressing rooms with running water, a safety curtain, wardrobe, workrooms and offices. A rehearsal room and a proper stage door were also added. The theatre could at last have its own wardrobe rather than paying rent. Mrs Newman, the wardrobe mistress, whom Joan Cross later described as 'taciturn and indifferent', continued to provide well-worn costumes of generic invention: gypsy skirts for *Carmen* and *Il trovatore*, 'vaguely medieval' for *Lohengrin* and *Tannhäuser*. For many years the cast continued to provide their own accessories, including fans and jewellery that were 'all strictly vintage Woolworth'.[35] The public areas and auditorium were unchanged, with the familiar non-alcoholic refreshments still provided.

With Morley College's departure there were new Orders in Council for the two separate organisations. But the main objective of the Royal Victoria Hall was still 'to provide high-class drama, especially the plays of Shakespeare, and high-class opera or lectures, musical and other entertainments and exhibitions suited for the recreation and instruction of the poorer classes of the former County of London'.[36]

Despite the Carey/Dent breakthroughs, and unlike the drama, the general standards of the opera improved rather slowly. From 1923, 'production' in the programmes was credited to Frederick Hudson, whom Joan Cross later described as a highly nervous and insecure man, a pessimist who, in his shiny black shoes, looked as if he would have been more at home as a bank manager in a small county town.[37] Hudson was in fact a stage manager, who had at his disposal only a tiny budget for costumes, props and scenery. He managed to get the shows on with only a part-time assistant, a stage carpenter, an electrician and nine hours' rehearsal. Sumner Austin recalled: 'You were told to come on *here* and go off *there*. The rest you filled in for yourself. There was no production whatsoever.'[38]

Although production standards were developing only sporadically, the singers were learning their trade and the company was beginning to develop its own 'stars'. The soprano Joan Cross, who had studied at the Trinity College of Music, joined the Vic in 1923. She rapidly became a hit with both audience and critics. Dent recalled the affection of the audience for the most popular singers, especially for Muriel Gough and Winifred Kennard. Fans would wait with flowers even in pouring rain for their favourites to emerge from the stage door. One young woman insisted on knitting a pair of green slippers for Carey, who had appeared as a barefoot Tamino.[39] Gough was loved, Dent wrote, for 'her charm of both voice and personality and her vivacious acting'.[40] Edith Coates, who had also studied at Trinity and with Carey, joined the company in the early 1920s.

Cross had been reluctant to join the Vic, having been put off opera by the productions she had seen there. 'I had seen opera', she wrote, 'and rejected it, considering it unbelievably stupid.' She continued: 'There was *Faust*, its demon figures strutting about in bright scarlet observed by a chorus of totally uninterested ladies and gentlemen – not only uninterested but uninvolved.' Cross nonetheless went to audition. She vividly remembered the conditions of the theatre: 'Here I was on a filthy stage piled high with broken flats and dirty rostra. A miserable light barely illuminating the surroundings.' Because of her complete lack of stage experience and Baylis's thriftiness, Cross was offered an unpaid job in the chorus.

Artistic development was severely limited by the company's meagre resources. Cross later described the performances as 'dreadful'. Scenery, props and costumes, she wrote, were 'shabby and used for each opera, and there were not enough wigs to go around (probably a blessing). Rehearsals were minimal – a single orchestral rehearsal on Tuesday mornings and a full stage rehearsal for chorus and principals with no orchestra on Tuesday night. Thursday was the first night and the first time that the full cast and orchestra met on stage!'[41] Dent wrote that the costumes were always 'eighteenth century "square cut", with wigs that never fitted'. The furniture in particular filled him with horror, as 'every scene seemed to take place in a kitchen'. He recalled the production of *La traviata* as the worst dressed and mounted that he had ever seen in his life.[42]

The repertoire grew only slowly. In 1920 the *Old Vic Magazine* explained that the Vic could not afford the royalties of Puccini. Consequently there was no Puccini till 1926, when *Madam Butterfly* was produced, followed by *La bohème* in 1928 and *Tosca* in 1929. Baylis remained faithful to English composers: her friend and colleague Ethel Smyth's *The Boatswain's Mate* and *Fête Galante*, together with Nicholas Gatty's less popular *Prince Fenelon* and *The Tempest*, remained close to the hearts of the Vic audience in their 'child-like directness'.* They did not, however, transfer to the company's new home, Sadler's Wells, in 1931.[43]

Charles Corri remained the conductor in charge of music. Cross recalled how 'the survivors of the ageing chorus continued to turn up ten times a month, rewarded by cake and lemonade'. His orchestra continued to be an ad hoc group, which he assembled week by week, when he lured them to come south of the river from other jobs. Corri was inflexible as an accompanist. 'He hated singers who

* Smyth was a composer and suffragette. She composed the suffragette anthem 'March of the Women', which she included in *The Boatswain's Mate*, an opera based symphonically on English folk songs and which, according to *The New Grove Dictionary of Opera*, 'forged a link between Romantic music drama and the realism of *Peter Grimes*'. Her other operas included *The Wreckers* (1906) and *Entente Cordiale* (1925).

paused or held a top note,' Cross wrote, and if they did, he proceeded without them to 'the general confusion of all concerned'. There was no coach and no music staff, and Cross taught herself by reading through scores at the piano.

Cross's first major role, as Cherubino in 1924, was a near disaster, her fragile confidence having been shattered by her costume – a much worn and stretched pair of breeches that looked like bloomers, and an ill-fitting velvet jacket, a 'bedraggled neck ruff and a cotton wool wig'. When she came off stage after the first act Baylis snatched off the ruff and said to her, 'You look hideous!' At the end she said, 'You sing nicely dear – pity about the acting.'[44] It took Cross time to establish a relationship with Baylis, and her acting skills developed slowly during the decade as she watched more accomplished actors rehearsing. By 1928 *The Times* had nothing but praise for her Cherubino: 'she combines the masculine and feminine traits of that ingenuous young man, looked the part and sang beautifully'.[45]

On 5 February 1925 Baylis offered Cross the role of Elisabeth in *Tannhäuser*, with a few hours of Collingwood's coaching and Hudson to take her 'through the stage business'. When she appeared on 26 February she was, she wrote, 'desperately ill-equipped' and in a state of rising panic. She had, however, the luxury of a partially new costume and the feeling that Baylis wanted her to do well. She was also praised by *The Times* critic, who wrote that the Vic had gained another most valuable recruit from the chorus. She was an assured actress and the purity of her voice remained unimpaired in the big ensembles. That same year she sang Aida, and a year later she was finally put on the payroll.

At a time of creation, when there was a sense of building something for the future, the hardship and sacrifices were manageable. The audience also made it worthwhile, as Joan Cross recalled:

They came regularly, paying their modest charge for their seats, admired, applauded, criticised, taking a deep personal interest in members of the company. With what was to become something of a tradition at the Vic and Sadler's Wells, little presents, letters and flowers were regularly handed in at the stage door. The last night of each season was an especially lively occasion. The presents assumed larger dimensions; baskets of fruit, boxes of chocolate, flowers . . . all subscribed for by the regulars in the audience.

Cross persevered. 'What is certain,' she later wrote, 'is that I was among a small pack pursuing a too often nearly lost quarry – "permanent" performances of opera in English.'[46]

The Shakespeare productions went on developing under Andrew Leigh, who took over from Atkins in 1925. Although there were still plenty of empty seats for both, Shakespeare took over from opera at the box office in mid-decade. Edith Evans was the first West End star to join the company, in the 1925/6 season, which broke box-office records with a profit of £4,500.

By 1926 it was clear to Baylis that her opera company, which was beginning to lose artistic ground to the drama, needed more space to develop. Baylis's choice for the new venue was Sadler's Wells theatre, a virtually derelict eighteenth-century theatre that had been converted into a cinema in 1896 but had not been used since 1916, set in the working-class neighbourhood of Finsbury. The expanding London Underground network was making it more accessible to audiences from further afield.

Reginald Rowe, an energetic, formidably able and philanthropically minded barrister who was already an Old Vic governor, became the honorary treasurer for the enterprise. In March 1925 the Duke of Devonshire, a keen patron of the arts, launched an appeal to purchase Sadler's Wells, reconstruct the interior and save both it and its historic traditions for the nation. Sadler's Wells was to be established as a foundation, not working for profit, under the Charity Commissioners, whose aim was to give an Old Vic to north London.* The Sadler's Wells Committee decided that the constitution of the new theatre would enable opera to be run on a much larger scale than at the Old Vic. The local council gave financial backing, public subscriptions poured in and plays and concerts were given to raise funds. Nellie Melba gave her farewell concert for the appeal in 1926, raising £300.

In July 1925 a gift of £14,000 from the Carnegie Trust enabled the committee to purchase the freehold of Sadler's Wells. The theatre was in a terrible condition, with £40,000 needed to repair it.

---

* The glittering Appeal Committee included four future and former prime ministers – Winston Churchill, Stanley Baldwin, Arthur Balfour and Herbert Asquith – as well as Thomas Beecham, George Moore, G. K. Chesterton and John Galsworthy.

Two external walls required complete replacement. The neighbouring residential buildings made expansion impossible and the renovation took five fraught years to complete. The long-suffering builder, F. G. Minter, frequently had to wait many months for payment. There was no hope of opening in 1926, as Baylis had intended, and work had to continue in the cramped Vic, which was also in need of substantial renovation.

Much to Baylis's consternation, the audience at the Vic was changing. From 1921 the stabilisation of the post-war British economy had benefited the middle classes, with schoolteachers in particular making clear gains in their earnings. For the working classes there were other attractions, especially the cinemas and cafes that were springing up throughout the city. At the Vic, as its reputation grew, the deserving and preferably local poor were being replaced by teachers, students and enthusiasts drawn from all over London and linked by the spirit of community and family feeling in the house in the 1920s. The audience demographic broadened further during yet more building work, again ordered by the LCC, in the 1927/8 season, when Baylis found a home for Shakespeare in Hammersmith and the opera did a tour of London music halls.* Twice nightly the opera company played abbreviated versions of *Faust*, *Il trovatore*, *La traviata* and *Daughter of the Regiment* at music halls in other areas, including Stoke Newington, Ilford and Kilburn.

When audiences returned to the Vic for the 1928/9 season, it was often to 'house full' signs outside the door. Corri gained seven string players for his orchestra, which still numbered only thirty-six when augmented for *Lohengrin*. In the February 1928 *Old Vic Magazine* he commented on how the Vic in particular, and British music in general, was supported by 'the workers', and on the devotion of the packed Saturday-night audiences. The critics, however,

---

* Owing to serious structural defects uncovered during the work, the final cost of the Vic's renovation was far greater than had been envisaged: £29,309 as opposed to the estimate of £16,000. The City Parochial Foundation gave £1,000, the Carnegie Trust £10,000. With savings and donations there was £10,384 outstanding by 1927/8. Harold Lloyd, the film actor, paid off the remainder of the Morley College rehousing, and a loan of £7,000 was made by the City Parochials to pay off the bank debt in 1928 (Old Vic annual report, 1927/8).

were beginning to take the Vic more seriously and to demand higher standards. *The Times* criticised *Tosca* severely: 'Mr Corri must do something drastic if it is to be worth while for an enterprising company of singers to undertake new productions . . . the score was shaken so as to be constantly on the verge of trembling to pieces altogether.' In the 1929/30 season Verdi's *The Force of Destiny* was heard in London for the first time since 1867. It was a great hit. The faithful filled the house, making it, according to Cross, 'tantalisingly difficult for the snob element from across the river who suddenly found an urge to see the piece'.[47]

Cross's work was constantly singled out for praise. Her sincerity and intelligence in the role of Elsa in *Lohengrin* in February 1928 and her Pamina of 'mellifluousness and charm, intelligent perception' were especially noted.[48] In April 1929 she sang and acted Desdemona in the Vic's first *Otello*, with beauty and a 'tender trusting bewilderment'. Hudson's control of the crowds on stage was erratic and Corri's conducting inflexible. Even so, the *Daily Telegraph* saw standards improving enough to make it possible to take a serious critical interest.[49] The paper also praised *Aida*, *Tannhäuser* and *Figaro*.

The mounting costs of the opera resulted in deficits and in 1930 the orchestra was cut for certain performances, although it was already well below strength for most of the repertoire. To enable Corri slowly to retire, Collingwood took control of three operas in the first half of the season. The governors' minutes noted: 'It was agreed that Mr Corri's age and failing grip brought the question of a pension fund to the fore.'

While the opera struggled, the drama flourished. From 1929 the Old Vic's new producer, Harcourt (Billie) Williams, was producing fewer Shakespeare performances, which were much better rehearsed. The productions were more subtle, with changes to the style of verse speaking and acting. Williams also brought in Martita Hunt and the twenty-five-year-old John Gielgud, already a star, although he had to be paid £20 a week.[50]

By the end of the season the box office was booming, with productions of *Romeo and Juliet*, *The Merchant of Venice*, *Richard II*, *Macbeth* and, finally, *Hamlet*, which became a wild hit and made Gielgud a matinee idol. 'Nothing justifies a producer's effort so much', Baylis wrote in the 1930 annual report, 'as a steady increase in the size of the audience . . . the Old Vic is pre-eminently the place for artistic experiment, even if some eggshells of prejudice have to be broken in the process.' Many were turned away for *Hamlet*, and Gielgud stayed for more successes in the 1930/1 season, with Ralph Richardson joining the company.

Not content with theatre and opera, Baylis created her trinity in 1926 when Ninette de Valois, who had experience with the Diaghilev ballet, opened her ballet school in South Kensington with the aim of training a company. She wanted to use the Old Vic as her base. The two women hit it off so well that Baylis agreed that de Valois should teach her drama students how to move, as well as to arrange dances for the drama productions and later the operas. From this initial arrangement the two women determined to create a full-time ballet company when Sadler's Wells reopened. Baylis 'recognised in Ninette de Valois a kindred spirit, both practical and visionary, a single-minded fighter with an indomitable will'.[51] In 1928 de Valois staged her first ballet, *Les Petits Riens*, as a curtain-raiser for the Christmas performance of *Hansel and Gretel*.

In December 1929 the governors decided to set up a special sub-committee to consider and advise on the operatic side of Sadler's Wells, which was to be on a much larger scale than at the Vic. It was agreed that the Vic could not bear any loss incurred by Sadler's Wells, and that the two foundations should be distinct entities in order to appeal to local patriotism. Their co-operation would be assured by a majority of governors being appointed by the Old Vic governors. There would be opera every night in one of the two theatres.[52]

On 21 October 1930 the governors decided that they would not allow the opening of Sadler's Wells unless the working capital could be brought up to £10,000. Captain Rowe succeeded in securing an advance of £3,000 without interest or security from the Duke of Devonshire. A further £2,500 from Harold Lloyd made the governors relent. A Finance Subcommittee was to take over from the hitherto informal meetings between Baylis and Rowe, and was to meet frequently.[53]

On 24 September 1930 Rowe wrote to George Bernard Shaw concerning the status of the two houses. Were Baylis, 'heaven forbid', to come to an untimely end, he wrote, their future would be legally assured by their status as charitable foundations. Even more important, Rowe believed that the Old Vic was now capable of an existence independent of Baylis; 'I have', he wrote, 'strong evidence that Miss Baylis has created not a Frankenstein monster but something that has come spiritually alive and will stay alive.' He would like to bet with Shaw, or 'some heavenly or post life bookie, that a hundred years hence the Old Vic and Sadler's Wells are carrying on strongly or more strongly than at present'. Behind the Old Vic, he explained, 'stand and work a body of enthusiasts who mean business'.[54]

# 3

# 1931–1937: 'A World of Awe and Wonder' – Lilian Baylis at Sadler's Wells

The new Sadler's Wells theatre opened on the foggy and frosty night of 6 January 1931. There was a packed house, with hundreds unable to gain admission. Edward J. Dent wrote in the renamed *The Old Vic and Sadler's Wells Magazine* that the opening of Sadler's Wells signified the 'establishment of a permanent English Opera House'. The singers would be able to spend more time with the company and so develop an even stronger *esprit de corps*. The tunes of *Madam Butterfly* and *Pagliacci*, he declared, would be hummed from Islington to Streatham Hill, and whistled by every errand boy from Peckham to Camden Town. It was always the popular audience that was the bedrock of a music-loving race.[1] 'We have a national opera,' wrote the music and drama critic Stephen Williams in the *Evening Standard*.[2]

Dent and Williams were overlooking the fact that Sadler's Wells actually opened with Shakespeare – *Twelfth Night* with John Gielgud and Ralph Richardson – and with speeches from the great and the good of the Vic and Finsbury. Baylis provoked much merriment when she dropped a basket of fruit that she had been given. The opera's sole contribution was the National Anthem, with Joan Cross singing the first verse and Constance Willis the second. According to Cross, the members of the opera company were duly offended that they had not been given a bigger role.[3]

In his memoirs Gielgud recollected how he and most of the musicians and actors hated the austerity of the 1,650-seat theatre and its unsympathetic acoustics. The theatre's architect, F. G. Chancellor, had been much influenced by cinema architecture. The result was an inelegant interior, and the small proscenium opening recessed from the pit exaggerated the sense of distance between stage and audience. Sumner Austin said there were only two good points on stage from which to sing, and much competition to get them. The backstage facilities were inadequate, and there were no boxes. Nonetheless, the extra space meant that the chorus could rehearse with the orchestra, and that opera could be staged for eight months of the year, and nearly every night of the week, in either the Vic or Sadler's Wells. The new British ballet company could also spread its wings.

It was not the last time that the company's move from one home to another would wreak havoc with the housekeeping. Sadler's Wells theatre opened at the height of a recession, £20,000 in debt, and turned out to be far more expensive to run than Baylis had anticipated. More singers, musicians, conductors and theatre staff were needed to cope with the increased workload. The repertoire had not been expanded to fill two theatres and the tired stagings of the Vic looked shabby and out of place in Sadler's Wells, just as those of Sadler's Wells would when the company eventually moved to the Coliseum in 1968.

The recession seriously affected the takings at the box offices, while the split programme between the two houses proved costly both in transport and in the enormous wear and tear on costumes and scenery as they were moved back and forth. The mixed programmes at both houses, Cross later wrote, proved a disastrous arrangement that staggered on for nearly four years. Frederick Hudson resigned shortly after the move. Then, after a splendid opening week, the box office began to suffer. On 14 January Rowe told the Executive Committee that although the drama company would pay its way with only moderately good attendances, opera would need much fuller houses to cover its £200-a-week expenses.

The audiences, however, did not materialise. The Shakespeare audience that had been cultivated over many years at the Vic did not transfer to Islington, and Sadler's Wells was rarely given a first night of its own and was unable therefore to benefit from the subsequent reviews and publicity. Sadler's Wells usually had the last drama week of a four-week run, which played to largely empty houses.[4] The opera audience that had filled the Old Vic two nights a week looked, in Cross's words, 'sadly meagre spread over five nights and a matinee'. The new theatre lacked the intimacy that Baylis had so ably developed at the Vic. It was, Cross wrote, a 'grim, cold, depressing struggle' for the opera company, who greatly missed the adulation of the crowded nights at the Old Vic.[5]

In May 1931, four months after the opening, it was agreed by the governors that Sadler's Wells would get some first nights in order to build up its audience for the drama. At the same time, however, it was learnt that an appeal to the Pilgrim Trust – a charity founded in 1930 by the American philanthropist Edward Stephen Harkness to support heritage and social welfare projects – had been unsuccessful. Consequently, the next Sadler's Wells season would open with a working balance of £4,000 and debts of £17,000 to the contractors and £3,000 to the architects. A campaign for funds was hastily launched, and in September it was agreed that Sadler's Wells should apply for a liquor licence.

Business at the beginning of the new season was 'deplorably unprofitable', largely because a production of *King John* was a box-office failure.[6] During her speech after the opening Baylis sought to maintain what Harcourt Williams described as the 'genuine optimism that flames like a torch behind her customary façade of financial ruin'.[7] In November 1931 she was concerned about the effect of the combination of the financial depression and the fact that London audiences could now choose from among an unprecedented number of operatic productions. Sadler's Wells and the Old Vic, together with Covent Garden's festival seasons, provided the equivalent of six performances a week. Although tickets at Sadler's Wells still cost only 5d to 5s, and Baylis cocked a little snook at Covent Garden's diamond tiaras, it was much harder to evoke local enthusiasm in Islington than it had been at the Vic in earlier days.[8]

The strain on both companies continued to be overwhelming. On 9 March 1932, when invited to a meeting of the Sadler's Wells Executive Committee to explain the catering system, Baylis sent one of the trustees, Miss Rowe, a note to say that 'the summoning of officials . . . to explain details of the working system involved an unreasonable strain on servants already overworked'.[9]

In April, in an effort to fill the stalls, Lady Hambledon, assisted by Lady Ottoline and Philip Morrell, formed the Sadler's Wells Society to encourage wealthy people to purchase books of admission vouchers. The society pledged to pay for the costumes and scenery for one play, one opera and one ballet each season. The first meeting raised £700 and the society made a £610 grant in its first season.[10] Despite these efforts, it looked as though the theatre would have to close, until in April 1932, at the eleventh hour, the Carnegie Trust agreed to cover the £8,200 debt for the equipment and running costs of the theatre during the previous and current seasons.

At the start of the 1931/2 season Reginald Rowe wrote a memorandum to the governors in which he said that it would be madness
to continue with the split system. Baylis, however, still refused to
concentrate drama at the Old Vic and opera and ballet at Sadler's
Wells, insisting instead on different combinations of planning. On
13 November it was agreed that there should be two weeks of
opera at Sadler's Wells and one of drama. The Vic would take over
production costs in return for Sadler's Wells handing over all box-
office receipts in excess of what was needed to keep the theatre
open.[11]

As well as the financial stresses, there was a vacuum on the production side. Edward J. Dent, Professor of Music at Cambridge, had
failed to get his friend Clive Carey appointed as Intendant or general director, since Baylis insisted that no one should be equal in
power to herself and the governors would not oppose her wishes.[12]
The lack of expertise sometimes caused a descent into farce: Cross
recalled a Marx Brothers-style mishap in 1931 when, shortly after
Hudson's retirement, the new stage manager hired an assistant who
simply pressed the button on the tab nearest to hand, so that curtains went up and down with irrelevant abandon.[13]

The novelist and writer Hugh Walpole recalled a cold wintry
evening when he went alone to a very poor performance of *Il trovatore*. The 6s stalls were empty, although the gallery was packed.
Walpole wrote: 'I heard that husky cockney voice in my ear, "'Tisn't
very good, dear, is it?" "No," I said, "it isn't." "If they had only
filled the six-shilling seats it would be better." "If the performance
were better they would fill the six-shilling seats." "Yes, it's a nasty
roundabout, dear," she answered.'[14]

In February 1932 the *Birmingham Post* pointed out that the
Sadler's Wells opera did not reach the standards of the Shakespeare
performances, and would not do so until the singers knew their
parts, the tenor could be persuaded not to walk off the stage in the
middle of a song, and the singers' rendering of the 'agony of death
no longer gave the impression of acute nervousness'.

Despite the financial difficulties, the 1931/2 season saw ten new
productions, five of which were prepared by Sidney Russell without
great distinction but which nonetheless provided a modest measure
of innovation and success. *Samson and Delilah* received 'a double

portion of first night enthusiasm', despite the low stock of Saint-Saëns at the time. According to *The Times*, Enid Cruickshank was an 'excessively luscious contralto' and de Valois provided an ingenious dance in the temple of Dagon. Even so, Percy Pitt was an inflexible conductor and not all the singers knew their parts.[15] The audiences were still 'lamentably small', according to *EK's Weekly* in November.

The main reason for the move to Sadler's Wells had been to enable the opera and the ballet to develop, and Baylis was determined that standards would improve. Henry Robinson, who had been a chorister with Carl Rosa and knew the repertoire inside out, took over as stage manager. He was efficient and devoted and, under his watchful eye, standards gradually began to improve, even, much to Cross's delight, the synchronisation between the last chord and the curtain. Lawrance Collingwood took charge of the orchestra in 1931, although Corri did not formally retire until 1935, when he received the first pension in the theatre's history.[16] Between them, Collingwood and Baylis set about forming a permanent opera company, enlarging the chorus and orchestra and providing regular rehearsals and coaching.

Joan Cross was herself a growing attraction at Vic-Wells. On 6 November 1931 she sang Dido in the first performance of *Dido and Aeneas* at Sadler's Wells, conducted by Constant Lambert. In March 1932 Sadler's Wells presented its first *Masked Ball*, with Cross as Amelia, in old bits of costume again. 'Figaro' [A. P. Hatton] in *Musical Opinion* now wrote of the 'sustained steadiness and quality' of her voice, while Tudor Davies sang with feeling and Edith Coates was a sturdy Ulrica. *Masked Ball*, and *Tannhäuser* later in the season, were packed out. In October 1932 Cross sang Butterfly for the first time in what was to become one of her signature roles.[17] As well as the quality of her voice and acting, her diction was always excellent.

On 29 April 1932 the *Radio Times* commented on the increasingly knowledgeable Sadler's Wells audience, scores under their arms, waving their coffee cups and arguing about the performance. Nearly everybody seemed to know everybody else.

In mid-1932 Thomas Beecham attempted to launch a National Opera Scheme, with the resources of Sadler's Wells included in the project. After many attempts since 1910 to found a permanent opera company as well as opera seasons, based on private subscriptions, Beecham had returned to Covent Garden as artistic director. The company he had founded in 1922, the Beecham Opera Company, had been taken over and absorbed by Covent Garden as the British National Opera Company and was to form the basis of the new seasons.

The conductor Geoffrey Toye, who had been a governor of Sadler's Wells since 1925, became co-director of the Wells for the 1932/3 season. Toye was also involved with Beecham in his endeavour to create a new syndicate with Lady Cunard to put on seasonal programmes at Covent Garden. American-born heiress Maud (Emerald) Cunard, Beecham's close friend, was a society hostess who held a salon of musicians, artists and writers. As a lover of grand opera, and a director of the Royal Opera House Company, she helped Beecham raise subscriptions from her wealthy friends for his Covent Garden venture. She herself took the 'Omnibus' box, entertaining guests to dinner before the performance. Emerald Cunard represented the social exclusivity that Baylis and Dent were determined to keep well away from Sadler's Wells.

When Beecham suggested greater co-operation between Covent Garden, the Carl Rosa and Sadler's Wells, the chairman of the governors, Reginald Rowe, was opposed and persuaded the governing body not to take a decision.[18] Baylis, on the other hand, pressured both by the financial difficulties and by calls in the press to unite all the operatic forces, was reported as telling the *Manchester Guardian* that she would like to see such a union with Sadler's Wells at the centre, under Beecham.[19]

*The Times* was adamant that amalgamation would make Sadler's Wells the poor relation of the 'grand season' and would be disastrous. What was needed was a cosmopolitan company giving masterpieces sung by the world's greatest singers, and at the same time a permanent establishment singing in English, developing home-grown talent.[20] It was an obvious, simple and sensible system but it only evolved after many vicissitudes and crises.

Dent was also determined that Beecham should not take over Sadler's Wells. He wished he could devote his life to Sadler's Wells, but he could not afford to give up his Cambridge professorship.[21] On 7 October 1932 he reported that during a visit to Sadler's Wells with a party of friends, Lady Cunard had upset Baylis 'dreadfully' by saying that the orchestra was shocking. Dent had consoled Baylis, determined not to have her confidence shaken. 'Cunard and Beecham would not have put their noses in the Vic ten years ago,' he wrote, and 'Beecham thinks of the company as a toy and must not be allowed to destroy it.'[22] Confidence was boosted in October 1932, when Rowe was able to report an encouraging increase in the takings of both theatres, despite a disastrous *Cymbeline*.[23]

Beecham continued his efforts to unite operatic forces. In November a 250-member National Opera Council was set up to promote agreement between Covent Garden, Sadler's Wells, Beecham's new syndicate the Imperial League and the BBC, with £25,000 from the BBC and £20,000 from Beecham himself. In December Toye became the managing director of the Imperial League, which enjoyed the patronage of some of England's wealthiest men. It sought to modernise Covent Garden and present opera seasons both of Beecham and his London Philharmonic and of visiting companies. In December Beecham was described as 'artistic adviser' to Sadler's Wells in *The Times*.

*The Times* continued to urge Vic-Wells to shun any association with Covent Garden, which was, it wrote, a 'dead weight in the neck of any progressive operatic movement in England'. It pointed out that of the two, Vic-Wells was the going concern and hampered only by lack of funds. The *Illustrated London News* also stressed that Vic-Wells were the only theatres in London with a 'consistent policy and artistic ambitions'.[24]

During the second Sadler's Wells season there was a definite improvement in the operatic fare, as Baylis came to accept the need for new producers who would help the singers to relinquish their cliché-ridden traditional poses. Carey believed that Sadler's Wells artists, who, like some of their German contemporaries, were now part of a permanent company and knew each other well, could bring a new and revitalised approach to their work.[25] Dent was the inspiration behind the Vic-Wells vision of creating a distinct entity for each opera produced, introducing several of his protégés to Baylis, including the thirty-four-year-old director John Barritt (Jack) Gordon, who was responsible for freshening up the productions at Sadler's Wells. Gordon, who was concerned with the detail of production and enabling performers to act, was a self-effacing man, given the unofficial title in the *Vic-Wells Magazine* 'The Producer Who Never Raised His Voice'. As well as supervising many revivals, he directed seventeen new productions between 1931 and 1942, starting with *La traviata* in October 1931. Dent, who saw it in February 1933, thought it 'altogether the most poetical' he had ever seen, and that Cross's Violetta was 'marvellously good'. He later said that Gordon's *La traviata* was the first time that it had been seen as a 'serious and beautiful work and deeply moving play and not just a Melba night out and a hopelessly vulgar and ridiculous opera'.* It was a shame, he thought, that there was no time to 'hammer it in' before it had to give way to drama, and the situation showed how essential it was for the drama and opera to be separated.[26] In November 1932 Gordon directed *The Devil Take Her* by Arthur Benjamin, and in February 1933 he directed *The Force of Destiny*.

In the *Vic-Wells Magazine*, Carey had warned the audience not to be horrified if Mephistopheles no longer wore scarlet tights or Micaëla 'a blue frock and high heels', but he need not have feared.[27] Baylis's concern that the new productions would lose loyalists proved unfounded. She admitted in the 1932/3 annual report that 'it now appears that the one thing they had been hankering after for years was just this new viewpoint'. She also recognised the need to expand the repertoire and get rid of some old favourites.

The improved standards, however, were proving too expensive to pay for themselves. Even though opera takings were up by 15 per cent, the Shakespeare had been disappointing.[28] In April 1933 Reginald Rowe insisted that there could not be another season without some form of endowment, as a result of which the BBC granted £6,000 for a season in return for broadcasting rights. Additionally, the Duke of Devonshire paid £6,000 towards the building debt of £20,000. In 1934, after much effort, Vic-Wells was relieved of its annual payment of at least £3,400 in entertainment

---

* Encouraged by Dent, Gordon had joined the staff of the Cologne Opera House after he left Oxford and the Royal College of Music in 1924. There he had worked with Hans Strobach, who was responsible for the visit of the Dresden Opera Company to Covent Garden in 1936. Gordon was very generous to Sadler's Wells, often anonymously donating gifts, including the dresses for *La traviata* and a gift of £2,500 in 1948 'in admiration of the work of Lilian Baylis'.

tax. Baylis claimed that she had told the Chancellor of the Exchequer, Neville Chamberlain, that she would have to close both theatres if he did not remove the tax and that she would then lecture in the States saying what a philistine he was.

The battle for independence from the Beecham incursion continued. Beecham's suggestion that Vic-Wells should stage *Salome* and *Siegfried* was, Dent thought, 'absurd', in terms of both the audiences and the resources available. He was supporting Baylis, who had 'naturally kicked violently', but considered that it was 'tiresome having these things foisted on us just when we are beginning to build up our own style'.[29] He was not, however, entirely confident of being able to maintain the direction in which Vic-Wells was going. He felt that he lacked influence with the board, which viewed him as a visionary with no head for the practical economic difficulties. Nor was he certain of Baylis's loyalty if it came to choosing between him and Beecham. She had, he told Carey, a genuine personal affection for him but no ability to estimate his, Gordon's and Carey's 'corporate value as a group of friends with the same ideals helping each other'. He feared that she might at any moment sacrifice their artistic ideals 'at the altar of Tommy'. By August, however, he reported that Baylis was getting suspicious of both Beecham and Toye, and was looking for someone strong on opera for the board.[30]

The company was definitely benefiting from Dent's vision and Collingwood's guidance, and was travelling in the right direction. From 1931 to 1937 Sadler's Wells staged fifty operas, compared with thirty at the Vic in the previous thirty years. *Così fan tutte* was produced in 1933 with Austin, Arnold Matters, Cross and Winnifred Kennard, and with Warwick Braithwaite conducting. In January 1933 *The Times* reported on the improvement of the company. Steadily, the more adventurous choice of repertoire and the slightly higher standard of production began to attract a new audience. That same month 'Figaro' in *Musical Opinion* wrote of the new *Otello*: 'At the Wells . . . they worship the job, which means they subordinate themselves to the composer.' The chorus 'struck the true dramatic note at the outset without hesitation and sustained it to the end'.[31] In September Gordon's *La bohème*, with Joan Cross as Mimì, showed the company's ensemble to good effect. It was sold out and the audience was delighted by it. The

*Yorkshire Post* commented on the renewed affection in the audience's relationship with the company, just two years after the opening of Sadler's Wells.[32]

A landmark production was Carey's *The Snow Maiden*, premiered on 12 April 1933. Collingwood, who loved the Russian repertoire, had been pressing to introduce Rimsky-Korsakov's opera to Sadler's Wells. Carey brought in the Russian designer Elizabeth Polunin, who provided 'a riot of colour mostly with painted hessian'. The company were able to fill all the roles except the title role, with Edith Coates scoring a marked success as Lehl, and with de Valois' ballet also involved. The production was recognised as setting a new standard, and the box office responded. Such was the success of *The Snow Maiden* that Baylis insisted that Rimsky-Korsakov's *Tsar Saltan* be put on while Chekhov's *The Cherry Orchard* was playing at the Old Vic in October. *Tsar Saltan* was well received by the press, with the scenery much commented on, but the audience was not so keen.[33] In November Carey directed Gluck's *Orpheus and Eurydice*, translated by Dent, who was determined to press for English to be used in the first Sadler's Wells production of the opera.

The following year Collingwood introduced Tchaikovsky's *Eugene Onegin* to Sadler's Wells on 12 December, with Cross as Tatiana, Coates as Olga, Henry Wendon as Lensky and Sumner Austin, who was too old, miscast as Onegin. Carey directed. Cross wrote of her wry affection for the Dent translation, giving as an example Gremin's immortal words: 'I should not be human/ if I did not adore that woman.' Ernest Newman in the *Sunday Times* called *Onegin* 'a gallant effort', despite being highly critical of Tchaikovsky's stagecraft and musical range, as well as of the orchestra and the singers for their age and their generalised, inappropriate operatic style. Only Cross and Henry Wendon received a modicum of praise. Nonetheless, *Eugene Onegin*, like *The Snow Maiden*, was a brave repertory departure, and began a tradition of Sadler's Wells introducing work that was virtually unknown to the British opera-going public.

Another noble and long-lasting, if less consistently positive, tradition also began at this time, with brave attempts to encourage new English compositions. In October of the 1934/5 season Charles Villiers Stanford's *The Travelling Companion* was given. It was kept in the repertoire for three seasons. On 17 October Collingwood's own opera, *Macbeth*, received its premiere.

When in 1933 Hitler came to power in Germany, the Sadler's Wells mission of developing an English opera tradition was set in sharper relief and faced a new rivalry with the arrival of refugees from Nazi Germany. In 1934 John Christie invited Fritz Busch from Dresden and Carl Ebert from the Städtische Oper Berlin to direct his new summer opera festival at Glyndebourne. Vienna-born Rudolf Bing, who in 1933 was assistant to the Intendant of the Charlottenburg Opera, Berlin, became the manager of the company. Glyndebourne was the antithesis of everything Sadler's Wells stood for, both in its social exclusivity and in its adherence to original-language performance. Nonetheless, even if the majority of the audience could not understand the text, the work of Ebert and Busch was an inspiring demonstration of the kind of rigorous collaboration between music and text that Sadler's Wells aspired to but rarely achieved.

From 1934 Sadler's Wells decided to continue on its own path, acutely aware of the potential effect of both the Glyndebourne and the Covent Garden powers on its future development. There was a growing rift between the parties, not least over conflicting social ambitions and the desire for status. Dent believed that Beecham wanted to make Vic-Wells the 'nursery garden' for the seasons at Covent Garden, which he hoped to run on a grand scale.

Collingwood seemed to Dent to be the most effective barrier to Beecham's ambitions; Baylis trusted him and he was 'an honest man and good musician, who knew more about opera than anyone else at Vic-Wells'. Dent urged Carey to assemble an informal committee with Gordon, Austin and Collingwood and Muriel Gough, who had retired from singing in 1931 and become a governor. They should meet regularly and press for their opera policy.[34] This advice was heeded; from October 1934 Collingwood, Sumner Austin and Gordon combined to support Baylis in the planning and casting of the repertoire. Sumner Austin together with Clive Carey and Gordon were in charge of production. They were known at Sadler's Wells as 'The Soviet'.

On 17 November 1934 Carey produced the company's first *Die Fledermaus*. The production had a classic mid-1930s Vic-Wells cast of Joan Cross as Rosalinda, Ruth Naylor as Adele, Arthur Cox as

Alfred and Tudor Davies as von Eisenstein. Warwick Braithwaite conducted. Dent could not bear the 'dreadful Viennese vulgar music' and hoped that Carey would dissuade Baylis from doing any more operettas, which he thought were 'undignified for our theatre'. However, he enjoyed and admired Carey's 'marvellously clever production', saying that 'we laughed like children at the comic business'.[35] *Die Fledermaus* soon became a staunch favourite with critics and audiences alike, starting a long-term tradition of operetta at Sadler's Wells.

In September John Barbirolli had conducted Gordon's production of *The Barber of Seville* in Dent's 'astonishingly alive' new translation. It was, according to the *Saturday Review*, worth going a long way to see and hear the show, as had been Barbirolli's conducting of Joan Cross in *Madam Butterfly* earlier in the month.[36]

The ballet under Ninette de Valois, with Constant Lambert as music director, was growing fast into a fine and respected company. From 1932/3 the company performed two evenings a week plus weekend matinees. The choreographer Frederick Ashton, together with Anton Dolin and Alicia Markova, who were already established stars, made guest appearances. New talents rapidly emerged, including Robert Helpmann and Margot Fonteyn. Artists and designers involved included Rex Whistler, Cecil Beaton, Duncan Grant and Sophie Fedorovitch. By 1937 the company numbered twenty women and ten men, with two resident choreographers, a resident conductor and forty students in the school. As the decade proceeded, the ballet was helping to pay for the opera.

There were also revolutionary developments in the drama department. Tyrone Guthrie had taken over from Harcourt Williams for the 1933/4 season. Guthrie, an Ulster Scot, was an imposingly tall thirty-three-year-old director who had been educated at public school and Oxford. His gentle voice, strong personality and sense of humour gave him great command and rapport with performers. His resolution, vision and integrity were also qualities that were of great value in the development of Vic-Wells. His background, however, was in experimental work with the Oxford Playhouse under J. B. Fagan and the Cambridge festival theatre, and he had had little experience of Shakespeare, with just one production, *Love's Labour's Lost*, under his belt.

In the 1933/4 season there were three months of drama at the Vic and one at the Wells. Baylis was hesitant to employ Guthrie, thinking him 'too West-Endy', and was fearful that he would exploit the Vic. She realised, however, that he had the energy she now lacked to direct drama at Vic-Wells. His enthusiasm, commitment, sense of humour and clear, vibrant commands soon galvanised the company, as did the clarity of his vision and his imagination. Before long, Baylis was telling Sybil Thorndike that Guthrie was 'one of the elect', that he and his wife Judy were 'beautiful people who make beauty wherever they go'.[37]

The time was ripe for change. Shortly after his departure, Harcourt Williams urged Baylis to change the split system and suggested that Vic-Wells needed to lose its parochial flavour. The audience, he wrote, had changed after 'fifty years of solid industry fired by the evangelical enthusiasm of those fine Victorian women'. Baylis no longer needed to speak just to the gallery, for in the body of the theatre there now sat 'middle class school teachers, the intellectual new poor, the typist clerks of both sexes, young women who work all day in the city, students of every kind'. These people wanted intelligent, well-thought-out performances.[38]

At the time of his arrival at the Vic-Wells Guthrie was reacting against naturalism and full sets. He described these as elaborate and careful pieces of antiquarian reconstruction that hovered 'uneasily between the realistic and the portable, alternating between the "front scenes" played against curtains, or pseudo-realistically painted drop scenes as in Vaudeville'.[39]

Having persuaded the Pilgrim Trust to give £1,750, Guthrie created a semi-permanent stage set which would offer the facilities supposed to have been available in the Elizabethan theatres. This consisted of stairs leading to a balcony, and underneath them a cubby-hole for intimate scenes and in which to hide props. The money saved would go into costumes, and although Baylis thought that having no scenery would be 'rather dreary' she approved of the economy and welcomed the new wardrobe stock. Guthrie recalled that she calculated with lightning speed that she could rig out the opera choristers for *Rigoletto* in the dresses that the Pilgrim Trust would provide for *Measure for Measure*. The permanent structure, however, was too obtrusive and clumsy to work as intended; neither Guthrie nor the architect had had enough experience. He was disappointed with his own *Tempest*.[40]

Much to Baylis's initial chagrin, Guthrie also brought stars with him, including Flora Robson and Charles Laughton, who was a tremendous success at the box office, although he was shocked to be asked to do more fundraising even though his performances in *The Tempest* were sold out. Guthrie's *Cherry Orchard* was also so successful that they had to extend its run. The writer Alan Pryce-Jones noted how the inhabitants of the Cromwell Road were being 'impelled into their peaceful Daimlers, driving into the dangerous purlieus south of the river'.[41] There was an immediate improvement in the box-office drama receipts to £6,083, while the opera was making a loss of £1,281 and the ballet a loss of £1,291. This improvement, however, did nothing to assuage Baylis's dislike of star actors or the resulting visits south of the river by 'West End' audiences.[42]

Baylis supported Guthrie against the governors, but her own relationship with him was volatile, and when she passed on attacking letters from some shocked members of the audience he was hurt and felt undermined that she should regard him as an untrustworthy 'irresponsible iconoclast'. 'What I think she did not realise,' he later wrote, 'was how much I admired her achievement.'[43] Furthermore, despite Guthrie's strongly argued plea to discontinue drama at Sadler's Wells, the governors refused in January 1934, arguing that it would 'break faith' with those who had worked to open the Wells.

Guthrie left after one season, the annual report commenting on his 'bringing into the theatre a great many of the younger generation'. Baylis was determined to wrest back control. Henry Cass, who was less controversial and equally young but less talented, took over. The paying customers, however, did not respond to him as they had to Guthrie.

During the mid-1930s Sadler's Wells began to be packed for the new opera productions, which gave the house an exciting atmosphere. One of the new offerings of the 1935/6 season was another important Collingwood contribution: the first performance outside Russia of the original version of Mussorgsky's *Boris Godunov*, produced by Carey in September. The vigour and fullness of tone of the chorus was commented on, as was Carey's creation of a 'stage illusion of much poetic aptness'.[44] Another innovation was Verdi's

*Falstaff*, which was rarely performed at the time. It opened on 11 March 1936. With its delicate, quicksilver 'point-making' and changes of mood, it was recognised as an ambitious undertaking for an English company. The orchestra and some of the principals were nonetheless praised, especially the Australian baritone Arnold Matters for his good articulation and 'admirable timing'.[45] It was the only 'lesser-known' opera to draw large houses, as a consequence of which it was decided to add only Wagner's *The Master-singers* and Verdi's *Aida* before Christmas.[46]

Too often there were half-empty houses for the regular repertoire, except for such favourites as *Faust*, *Lohengrin* and *Carmen*, although the temperament of the company proved to be almost insurmountable in *Carmen*. Baylis was constantly worried. Joan Cross later recalled overhearing her mutterings about how to pay the week's salaries.[47] The 1935/6 annual report noted the enlargement of the orchestra to forty-eight, which was twice the size of Corri's original group, the expense of which was frightening to Baylis. She missed her old favourites, such as Michael Balfe's *Bohemian Girl* and Julius Benedict's *Lily of Killarney*.

With great reluctance, Baylis was finally forced to recognise that opera was more popular at Sadler's Wells and drama more popular at the Vic. From the 1935/6 season, the charity commissioners changed the terms of the trusts, making it possible to present opera and ballet exclusively at Sadler's Wells and drama at the Vic. Prices still had to be kept low under the terms of the Sadler's Wells Foundation; artisans and labourers should still be provided with 'recreation and instruction'.

Chastened and exhausted, Baylis welcomed Guthrie back for the 1936/7 season after the governors agreed to his condition of runs of not less than three and no more than six weeks. She decided he should be appointed director of drama in November 1936. Although Guthrie was taking a considerable drop in salary, he was pleased by her offer and after his return was staunchly supported by Baylis. Each had learnt to appreciate the other during the intervening season. Guthrie later wrote: 'The interim had taught me the difference between a theatrical institution with a policy and the haphazard conditions of the commercial theatre, where no manager, not even Beaumont [the West End impresario], seemed to have much more of a plan than to produce "a success".'[48]

When Baylis was honoured at a Foyles literary lunch on 26 April 1936, Guthrie described her as a human dynamo and explained how the lively atmosphere of the theatre resulted from the low prices that encouraged a young audience. Baylis, by then very famous but ill and tired, began to see Guthrie as a potential successor in charge of the whole operation. His gradual taking over of the mantle marked a change in the role of Vic-Wells, despite the terms of the trust agreement. For Guthrie, Shakespeare was not there to be a moral, social or political platform, or 'educative' in the sense that Emma Cons would have understood it. The audience at the Old Vic had long since ceased to consist of 'the good poor waiting humbly for evangelical peers to lift them out of the gutter'. Guthrie was determined that the last vestiges of the Old Vic's great tradition of social service should give way to a highly professional outfit. He brought with him George Chamberlain as stage manager and insisted that the two theatres should have separate staff and finances, so that the drama no longer subsidised the more expensive opera.[49]

During the 1936/7 season Guthrie clearly stamped his authority on the drama company, which included Alec Guinness and Laurence Olivier – at twenty-nine already a romantic film lead – whom Guthrie persuaded to do a Freudian Hamlet. Also appearing were Michael Redgrave and Edith Evans in *As You Like It*. *Twelfth Night* included Olivier's Sir Toby and Guinness's Sir Andrew. There were, however, empty seats even for Olivier's Hamlet, and some of the old guard resented the importation of a film star. Guthrie successfully took the Vic's *Hamlet* to Elsinore in 1937 as part of the King of Denmark's silver-jubilee celebrations. He also took Ibsen's *Ghosts* and *Measure for Measure* to the Buxton summer festival.

The opera progressed in the autumn of 1936 with *Falstaff*, Gordon's new *Carmen*, *Madam Butterfly* and *The Mastersingers*, and Carey's *Aida*. In the cast of *La bohème* in September were Cross and a new tenor, D. Morgan Jones. The new *Aida* opened a month later, directed by Carey and designed by Powell Lloyd, Edith Coates's husband, after research in the British Museum. Together they contrived to create a feeling of spaciousness in the physically restricted conditions of Sadler's Wells. *The Times* thought it an exhilarating evening despite a lack of both pomp and magnificent singing, with Molly de Gunst a young and fresh-voiced Aida.

Carey produced Dent's new version of *Figaro* in January 1937 with Arnold Matters. He also directed *The Magic Flute* in March and *Hugh the Drover*, a Ralph Vaughan Williams ballad opera, in April. Sumner Austin's *Rigoletto* had benefited not just from the Pilgrim Trust costumes but also from Dent's new translation, which he had prepared in 1936. He had continued to press for every word of the text to be clear and meaningful and had written to Carey while he was translating to say that he hoped he would not mind the 'deliberate brutality' of Sparafucile's and Maddalena's language, and the places where the audience might laugh. He had seen enough Shakespeare not to be afraid of laughs in tragedy.[50]

In November Gordon directed *Fidelio*. Carey thought that the intimacy of the theatre and Gordon's direction were both excellent, and the dialogue carefully spoken, but that Braithwaite did not get the singers or players to reach the 'deep *intimate* soul of it'. It nonetheless had good houses.[51] The lesser-known works were, however, still viewed with suspicion, although this was not true of the theatre and ballet, where modern work was more popular. The year's loss of £7,590 was made up by anonymous donations and gifts.

Baylis has been accused of demanding too much from her singers and musicians for the paltry salaries she continued to pay. Opera, however, was clearly never going to pay for itself in the way the theatre was beginning to. In July 1937, in offering Cross her contract for the next season, Baylis reluctantly but firmly rejected her request for a higher fee. 'I am really honest when I say I would like to give you more money and would do so gladly if there were any,' she wrote. Cross was, she confided, paid more than anyone else in the company per performance and, although she valued her work tremendously, she felt that if there were any money to spare, then 'some of the poorer paid artists should get a little more, so that they could afford lessons, and give up the endless outside work which wearies them, and spoils their voices'. Management had tried to improve salaries for the new season, but only on a very small scale. 'My dear,' she concluded to Cross, 'I do hate not agreeing to any suggestion of yours. I know you are so truly one of us, willing to help in all our work whether you are in the cast or no . . . but if those who work for us thought first of money, our work would not be alive.' The season had at last seen the debt of the theatres wiped out, but this, she explained, was because of the plays and 'Olivier losing many thousands by helping us'. The financial sacrifice would continue until there was a 'really good subsidy given for opera'. She added: 'God bless you and continue to help us.'[52]*

In the autumn of 1937 Baylis, then sixty-three, told Father Andrew: 'I know if I go on as I am going my work will kill me, but I don't see why it should be otherwise.'[53] As her health declined, she was looking for someone to take over the opera company. She asked Carey in 1937, but he declined, feeling that he lacked the ruthlessness required to run such an organisation.[54] At that time Vaughan Williams suggested to Baylis that Dent himself should be the new director of the company, but Dent felt that he was too old, not good at business and could not afford to lose his Cambridge pension.[55] The problem remained unresolved.

For the new drama season, Guthrie brought Michel St-Denis to direct Shakespeare's *Macbeth*, which was due to open on 23 November. Just before its planned opening Guthrie decided that it was not ready and postponed it. This was a great shock to Baylis, as was the death of one of her beloved dogs, run over by a car. She had a heart attack on 23 November, although she recovered sufficiently to express her wish that *Macbeth* should open as planned and that performances of *Tabarro* and *Gianni Schicchi* should not be cancelled before sending reassuring messages to her staff. The recovery was brief, however, and she died after a second heart attack at her home in Stockwell on 25 November 1937.

Sybil Thorndike described Baylis as the 'most courageous woman that was ever associated with the theatre'. Even during the war

---

* In conversation with the author, the designer Timothy O'Brien spoke with some vehemence about Baylis's taking advantage of the people who worked for her by quoting God's purpose. It should not be forgotten, however, that all experimental and non-commercial theatre, without state subsidy, suffered from the same dilemma. Norman Marshall in *The Other Theatre* (London: John Lehmann, 1947) tells many stories of penury and eventual disbandment of non-commercial theatre before the war. The Gate Theatre, for instance, was often forced to pay the cast a few shillings a week, and the directors used to come in early and clean the theatre: 'Even a charwoman was a luxury which the theatre could not afford' (p. 43).

Thorndike never saw her 'give in to tiredness or discouragement.'[56] With her faith and singleness of purpose she not only focused her energy but also, in the words of Reginald Rowe, succeeded in firing up others with 'her white-hot zeal' to devote themselves whole-heartedly to her cause. Combining ruthless frugal determination with generosity and kindness, she commanded dedication and service without which the three companies would not have existed. The year before her death W. H. Auden had written that the two theatres of Sadler's Wells and the Old Vic were amongst 'the best and strongest civilising influences to be found in London'. It was, he said, 'a tribute to Miss Baylis that this steady and immense progress has taken place'.[57]

Dent was ambivalent about the loss of Baylis, as he felt that she had in some ways hindered the great project and that much energy had been expended in convincing her to do things that ultimately proved immensely successful. He and Carey were endeavouring to educate audiences, critics and casts to the subtleties and humour of works, even those as well known as *Don Giovanni* and *Figaro*. Dent felt that the younger generation, including Guthrie, understood this ideal better than did the older, more experienced types at Covent Garden, the British National Opera Company and Carl Rosa.[58] He was not entirely fair, as Baylis had in fact been open to new ideas and especially to new talent. In March 1938, six months after her death, the governors allowed Guthrie to do *Hamlet* in modern dress despite their own misgivings, acknowledging that Baylis 'had always been prepared to support her producer even against personal inclination when she felt that his point was a matter of conviction and sincere thought'.

Baylis had provided her own obituary in a speech on the radio in which she articulated her belief about the theatre:

The theatre isn't an excuse for wonderful evening gowns and jewels,' she said. 'It isn't a fad of people with long hair and sandals, or a perquisite of varsity men and women; good drama isn't only for the students of training colleges and boys and girls swotting for the Oxford and Cambridge Locals. It is a crying need of working men and women who need to see beyond the four walls of their offices, workshops and homes into a world of awe and wonder. Furthermore all art is a bond between rich and poor; it allows of no class distinctions . . . the theatre is perhaps the most easily understood branch of art for the man and woman in the street.[59]

Baylis had built up and educated her audience, and she had also created the basis for an infrastructure in which talent could grow. Cross recognised Baylis's support, friendship and faith in her over the years: 'She put up with what she considered my dreadful acting, all the time trying to create the circumstances in which I could improve. And what she did for me she did for countless others . . . I grew to love her dearly, while my respect for her increased with the years that I worked for her.'[60]

Above all, as *The Times* recognised in December 1936 in its review of Gordon's new *Mastersingers* – with Arnold Matters as Sachs – it was the ensemble Baylis had created that allowed for such progress. 'Ambition has not vaulted too high,' it said, and the production 'proved the value of a permanent company in a permanent theatre, for without these conditions such excellent results could hardly have been achieved. For the merit of the performance lay not in any outstanding individual performers but in the high standard of the ensemble, the careful study of minor parts, and in the unusual vitality of the whole action.'

# 4

# 1937–1945: A Heroic Struggle – Joan Cross and the War

The spirit of Lilian Baylis lived on long after her death and remained a constant and lasting inspiration for the company she created. Hugh Walpole described a long queue outside Sadler's Wells for a revival of *The Mastersingers* on 5 January 1938. Inside there was 'so much enjoyment radiating from the stage out to the audience and back from the audience to the stage again'. Baylis had made it 'very easy and simple for an onlooker to feel he is sharing in a creative art'.[1] On 18 March it was reported that the Lilian Baylis Memorial Fund had raised £15,261. One elderly woman from the Old Kent Road, who had been a galleryite for seventeen years, had sent £3 she had saved up. The work continued to develop, with the company performing its first *Valkyrie* on 8 December.

It took some time for the companies to find their new leadership. Meanwhile, Sir Reginald Rowe became temporary head of Vic-Wells, with Clive Carey, Sumner Austin and Jack B. Gordon remaining in charge of the opera company. Professor Edward J. Dent continued to exert influence in the background, in the hope that the governors would remain satisfied with the 'Soviet'.[2] In March 1938 he was keen to maintain the work of the last twenty years, which had built up a real tradition of opera in English – singing, acting, ensemble and production. The companies should plan ahead, lead opinion and send out tours. Even though he was not much in favour of Wagner, he recognised that Sadler's Wells was still the only place in the world where people could see *The Mastersingers* or *The Valkyrie* for 6d. Dent advised a repertory based on British opera: one new work a year in addition to the 'classics' such as Mozart, Gluck and Beethoven, the 'indispensables' such as *Faust* and *Carmen*, and 'prestige operas' such as either *Oberon* or something modern such as *Jenůfa*. The company should stay at Sadler's Wells for five or ten years, but if it moved to a central theatre – for example, Covent Garden or Her Majesty's, Haymarket – it would have to reconsider its policy. The ideal would be a pair of houses, large and small 'as in Munich or Stuttgart of old'.[3]

Not all Dent's advice was heeded. When Carey planned *Der Rosenkavalier*, Dent warned him against the tendency towards 'heavyweight opera', for which he feared the scenery would be a great difficulty. He urged Carey to consider Janáček's *Jenůfa*, which he had seen in Prague in 1935 at the German Opera.[4] Dent was determined to maintain the principles of Sadler's Wells. When fellow governor Muriel Gough reported to the board on 18 March that Busch and Ebert wanted to do an opera at Sadler's Wells, the board minutes recorded that 'it was felt that the employment of foreigners would require careful consideration'.

Dent's new translation of *Don Giovanni* was heard on 9 February 1938. His intention was to convey the impression that 'rape and murder, adultery and especially sacrilege' were 'great fun'. Cross not only sang Donna Anna with 'coloratura and dramatic force', as he told Carey, but also looked slim in her new costume, proving his concern about her weight to be unfounded.[5] He found Charles Reading's tinted serge curtains and pale buff masonry dingy and boring; without traps through which to drag Giovanni to hell, he thought the devils unconvincing. Nonetheless, it had been a sellout, with the theatre so crowded as to be uncomfortable. On 22 February *Fidelio* proved popular with the gallery, though less so with the stalls.[6]

The crisis in Europe was intensifying. It was from the Berlin Kroll Opera House – now serving as the political assembly following the burning of the Reichstag – on 20 February that Hitler not only warned of the imminent Nazi takeover of Austria but also threatened the rights of the 10 million Germans living outside the Reich. On the night of 11 March Hitler's troops crossed into Austria. In the weeks that followed, all those who had opposed the *Anschluss* were systematically arrested and sent to concentration camps. Anti-Jewish laws were introduced and brutally enforced. The stream of refugees from eastern Europe grew as Hitler built up pressure on Czechoslovakia.

The MP and writer A. P. Herbert made an appeal on behalf of Sadler's Wells in the *Sunday Pictorial* on 20 March. In it he linked the perilous international situation to the insecure financial state of Sadler's Wells. By the time his appeal was printed, he wrote with irony, another small country might have 'surrendered joyfully to a benevolent dictator'. Supporting Sadler's Wells was an 'assertion of sanity at a crazy time'. Salzburg, famed as a free centre of international art, would become a closed preserve of Aryan music and Nazi thought. 'Let us be grateful', he wrote, 'that at Sadler's Wells the tenors and ballerinas are not judged by their political thoughts.'

The threat of war loomed throughout the summer of 1938. In late September Prime Minister Neville Chamberlain delayed war by sacrificing Czechoslovakia, but not before trenches were dug in London parks and gas masks fitted throughout Britain. It was not long before the international crisis began to take its toll on the Vic-Wells companies. Underground stations were closed and the governors reported that takings were well down in October. Even the modern-dress *Hamlet* with Alec Guinness was losing money, despite its beauty. The continuing international crisis, combined with losses of £2,500 in the previous season, put the two theatres into a difficult situation. In November a shocked Rowe reported that 'the opera company was far from paying for itself', even with the BBC subsidy: the total receipts for the opera the previous year had been £25,000, while the expense of salaries alone had been £32,000 – figures that Dent thought 'fantastic'.[7]

It was decided that Lord Lytton would canvas the government for a grant for both companies. On 10 February 1939 the governors decided to institute savings of £800 by cutting down the orchestra and by not paying a proposed £100 salary increase to producers and conductors. There would be no more than three new productions in the 1939/40 season, with the cost of each not exceeding £600.[8]

The lack of leadership within the opera company was also causing difficulties. Carey was so unhappy that he was considering leaving. He told Dent on 5 November that his new production of *Tannhäuser* had 'really crashed' as a result of the extremely reduced rehearsal time: Sadler's Wells, he wrote, could not be run by committee. Although he had the right sort of artistic vision for an Intendant, Carey did not think that he had enough business sense or hardness. While he had gained confidence with age, he felt he had 'lost the drive'.[9]

Meanwhile, Dent was concerned that on the board only Muriel Gough and Dent himself were standing up for the opera. Rowe,

having taken the place of Baylis, knew a great deal about legal matters and business but was more interested in the drama and ballet.
Dent was also worried about the lack of direction in the opera company: stagnation was caused by the producers trying not to hurt
each other's feelings, and Collingwood, who was a good musician
and knowledgeable, lacked leadership quality.[10] After Dent saw
*Tannhäuser*, however, he informed Carey that the only thing wrong
with it had been the puritanical Venusberg. He suggested to Carey
that he tell Ninette to follow Baylis's example and to 'pray before
she goes to bed that God will send her lustful thoughts'.[11]

A Vic-Wells Mediterranean tour in December 1938 had been
arranged by the British Council, despite threats of anti-fascist agita-
tion if Italy were included. The governors, refusing 'to be drawn
into politics', had agreed to the tour. The modern-dress *Hamlet* was
so popular in Milan that Guthrie received an invitation to direct
*Caesar and Cleopatra* at the Manzoni theatre in Milan the following year, which he hoped to be able to accept.[12]

The third new production of the 1938/9 season was the new Jack
Gordon/Powell Lloyd *Il trovatore*, which opened on 25 January
1939. Dent had translated it with great difficulty, laying on the
melodrama as 'hot and strong' as he could. During his work he had
urged the directors to try to make it clear that there was a civil war
going on, with Manrico on the rebel side and Luna on the royal-
ist's.[13]

On 24 February Guthrie became the director of the Old Vic and
Sadler's Wells in charge of general policy for both theatres. The governors believed that he had the right 'qualities of leadership and a
whole-hearted interest in the aims of the two theatres'. He would
receive an annual salary of £1,000 and a car allowance. After his
appointment, Guthrie moved the offices to Sadler's Wells. Although
Dent stressed the need for an opera Intendant, the governors
decided that 'part time' directors were more valuable.[14]

Guthrie's ambition was for the Old Vic to become the basis for
the country's National Theatre. On 10 March he sought and
received assurance from the governors that they supported his
vision for the future. He believed that the players of the Old Vic
would become the National Theatre Company, and when the Vic
itself was demolished, whatever building replaced it would be called

the National Theatre. The Vic would provide 'trained personnel, tradition and good will'. Under this arrangement, Sadler's Wells would be divorced from the Vic altogether.[15] That same day agreement was reached with the Shakespeare Memorial National Theatre Committee that the Old Vic company would be the planners and its theatre the building for the future endowed National Theatre. At that time the £75,000 site for the National Theatre was in Kensington, but it was agreed that the site might be sold and two theatres built on the river instead. There would be an appeal to raise £100,000.

At that same meeting, Dent said the BBC grant was insufficient for the demands of the rapidly improving standard and ambition of the opera company. *Der Rosenkavalier* on 8 March 1939 was the most daunting venture yet undertaken at Sadler's Wells, given the memories of Lotte Lehmann and Elisabeth Schumann at Covent Garden in the late 1920s. Cross had baulked at the stultified Alfred Kalisch translation, which included such lines as 'Smile I at thee', but Clive Carey helped her make alterations. On 19 April eighty-year-old Ethel Smyth's *The Wreckers* was the last new production of the season. *The Times* praised Sadler's Wells for taking risks, persevering with British work and presenting everything it did with conviction, finding the way to interpret and deal with different styles and new works. It was, they said, a sure route to first-rate performances and thence to first-rate audiences. *The Wreckers* was the last new production before war was declared on 3 September.

After the outbreak of war all entertainment was suspended. The Old Vic temporarily closed and Sadler's Wells staff were given two weeks' notice. Those who were not called up worked out their notices. A letter went out to the staff to say that if they could work for their basic salaries it might be possible to arrange future dates. Guthrie was retained on a salary of £7 a week.

Just under four weeks later, on 29 September, Sadler's Wells was able to reopen with a Saturday matinee of *Faust*. A photograph in *The Bystander* showed long queues waiting for tickets, while Cross was shown putting up posters with information about the reopening and other shows to come.[16] At first, performances had to finish before blackout time, but after the initial shock subsided, and for the rest of the 'phoney' war before European hostilities began in earnest, government regulations about opening times were relaxed and theatres began to resume their programmes.

On 13 October it became clear that the BBC would pay the grant it had promised Vic-Wells, but the overdraft still stood at £9,127 17s 2d. Guthrie told the governors that all activities had to be regarded as short-term and that all the staff had taken a substantial cut in their salaries. He also told them that the wardrobe was being eaten by mice and should be moved to the country. The performances were sold out and *The Times* commented on the most intelligently responsive audience for an Arnold Matters/Joan Cross *Figaro* that even Sadler's Wells had ever known. There could be no question, *The Times* wrote, about the demand for opera. So successful were the Saturday matinees that Thursday evenings were added and, soon after, a third evening.

Guthrie was not entirely convinced of his role, offering to take control of the drama and resign his directorships of all three companies. On 28 November he told the governors that he been made a very good film offer and was prepared to give up his Old Vic salary. He also offered to hand back £800 to the Old Vic as a guarantee against loss for the reopening of the Old Vic, as the blackout and the closure of Waterloo Underground station were making things very difficult. The governors, however, did not accept Guthrie's generous offer. They were wise to have faith in him, for his vitalising influence and generosity did much to keep the flame of the companies burning during the war.

Soon after the outbreak of war Carey went to Australia, where he stayed, teaching in Adelaide. He was somewhat bitter, perhaps jealous, at the thought of the Vic-Wells being under Guthrie, whom he described as a 'self-conscious and mannered dilettante'. He was nonetheless glad in the new year that Sadler's Wells was 'keeping its head above water with Jack Gordon'. Despite his disappointment, Carey felt that there were plenty of people to carry on the production of opera, whereas when they started there was 'really no one with any intelligent ideas on it'.[17]

Despite the worries about costs, the company managed to produce four new productions in the winter of 1939–40, with a new *Otello* and a new *Die Fledermaus* in the repertoire in December 1939. Carey was angered that Guthrie brought in Hedley Biggs to direct *Die Fledermaus* with 'lots of scenery' and no production –

just using some of Carey's own stage 'business' from his 1934 production.[18] On 1 January 1940 there was a Jubilee Performance of Wartime Opera at Sadler's Wells attended by Queen Elizabeth and Princess Marina of Kent. On 12 January the governors learnt that Guthrie had given up his film work in order to devote all his energies to Vic-Wells.

In the first months of 1940 Sadler's Wells continued to perform to good audiences. The new *Barber of Seville* in February, Dent informed Carey, was a great success. He sought to reassure him that Jack Gordon was 'incredibly patient and forbearing with everybody', and he was confident that in the long run the place would be run in the way they envisaged.[19] Unlike Carey, Dent appreciated Guthrie, believing him to have 'immense keenness and a certain vision and imagination, which he is only too keen to devote now to the opera side as well, now he is director of the lot'.[20]

Dent was pleased that Guthrie shared his belief that operatic performance could only be reformed when the text took on equal weight with the music. Just after the war Guthrie explained, in one of the booklets written for the new post-war Sadler's Wells audiences, *Opera in English*, why opera had never been part of the 'native cultural tradition'. Like an exotic import from Italy, it had flowered 'often magnificently in the conservatories but putting no roots in our soil, making no adaptation to our climate'. This was because British opera companies since the seventeenth century had depended on foreign classics with foreign imported stars performing in tongues other than their own, which had resulted in opera being judged on a minimal understanding of the text. The consequent emphasis on the musical values at the expense of the dramatic had led to stylisation that had been pushed to such extremes 'as often to be quite absurd'. When the musical side entirely outweighed the dramatic, he wrote, it was reasonable enough not to bother if the young lovers were impersonated by 'middle-aged heavyweights, with no acting talents whatever, provided they make the right noises'.[21] He was not unhappy at the prospect of concentrating on the dramatic aspect of opera during the war.

In January 1940 the Council for the Encouragement of Music and the Arts (CEMA) had been founded jointly by the Board of Education and the Pilgrim Trust, with a mandate to bring music, drama and art to the whole country. As the war progressed, with entertainment in a state of general collapse, workers concentrated in new factories, doing repetitive work for long hours, and with many bombed out of their homes and evacuated from London, the need and opportunity to support cultural activity and bring colour into drab lives seemed irresistible. The government was engaged in an effort to maintain the pursuits of peacetime, which were part of a way of life in a society based on democracy and freedom of choice. An initial grant of £25,000 from the Pilgrim Trust was raised to £50,000 shortly after. CEMA was a valuable support for the development of Vic-Wells during the war.

Guthrie's developing concept of a mobile company, with all three of its branches touring, received enthusiastic support from Lewis Casson, the drama director of CEMA. It was agreed that Ninette de Valois would maintain the nucleus of the ballet in a mobile touring unit. The spirit of the opera company and the desire to carry on was extraordinary. Artists suggested that their salaries be cut to £2 a week rather than undergo any reduction in their numbers. Guthrie rejected their offer as 'too generous' and endeavoured to maintain salaries of no less than £3. The orchestra's offer of a 50 per cent cut was, however, gratefully accepted. Warwick Braithwaite reported: 'rather than imperil the continuity of the tradition and ensemble of the company, artists were prepared to work in the autumn for subsistence wages, or even without a fee'. The governors in response were 'deeply appreciative of the spirit shown by the company' and placed it on record that it was their intention to have an autumn season.[22]

On 13 March 1940 Gordon's new *La traviata* opened. The summer season included revivals of *The Barber of Seville*, *The Marriage of Figaro*, *Don Giovanni* and *La bohème* – in Dent's words, a Carl Rosa-style repertoire which was performed with a 'certain professional competence and integrity'. According to Dent, the main problem was that so long as Guthrie professed his ignorance of opera, the directors went on in their 'old stodgy way', with things in the same old rut. Dent later wrote that although Guthrie, 'like Miss B, could not visualise an opera from a score', in fact he was musical enough to read one.[23]

In May 1940 Hitler, having bombed and slaughtered his way through Poland in September 1939 and overrun Denmark and Norway in April 1940, turned his army towards the Low Countries and France. The progress of his forces was rapid. De Valois' ballet company were in Holland during the German invasion and sought sanctuary at the British Legation in The Hague. They were evacuated, minus scenery, costumes and music, after four days, first by bus, dodging parachutists, and then in a crowded cargo boat. They had lost the costumes and scenery for several ballets. The reopened Vic struggled on with a short theatre season in 1940, which included productions by Granville Barker and Casson. On 14 June – the day on which German troops entered Paris – Guthrie reported to the governors that the Vic was running at a loss and that only by further cutting salaries would it be possible to finish the season, which included the George Devine/Marius Goring *Tempest*.

*The Tempest* closed at the Vic on the night of 22 June, four days after France surrendered. The theatre did not open again during the war and on 10 May 1941 was badly damaged in an air-raid which destroyed the roof, the back stage walls and the lift.

Already by May 1940 the opera had an overdraft of £8,000, even though they often played to full houses during the summer season. Guthrie dispensed with Jack Gordon after the opera season. Gordon, a modest and generous man, took a post as an inspector of ordnance at a munitions factory. After Gordon's departure, the more forceful Guthrie gave Sumner Austin greater executive powers for opera and there were plans to reopen in September.[24]

Hitler's offensive prior to his planned invasion of Britain was launched with a full-scale air attack on 9 August. The Battle of Britain, by which Hitler endeavoured to destroy Britain's air defences, continued throughout August. The first night of the Blitz, the concentrated bomber offensive against British cities that Hitler hoped would destroy public morale, began on 7 September. The final wartime performance at Sadler's Wells took place that night. Guthrie later recalled that he and some colleagues went onto the roof of the theatre, where they counted 'seventeen conflagrations, turning the night sky to crimson, while from below the "Jewel Song" from *Faust* incongruously tinkled'. They wondered, he recalled, 'if this was the end of Sadler's Wells, the end of this particular experiment in national expression, just as it might be the end of a good deal else in our national life'.[25] By the end of the week 976 Londoners had been killed.

The Blitz continued remorselessly. Guthrie was bombed out of his home, as were Annette Prevost, Baylis's former chauffeuse and personal assistant, and Evelyn Williams, Baylis's former secretary. On 7 September 1940 Cross reported in her diary that they had moved into Sadler's Wells 'surrounded by a few bare necessities'.[26] The homeless were sleeping on mattresses between the rows of seats and under the stage, with Guthrie, his wife and members of the company acting as waiters and peeling potatoes for meals. On 10 September Guthrie wrote to Cross to inform her that the season was to be postponed and asked her to give temporary voluntary service at the theatre.[27]

Guthrie told the governors on 13 September 1940 that the borough of Finsbury had commandeered Sadler's Wells as a reception centre for a hundred air-raid victims who had been made homeless. He asked for permission for the staff and their families to use the theatre as a shelter and for those working there to receive £3 5s. There was a bomb explosion and air-raid warning during the meeting and it had to be completed in the basement.[28]

The climax of the Blitz was reached in the air battle of 15 September, when every available fighter plane of the RAF was deployed and after which Hitler postponed the invasion indefinitely. The Blitz, however, continued and it soon became obvious that there would be no more performances at Sadler's Wells, not least because people retired to their air-raid shelters at what Cross described as a 'ridiculously early hour'.[29] It was clearly time for the companies to leave London. The newly formed CEMA agreed to guarantee the companies against loss for their new touring role. The Old Vic took the Lewis Casson/Sybil Thorndike *Macbeth* to audiences in the West Country, the mining areas of South Wales and the industrial north-west. The company went from strength to strength on tour and in 1942 made the Liverpool Playhouse its base.

In order to keep the opera alive, Guthrie experimented with a tiny cast of singers accompanied by an orchestra of five, to perform in small mill towns off the normal touring circuit in Lancashire and Yorkshire. Cross was invited to join the tour by Guthrie, who warned that it would be rather 'humble' and that they might have to be prepared to sleep nine in a bed. Sumner Austin was put in charge of twenty people, including Collingwood, Edith Coates and her husband Powell Lloyd, Henry Brendon, Ruth Naylor and John Hargreaves. Collingwood's 'orchestra' consisted of two first violins, one second, a clarinet and a bassoon.

It was not possible to employ more than a handful of the 150 members of the pre-war opera company. Four choristers symbolised a chorus and understudied the principals, while looking after the props, scenery and lighting. Lawrance Collingwood presided at the piano, conducting simultaneously. Powell Lloyd was stage manager and singer. The settings were provided by the Harris sisters Margaret (Percy) and Sophie, together with Elizabeth Montgomery, known collectively as Motley, who were later to play a major part at Sadler's Wells both designing and teaching. For a production of *The Marriage of Figaro* they fabricated easily portable tri-fold screens instead of scenery. Much influenced by the British artist Claud Lovat Fraser and Diaghilev's ballet at the Coliseum, they were amongst the first designers to 'dispense with brocade and rabbit hair, and do things with a sharp clear outline'.[30] For *Figaro*, two chairs and a sofa were the props. It was decided at the last moment that as well as Guthrie rehearsing *Figaro*, Powell Lloyd would rehearse *La traviata*.

On 30 September Guthrie informed Dent that the opera company was to open in three weeks' time in Buxton, which had been one of the most receptive towns already visited, and asked him to help by writing two articles for the local papers about Sadler's Wells and the operas. 'If you do this,' he wrote, 'you will earn yet again the real gratitude of this demanding old firm; one more star in your crown.' Guthrie added: 'We are a madhouse. Five tours either in the country or being organised, 160 homeless people living in the theatre and giving a lot of trouble.'[31]

In mid-October, as the Blitz continued, because of the strain and the difficulty of communication in and with London, Guthrie suggested that the headquarters should also leave the capital.[32] He decided to make Burnley the company's headquarters, as the manager of its Victoria Theatre was keen to have the company there. By 21 October five Vic-Wells companies were on tour, with the opera performing *Figaro* and *Traviata* in Lancashire, and the ballet and theatre companies also on the road. Concerts were given on Sundays, as well as some ballets, including the premiere of Ashton's *Dante Sonata* with Michael Soames and Fonteyn.

After gathering at Sadler's Wells on 21 October 1940 the diminutive opera company left for Buxton on a brilliantly sunny autumn day. Guthrie and his wife had gone ahead the previous Friday to make arrangements, and some time after the group arrived, suit-cases piled high, Cross saw the large and imposing figure of Guthrie swinging down the road with a broad smile on his face. Cross described the ensuing scene: '"The worst possible news," Guthrie announced (with what I have since discovered is his real passion for making the most of the opening situation, you can always work back to something) with gusto. "There simply isn't anywhere to stay." The town was packed with refugees.' It emerged that Guthrie had arranged for the hospital to give them two wards, an arrange-ment with which they were delighted: 'We had warmth and com-fortable beds & oh! to go to bed without chance of a gun or a bomb! We slept like logs all of us.'[33]

During the war Cross and the company toured extensively. From 1942 to May 1945 they visited eighty-seven venues without a break. The schedule was gruelling: one four-week period saw the company move from Exeter to Brighton to Hull and then to Llandudno. The conditions were primitive, with performances tak-ing place in small theatres and halls, but the response was reward-ing. In October 1940 *La traviata* played in Stockport and Burnley. *Figaro* had a good audience in Burnley in October and November, and played in Stockport and Accrington in November. On 18 November Cross noted that her main impression of the week was one of 'acutely uncomfortable theatres' and of singing to the best of her ability 'over the cries of the attendants showing latecomers into the performance'. Being only used to films and variety, she wrote, they behaved as usual, and 'were staggered to learn that all the music was important'. They also had to compete with rain on the roof on the Saturday.

But there were also pleasures. The company were delighted by autumn in the Lake District, which some members were seeing for the first time. In Keswick, however, they played on such a small stage that there was no room to make some of the exits and entrances. Not surprisingly, in November 1940 the governors paid high tribute to the 'financial sacrifices' and to the work that Guthrie and the staff had done in circumstances of 'considerable difficulty'.[34]

Mary Glasgow, the secretary to CEMA and later the first secre-tary general of the Arts Council, from 1946 to 1951, wrote to Guthrie on 7 November 1940 with little but hope and encouragement to continue planning the tours: 'We are living on faith, and personally I have not the slightest doubt but that we shall go on.'[35] On 19 January 1941 the governors learnt that the Carnegie Trust was to guarantee the opera tour up to £100 a week for ten weeks and up to £500 in the event of serious loss. In the event the performances proved so popular that neither the Carnegie nor the CEMA guarantees were much called upon.

Guthrie later wrote that as the drama companies visited small towns and villages, artistic standards had, 'to some extent, to be subordinated to social service'. He was quick to recognise the long-term potential of the current difficult circumstances. De Valois' ballet company would be the only branch of Vic-Wells to maintain its high artistic standards, which, he decided, would never be so subordinated, even if that meant not receiving subsidy. He believed that if the standard of the ballet were lowered, 'the company would dissolve'. The scaling down of the drama and opera companies, however, was valuable in creating goodwill and 'closer contact with provincial audiences and education authorities everywhere'. Furthermore, this work, Guthrie noted, was achieved for the first time with the safety net of public subsidy.

The company members were stoical but sorely tried. A brief respite over Christmas and the new year of 1941 saw Cross at home in London 'feeling terrible', with a bad cold, headache and a high temperature. 'What a business travelling is,' she noted in what is an almost unique complaint in her diary. During the Christmas break she watched the city burn from her window and reported bombs dropping around Sadler's Wells, where friends were once again camped out. Suffering from chickenpox, she was too ill to take part in the first night of *The Beggar's Opera*, which opened in Burnley on 16 January.

Dent scored *The Beggar's Opera* for a 'very chamber' band of one flute, one oboe, one clarinet, one bassoon, two horns, strings and piano.[36] Cross rejoined the troupe for *The Beggar's Opera* in Huddersfield on 7 February. It was a bitterly cold winter of heavy snow and cold railway platforms. 'Miserably cold,' Cross wrote. 'Stayed in boarding house inhabited wholly by v. old ladies and gentlemen. They make a complete circle round the useless fire.' The show, however, was 'terrific'.

January 1941 found the company in Burnley, Huddersfield and Harrogate, with a less successful visit to London in February. During this period principal singers could be required to sing as many as six performances in a week and often had to shift scenery themselves. By March everyone was ill. Tudor Davies was singing six shows in one week. The mezzo-soprano Valetta Iacopi, who had joined the company in 1934 and who had a contract to sing Azucena and Amneris with Tullio Serafin in Rome when war broke out, remained with the company and found herself cleaning and doing the laundry as well as singing for £1 a week.[37] Not until 1942, when the stage staff increased, did things improve.

A season in Glasgow in March 1941 was conducted by Warwick Braithwaite with the Scottish orchestra. *Madam Butterfly* was performed to the accompaniment of a Luftwaffe bombardment. Clydebank, home of the shipyards, was in ruins, according to Cross, and a 'horrid sight'. They sat up all night. 'It was a wretched raid & I fear will kill business,' she wrote. The season was indeed a 'dismal failure', but apart from the Blitz, it was a very pleasant visit, thanks partly to the Scottish orchestra and the use of the Theatre Royal, the first big venue they had visited since they started touring. Guthrie arrived 'in tremendous form' along with an amateur chorus for rehearsals of *Die Fledermaus* and *La bohème*, providing both a boost to morale and a cause for merriment.[38]

On 18 March 1941 Guthrie urged two of the governors, Lord Lytton and Reginald Rowe, to allow an overhaul of the companies' management. The workload for the available staff was too heavy and he was spending time on routine and office work that would be 'better employed in dealing with questions of policy'. Sumner Austin was over-extended trying to sing and direct while acting as general manager of the opera company. Guthrie urged the appointment of an opera manager with specialist knowledge, suggesting Rudolf Bing, who had been Carl Ebert's assistant at Darmstadt in the late 1920s and Intendant of the Charlottenburg Opera in Berlin from 1930 to 1933 and who was willing to take on the task. Dent gave that idea short shrift, telling Guthrie that Bing was an excellent clerk or servant but knew nothing of English opera or traditions. As a result of Dent's letter Bing was rejected by the governors, while Guthrie continued to press for the opera to have someone constantly present who was knowledgeable enough to take decisions and had a personality strong enough to 'bang heads together'.[39]

Dent was afraid that the opera company would disintegrate and a new order come along with – as he wrote – John Christie and his German refugees, and that after the war all the Jews would return to Germany. He also foresaw that one day everything would be moved from Sadler's Wells and an English opera established at Covent Garden.[40] Despite their rejection of Bing, the governors approved the concept of an opera director in April.[41] That same month, Guthrie reported that CEMA was so pleased with the Vic's work that they wanted it expanded. From 1941 Guthrie decided to make the plays available in London by playing at the New Theatre, St Martin's Lane, where Bronson Albery was the managing director. The opera and ballet would also play at the New Theatre.[42]

In May 1941 the company were in Hull, which suffered greatly in the last few weeks of the Blitz before Hitler turned his attention to the invasion of the Soviet Union. Joan Cross recorded the night of 7 May in her diary:

We had just gone to bed when the siren went – a few moments after which we could hear incendiaries. We dressed hurriedly & foregathered in the lounge & decided that we wouldn't go to the basement . . . a few moments later a violent explosion broke all the windows . . . we all clung to each other and went rather green . . . one of the rooms of the hotel caught fire but was put out at about 4.30. After 6 hours of concentration bombing . . . we came upstairs.

In the morning there was such devastation that she could not believe that anyone would find their way to the theatre. One by one, however, the company members, each with their own story of survival, staggered over the tangle of fire hoses that bisected the roads. Some had sheltered in the theatre, some had had roofs fall down on them and two had sheltered under a staircase, but all were alive. The costumes had to be fished out from the debris with a long pole for the matinee of *La traviata* that afternoon, when they were astonished by an attendance of almost 200 people.[43]

After the terrors of Hull the company moved on to London, where they performed *Madam Butterfly*, *The Beggar's Opera* and *The Marriage of Figaro* in May and June at the New Theatre.

When Sumner Austin was called to work at the War Office on 11 July, Guthrie insisted that Joan Cross take over from him. She was prepared to give up her singing to concentrate on the administrative needs of the company. Although her contract stated that she was no longer to sing, she was often called upon to do so in emergencies, or to take on small parts.[44] Three months later Guthrie told the board that she was 'proving very efficient in her new duties'.[45] Dent was sorry that Sadler's Wells had thrown away their best singer, but he was impressed both by Cross's willingness to renounce singing for a small stipend and by how she had begun to secure some good singers to take on her parts. He found her intelligent and clear-headed and saw how the singers liked working under her. She was, he informed Carey, 'genuinely public spirited'.[46]

From February 1941 *Madam Butterfly* was constantly in the repertoire, but proved more popular later when it was possible to employ more orchestral players. In July, Dent thought *Dido and Aeneas* was thoroughly well rehearsed by Collingwood. Cross, who was standing in, was 'really first rate' as Belinda, and Edith Coates was a juvenile Dido in a red wig. Scenery was rudimentary, just wings and a backcloth, with costumes adversely affected by the recent rationing of clothes.* Sumner Austin's idea about production, Dent reported, was 'not very good', but the sombre lighting did something to hide the 'inadequate dancing and acting'.[47]

In August and September *Dido and Aeneas* played in Leeds, Halifax, Kendal and Keighley. Both Cross and Dent were delighted that the 'two Lascelles boys came every night'. They were referring to the eighteen-year-old George Lascelles, later the Earl of Harewood and managing director of Sadler's Wells and ENO, and his brother Gerald, who were already devoted to opera. Cross reported the possibility of a command performance of *Figaro* at their home, Harewood House, in August 1941.[48] It took place in September. During the war Harewood House was a convalescent hospital and ambulances were sent to collect the company. The performance, which was attended by the Lascelles brothers and their mother the Princess Royal – daughter of George V – was, according to Cross, 'very "scratch"', the stage so small that there was only one entrance and exit, which lost the point of the conceal-

---

* Clothes rationing was introduced on 1 June 1941. The annual coupon allowance was the equivalent of one complete outfit a year. Second-hand clothes did not require coupons if sold privately.

ment of Act II. The company were given supper after the performance.[49]

Guthrie was a great optimist and visionary, telling Dent in the summer of 1941 that he believed that after the war there would be a
huge demand for music and English opera all over the country.[50]
Dent himself was increasingly worried that at the first opportunity
after the war either Glyndebourne or Covent Garden would emerge
with a ready-made scheme for foreign opera. Dent hoped that
Carey, whom Guthrie admired, would return from Australia, and
that together Carey and Dent would run Sadler's Wells.[51]

Meanwhile, the company was slowly but surely growing. By
November 1941 it numbered fifty. Cross was delighted to have a
secretary that autumn. Productions were also being spruced up. *The
Barber of Seville*, directed by Powell Lloyd and with new costumes
and scenery, played in Harrogate in September. Preparations for a
new *La traviata*, to be directed by Guthrie, were also progressing.

Cross had suggested to Guthrie that Sophie Fedorovitch, an
expert in the art of suggestion and economy of means, should be the
designer. Together the two women agreed that as long as the productions were unable to employ full-sized scenery, the clothes must
supply the decoration of the stage. There would be virtually no furniture, but the 'frocks of the girls were to be immense crinolines',
which they hoped would fill up the wide-open space of the stage. By
August 1941, however, they were also faced with 'the coupon situation', which was only overcome by Fedorovitch's ingenuity in
making the greater part of the frocks out of unrationed net. Cross
was nonetheless appalled by her insistence on long gloves for each
of the girls, but the excitement at some luxury in the midst of priva-
tion was palpable. 'I am enraptured,' she wrote in October 1941,
'particularly with the second act frock for Violetta: a symphony in
grey and black . . . Sophie has found some lovely bits & pieces in
old paste & a really beautiful collection of jewels for the girls,' who
were 'fearfully excited to wear such things'.[52]

In November Cross appealed to Edward Johnson at the
Metropolitan Opera in New York to send a 'Bundle for Britain' –
including 'tights, shoes, stockings, gloves', all of which by that time
were virtually irreplaceable. She appealed to 'a feeling amongst the
very great for their younger and weaker friends in the world of

opera now under such exceedingly trying circumstances'.[53] The bombing of Pearl Harbor was less than a month away.

The tour continued to be gruelling. In October Cross had been shocked by the state of Liverpool, which had been 'very thoroughly bombed', and the grim weather made it even more depressing. But their work was not in vain. The *Burnley Express and News* greatly appreciated the stoic efforts of the small company. On 3 January 1942 it reported on the three-week tour with *Figaro* and *Barber*, during which Herbert Menges and Lawrance Collingwood conducted without a break. John Hargreaves sang eighteen times and many artists were singing in every show.

When Hargreaves and fellow baritone Charles Miller were called up in January 1942, there was a feeling of despair in the company, as their loss would threaten the whole operation.[54] Dent at the governors' meeting insisted that the Ministry of Labour should be told that 'the survival of a unique cultural organisation' hung upon their decision. In May their call-up was deferred for six months after Guthrie spoke to the government's economic adviser John Maynard Keynes, who had been made chairman of CEMA in April 1942. It was agreed that in future CEMA would handle all applications for deferment.[55]

Keynes, who believed strongly that professional enterprises should maintain high standards of quality, was, together with the Treasury and Carnegie, keen to see the creation of a national council for opera. Aware of these developments, the governors, with additional backing from Bronson Albery and Sir George Dyson, were finding it increasingly hard to maintain the independence of the Old Vic and Sadler's Wells. Dyson, the son of a Yorkshire blacksmith who played the organ at the local Baptist church, was himself a composer, and from 1937 the director of the Royal College of Music. He was also a man of great administrative skill and financial acumen, and under his directorship the college had become a high-quality training ground for professional musicians.

Dyson clearly saw that state subsidy would inevitably replace private patronage after the war. Like Albery, he was insistent that Sadler's Wells should be well represented on any newly created national body in order to preserve its identity. Dent sought to reassure the board that all would be well so long as Keynes was chairman of CEMA and Eric Walter White and Mary Glasgow were involved, since they were all devoted to Sadler's Wells. Dent stressed that the Old Vic and Sadler's Wells should become the centres of national drama and opera after the war and that a CEMA subsidy for opera and ballet should be established.[56]

With the company's two leading singers safe from call-up, Cross and Guthrie felt able to embark on some new productions that would be suitable for the larger centres. In 1942 the orchestra was increased to twenty-four players, which made it possible from 12 January 1942 to perform *Rigoletto*, directed by Powell Lloyd with Alix Stone designs. It played all over the country from January to August, from Blackpool to Swansea to the Arts Theatre, Cambridge, which Keynes had founded before the war. Many local newspapers followed the work of the company enthusiastically, explaining the plots and background to the operas. The Norwich-based *Eastern Evening News* declared on 10 February that there were to be four weeks of the best Italian opera, which belonged to a golden age 'long before Mussolini was ever thought of'.

The new *La traviata*, directed by Guthrie with Powell Lloyd, opened in Burnley in January 1942. The result of their efforts was described by Cross as a *Traviata* that was light, adaptable, easy to transport and balanced between elegance and economy, with 'rich and extravagant-looking' costumes for the chorus and principals.[57]

The Sadler's Wells opera tradition, even in the midst of war, impressed Guthrie, who later wrote:

It was my first and last experience of an opera production when there was enough time for the dramatic preparation. In this case all the principal singers were not only thoroughly familiar with the work, they also had long experience as a team. Joan Cross, who had sung and acted Violetta with immense acclaim at Sadler's Wells before the war, was not only a top ranking singer and musician but also an admirable actress. The rest of the cast were well-suited. We had time for some discussion of the meaning of the work and how we might try to express it with the simplicity and economy which wartime production demanded. We even had time to try things this way and that, adapting the stage business to the various personalities of the artists. Sophie Fedorovitch designed the scenery and dresses of masterly simplicity and elegance; the result was an effort upon which I look back with some pride.[58]

The *Cambridge Daily News* was delighted, describing *La traviata* as a 'great success for this courageous organisation'. Fedorovitch had created a bright and spacious set enacted before a large window and balcony with railings that would have gladdened the hearts of the salvage people had they been real.[59] Dent found the new *Traviata* enchanting, save for the translation, which forced the singers to bawl. Guthrie asked him to prepare a new version.[60] There was also a new set for *Madam Butterfly*, and by the end of the year there were four new productions.

The hardships were nonetheless enormous. The winter of 1941–2 was again bitterly cold, with an ENSA* tour before the well-earned Christmas holiday, impassable roads over the moors and more illness in the new year. Digs were universally deficient, and in February Collingwood nearly froze to death sleeping in a converted conservatory. Not only were dresses rationed, but there was a shortage of wood and other materials. Joan Cross later recalled the tired costumes and accessories, many of which still had to be provided by the singers. She also recalled a costume parade in 1942 at which 'the long-suffering' Tyrone Guthrie sighed: 'Let's get rid of the diamanté dogs, dear?'[61] Guthrie was keen to prepare more shows that were likely to adopt scenery by 'suggestion' – something Carey called 'stunts' but which Dent reminded him had its precedent in the 1920s German–Russian '*Expressionismus*', which had also resulted mainly from 'poverty of resources'.[62]

On Dent's suggestion, and under his general supervision and approval, another of his protégés, Kurt Joos, directed the new *Magic Flute* at the Arts Theatre, Cambridge, on 10 March 1942. Joos was a dancer-director whose Youth Ballet Company had performed at Cambridge in the late 1930s when he had sought refuge in England from Germany. Dent was keen for Joos to bring some movement into the productions and to stress the importance of getting the words across. Joos was liked by the company, who learnt much from him in rehearsals and as a result of his efforts were moving better. This was especially true of the often stiff and awkward Hargreaves, who became a lively Papageno. Dent was also

---

* Entertainments National Service Association for entertaining the armed forces. ENSA came under the National Services Entertainments Board, which operated under the Ministry of Labour and National Service. Its purpose was to provide entertainment for HM forces and for munitions workers. ENSA was controlled financially and administratively by NAAFI (Navy, Army and Air Force Institute) on the entertainments side.

impressed by Cross's recruitment of young singers, especially a very 'good-looking' young Yorkshireman – Arthur Servent – as Tamino.

After much battling, some decent scenery and costumes for *The Magic Flute* had been acquired. These were more elaborate than those of the famous 1911 Cambridge production, in order to help explain the story to the new audiences.[63] Painted cloth was the order of the day, and the lack of canvas, which was usually sourced from Japan, resulted in the need to double up such scenes as the *Madam Butterfly* 'sky' cloth with Pamina's bedroom.[64] The Cambridge Arts Theatre had contributed £300 to the cost of the costumes, but Norman Higgins on behalf of the Cambridge Arts Theatre trustees questioned the £500 for scenery as they had believed most material would be coming out of old Sadler's Wells stock. Higgins relented after Guthrie explained that most of their old stock had been cannibalised already, and that no more than £75 worth could be used for *The Magic Flute*.[65]

The show sold out every night. *The Times* was appreciative: 'Here, in the time of our utter operatic bankruptcy, our one surviving opera company is still enabled to present one masterpiece, perhaps the greatest of all, in a spirit befitting its theme, the abode of wisdom and light.' Above all, every member of the cast made the words intelligible.[66] At the opening, Joan Cross referred to the 'Sarastro of Sadler's Wells' living in Cambridge – Edward J. Dent. Dent himself was beginning to realise that his mission was in the process of being accomplished, as audiences now wanted and expected to hear and understand the words.[67]

Cambridge's 'Sarastro', Dent was nonetheless still liable to use injudicious language. In March 1942 he expressed his concern that John Christie intended to open Glyndebourne after the war with *Die Zauberflöte*, 'of course in Yiddish', and that American companies were beginning to do translations in Brooklynese 'refugee'.[68] Off-hand prejudice such as Dent's was not an uncommon pre-war phenomenon, nor did the events of the war lessen its rough edge. It was not until December 1942 that the joint Allied declaration, solemnly announced in the House of Commons, condemned Hitler's 'cold-blooded extermination' of the Jewish people.

By May 1942 the company numbered eighty, and the new productions filled seasons at the New Theatre in April, September and December. In the spring of 1942 the ballet was doing rather better than the opera, and seemed to have sufficient coupons to employ the artist Oliver Messel to design their costumes. To Dent the opera seemed, in comparison, 'hopelessly second class', although both Guthrie and Powell Lloyd were having much success in getting the company to enunciate clearly. The strains of war were beginning to affect Collingwood, who was bored, utterly weary and negative. The German refugee Peter Gellhorn had joined the company as co-répétiteur. Dent found him an intelligent teacher and 'not at all unpleasantly Jewish – indeed he does not look Jewish at all and does his best to be English'.[69]

Audiences were growing in number and enthusiasm. They were delighted to hear the words of *The Barber of Seville* in April, and Edith Coates was proving to be a fine Rosina, a real contralto with beautiful coloratura. Although the company did not have enough time to learn Dent's new translation of *La traviata*, he provided them with notes on the secondary characters. In August Cross reported sold-out houses in the small theatre in Swansea. Wales, she wrote, was 'a wonderful place to give opera'.[70] In October Cross described a full house at the Bristol Hippodrome. In the interval, she and Guthrie gave a broadcast talk on the opera from a box. It was not a simple task for the six-foot-four-inch Guthrie, who had to be 'folded in half & pushed inside'. *La bohème* in the New Opera House in Blackpool, a town crammed with civil servants and air-force personnel, was described by Cross as a 'wow'.[71]

In what was an exciting development, Wigan's Education Committee asked in July 1942 for the whole of their Hippodrome Theatre to be devoted to matinees for 1,200 schoolchildren. The Vic-Wells management thought the idea the most progressive and exciting action to be taken by an education committee in connection with the theatre. In September *The Magic Flute*, *La bohème*, *The Barber of Seville* and *La traviata* played there. On 12 September the *Wigan Examiner* reported: 'the operatic festival is one of the few good things this war has brought about', the *Barber* producing a full house with a 'rapt and enthusiastic audience'. The *Sunday Observer* reported that Wigan had been deprived of theatre and music in the past only because of prejudice and 'commercial obstinacy'.

The relationship between arts institutions and the state was evolving rapidly. CEMA had received a grant of £25,000 from the

Treasury, and early in 1942 the Board of Education took over financial responsibility for the arts. It was becoming accepted that the need for CEMA would continue after the war. From the early days of the packed Myra Hess lunchtime concerts at the National Gallery to the later visits of the London Symphony Orchestra and the London Philharmonic to the munitions factories, it was clear that classical music, together with drama, ballet and opera, could be appreciated by a far wider public if they were given the opportunity. When R. A. Butler took over responsibility for CEMA at the Board of Education in July 1941, he was determined to give CEMA a more permanent role and invited Keynes to make a long-term plan for state policy for the arts.

In August 1942 the *Observer* wrote that the war had made 'recreation more than ever a matter of public policy', and *The Times* pointed out the 'vital importance of the arts on public morale'.[72] From 1934 Sadler's Wells was amongst some two thousand organisations that had been exempted from paying entertainment tax 'with a view to the education of public taste'. In June 1943 the commercial theatrical managers also approached the Treasury, asking to be relieved of the entertainment-tax burden. In November HM Customs and Excise decided that state subsidy by way of remission of taxation was not 'sound' in principle but should rather be achieved through CEMA. On 12 November it was decided that CEMA should distribute £115,000 that had been set apart to ensure that the wartime blackout did not result in the obliteration of music and art.[73]

The Cambridge Arts Theatre had been so pleased with *The Magic Flute* that it soon approached Guthrie for another production, a full-length *Figaro*, again directed by Kurt Joos. It opened on 27 November 1942, with scenery and costumes by William Chappell, who, like Messel, was an artist who designed mainly for the ballet. Dent was charmed by the production in July 1943, even though only Edward Donleavy as Figaro was truly up to standard vocally. He thought that Rose Hill, 'a little Jewess', was a charming Susanna who acted very well.[74*]

In April 1943 Guthrie directed *La bohème* at the New Theatre;

* Rose Hill played the role of the bedridden Madame Fanny in seventy-seven episodes of the BBC sit-com *'Allo, 'Allo* from 1982 to 1992.

*The Times* critic, while nostalgically recalling being transported to Italy during the Covent Garden performances before the war, was delighted to recognise Guthrie's discovery of a 'dramatic truth' and homogeneity and to see a reading of the opera in an English style for an English audience. Guthrie also brought out a winsome, convincing, English-style performance of Mimì by pretty Australian soprano Linda Parker, who sang with a good, clean, firm line.[75] The badly lit Bagnell Harris scenery and the dated translation were more heavily criticised.

In the programme Guthrie wrote that the season made no pretence to be grand opera. The prevailing circumstances meant that 'opera cannot be grand', and yet he hoped the performances would be welcome. The experience in Lancashire had encouraged the belief that it was worth keeping Sadler's Wells alive and that the company might form the basis of a future National Opera. It was 'the isthmus, small but strong, linking the continents of the past and the future'.[76]

In October 1942 Bronson Albery had become joint administrator of the Old Vic and Sadler's Wells to help with the business management so that Guthrie could concentrate on artistic policy. The Shakespeare company was playing to varying audiences, with Oxford doing the best business. By 1943/4 Sadler's Wells was the largest touring opera company in the country, with a hundred personnel and three fifty-foot trucks. New singers were joining the company, including Peter Pears in June 1942, after his return from America. Pears had been a pianist and organ scholar at Oxford, and after free singing lessons at the RCM for two terms had joined the BBC chorus in 1934. It was while he was with the BBC singers from 1936 to 1938 that he met Benjamin Britten, with whom he went to the USA at the beginning of the war. The critic Hans Keller later described Pears as having a voice 'unsensuous and unvoluminous enough to be absolutely dependent on musical expressiveness, on sharp delineation, subtle modulation, on intensive, individual shaping, on what Pears himself would call "characterisation"'.[77]

Pears sang his first Tamino on 19 January 1943, and it was not long before he was feeling the strains of overwork. When he sang the Duke in *Rigoletto* in June 1943, *The Times* noticed that the golden quality in his voice had changed, 'hardening up for carrying power and brightness', while admiring his professionalism and his 'unfailing mastery of diverse styles of singing'.[78] On 22 May Benjamin Britten wrote to a friend: 'His throat is troubling him too. It is all the trouble of too much work – Sadler's Wells love him so & want him for the *Barber* (as well as *Magic Flute*, *Traviata*, & *Rigoletto*, each learnt in two weeks).'[79] Dent thought him a charming, young, good-looking Alfredo in *La traviata* in July 1943 at the New Theatre.

Cross was saddened in August when a new production of Tchaikovsky's *Queen of Spades*, with beautiful and exciting designs by Oliver Messel, had to be abandoned for financial reasons. The company, thoroughly bored by their limited repertoire, were 'disappointed and defeated' by the decision.[80] They soon recovered their spirits, however; Dent reported them keeping going 'marvellously' in November.[81] On 20 October 1943 *Hansel and Gretel* at the New Theatre was a full-size production by Powell Lloyd. To replace the Tchaikovsky, Cross and Collingwood invited Eric Crozier, on Guthrie's suggestion, to direct *The Bartered Bride,* which opened on 10 November.

Crozier was described by Dent as a very clever, attractive and intelligent young man from the drama side.[82] Crozier remodelled the dialogue, which was spoken, not sung to what Dent considered Smetana's rather dreary recitatives. This, he thought, 'really brightened up the opera immensely'. Encouraged by Dent to give full emphasis to the ballet, Cross arranged for the Czech government-in-exile in London to release their ballet master, Sasha Machov, to coach the ballet.[83] Even 'Ninette graciously permitted her back row to appear', Dent told Carey. Machov helped to imbue *The Bartered Bride*'s rural and 'real people' origins with a distinct anti-German, pro-Czech flavour. The production was quite unlike the last Teutonic Covent Garden revival and other pre-war productions that had reached the outside world via Germany. They had been full of parody approaching burlesque, reflecting German attitudes to Czech 'racial cultural aspirations'.[84] The result, Dent wrote, was 'most effective and spirited'. A much improved Arthur Servent was a good Jeník, Donleavy was amusing as Kecal and Peter Pears as Vašek scored a great hit, despite Dent finding him 'absurdly feminine'.[85]

Much to the delight of Guthrie, the show, which had taken ten weeks to prepare, was a 'roaring success' that took London by storm and, 'contrary to expectations', Crozier's production became 'the most popular work in the repertory'.[86] For the second perform-ance the entire theatre was taken over by the Czech government-in-exile for their soldiers, who were 'wildly enthusiastic'.[87] Carey wished the British government would offer the encouragement given by the Czechs. 'One wonders if that frame of mind can ever be cultivated in our solid people,' he wrote to Dent.[88]

Despite the great success of *The Bartered Bride*, the company was faced by yet another autumn and winter of touring, accompanied by illness, deprivation and growing weariness. 'There is nothing to recommend Bolton,' Cross wrote in October 1943. In December the journey to Dudley was bitterly cold and the digs situation 'frighten-ing', with some members of the company sleeping in the local police station. No one came to see *The Barber of Seville* in Dudley because they were saving up for the Christmas pantomime.

As Dent wrote in January 1944, plans for the long-term future of the Sadler's Wells company and opera in English were swallowed up in the daily struggle of 'actually running the company in wartime'. Having given up his Cambridge duties, Dent had moved to London in order to become more involved in Sadler's Wells, CEMA, ENSA and the BBC. In the new year, his was the most urgent voice at the Sadler's Wells Board meetings, where the governors seemed terrified of taking on commitments or planning ahead without a guarantee that CEMA would continue to subsidise Sadler's Wells. Even if CEMA did guarantee them, they were afraid that the West End managers would be 'furiously jealous'.[89]

While the governors procrastinated, it was becoming more urgent to prepare for the future, as those making post-war plans for both Covent Garden and Glyndebourne were progressing with their schemes. Dent feared that they wanted opera in 'any language other than English'. Sadler's Wells was faced with the choice of sticking to 'the ghost of Miss Cons' and returning to Islington or becoming 'the Royal and English National Opera' on a really big scale in the most suitable West End theatre.[90]

Guthrie, although he was prepared to plan for the long term, was more concerned about drama than opera. He also doubted whether there were enough singers available. Dent assured him that there were, although they needed to be found and trained. He urged the board 'with some heat' to give Guthrie a free hand in drawing up a long-term plan. The Trust, however, which was tied to the bricks and mortar of Sadler's Wells and the Vic, was determined to limit its terms of reference to its articles of association. Meanwhile, Cross had produced a plan for Sadler's Wells that included a junior company to tour smaller towns and a national opera school. Carey agreed that an opera school was essential – it would, he wrote from Australia, save time spent on having to teach how to act while producing.[91]

The company was indeed struggling. The severe strains of the four-year tour as well as the bombing were taking their toll. It was clear that Collingwood's fatigue was adversely affecting both standards and morale. On 11 May 1944 Pears wrote to Britten after a performance of *La bohème*: 'Vic Sladen as Mimi – not bad at all and no bad mistakes but Collingwood really stinks.'[92] Joan Cross's handwritten cast books for the war years show constant replacements of cast and conductors because of illness.

In June 1944 the V-1 pilotless bombs began to strike London, followed by the V-2 rocket bombs in September. The threat of attack was constant until March 1945. It was estimated that the alert was sounded in London 1,224 times during those nine months. Cross described the fortnight spent in Wimbledon in the second week of June 1944 as a nightmare, with constant flying bombs and not a single show without its warning. Somehow, she noted wryly, the attacks always came in the quiet passages. It had been anxious work waiting for the cast and orchestra to turn up and they counted themselves 'singularly fortunate' that there had been no casualties. 'A bomb dropped *behind* the train that Edith & Harry were in', she wrote, '& ahead of one that several others were in. Not surprisingly, the audiences were terribly poor.'[93]

Undeterred, Cross was about to sing Fiordiligi in *Così fan tutte*, which Dent was cutting down to under three hours. It was to be set in 1790 by designer Kenneth Green.[94] It opened at the Princes Theatre, London, on 29 August. Sasha Machov directed, with Crozier as stage manager. Dent thought it 'over-balletified, over-decorated and altogether affected and "precious" and not very well done in that genre'. Joan Cross sang Fiordiligi well, but the horns played 'abominably'. Owen Brannigan, the thirty-six-year-old

Northumberland bass, was a rather Irish Don Alfonso, Hargreaves was 'clumsy' and Pears amusing, but 'hardly adequate as a singer for "Un' aura amorosa"'. *Così* was, however, 'for the first time within living memory, a real popular success – the house full every night'.[95] Pears was much praised. The critic Hans Keller later recalled how he was lying down in the gallery during *Così* because 'one production was as bad as another', when he heard a tenor who made him 'literally, sit up'. Pears, he wrote, was a musician who instinctively acts the music, with plenty of humour, but no fooling.[96]

Dent and Guthrie had decided to draft a memorandum for a post-war scheme for opera. Guthrie, who wanted the Vic to become the National Theatre, was also planning to take over the New Theatre to form a permanent drama company.[97] At the same time, the other forces engaged in 1944 in post-war opera plans were making progress. The Covent Garden Trust had been created, consisting of classical-music publishers Boosey and Hawkes, classical-music agent Harold Holt and CEMA's representatives Sir Stanley Marchant and Sir Kenneth Clark, whom Dent described as 'absolutely honourable' and loyal to Sadler's Wells. In May the Covent Garden Trust secured a five-year lease directly from Covent Garden Properties Ltd to produce opera and ballet, a single letter from Keynes to his Treasury colleague Sir Anthony Barlow being sufficient to secure the necessary funds for a sub-lease from Boosey and Hawkes.[98]

The Covent Garden Trust invited Sadler's Wells to join them, Dent informed Carey, but 'our worthy governors refused'. Dent was not sorry to lose Covent Garden, as two thirds of the audience could not see the stage and it could be run only on 'old Italian lines'. Furthermore, Boosey had told him that 'they really had no use for English opera or opera in English sung by English singers at all'.[99] After the war they wanted to revive the glories of the Royal Italian Opera House, with singers mostly from New York. They were hinting that they wanted to give English opera a chance, but although feelers were going out for the ballet they felt that Sadler's Wells opera was not good enough.

Sadler's Wells was indeed suffering in the latter stages of the war. Some members of the orchestra, including two flautists and the first horn, had decided to leave because of the flying bombs, and Collingwood was having a difficult time replacing them.[100] There was also a shortage of singers, Dent explained, as all the young people of both sexes were being called up, and it was impossible to get anybody released. The Ministry of Labour was begging for stage carpenters to repair damaged buildings.[101]

On 4 August Boosey invited Dent to join the Covent Garden Board, explaining that they were most anxious to avoid any feeling on the part of Sadler's Wells that they were in any way outside the scheme or that any rivalry was intended. Two weeks later Dent told Carey that at the first Covent Garden Board meeting he had met David Webster, a businessman with an interest in music and theatre and chairman of the Bon Marché department store in Liverpool, who was to be the general manager. Webster appeared to agree with Dent about 'building up a really first-rate opera to sing in English' and 'in disapproving of the old Covent Garden system of miscellaneous stars all singing in German or Italian with English singers allowed to do small parts, with no proper rehearsal or production'. He found Webster extremely genial and agreeable, 'fat and prosperous looking' and 'pink with high polish', who should be Lord Mayor of some big provincial town.[102]

Dent was beginning to look more favourably upon co-operation with Covent Garden resources, not least because Sadler's Wells was, he admitted to Carey, at a very low ebb. Collingwood was exhausted: 'one might as well talk to Gilda in the sack'. He was practically a corpse, galvanising himself into action on the conductor's desk and taking everything twice as fast in order to make the orchestra sound as if it were twice the size. There were areas of agreement with the Covent Garden Board, as no one wanted Beecham as director or anything to do with Christie. Policy would stay in the hands of the committee, which Keynes would chair. Mary Glasgow of CEMA was already there, and there seemed to be a nucleus of a group of good friends who could work together. Dent thought that Webster seemed fine. He had warned him 'against the German Jews who were ready to muscle in everywhere . . . and spread the notion that England was not a musical country'. Webster himself was not a Jew, which was 'a good thing' for Dent. First, he wrote, 'we need peace – then a period of two to three years to train people and build up a first rate company'.[103]

That autumn Guthrie and Dent were completing their memorandum about the future of opera policy at the Wells. The two men, so very different in character and training, made a strong team. They shared a vision for the lyric theatre that was both practicable and realistic. Dent informed Carey: 'I said to Tony – and Tony did understand – "What we are aiming at is something that has not yet been seen anywhere, and which only exists in our imagination, even if yours and mine don't exactly coincide, but these Covent Gardeners can't imagine anything; they can only remember what they have once seen, either at C.G. or at Vienna or elsewhere and want to set up that as a standard."'[104]

The problem in Dent's view was that Sadler's Wells singers could not fill Covent Garden and could not sing the sort of operas that its large stage required, nor dominate an orchestra of eighty. The lack of voices at Sadler's Wells meant that collaboration with Covent Garden was impossible and that they would have to stick to *opéra comique*. He also considered Covent Garden to be useless for the future as it was built for 'Italian opera and tiaras in the boxes'. The early-Victorian décor 'suggested crinolines at once', with no place for regency waists or modern flannels. Guthrie wanted better acting and better translations and was waiting for new native repertory so that they did not have to 'waste any more time in performing the stock Italian operas in English'. They were, he said, 'foreign to the English temperament'.[105]

Their memorandum was logical and coherent. Had it been adopted it might have saved many tears later. 'In a nutshell', Dent wrote, it amounted to Sadler's Wells being the Opéra Comique and Covent Garden the grand opera. It was also a definitive statement on behalf of opera as drama in English, and for the role of opera in the new world order following the upheavals of the Second World War. The memorandum of Guthrie and Dent declared that 'the revolution in financial and social values caused by the war creates a unique opportunity to demolish the demonstrably false preconception that opera is solely for the wealthy and aristocratic'.[106] The war had made people value their cultural heritage. CEMA and Sadler's Wells combined disinterested patronage together with practical experience and public goodwill.

Guthrie and Dent envisaged that foreign works would also be produced with a view to developing a style in which music and theatre were balanced, and where singers must be able to act and look their parts, not be chosen for big voices: 'Ensemble and teamwork will tend to be emphasised rather than individual brilliance and virtuosity.' Hitherto drama had suffered as the repertoire had consisted mainly of foreign works 'sung in execrable translations, so that the inadequacy of the literary element has highlighted the musical'. It was necessary to draw out the natural British ways of speaking and singing, and of the British tradition of poetry and drama. Singers did not need to make a 'big noise like a foreigner'. Successful Sadler's Wells productions of *The Marriage of Figaro*, *The Bartered Bride* and *The Barber of Seville* were a 'conscious adaptation of style to suit the temperament of native artists and our native traditions of art and manners'. It was not clear that they could achieve the 'Nordic mysticism of *Götterdämmerung*' or the 'Mediterranean abandon of *Rigoletto*'. Sadler's Wells would create a native opera ensemble. School and training were needed for local singers, who must be encouraged and enabled financially to make opera a career. There were some exceptional young composers, and the aim of Sadler's Wells should be to provide a mechanism whereby the native gift for music, poetry and acting could find a joint expression in the lyric theatre.

Dent and Guthrie also set out a founding principle of Sadler's Wells – the 'special relationship' with the audience. Sadler's Wells had always been, and always should be, they wrote, animated by ideals which were not solely aesthetic but also partly social and humanitarian, with 'a more affectionate and vital relation between stage and audience than could ever exist where the theatre's policy is guided by aesthetic principles unmixed with baser matter'.[107]

When the governors received the memorandum, they were impressed. 'Dear good Lytton', wrote Dent, 'approached it in the spirit of a commission in Manchuria, and was delighted, I think, at the prospect of delimiting frontiers and embodying everything in a solid diplomatic instrument.'[108]

While Sadler's Wells was planning its future, the Covent Garden Trust was also developing its plans. When Dent and Guthrie visited Covent Garden, which was used as a dance hall during the war, it looked to Dent like a 'dream film in Technicolor', and he could not but feel 'slightly intoxicated by the strange effect of the light and the sound of saxophones etc. through amplifiers'. Apart from its perfect acoustics, however, Dent wanted Webster to be able to strip the inside and remove the boxes, 'on democratic lines'. Webster had told them that there was no money and that the building would have to be pulled down when the government got round to building a real national opera house.[109]

Signs of tensions between the Covent Garden and Sadler's Wells forces were already beginning to appear. Dent feared that Covent Garden would go back to the old system that he and Guthrie had been fighting to replace, with foreign stars, English singers in small parts, and all singing in 'Covent Garden' Italian. He told Guthrie that Sadler's Wells must pursue its own course, choosing repertoire very carefully, building up the singers and doing serious scholarly work with plenty of rehearsal. 'We can beat them on ensemble any day,' he said.

At Covent Garden, Dent told the unamused committee that *Figaro* should not be played there at all. William Walton was horrified by the thought of asking native composers to write operas on the scale of Sadler's Wells. At the meeting Guthrie suggested that Sadler's Wells pursue its policy of *opéra comique* in English at popular prices, and that Covent Garden should stick exclusively to foreign ensembles. Webster, however, wanted to have a grand-opera season the following August in English, using Sadler's Wells singers, even though few of them other than Joan Cross could project their voices sufficiently in Covent Garden. Many older singers had left under Guthrie, who found them 'quarrelsome and insubordinate'. Dent thought that they 'did not take to Tony's standard of rehearsing' and that they needed better pay.[110]

Despite the growing differences, on 5 January 1945 Dent informed Carey that the 'treaty' with Covent Garden would be ratified the following week. Sadler's Wells would lend its company to Covent Garden from September 1945 for five years, with two or three Sadler's Wells members on the Covent Garden Board, Dent and two others. Care would be taken that they were not submerged and did not lose their identity, even though artistic control would be under the Covent Garden committee. Sadler's Wells would remain under the same artistic direction, with Crozier possibly part of the artistic team.[111] Dent, having spotted that Webster was going to be the most powerful person, decided to stay close to him and to encourage him in his love of power in order to influence him. He had made a list of possible repertoire for Webster, including many English works, but preserving works like *Figaro* and *Don Giovanni* for the smaller house. 'The curse of the Wells', Dent warned, was 'indecision'.[112]

Sure enough, at the last moment the Sadler's Wells governors became very worried about the legal obligations of their charter, as well as their responsibilities to the staff, many of whom would not be taken on by Covent Garden. Guthrie pressed the governors to accept the scheme, arguing that 'since the Old Vic charter was granted in 1880, social conditions had changed'. The theatre's most valuable contribution was to be made in high artistic standards, 'not in cheap seats as a form of social service'.[113] On the other hand, Covent Garden did not understand the responsibilities of Sadler's Wells to 'its supposed proletarian audiences'. By 27 March Dent was urging that Sadler's Wells must have an alternative plan 'in case it did not work, or the war went on beyond the B&H lease!!'[114]

There was no progress with the Covent Garden representatives, despite their assurances to the governors that there would be 259 cheap seats. It was now quite clear to Sadler's Wells that Covent Garden wanted to take over the 'goodwill' of their name but practically none of the people belonging to it, and hoped to scrap the company and use Sadler's Wells as a school. A Covent Garden archive document of April 1945, probably written by Webster, suggested that only Goodall, Cross and a few of the Sadler's Wells personnel, chorus and orchestra would be kept on.[115]

The governors remained concerned about their responsibilities to Collingwood and the staff. Dent had also come to realise that Covent Garden, in association with Sadler's Wells, might easily become just Covent Garden – 'like the *Nation* melting into the *New Statesman*'.[116] At the same time he feared that there were not enough singers for two opera houses. On 18 May Carey told Dent that it was 'nonsense about the voices': it all depended on 'carrying power not size of voice'. There were plenty of capable singers, including Edith Coates, Hargreaves and Arnold Matters, although Matters was keen to go back to Sydney. Nor were the scenery and the conductors any good, except possibly Goodall in a subordinate capacity. Guthrie always had some other career in view, although he remained very loyal to the opera.[117]

On 7 May 1945 Germany surrendered. Londoners started to pour into the streets in celebration, becoming a massive throng of joy and relief the next day, official VE Day. Britain after the war was a very different place from 1939 and further readjustments in society and the economy had to be faced. The state had taken on responsibilities unimaginable before the war, in every area of life, and had instilled the potent idea of a much fairer, more equal society. The Ministry of Food, which was in control of rationing, had enforced a centralised system of fair distribution that was the main weapon in winning acceptance for the deprivations and difficulties that rationing imposed. By 1941 the poorest members of society were receiving better nutrition than before the war, with vitamins and free milk. Not only was the system centrally organised, it was also a great leveller. At the same time, the Minister of Labour, Ernest Bevin, who had been brought into the Government of National Unity by Churchill to mobilise national manpower, contributed to the recasting of social values and changing the status and conditions of the industrial worker. The Beveridge Report of late 1942, which formalised the concept of a complete welfare state, became a best-seller, capturing the public mood and focusing attention on the ills of society and how to put them right.

Professor Richard Titmuss, the official historian of wartime social policy, wrote in 1950: 'It was increasingly regarded as a proper function of Government to ward off distress and strain amongst not only the poor but almost all classes of society.'[118] The evolution of centralised funding for the arts and a fairer distribution of its benefits was one of the great social changes generated by the war effort, with the wartime Vic-Wells playing a major part in the development.

Guthrie was quick to recognise the change. He believed that the role of Sadler's Wells was no longer to take part in poor relief but to strive to improve standards of performance for a wider audience. He pondered on the changes in attitude to the arts in general, and opera in particular, that had evolved during the war, writing in 1945:

It does not seem to me unreasonable to suppose that the war has awakened in many hundreds of thousands of people a realisation that many things which formerly they had considered too high brow or too grand for them are easily within their imaginative and financial grasp . . . the pleasant amenities of a fortunate few should rightly be regarded as universal necessities.[119]

# 5

# 1945–1959: Norman Tucker, 'The Cuckoo in the Arts Council Nest'

In the immediate aftermath of the war it was not clear whether Sadler's Wells would survive to benefit either from the great social changes taking place or from its own historic struggle. Not only were the developments at Covent Garden casting the future into doubt, but at Sadler's Wells itself the stoic leadership of the war was unravelling. Ironically, it was to be one of the greatest achievements in the company's history that nearly resulted in its demise.

In January 1944 Benjamin Britten had started composing *Peter Grimes*, after having hammered out the libretto with the playwright Montagu Slater.* The publishers, Boosey and Hawkes, had initially wanted the premiere for the opening of Covent Garden. Britten had agreed, as he 'deplored the low musical standards of the Wells in general and of the orchestra in particular'. Covent Garden, however, did not look as though it would be ready for some time.[1]

In the course of his work, Britten had become closer to Sadler's Wells, having sought and received advice about the technicalities of opera staging from Eric Crozier and also having discussed the libretto with him.[2] He remodelled many of the roles on Sadler's Wells singers: Ellen Orford on Cross, Auntie on Edith Coates, and after changing the role from baritone to tenor, Peter Pears as Grimes. When Britten played them the first part of *Peter Grimes* on the piano in Liverpool, Guthrie, Cross and Collingwood immediately agreed to stage it.[3] Cross wrote in her diary on 19 March 1944 that they had all been 'greatly excited'. The music was 'vivid and virile with moments of great beauty, superior to my mind to anything he has yet invented'.

---

* Britten had received the commission from Serge Koussevitsky, the conductor of the Boston Symphony Orchestra, and its premiere was to have been in the United States, at Koussevitsky's Tanglewood festival. When Britten's relationship with Sadler's Wells developed, Koussevitsky gave his permission for *Peter Grimes* to be premiered there.

In December 1944 plans for staging the opera had begun in earnest, with Reginald Goodall, who had joined Sadler's Wells on 24 September 1944 as a répétiteur, in charge of the musical preparation. After performances of *The Bartered Bride* in December, Goodall had been made assistant conductor, and Britten decided he wanted him to conduct *Peter Grimes*. Collingwood agreed, and Guthrie also accepted that Crozier would direct.

Crozier recalled in an article for *Opera* in 1965 how preparations for *Peter Grimes* contributed to the break-up of the Sadler's Wells management after the war. As soon as the copies of the first act of *Peter Grimes* were made available in February 1945, a group of singers had started a campaign 'against those responsible for holding the company together during recent years' and against the work itself. There was an accusation that Cross's participation was the reason for the opera being produced, and there was much complaining about the music's cacophony.[4] Cross recalled groups of singers gathering in dark recesses of the theatre, 'muttering discontentedly'. Not only did the principals and chorus hate the new opera, 'they resented the fact that Peter Pears and I were taking the principal roles'.[5]

The company had believed that they would return to Sadler's Wells, perhaps in *Il trovatore*, with company favourites in the leading roles. Not only was *Peter Grimes* to be conducted by Goodall, but many stalwart company members were excluded from the cast.[6] The soprano Elizabeth Abercrombie had originally been chosen to alternate with Cross, but Britten changed his mind and Cross alone was to sing, much to the anger of Abercrombie and her friends. Cross's return to a singing career threatened the jobs of other sopranos; rumours of the Covent Garden plans were also making everyone anxious for their futures.[7]

John Hargreaves, who had been a true stalwart of the company throughout the war, was offered no part at all and became a focus for dissension. Goodall was too conscientious an accompanist for some of the singers, who had acquired slovenly habits during the war and resented his accusations of inaccuracy. For his part he knew how hard it would be for most of them to master the difficult new idiom of Britten's opera.

As the war drew to its close, Cross was exhausted from the tour and drained by the continuous bureaucratic work necessary to keep singers out of the army and to obtain coupons for costume material.

In March she had handed over the job of opera director to Guthrie in order to defuse the row over *Peter Grimes*. She too was worried about the vocal resources of Sadler's Wells, and she did not think that the sopranos, other than Victoria Sladen, were a match for the men or for the mezzos and contraltos. No one, however, paid attention to her offer to resign.[8]

Serious trouble had begun when the eleven-week period of rehearsals began on 22 March 1945 in Liverpool. 'Simmering resentment', Cross later wrote, 'boiled up into open hostility.' Tom Williams, who was supposed to sing Balstrode, pulled out, claiming he could not learn the part. Cross replaced him with Roderick Jones. The orchestra and chorus struggled with the work and remained, in Cross's words, 'stubbornly antagonistic towards the piece as well as towards Peter [Pears] and myself'. Britten and Pears 'were sneered at as Joan's pansies'.[9] Leading singers had also complained that the composer, leading tenor and producer had been conscientious objectors – something that was intentionally reflected in the character of Grimes, the 'tortured idealist'.[10] It was a terrible time for Cross, who recalled being in a trance-like state of emotional and physical exhaustion, exacerbated by the unpleasantness and resentment.[11]

Rehearsals for *Peter Grimes* continued in church halls and hotels, while the company performed nightly in Hammersmith, Wimbledon or Birmingham. Goodall coached the singers, and the new chorus master, Alan Melville, tried to prepare his baffled choristers. The company finally reached Sadler's Wells on 19 May, when Goodall was able to conduct the dress rehearsal with an augmented orchestra of fifty players. In an interview with Alan Blyth in *Gramophone* in June 1970 Britten recalled that at the dress rehearsal he 'thought the whole thing would be a disaster'.

Guthrie endeavoured to dampen the flames of dissent, telling Dent on 25 May that the barrage of rumour concerning Covent Garden – most of which was unfounded and fantastically exaggerated – was having 'quite a disintegrating effect'. He was preparing plans for a major reorganisation of the company and wanted Dent to scrutinise them. He was not happy that members of CEMA were on the Covent Garden Board. Dispensers of the state support, in his opinion, 'should be above, not concerned with, contemporary artistic policies'.[12]

The crisis came to a head just before opening night, when the governors told the company that new contracts would be issued for only the six-week London season. The Equity trade-union representatives, Hargreaves and Abercrombie, formed a committee and confronted the governors. Making it quite clear that the company did not wish to go to Covent Garden and that it was essential to maintain Sadler's Wells in order to develop the careers of young singers, they threatened a boycott of the season by Equity members.[13] They were supported in their wish to maintain the independence of Sadler's Wells by Sir George Dyson, who had replaced Sir Reginald Rowe as chairman of the Trust after Rowe's death in January 1945. The Earl of Lytton soon joined forces with Dyson to put an end to the Covent Garden plan. David Webster was so informed on the day that *Peter Grimes* opened.

While the future of Sadler's Wells was hanging in the balance, the premiere of *Peter Grimes* symbolised the birth of a truly native opera after a long and devastating war. Shortly before its premiere on 7 June 1945, Tyrone Guthrie wrote that the work put to the test an operatic policy that had been doggedly pursued for many years, which aimed at the creation of an operatic ensemble that could 'give authentic expression to new British works, if and when the occasion arose'. He believed that the company would show itself to advantage in a piece that was not a 'tepid translation of torrid specimens of Mediterranean art'. The new opera was 'traditionally, instinctively, sub-consciously native rather than alien'. It was a symbol, an act of faith, the result of 'five gruelling years' of trying to hold something together from the past, making it the 'very opening of the new era, a gesture of innovation'.[14]

Queues for the gallery formed from 10 p.m. the night before the premiere. On the night, the house was full, with the great and the good of the musical world present. The loyal audience of Sadler's Wells returned to the galleries, wheelchair-bound Doris Perrot telling the *News Chronicle* that music was her whole life.[15]

Cross described the immediate response of the audience. 'At first we didn't know,' she wrote. 'There was silence at the end and then shouting broke out.' The stage crew were stunned, thinking it a demonstration. 'Well, it was,' she wrote, 'but fortunately it was of the right kind.'[16]

Critics immediately recognised that *Peter Grimes* was a landmark for British opera. On 8 June Frank Howes wrote in *The Times* that it had ranked as one of the 'small number of works that will hold the stage and add something new to musical experience'. It was a happy augury for Sadler's Wells Opera that Britten's *Peter Grimes* should mark the company's return to its old home after five years of itinerant exile. It was also a 'good omen for British opera that this first fruit of peace should declare decisively that opera on the grand scale and in the grand manner can still be written'. Expectations ran high and were not disappointed.

Howes described how *Grimes* fulfilled all the requirements of opera. Its dramatic appeal 'comes straight off the stage to the listener'. It proceeds 'by sharp turns of the dramatic screw, to situations of great power, intensified by orchestral music of diabolical cunning'. Opportunities for fine singing, especially from the chorus who make up the character of 'Public Opinion', were provided in profusion by Britten, 'from the intonation of the general confession' to crowd scenes 'unparalleled outside the Russian operas'. For Howes the sea was another character: 'In the entr'acte Britten has written salt-water music of unequalled intensity – a universalised image of the sea in tempest.'[17]

Reginald Goodall's conducting and the performances of the artists also received high praise. Howes wrote that in Goodall the company had discovered an operatic conductor with a talent for dramatic music. His piloting of chorus and orchestra through a complex score was the chief factor in the opera's successful performance. William Glock in the *Observer* wrote of Goodall's 'musicianly appeal, which sometimes rose to the level of evangelical zeal'. He thought that Joan Cross sang Ellen Orford with ardour, dignity and a beautiful quality of tone.[18]

On 18 June Britten told a friend: 'It looks as if the old spell on British opera may be broken at last.' To Imogen Holst he wrote on 26 June: 'Perhaps it is an omen for English opera in the future.' He hoped that many composers would 'take the plunge' and find that the water was 'not quite so icy as expected!' He added: 'I think that the occasion is actually a greater one than either Sadler's Wells or me.'[19]

The premiere of *Peter Grimes* was to prove a happier 'augury' for Britten than for Sadler's Wells. The wartime leadership was dissolving and *Grimes* proved to be a unique event in the annals of the company. A new work of such enduring potency and genius was never again premiered there, despite much effort and endeavour over many years. After its run had ended, Sadler's Wells lost not only its close links with the composer but also many of the outstandingly talented personnel that it so badly needed.

Ernest Newman had devoted articles to *Peter Grimes* in the *Sunday Times* on three consecutive weeks from 10 June. While he recognised the importance of the work, the third article was a sustained discussion about the unsatisfactory nature of the theatre's acoustic and its detrimental effect on the singers' tonal values and articulation. He argued for the work's transfer to Covent Garden as soon as possible.[20]

Not only the future of the theatre but that of the company itself was in doubt. The events leading up to the premiere had left the battle lines clearly drawn and the great success of *Peter Grimes* had not assuaged the ill feeling of company members towards Cross. In July there were unofficial reports in *The Stage* that she had offered her resignation.[21] Cross later wrote that apart from two flattering lunches, no one paid attention to her resignation. It was not announced in the press and Guthrie, who was himself losing control of the company, chose to ignore it, hoping that the success of *Grimes* would make her change her mind; instead, she refused to go to company meetings. The next few months were dismal for Cross; she had no money and her housekeeper had to take a job elsewhere.[22]

Guthrie's own hopes, expressed just before the opening of *Peter Grimes*, were to be bitterly disappointed. Had he been surer of himself and his beliefs, he would have been able at the end of the war to turn the companies – ballet triumphant, opera and drama battered but intact – into 'a real British National Theatre'. They were, he wrote, the 'repositories of certain indispensable skills and traditions'.[23]

Guthrie's authority was seriously undermined when a company member, the baritone John Hargreaves, organised an ENSA tour under Walter Legge's management behind his back.[24] This meant that a planned Decca recording of *Peter Grimes* would not go ahead. There were also clashes in the Old Vic Shakespeare company. Guthrie was unhappy when in June 1945 it was decided by the governors that the company's West End season was to be run by Olivier, Richardson and John Burrell, who had been his deputy. He was worried that Burrell would be overawed by his powerful fellow directors. On 27 July Burrell became responsible for all the Old Vic's dramatic activities.

That same day an emergency meeting of the Sadler's Wells directors discussed letters from Hargreaves, Abercrombie and Braithwaite in which the two singers urged that the direction of the opera company should not be vested in one person. Braithwaite was engaged as a conductor during the ENSA tour. Dyson proposed to offer the company six-month contracts before they went overseas, giving them a definite date by which they must accept. He also reported deadlock in the negotiations with Covent Garden after he had asked for £30,000 (based on two-year profits) for the goodwill of the company. Keynes and Glasgow had thought it a reasonable offer, but Covent Garden had turned it down – instead suggesting four annual payments of £3,500.[25]

Sadler's Wells was on tour in Belfast on 1 August when Britten wrote to Pears: 'I do so hope this lousy tour isn't being too hellish for you.' He advised Pears not to take any notice of 'those ludicrous fools' (the insurgents) and to spend his time with Cross, Goodall and Collingwood. On 4 August Pears replied that he was seeing little of the rest of the company. On the contrary, he was looking for talent to join the new company that he and Britten were planning to create. One possible candidate was Roderick Jones, the original Balstrode, who was 'genuinely sick' at not being allowed to record *Peter Grimes*. The singers were not quite ready to leave Sadler's Wells, however, as they did not dare 'cut off from a sure job yet'.[26]

In August Dyson himself took over responsibility for the company, trying to maintain discipline and mend fences. On 18 August the baritone Edward Donlevy wrote to the manager of the companies, George Chamberlain, that 'the elements of quarrelsomeness, overweening ambition, envy, fear of unemployment, hysteria' which had appeared during the previous six months had done 'more to damage the artistic standard of the company's work than anything else could possibly have done'. On the 21st Dyson himself wrote that in the aftermath of war the company was in a terrible state: a 'nightmare of division'. If the singers did not agree to the contracts for the 1945/6 season, the company would have to be disbanded.[27]

In an attempt to lessen the ill feeling, Dyson persuaded Collingwood to stay on as music director and invited Cross and Pears to
appear in a revival of *Peter Grimes* in the new London season.
Cross agreed, and so did Pears, provided that Crozier and Goodall
were involved.[28] On 22 August, however, Cross wrote her final letter of resignation to the chairman of the governors, Sir Ernest
Pooley. She expressed her regret that her term of direction had come
to such an 'ignominious end' and that 'sound policy should have
failed so ingloriously'. The opera company had been without leadership for more than six months and the internal conditions were
chaotic. The standard of performances had fallen alarmingly and
the ENSA tour could only aggravate the situation. Her whole professional life had been dedicated to Sadler's Wells and she would
willingly have stayed on the list of artists. But now that a fresh start
was needed in the face of overwhelming difficulties her enthusiasm
was exhausted.[29]

On 5 September the governors accepted her resignation, with
some voices regretting her loss and expressing the opinion that 'the
direction of the company which had achieved the production of
*Peter Grimes* was more important than any other consideration for
the future of opera'. Violet Bonham-Carter, a Liberal politician who
joined the Old Vic governors in 1945, suggested that Cross's 'long
and valued service' entitled her to more consideration than 'any
other artist who might choose to resign'. Dyson, however, felt that
all artists must 'accept contracts without conditions' and recommended Clive Carey to replace her.[30] He urged CEMA to give
Sadler's Wells a grant rather than a guarantee against loss so that
the company's resources might be more easily assessed.[31]

It was a sorry end to a heroic story. Lord Harewood greatly
admired Cross. She was, he wrote, 'one of the might-have-beens of
operatic life in our time' in that she spent the best years of her career
touring and administering in wartime, 'not spreading her talents
through the world in peace'.[32]

While the future of Sadler's Wells was uncertain, state patronage for
the arts was being formalised. In July 1945 Keynes had launched
the Arts Council in a BBC broadcast, declaring that at last the government had recognised its duty to patronise the arts. Keynes did
not believe, however, in an open-ended purse; rather he saw patron-

age as providing endowments, loans or a guarantee against loss, such as Sadler's Wells had received in the war. His ideal was a mix of private and state patronage, but he gradually came to realise that private patronage would be destroyed by high taxation and the arts might become extinct. This dilemma remained at the core of arts-funding policy, first as the Treasury came to comprehend the growing nature of the demands that would be made by developing arts institutions and then, in the 1980s, with the return to a greater degree of private patronage as an objective in government thinking.

Keynes had drafted the Arts Council's constitution in September 1944. It consisted of a permanent council of eleven members, five of whom were to serve as an executive committee to chair panels of outside experts. There was to be a director general with a small staff. Under R. A. Butler's Education Department and with Keynes its first chairman, the Arts Council was very much in harmony with the model of the BBC as an educational enterprise promoted by its director general, Lord Reith. 'We look forward very much to the time when the theatre and concert hall and the gallery will be the living element in everyone's upbringing, and regular attendance at the theatre and concerts a part of organised education,' declared Keynes.[33] The Arts Council's remit was about developing 'excellence' and improving standards of execution, as well as increasing accessibility. It was intended to foster opera and ballet, but it was Covent Garden that lay at the heart of Keynes's hopes for making London a great artistic capital. Covent Garden received £25,000 in the Arts Council's first year; Sadler's Wells received £10,000.

The opportunity had at last arrived to establish an operatic culture in England. An Arts Council report of 1967 paid tribute to the work that had preceded the momentous change in circumstance: 'The wonder is that, with such daunting conditions of work, two companies [Sadler's Wells and Carl Rosa] bred generations of artists who were capable of responding successfully when opportunities came.'[34]

Whether those 'artists' would be part of a vibrant Sadler's Wells was by now very much in question as the company disintegrated, losing some of the most gifted and devoted of its component parts. On the day that the company went on the ENSA tour to Europe on 28 August, Pears wrote to Britten to say that it looked as if 'the powers of evil' had won and that the recording of *Peter Grimes* was off.[35] Sixty-six members of the company travelled by land and sea, while the cast of the first opera performance in Hamburg flew out earlier in order to have time to rehearse with the local orchestra. All in all the company consisted of ninety-six artists and staff.

The eight-week tour was a shattering experience for the company as their train wound its way slowly through Holland, which was celebrating victory, and then through Germany. One member, Bruce Worsley, was struck by the sight of towns and cities 'each consisting of a circular area of rubble', with the Germans apparently not doing very much to clear up the ruins, living in cellars and whatever was left of the buildings. Hamburg had been 'blasted to destruction' and all the cities looked strikingly alike.[36]

The company performed *Rigoletto*, *La bohème*, *The Bartered Bride*, *Madam Butterfly*, *The Marriage of Figaro* and *Così fan tutte*. There were problems with casting as many company members had to return to England to fulfil engagements to which they had committed before the tour was organised. Amongst those who filled the gaps were David Franklin, who was released by the RAF, John Barbirolli and Joan Hammond, who joined for two performances of *Madam Butterfly*. The scenery did not arrive until ten days after their first performance and makeshift replacements had to be borrowed from local municipal operas in the meantime. Powell Lloyd was in charge of rehearsals; Goodall joined later. Many members of the company went down with bronchitis caused by the rubble and dust, and Edith Coates had to be admitted to hospital after reacting badly to a typhus vaccination.

The company were in Hamburg from 5–11 September. On 23 September they were taken to Belsen, where the horror 'cast a gloom over the company'. Warwick Braithwaite was sickened and overwhelmed by what he saw, including 'huge mounds of earth and sand piled above the graves of thousands of unknown dead'. He arranged for some of the Sadler's Wells singers – Edith Coates, Arthur Servent, Linda Parker and Ronald Stear – to give a concert to the displaced persons. Together with Walter Susskind at the piano, they gave of their best and were much appreciated by their audience.[37]

On 1 and 2 October the company performed in the British sector of devastated Berlin at the Theater des Westens – the temporary home of the Deutsche Oper, whose building had been bombed out.

They reached Düsseldorf on 22 October, returning to England on 28 October via Ostend.

On 12 December Guthrie finally resigned, and it was decided that Carey was to be asked to direct the opera company for six months. That same week, Cross failed to persuade the governors to support the intimate opera group she was forming with Britten, Pears and Crozier, which shortly after became the English Opera Group. At this moment the company's existence was hanging by a thread and, with Covent Garden in the process of creating an opera company based on English-language performances, artists and composers, the struggle for survival seemed an almost hopeless task. Somehow the forbearance and determination of a few individuals kept Sadler's Wells going for long enough for the two houses eventually to pursue something resembling the logical path set out by Dent and Guthrie in 1944. In true British fashion, however, the outcome was more the result of individual personalities and events than planning.

Some of the governors were wary of Carey's appointment, Evelyn Williams suggesting that Carey's age and his six-year absence in Australia during the war might mean he was out of touch with the younger and more forward-looking musicians. They unanimously accepted him, however, for six months.[38]

Carey was faced with the great problem of getting the company functioning at a reasonable level once more. Dent sought to encourage and advise him, urging him to find new singers quickly, to keep an eye and ear on everything and ruthlessly tell everybody, including stage managers and conductors, what they ought to do. He advised Carey to tell his singers: 'The softer you sing, the more care you have to take with articulating your words, so as never to let down the intensity.' If Carey hesitated or appeared undecided, dangerous outside forces would get in, but if he kept a firm hand on things and had a clear policy, Dent believed Dyson would support him.[39]

On 10 December Dent wrote to Carey to say that he had dissuaded critic Desmond Shawe-Taylor from writing a provocative article about Sadler's Wells in the *New Statesman*. Shawe-Taylor believed that Sadler's Wells had sacked Cross and Pears or that they had been forced to resign. Dent had put him right and urged him to concentrate on the future of Sadler's Wells and to foster it.[40]

Despite Dent's support for Carey, there was pressure to have him replaced. A memorandum was circulated amongst the Trust in which it was pointed out that it was unlikely that he could re-establish links with the lost members of the company or improve standards of production, when before the war the general level of performance had not been high enough.[41] Violet Bonham-Carter wrote to Dent on 23 January 1946 to defend her sponsorship of Rudolf Bing, whom she knew personally and admired, to run Sadler's Wells. It was not her aim to make Sadler's Wells more like Glyndebourne, she wrote – 'the preserve of a small, rich elite' – but rather to transmit its 'quality and musical standard'. To the argument that Sadler's Wells was sold out, she retorted that all theatres were – 'good bad and indifferent'.[42]

Dyson and Dent united to prevent what Dyson believed to be an attempt to create a 'pale imitation' of Glyndebourne or Covent Garden. Were they going to be 'a people's opera or not'? Dyson asked. A small group should be chosen to discuss policy, names and conditions.[43]

On 23 February 1946 a major component of Sadler's Wells, the ballet company, moved to Covent Garden on the suggestion of Keynes. Ninette de Valois remained the director of the Sadler's Wells ballet, with Peggy van Praagh as her assistant at the newly created Sadler's Wells Opera-Ballet. De Valois was based at Covent Garden, making frequent visits to Sadler's Wells. The ballet company's departure with no compensation entailed a loss of income to Sadler's Wells of £15,000. The Wells company's reserve funds after the war were soon used up as costs rose.

It was up to Carey to salvage what he could by painstakingly rebuilding the company with new singing talent. Tenor James Johnston, the son of a Belfast butcher, joined Sadler's Wells in 1945 and remained a mainstay of the company until his retirement in 1958. Charles Mackerras, who would later become the company's music director, described him as a 'great sort of quasi-heldentenor' who was at home in Italian opera. In January 1946 Johnston sang the Duke in *Rigoletto*, giving a 'grand full-blooded display of real tenor tone'.[44] He also sang Rodolfo in *La bohème* in 1946 to packed houses, audiences queuing up round the block for tickets – many at their first *Bohème*.[45]

The 1945/6 Sadler's Wells season had begun late, on Boxing Day, with *The Bartered Bride*, conducted by the Czech émigré Walter Susskind, who had a natural feel for the Czech rhythms. It was then back to the 'torrid' Mediterranean with *The Barber of Seville*, which opened on 2 January 1946. Dyneley Hussey wrote in *The Spectator* that Michael Mudie conducted with a 'feel for Italian melody', although the violins were 'wretchedly out of tune'. The production was supervised by forty-year-old director John Moody, who was to have a distinguished career at Sadler's Wells and Welsh National Opera as director and, with his wife Nell, translator. *The Barber of Seville*, however, seemed to Hussey to be a bit of a muddle – instead of organised and concerted movement there were 'free-for-all scrambles'. Nonetheless, the critic wrote, Carey was wise to hurry slowly, recruiting young singers like James Johnston and Howell Glynne, who impressed Hussey as a promising and true buffo.[46] On 1 February Philip Hope-Wallace wrote that Carey was beginning to make a difference, but Sadler's Wells needed a 'big heave to get out of mediocrity'.[47]

Pears and Cross returned to Sadler's Wells for a revival of *Peter Grimes* on 7 February. When Britten appeared, he was cheered 'as if he had just scored for Chelsea'.[48] Shawe-Taylor wrote that Britten's work required larger forces to do it justice and suffered 'lamentably from the shortage of strings', particularly in the interludes.[49] Jennie Lee, Labour MP and a future minister responsible for the arts, had attended the revival and revealed a certain lack of discernment, writing in *The Tribune* that she had been disappointed and alarmed that a work she found to be an affront to the eyes and an 'outrage' to the ears should be given a boost because it was British. If there was going to be a National Theatre, there could be no place, she warned, 'for the taint of nationalism. Works must be judged solely on their merits.'[50]

In March Bing was interviewed by the governors to take over from Carey, after he and James Robertson had been identified as the most suitable contenders. Bing told them that he regarded Sadler's Wells as of great importance and would willingly accept the position but would not give up his Glyndebourne work. The governors' ballot was consequently six to three in favour of Robertson.[51]

Robertson, who had served in the RAF during the war, spoke excellent German. Mackerras, who worked with him from 1947, considered him a fine musician, although not as good a conductor as Michael Mudie, who was 'first conductor'. Robertson joined the company after experience as répétiteur on the music staff at Glyndebourne, where he had learnt, under Fritz Busch, 'the good old German way of doing Mozart' with no appoggiature.[52]

In April 1946 Sumner Austin produced Ralph Vaughan Williams's *Sir John in Love*, with Bagnall Harris's décor. The *Observer* praised it as 'genuinely, innocently and magnificently national' – the music 'completely of its period and completely of its time'. Vaughan Williams's Falstaff was a rich musical portrait with an 'autumnal glowing aria in the second act, a swaggering march to his discomfiture' and recovery in a glorious tune. Roderick Jones was Falstaff and Howell Glynne, Ford.[53]

Wolf-Ferrari's 1906 *I quatro rusteghi*, translated by Dent as *The School for Fathers*, opened on 7 June. It was directed by the forty-eight-year-old Dennis Arundell, who had studied music and classics at Cambridge just after the First World War and had become an influential figure in music theatre since his first Cambridge productions in the early 1920s. Dent had been busy for some months revising his earlier translation of the libretto, and by January was having difficulties with Arundell, who wanted to transfer the play from Venice to London and give everyone English names. Arundell was keen that the thoroughly middle-class and vulgar atmosphere of the play should come across. Dent mischievously reassured him that Sadler's Wells could do 'all that' for him 'without any coaching'. Arundell's only problem, he suggested, would be to turn Morgan Jones into a fop, although dress and make-up would help.[54] Arundell won the argument – the scene was set in a London of corn chandlers, apothecaries and cutlers. St Paul's was prominent in the décor of the young artist Michael Whittaker. Arundell also set a real cat alone on the garden wall to end the first act, in order, as he explained, to strip 'the bourgeois comedy of any falsely romantic association'.[55]

The show was much enjoyed by the public, although many of the singers struggled with some of the ensembles and the production met with a mixed critical response. *The Times* critic said that by locating the piece in London, Arundell tilted what was a comedy of manners 'uncomfortably towards farce'. He did, however, praise Sadler's Wells for pursuing a 'progressive policy' and greatly enjoyed the good humour and tunefulness of the work.[56] Not long after his pep talk from Dent, Shawe-Taylor in the *New Statesman* praised *School for Fathers* as the most polished production since before the war. It showed, he said, that a new broom had been at work. Arundell had got the cast to act with ease and lack of exaggeration; Howell Glynne received particular praise. The new music director, James Robertson, managed the many ensembles with 'lightness and precision'.[57] Robertson and Arundell were central to the revival of Sadler's Wells at this time.

The Arts Council, having given a guarantee against loss of £5,000, were faced by a Sadler's Wells deficit of £6,516 in August 1946. *School for Fathers* had cost £1,837 and *Sir John in Love* £1,307. Someone noted on the Arts Council accounts next to *Sir John*: 'Some of this money was disgracefully ill spent.'[58] The deficit did nothing to help Carey gain the long-term confidence of the trustees, despite Dent's encouragement, and he was not sorry to hand over responsibility to James Robertson before the 1946/7 season. Sumner Austin was technical director, John Moody the resident producer, with Arundell as guest director.

Productions in the early post-war years were concerned with the need to familiarise new audiences with the repertoire, new and old. *Tosca*, directed by Dennis Arundell and designed by Michael Whittaker, opened on 18 December. Arundell wrote that in an attempt to make the story clearer to those who did not know it – and there were many – he had ill-advisedly introduced the Marchesa Attavanti hiding the key at the beginning of the opera.[59] Victoria Sladen's Tosca was slightly more convincing vocally than dramatically. James Johnston was Cavaradossi and Roderick Jones Scarpia. Douglas Jones, who later directed opera as Douglas Craig, was Angelotti. According to *The Times*, the string tone under Michael Mudie's direction was not adequate for Puccini's melodies.

In July 1947 *Musical Opinion* was saddened to find Sadler's Wells sounding 'more than a trifle fatigued', which it ascribed to the strain of singing in such an unresponsive acoustic. Encouraging though they were, the senior critics also pointed out the distance that Sadler's Wells had yet to travel if it were to catch up with the standards of provincial houses in Europe. Shawe-Taylor wrote in the *New Statesman* on 9 August that the BBC's Third Programme was familiarising English listeners with both foreign languages and a high standard of singing and added that until such time as singing was remunerated as a full-time occupation, there would be no chance of emulating such standards.[60] For Germans, unlike the English, opera was a necessity. The *Coventry Evening Telegraph* reporter had been astonished to see in Hamburg the 'loyal, reverent, understanding audiences' travelling through 'acres of devastation, under conditions which make the London underground at rush hour seem like a luxury cruise'. There were, however, changes afoot even in England, with new groups of enthusiasts resulting from the troops' exposure to opera in Italy. The *Daily Telegraph* reported that opera parties of more than two hundred people were being organised by factories, offices and shops, Whitehall and the offices of the London County Council to visit Sadler's Wells. Almost all of the promoters were, the report said, ex-servicemen who had served in Europe.

Attempts to renew the old, tired and tatty core repertoire continued with Dennis Arundell's *Faust* on 14 October 1947. It was the first time it had been seen at Sadler's Wells since the fateful Saturday of 7 September 1940. The new *Faust* did not look tired but it did appear rather poverty-stricken, costing £1,400. Joseph Carl's unusually deep backcloth showed a dark sky when let down and the elongated houses of the Kermesse when raised. The sets were not only ugly but also shuddered alarmingly when doors were slammed.[61] Pauline Grant choreographed the *Walpurgisnacht* ballet, which, in Norman Tucker's words, 'verged pleasantly on the erotic'.[62]

Arundell's aim was to recreate what he called the 'psychological' Covent Garden premiere of 1863 planned by Gounod, who had despised the simultaneous realistic Haymarket version. Newman acknowledged his success in replacing the usual crude realism by a 'general atmosphere of mystery, sometimes almost of mysticism'. Mephistopheles was a dark force of evil instead of a pantomime Demon King.[63] Sometimes the darkness was too literal and the performers were obscured. James Johnston was Faust, Marion Lowe Marguerite, Howell Glynne Mephistopheles. Michael Mudie conducted. The production packed the house at first and it remained in the repertoire until March 1956.

Before the end of the 1946/7 season, the exhausted Robertson appealed to his old friend Norman Tucker to come and help run the company. From December 1947 Tucker, with Robertson and Mudie as resident conductors, formed an unofficial triumvirate, known in the house as the 'Three Norns'.* Their task was to keep Sadler's Wells alive, while the Arts Council regarded it, in Tucker's words, as an 'embarrassment'.

Tucker was a fine pianist but had given up hopes of a professional career, realising, as he put it, that he would never be more than an 'also-ran'. He had been an opera lover ever since spending time in the amphitheatre of Covent Garden with his school friend Isaiah Berlin in the early 1930s. He also appreciated the Sadler's Wells company, having been a frequent member of the audience during the war and having seen the first five performances of *Peter Grimes*. He had had a classical and musical education at St Paul's and Oxford, studied piano and performance at the Royal College of Music, and worked at the Treasury during and just after the war under three chancellors – Kingsley Wood, John Anderson and Hugh Dalton. His talent, education and experience stood him in excellent stead when he decided to work in the arts. A quiet and introspective man, though with a keen sense of fun, Tucker was to prove to be a man of steely determination, total commitment and an unwavering sense of purpose.

Before responding to Robertson, Tucker went to see Steuart Wilson, music director of the Arts Council, who warned him not to accept, as he regarded Sadler's Wells as a dying institution. Tucker nonetheless decided to take the job, despite the low morale and standards of the company.[64] The company's survival after the war can be substantially ascribed to his determination and skill. Tucker joined the company at the end of the 1946/7 season when it was on tour in Belfast. It was, for him, a crash course in opera administration.

The shape of the post-war arts world was undergoing profound if gradual changes, the ultimate outcome of which remained unclear for some time. The civil service and government were slowly and somewhat reluctantly coming to terms with the concept of state funding and the open-ended nature of the demands that would be made by uncompromising arts administrators and their enterprises,

* Three virgin goddesses of destiny in Scandinavian mythology that open Wagner's *Götterdämmerung*.

and by their boards, whose members were themselves part of the establishment. The artists and their boards proved wily, utterly determined and ambitious in their efforts to extract funds from the government and develop their institutions. The one thing that was not intended was the development of two opera companies and two national theatres, but the story of the post-war arts world is the evolution of just such a dual set-up.

During the 1947/8 season there were changes on the Sadler's Wells Trust. Two governors, the devoted and long-standing chairman Lord Lytton and Lord Hambledon, died and it was decided to separate the governors of each foundation, with each meeting separately. The government thought it advisable to appoint independent directors interested in opera because of the investment of public money. James Smith, later described by Arnold Goodman as 'an immensely amiable, kindly and gentle figure',[65] became the chairman of the Sadler's Wells Trust, which dealt with all the artistic activities.* Viscount Esher became chairman of the Old Vic governors, who dealt with the bricks and mortar of the two buildings. Dent stayed on the governing body of Sadler's Wells.

While the governance was being reorganised, Michael Mudie, the principal conductor, was endeavouring to define the company's role in relation to Covent Garden. He wrote a memorandum on Sadler's Wells policy in December 1947, which was based on the belief that with continued subsidy and the assistance of the BBC, an audience large enough to fill both houses would develop. Sadler's Wells, he wrote, 'should probably always retain the character of a people's theatre with relatively cheap seats'. It had to keep a broad basis of popular repertoire, perform lesser-known masterpieces and encourage new English operas. Immediate objectives included control over principals taking outside engagements, improving standards of acting and giving long-term contracts to young principals so they would not be tempted away. With these aims in mind the Arts Council was to be asked for a larger subsidy of £40,000.[66]

As well as defining its mission, the company was also beginning to absorb new talent. In the spring of 1947 the twenty-two-year-old Charles Mackerras, who had been principal oboist with the Sydney

---

* Smith was also a trustee of the Covent Garden Opera Trust from February 1946 until April 1950 and then on the board until resigning in 1954, though he returned for a second period from 1955 to 1957.

Symphony Orchestra, joined Sadler's Wells. Mackerras had seen Mudie about a vacancy for a second oboe and cor anglais, after which he was offered a job for the thirteen-week tour. On hearing of Mackerras's interest in conducting, Mudie also appointed him as a junior répétiteur and off-stage conductor, despite the fact that he had had no previous experience in these areas.

Mackerras's Sadler's Wells career began on 21 May 1947, in the King's Theatre, Southsea, in *La bohème*. It was his first job in opera, and throughout the tour he was sight-reading. He was soon conducting off-stage choruses. In those days, he later pointed out, there were no television monitors and he would leave the orchestra to conduct the Te Deum of *Tosca*, looking through a hole in the scenery, relaying Mudie's beat. In the third act, he would go again to play the bells. In the orchestra, also sight-reading, was the young clarinettist Judy Wilkins, with whom Mackerras immediately struck up a friendship. Their love and intimacy, he recalled, grew during the thirteen-week tour and they were married in August 1947.

At that time, according to Mackerras, the orchestra was about forty pieces, with twenty strings, double woodwind, four horns and five brass. When it was in London, it used to do operas like *Tosca*, which is scored for triple woodwind and three trumpets, with its full orchestral complement. The moment they went on tour, Mackerras noted, the numbers 'went right down', since the Sadler's Wells ballet company were on tour at the same time, with another, smaller section of the Sadler's Wells orchestra. With performances every night plus a matinee on Saturdays, the tour was 'very hard work' and also rigorous training.[67]

In September 1947 the company were back at Sadler's Wells performing *The Barber of Seville*, with Mackerras still hopping in and out of the pit. He was also coaching singers in their parts in the mornings. Mackerras won a scholarship to study in Prague with the conductor Václav Talich and went away for a year, accompanied by Judy.

On 17 December Hedley Briggs produced and designed a new *Die Fledermaus*. It was set in the 1870s: 'mahoganoid, effulgent with gas globes, ruched, bustled, pink waistcoated', with Valetta Iacopi as Prince Orlovsky and Arnold Matters as the Governor – both reprising their pre-war roles. Howell Glynne was Frosch. Conducted by Robertson, it was musically a lively and amusing show.[68] On 29 January 1948 Clive Carey directed with great animation what Mackerras later called a wonderful production of *Così fan tutte*, in the 'funny old Marmaduke Browne translation'.[69] A new *Il trovatore* directed by John Moody on 18 February, however, showed up the weaknesses of the company. For *The Times*, Johnston, Joyce Gartside and Redvers Llewellyn lacked any element of dramatic excitement: 'Their anglicised manner would be sufficiently satisfying if they had in themselves more power of emotional contagion.'[70]

In the autumn of 1948 Mackerras was back at Sadler's Wells as répétiteur and assistant conductor. Shortly before he left Prague he had written to his mother: 'I feel misgivings about going back to England. It will seem a bit tame and I'm sure the insular narrow minds of many English will drive me mad. However, I am really looking forward to beginning in Sadler's Wells.' When he got back, he was duly depressed by the drabness as well as by 'the extreme ordinariness and undistinctiveness of the English'.[71] It was indeed a grim time in the country at large, with fuel shortages, long queues for scant produce in the shops, inflation and a feeling of acute disappointment that the end of the war had not brought an end to deprivation and gloom.

The first thing Mackerras conducted was *Die Fledermaus* on 20 October 1948. 'One three-minute rehearsal with the orchestra and an hour with a few principals,' he wrote to his mother. Mudie had been 'quite astounded' by his performance, at the same time as taking him through his mistakes.[72] 'I conducted hundreds of performances of *Fledermaus* after that,' he recalled, 'because that was the opera that James Robertson and Michael Mudie were bored with.'[73]

On 27 October Norman Tucker was given sole control of Sadler's Wells, formally assuming the title of director in 1950. He was knowledgeable about music and planning, sensitive with artists and possessed a keen eye for talent. He also had a rare skill in translation, taking over the role of Dent in providing singable translations of both familiar and unfamiliar work, in particular of Janáček, as well as revising earlier translations that were no longer idiomatic.

Schooled in Greek and Latin, he was fascinated by the manipulation of words and delighted by bringing into play his musical imagination. Since opera in English lay at the core of the Sadler's Wells mission, the importance of this particular expertise cannot be overestimated.

Tucker was also well informed about business and finance, and his wartime Treasury experience proved invaluable in the delicate negotiations with the Arts Council. In his memoirs he described the 'strictly unethical' methods of getting money out of the Arts Council. In general, keeping the company 'in the black' was not his objective; it was preferable to be 'healthily in the red' and thus keep the subsidy as high as possible for the next year. It was, he wrote, 'a nice point of judgement how far we could inflate our legitimate and essential demands without sacrificing credibility'.[74]

It was not long before Tucker's strategy became a necessity, since Sir Stafford Cripps had taken over from Hugh Dalton as Chancellor of the Exchequer on 29 September 1947. Dalton had been an ally of both Covent Garden and the Arts Council, which had been able to increase the 1947/8 grant to Sadler's Wells to £23,000. This enabled Sadler's Wells to show a surplus of £4,180 that year. In July 1948 the next season's grant was raised to £40,000, although the theatre's ballet company and school cost £6,500 more than the grant allocated for them. On 7 December, shortly after Tucker took over, the Finance and General Purposes Committee noted that the Arts Council must be made aware that the repertoire was growing and that this necessitated an increase in the number of principal singers.

In March 1949 Sadler's Wells' application for a grant of £74,000 for the following season was reduced to £47,000 by the Arts Council. Tucker armed the Trust with arguments and questions for the Treasury. How, he asked, could the low prices of Sadler's Wells sustain work comparable to that of Covent Garden and compete for English artists on a subsidy a fraction of that of the younger company? Although Sadler's Wells ticket prices had increased slightly since the 1930s, with top prices up from 6s to 9s and the lowest from 6d to 1s, they still remained both affordable and much lower than those of Covent Garden, whose top price was 17s 6d and lowest 2s 6d.

It was Covent Garden, however, that was to be protected. On 17

March a special appeal from James Smith to Stafford Cripps received short shrift. Cripps wrote that the Arts Council was an autonomous body into whose decisions he could not intervene. There was a hint of embarrassment in his explanation, however, that the 'special consideration' for Covent Garden was because of the 'magnitude of the undertaking'. Covent Garden was a special case and had to remain so, if the Treasury were not to find the floodgates opening up.[75] Cuts would have to be found at Sadler's Wells.

Tucker, as well as fighting the Treasury, immediately set about the task of reviving the vigour and morale of the company and giving a boost to the steadily improving box office. Having decided to prepare Verdi's *Simon Boccanegra*, he embarked on creating a version and translation that would, as he put it, make 'intelligible to English-speaking audiences a plot of the profoundest obscurity'. This particular translation was an example of a licence with the original that would soon be considered unacceptable. His version included an interlude that he composed between Acts III and IV to shorten and make more intelligible the interval between the taking of the poison by the Doge in the middle of Act III and his long-delayed death scene at the end of the opera.[76]

The British premiere of *Simon Boccanegra* on 27 October 1948 revealed the powers of recovery of Sadler's Wells. Directed by John Moody and designed by the artist John Piper, *Boccanegra* was one of the great achievements of the era. Arnold Matters, then at the height of his career, was Boccanegra, Howell Glynne was Fiesco, James Johnston Gabriele, Joyce Gartside Amelia. Piper's sombre but rich settings created a grand-opera scale 'as if by magic' and John Moody gave an impression of crowds and movement within his limited space and resources.

The company were galvanised by the production and audiences packed the theatre. Extra performances had to be put on. For the critic Andrew Porter, the production was one of the most important events in the revival and re-evaluation of Verdi's lesser-known works.[77] Most critics welcomed with delight the introduction to the repertoire of such a masterpiece.

A steady improvement in the dramatic aspects of production was also making an impact. Guthrie believed that his *Carmen* in February 1949 was controversial because he had encouraged

Anna Pollak not to be afraid to make Carmen the vulgar, violent slut that Mérimée's story demanded. She played, he believed, with 'great verve and authority'. Guthrie wrote of his own production:

The first act was set in quite a squalid, sordid sort of environment and the factory girls looked like factory girls, not like operatic choristers whose sole concession to the warm South is to sling embroidered Spanish shawls over themselves, as if they were suburban grand pianos.[78]

*The Times* recognised the care 'normally lavished on a stage play' and was impressed by the power and drive of the producer, which had affected the cast, all of whom had been inspired both in singing and in acting.[79] Mackerras later remarked on the skill with which Guthrie used the chorus as individual people, especially when the girls came in and during the quarrel. It was, he said, 'just a sensational production' which was 'extremely revolutionary at the time'.[80]

Dent, who resigned from the governing body in 1949, was pleased that it had been a very sordid *Carmen*, and accused the old guard of wanting things too 'drawing roomy'. He had been brought up in an atmosphere of very strict class distinctions and had had to learn all the rules of the game, but those attitudes, he said, belonged to Queen Victoria and not to 1949.[81]

Mudie, a young man in his thirties, had fallen ill with disseminated sclerosis, which became increasingly debilitating. During the 1949/50 season Mackerras sometimes took over from both him and Robertson in London and also on tour without rehearsal, which was both a frightening experience and excellent training. Mudie continued to help and train Mackerras as his health deteriorated.[82] When in March 1949 he conducted *Rigoletto*, *The Times* critic wrote: 'The chief point of interest was the emergence of Mr Charles Mackerras as a conductor of promise. He kept the music flowing, secured a good ensemble' and brought out such refinements as there were in the score.[83]

As the public were introduced to the expanding repertoire, standards slowly improved and, above all, the singers were making sure that their words were audible. Mackerras later recalled that company members were not always 'the greatest singers, but by hell you could hear what they were singing'.[84] Mackerras conducted *Così fan tutte* on tour in Oxford on 23 May. At that revival Marion Lowe was Fiordiligi and Anna Pollak was, in Mackerras's words, 'incomparable as Dorabella'. He hugely admired Pollak. She was 'just superb in more or less every role I heard her sing'. Her every word was audible: 'Talk about diction!'

On 1 October another fine young singer, Amy Shuard, fresh from her first stage experience in South Africa, joined Sadler's Wells. When Shuard made her debut as Marguerite in *Faust*, Harold Rosenthal of *Opera* magazine pointed out that even a standard repertory revival could be not just rewarding but even exciting at Sadler's Wells, when young talent emerged. Shuard possessed a 'truly thrilling voice of the kind that becomes fuller and more powerful in its upper reaches; the tone is round and vibrant'. She also had a charming stage presence and natural acting ability.[85*]

Guthrie's production of *Falstaff* in December also added to the reputation of Sadler's Wells, with Guthrie himself suggesting that the direction 'had more variety and zest' than was usual on the operatic stage. He later wrote that he believed that it had gained much from the comparative intimacy of Sadler's Wells and from the admirable teamwork of its company. Arnold Matters had neither sufficient voice nor personality to dominate La Scala, Covent Garden or the Met, but his musicianship and the deft economy of his acting were perfect for the Wells.[86] *The Times* was impressed and very much liked the bustle and 'the organised disorder' that Guthrie mustered and the growing ease of the ensembles.[87] The company's morale was very much in the ascendant. Mackerras remembered that when the Scala came to Covent Garden with *Otello* and *Falstaff*, 'we all thought that our *Falstaff* was better than theirs'.[88]

The critics also greatly appreciated Joan Cross's musicianship in her intimate and moving production of *La traviata* on 21 February 1950. Lord Harewood praised the production in *Opera* for its many unobtrusive yet telling details and wrote of the tradition that Cross had handed down to her Violetta, Marjorie Shires, helping her to develop her potential. He nonetheless criticised Mudie,

* Born in 1924 in London, Shuard had studied at Trinity College of Music under Ivor Warren and later under Eva Turner.

whose health was deteriorating, for conducting badly with erratic tempi, his orchestra uncertain.[89] On 9 May a new Powell Lloyd production of the Vaughan Williams ballad opera *Hugh the Drover* found James Johnston fully and charmingly at ease in the Cotswolds.

There was growing concern at the Arts Council as to whether Covent Garden and Sadler's Wells should remain independent or be merged. Sadler's Wells was clearly showing no signs of giving up the ghost, and both were demanding more and more resources as their standards improved and their identities developed. On 12 April 1950 Tucker appeared before the Arts Council's Opera and Ballet Subcommittee, which was deciding on opera policy for the next five years. He trod on eggshells, fearful of saying the wrong thing about co-ordination with Covent Garden in response to the chairman's pronouncement that in the long run the country was 'not going to stand the idea of two rival organisations being financed out of public money'.[90] The criticism of duplication was growing. In August 1951 *Opera* magazine's editorial complained that in the 1949/50 season *Carmen, La traviata, La bohème, Tosca, Il trovatore, The Marriage of Figaro, Rigoletto* and *Madam Butterfly* were given at both houses, sometimes at the same time. Even press nights occasionally clashed.[91]

Covent Garden remained the favoured child. Tucker was having difficulty keeping his singers and orchestral staff together because of the poor pay, and by November the chorus was very restive. He had to give up the premiere of Britten's *Billy Budd*, which had been commissioned for Sadler's Wells as part of the Festival of Britain in 1951. Tucker said the reason was entirely financial, later writing that it was impossible for Sadler's Wells to supply a double male chorus. Britten, who in any case was not happy about the musical direction at Sadler's Wells, did not believe Tucker's explanation. Nonetheless, it was feared that the deficit to September 1951 might be as high as £54,000 and the Sadler's Wells Finance and General Purposes Committee agreed that *Billy Budd* was beyond the financial and numerical resources of the company.[92]

The loss of revenue resulting from the transfer of Sadler's Wells ballet to Covent Garden was also proving damaging. In February 1951 George Dyson wrote to *The Times* stressing the serious losses incurred by the parent theatre since the transfer of the senior company four years before, without any compensation. Sadler's Wells had lost a principal source of income, while the Sadler's Wells Theatre Ballet continued to nourish the ballet at Covent Garden, training and providing new talent for it. The lion's share of the ballet subsidy went to Covent Garden – the mother was being starved to feed the child.[93]

The Arts Council was unmoved. Sir William Emrys Williams, the Arts Council secretary general, responded on 29 March that the grant would be £60,000 for 1951/2 and would remain at that level for three or four years. The cost of the ballet school would have to come out of the grant and its future be negotiated directly with Covent Garden.

The question of improving the dramatic skills of the company was exercising Tucker. Guthrie himself thought his production of *The Barber of Seville* was 'a poor effort . . . at once galumphing and stark'. It opened on 28 November 1950. He felt he had demanded more virtuosity from the singers at Sadler's Wells than they could supply at that time.[94] The critics complained that it was too busy and over-produced.

Tucker was keen to bring theatre talent to Sadler's Wells, as Covent Garden had done with the dynamic young Peter Brook in 1947–9. He told Arundell: 'There are some fine producers in the "straight stage" but few of them are adequately qualified to produce opera.'[95] He was determined to remedy the problem, helped by his friend Stephen Arlen, who was the general manager at the Old Vic. Arlen introduced him to the 'famous Old Vic dissident triumvirate', the inspirational French director Michel St-Denis, George Devine and Glen Byam Shaw, and they all directed at Sadler's Wells from the 1950s.

Instead of being in charge of the evolving plans for a National Theatre after the war, the trio had fallen victim to the growing rivalries. On 29 January 1949 Oliver Lyttelton, of the Shakespeare Memorial Theatre, and Lord Esher, an Old Vic governor and, like Lyttelton, a member of the National Theatre Committee, had announced an agreement with the approval of the Arts Council to work together towards a National Theatre on the South Bank. It was to be built midway between Waterloo Bridge and Hungerford

Bridge.* Esher declared: 'This is the first artistic venture of our new young educated democracy and the beginning of a new period in our national life.'[96] In February 1949 legislation was passed: the London County Council was to provide a South Bank site and the government a million pounds.

Meanwhile, the leadership of the Old Vic company had been undergoing changes. After the Vic's dramatic activities had been put under John Burrell, Laurence Olivier and Ralph Richardson in June 1945, the company had successfully played in the New Theatre in the West End. In January 1947 St-Denis, together with George Devine and Glen Byam Shaw, and with the support of the governors and an Arts Council grant of £9,500, opened their Old Vic Theatre Centre.[†] As a branch of the venture, Devine opened the Young Vic company at the Lyric Hammersmith, and Byam Shaw opened the theatre school.

The great London plan, however, was threatened when the 1947/8 season of the company at the New Theatre, in the absence of Richardson and Olivier, who were on an Old Vic tour to Australia, went into serious deficit. Lord Esher, the new chairman of the Old Vic governors from March 1948, together with the governors decided not to renew their contracts and that the company should leave the expensive West End and return to the Old Vic. Llewellyn Rees was appointed administrator and Hugh Hunt artistic director.

With the Old Vic company back in the theatre, the school had to move to Dulwich in 1949. Although St-Denis, Byam Shaw and

* Oliver Lyttelton was created Viscount Chandos in September 1954. He was an old friend and ministerial colleague of Winston Churchill, who had made him Minister of Production in 1942 and Colonial Secretary in 1951. He was known for his wit, talent for mimicry and his dark sense of humour. After resuming his business career in 1954, he devoted much of his time to the National Theatre. He was chairman of the National Theatre board from 1962 to 1971.

† St-Denis, who had trained at his uncle Jacques Copeau's experimental theatre in Paris in the 1920s, was the senior partner in the London enterprise. With Devine and Guthrie, he had founded a radical stage-training school, the London Theatre Studio, in Islington in 1935. During the war he oversaw the Free French radio broadcasts. St-Denis, with his belief in the need for clarity of text, technical skill and ensemble work, was the inspiration and mentor for a generation of directors, including Devine at the English Stage Company and Byam Shaw and Peter Hall at Stratford-upon-Avon.

Devine were still directors of the Old Vic company, there were growing tensions with Hunt and they were gradually edged out. Hunt
and his general manager, Stephen Arlen, suggested that Guthrie be
asked back to the Old Vic, which began to stake a claim to become
the new National Theatre. On 7 May 1951 Esher accepted the trio's
resignations. Guthrie, who had not spoken up for the three men,
together with Esher and Hunt became the villains of the piece for
theatre people, who greatly admired the work of St-Denis at the
school. Although St-Denis was probably the best-qualified candidate, it was believed by many that Esher could not countenance the
thought of a Frenchman running a future National Theatre, so had
taken steps to remove him from the scene.

St-Denis was unable to find funds for the school and it was closed
in 1952, despite a press outcry and parliamentary questions.
Having lost their place in the National Theatre scheme, the trio
went their separate ways. St-Denis based himself in France, where
he worked and taught, Devine went freelance until he became the
artistic director of the English Stage Company in 1955, and Byam
Shaw went to Stratford, where he became the artistic director in
1957. Tucker quickly took advantage of their availability to bring
them to Sadler's Wells.

Although none of the three had musical backgrounds, they were
helped, according to Tucker, by the 'assiduous study of gramophone
records',[97] and succeeded in providing work that was to help define
the future of Sadler's Wells as an ensemble opera company. Devine
directed five shows at Sadler's Wells between 1951 and 1955. He
was aware that final authority must lie with the conductor and that
it was the conductor who not only led the company during the performance but also was the primary interpreter of the composer. The
director should operate within the framework of the score and his
inspiration spring from the music. For Devine, Sadler's Wells was a
real company, with a 'fine co-operative spirit' that meant it was possible to achieve fully integrated performances.[98]

It was Arlen who persuaded Devine to direct Tucker's translated
and shortened version of *Don Carlos*. Devine, in Tucker's words,
'was fond of music but had no knowledge of the functioning of
opera', but Tucker was able to familiarise him with the work by a
sing-through with piano accompaniment and tapes. *Don Carlos*,
which was still far from being recognised as a masterpiece, opened

on 16 January 1951. Tucker, 'intoxicated by the success of *Bocca-negra*', restored part of the Fontainebleau act and Schiller's ending, but cut the Veil Song and the *auto-da-fé*, which was difficult for Sadler's Wells to stage and also was not in Schiller. In a five-page review in *Opera*, Harewood criticised each of Tucker's omissions and rearrangements, concluding that they constituted an 'operatic heresy' and destroyed the musical development of the drama. He thought that the whole level of musical achievement was on 'a lower plane' than that of *Boccanegra* two years earlier.[99]

Harewood and *The Times* criticised Devine for hurling his characters 'to the dirty ground in their best clothes at moments of emotional stress'.[100] Shawe-Taylor and Felix Aprahamian, however, were more appreciative of the skill and soundness of the production and Devine's creation of impressive theatrical moments. Aprahamian was greatly impressed both by his achievement in contriving 'a vivid popular insurrection on a few square feet of stage' and Tucker's skill in compressing the work.[101] Although most critics were delighted to be given the opportunity to encounter even Tucker's reconstituted version of what was a little-known work, it proved too great a challenge for the company's resources. Mackerras later recalled that the theatre was just not suitable for such grand operas as *Don Carlos*. The omitted *auto-da-fé* scene was, after all, he mused, 'one of the biggest scenes in the whole of Verdi'.[102] Nor was the singing up to standard. Harewood thought that, great singer though she was, Joan Hammond's Queen was 'pushed and shrill' and that James Johnston was not at his best as Don Carlos. Only Frederick Sharp's Rodrigo and Amy Shuard's Eboli were worthy of the piece.

An epidemic of flu, which attacked the company just before opening night, affected the performance, but morale was bolstered by the unflappable Devine, who carried them through the crisis. He was respected within the company as a calm, true professional who could be relied upon to leave nothing to chance. Although he could be brusque with the artists, Tucker noted that he was 'generally liked and respected'.[103]

While *Don Carlos* was a disappointment, Tucker's next venture was an outstanding achievement. On 10 April Leoš Janáček's *Katya Kabanova* received its English premiere. Mackerras had heard *Katya* for the first time at the Czech National Theatre on 15

October 1947, during his year in Prague. In 1948 he wrote to his mother after the Prague spring festival: 'It is a terrible shame that these works are quite unknown outside this country. They are certainly in the front rank of modern opera ... when I get back I will do my utmost to persuade Sadler's Wells to perform one of them, though I don't suppose they will.'[104] After his return, one of the first things he did was to draw *Katya* to the attention of Tucker, who was 'immensely interested in the idea' and decided to include it in the 1950/1 season. Tucker translated with the assistance of a friend of Mackerras, Arnošt Propper, who provided him with the literal meaning. 'That's what originally started the Janáček specialisation by Sadler's Wells/ENO,' Mackerras later reflected.[105]

Arundell was to produce *Katya*, and it was intended that Mudie, who was most insistent, would conduct the premiere, while Mackerras was to coach and teach the singers. Mudie's health, however, was rapidly and obviously deteriorating, and Tucker later admitted that he had erred in acceding to his request. Relations between the ailing Mudie and Mackerras reached a crisis during the *Katya* rehearsals when Mudie began to lose his sight and control of his movements. Mudie, supported by Tucker, was 'determined to soldier on' with *Katya* when it was quite obvious to Mackerras that he could not do so. As Mackerras took over more of his work, his frustration with Mudie grew. Mackerras later reflected that he might have been too intolerant of his mentor. 'I think they thought that I had bitten the hand that fed me,' Mackerras recalled. 'There were faults on both sides – he was still in his thirties – suffering from a terrible affliction.' Mackerras's judgement was proved right and he had to take over *Katya* at short notice. Thus it was, as he later reflected, 'that I not only introduced Janáček to this country but also conducted it'.[106]

Most critics were deeply moved by the poetry and humanity of the opera. Shawe-Taylor was immediately struck by its 'undiluted strength and purity of human feeling' and expressed his gratitude to Sadler's Wells for enabling the English public to make acquaintance 'with a work of art unlike anything in our operatic experience'. It was, he wrote, their most impressive and courageous achievement since their production of *Peter Grimes* in 1945.[107] Ernest Newman in the *Sunday Times* was the only critic who failed to recognise the genius of the work, describing Janáček as 'rather a scrap by scrap composer' who found it 'difficult to think consecutively for more than two or three minutes at a time'.

Harewood called *Katya* the operatic highlight of the season and 'one of the most moving experiences' he had had in an opera house for a long while. As Katya, Amy Shuard had 'intensity', although she lacked experience. Harewood urged people to go and see it twice, but the audiences still did not materialise.[108] *Katya* was only repeated twice in November and then dropped from the repertoire until Rafael Kubelík conducted a revival in June 1954 with blazing intensity. In April 1955 Shuard brought in audiences for a revival, but she then moved to Covent Garden for the 1955/6 season, when the Australian soprano Elizabeth Fretwell took over her repertoire.[109] Over the next few years, entirely due to Tucker's determination and perseverance, and with Shawe-Taylor's constant support, there was a slow but steady increase in the audience for Janáček.

Mackerras was depressed and frustrated. In a letter to his mother he wrote that he was 'rather expecting some squalls over the success of *Poll* and *Katya*'. On 13 March 1951 Mackerras's *Pineapple Poll* was first performed for the company's Festival of Britain programme, after the copyright of Sullivan's music expired. South African John Cranko was the choreographer. It was very well received by audience and critics, *The Times* referring to its 'exuberant good humour'. It was recorded the same year. Although Mudie's conducting had deteriorated, he kept his job, Mackerras recalled, because everyone felt so sorry for him in his suffering. Mackerras, however, wanted to develop his outside connections and leave the Wells within the year unless there was a significant improvement in his position.[110]

In early 1951 Tucker decided that he needed more assistance in the day-to-day running of the organisation. His general manager George Chamberlain, Baylis's loyal lieutenant, was also still general manager at the Old Vic, which was, in Tucker's opinion, his first love, and the demands made by the two theatres meant that he was overburdened with work. Tucker asked Stephen Arlen, who was at that time working for Chamberlain as stage manager at the Vic, to come and help him at Sadler's Wells.

Arlen, a great enthusiast in all he did and a man of great energy, had been brought up in the theatre. His father had been a comedian and he himself had joined a touring repertory company after leaving school. He put on plays in the army, returning to the theatre after the war to become manager of the Old Vic centre under Byam Shaw, St-Denis and Devine. Later he had worked for the impresario Prince Littler at the Coliseum as stage manager. He maintained close contacts with European impresarios and theatre directors from his days arranging the Old Vic tours.

Tucker recalled that he and Arlen took to each other at once and became close friends. Arlen, he observed, was everything he was not, and a true man of the theatre. At first Arlen was reluctant to take up the position. He was deeply suspicious of opera and recalled demanding his money back after a production of *Lohengrin* in the 1930s when he had considered the 'waddling on' of the swan to be an 'absolute disgrace'.[111] Yet Tucker persevered, regularly entertaining him to lunches at Simpsons and enlisting Guthrie's support.[112] He became general manager for the 1951/2 season. Together Tucker and Arlen were a formidable team, complementing each other's skills and talents.

Dennis Arundell continued to be the mainstay of the Sadler's Wells directorial team, despite his erratic temperament. Mackerras, who conducted the new Arundell *Figaro* on 23 October 1951, was quite able to stand up to his interference in the musical direction. Elsie Morison was Susanna, Anna Pollak Cherubino, Matters Figaro, Denis Dowling the Count. Harewood praised Arundell's *Figaro* for dispensing with traditional stage business, for clarifying the action and for its 'entirely engaging unforced quality'. He nonetheless did not care for the 'suburban rooms' of Acts II and III, nor the unprepossessing pine wood of the last act, designed by John Glass, the head of Sadler's Wells production department.[113] *The Times* critic acknowledged that 'thanks to the Eberts, Guthries, and Arundells the art of the director is now accepted'. No longer did singers 'bundle on to the stage with some faded scenery, using a few stock gestures'. Even if these directors sometimes went wrong, they had successfully established that the dramatic element in opera must be properly served.

For the first half of the season the average attendance was 81 per cent of capacity, and new productions were beginning to flow.[114] Arundell also directed Massenet's *Werther* in February 1952, translated by Tucker and designed by Ernest Stern, who had previously worked with Max Reinhardt, the Austrian director who was one of the founders of the Salzburg Festival. *The Times* commented that *Werther*, which had not been produced in England since 1910 and had been regarded as 'sugar, sex and water', was now seen as possessing 'sensuous charm'.[115] Arundell produced the opera in keeping with the romanticism of its period, and according to Harold Rosenthal handled the build-up of tension in the last act in a masterly fashion.[116]

George Devine's second production for Sadler's Wells was *Eugene Onegin* on 22 May with Motley designs and Cranko's choreography. Both scenery and direction were natural and sincere, the production charming and intimate. Orchestra and chorus, however, had rough and untidy moments under Robertson. Amy Shuard sang Tatyana after her return from Italy, where Tucker had arranged for her to go for coaching.

The first new production of the 1952/3 season was Sadler's Wells' first *Seraglio* on 2 October, directed by Clive Carey with Dent's translation. *Seraglio* fitted 'happily into the spirit of our *Volksoper* Sadler's Wells', said the *Times Educational Supplement*.[117] Basil Coleman's production of *Samson and Delilah* on 20 November did not fit so well.* Cranko's choreography for *Samson* could not compensate for the small scale of Sadler's Wells and 'meagre-looking Philistines'. Nor did Mudie's conducting help. Shawe-Taylor described the music as 'pedantic and dull . . . like a Mendelssohn score left out in the rain'.[118]

*Samson* was, however, the beginning of a long and creative association with Sadler's Wells for twenty-eight-year-old designer Ralph Koltai. When still a student Koltai had been spotted by Joan Cross, who introduced him to Coleman. She remained his mentor, teaching him how to focus on the important things in the staging. Inspired by the 'exciting visual abstraction' of Roland Petit's Ballet des Champs Elysées, Koltai brought his own abstract, 'vaguely cubist', sculptural approach to Sadler's Wells for *Samson* at a time when Motley's highly professional and polished work was more naturalistic in approach. Koltai remained a designer more concerned with 'what it is about, rather than where it is', in a manner later described as 'looking for the metaphor'.[119]

* Coleman worked extensively with the English Opera Group from 1949 through the 1950s. He collaborated with Britten on the first stagings of *The Little Sweep*, *Billy Budd*, *Gloriana* and *The Turn of the Screw*.

Harewood again questioned the choice of repertoire when Sadler's Wells presented a cramped and undistinguished *Il trovatore* in January 1952. He was particularly struck by the convent scene, when both di Luna's and Manrico's men had to enter the convent by means of the same tricky flight of steps. 'The resulting scramble', Harewood wrote, 'was a perfect example of satisfying the claims of realism while denying those of plausibility.'[120] It was the end of the road for the ailing Mudie, whose contract was terminated shortly after.

A Ralph Vaughan Williams double bill ended the season in June – the Sadler's Wells premiere of *Riders to the Sea*, based on a play by J. M. Synge, which was paired with *Hugh the Drover*. *The Times* called *Riders* a 'little masterpiece of half-tones', combined with soaring phrases of compassionate beauty.[121]

The 1953/4 season opened on 1 October with the first night of Verdi's *Luisa Miller*, after practically a century of neglect. John Hargreaves was Miller – Luisa's father; Victoria Elliott was Luisa. Alix Stone designed with an eclectic range of costumes: 'Elizabethan, Jacobean, Tyrolese, that looked as if they had been assembled casually from a warehouse'.[122] The translation was by Tom Hammond and Tucker and invoked occasional 'audible sounds of merriment', as when Oreste Kirkop's Rodolfo sang of plunging his sword into his 'boo-oo-som'.[123]

Tom Hammond had joined Sadler's Wells as a répétiteur in 1946. He became a much-loved and, with his encyclopaedic knowledge of opera, indispensable part of ENO until his death in 1981. As personal assistant to Tucker and after 1968 music consultant at the Coliseum, he was, in Mackerras's words, 'a wonderful man who was really Tucker's great adviser on voices'. He was sent off as a travelling talent scout by Tucker, particularly to Australia, where he found many fine singers. Although he was a tremendous Francophile and a fine linguist, Hammond cared passionately about opera in English and, both in collaboration with Tucker and on his own, produced a number of excellent translations. He hated changing note values and tried to use modern speech without inversions – 'thees and thous', he warned, would put young people off. Hammond's translations of Rossini, where he strictly and with great skill adhered to rhyming couplets for comic effect, made a significant contribution to the growing appreciation of the composer.

*

Progress was steady. *Hansel and Gretel*, conducted by Vilem Tausky and designed and produced by Powell Lloyd, was described by Porter as 'consistently stylish, consistently right'. Porter praised the beautifully sung and naturally acted children of Marion Studholme and Anna Pollak.[124]

In 1954 both Robertson and Mackerras left the company – Robertson in January to become the principal conductor of the New Zealand Broadcasting National Orchestra and Mackerras to work at the BBC as the full-time conductor of the BBC Concert Orchestra. Later he joined Britten's English Opera Group. Mackerras had been taking on more work outside Sadler's Wells, both for the BBC and with Cranko, with whom he prepared another ballet in 1954, the *Lady and the Fool*, using music from early Verdi. Mudie too had retired, leaving Sadler's Wells without a music director for three years, despite efforts to find a suitable candidate.

At the start of the new season, on 22 September, Lennox Berkeley's *Nelson*, with libretto by Alan Pryce-Jones, received its stage premiere. Berkeley's style was tonal and the work heroic and romantic. The composer displayed sympathy for the voice and for the English language, but critics felt that the fine music needed strong revision in order to tighten up the plot. George Devine directed with 'deftness' a cast that included Victoria Elliott as Lady Hamilton, Pollak as a splendid Lady Nelson and Matters as Sir William Hamilton.[125] Vilem Tausky, who later wrote of its 'marvellously touching death scene', conducted.[126] The work's premiere was timed just a month before the English Opera Group brought Britten's *Turn of the Screw* to Sadler's Wells, conducted by the composer. Joan Cross was Mrs Grose, Peter Pears was Quint, David Hemmings was Miles, Olive Dyer was Flora and Jennifer Vyvyan was the Governess. Andrew Porter reported that it was harder to obtain seats for *The Turn of Screw* than for the latest musical.*

On 24 February 1955 the Devine production of *The Magic Flute*, designed by Motley, was seen as the work of a fresh and inventive

* London had five opera premieres in the 1954/5 season. As well as Britten's *The Turn of the Screw* and Berkeley's *Nelson*, there was Berkeley's *The Dinner Engagement* and, at Covent Garden, Walton's *Troilus and Cressida* and Tippett's *The Midsummer Marriage*.

mind, and was praised for its enchanting treatment of the animals as well as the technical prowess displayed in the scene changes. The Queen of Night was June Bronhill's first important role after coming to England from Australia. It was conducted by Rudolf Schwarz, whom the management were considering for music director.

The next few years were to decide whether there were to be two opera houses in London, once it had become clear to the Treasury just how expensive it was going to be and just how much the public appetite grew 'upon the feeding'. It was increasingly clear that Sadler's Wells was woefully underfunded for its task. The Arts Council grant increased from £15,000 to £100,000 in the years 1945/46 to 1954/5, and ticket prices increased from 9s to 12s 6d top price, and bottom prices from 1s to 2s. In October 1952 the Trust's overdraft was £28,000 and cash payments were exceeding cash receipts by £100 each week. The board noted with alarm that 'there was a danger that the moment might come when it would be impossible to meet essential weekly outgoings'.[127] The deficit by February 1953 was £99,763 and the reserves £3,000. Tucker's brinkmanship was becoming all too real.

On 30 April Emrys Williams at the Arts Council gave Sadler's Wells a loan of £20,000 as part of the first instalment of the next year's grant to keep them solvent and insisted that in future the Arts Council music director, John Denison, would sit in on the Trust meetings.[128]

Various subterfuges had kept the Sadler's Wells deficit from reaching levels unacceptable to the Arts Council: in 1953 one third of the special Festival of Britain grant had been diverted to normal running expenses.[129] By March 1955, however, the following season's budget was proving impossible to balance with an estimated £130,000 shortfall. Arlen continued to ask the Arts Council for advances.[130] Problems were exacerbated by the constant loss of artists to Covent Garden after they started to draw the public.

Despite the difficulties, the momentum for improvement was unstoppable. During 1954 Tucker decided that it was crucial for the company to move out of Sadler's Wells. He wrote in the annual report about the conditions in the theatre and the wear and tear resulting from its 290,876 visitors during the year. The corridors backstage were not wide enough to allow one person to walk with a crinoline, let alone two to pass. The backstage facilities for principals were terrible – there was one room for eleven sopranos. There were no showers or WCs in the dressing rooms. 'If a prima donna wishes to spend a penny before her entrance,' Tucker wrote, 'she has to climb two flights of stairs to do so. Small wonder that the possibility of having a new theatre with adequate facilities and accommodation is the fulfilment of our wildest dreams.' The Trust and governors supported the plan.[131]

It was at this time that *The Times* pointed out how Germany had already rebuilt nearly all its opera houses. Hamburg, one of the few houses not to have been completely destroyed, resumed performances immediately after the war. There were new houses in Essen and Bochum, and in Aachen a modern theatre had been put inside the shell of the old one. Plans had been approved for new houses in Cologne and Münster.[132] By 1954 there were fifty-six theatres regularly giving opera in West Germany, of which eight were Staatsoper organisations and the rest supported by their cities or provinces.

Tucker, in his quest for a new theatre to house Sadler's Wells, found his greatest friend and advocate in Sir Isaac Hayward, the leader of the London County Council. His aim was to offer a site on the South Bank of the Thames, between the Festival Hall and County Hall.

The Arts Council, hard pressed trying to support the work of Covent Garden, Carl Rosa and Sadler's Wells when it had scarcely enough resources for one company, was less enthusiastic. The provinces were being starved of opera in comparison with their wartime experience, with visits from a much-depleted Carl Rosa company, short Sadler's Wells summer seasons and occasional visits by Covent Garden to the few centres where the theatres were big enough. Tucker wrote of 'cries of woe from the provinces', which touched the Arts Council on a tender political nerve. The Council supported a Covent Garden of international repute and a touring company strengthened in quality and able to take to the road for longer periods. Mergers, Tucker wrote, 'were in the air'.[133]

The debate soon became focused on whether Sadler's Wells should be merged with Covent Garden or rehoused on the South Bank. On 17 May 1955 the board chairman, James Smith, told the Trust that the company was faced by two possible courses in the light of its ongoing financial problems. The hoped-for course was a 'developing future' in a new house on the South Bank, funded by the Arts Council. The other was to stay at Sadler's Wells with a similar level of grant to the current one, based on a policy of lowered standards. Smith met Kenneth Clark, the chairman of the Arts Council, who, while expressing great sympathy, let it be known that their preference was for a smaller concert hall and art gallery before an opera house. Smith told Clark that if a grant of £130,000 were not forthcoming, Sadler's Wells would close down. The Arts Council agreed to convey this to the chancellor, Harold Macmillan. John Denison, the Arts Council representative at the Trust, suggested another theatre in the West End, but this was felt to be a compromise that 'might not be to anyone's advantage'.[134]

There was support for Sadler's Wells on 29 April when Eric Walter White wrote a paper for Douglas Lund of the Arts Council's Opera Subcommittee in which he stressed that both metropolitan companies should have the first claim on Arts Council attentions as London should maintain standards and was now an international centre of music. The use of English, he pointed out, required no defence in the case of Sadler's Wells, but in the case of Covent Garden it had come in for some comment, as it had been 'built as an Italian opera house'.[135]

On 16 December Tucker told the Trust that a decision on the South Bank was urgent as he needed to know if he was pursuing a policy of cuts and retrenchment or one of development for the 1956/7 season. There was still no music director and negotiations with Rudolf Schwarz depended on the outcome of the South Bank decision, as he was only interested in taking up the post in conjunction with the new theatre.[136]

On 6 April 1955 Anthony Eden had succeeded Churchill as prime minister, with R. A. Butler his chancellor. Butler had been forced to introduce an emergency budget in the autumn of 1955 during the balance-of-payments crisis, increasing purchase and profits tax and cutting local-authority building. Out of favour with Eden, Butler was replaced on 20 December by Harold Macmillan, who was more willing to increase public expenditure.

The change came not a moment too soon for Sadler's Wells. On 18 January 1956 Tucker told the Trust that the Arts Council, which itself would not receive any increase for two or three years, had granted Sadler's Wells an increase of £17–25,000 less than requested. Tucker warned that not only would the planned production programme have to be cut, but that there would also have to be cuts in the chorus, orchestra and principal singers. He agreed with the Trust that they would resign at the end of the year, with only Lady Dalton dissenting, in the light of the Suez crisis and the slight Arts Council increase. The Trust decided to prepare a draft press statement.

The Trust agreed two weeks later that Kenneth Clark should be urged to impress upon the government, 'in the most uncompromising terms', that Sadler's Wells would have to be put on a sound financial footing if it were not to close down completely.[137] Smith also reminded the Arts Council of the already crucial interrelationship between Covent Garden and Sadler's Wells – not least in the 'traffic of artists'.[138] The pressure was successful for the time being. When Kenneth Clark saw the 'hard-pressed' new chancellor, Macmillan, on 8 March, he was given what he described as a patient hearing.[139] The next day Sir William Emrys Williams told the Trust that the Arts Council would increase its grant by £5,000, to £115,000, and that the Treasury had agreed to reconsider the grant for the 1957/8 season. The directors would have been most heartened, he said, had they heard 'the unanimous and emphatic view of the Council that Sadler's Wells must on no account be permitted to close'. The Trust agreed that Tucker should continue to plan for the first six months of the 1957/8 season, at which point the possibility of closure would be looked at again.[140]

Between 1 and 16 June the Trust received an advance of £10,000 from the Arts Council, but by September the crisis was still looming and it seemed that there might not even be enough money to wind up the organisation by the following spring. In July Tucker and James Smith discussed with Sir Isaac Hayward, the leader of the London County Council, how the council might help Sadler's Wells until the question of the new house was resolved.[141]

On 9 January 1957 Anthony Eden resigned after the Suez crisis and a new Conservative government was formed under Harold Macmillan, whose chancellor was Peter Thorneycroft. The economic situation continued to deteriorate during 1957, with sterling declining in value and the bank rate raised to 7 per cent on 19 September.

The Treasury had decided that a Sadler's Wells' merger with Covent Garden was the only solution to the unending deficits and demands – an opinion conveyed by Sir Alexander Johnston, Third Secretary to the Treasury, to Emrys Williams at the Arts Council on the day after Eden's resignation.

Emrys Williams was in full agreement, having failed to get the LCC to underwrite Sadler's Wells completely, even though they were prepared to provide a site for a South Bank theatre. On 23 January Emrys Williams informed Johnston that the Sadler's Wells Trust would resign at the end of the season but that the Old Vic governors had reacted with 'robust indignation' and would run Sadler's Wells themselves or appoint a new Trust. He thought it would work out well, since the junior ballet company could go to Covent Garden and tour, which would please both de Valois and Webster, who complained that the ballet was underemployed at Covent Garden.[142]

Emrys Williams was forming his opinion based on information received from Covent Garden. On 20 February he informed Johnston that Webster and his accountant, Douglas Lund, had already offered their opinion, 'after scrutiny of the expenditure of the two theatres, that savings of around £25,000 might be secured if the two theatres were governed by one body and administered by one management'.[143] Since Lund was the accountant both of Covent Garden and the Arts Council, the figures might have been over-optimistic.

When the governors of Sadler's Wells demanded reductions of £37,000 in the operational budget on 17 February 1957, Tucker agreed to try to work out a plan. The theatre ballet would be 'amalgamated with the senior company', which would make a £3,000 saving, and seat prices would be increased by 50 per cent.[144] A letter from Emrys Williams on 8 March demanded: 'You will cut your coat according to your cloth.' Board member David McKenna was furious and wrote a tough letter to Clark threatening to cancel the entire programme.[145]

At the Arts Council, Kenneth Clark had decided to try to resolve the 'opera drift' situation and to lift the matter 'out of the sphere of personalities and day-to-day jealousies'.[146] He presided over a meeting at the Arts Council on 8 April which was attended by Smith, McKenna and Mrs Strauss of Sadler's Wells, and the Arts

Council chairman Lord Waverley, together with Professor Lionel Robbins, Professor Franks and Garrett Moore (later Lord Drogheda) of Covent Garden, to discuss the suggestion of a merger. There was polite general agreement that there was a place for two opera houses in London performing rather different functions, but 'considerable divergence of view between Sadler's Wells and Covent Garden as to future organisation'. Lord Waverley and Professor Robbins, as it turned out somewhat disingenuously, 'recoiled from unification' and spoke of a federal structure, giving no details. Some members of the Sadler's Wells Trust favoured unification with one administrator and one board, whose directors would be responsible for artistic planning.[147] The drift continued, with the debate wavering between total amalgamation or a much reduced role for Sadler's Wells.

In the discussions with the Arts Council the Covent Garden Trust revealed its preference for a very cut-down Sadler's Wells. On 6 May Lord Waverley expressed the opinion that economies would come from 'less ambitious productions and economical use of singers at Sadler's Wells', rather than from administrative reorganisation. Robbins proposed that cuts to the Sadler's Wells music staff and artists, orchestra and chorus could save £22,000. Sadler's Wells' chairman James Smith, who also sat on the Covent Garden Trust, suggested that Sadler's Wells should become a 'folk opera', staging operas with small forces and operettas. Waverley, playing a double game, said he thought it would be best to preserve the identities of both houses. 'Amalgamation would result in artistic loss far outweighing the small economies that were likely.'[148]

At the Arts Council, Emrys Williams strongly supported the folk-opera policy at Sadler's Wells. Most knowledgeable opinion, he argued, agreed that folk opera does not need an orchestra of fifty-seven. A reduction to, say, forty-five would save £10,200 a year.[149] The Treasury, not surprisingly, strongly favoured total merger. On 10 May 1957 Johnston wrote that 'no-one in their right senses, if they were starting afresh would set up two separate organisations to administer such a large government grant'.[150]

While the destiny of Sadler's Wells was being debated, the artistic management persevered in improving the company. On 1 May 1957 a new *Il trovatore* translated by Tucker and Tom Hammond was distinguished mainly by developing the careers of some future stars of Sadler's Wells, including Australian tenor Ronald Dowd, a 'musicianly Manrico', and a warm if unpolished Peter Glossop.[151] Glossop, after returning from military service in Germany, had been a member of the Sheffield Operatic Society and then auditioned for Norman Tucker, who offered him a place in the chorus in 1952. Until 1963, when he joined Covent Garden as a principal, he sang all the leading baritone roles in the Sadler's Wells' repertoire, to the approval of the critics and the delight of the audience. He later went on to sing leading baritone roles internationally.

On 24 May *The Moon and Sixpence* by John Gardner, based on the novel by Somerset Maugham, with a Patrick Terry libretto and designed by Leslie Hurry, was Peter Hall's first opera production. It impressed more for its integrated production than for its music, Hall eliciting fine performances especially from Pollak, Coates and Rowland Jones. Bronhill was the young girl. It was well conducted by Alexander Gibson, a protégé and friend of Tucker, who had engaged him with a view to appointing him music director from 1957. Gibson, a well-liked man, quickly became a first-class opera conductor for Sadler's Wells until he returned to Scotland in 1960 to take over the Scottish National Orchestra, and later founding Scottish Opera.[152]

The growing confidence and cohesiveness of the company was evident in the revivals. In November 1957 Andrew Porter was delighted by a revival of Basil Coleman's 1953 *Don Pasquale*, whose constant wit and fun was now accompanied by 'a new musical stylishness'. Bronhill, Gwent Lewis, Denis Dowling and Owen Brannigan sang with a care 'for refinement and distinction'. Bryan Balkwill, who had worked at Glyndebourne, showed that he knew how to produce 'colourful, well-balanced playing' that 'enhanced the action on the stage'.[153] Dent's witty translation, well articulated, while tending to broadness of humour, lay behind an increasingly confident national style of opera while also embracing its Italian credentials.

The warm appreciation of Dent's 1946 translation of *Don Pasquale* was a fitting memorial to the man who had been in the vanguard of creating an operatic culture in the UK. Dent, who had been plagued for many years by stomach ulcers, died in August 1957, aged eighty-one. At the time of his death he was virtually blind and completely deaf and for four years had been unable to hear the operas he had helped to produce.

Dent's vision of an English-language ensemble company was being threatened by the Arts Council, just when it seemed as though it might finally be realised. The amalgamation talks were becoming more threatening. Johnston at the Treasury was prepared to get tough with Covent Garden, telling Emrys Williams that Covent Garden would 'come quietly' if amalgamation were made a condition of their grant. He hoped the Arts Council would support such an approach, even though Clark was not taking a very strong line. Lord Moore, acting chairman of Covent Garden and chairman from January 1958 (he inherited the title of Earl of Drogheda on 22 November 1957), had said he would trade independence in exchange for the Treasury agreeing to pay off the deficits.[154]

Covent Garden finally 'came clean' with the Arts Council on 28 May 1957, when Robbins admitted that the members of the Covent Garden Board had taken up such a position because they were concerned that it would be put about that they had 'contrived the death of Sadler's Wells out of envy and hatred', since the merger would largely consist of their swallowing up Sadler's Wells. Robbins now told Johnston that the Sadler's Wells Trust had not been running their affairs economically and efficiently and that the only kind of merger they would even contemplate was one whereby Covent Garden continued 'more or less as at present', with perhaps two places on the board for Sadler's Wells, 'which would then go out of business'.[155]

While Covent Garden was pressing for its demise, Sadler's Wells was fulfilling its commission, and the public were responding. The Arts Council report of 30 May 1957, *Opera in London*, pointed out that there was now an audience for two houses: 'One of the ironies of the situation is that despite their anxieties and disappointments both companies are manifestly presenting works of increasing merit and securing exceptional box office results.' London had 'abundantly demonstrated its appetite for opera'. The Arts Council was involved in the crisis 'up to its neck'. It was a trustee and had gone bail with its bankers Coutts for Sadler's Wells in the case of bankruptcy. As a consequence, the Arts Council could find itself spending its entire annual budget for opera on the costs of closing down Sadler's Wells and Covent Garden. Ministers and advisers believed that opera was 'getting out of hand' and that there was not a clear enough distinction of purpose between them at present. There were many arguments for and against amalgamation, and the root of the problem was insufficient subsidy at both. As always, the heaviest costs were wages and salaries.[156]

The true meaning of government subsidy was slowly dawning on an alarmed Treasury. On 6 June Johnston wrote to Emrys Williams at the Arts Council, asking him to set out the 'financial horrors that face us' if nothing were done about opera in London and 'we drift on as at present'. He did not agree with the Arts Council's assessment of audiences: London's 'appetite' was only at a 'subsidised price', he argued. Six days later Emrys Williams pointed out the new world order to Sir Alexander Johnston: 'The appetite for reading and swimming has also been subsidised . . . whether we like it or not we are living in a Welfare State where the expectancy of a subsidy rouses no alarm even amongst Tories!' It would not be possible to peg expenditure even if the upward spiral of Sadler's Wells spending were arrested. He agreed that there would have to be a single administrator, but they should soft-pedal so that the bodies could be 'coaxed' into acceptance.[157]

On 17 June Sadler's Wells announced to the press that there would be no new productions the following season.[158] Two days later Johnston informed his colleague at the Treasury, Roger Makins, that the positions of the two companies were now reversed: Covent Garden accepting the merger but half of the Sadler's Wells Trust threatening to resign. As Webster would be the chief administrator, Tucker might refuse to serve under him and also resign. In June the Arts Council would announce quite firmly and categorically that Sadler's Wells and Covent Garden would receive a grant of £450,000 only on condition that they amalgamate. Johnston reported that Emrys Williams was confident that he could get the press behind the merger.[159] He was not so convinced and suggested to Emrys Williams that the proposed grant was so large that maybe the present arrangement could continue on condition that both trusts cover their deficiencies by raising seat prices or making economies.[160]

It was announced on 25 July 1957 that a committee of two representatives each from Covent Garden and Sadler's Wells and three Arts Council members would prepare a Covent Garden/Sadler's

Wells fusion plan. Sir Kenneth Clark was not happy. He said bluntly that it would be 'too high a price for the benefits of fusion if the result were Mr Webster and the Covent Garden Board with two guinea pig directors from the Wells controlling both houses'.[161]

At a meeting at the Arts Council on 8 August Clark conveyed the 'guinea pig' plan to representatives of the two houses. There was to be a single governing body which would consist of the present Covent Garden Board and two further representatives of Sadler's Wells, since there were already two members of Sadler's Wells on the Covent Garden Trust, Isaiah Berlin and James Smith. There would be a unified administration with a central planning office under a general administrator and there would be a deputy general administrator to oversee Sadler's Wells. Amalgamation could be achieved only with the willing consent of the governing bodies.[162]

The Sadler's Wells Trust agreed to continue with talks but were not unaware of the plot afoot. At their 19 August meeting it was pointed out that one of the two Sadler's Wells members already on the Covent Garden Board, Isaiah Berlin, had not been a regular attender at Sadler's Wells meetings. They resolved that Sadler's Wells should nominate four representatives to the new governing body, not two. It was also agreed that there was no point in the amalgamation if the Treasury did not write off the chronic deficits.[163]

Berlin, who had little interest in opera in English, admitted to Moore on 3 October 1957 that his position on the Sadler's Wells Board was 'embarrassing' and that directors of Sadler's Wells were not keen that he be regarded as one of their representatives when amalgamation occurred, in view of his 'intermittent interest in their affairs'. They did not regard him, he wrote, as 'quite flesh of their flesh' and he had been dissuaded from resigning only by James Smith, who felt it would weaken his hand in the negotiations. His preference was to stay on the board of Covent Garden now it was becoming more of an international house. Although he thought that the demand of Sadler's Wells for six places on the joint board was 'monstrous', he suggested a compromise: that they could add two of their number in addition to Smith and himself, and when the 'next lot' of Covent Garden directors retired, one or two further Sadler's Wells representatives could be added.[164] On 7 October Garrett Moore responded: 'I think the Sadler's Wells people are being very tiresome and I would certainly not be in favour of appeasing them in the manner you suggest.' The Arts Council had suggested fusion, 'and it is for them to sort out the resulting difficulties'.[165]

While local rivalries raged, the wider picture was discussed in the press. On 10 October 1957 *The Times*, in an article discussing the Arts Council's annual report, pointed out that if they received just £250,000 more, all the chronic crises – including that of the orchestras – could be solved overnight. 'Having created a public,' they wrote, 'it is all the more necessary to ensure that the public gets what it wants and needs.' It was time to stop glorifying British philistinism 'as though it were a symptom of concentration upon the brisker arts of getting and spending'.

The Carl Rosa company was also in dire financial straits. Its director, Mrs Phillips, was resigning due to ill health, and its members were contemplating joining forces with Welsh National Opera. On 24 June the Arts Council had discussed the possibility of Carl Rosa having to close for three months at the beginning of the following year if the Council did not receive a supplementary estimate from the Treasury. The Arts Council was 'not prepared to shed any tears over the Carl Rosa' but agreed to consult the Treasury.[166]

On 14 October, after meetings with the Arts Council, the Sadler's Wells Trust unanimously decided that amalgamation with Carl Rosa rather than Covent Garden was the 'right step to propose in the circumstances'.[167] Norman Tucker prepared a memorandum setting out coherent plans for a future national opera policy: Sadler's Wells would close for a few months in order to restore a full production programme of a minimum of four new productions a season, aiming at standards of metropolitan excellence. Sadler's Wells would have an October-to-April London season, a tour of eight to ten weeks and a short summer season of operetta. Carl Rosa would play in London for a month during the Sadler's Wells tour. He pointed out the disadvantages of amalgamation with Covent Garden. From starting out as a localised venture, Sadler's Wells had developed into the 'people's or municipal opera . . . a popular opera house in the best sense of the word', with cheaper seats and a fundamentally different audience. Covent Garden was a child of the 'golden age of opera', Sadler's Wells a 'child of our times'. Problems of repertoire could be dealt with quite well by a small committee. On 21 November the Trust told the Arts Council that they recommended joining up with Carl Rosa on the basis of Tucker's plan.[168] On 9 December the Arts Council decided to support their proposal.

The 1957/8 season saw the third ticket price rise in three years. Top price went up to 12s 6d – from 12s in 1953/4 – and bottom prices up to 3s 6d from 2s.[169] It was not a good year at the box office, which faced apathy due to the lack of new productions. There was an average attendance of 53 per cent.[170] New singing talent was the main attraction. Peter Glossop and Charles Craig sang in *Il trovatore* on 26 November 1957. They were, *Opera* wrote, 'strong acquisitions to the company'.[171]

The few new shows that did go on showed a steady improvement. On 20 January 1958 *The Merry Widow* opened, translated by Christopher Hassall, produced by Charles Hickman, with décor by Thea Neu. After many meetings to secure the rights for the production from their owner Jack Hylton, Sadler's Wells was able to present an authentic version. Although the production disappointed some critics as lacking in Viennese style, Alexander Gibson, according to the *Daily Telegraph*, 'kept the lilting score continuously on the boil'. June Bronhill was the Widow – a role she sang for more than two hundred performances. In Tucker's view she had brilliance and agility, with 'an acting ability that moved easily from sentiment to comedy'.[172] The Sadler's Wells singers adapted to a new style with aplomb. Howell Glynne became a broad operetta-comedian 'as to the manner born',[173] and Thomas Round, ex-D'Oyly Carte, was a dashing Danilo. The production proved very popular with audiences and was often sold out. Arlen, a friend of the Coliseum's owner, Prince Littler, was able to arrange for it to be transferred to St Martin's Lane.

The same month that *The Merry Widow* opened, the Carl Rosa crisis reached a climax. The new chancellor, Peter Thorneycroft, had promised Clark at the Arts Council that 1957/8 would be an exceptional year and that he would be more generous in the future. Just after Christmas, however, he had informed Clark that he was again putting the same ceiling on the following year's grant-in-aid, as a result of which the Arts Council found itself £250,000 short. Clark had protested that one or more opera companies would have to close down, but Thorneycroft was adamant. Covent Garden would get £305,000, which was much less than it had asked for, and Sadler's Wells £100,000. Carl Rosa would receive £45,000 instead of the current year's £60,000. All three representatives said they would have to close down under these allocations. 'In a personal capacity', David McKenna suggested to Clark that Covent Garden be closed down as a permanent British company but retained as the home of the Royal Ballet.[174]

On 5 January 1958 Chancellor Thorneycroft, having lost the battle for general spending cuts, resigned and Macmillan, who had supported the spending departments, replaced him with Derick Heathcoat Amory. Economic expansion could proceed, with income tax steady at 8s 6d in the pound and inflation seemingly under control.

As yet, Sadler's Wells did not benefit from this political change, and plans for amalgamation with Carl Rosa gathered momentum. On 31 January the Arts Council offered £215,000 for joint activities on condition that all their debts were repaid. The new company should be called the Sadler's Wells Carl Rosa Trust. A week later the Arts Council, Sadler's Wells and Carl Rosa discussed the offer. It was clear that by the time the debts had been paid and the Carl Rosa spring tour completed, there would only be £130,000 left for the September 1958 to March 1959 season. It was not enough to maintain separate companies. It was suggested by the Arts Council that if some plan could be made to get through 1958/9, some expansion of one company might be possible in 1959/60. Tucker argued that standards could not be maintained if thirty weeks of opera were given outside London.[175]

Tucker later described this Arts Council offer of just seventeen weeks' opera at Sadler's Wells and the rest on tour as the 'Denison plan' after its architect John Denison, the Arts Council music director. As far as Tucker was concerned, it entailed 'a strengthened and augmented Carl Rosa (from our ranks), presumably still run by the ageing Mrs Phillips, which would tour for thirty weeks a year, leaving what remained of the Wells to fend for itself as best it could in London'. Together with Gibson and Arlen, Tucker sat quietly at Trust meetings, having earlier expressed his opposition to the plan while holding his fire and 'leading Denison gently up the garden path'.[176]

Tucker, however, had no intention of being associated with such

a merger.[177] On 10 February he told a special meeting of the directors that thirty weeks' touring was not possible. One metropolitan
company should do between sixteen and twenty weeks' touring,
with a second company being formed after three years. Arlen supported Tucker: 160 people would have to be sacked, especially the
chorus and staff producers and wardrobe. Standards would
inevitably drop.[178]

Even the Treasury was uncomfortable with the arrangement,
despite the Arts Council secretary general's argument that opera
had come to occupy too large a part of the Arts Council budget.
Thomas Padmore, an amateur musician and second secretary at the
Treasury, was concerned that it would be said that his ministry had
'slaughtered Sadler's Wells to achieve a petty economy'.[179]

Matters were brought to a head on 25 February, when Tucker
offered Smith his resignation, together with those of Arlen and
Gibson. The Trust had 'clearly not read the signs of fire raging
within us', he later commented.[180] In his letter he stressed that, had
Carl Rosa rested for six months and not organised a spring tour
before they knew what their grant was going to be, there might have
been enough money to do a beneficial amalgamation. 'I cannot', he
wrote, 'accept the dismemberment of a company which has been
carefully built up over a long period'.[181]

Three days later, 'at zero hour, when the directors were about to
sign on the dotted line', Tucker announced the merger proposals
and his resignation to the shocked assembled company, warning
that some of them would not be re-engaged after July. His resignation letter was handed to the press and the debate was thus brought
into the public arena, where there was strong support for Tucker
and Sadler's Wells. The company formed a fighting committee with
Hargreaves as chairman, and insisted on meeting the board of directors, to whom they gave an unpleasant half hour, demanding their
resignation.[182] At the same time, Lord Esher set up a committee to
raise £35,000 to maintain Sadler's Wells as a metropolitan company.

The Treasury representatives felt that Emrys Williams at the Arts
Council had behaved badly and were not happy that it fell to them
to prepare the answers to parliamentary questions about the fate of
Sadler's Wells. They had been told that the extra £100,000 they had
given would keep Sadler's Wells alive, but the present scheme

entailed the virtual disappearance of the company. Padmore observed that this was 'a lamentable thing' for which the Treasury would get the blame.[183] They were determined to ensure that the Arts Council should take responsibility for what was proving to be a controversial decision.[184] The Treasury prepared arguments for the government's answers to Parliament on 5 March, proclaiming the generosity of the growing subsidy and placing opera in the context of the general financial picture. The Treasury grant to the Arts Council had gone up from £235,000 in 1945/6 to £985,000 in 1957/8. For the following year the chancellor had agreed a figure of £1.1 million, which was an 11 per cent increase and one which the Arts Council had said was enough to keep Sadler's Wells going. The opera companies had to pay their overdrafts. 'Admittedly opera is always expensive,' Johnston in the Treasury wrote, 'but it has tended to become the cuckoo in the Arts Council nest which throws all the other fledglings out.' Opera now accounted for 65 per cent of the Arts Council budget, and even Covent Garden, the maintenance of whose standards was the Arts Council's 'first objective', was having to make cutbacks.[185]

Padmore, a classical-music lover and later chairman of the Handel Opera Society, now proved to be the champion of Sadler's Wells. He stressed that the Chancellor of the Exchequer and the government should not support the Arts Council. It was impossible to provide decent opera without subsidy, he argued. Carl Rosa standards had for a long time been 'not much better than contemptible', while those of Sadler's Wells had been 'high and continuously rising'. The Arts Council had decided to throw away the latter while retaining the former. Their decision would also probably prove to be very expensive, as touring was always costly. He was dismayed that the Arts Council was 'letting the anti-London pro-provinces faction' push them into something he believed to be nonsense. He penned 'cries of anguish not particularly suitable for the file', and definitely not very civil-servant-like, at the prospect of 'losing Sadler's Wells in which so much had been invested and of which the country had to be proud'.[186]

Meanwhile, as a result of huge public support and the fundraising efforts, Tucker had not finalised his resignation. The chairman had received a promise of an anonymous grant of £15,000, and the mayor of Finsbury was hopeful that the LCC might help. Arlen told the Trust that he was convinced that the support that Sadler's Wells had received both from the press and the public made it unlikely that there would be any trouble raising sufficient funds for this year. Arlen's spirits were undaunted: 'Given proper support the company could achieve an eminence that the ballet company had already achieved.' He also told the Trust that he considered Tucker irreplaceable. If amalgamation went through, support would be dissipated. Tucker had prepared a press statement for next season based on a full programme and with Sadler's Wells retaining its separate identity.[187]

Thus it was that on 24 March the Trust asked Tucker and Arlen to prepare a full programme while working in close liaison with the Appeals Committee. The Treasury accepted the Trust's decision to abandon the merger plans and continue to plan for full-scale operations as a separate company.[188] Denison for the Arts Council, however, remained discouraging, telling Sadler's Wells that they should regard themselves as 'going it alone'. Four days later Emrys Williams informed Smith that the sum of £215,000 would be the same no matter how it was divided between the Carl Rosa and Sadler's Wells.[189]

The Appeals Committee formed by Smith and McKenna and chaired by Lord Esher began its work the same day. The national press strongly supported Sadler's Wells. The Finsbury borough librarian Reginald Rouse wrote: 'London pride can surely afford a trifling subsidy to keep its opera going' – a mere tenth of a penny rate for all London would provide £38,000 to save the Wells.

On 28 April the Trust formally ditched the amalgamation plans and Tucker rescinded his resignation for at least a year. That same day, Denison informed Emrys Williams that Tucker had agreed to stay on the basis that the Trust accepted a budget with a deficit of £189,000, and on the understanding that production costs would be cut if they did not get their extra £40,000. Sadler's Wells would pay off £10,000 of debt and had high hopes of the London County Council. They were seeking Arts Council reassurance that their present grant of £150,000 per annum would not be cut. They would restore a full programme with three and a half new productions and five weeks' touring.[190] On 4 June the Arts Council formally made the offer of £150,000.

Arlen prepared plans for Sadler's Wells and touring, and

transferred the production of *The Merry Widow* for the month of August to the Coliseum, where his old employer, Prince Littler, was keen for Sadler's Wells to produce operettas between his pantomime seasons. This move was intended to give the company contact with the West End and facilitate the absorption of Carl Rosa. There would be two companies, one giving opera at Sadler's Wells and on tour, and one showing operetta at the Coliseum. All artists would be contracted by Sadler's Wells. The time had come, he wrote, to bid 'an honourable farewell to the name of Carl Rosa'.[191]

In July the LCC agreed to a £25,000 grant as an emergency measure for one year and to set up an independent committee to see whether they could continue to contribute to Sadler's Wells from the rates. Tucker's and Arlen's plan for the next season was accepted by the Trust on 8 September, and announced by the Arts Council seventeen days later. There would be no further grant to the Carl Rosa. Sadler's Wells would present opera in London and in the provinces, and operetta at the London Coliseum. There would be two companies with one pool of principal singers, and twenty-five to thirty weeks of touring by each. Sadler's Wells would invite provincial representatives to sit on its board.[192]

Lord Esher wound up the Appeals Committee on 22 September. It was, he announced, one of the few projects with which he had been associated which had been able to close down because it had achieved its objectives. On 8 December 1958 the directors heard reports of the 'high standards, efficiency and morale of the company', which had received much assistance from Professor Procter-Gregg, director of Carl Rosa. All but six of the chorus had been offered employment and all but five of the orchestra.[193] Stephen Arlen became administrative director, and detailed planning for the 1958/9 season went ahead.

The future looked promising. *The Flying Dutchman* opened on 29 October. It was produced by Dennis Arundell, who had decided he wanted to work with a new designer. He turned to Timothy O'Brien, who was very much of the new generation of theatre talents, having been influenced, like Peter Hall and John Barton at Cambridge, by the literary critic and academic F. R. Leavis, a man who 'pursued textual analysis and moral purpose with fundamentalist fervour'.[194] Like Hall and Barton, O'Brien was slowly coming to favour a new style of production that was not dependent on the social manners – or connections – of the previous generation.*

Unknown to O'Brien, Tucker had suggested a Wieland Wagner-style set with an empty stage and projected 'magic-lantern' scenery, explaining that the opera is 'difficult to mount at the best of times but given our severe limitations of space, it called for imaginative treatment of the highest order'. Arundell, however, decided that he wanted 'to help the audience more than present them with an abstraction', and consequently needed a solid ship. O'Brien, 'happy to oblige', provided him with a storm and a ghost ship.[195] Tucker described the gradual appearance of the ship out of the depths until, in a '*coup de théâtre*, depending on split-second timing', a total blackout was replaced by the revelation of a fully-rigged vessel. The Victorian effect of the arrival of the ship, the critic Rodney Milnes later recalled, 'hit you between the eyes; it was just amazing'.[196] The gaunt figure of the Dutchman came ashore on the high rocks, where every foothold had needed constant rehearsal. David Ward made his name in this production. Alberto Remedios, who had joined Sadler's Wells in 1956/7, was the Steersman. William Reid conducted because Gibson was ill. The production was brought back at the end of the season by public demand.

According to the tolerant Tucker, Arundell was 'a brilliant, difficult man'.[197] He berated Elizabeth Fretwell during the curtain calls on the first night of *The Flying Dutchman* in front of the whole cast, and, being himself a sound musician, interfered in the sphere of all but the most confident conductors. His asperity, O'Brien later explained, may have come from his having been a 'gilded youth, a person of high promise, who in the end was a disappointed and embittered man because the promise was not always fulfilled'. Although O'Brien enjoyed the task at the time and his design was much praised by the critics, his friends told him it was not very good. He quickly moved into a new style and sensibility when he

---

* Direction and design at the end of the 1950s reflected a tougher, more cynical, socially aware approach, much evident in the work of the English Stage Company under George Devine at the Royal Court and Peter Hall's Royal Shakespeare Company at Stratford. Hall, a brilliant and ambitious young Cambridge English graduate with a working-class background, made Stratford in the early 1960s a centre of excellence in direction, acting, writing and design. He was joined by St-Denis and Peter Brook in 1962, with John Bury as the resident designer.

joined the Royal Shakespeare Company shortly after *The Flying Dutchman*. He found that his Cambridge-educated colleagues regarded opera as 'something a little self-indulgent' and that for them 'operatic' was 'a dirty word'. Looking back, he felt that Sadler's Wells was small and friendly but a little underpowered, and its productions at that time 'creaky, illustrative and orthodox'.[198]

It was a hard enough battle for the Sadler's Wells team to improve musical standards, increase its audience and survive. Innovations in design had to come second. Although O'Brien and Arundell had hoped to stage *The Flying Dutchman* without an interval, it was decided the drop in the bar profits would have been too great.

On 26 November 1958 *Seraglio* was conducted by Colin Davis so successfully that Tucker decided to appoint him music director after Gibson announced his plans to return to Scotland in 1960. William Glock, in his review of *Seraglio*, wrote that Davis had 'reflected on every problem and every nuance of character' and had gained in control and assurance. 'Let us not be silly and hail a new master of world rank, just because we need one; but the promise is there.'[199]

Sadler's Wells seemed safe at last and to be moving forward artistically. The combination of public support with a resolute and successful artistic leadership had saved the company once more. At the same time, the Treasury had reluctantly come to accept the concept of opera as an integral part of the welfare state, no matter how insatiable its demands. The door to local government support had also been opened. The fighting cuckoos had established their places in the nest and their hungry demands and growing appetites would prove an unending headache for the Treasury and the Arts Council.

# 6

# 1959–1966: A Home on the South Bank?

After the demise of Carl Rosa, the horizons of Sadler's Wells widened and its reputation grew both at home and abroad. Having taken on responsibility for the bulk of opera touring throughout the United Kingdom, Sadler's Wells found the amount of time spent on the road increased from nine weeks in 1957 to forty-two in 1960, the year in which the tour included Australia. In 1962 the company was split into two, with two orchestras and two choruses and a pool of singers, equal in stature and each with its own repertoire. Originally they were known as S and T companies, and after 1964, T became W company.* One or other company was on the road the whole year round, taking it in turns to be based at Sadler's Wells. This pattern of touring in the United Kingdom was maintained until 1967, when the schedule was reduced to twenty weeks. Although expensive to sustain and challenging to organise, the tours were not only in the tradition of Sadler's Wells but were enjoyed by the company and regarded as a positive contribution to its camaraderie and *esprit de corps*. They also gave opportunities for new members to gain experience.

Stephen Arlen, with his European connections, also organised substantial foreign tours. In 1962 and 1963 the company visited Germany for two weeks, and in 1965 there was a four-week tour of Europe, visiting Zagreb, Prague, Vienna, Hamburg and Paris. Tucker was conscious of 'trespassing on territories with long healthy traditions of opera and showing our modest wares', and chose the repertoire with care, to include such works as *Peter Grimes*, *The Rake's Progress* and *Iolanthe*, all of which had original English texts. The company scored a particular success in Munich

* S stood for Sadler's Wells Theatre, as in resident company, while T was the company on tour. This changed to S and W – Sadler's and Wells – as the two companies then started to swap round and one would be at Sadler's Wells Theatre while the other was on tour.

with *The Rake's Progress* and *Peter Grimes*. In Prague, with Charles Mackerras as their guide, the travellers admired the beauty of the city but were constantly aware of surveillance by the oppressive Soviet-backed regime. Tucker was delighted by the growing reputation of his company at home and abroad.[1]

Sadler's Wells was also extending the range of its activity within London. Another operetta in the West End, *Die Fledermaus*, opened at the Coliseum on 17 April 1959. Wendy Toye, originally a dancer, choreographer and director of film comedies, was in her element. Andrew Porter described her production as stylish and 'sparkling with charm and spirit' – choreography, stage patterns and effective detail all gave unfailing pleasure. Christopher Hassall's translation was sung distinctly and with command by both first and second casts, which included Anna Pollak, Victoria Elliott, Rowland Jones, Alexander Young and June Bronhill. Vilem Tausky conducted. The financial results were disappointing because the expenses of the production had been underestimated, but the experiment continued.[2]

As a result of the disruption and uncertainty of the previous year, *Rusalka*, on 18 February 1959, was one of only two new shows in the 1958/9 season at Sadler's Wells. It was also the opera's first professional production in Britain. Desmond Shawe-Taylor was delighted by James Bailey's enchanted lakeside flickerings, but was less beguiled by the 'too solid nymphs' capering around in Wendy Toye's 'rather restless and uncertain production'. A stately Joan Hammond made one of her rare London stage appearances, conducted with affection by the Czech conductor Vilem Tausky, who was a frequent guest conductor at Sadler's Wells in the 1950s and 60s.

At this time, Covent Garden, under the influence of board members Isaiah Berlin and Walter Legge, was moving towards original-language performances with international performers. Maria Callas had been singing regularly at Covent Garden since 1952, and Luchino Visconti's production of *Don Carlos* in May 1958, conducted by Carlo Maria Giulini and with an international cast, had laid to rest the concept of Covent Garden as an English-singing company. The Franco Zeffirelli *Lucia di Lammermoor* had made Joan Sutherland an international star and brought Zeffirelli into the house as a regular contributor. Georg Solti's appointment as music director in May 1960 set the final seal on Covent Garden's role as the international house.

Tucker was determined to differentiate Sadler's Wells from Covent Garden by using his own, Tom Hammond's and Stephen Arlen's skills and boldness in recognising new young British and Commonwealth singing talent and in identifying a new generation of directors and designers. On 30 April 1959 Tucker told the board that he wanted to encourage the younger generation of directors.[3] One was the thirty-five-year-old Anthony Besch. After wartime service, Besch had completed an English degree at Oxford, where he directed *Idomeneo* at the Opera Club. He started his professional career in 1950 at Glyndebourne as assistant to Moran Caplat and had then worked under Günther Rennert and Carl Ebert. His first production for Sadler's Wells on 13 October was a work little known in Britain, Giordano's *Andrea Chénier*. Most critics dismissed the *verismo* blockbuster as a 'blood-and-thunder piece' for big star singers, and noted that the forces of Sadler's Wells were insufficient for the task. Harold Rosenthal, however, wrote of the care lavished on the production by Besch, who 'marshalled his limited forces with skill'.[4] Peter Glossop was a forceful Gérard. Tausky conducted.

At the same time as introducing unfamiliar repertory, there was an inclination to ignore the physical limitations of the house, and perhaps even to tread on Covent Garden's toes. On 9 December 1959 Besch directed *Tannhäuser* in the translation of Ernest Newman, who had died on 7 July. Colin Davis, who conducted, later observed that not only was *Tannhäuser* 'a very, very difficult piece' but that operas on such a scale 'were not really suited to Sadler's Wells at all'.[5] The still dry and unsympathetic acoustics of the theatre told against it, wrote Philip Hope-Wallace.[6] *Tannhäuser* was designed by Motley, who set the realistic action, Andrew Porter wrote, in 'square, ugly unrealistic décor'.[7] Colin Davis's youthfully buoyant conducting, however, was aided by Besch's tactful production and the noble performance of Ronald Dowd. Davis himself had already been chosen by Tucker to take over from Gibson as principal conductor from August 1960.

Tom Hammond was the inspiration behind the production of Rossini's *Cinderella*, which was staged in October 1959. The future distinguished critic and editor of *Opera* magazine, Rodney Milnes, soon to start his career as a journalist, recalled: 'It was Tom Hammond who woke us all up to Rossini.' Hammond later planned *Count Ory* (20 February 1963) and *The Thieving Magpie* (27 January 1966), both of which lasted well into the Coliseum era. *Cinderella* had become familiar to Glyndebourne audiences, but London had seen very little Rossini, since even *The Barber of Seville* had left the Sadler's Wells repertory in 1953. Audiences were delighted by the high spirits, tenderness and inspired melodies of what Porter described as 'a beautifully made piece'.[8] Douglas Craig directed deftly and wittily, with a light touch. Arthur Jacobs translated. If the production invested the opera with a fairy-tale element that Rossini had deliberately eschewed, it also captured much of its sparkle and did not distort the characterisation. Denis Dowling as Dandini, Anna Pollak as Clorinda and Howell Glynne as Don Magnifico won plaudits for comic timing as well as vocal assurance. Patricia Kern was a gentle Angelina whose vocalisation was adept and technically secure, her phrasing 'musical, free and often most affecting'. Porter considered Kern one of the great British mezzos, sharing with Janet Baker 'flexibility of divisions, stamina, clarity of emission and beauty of tone'.[9] Bryan Balkwill conducted crisply and with spirit, according to Shawe-Taylor.[10]

The extent of Sadler's Wells' artistic development was revealed on 15 January 1960, when it gave the British stage premiere of Stravinsky's 1927 opera-oratorio *Oedipus Rex* in a double bill with the 1957 production of Bartók's *Duke Bluebeard's Castle*. *Oedipus* was directed by Michel St-Denis and conducted by Colin Davis. The spoken narrative was in English, and the chorus, with whom St-Denis spent two thirds of the rehearsal time, sang in Latin. The twenty-two-strong tenor and bass chorus, masked and dressed alike in long, dark clothes, was still when the principals were singing but involved in slight movement the rest of the time. Their movement was, Tucker wrote, 'like corn lightly stirred by a summer breeze'. It took hours to achieve this perfect unanimity of ensemble.[11] St-Denis and his designer, M. Abd'elkader Farrah, created splendidly ominous masks, a tiered chorus and formal movements. Together they captured the ritual style of the opera with 'savagery and stylistic decisiveness'.[12]

In a dinner jacket, Michael Hordern proclaimed the English narration with a heightened mode of delivery that Philip Hope-Wallace thought a good equivalent for the French original, which had been written and delivered by Jean Cocteau. Raimund Herincx gave an impressive double, as Creon and Messenger, David Ward a fine Tiresias. Ronald Dowd sang Oedipus powerfully, with 'splendid firmness and ringing tone', wrote Peter Heyworth.[13] Davis believed St-Denis to be a master who was working in a very stylised and precise way, with the characters in masks the 'puppets of the gods'. It was, he said, 'a very ferocious piece that works when done with crazy intensity'. According to Heyworth, Davis responded to and matched the production 'with incisive rhythms, hard orchestral textures and fine internal balance', drawing out all the score's 'fierceness, lucidity, and remorseless momentum'. The critics found *Oedipus* an overwhelming theatrical event – a triumph both musically and dramatically. David Cairns thought it one of the finest musical ensembles in the company's history.[14]

Ronald Dowd – Sadler's Wells' Oedipus – was one of the Australian contingent who contributed so much to Sadler's Wells after the war. He was an emotional, volatile and nervous performer. Tucker later wrote about his uncontrolled rage after the final dress rehearsal of *Oedipus*, which he had managed to soothe. Dowd nonetheless had the ability to 'set alight a dull *Fidelio*' and raise Samson to epic stature 'by the power of his noble, tormented presence and impassioned declamation', David Cairns later wrote.[15] On 18 January 1960, however, the Trust was informed that Dowd no longer wished to be a member of a permanent organisation, although he agreed to make guest appearances. It was a great loss to the company, as he was considered indispensable for many dramatic tenor roles.[16]

The innovative programming was coming at a price. Neither the critical nor the artistic triumph of *Oedipus Rex* helped it at the box office. The increased amount of touring since the demise of Carl Rosa was also proving a drain on resources. Sadler's Wells had requested an extra £36,500 in order to expand touring and repertoire and employ more top-ranking British singers, but on 11 November 1959 the Arts Council had decided not to make an increase on their promised £260,000 for the following year. Furthermore, at the urgent meeting held at the Arts Council on 28

January 1960, Williams, Denison and Lund warned McKenna and Tucker that if Sadler's Wells could not provide a comparable amount of touring to that of Carl Rosa, they would be in 'considerable political difficulty'.[17]

Both for financial reasons and because of their touring responsibilities Sadler's Wells felt justified in expanding into repertoire hitherto considered Covent Garden's preserve. As Sadler's Wells saw it, since they were the only company providing English-language performances and most of the touring, they should be producing all the popular basic repertory as well as continuing to produce new and lesser known works and their own familiar repertoire.[18] They also had to fill the house. On 14 December 1959 the Trust decided the company should prepare a new *Tosca*.[19] Tucker told the Opera Subcommittee on 18 February 1960 that it was essential to increase the number of productions of the standard repertoire alongside shows like *Rusalka*, *Oedipus* and *Andrea Chénier*. Sadler's Wells must produce a new *La traviata* and *Barber of Seville* for the tour, despite Covent Garden's claims to be solely responsible for touring such repertory.[20]

Arundell was chosen to replace his own production of *Tosca*, with Davis conducting. When the new production opened on 2 April, Marie Collier was a superb Tosca, in transparent skirts, emerging as softer and less self-assured than usual, which intensified the drama of Scarpia's murder. She was, said *The Times*, a 'highly strung, highly sexed Tosca'.[21] Charles Craig was Cavaradossi and Peter Glossop Scarpia.

Because the repertoire was overlapping, it was decided in January 1959 to set up a formal structure to co-ordinate the two houses' plans. The Covent Garden/Sadler's Wells Co-ordinating Committee sat for the first time a month later, on 25 February, when it was agreed that efforts should be made to avoid duplication, particularly of routine works. John Tooley, Webster's assistant general administrator at Covent Garden, and Stephen Arlen were both willing and able to make things run smoothly at that level.[22]

This development did not, however, remove the tensions entirely. In June 1960 Covent Garden expressed its irritation that Sadler's Wells was demanding a share of the larger operas. In a letter of 25 May to Isaiah Berlin, Covent Garden Board member Edward Sackville-West wrote that it was 'time a halt was called to these "brave efforts" for which Sadler's Wells is invariably applauded (in true English fashion) whereas Covent Garden is blamed for everything short of perfection (eg *Don Carlos*)'. *Dalibor*, which Tucker was considering, was far too large an opera for the resources of Sadler's Wells and he should not be allowed 'to fob us off with *Forza* . . . it must be *Boccanegra* or nothing'. Sackville-West was also unnerved by the success of Sadler's Wells in finding talented English directors.[23] Co-dependence, rivalry and occasionally jealousy were already established as sometimes destructive, sometimes stimulating features of the relationship between Covent Garden and Sadler's Wells.

Davis conducted the new *La traviata* when it opened on tour in Manchester on 5 September, after which it reached London in October. It was the first opera production of Frank Hauser, the director of the Oxford Playhouse, who displayed his theatrical skills and preference for realism alongside a certain awkwardness with operatic convention. Soliloquies, such as that of Violetta in Act I, were over-embellished with stage business – Violetta singing to a doll.* Desmond Heeley set the action with sociological truthfulness in a Paris salon of the 1830s, stuffy and hypocritical, in silk and satin crinolines that raised applause as the scenes were revealed. Raimund Herincx was a convincing Germont, Elizabeth Fretwell a Violetta of spirit and nobility. It was both a freshly thought-out production and, together with Davis's brisk attack, a somewhat stern and rightly angry *Traviata*.

In April 1960 Wendy Toye's production of Offenbach's *Orpheus in the Underworld* continued to establish a happy central role for operetta at Sadler's Wells and later for ENO. Toye created with 'inexhaustible comic invention' a show that was revived every year until 1978. Andrew Porter loved the 'brightness of invention and irresistible urge of high spirits' that Toye captured so well and with such style. He was, he said, 'simply whirled away into a state of happy, helpless frenzy'. Anna Pollak was a splendid Public Opinion and June Bronhill outstanding as a 'bright, naughty' Eurydice. Eric Shilling, a stalwart member of the company for over thirty years,

---

* Ingmar Bergman in an interview in *Opera* in October 1962 spoke of the reluctance of modern directors 'in revolt against the old-fashioned stand-still concert in costume' to allow singers to stand still at all. The aria, he said, was a 'moment of rest: a natural rhythmic accent in the performance'.

made the role of Jupiter famous in England.* Newcomer Jon Weaving was a 'personable Pluto', and altogether it was a 'sparkling ensemble', which Alexander Faris conducted with verve.[24]

The ensemble company that was being built up in the 1960s benefited the operetta repertory. Rosenthal, when reviewing the recordings of the operettas, which were released in 1981, described them as 'a wonderful mixture of young blood and more experienced "pros"'. Amongst them were ex-D'Oyly Carte tenor Thomas Round, together with Derek Hammond Stroud – later Sadler's Wells' Alberich – and their Italianate tenor Charles Craig.[25]

From July to October 1960 the company made a highly successful operetta tour of Australia, negotiated by Arlen. Some local singers were auditioned for parts, since performances were continuing at home. The company started in Melbourne in October, reaching Sydney in December. Bronhill's fine notices resulted in her being invited to sing Maria in *The Sound of Music*, and by 1962 she was lost to the company. Iris Kells took over many of her roles. The success of Bronhill, Ronald Dowd and Elsie Morison further encouraged more singers to come from Australia. These included the tenors Gregory Dempsey and Donald Smith and baritone Neil Easton.

Productions were uneven and not all works were worthy of excavation. Edward German's *Merrie England*, written in 1902, was directed by Arundell on 10 August 1960 and described by Edmund Tracey in the *Observer* as 'chest-beating tush-mush'.[26] William Mann thought it full of 'squishy vocal quartets and solos that evoke memories of bosomy contraltos, piping soubrettes and clammy-handed tenors'. Arundell did his best to make it a piece that audiences in 1960 'need not blush at', and his fine operetta ensemble again shone: Patricia Kern, Joan Stuart and Anna Pollak's Queen Elizabeth, who flounced and spoke her lines beautifully, singing 'oh peaceful England' with dignity and restraint.[27] The *Times Educational Supplement*, while deploring Edward German's jingoistic 'inane farrago', saw the production as a good omen of the pos-

---

* Alan Blyth in his obituary of Shilling described his versatility in roles ranging from Dr Bartolo, Leporello and the Lord Chancellor in *Iolanthe* to Dr Kolenaty in the *Makropoulos Case*. He was a great favourite of audiences who 'liked to see their singers disport themselves in a varied repertory', and 'all his assumptions were adorned by impeccable diction' (*Guardian*, 22.2.06).

sibilities for Sadler's Wells doing Gilbert and Sullivan once the D'Oyly Carte's monopoly expired the following year. Audiences seemed to be made up of 'Suez groupies and colonels of both sexes . . . who cheered every insular swagger to the echo'.[28]

The Trust expressed its displeasure at the drab costumes and scenery of *Merrie England*, which were not considered worthy of Sadler's Wells.[29] Arlen explained that the fault lay with Arundell, who found it hard to work with designers and had little visual sense of his own. He was proving a difficult colleague and Arlen suggested that his talent did not compensate for his personality problems or the administrative difficulties he created. Davis later said that he had found Arundell 'a curiously sardonic character – he had a rather superior voice – didn't smile often, but very clever and a very good producer, he got people into the piece'.[30] Arlen suggested that Frank Hauser should take on the role of director of productions to work alongside Davis, who felt that he needed someone 'of similar status' to himself.[31] Hauser, however, declined the offer.

On 25 January 1961 Sadler's Wells gave the first performance in English of *Ariadne on Naxos*, clearly directed by Anthony Besch with Peter Rice's ingenious and delightful set. Tom Hammond's translation helped the comprehension of the audience in the prologue, although articulation was occasionally lost later. Fretwell was an opulent-voiced and regal Ariadne, while Bronhill as Zerbinetta threw off her fiendish coloratura with 'coquettish zest'. Shawe-Taylor felt that Davis, while eliciting a fine performance from the orchestra, conducted with less feeling for the music than he had with *Oedipus* and lacked the Viennese lilt. *Ariadne on Naxos* was very well received by audiences, and its surprisingly good attendance was ascribed to more exposure to the piece, especially from records.[32]

The twenty-nine-year-old Colin Graham, who had worked with the English Opera Group, was the next young talent to work at Sadler's Wells. His contribution to the company's development over the next two decades was of lasting significance in raising the standards of professional stage direction. Andrew Porter later described his particular talent as the 'ability to trace the long line of the drama without neglecting or falsifying the incidental representational detail'.[33] His first opera for Sadler's Wells was Janáček's *The*

*Cunning Little Vixen*, then unknown in England. It opened on 22 March. Shawe-Taylor was again 'bowled over' by the beauty and originality of the work – 'so terse and laconic, yet so ripe and humane'. Something, he felt, must be right about the production, which was not very imaginative but equally was not coy. Later visits confirmed his response, as did the full and enthusiastic houses. The lack of critical enthusiasm for the production might have been the result of Barry Kay's scenery, which was flimsy, bare and dully lit. Newly recruited Australian baritone Neil Easton was a robust and genial Forester, though lacking in poetry and wonder. Bronhill, in her last role at Sadler's Wells, successfully shed her operetta habits to sing clearly and act convincingly as the Vixen.[34] Audiences were responding to the new work and careful preparation, with attendances at *The Cunning Little Vixen* and *Merrie England* sometimes reaching capacity.[35]

In October the New Opera Company's production of Stravinsky's *The Nightingale* was staged at Sadler's Wells under an arrangement whereby the company put on its best shows at Sadler's Wells using the senior company's resources.* With Leon Lovett as their music director, Anthony Besch their artistic director and Peter Hemmings their administrator, they played a substantial role in presenting new works to the London opera public. Later productions at Sadler's Wells included Prokofiev's *The Love for Three Oranges* in March 1963 and Henze's *Boulevard Solitude* a month later.

In late 1959 political changes and economic problems meant that there was once again pressure on the development of Sadler's Wells. In October 1959 Macmillan's Conservatives had won the general election with 365 seats to 258 for Gaitskell's Labour Party. Macmillan's expansionist economic policies, intended to improve the lot of working people, led in 1959 to a dangerous fall in the currency reserves. Full employment was leading to increased wage claims and higher inflation – 5–6 per cent was viewed with dismay in 1960. By February 1960 public expenditure was £340 million more than the Treasury considered wise. The bank rate was

---

* The New Opera Company had emerged from the Cambridge University Opera Club's production of *The Rake's Progress* in 1956 and mounted short London seasons of unfamiliar twentieth-century works from 1957. Its first season saw the stage premiere of Arthur Benjamin's *A Tale of Two Cities*.

increased to 5 per cent and a period of what was termed 'stagfla-
tion' – economic stagnation accompanied by inflation – was accompanied by an increasing need to prop up the nationalised industries.
Selwyn Lloyd, who was close to Macmillan on economic policy,
became chancellor on 27 July 1960. In July and August strikes by
the power workers and seamen led to inflationary wage increases,
and the balance of trade deficit rose to £122 million in October. At
the end of July the bank rate was increased to an unprecedented 8
per cent and the government introduced a not very successful 'pay
pause' in September. By the autumn of 1960 it was clear that there
would have to be a reduction in public spending.

The warning signs of impending belt-tightening had been apparent the previous year. Although the Arts Council had received an
extra grant, Sadler's Wells had not been a beneficiary. On 6 March
1959 Emrys Williams of the Arts Council had informed Norman
Tucker that Sadler's Wells would not be getting any extra funding.
The outlook brightened three days later, however, when the support of the London County Council was given official sanction
after an independent committee of enquiry under Sir Frederick
Hooper recommended substantial and continuing assistance from
the London rates. It was intended that support should be sufficient
not just to ensure the survival of Sadler's Wells but to enable it to
develop standards appropriate to a metropolitan house. He recommended a grant of £35,000 a year for three years and an initial
£15,000 for immediate maintenance, in order to keep ticket prices
at a level that would not depart from the spirit of the charter or
lose any of the audience, especially students. The report underlined
the interdependence of the two houses: Sadler's Wells was a well-
run organisation that complemented Covent Garden and was
essential as a training ground for young singers. Not for the last
time, an independent report argued that there was an audience for
both houses which one alone could not satisfy.[36] It was, however,
the first time that local government had declared its recognition of
its role in supporting a major cultural amenity for the people of
London.

The first concrete result of the LCC's support was revealed at the
beginning of the 1959/60 season, when their £15,000 funding of
the theatre's redecoration was unveiled. The house had the air,
according to Harold Rosenthal, of a 'modern super cinema'. He

bewailed the loss of the 'individual dowdy atmosphere' in which he and so many others had spent their operatic infancy in the 1930s.[37] The altered proscenium arch and enlarged pit had not improved the acoustics and they had to be drastically altered at a cost of a further £1,200 the following year.

The two-company touring policy, established after the demise of the Carl Rosa, was causing serious financial difficulties for Sadler's Wells. The accumulated deficit would be £90,000 by the beginning of 1961 and could only be sustained if the bank agreed to accommodate the overdraft.[38] In February 1961 Arlen informed the Arts Council that its offer of £325,000 for 1961/2 would not cover the two companies for the whole year and that one of the two touring companies, T company, would have to be disbanded.[39] At this time the Arts Council was a largely supportive institution, and his appeal elicited a positive response. On 7 March Lord Cottesloe, the new chairman of the Arts Council, hinted that support would be forthcoming in the shape of a supplementary grant to cover salary increases if there was a crisis.* The Trust decided to carry on with the company's planning.[40] It was also decided that ticket prices would have to be raised. In the 1961/2 season the top price went above £1 for the first time and the bottom price went up from 3s 6d to 5s. Prices nonetheless remained inclusive throughout the 1960s. Rodney Milnes, whose first flat in London in 1961 was within walking distance of Sadler's Wells, had felt 'incredibly lucky' to be able to sit in the gods for 'pence'. The saying went that the cheapest price should never be more than a packet of ten Woodbine cigarettes. It was, he said, 'the sense of mission that kept it going and that sense of mission remains absolutely critical'.

Hopes for the new opera house faced a setback in the spring when, after years of stalling on the issue of a National Theatre, the Arts Council's report, *Housing the Arts*, published on 22 April 1959, suggested that it was desirable but not urgent for Sadler's Wells to move to a more metropolitan site. At the same time the report recommended capital expenditure of £1 million and urged

---

* John Fremantle, fourth Baron Cottesloe, was, like Oliver Lyttelton (Lord Chandos), an old Etonian. After wartime service he sat on the LCC and the Port of London Authority Committee and was a governor of the Old Vic/Sadler's Wells Trust from 1957 to 1970. The eventual building of the National Theatre was in large part due to his determination and persistence.

immediate progress on the proposed theatre on the South Bank as well as the building of a medium-sized concert hall and an exhibition gallery. Selwyn Lloyd allowed the Arts Council to publish its report, although the government made no commitment to implement its findings.

It was dawning on a somewhat horrified Treasury that a National Theatre would result in a new relationship between the state and the arts. English theatre had hitherto been treated as independent and commercial, with occasional small grants for deserving causes. A National Theatre would in effect be a state-run and state-owned enterprise, with an ever-growing annual subsidy. So far, it had been explained that only Covent Garden would receive such 'special treatment', because, being such an 'exotic growth', it could not otherwise establish itself. The potential demands of three national companies was a worrying prospect for the government, and Sadler's Wells was soon drawn onto the political battlefield.

Despite Treasury concern, the impetus for a National Theatre did not diminish, while competition amongst contenders for the role became fiercer. The Old Vic governors were determined that the Old Vic organisation would be its nucleus and passed a resolution to that effect on 16 April 1959. The Joint Council for the National Theatre – chaired by Lord Chandos* – included members of both the Old Vic and the Stratford governing bodies. In 1960 Laurence Olivier was unofficially chosen to be the director of a future National Theatre by Chandos and Kenneth Rae, the secretary of the Joint Council.

Meanwhile, Peter Hall, who had taken over from Byam Shaw at the Stratford Memorial Theatre, had been rapidly expanding the activities of the theatre and was making a bid for his own company – to be renamed the Royal Shakespeare Company in 1961 – to become the National Theatre under his stewardship. Olivier, however, wanted nothing of the kind – it was to be *his* National Theatre.[41]

In June 1960 the Joint Council urged the chancellor to agree to the implementation of the plan for a National Theatre based on the amalgamation of the forces of the Old Vic and Stratford. In

---

* Formerly Oliver Lyttelton, who had been elevated to the peerage in 1954.

November Hall took a three-year lease on the Aldwych Theatre for his company. Meanwhile, the government came to envisage the National Theatre as consisting of three elements: one in the new building on the South Bank, one in Stratford and an experimental theatre at the Old Vic.[42]

Despite the *Housing the Arts* report, Tucker was determined that his company should leave Sadler's Wells. On 16 October he told the *Sunday Times*: 'Unless we can have a new home, we shall soon reach a dead-end with audiences and with artistic development.' The entire South Bank scheme seemed to receive a mortal blow, however, on 21 March 1961, when Selwyn Lloyd announced that the government would no longer support it. Instead, it was decided to give more support to the Old Vic, the regions and Stratford.

The momentum for a bricks-and-mortar National Theatre was not going to diminish, and Sadler's Wells now emerged as a crucial piece in the jigsaw. The Treasury saw a possible solution both for building the theatre and relieving itself of supporting two opera houses when Chandos suggested that if Sadler's Wells were involved in the scheme, the LCC might pay a higher subsidy to Sadler's Wells. Sadler's Wells would be the metropolitan company – an *opéra comique*, as in France, doing small-cast operas – supported by the local authorities, and Covent Garden the national company. Even if the government had to support touring to some extent it would still be a relief to the Exchequer. The 'alarming trend' upwards of the Sadler's Wells subsidy made it well worth 'serious investigation'. There could be one theatre with two auditoria on the South Bank, and Sadler's Wells and the Old Vic could be sold off to help pay for the new theatre.

The government had to be squared. In April the Treasury noted that the Cabinet was changing its mind, not really believing that Stratford in London, the Old Vic and Sadler's Wells could really fit under one roof, 'even if allowance were made for a suitable amount of deflation of RST [Royal Shakespeare Theatre] ambitions'.[43]

A concerted effort was made by the supporters of a National Theatre to shame the government into reversing its decision, Chandos leading the campaign by putting pressure on Tory ministers. The House of Lords debate on 20 April showed powerful support for a building worthy to house an English national drama. Britain remained one of the few great nations that did not possess a National Theatre, Lord Silkin stated, and the government ought to take the lead in such matters. Lord Cottesloe, the new chairman of the Arts Council, pointed out that it was the LCC, not the government, that was providing London with concert halls, galleries and works of art from sculptors to 'embellish' new schools and housing estates.[44]

The LCC under Sir Isaac Hayward was indeed leading the way. Hayward took a delegation to the Treasury on 6 June, offering £1.3 million if the government would provide the £1 million to which it was legally committed by the 1949 National Theatre Act. Hayward proposed to raise this sum by levying a penny rate over three years. He told Selwyn Lloyd that the LCC had no objection to Sadler's Wells being rehoused.

Sadler's Wells was becoming an intrinsic part of the scheme. On 15 June Chairman James Smith wrote to Covent Garden Board member Isaiah Berlin to inform him that Sadler's Wells intended to sell the site and use the proceeds for the National Theatre scheme and to settle their outstanding debt. The Sadler's Wells company would continue to operate in the new building under its own name.[45] Meanwhile, the chancellor, Selwyn Lloyd, was urged by the music-loving Thomas Padmore at the Treasury four days later to encourage his 'old friend' James Smith to come into the scheme. Stratford and Sadler's Wells were agreed that both companies would use both auditoria and 'Box and Cox' between them. The chance of controlling the growing deficits of all three companies – Sadler's Wells, the Royal Shakespeare Company and the Old Vic, together with the possibility of the London County Council shouldering a large part of the burden – was irresistible.

The Cabinet also came on side when it began to see the new scheme as a way of delaying the day of reckoning. In June it was agreed that in view of its offer, the LCC should be asked to submit a scheme. 'These tactics', they decided, 'would ensure some considerable delay before it became necessary to undertake a definite commitment.' They could not give an immediate undertaking because of the 'economic situation'.[46]

Selwyn Lloyd therefore wrote to Hayward on 23 June agreeing to release the £1 million. He invited the Joint Council to submit a scheme that would include the Old Vic, the Royal Shakespeare Company and Sadler's Wells. The government would commit an annual subvention of £230,000 for drama and £170,000 for opera, for expenditure at both the new theatre and at Stratford, but not at the existing York Road or Rosebery Avenue sites, and not for touring. If any party pulled out, the subvention would be reconsidered.[47]

In thanking Selwyn Lloyd, Chandos wrote that Hall, the Stratford chairman Fordham Flower, Olivier and Kenneth Clark believed that the scheme, far from being a compromise, was 'a great advance on anything that had yet been thought of'. They hoped Olivier would oversee the artistic side of the operation. The chancellor told Smith on 30 June that he was particularly keen that Sadler's Wells should be part of the scheme. That same day, the Treasury sounded a note of warning that if the Old Vic were left out in the cold, they would demand more money, and four days later the chancellor suggested to Chandos that the Old Vic should also be involved. On 7 July Chandos therefore pressed for all three bodies to come under a supreme board of twenty people. Olivier would be assisted by George Devine and Hall, with a single budget. Sadler's Wells would contribute with the sale of its Rosebery Avenue theatre, and the LCC would be asked to increase the annual grant to the company from £45,000 to £100,000.

The Treasury thought they had solved the problem. They did not want three companies competing for funding and still wanted the Royal Shakespeare Company to continue mainly in Stratford, in which case one theatre in London would be able to contain the three companies. The present situation, they noted, had without doubt been brought about by the RSC 'holding out for their self-appointed goal of a permanent London home in addition to Stratford'. Richard Cerdin Griffiths, Assistant Secretary at the Treasury, spotted the crucial element in the new situation: 'They all see that once they are housed the government will have to cover any deficits!' Covent Garden had led the way: 'They will point with some justification to the grim history of the Covent Garden subsidy position over the last ten years.'[48]

The Treasury thought they had come up with a perfect solution, but they had reckoned without the jealousies and opposition that it would arouse. The Covent Garden/Sadler's Wells planning disagreements and rivalry had been growing steadily. In March 1961 Covent Garden was refusing to allow Sadler's Wells to produce *Un Ballo in maschera*, *La forza del destino* or *Simon Boccanegra*. Berlin reported to the Royal Opera House director Burnet Pavitt that Tucker by now detested Covent Garden 'openly, violently and continuously'.[49] For its part, Covent Garden was having none of the Treasury plan. On 13 July Covent Garden's chairman, Garrett Drogheda, wrote:

Dear Selwyn: I cannot help feeling concern over your decision to incorporate Sadler's Wells into the National Theatre project. By your decision you are in effect saying that Covent Garden, which since the war has been upheld by the state as the national Opera House and which is exclusively responsible for the National Ballet, no longer holds the position of National Theatre concerned with the arts of opera and ballet. Unless clearly stated people will think as I do and it will have a very unsettling effect on the people employed at Covent Garden.[50]

The Treasury gave Drogheda short shrift, suggesting that Covent Garden should join in with Chandos and the Joint Council. Drogheda was not amused, replying on 9 August that due to 'most difficult problems of conflicting personalities' it would only be possible if there were a joint Sadler's Wells/Covent Garden administration, which had been discussed some time before.[51]

Drogheda's anger grew in proportion to Tucker's confidence and excitement. On 18 July Tucker released a press statement. Although the new building would not be a purpose-built opera house, it would be 'designed to take account of the most modern ways of presenting theatrical performances and equipped in the most modern way'. All the lyric arts would be presented in it, with unique opportunities for 'inter-communication between the arts'. There would be two auditoria, one mainly to house the opera and one the drama company. It was a moment of opportunity:

We believe that a new theatre is required to house the complete lyric Arts, i.e. drama, opera, ballet and anything else that can be suitably represented in a theatre, and that this is one that will accord with modern thought and will appeal to the younger generation. This theatre will be completely modern in conception and execution.[52]

Sadler's Wells' existing home at Rosebery Avenue would be sold to pay for the new theatre, and he hoped that Sadler's Wells would become a 'genuine theatrical opera school', vastly superior to the London Opera Centre.[53]*

On 13 July Smith wrote to Chandos to convey the Trust's acceptance of the scheme, by which Sadler's Wells would retain its name and the company would have the use of one or other auditorium throughout the year and representatives on the National Theatre body.[54]

The 1960/1 annual report was the last prepared by James Smith after fifteen years as chairman. David McKenna, who took over in November 1961, described his predecessor as an essentially practical man who believed in the evolutionary approach. And at the same time he had held on passionately to the principle that if an artistic enterprise is to succeed, it must be of high quality.

Tucker was not alone in his enthusiasm. On 19 July the LCC adopted the motion to participate in the establishment of a National Theatre on the South Bank. In his speech Sir Isaac Hayward said he hoped that it would be ready in time for the 400th anniversary of Shakespeare's birth in April 1964. On 24 July the LCC said that if more space were needed, they might provide a bigger site.[55]

The National Theatre owed a huge debt of gratitude to the LCC under Hayward, Lord Esher said in the House of Lords on 20 April. It was his team that had provided the full enthusiasm and support for 'intellectual and artistic things' over the years. In the same debate Lord Cottesloe, who had taken over the chair of the Arts Council from Clark, said that at the age of sixty-eight he could see more clearly than the government that in an era when England had

* The London Opera Centre was an institute for opera training set up in 1963 with an Arts Council grant. Housed in the former Roxy cinema in Commercial Road, east London, it also served as the rehearsal stage for the Royal Opera House. David Webster was responsible for the appointment of Humphrey Procter-Gregg as director rather than Anne Wood and Joan Cross, whose own National School of Opera, founded in 1948, was fatally undermined by its creation. Cross and Wood, who were Procter-Gregg's assistants, resigned in 1964, together with board member Lord Harewood, as they believed that the relationship with the Royal Opera House – whose rehearsal time got preference over the school's needs – was not beneficial. They also believed that the cinema rent took up too much of the Arts Council grant. Procter-Gregg was himself replaced by James Robertson, who remained the director until the centre closed in 1978. Amongst its most illustrious students were Kiri Te Kanawa and Ann Murray.

no empire, air force or army, supremacy could only be pursued through its outstanding judges, its imaginative politicians and its writers, artists, dancers, painters and musicians.

Amidst the excitement Tucker was fully aware of the opposition that the plans for the South Bank would provoke, particularly from the local Finsbury and Islington regulars and the Vic-Wells association. Above all, Covent Garden, which had no leg to stand on, would fear an 'encroachment of their royal rights'. Sections of the Arts Council were hostile, 'partly because they would not have approved of the idea anyway, and partly because they were not consulted'. Equity, the performers' union, had not understood the scheme and feared job losses. The Charity Commission was 'ill-informed and unfriendly', as were the 'more sentimental members of the public generally'.[56]

Equity indeed proved to be strongly opposed to Sadler's Wells becoming involved with the National Theatre. They feared a monopoly, arguing that 'rivalry between entirely separate dramatic companies is an incentive' and that amalgamation would exclude anyone who did not see eye to eye with the management. Arlen's correspondence with the assistant secretary general of Equity, Hugh Jenkins, proceeded in amicable disagreement, with the latter writing on 13 September: 'I hope you get a nest of your own on the South Bank. You are too big a cuckoo for the National Theatre one.'

Meanwhile, Arlen was vigilant and lively in answering the letters of the 'sentimental' critics. Writing to Harold Rosenthal, editor of *Opera*, he recalled the standards of the Baylis era: 'Lord knows you are stuffy enough as a rule about what we do. I hate to imagine how you would be if we not only put the prices down but also gave you some of the sort of things I remember hearing here, and walking out of, in the days of the great lady.'

On a more serious note, there were friends who feared Sadler's Wells was being used. On 22 August Evert Barger, a businessman who worked for the UN, was a friend of Arlen and had been on the board from 1958 to 1960, wrote to warn Arlen of the vipers' nest he was being drawn into. If there was any prospect, he wrote, 'of building an opera house on the South Bank, I would, as you and Norman know, be one of the strongest supporters of the plan'. But he believed that there was no such hope, and that Tucker and Arlen were being taken for a ride. The National Theatre, when built, was going to be run by Peter Hall, and the opera would take second place. How, he asked, could they agree 'to the division of an annual budget (I mean subsidy of £400,000 roughly in the proportion two thirds for drama and one third for opera)?' Barger continued:

A few years ago Norman told me he hoped to take over Covent Garden and that Webster would retire. It would of course be far and away the best thing, and it may yet come to pass. You are, I must tell you, making a great miscalculation in the middle of your lives. The NT is for Shakespeare and Shaw, in the public mind, and will not be an opera house. You should not sell up Sadler's Wells, however clever the scheme, which the Arts Council has put up to the London County Council. You are trying to mix blood and oil. It will, I think, be of great disservice to opera in London and the provinces. You and Norman will have little control, whatever gentlemen's agreements you may think you have entered into over a National Theatre on the South Bank.

Barger concluded his plea: 'Norman is the greatest opera director the country has, and I would hate to see him taken for a ride. He will get on worse with Peter Hall than he has with Webster.'

Arlen was not dismayed, replying to Barger on 25 August that 'it is not going to be run by Peter Hall', and explaining that there was 'no question of division of annual budget. In any case, the new Knight [David Webster] is, I fear, immortal.' He shamefacedly admitted to Barger that it was he and Tucker who had thought of the scheme. The opera house would be for Sadler's Wells and 'no-one else unless we chose to let them have it'. He added: 'You are wrong that he would get on worse with Peter Hall than Webster but the real point is that he does not have to get on with Peter Hall if he does not want to; assuming that Peter Hall is the Director.'[57]

Arnold Goodman, who later sat on the Covent Garden and ENO boards and was chairman of the Arts Council from 1965 to 1972, worked at the time in the offices of Rubinstein Nash, solicitors to the Old Vic governors. He had been asked by Lord Chandos to prepare a draft scheme that would not cause offence to any of the parties.[58] As the Trust put it, he was preparing 'constitutional requirements and safeguards'.[59]

The National Theatre power struggle was reaching a climax. On 16 August the Arts Council chairman, Lord Cottesloe, told Hall that Stratford could not expect a subsidy, for which they had been campaigning since 1958, unless they agreed to Chandos's plans for amalgamation. This was a declaration of war in the eyes of Hall and his chairman Fordham Flower. They expressed their dissent to the Joint Council on 20 September, when they said they were frightened of becoming the poor relation and, 'to put it very bluntly, we don't like the set up'. Five days later Flower told the Joint Council: 'Larry wants to eliminate Stratford as a competitor.'[60]

Goodman wrote that when he delivered his draft constitution to Stratford, they looked at the document with 'lack-lustre eyes and minimal interest'. When asked who would be the head of the organisation, Goodman, who had not been informed, 'opined' Olivier, at which point their faces became 'rather distant'. It was clear to Goodman that he had 'seen the last of them'.[61] In October the Treasury noted that it was becoming apparent that Stratford were thinking hard about coming in, since it looked as if they were beginning to lose their identity.[62]

As far as Sadler's Wells was concerned, the Arts Council, the Joint Council and the Treasury were agreed about one thing: the new opera house must in no way 'compete with Covent Garden'. It should seat no more than 800 and its productions should be easily transplanted to provincial theatres.[63]

On 8 November Sadler's Wells announced the appointment of Colin Davis as music director for four years. Davis's relationship with Tucker did not prove to be an easy one. According to Davis, Tucker was very clever but 'very withdrawn' – a homosexual at a time when it was still illegal and dangerous to be identified publicly; he was 'a very lonely man' who maintained emotional barriers which Davis found difficult to overcome, even when talking to him about music. Davis ruminated: 'I think I was too young and brutal to know how to handle him.'[64] For his part, Tucker acknowledged that they were both 'strong willed in their own preserves', describing Davis as a 'brilliant, likeable, often difficult young man'.[65]

It was specifically stated in the press announcement that Davis would be preparing the two Sadler's Wells companies for their rehousing on the South Bank. In November 1961, however, Arlen started to be concerned that the situation was deteriorating, asking the secretary of the Joint Council, Kenneth Rae, for clarification. Arlen used Davis in his argument. The Music Director, he wrote, had made 'considerable personal sacrifices and refused one very attractive offer in order to join us'.[66*]

The tension between Olivier and Hall reached a climax in the winter with fierce competition for actors, as Olivier tried to cast his 1962 Chichester season. So long as Olivier was considered to be the head of the National Theatre, Stratford was not interested in the marriage. By December news of dissension in Chandos's committee – about the Old Vic/Stratford amalgamation and the size of the Sadler's Wells theatre – was reaching the Treasury, and on 28 December it was noted in the Treasury that Stratford had finally pulled out altogether, feeling both double-crossed by the Old Vic and 'elated by the success of their venture at the Aldwych Theatre'.[67] In February 1962 Olivier wrote a twelve-page letter to Hall, accusing him of scheming to hijack the National Theatre for Stratford, of creating an empire and trying to outmanoeuvre the organisation that had been working on the scheme 'long before Stratford ever thought of it'.[68]

Meanwhile, the Joint Council's plans were becoming more ambitious. In January 1962 Sadler's Wells joined the Joint Council Committee, which was still chaired by Lord Chandos and included Lord Esher, the erstwhile chairman of the Old Vic governors, and Lord Cottesloe, the chairman of the Arts Council. Olivier regularly attended, gallantly supporting Sadler's Wells.[69] On 15 January the new Sadler's Wells chairman, David McKenna, reported on his meeting with the Joint Council at which an alternative scheme had been discussed. There should be an amphitheatre for drama in conjunction with an opera house for Sadler's Wells, although 'not necessarily under the same roof', and the Old Vic would be the proscenium stage. The LCC was not willing to provide two sites but would consider a larger single site. McKenna warned that the government's subvention would not be enough for such a plan and that the withdrawal of Stratford meant a reduction in the annual grant from £400,000 to £300,000. The final decision lay with the chancellor.[70]

---

* Davis has a different recollection of events: 'This is new to me,' he said. 'Probably Arlen playing politics,' although he vaguely recalled 'something about [a job in] Liverpool' (interview, 18.9.06).

Sadler's Wells, firmly established, now faced greater demands from the critics. When, on 2 February 1962, Colin Davis collaborated with Byam Shaw on Stravinsky's *The Rake's Progress*, Andrew Porter described it as a 'dun-coloured performance', both musically and visually – with Motley's fixed planks on a trestle set 'against wings and background of pale coffee'. Sadler's Wells, he explained, was no longer 'a company we need make allowances for'. He was also unimpressed that Byam Shaw had dispensed with curtains, as it removed all sense of formal structure from an opera conceived in closed forms and destroyed the finales of each scene. Davis, however, became more relaxed with the score and his 'care more complete' as the performance progressed. All the critics were impressed by the depth of the Graveyard and Bedlam scenes and the vivid choral singing.[71]

Davis himself found it terribly exciting, learning 'all this new music we did not know'.[72] By the time of its revival in January 1963 he had firmly secured 'the weight of Stravinsky's pulses and rhythmic ambivalences' so that each number exhaled its particular character *ab initio*. Byam Shaw's production was also more appreciated at its revival and the cast had gained in confidence – Alexander Young's Tom Rakewell, 'strong of voice, weak of character', Herincx's blacker, sleeker, more baleful Nick Shadow and Edith Coates's 'unspeakably debauched' Mother Goose.[73] Heather Harper had taken over from Elsie Morison to sing an even warmer and more appealing Anne Trulove.

Tucker had introduced Byam Shaw to Davis, and they immediately got on well. In rehearsal, Tucker wrote, Byam Shaw would 'sit quietly through the scene, only interrupting if absolutely necessary, and then in general tones make his comments'. He was, Rupert Rhymes, ENO's director of administration in the 1970s, later recalled, 'the perfect English gentleman, but his command of the trooper's language was second to none'.[74] He was also an encouraging director for singers.

On the day of the premiere of *The Rake's Progress*, McKenna told the Trust that if the company were to progress artistically, Byam Shaw should be in charge of productions, to advise on repertoire, producers, designers and all aspects of work on the stage. He would also take special responsibility for young artists and keep an eye on touring productions. Davis said that if Byam Shaw signed on, he would like to extend his contract.[75]

On 7 March Tucker announced Byam Shaw's appointment as director of productions to 1967, outlining his previous work at the Old Vic and Old Vic school, as well as his eight years at the Stratford Memorial Theatre. With the appointment of Byam Shaw confirmed, Davis also extended his contract, due to end in 1964, to 1967. The appointments of John Blatchley as Byam Shaw's assistant and Margaret Harris of Motley as head of design were also announced. 'Apart from their eminence in the world of theatre,' Tucker wrote, 'they have been connected with teaching, both on the dramatic side and design.' This would create a permanent team at Sadler's Wells for the first time.[76]

Blatchley was currently George Devine's assistant at the Royal Court, where much of the most radical theatrical work was taking place. He was also from the Old Vic school, and had worked with Michel St-Denis at Strasbourg. These new colleagues, all of them friends of Arlen from his Old Vic days, would be, said Tucker, 'of inestimable value to an organisation that relies to a large extent on young singers'. They would also be able to offer their experience and advice to young designers and producers employed from the outside. The preparations would ensure that Sadler's Wells would be of the right quality to occupy their new home on the South Bank.[77] Theirs was a real vision of a training ground for young talent.

The 1961/2 season opened on 1 September with John Barton's production of *Carmen*. The original version, with spoken dialogue, was used, much to the excitement of Porter, who thought it helped the action proceed more smoothly and sensibly. It did, however, expose the singers to charges of not delivering the dialogue as skilfully as trained actors might, and Barton – an academic and colleague of Hall's at Stratford – was blamed for failing to improve their delivery of the text. Their stage movement was 'stilted and monotonous', the characterisation weak. Patricia Johnson remained 'a nicely brought up girl trying to ape a Spanish guttersnipe'.[78] Davis thought Barton was 'a little bit at sea – very young'.[79] The new Sadler's Wells recruit, Australian Donald Smith, had, in Porter's words, 'a thrilling vocal instrument, warm and flexible' but lacking heroic volume. Colin Davis drew from his orchestra a 'spontaneously joyous rhythm and sunny sonority' that matched Ralph Koltai's 'blotchy sun-baked slabs'.[80]*

At its revival in November Blatchley tightened up the action. The new Carmen, Joyce Blackham, was 'excitingly near the mark', voluptuous and with a thrilling, rich chest voice. Davis thought her 'temperamentally very well suited', while Charles Mackerras, who conducted Blackham as Carmen in October 1965, recalled her as a 'sexy creature'. Don Smith, he added, was 'not very romantic' but had a 'gorgeous voice'. Together, he observed with a twinkle, they were 'the reigning divas'.[81]

After the great success of *Orpheus in the Underworld*, Tucker lost no time in establishing that Gilbert and Sullivan should be brought into the repertory as soon as the D'Oyly Carte copyright expired on New Year's Eve 1961. *Iolanthe* was chosen, since Guthrie was putting on *The Pirates of Penzance* and *HMS Pinafore* in the new year in the West End.[82] It opened on 1 January 1962 at the Royal Shakespeare Theatre in Stratford, directed by Frank Hauser and designed by Desmond Heeley. The first non-D'Oyly Carte productions were given much coverage in the press and Sir Malcolm Sargent conducted some special D'Oyly Carte perform-ances at the Savoy, determined to show that there was life yet in their old ritualistic shows. Cairns, however, wrote of the Savoyard die-hards: '1961 can be ignored because it is really 1901.' A visit to the Savoy Theatre was a 'return for an evening to an age when the Empire is big and red on the map, income tax is 1s in the £ and America has not yet been invented'. The old formula kept their 'nostalgia green and fresh'.[83]

Sadler's Wells, while not entirely convincing audiences that D'Oyly Carte's days were over, managed to provide delectable Arcadian landscapes designed by Desmond Heeley and a measure of delight with its modern lighting by Charles Bristow, the first lighting designer to be named in Sadler's Wells programmes. There were also some excellent performances: Denis Dowling as Lord Mountararat, Elizabeth Harwood as a very pretty Phyllis and the unfailingly musical Patricia Kern as Iolanthe. Eric Shilling, accord-ing to Cairns, was the '*sine qua non* and *ne plus ultra* of Lord

---

* Koltai recalled that Tucker had employed him as a 'safety factor' for the opera novice John Barton, as a result of which began Koltai's association with the Royal Shakespeare Company (interview, 29.10.07).

Chancellors, practised to the last twitch of the tapir nose smelling trouble, the expertly timed emphasis of dubious jaw or questioning eye'.[84] Hauser, who professed to never having seen a Savoy production, directed with 'wit, taste and invention'.[85] *Iolanthe* was a huge success at home and abroad and marked the start of Gilbert and Sullivan becoming an integral part of the Sadler's Wells' repertory, despite intermittent expressions of board distaste. Operetta was good for the box office and relieved the singers and chorus of some of the strenuous daily grind in what Davis described as an 'opera factory'.

At the end of August 1962 Rolf Liebermann's Hamburg State Opera company visited Sadler's Wells with Wieland Wagner's production of *Lohengrin*, Hans Werner Henze's *Der Prinz von Homburg*, Günther Rennert's 1957 *Wozzeck* and his *Lulu*. The Hamburg company's ensemble revealed its strength and identity in a series of theatrically and musically powerful performances. It was hoped that they would be an inspiration for Sadler's Wells as the company endeavoured to reach such heights itself. For Davis the visit was a 'big event' – his first encounter with *Lulu* and *Der Prinz von Homburg*.[86]

The Handel Opera Society also visited Sadler's Wells that summer, as it had done regularly since 1959. They presented *Jephtha* in July, directed by Besch with Janet Baker as Storgé and Ronald Dowd in the title role. *Radamisto* was not one of the society's finer shows, although another future English star, Josephine Veasey, sang the title role.

As planning for the construction of a National Theatre moved ahead in the new year, the concept of a separate opera house began to gather momentum. This would entail two sites, the original National Theatre site for Sadler's Wells and a new site next to Hungerford Bridge for the National Theatre itself. The LCC would build car parks on both sites and walkways would be constructed around each building to connect the various arts institutions.[87]

On 21 March the Equity assistant secretary general Hugh Jenkins wrote to Arlen: 'You will be glad to know that for some time I have been advocating that you should have a new nest by the water all to yourselves. This notion has caught on in influential circles as I expect you know, and I hope that it may still be possible to save you from becoming a cuckoo.'[88] The Arts Council having informally approved the scheme, Sir Isaac Hayward would shortly announce the provision of two sites, and the chancellor release the money.[89]

The Joint Council's plan was published on 17 April: there was to be an amphitheatre auditorium for drama at Hungerford Bridge on a site large enough to build a proscenium later; on a separate site adjacent to County Hall an opera house would be built provided by the London County Council. In responding to the Joint Council scheme, the Arts Council made it very clear that 'the Opera House was to be designed to serve as complement and not a rival to the Royal Opera House, Covent Garden'.[90]

The new South Bank Theatre and Opera House board, under Lord Cottesloe's chairmanship, would be joined by two Sadler's Wells nominees, Tucker and McKenna. They, together with the two National Theatre representatives, Lord Chandos and Laurence Olivier, would be responsible for the planning and building. Olivier's directorship of the National Theatre was announced at the same time. His Chichester ensemble would be housed at the Old Vic until the National Theatre was ready. The development was to be funded as before.[91]

The scheme was at last perfect, but the Cabinet had to take the final decision and the financing of it was left unclear. On 11 May Cottesloe wrote to the Treasury that the annual subvention for the National Theatre would not be sufficient, but 'he did not think it desirable to pursue that issue at that moment'. Henry Brooke, the Paymaster General, reported to the Treasury that doubts had been expressed in the Cabinet as to whether there was 'really any need – or at any rate any hurry – to spend a lot of money on replacing Sadler's Wells'.[92]

Three days later the Treasury, realising that they were in danger of losing a unique opportunity to pass the burden of supporting Sadler's Wells over to the LCC, prepared a memorandum for the chancellor urging the Cabinet to take '*the* decision'. There might never be, they argued, 'a better moment after half a century of history and two years of active negotiation'. They strongly supported the construction of a new opera house. Although the case for Sadler's Wells moving was 'not very strong', the theatre was obsolescent, 'and with every year that passes this will become truer'. If this opportunity were missed, they wisely pointed out, Sadler's Wells would continue to exert pressure and the Exchequer would end up carrying the financial burden, whereas under this scheme the London County Council would pay for both and might even give more to Sadler's Wells. The LCC was anxious to go ahead as soon as possible, and its attitude owed much to the personal interest and enthusiasm of Sir Isaac Hayward, whose term of office was coming to an end. The Charity Commissioners could be relied upon to safeguard the 'poor man's opera house'.[93] The Cabinet approved the plan on 15 May and it was announced on 3 July.

On 9 August Arlen was focused on the inadequate funding for both the scheme and the running costs, coming up with the idea of a national appeal. Tucker, however, felt it was too soon for the public, since an Art Fund appeal to save the Royal Academy Leonardo cartoon for the nation had only recently raised £450,000. He also foresaw that the RSC would 'go mad' if Sadler's Wells started such an appeal with £1.3 million in the kitty, while the RSC had nothing as yet.

Sir William Hart, clerk to the London County Council, strongly supported Sadler's Wells. He had been a law tutor at Oxford before moving into local government in 1947. He was well liked and greatly respected as a formidable intellect, a fine and devoted public servant, and one who was extremely knowledgeable about town planning and public administration. At a meeting on 11 August Hart advised Sadler's Wells that 'detailed questions' about finance 'should be ducked' and every effort should be made to get the board working and get as many people committed as quickly as possible. His advice was: 'Get everything going and, having done so, solve the problems later.' He added that they should do 'nothing controversial until it is too late, and then the Lord will provide'.[94]

Two days later, however, at the South Bank Theatre and Opera House board meeting, Hayward fired a warning shot across the bows of Sadler's Wells. If there was a shortage of money, he warned, priority would have to be given to the National Theatre and the opera house delayed in consequence. Arlen had been perturbed about this possibility, but had been reassured by Hart that he was not to worry. 'Brick for brick,' he advised. Small wonder that Arlen felt that Sir William Hart was 'the key to the whole business'.[95]

Fighting arguments were quickly prepared by Arlen to counter potential opposition. A policy statement would suggest that unless the whole treatment of opera was reconsidered and opera itself 'given a shot in the arm, it may well be that in fifty years' time the tradition will be a dying one'.[96]

On 19 November the National Theatre board asked if Arlen would become their administrative director to assist them in building up their organisation. Although he wanted to stay full-time at Sadler's Wells, he accepted for a limited period, believing that the speed of building the opera house depended on the speed of building the National Theatre. It might also help create a strong, confident and sympathetic administration there.[97] His widow Iris recalled that Arlen was reluctant to leave Sadler's Wells. He 'could not live without' his singers, for whom his door was always open and who reciprocated his affection.[98]

The 1962/3 season reflected the growing excitement within the company. Exhilaration could be sensed in its wide range of unfamiliar works and new productions. On 11 October Byam Shaw's new *Idomeneo* was the opera's first fully professional production in London, and an important collaboration for both Davis and Byam Shaw. Motley designed a timeless set consisting of vertical black panels as background. In order to free it from a traditional classical setting it had a mixture of styles and 'stern Minoan, utterly unbaroque costumes'.[99] Byam Shaw's production was partly realistic, partly stylised, with an 'effective handling of crowds and exciting choral groupings'. Under Davis's direction the chorus excelled itself, despite the cramped space which diminished the epic qualities of the opera.[100] In Stanley Sadie's opinion the orchestra lacked 'rhythmic flow and through-phrasing'. Ronald Dowd was a heroic Idomeneo, Elsie Morison a tender Ilia.[101]

In December John Blatchley and Timothy O'Brien gave life to Puccini's *The Girl of the Golden West*. Theirs was a fine partnership, although the concept and design – with a large free-standing electric log fire and huge mining sluice in the last act – were more naturalistic than O'Brien considered acceptable after his work at the Royal Shakespeare Company. It nonetheless worked well, he reflected, for a 'genre piece, with its mines and mists and snowy wastes'.[102] Raimund Herincx was a 'suitably dark voiced' Jack Rance and Elizabeth Fretwell a splendid Minnie. Donald Smith was

Dick Johnson and Warwick Braithwaite conducted a 'rousing performance', with a strong 'sense of drama and pace'.[103]

*The Rise and Fall of the City of Mahagonny* on 16 January 1963 made an overwhelming impact. 'The moral of the soulless pleasure-town continues to strike hard in our Affluent Society,' wrote Shawe-Taylor, who found the 'racy Berlin cabaret style, the zip and pungency of the text, the hit tunes and jazz rhythms' exhilarating.* Michael Geliot directed a project he and his friend Ralph Koltai had long since dreamt of doing together, and they were united in their desire to convey the relevance of the political and humanist message of the work.[104] *Mahagonny* was, Koltai later reflected, the one labour of love of his career and he was instrumental in securing both the support and music rights from Lotte Lenya and the English rights from Brecht's son, Stefan.[105] They set the work in contemporary London in a 'do-it-yourself' design 'cunningly assembled from the contents of an old lorry and from *actualité* photographs projected on a screen'. Colin Davis, in his element, gave such vigorous and pointed musical direction that the greatness of the music was fully revealed.[106] Both April Cantelo as Jenny and Dowd, a slightly too mature and grizzled Jimmy, mastered their tricky roles with conviction and intelligence. Particularly powerful was the scene of the death from gluttony of Jake, sung by Alberto Remedios, accompanied by Weill's sentimental waltz under Oxfam-type famine projections. All in all, *Mahagonny* was a brave and remarkable venture; Rodney Milnes later reflected that he had never seen it better done, admiring the way the curtain rose on an empty stage onto which a rusty old truck pulled up and from which the whole design gradually emerged.

In February Rossini's *Count Ory*, translated by Tom Hammond, also sprang into dramatically sharp and inventive life in the hands of Anthony Besch and Peter Rice. Hammond was praised for capturing both Scribe's formal and artificial rhyming scheme and the ambiguity of the work. Shawe-Taylor enjoyed Rice's fleur-de-lys backcloth and gold pepper-pot castle. It was, he wrote, a first-rate musical performance, with Patricia Kern and Elizabeth Harwood in particular providing same dazzling vocalisation under Bryan

---

* The Lord Chamberlain had found it racier still, insisting that the words 'shit' (three times) and 'pissed' (once) be cut from the text (Lord Chamberlain's Office to ENO, 20.12.62, ENO Ad 85 Box 61).

Balkwill's admirable direction and, in Besch's hands, dashing characterisations.[107] *La Belle Hélène* in May was another excellent
operetta for the Sadler's Wells ensemble.

On 23 April a new *Peter Grimes* directed by Basil Coleman
showed the critics that they had not been justified in focusing on the
lack of size of Sadler's Wells in 1945. The advantages of a small
house production were apparent in the force of the characterisation,
especially that of Ronald Dowd's Grimes, 'as deep and sad as the
sea itself', and Elizabeth Fretwell, an Ellen of lustrous tone and
grandeur of phrasing. The portrayal of Bob Boles by Gregory
Dempsey, another of the Australian recruits, was galvanising in its
'consuming hatred of Grimes', thought Cairns.[108] Mackerras's
dynamic direction of chorus and orchestra and principals more
than compensated for the dry acoustic, which weakened the force of
the storm and moonlight music.

Shawe-Taylor had written in his review of *Mahagonny*:

Despite all its shortcomings this first English production of an entirely
novel and unique opera achieved a remarkable measure of success, coming
as it did from a repertory company in between revivals of *The Bartered
Bride* and *Rigoletto*; and none should miss it. Let me add a word of admiration for a management that can give us in one season *Idomeneo*, *The
Girl of the Golden West*, *Mahagonny* and *The Rake's Progress*, *Count Ory*,
*Boulevard Solitude* [New Opera Company] and a new production of *Così
fan tutte*. Even Brecht, who liked to gibe at 'culinary opera', could scarcely
have denied the enterprise and variety of such a menu.[109]

Davis had greatly enjoyed *Mahagonny*. These were indeed exhilarating days both for him and for Sadler's Wells.

Together with the artistic excitement there was a growing sense of
future possibilities. In July 1963 Tucker and Arlen hit on an exciting idea, which Arlen described as 'dynamite': one of the Sadler's
Wells companies should be housed in Manchester, which would
solve the problem of the need for a provincial house as well as the
problem of the two companies. If the LCC built the South Bank
theatre, it could be called the London Opera House.[110] On 12 July
the board formally welcomed the opportunity of being rehoused on
the South Bank and would co-operate in any agreed scheme.[111]

On 15 June the last performance of the Old Vic company had
taken place, and in October the National Theatre officially opened

in its temporary home, the Old Vic, with Peter O'Toole's *Hamlet*. Sean Kenny had designed a new stage with a revolve known as Kenny's Revolt. For the next ten years Olivier set his imprint on the growing company, developing an ensemble of fine young actors.

Weber's *Der Freischütz* at Sadler's Wells on 12 September was the opening production of the 1963/4 London season. Byam Shaw's direction was 'transparently honest in its simplicity and tact, devoid of affectation or mannerism'. The chorus emerged as a real village crowd and the Wolf's Glen had distinct eeriness. *Der Freischütz* marked the 'dawn of vernal romanticism', wrote Peter Heyworth, and Davis conducted with exceptional insight into the music's 'spring-like lyricism and buoyant rhythm'.[112] Cairns wrote of the orchestra's vigour but criticised the quality of tone and phrasing, which he found well below 'the fairly modest best that Sadler's Wells are able to attain with their present subsidy, acoustics, and orchestra pit'. Motley's simple setting caught the horrors of the Wolf's Glen better than the sunlit forest slopes, which were represented by a 'grim parade of sentinel like fir trees'. According to Heyworth, Donald McIntyre was a 'big, black, firm-voiced Caspar', Elizabeth Robson a deliciously fresh Aennchen with a warm and agile soprano, and Remedios a well-sung if unrelaxed Max.

One of the most intensely exciting British premieres of these rich seasons was Janáček's *The Makropoulos Case*, on 12 February 1964, nearly forty years after its first performance in Brno. Translated by Tucker, it was conducted by Charles Mackerras, whom Tucker was bringing back into the Sadler's Wells fold. Both the opera and its production more than fulfilled expectations. The directness and dramatic intensity of Janáček's music, his empathy for his ice-hearted 300-year-old heroine, the dramatic imagination of the design, the precision and characterisation of Blatchley's production and Mackerras's love, insight and enthusiasm for the music added up to great music theatre.

The artists vividly personified Janáček's penetratingly drawn characters. Marie Collier's Emilia Marty was an astonishing achievement – at the same time irresistibly beautiful and arrogant, melancholic and immensely moving in her utter weariness. Gregory Dempsey was the tortured lover, Albert Gregor; Raimund Herincx the power-loving Prus and Eric Shilling the lawyer.[113] Shawe-Taylor called *Makropoulos* a 'stunning achievement in the middle of a season that offers so bold and varied a repertory'.[114]

Mozart fared less well. Basil Coleman's production of *The Seraglio* in April was found to be overambitious, even 'pretentious' by Porter. The 1964/5 season also saw new productions of the more popular repertoire, including on 16 September Glen Byam Shaw's very revised *Faust* in Motley designs, and in November Ava June took the title role in Colin Graham's unsentimental *Madam Butterfly*.

While the artists expanded their horizons, the probable cost of the South Bank project had begun to worry the Treasury. In November 1963 the National Theatre architect Brian O'Rorke had been replaced by the forty-nine-year-old Denys Lasdun, after a selection process that had involved Olivier, Peter Brook and George Devine. When it became apparent that £2 million would be nowhere near sufficient for the project, Lasdun sought to reassure the Treasury that he was very 'familiar with cost control' and that there would be no 'marble, brass or gold knobs'. The National Theatre plans involved a large adaptable auditorium and a small experimental one, and the Treasury noted that the South Bank board should be reminded that only one auditorium should be built in the first instance.[115]

The National Theatre and Opera House (NTOP), the plans for which Lasdun developed between 1963 and 1964, was finally set between County Hall and the Festival Hall, between the Thames and the Shell Tower, which the architect sought to neutralise visually while not obscuring its views of the river. The NTOP was based on Lasdun's concept of an urban landscape of artificial rivers and valleys, its strata theme using a series of interpenetrating social platforms and the two fly towers of the houses creating a valley between the theatres – Theatre Square – for public use. A large stretch of the river bank would also be opened up for public use, and the whole scheme was intended to make the outside public areas part of the excitement and festive spirit of attending the theatres.[116]

As the plan developed, so did the realisation of the likely cost of both building and running the theatres. In October Chandos told Tucker that he was 'softening up the Treasury' by warning them that the £130,000 annual subsidy was not going to be enough to build up and maintain a 'worthy National Theatre' and that £1 million would be insufficient to build it.[117] By December Hart was discussing a likely cost of £10–11 million for the project. The Treasury was not so easily softened. On 15 January 1964 they told Chandos that they were not prepared to see either two National Theatres competing with one another or an amalgamation with Stratford that would result in the necessity for two full-scale auditoria.

A week later Cottesloe told the Treasury Chief Secretary John Boyd-Carpenter that the tentative figures were £3–4 million for each building. The Gelsenkirchen opera house near Essen, in North Rhine-Westphalia, had cost £1.5 million, but building costs were lower in Germany and it was built on 'rather stricter standards of austerity'. He hoped that the LCC would increase their capital contribution. Since 1949 building costs had increased by 74 per cent. The architect, it was agreed, should be told that a second auditorium might be built later.[118]

While the Building Committee of the National Theatre had endless discussions as to whether the theatre should have a proscenium or an open stage, Sadler's Wells was formulating its own requirements. Its theatre should seat 1,600 and have a proscenium forty feet wide, with the overall width behind three times that to accommodate personnel and scenery. The new Hamburg opera house, where all major problems had apparently been satisfactorily solved, was to be the prototype.[119]

The excitement was palpable. After receiving Lasdun's first drawings of the stage layout, Arlen wrote to him on 16 April 1964 to say that he personally would like to see the highest grid that could be got past the LCC or GLC Elevations Committee. He refused, he exclaimed, 'TO DISCUSS A PROSCENIUM ARCH'. The 'John Burys, Ralph Koltais and Peter Brooks of this world' were trying to do away with borders.* On 27 May the Technical Committee

---

* It was an exciting period for theatre design, with Koltai and John Bury introducing different materials, such as scaffolding, real wood and cement into their sets, at a time when sets were still usually composed of traditional painted flats. John Napier was a pupil of Koltai at the Central School of Design and described Koltai, along with Bury and O'Brien, as the fathers of modern British theatre design. 'Pure design', writes Napier 'is about the manipulation of abstract objects in a space in order to give that space an atmosphere or mood that enhances the atmosphere of what is happening in that space' (John Napier, *Ralph Koltai: Designer for the Stage*, London: Nick Hern, 2003, p. 12).

agreed that there 'should be no permanent false proscenium'; designers 'could add one for individual operas'. Tucker informed Lasdun in June that Sadler's Wells reckoned to have a repertoire each year of about thirty works, of which eight ought to be new productions and one or two of them brand-new works.[120]

Amidst all the planning excitement there was a moment of sobriety when at the 20 July meeting the Trust was told that average attendance had dropped by 9 per cent over the last four years and takings had dropped by £29 per performance in 1963/4. Arlen was 'at a loss to know where to place advertising' and had asked the consultancy firm Martech for advice. McKenna stressed that the most important consideration was that the company going into the new opera house should be of a 'suitable standard and size to fulfil their duties'.[121]

In the 1962–4 biennial report McKenna wrote that the new South Bank theatre would be ready in 1970. The task of the existing organisation, he wrote, would be 'to strengthen itself and develop so that the move would not be an upheaval, but merely a continuation'. Wage rates and the increased cost of touring meant that by 16 December 1963 the accumulated deficit had reached £90,000 – as high as it had ever been.[122] 'We thus started the present financial year in a very precarious position,' McKenna wrote, continuing with a charmingly mixed metaphor: 'We travel two roads and work on two floors; the top floor provides the excitement of planning the new theatre, and the basement the struggle for survival.'

At the start of the 1964/5 season, on 21 September, the Trust learnt that both roads were to lose the guidance of their music director. Colin Davis did not wish to continue in the post, although he did want to fulfil his conducting obligations and maintain his connections with the company. He was finding that the amount of outside work he was undertaking made it difficult for him to maintain the standard of his administrative work. On 19 October he agreed to stay on until the end of 1965.[123]

Tucker later wrote that his relations with Davis had become strained, a situation for which he largely blamed himself.[124] Davis remembered: 'I was falling out with Norman Tucker quite severely . . . I irritated him beyond belief and I could not understand why he would not sit down and get on with it.' Byam Shaw was, according to Tucker, 'deeply hurt' as he had found an ideal collaborator in Davis and had hoped to work with him for many years. He told the Trust that he found the loss of Davis to be a 'very serious matter' and believed he could have been pressured into staying.[125] Arlen and Tucker did not feel it appropriate to ask Davis to change his mind when his career was developing fast and he wanted to 'spread his wings'. Later, Davis recalled, 'Arlen tried to persuade me to go back when they moved – you can't go back on things.'[126]

There were about to be changes in the political firmament that would have ramifications for the arts in general and for Sadler's Wells and the National Theatre project in particular. Unemployment and inflation had been rising, and Macmillan's authority and popularity steadily declined after a by-election defeat at Paisley in May 1961. In July 1962, in a major Cabinet reshuffle, he replaced Selwyn Lloyd with Reginald Maudling, who also believed in an expansionary economic policy. But in January 1963 the French vetoed Britain joining the Common Market, and the economic situation deteriorated in the harsh winter of 1962–3, with frequent power cuts and unemployment reaching 4 per cent. Macmillan at sixty-nine was tired and, after a series of sex and spy scandals affected the standing of the government, he resigned in October 1963. Lord Home took over.

On 16 October 1964 Harold Wilson's Labour Party came to power with James Callaghan as chancellor. Jennie Lee was asked to prepare a White Paper defining government policy on the arts and, if the Cabinet supported it, the prime minister was to create a ministry. Lee was made a parliamentary undersecretary on 24 October 1964 – the lowest of the ministerial ranks – with responsibility for the arts, with the explicit brief of expanding government support. Her two secret weapons were to be the personal support of the prime minister and her alliance with Arnold Goodman, whom she planned to appoint as head of the Arts Council, in place of the patrician Lord Cottesloe.

The new Labour government and Jennie Lee's appointment seemed to bode well for the new opera house until the details of the planning and financing began to emerge. The same day as the general election Lasdun and Cottesloe discussed the growing problems with the Treasury as costs mounted. Cottesloe prepared to launch the battle with the Treasury when it was learnt by the South Bank board five days later that the figure for the proposed National Theatre was £10–12 million.[127]

Arlen was getting nervous. On 23 October he told Lasdun that the Treasury was keen to draw a line between the opera and the theatre so that one of them could be deferred. He therefore hoped that Lasdun would 'lock everything together indissolubly'.[128] On 10 November Mary Loughnane at the Treasury confirmed that the figure was now £10 million plus £2 million for car parks. She believed that Hayward's London County Council would probably 'quite cheerfully' vote substantial additional sums, but from 1 April 1965 the LCC would become part of the Greater London Council, which did not feel the same enthusiasm for the scheme and had expressed horror at the proposed expense.*

Although the Treasury told Cottesloe that a cost of £10 million was 'quite unacceptable', they had not yet given up the project entirely. They planned to wait for the Greater London Council to get used to the idea and then agree to meet 50 per cent of the cost if the GLC would provide the other 50 per cent. Despite this surprising if unexpressed support from the Treasury officials, the scheme was unravelling. K. E. Couzens at the Treasury noted on 12 November that the Arts Council had never liked the idea of the National Theatre building, and this was especially true now the Royal Shakespeare Company had set up in London at the Aldwych – a rival theatre of 'about equal quality'. Jennie Lee had been heard to say of Sadler's Wells 'that she wonders whether its transfer to the South Bank is a top priority'.[129]

At Sadler's Wells planning nonetheless continued to run ahead with blind optimism. On 25 November the Sadler's Wells Technical Committee saw a stack-up model of the opera house. They were hugely enjoying planning the country's first purpose-built modern opera house. It would have facilities as yet undreamt of: dressing rooms, offices, canteens, fitting rooms, a paint frame, rehearsal and music ensemble rooms – all of the right size and scope and placed in the ideal position for ease of work. On 27 January 1965, on Arlen's

---

* The Greater London Council, although still Labour-controlled and supportive of the arts, was something of an unknown quantity. From 1 April 1965 it would be responsible for the National Theatre project.

suggestion, Lasdun brought to the Sadler's Wells Technical Committee a design for an experimental area within the opera house.

The new house would also have additional artistic strength. In late 1964 Arlen invited Edmund Tracey, who was a music critic at the *Observer* under Peter Heyworth, to come and help Sadler's Wells. Since the National Theatre was employing Kenneth Tynan as a dramaturge, Arlen believed that Sadler's Wells should have one. Tracey agreed to be the senior officer in the PR department and was responsible for introducing more detailed and academic essays into the programmes. He became a much-loved colleague for many years. With a great sense of humour, Tracey was, in Cairns's words, 'a wise friend, and captivating companion, with a native Irish genius for storytelling, a near-perfect memory, a natural talent for attracting bizarre happenings and strange encounters, a mind full of unpredictable ideas and a rare way with words'.[130] For his part, Tracey described how he had been impressed by 'the direct abruptness' of Arlen's first enquiry, 'the rapidity with which it was followed up, the vigour and charm which finally persuaded me'. They were a formidable team.

Sadler's Wells was attaining new operatic heights just as its hopes of a new home hung in the balance. On 24 February 1965 Richard Rodney Bennett's commission *The Mines of Sulphur*, with libretto by Beverley Cross, was premiered. It was conducted by Davis, and Colin Graham directed a cast that included Catherine Wilson, Gregory Dempsey, Joyce Blackham and Ann Howard, whose Sadler's Wells/ENO career was to span over thirty years and who would become a great favourite amongst audiences. Bennett's ghostly Gothick romance with its strong musical atmosphere, theatrical strengths and technical assurance was a fine achievement. It was superlatively acted and directed, and Sadler's Wells was praised for its confidence and conviction in staging the work. In 1965 the Gulbenkian Foundation announced a grant of £4,500 to 'help encourage young composers and librettists to devote their talents to the composition of operas, which, it is hoped, will eventually be heard at Sadler's Wells'. This led to Malcolm Williamson's *Violins of St Jacques* in 1966, Richard Rodney Bennett's *A Penny for a Song* in 1967 and, in 1974, Gordon Crosse's *The Story of Vasco*.

Mackerras's famous edition of *The Marriage of Figaro* on 9 April 1965 was immediately recognised as an important landmark not just for Sadler's Wells but also for Mozart performance, as had been the Busch/Ebert *Figaro* at Glyndebourne in the 1930s. Mackerras was not only a scholar and conductor but possessed acute dramatic sensibilities. Nor was *Figaro* a mere historical exercise or festival event, but rather 'a mid-season popular piece enjoyed by a large audience'. Porter heard the work as if new because of the conductor's 'sense of tempo and inner balance, and phrase weight'. Mackerras, he wrote, was a 'born Mozartian, as well as a born man of the theatre'.[131] The *Times Literary Supplement* was delighted that at last a Mozart production at Sadler's Wells showed 'all the freshness, brio and intelligence' which made the theatre so enjoyable a venue at the time.[132]

Mackerras had learnt a Germanic Mozart style from James Robertson, who had worked with Fritz Busch at Glyndebourne, but his fascination with autograph scores made him rebel against what he saw as the lack of freedom in interpretation.[133] In the 1950s, as did other musicians at the time, Mackerras pursued his interest in authentic performance practices. He researched at Donaueschingen, in south-west Germany, where he found the individual part books of singers from the 1780s and 1790s, in which there was heavy ornamentation in the arias and lavish cadenzas had been inserted at all the *fermatas*. At the time of his researches, the use of appoggiatura was exceptional and ornamentation not practised at all. In a 1965 article entitled 'What Mozart Really Meant' Mackerras explained that vocal appoggiaturas had rarely taken written form, being understood and supplied by the singer. Modern conductors, anxious to do away with the vocal excesses of nineteenth-century singers, had 'thrown the baby out with the bathwater', and had in consequence lost the 'essential melodic style of all vocal music of the eighteenth and nineteenth century, particularly in the recitatives'.

Mackerras explained his findings and the problems encountered in Mozart's many revisions. One such problem was that of the extra arias that Mozart had provided for his different Susannas – Nancy Storace, his first Susanna, a fine singer-actor for whom he wrote 'Venite inginocchiatevi' and 'Deh vieni non tardar', and Adriana Ferrarese, for whom he wrote 'Un moto di gioia' and 'Al desio'. Mackerras believed that Mozart's original music for the Countess, who had the higher line in ensembles, was typical of his aristocratic heroines with its 'soaring, grandiose, but slightly hysterical passages' and it made more dramatic sense. He gave the example of the trio in Act II, where it was clear to him from reading the autograph score that Mozart intended the coloratura passages for the Countess to be sung *fortissimo*, proudly and defiantly by the Countess, and not in an 'arch and pretty' manner by Susanna, in order to make sense of both the music and the dramatic situation. Mackerras discussed other puzzles in his article and concluded, 'The musician can only use his good taste and feeling for history,' both of which he had in abundance.[134]

Tucker, who agreed to present Mackerras's version of *Figaro* with his appoggiaturas and embellishment findings, grew in enthusiasm as he heard each new cadenza or variant that Mackerras had found in Vienna, Florence, Prague, Paris, Hamburg, Berlin or Donaueschingen. Mackerras remembered the whole cast, including Elizabeth Harwood, Donald McIntyre and Raimund Herincx, being 'very interested in what I had to say about the recits and appoggiaturas. The orchestra were less interested but that came with time.'[135]

The critical reception was on the whole wildly enthusiastic. Shawe-Taylor found the blend of voices in the runs introduced by Mackerras in the final stages of the letter duet, and the 'little garlands' of thirds and sixths, 'ravishing and perfectly in place'.[136] The *TLS* was also delighted by the ensemble performance and by Blatchley's production, in which each situation and character was rethought afresh, with exemplary articulation in Dent's translation. Ava June's Countess in particular emerged as the 'high-spirited, sentimental, impulsive' Rosina rather than either the familiar Edwardian grande dame impersonation or a drooping lily. Both music and direction threw off the 'dead Viennese chrysalis and restored *Figaro* to its pristine comic freshness'. Although there was criticism of Blatchley for understating the social protest and revolutionary implications of the work, the *TLS* welcomed the chance for Mozart's 'profoundly humane yet irresistibly comic' voice to shine through.[137] Cairns wrote that Mackerras's 'natural sympathy for Mozart and Mozartian comedy, the loving way he gives its full value to every phrase, the slightly rough musical surface that distinguishes real from camp Mozart, the preference of warmth to elegance', made this *Figaro* not only revolutionary but also unforget-table.[138]

During the 1964/5 and 1965/6 seasons Mackerras was a frequent guest at Sadler's Wells. On 22 April 1965 he conducted *Peter Grimes* with Dowd, whose interpretation he greatly admired. On 28 October a production of Janáček's *From the House of the Dead*, the first in the UK, was also striking in its intensity. Porter wrote that the performance was not just great music but also great thea-tre. Rigorous rehearsal and the sense of security that Mackerras gave the singers enabled them, under Graham's direction, to act and react to each other with minimal focus on the conductor and to give life to each individual character: David Bowman's Shiškov, Gregory Dempsey's Skuratov and Ronald Dowd's Luka. Koltai designed a realistic décor based on photographs of Siberian prisons. An act drop of a huge wall on which the prisoners had scrawled their names was raised to reveal a prison courtyard in which all the chained prisoners sang and played out their stories. Mackerras brought out the depth of the humanity in Janáček's score: 'the light shining even in deepest darkness, the "spark of God in every crea-ture"'.[139]

Monteverdi's *Orfeo* on 21 September was the only opera not sung in English apart from *Oedipus*, which had been sung in the original Latin. An exception had been made for *Orfeo* because of special pleading for Italian from Raymond Leppard, who con-ducted.[140] The resulting poor Italian helped to keep the use of English sacrosanct thereafter. The slight detour of the Italian-language *Orfeo* did not distract Sadler's Wells from its illuminating and innovative path. *The Thieving Magpie* in January 1966, accom-panied by Tom Hammond's educational article in *Opera*, was given its first Sadler's Wells performance and conducted with accom-plished Rossinian style by Mario Bernardi.

In May and June 1965 Mackerras had accompanied Sadler's Wells on a European tour to Amsterdam, Paris, Lausanne, Geneva, Prague, Zagreb, Bratislava, Vienna and Hamburg, with *The Mines of Sulphur, Iolanthe, Peter Grimes, Makropoulos* and *The Rake's Progress*. The British Council later acknowledged the role of Sadler's Wells in presenting British opera to Europe: 'It is we think only now that foreign audiences are beginning to appreciate the spe-cial qualities of British contemporary opera. Much of this is a direct result of extensive touring in the last four or five years by Sadler's Wells and the English Opera Group.'[141]

The great progress of the company seemed to be threatened when at the end of 1965 Colin Davis resigned from Sadler's Wells, leaving Byam Shaw feeling badly let down.[142] At the same time Mackerras was going to Hamburg as first conductor for three years from the 1966 season. At least Mario Bernardi, when approached to be music director, seemed interested.

Hopes for the new opera house were also beginning to recede. The discussions inside the South Bank board were becoming a combination of visionary dreaming and increasing insecurity. On 24 February 1965 Lord Chandos told Lasdun that he could see London becoming the 'cultural Athens of Europe', but at the same time he warned that Jennie Lee could not be relied upon to be sympathetic as she was 'too provincial'. He agreed with Lasdun that Aneurin Bevan would have been far better for their purpose.[143]

Jennie Lee's White Paper was published in February 1965 and, as suspected, recommended greater support for regional activity, especially in housing the arts. It also omitted the opera house from the South Bank scheme. Preparing the White Paper had been a major task – the election manifesto had done little more than suggest that the growth of technology would generate more leisure time that should be filled with suitable pursuits. The arts, supported by the Arts Council, were viewed very much as the 'posh' end of the cultural spectrum. The White Paper was non-prescriptive, stressing that state patronage should in no sense define public taste, while recognising that if artistic achievement were to be maintained and the best made more widely available, more generous and discriminating help would be needed. In order to encourage a wider public it was necessary to create a new social as well as economic climate so that the cheerless, unwelcoming environments of arts institutions no longer alienated all but the specialist and devotee. The White Paper stated:

Too many working people have been conditioned by their education and environment to consider the best in music, painting, sculpture and literature outside their reach. A young generation, however, feeling more self-confident than their elders and beginning to be given some feeling for drama, music and the visual arts in their school years are more hopeful material.

The younger generation, the White Paper argued, wanted 'gaiety and colour, informality and experimentation'. Greater emphasis would be laid on regional policy. In local government only Birmingham, Manchester and the LCC had hitherto shown an enlightened arts policy, and more local councils needed encouragement, money, buildings and advice through regional arts associations. It was also decided that since expenditure was set to increase substantially, the Department of Education and Science should take over from the Treasury all government support for the arts – from museums to the Arts Council.[144]

Lasdun noted the response of 'general gloom' in his office to the White Paper on 23 March. The opera house was an intrinsic part of his design. The next day he noted that he would regard the 'omission of opera as a change of brief with all that that implied . . . no opera, no theatre by DL&P [Denys Lasdun and Partners]'.[145] Until they were officially informed of the removal of Sadler's Wells from the scheme, however, Lasdun would continue to work.

Arlen also battled on, even though it was made clear to Bill Fiske, Cottesloe, Chandos and McKenna on 20 July that the government would share the costs of the theatre with the Greater London Council but not those of the opera house.[146] Arlen wrote on 24 September to N. J. Abercrombie, who had become the secretary general of the Arts Council in 1963, to point out that Sadler's Wells had not been given the opportunity to reduce any parts of the plans, and that Lasdun had not been given a new brief. Arlen believed that there were political reasons for the impasse – because of what had been mistakenly called the 'second Covent Garden'. Without the new theatre the whole scheme for English opera would collapse. He tinkered with the costs, trying to reduce his ideal plans to something more realistic, but Arlen told the Trust on 18 October that Lasdun did not think there could be substantial economies unless intrinsic elements were removed from the plans. At the same meeting Tucker warned that it was not clear whether the government would even contribute to a cheaper scheme.[147]

The support that Sadler's Wells had enjoyed at the Treasury was not going to be replicated at the Department of Education and Science. On 15 October the DES noted: 'I very much hope that it will be possible to dissuade Sadler's Wells from moving from Islington, where they bring so much light into an otherwise dim part of London!'[148]

Meanwhile, the Opera House plans were reduced from £4.85 to £4.4 million, and the whole project to £12.65 million (a reduction of £1.85 million). At a meeting of the South Bank Theatre and Opera House board on 20 October Bill Fiske, Labour leader of the newly created GLC, said it was too much for the Council to shoulder half of the National Theatre and all of the opera house, but it was decided to tackle the government again.

In 1965 Lee appointed Arnold Goodman chairman of the Arts Council, replacing Lord Cottesloe, 'the arch Tory', who had not taken her appointment seriously.[149]* In July that year Goodman became a life peer. Lee's and Goodman's partnership was staunch and energetic in the service of the arts in general, but was to have long-term repercussions for Sadler's Wells. On 22 October Sadler's Wells was able for the first time to explain directly to the minister its role in London and the provinces. The minister, however, reiterated the July decision, even though Tucker warned that there was a danger of 'deterioration in standards' if they did not move. It was at this meeting that Lord Goodman suggested that Sadler's Wells should move to a West End theatre, if 'there was a time lag' before the theatre was built. McKenna agreed to consider the idea. Arnold Goodman and Lee said Sadler's Wells should remain a theatre and the proceeds from its sale should not be counted in the financing of Sadler's Wells projects. It was 'one of the few suburban theatres in London', Lee argued.[150]

An angry Lasdun demanded on 1 December that if there were no decision by the end of the month he would abandon all work on the project.[151] At 10.30 a.m. on 15 December Lasdun noted a conversation with Lord Cottesloe: 'HMG wish to persuade drop Sadler's Wells. Ministers and officials in agreement pending final decision therefore CONTINUE.' On 23 December the South Bank board told Lasdun to carry on working, on the basis that he would be paid for the work he had done if the scheme were dropped.

---

* In 1963 Kenneth Robinson and others in the Parliamentary Labour Party's Arts and Amenities group had persuaded Harold Wilson 'how big an impact could be made in an important field by an injection of resources which would be trivial in terms of total expenditure'. Robinson partially ascribed Lee's appointment, and that of Arnold Goodman to the chair of the Arts Council in May 1965, to that encounter (Robinson to Harold Lever, 8.10.75, ENO Ad 5 Box 7).

News of the fading government support for the new opera house reached the *Sunday Times* on 17 January 1966. Arlen responded in the *Observer* by saying that it was time to state the case clearly, focusing on the importance of having a London centre to help support the artistic policy of places such as Manchester, where it had recently been announced that an eighteen-acre site had been set aside by the city for an arts centre with an opera house.[152]

Unknown to Arlen, on 18 January 1966 a meeting between Lasdun and Lord Cottesloe confirmed that the Treasury endorsed Jennie Lee's statement that they were not committed in any way, nor ever had been, to the opera house. They were particularly fearful of the possibility of the need for increased subsidies. Lasdun noted that a decision to abandon the opera house would 'leave a gap to be filled' and a decision to be taken as to what should be put in its place.[153]

Bill Fiske of the GLC still thought he could get the whole site plus the opera house if the cost did not exceed £10 million, at which point Arlen agreed to cut out the paint frame.[154] There ensued strenuous bargaining about the price and content of the development, with Arlen arguing that the cheapest model would be Sadler's Wells on the South Bank combined with a Manchester company. His papers included a careful study of the needs of Manchester and the provinces, with ambitious plans for the Manchester opera house, which would be smaller than Gelsenkirchen's but have better stage facilities than the Royal Opera House.[155]*

At a meeting with the Department of Education and Science and the Treasury on 28 January, Arnold Goodman, the new chairman of the Arts Council, was expressing his personal view that the opera house was not necessary, although officially this was a matter for the South Bank board. He suggested that if the Arts Council wanted to discuss the basic question as to whether 'it wished Sadler's Wells to be retained or disappear', they could do so at their next meeting.[156]

Three days later Arlen and McKenna fought for their scheme at the GLC, trying to convince them that they would not need a greater subsidy than Covent Garden, as was being suggested. There were some

---

* At the time the combined London grant of Sadler's Wells from the GLC and the Arts Council was £243,000. If the GLC decided to 'go it alone', with the Arts Council maintaining its current levels, it would have cost them a further £81,000.

penetrating questions from W. L. Abernethy, the GLC controller, and the lawyer Victor Mishcon, Labour councillor for Lambeth, suggesting that Arlen's figures for expenditure were 'grossly underestimated, and their potential audiences overestimated'. Arlen argued that the excitement of the new house would keep audiences up to 80 per cent. Fiske pointed out that the whole GLC budget for the arts was £650,000 a year, of which £500,000 would be taken up by opera. Arlen and McKenna were very distressed and incredulous when Fiske said that he had heard from the Arts Council and government sources that Sadler's Wells would lose their subsidy altogether if they moved. This would place too great a burden on the GLC, which would make its decision during the next few weeks.[157]

On 16 February Lasdun asked Fiske straight out whether the GLC could face the burden of £9.5 to £10 million to bring this imaginative scheme into being now that the government had definitely pulled out of the opera-house scheme and would not make any contribution to additional running costs if Sadler's Wells moved. Should the site be changed, he warned, the whole plan would have to be rethought. The National Theatre would cost £7,353,023, the opera house £5,412,477, the car park £818,502, the furnishings £570,000. The whole cost, plus fees, was £13,781,000.[158] Any re-examination of the plans to include reductions in the opera-house scheme would, Fiske said, mean an unacceptable delay for the National Theatre. Lasdun said he could start working on the theatre, provided that the 'wind of probability' was favourable to the opera house, which could be delayed to 1971/2. Fiske's response was that the 'wind of probability' was 'not blowing favourably'.[159]

On 25 February Lasdun was told to go ahead with the theatre but the opera house was to be deferred. Three days later a press statement was prepared to announce that the Arts Council had set up a committee to look into the needs of regional opera and that no decision could therefore be made about the South Bank opera house. The National Theatre was to go ahead, the costs jointly shared between the GLC and the government.[160]

On 28 March Lasdun was formally authorised by Cottesloe and the South Bank board to continue to the design stage of the National Theatre, without waiting for a decision on the opera house.[161] On 9 August an angry Lasdun was on the verge of resigning and issuing a statement to the press. He noted:

The Department of Education and Science, which came into the picture around 1965 under the Ministry of Miss Jennie Lee, has to date been responsible for non-productive work: for going back on the decision on Opera; for tampering with the current brief on the nature of Theatre and its capacity for frustrating the architects both in their work and in their agreements . . . it is Miss Lee's department that is wasting public money, and that she is responsible for the interference of politics in architectural matters, which will be shown to be prejudicial to standards in excellence for the NT.[162]

It was to be another three years before work began on the National Theatre and nine years until the South Bank theatre opened on its fourth and final site east of Waterloo Bridge. By 1974 Peter Hall had taken over from Olivier to bring the National Theatre into the promised land. A new opera house for Sadler's Wells was not to be part of the great scheme.

Tucker placed the blame for the loss of his opera house squarely on Covent Garden, later writing that the whole South Bank scheme was 'anathema to David Webster, his chairman Lord Drogheda and other members of his board'. He wrote of 'skulduggery with notes dropped into Ministers' pockets and the like'. The Arts Council had always been ambivalent about the scheme as it entailed competition with Covent Garden, 'which they had been nurturing over the years' and supplying with 'liberal slices of the Government money available for the arts'.[163]

In truth, it was not only Covent Garden's hostility that had put paid to the Sadler's Wells dream of a modern purpose-built home of its own, in what was to be the heart of the performing arts in London, reunited with the drama as in the early Old Vic days; a place where its future would have been secure and where its development could have been planned in a rational way in relation to the 'senior' house. The original inspiration for including Sadler's Wells in the South Bank plans had been the hope of reducing the growing demands being made on the Treasury, but with the emergence of a more ambitious and exciting scheme, the government and Arts Council had been faced by something much more challenging in terms of short-term funding and more threatening in terms of long-term commitment. Ironically, shortly before Lee, who was more committed to the provinces and Covent Garden than to Sadler's

Wells, removed the arts to the DES, some Treasury officials had begun to see the potential of such an ambitious scheme to be undertaken jointly with the London County Council.

For Tucker, the collapse of his long-term hopes had a deleterious effect on his health and on his increasingly serious drink problem. He took the failure very much to heart and was, he wrote, 'depressed, discouraged' and unwell.[164] On 8 March 1966 his contract was terminated 'abruptly' and he was deeply hurt to find his office cleared when he came back from an enforced holiday. It was announced that Arlen would be the managing director and Bryan Balkwill and Mario Bernardi the music directors.

Barger had warned Tucker and Arlen: 'You are, I must tell you making a great miscalculation in the middle of your lives.' His warning had proved sadly true for Tucker, whose achievements were nonetheless formidable. Apart from bringing Sadler's Wells back from the brink of extinction on more than one occasion, he had prepared the company for a consolidated and powerful artistic future. There was an ensemble of fine singers and a body of directors who had established the concept of opera as drama once and for all at Sadler's Wells, however frustratingly limited the resources. He had placed unfamiliar work, especially Janáček, before the public with devoted consistency. Amongst his translations were those for *Simon Boccanegra, Luisa Miller, Don Carlos, Katya Kabanova* and *The Cunning Little Vixen*; his translation of *Makropoulos* was still being used in 2006 in a new production for Mackerras's eightieth birthday. In preparing the company for their new opera house he had ensured that it was ready to reach great heights in the next decade. In 1993 Edmund Tracey was able to hold Tucker up as an example of a true revolutionary in all that he had achieved.

# 7

# 1966–1972: 'Arlorium'

On 8 March 1966 Stephen Arlen became the managing director of Sadler's Wells at the age of fifty-three. He combined administrative talent and tough negotiating skills with imagination and vision, and although he was not a musician, he had, according to Edmund Tracey, a flair for recognising what was good or bad in a musical performance as well as a shrewd understanding of what worked on the stage. Lord Goodman greatly admired his energy and determination, describing how he planned and bullied, 'cajoled and wheedled, with a total lack of concern for his own welfare or health'. Ideas shot out of him 'like bullets from a machine gun', Tracey later wrote.[1]

At the time of Arlen's appointment Tracey was appointed director of drama and text. He was central to Arlen's team, responsible for repertory planning, for what happened on the stage and for the 'words the singers actually sing'.[2] Mackerras recalled that Tracey was not only extremely erudite but was also a very calming influence upon his colleagues. Amongst his many and varied contributions to Sadler's Wells/ENO over the next thirty years were the many new translations he prepared, including *The Tales of Hoffmann, La traviata, Manon, Aida, The Sicilian Vespers* and Gounod's *Faust* in 1985 – in the original version with dialogue. He also provided new dialogue for *Fidelio, La Belle Hélène* and *Seraglio*.

The leadership was completed on 21 March, when Bryan Balkwill and the thirty-five-year-old Canadian conductor Mario Bernardi jointly accepted the music directorship to oversee the two companies W and S, which would continue to perform in equal strength at Sadler's Wells and on tour.

Arlen quickly recovered his strength after the bitter disappointment of the loss of the new opera house. On 18 April he told the directors that he did not accept that the Arts Council's demand for a balanced budget for 1966/7 should entail a reduction in either activity or standards, and he stressed that the Trust had not approved such a course. The repertoires of both companies needed building up during the next season.[3]

The compulsion to press for ever greater artistic achievement at Sadler's Wells was not entirely without support in the artistic establishment. Arnold Goodman was both a friend and an ally, and within the Arts Council executive John Cruft, the Arts Council music director and ENO assessor from 1967 to 1980, was also a staunch advocate. He was a true professional with an impeccable musical pedigree, a staunch believer in and judge of excellence and always on the side of the creators. Described as 'modest to a fault, wise and witty', Cruft was the facilitator of much of the expansion of operatic life in the UK over the next two decades. On 10 May he helped Arlen explain his deficit to the Arts Council by arguing that the budget had been worked out before the imposition of selective employment tax.

Another crucial ally for Sadler's Wells continued to be the Greater London Council, whose representative, W. L. Abernethy, informed Arlen that the GLC grant would be raised by £25,000. It was hoped that this sum, plus the Arts Council's contribution to reduce the deficit, would make the organisation's finances more secure.[4]

The question of the South Bank theatre was part of a wider debate about whether opera might ever become a more deeply rooted and popular art form in the UK. From the 1960s, when the concept of arts funding had finally sunk into the consciousness of both government and arts administrators, to the 1980s, when the level of funding was brought into question, there were valiant efforts by opera practitioners to make opera as popular as it was in many other parts of Europe. It was to prove an uphill and ultimately not entirely successful struggle, despite some periods of expansion during which there was an enthusiastic response from the public, the Arts Council and the political establishment.

In the summer of 1966 the Arts Council set up the Opera and Ballet Enquiry to look into the future of opera in the provinces and advise on the balance between touring and regional opera. Unlike later enquiries, such as those of Dennis Stevenson in 1994 or Richard Eyre in 1997, whose remit was to question the level of provision, the purpose of the 1966 enquiry was to report on how best to *increase* provision and further develop audiences for the lyric theatre.

On 25 July Arlen attended a session of the Arts Council Enquiry chaired by George Harewood, who was the chairman of the Arts Council's music advisory panel from 1966 to 1972. Harewood pointed out that the government favoured the development of opera in the provinces, reporting Jennie Lee as saying that 'a pay pause did not imply a planning pause and that to restrict opera planning was "political illiteracy"'. It was made clear, however, that this statement referred only to the provinces and not to the South Bank scheme. Arlen was now opposed to the building of a new opera house in Manchester, which had, as far as he was concerned, depended on the South Bank opera house going ahead. The amount needed to build in Manchester, he argued, was enough to buy four or five theatres at present owned by the management company Howard and Wyndham that would serve the country as a whole.

Arlen and Harewood were nonetheless agreed that the future pattern of opera provision would have to be based less on touring and more on the provision of local theatres. Touring opera, Arlen argued, 'did not truly educate; a week in each town satisfying the addict rather than improving the level of appreciation'. He added that in other countries opera companies did not tour. Harewood pointed out that although touring opera outside London had hitherto been integral to British opera, a different pattern was emerging with the development of state patronage. It was the role of the enquiry to see what already existed and how it could be improved.[5]

With or without the South Bank opera house, Arlen was determined to rehouse Sadler's Wells as soon as possible. He was worried that the disappointment over the South Bank, the planning of which had aroused great enthusiasm, would lower the morale of the company. He was looking at various West End theatres, the most promising of which was the London Coliseum, not only in view of its known staging and acoustic qualities, but because its lease was held by Prince Littler of the Stoll Moss Empires chain, who was a friend of Arlen. On 6 September Arlen wrote to Goodman for help, keen to strike while the 'iron was hot'. He also turned to the Greater London Council architect Hubert Bennett, to whom he appealed as a potentially key figure. He hoped that if Bennett were involved in the conversion of the Coliseum, 'the money would be that bit easier to come by', since, he explained, Bennett would not like it 'to come off at half cock'.[6]

Arlen was now opposed to the Manchester scheme because he was afraid that Sadler's Wells might be abandoned completely and because he still had a glimmer of hope for the South Bank theatre.[7] On 26 October he explained to Harewood that he was in despair to think that no support might be given for the company to move anywhere. It was impossible to maintain standards in Sadler's Wells, where the conditions of work were 'nothing short of disgusting'. He felt 'bitter in the extreme' that the Manchester project might move forward without at the same time assurances being given to Sadler's Wells, which as a historic institution was not a 'dream but a living entity'.[8] Two days later Arlen wrote to Denys Lasdun complaining that Sadler's Wells theatre was 'an ant-heap, insanitary and unsafe'. It was, he added, 'intolerable – for me, I despair'.[9]

When Harewood replied to Arlen on 15 November, he expressed his own surprise that the Sadler's Wells opera house had hardly been mentioned at the meeting, but felt that the new suggestion of moving to the Coliseum, which had come as a surprise to most of those at the meeting, was an attractive one. He thought Lord Goodman did too, since it seemed to provide a compromise solution that would not require government sanction, as it involved spending on a lesser scale. Harewood offered to put the South Bank scheme on the agenda of an early meeting, so that its non-discussion would not 'become a sort of time-bomb lurking beneath all our considerations'.[10]

Arlen explained to Harewood that Sadler's Wells had kept the new opera house off the agenda 'because it was obvious that the whole scheme had become anathema to everybody, and we feared that to flog it would land us with absolutely nothing in the end, not even a consolation prize'. The Coliseum was a good solution because it would be quick, and, if the South Bank scheme went ahead later, it could be a halfway house. A speedy decision was needed.

The Greater London Council remained supportive of Sadler's Wells. On 21 November Hubert Bennett agreed that the Coliseum was well suited to the company's needs, but that it should still be made clear to the South Bank board that a South Bank opera house was the ultimate aim.[11] On 6 December Harewood informed Arlen that the Coliseum had appealed strongly both to himself and, even more importantly, to Goodman. Six days later Arlen made one last appeal for the South Bank opera house to Harewood. Sadler's Wells was, he wrote, the 'national opera' and the Coliseum was a 'sensible stepping stone'. But he added: 'Or am I mad?'[12] Harewood sought to dissuade him. His idea of a national opera would 'create opposition', particularly from Covent Garden.[13]

Operetta had ended the 1965/6 season, when Byam Shaw's new production of *Die Fledermaus* on 29 March replaced Wendy Toye's much-loved staging that had played at the Coliseum in 1959. Arthur Jacobs still enjoyed Christopher Hassall's witty translation, now accompanied by well-paced spoken dialogue prepared by Tracey. He also enjoyed Eric Shilling repeating his prison governor and Emile Belcourt's dashing Eisenstein.[14] In May 1966 a new production of Offenbach's *Bluebeard* was produced by dancer Gillian Lynne, with some extravagant and amusing choreography. Joyce Blackham was a triumphant 'nymphomaniac hoyden Boulotte'.[15]*

*The Queen of Spades*, produced by Anthony Besch, designed by Leslie Hurry and conducted by Alexander Gibson, opened the 1966/7 season on 14 September. *The Times* thought the performances of Ava June as Lisa and William McAlpine as Hermann lacked passion and that nothing in the production matched the richness and colour of the score. This was especially true of Hurry's drab utility scenery for the first scene, which consisted of two

---

* For Arlen operetta was central to the repertoire of Sadler's Wells, and he was consequently concerned at the lack of choice, explaining to Guthrie on 8 February 1967 that he felt that they had done the best of Offenbach, that the 'slush-lush Lehars' appealed to neither them nor the public and that they felt 'sad' at the thought of doing *The Merry Widow* again. They had considered *Candide*, *Kiss Me, Kate!* and Gilbert and Sullivan but, he told Guthrie, the idea of a pantomime of *Dick Whittington* appealed to him most. It would be composed by Malcolm Williamson and written by Tracey and have 'gorgeous music, lots of tunes, and yet be appropriate to the opera house'. Even the board favoured the idea, to his astonishment. On 10 February 1967 Arlen wrote to Leonard Bernstein asking him to write an operetta: 'We feel ourselves at the end of the line,' he wrote (ENO Ad 65 Box 55).

grotesque statues and a dull green backcloth and did little to convey
St Petersburg in spring.[16]

Malcolm Williamson's *The Violins of St Jacques* was the last of
four Gulbenkian Foundation commissions. It was conducted by
Vilem Tausky, its dedicatee, on 29 November and was directed by
William Chappell and beautifully designed by Peter Rice.
Williamson's music was melodious and singable, and Porter found
both production and opera highly enjoyable, with the company
shown at strength.[17]

It was clear to Arlen that the artistic team needed strengthening.
On 9 August Tracey had written to Arlen that they must get Charles
Mackerras back into the house, especially because it would be good
for the continuance of Sadler's Wells' good reputation for presenting Mozart.[18] At the time Mackerras was commuting between
Hamburg and Covent Garden, hoping to take over from Solti when
he retired from Covent Garden in 1971. In August Arlen had also
turned his attention to the question of improving the standard of
staff producers by having more 'resident producers of the calibre of
Mr Byam Shaw and Mr Blatchley'. He was hoping that Colin
Graham would join the following year, as there could be no new
expenditure this year.[19] After its inauspicious first airing at Covent
Garden in 1953, Graham did a fine job of redeeming *Gloriana* at
Sadler's Wells on 21 October, with a magnificent performance by
Sylvia Fisher and the young tenor John Wakefield. In December
1966 Graham joined the staff.

Early in 1967 a decision on the Coliseum became urgent because
the current lessees, Cinerama, were about to take up an option for
a further three years' lease. On 20 February Arlen received a letter
from Prince Littler saying that the Coliseum could be available for
seven years.[20]

Unknown to Arlen, on 16 February Lord Cottesloe had given
Lasdun final confirmation that there was to be 'no opera'. It was to
be the Waterloo site without the opera house, Lasdun noted, and it
was 'superior to former site'.[21] A month later the decision was made
public when, on 14 March, Victor Mishcon announced at a meeting
of the GLC, where he was chair of the General Purposes
Committee, that because of the higher priority given by the government to building outside London, there would be no opera house.

Mishcon sought to reassure Sadler's Wells by telling them that it was recognised that they were meeting a vital need in London's artistic life by providing opera in English for the people at popular prices.[22] The Trust immediately agreed that Sadler's Wells should press for rehousing as soon as possible.[23]

In the 1964–6 report Stephen Arlen wrote of the loss of the South Bank opera house:

Over the last four or five years everyone at Sadler's Wells employed in the technical branches has spent a disproportionate amount of their time planning the opera house that is no longer to be. It is all on paper and could be said, even now, to be as far if not further advanced than the National Theatre plans . . . One wonders how much of this time could have been utilised in normal work to the immediate benefit of the people who watch the works of Sadler's Wells in the provinces.

The reorganised Greater London Council, faced with an election on narrow margins, had ducked the responsibility of spending £7 million on 'an artistic venture of minority interest'. The government had given way to the pressures of the provinces and Scotland, where Scottish nationalism was growing. 'It is interesting to note', Arlen added, 'that the very pressures that have built up regarding the operatic development outside London have probably been due in some measure to the fact that for the last five years Sadler's Wells has been sweating out its lifeblood to provide the viper with its venom.'

Arlen was not one to stay downhearted for long, and immediately sought to address weaknesses in Sadler's Wells' planning in his memorandum 'After One Year' on 23 March 1967. The casting of new productions should assume number-one priority, he wrote, and be arranged at least eighteen months ahead, with conductor, director and designer also chosen well in advance. He pointed out weaknesses in the various departments, especially the general manager's office, where the call sheets were 'in disrepute', and the touring and press department. He was 'browned off' and bewailed the growth of paperwork, and felt the two previous years had taken their toll on him.[24] He was not, however, defeated and his next move was to plan a major new production that would be of great value both for the 'prestige and morale of the company'. On 16 January the Opera

Subcommittee agreed that Reginald Goodall should conduct a carefully prepared new *Mastersingers*.[25]

Tracey later recalled the origins of the great project.* Arlen was getting tired of having the two S and W companies – each with its chorus of forty-eight and orchestra of fifty-six – and wanted to conflate them. Tracey therefore hit on the idea of doing *The Mastersingers*, for which both companies would be needed. Mackerras later pointed out that a chorus of over ninety in Sadler's Wells was huge.[26] *The Mastersingers* was to prove instrumental both in improving morale and in consolidating the forces of Sadler's Wells into the great company it became at the Coliseum for the next twenty years.

According to Tracey, Arlen was exercised about who should conduct *The Mastersingers*, as neither Balkwill nor Bernardi was a Wagner specialist. Tracey suggested that the right person was Goodall. Arlen 'immediately took the idea up, not least because his wife Iris Kells idolised him'. Lord Donaldson, who was on both the Covent Garden and Sadler's Wells Boards at the time, and David McKenna were both keen on the idea.† When Goodall accepted the invitation in February, Covent Garden agreed to release him. Tracey described how Goodall had become fascinated by Arlen's approach to him. 'I'll need a lot of time, dear,' he said, and asked who would be singing. It emerged that Norman Bailey's participation in the great project was important for Goodall, since he was the only person who knew the part and had sung major Wagner roles on stage in Germany, whereas everyone else had to be taught from scratch.

Negotiations with Bailey to join Sadler's Wells had begun in December 1966. In May 1967 Tracey, who had decided to recruit him after a tour of German opera houses, reported him well pleased with the potential roles being offered him, including Sachs in *The Mastersingers*.[27] Arlen and Tracey insisted that Alberto Remedios

* Tracey, together with critics Andrew Porter, David Cairns, Peter Heyworth and John Warrack, had formed a kind of club to support Goodall after hearing him conduct Wagner in the 1950s.
† John (Jack) George Stuart Donaldson (created a life peer in 1967) was on the Covent Garden Board from February 1958 to March 1974 and on the Sadler's Wells/ENO Board from 1960 to 1974. It was felt at the time that rather than creating a conflict of interest, by sitting on both boards he would be able to help iron out potential difficulties between the houses.

sing Walter – the 'total innocent'. Tracey recalled that 'the first time Alberto sang the prize song with the chorus, it was so beautiful, so moving' that those who heard him 'were crying'.[28]

Byam Shaw, according to Tracey, immediately fell under Reggie Goodall's spell, to which some, including Bailey, were immune. Blatchley was originally to have prepared just the staging of the chorus, but in the end the work was divided. Every aspect of the production was carefully considered. Tracey, determined to ensure a set designed with a 'strong masculine style' and costumes with a 'very accurate sense of historical period and colour', approached John Bury and then Tanya Moiseivitch with the design commission.[29] After both declined, the task fell to Motley and David Walker.

As plans for *The Mastersingers* progressed, it was learnt that Cinerama was willing to relinquish its option on the lease of the Coliseum. The GLC was not 'unfavourably disposed' and Goodman was supportive, telling Arlen on 21 June to 'let me know in good time when you are going to need more money'.[30] There were rumours in the *Sunday Times* on 21 August that Sadler's Wells was to close and the company move to Manchester. Arlen, perturbed that there was no reference at all to London in the draft of the Arts Council opera report, turned to Harewood stressing that he had the Coliseum at 'the tip' of his fingers. Goodman, in the chair of the Arts Council Enquiry, agreed that the removal of Sadler's Wells to a larger theatre should be noted in the report. 'There was discussion on the proximity of the Coliseum to Covent Garden but it was agreed that in the West End of London no difficulties would be caused to either company.'[31]

Work at Sadler's Wells was in a slight trough. The 1967/8 season had opened with a dull *Magic Flute* on 9 August 1967, directed by Frank Hauser and conducted by Bryan Balkwill. On 4 October Gluck's *Orpheus and Eurydice* in the Paris version, directed by Byam Shaw and designed by Jocelyn Herbert, fared little better.

On 31 October Sadler's Wells gave the world premiere of Richard Rodney Bennett's *Penny for a Song*, based on John Whiting's play. Alan Blyth noticed how Colin Graham was gradually bringing out the best in the Sadler's Wells team, with characters lesser and minor moving naturally and reacting to each other throughout. Alix Stone designed a warm and peaceful Dorset country house, and Blyth thought that Bennett and Graham obviously felt immense sympathy with the play's blend of 'lighthearted comedy and elegiac sentiment'. It was not, however, a winning combination for the public and the opera was a flop, with an audience of 22.5 per cent capacity.

In November 1967 the editor of *Opera*, Harold Rosenthal, complained of lowered standards since Arlen and the two music directors had taken over Sadler's Wells, suggesting that the two-company plan was resulting in a dilution of vocal talent. He urged that Sadler's Wells be rehoused as soon as possible.[32] The problem of musical standards was all too apparent to management. On 19 August Arlen had informed Tracey that the music directors would in future have greater responsibility for programming and casting: 'We are an opera house and we live or die by our music,' he wrote. Revivals would be decided in concert with the dramaturge, Tracey.[33] The need to replace the two-company system was also glaringly apparent and he proposed that after the move, one of the two companies should be of the right size and standard to move into the new theatre and the other geared to touring.[34]

Arlen wanted to form an inner group of singers who would be given longer contracts, more pay and tuition, both vocal and dramatic.[35] Colin Graham welcomed Arlen's suggestion as 'splendid, vital, and vitalising'. At the same time he expressed the view that the press was hostile because it was forgetting that the Sadler's Wells was an ensemble company and 'not a canary cage'. He nonetheless agreed that new singers must be found, because the existing ones were moving on when they became successful and they could not depend solely on Elizabeth Fretwell and Donald Smith.[36*]

*

* Tom Hammond continued to talent-scout for the company in England and abroad, sending witty and perceptive accounts of singers to the directorate, as well as detailed analyses of productions, translations and sets. On 22 September 1970 he sent a report on Welsh National Opera's *Simon Boccanegra*, in which he described the young Thomas Allen as Paolo: 'a good actor of excellent appearance' who 'has class vocally' and should be watched as a potential Verdi baritone. In the same memorandum he described Josephine Barstow as an 'impeccable musician and stylish performer whose voice is an acquired taste . . . tall, slender and feminine'. On 29 September 1972 he reported on John Tomlinson's Colline in Glyndebourne Touring Opera: 'useful young bass too boyish for bass roles in a big theatre. He must be watched however' (author's collection).

The Arts Council Enquiry was ready with its recommendations: together with Scottish Opera and a further developed Welsh National Opera there should be a new opera house in Manchester, and key theatres should be bought by the nation. As part of the plan, Sadler's Wells would move to the Coliseum. The decision was urgent as Littler was now offering Sadler's Wells a ten-year lease, which, if it were not accepted immediately, might mean that the Coliseum would not be available for at least five years. Arlen told the Trust on 30 November that the moment had come to make 'virtue of necessity'. The Greater London Council was also keen to free the Royal Festival Hall of the Festival Ballet, which could be housed at the Coliseum. Warning voices on the Trust feared that the move might change the nature of Sadler's Wells and bring it into starker competition with Covent Garden. Arlen was unstoppable, arguing that the decision was only one of venue and did not affect the nature of the work.[37]

Tracey was as enthusiastic as Arlen. 'It's a fine, exciting theatre,' he wrote, 'with all the glamour that Sadler's Wells lacks.' And, he continued, 'the move there could be stunningly successful – and every string should be pulled and every stone upturned to make it work'. The preparations must not be done on the cheap and they must 'start with glamour' in order to bring the audience with them. This was especially true of the decoration of the upper levels and the bars. The working conditions of the company were a priority. They needed an enlarged pit, an overhaul of the stage machinery, a false proscenium, a new switchboard and redecoration of the galleries. The architect thought £100,000 would be needed and the owners might help. Tracey suggested that the illuminated dome should include the 'magic word "ARLORIUM" revolving over the rooftops'.[38] There was the additional connection in that Byam Shaw's father had illustrated the original drop curtain of the Coliseum with personalities of the stage and music hall in 1904.

The move to the Coliseum was being planned in an extremely unfavourable economic climate. When Arlen set out the detailed proposals for the move in January, he started with the statement that the country was in the grip of a serious economic crisis and that a rebuilding scheme of £2 million was therefore impracticable. It would only be possible to improve the basic essentials, but the Coliseum was structurally sound, of remarkable quality and could house everything but rehearsals. Although the move would necessitate higher prices – top price at the Coliseum would go up to £2 5s from £1 12s at Sadler's Wells – they would not be as high as those of *The Mastersingers* at the Wells, and there would be 500 tickets available at the same prices as before. Gallery tickets would be sold at 5s in the 1968/9 season – the same price as at Sadler's Wells. Expenses would be kept down by using old productions and, with the Arts Council's agreement, a reduction of nine weeks' touring in the first year.

The new *Mastersingers* opened at Sadler's Wells on 31 January 1968. It was an instant sell-out, and provided the impetus to the company's flagging fortunes that Arlen had hoped it would. Critics were delighted that Goodall was able 'to display his serene and noble Wagnerian style' and provide a 'mellow, expansive, tender' account of the score. Glen Byam Shaw and John Blatchley ingeniously concealed the limitations of the small stage and rightly stressed the humanity of the characters, according to Shawe-Taylor.[39] Cairns thought Norman Bailey's Sachs was a character of strength, integrity and warmth, and that Alberto Remedios as Walter spun 'rapt, beautifully shaped lyrical phrases'. Both Gregory Dempsey's painfully real and awkward David and Derek Hammond Stroud's Beckmesser were articulated with the utmost clarity and individuality.[40]

The production was, in Harewood's view, a 'revelation' – the combined effort of the individuals so much greater than the sum of its parts.[41] Critics were deeply moved by what was so obviously a formidable company effort, and David Cairns stressed that as a 'true corporate achievement' it was the ultimate retort to those who criticised the uneven standards and periodic disasters of the current regime.

Goodman was now ready to put the Coliseum plans scheme before Jennie Lee, and budgeting for the move became the main preoccupation for Arlen and the Arts Council.[42] On 4 January 1968 the secretary general telephoned Arlen to tell him to budget within a subsidy of £632,000.[43] On 6 February Arlen estimated that the deficit in the first year of the move would be £847,000 and would necessitate an increase in the grant of £107,000.[44] The ministry agreed to the move but doubted whether the grant could be increased to cover such an increase in operating costs.[45] On 20 February Cruft noted that Arlen had done the costings for work at the Coliseum and thought that a possible deficiency of about £51,000 might be covered by deferring one new production to April 1970.[46]

A month later it emerged that there might be a deficit for the current year of £70,000. The Trust was told that it might be due to patrons who had paid more than normal for *The Mastersingers* deciding to compensate by going to fewer other performances. Arlen was undeterred by the financial worries, and the outstanding success of *The Mastersingers* soon led him to the next great Sadler's Wells project. On 5 March he told the Trust that he was keen to employ Goodall again and preferred *The Valkyrie* because it was Goodall's heart's desire to conduct *The Ring*. Donaldson warned that Covent Garden would regard the *Valkyrie* suggestion as an encroachment, but it was pointed out in reply that Covent Garden turned away thousands of people for *Ring* performances for lack of seats.[47] Although they might well consider the idea an intrusion on principle, it was known that Covent Garden would not be performing *The Ring* between 1968 and 1970. Arlen told the Trust that the company were ready the minute they were given the go-ahead and stressed that Goodall was no longer young or well.[48]

Throughout the spring intense efforts were made to make the move to the Coliseum financially feasible. Goodman, who was ready to rap artists on the knuckles for deficits, remained constant when it came to giving substantive support. At a meeting at the Arts Council on 27 March, in his presence, it was agreed that the Arts Council would make a £70,000 supplementary grant to pay off the overdraft. At the same time Sadler's Wells must be asked how they intended to reduce their deficits. Goodman made the dry comment that all theatre people were 'incurably optimistic on the success that lay round the corner'. From March to May all were agreed that Arlen's estimates about the takings at the Coliseum were very optimistic.[49]

The next step was to apprise Covent Garden of developments. The day after the meeting at the Arts Council Sadler's Wells informed Covent Garden that they were virtually in a position to complete their arrangements for taking over the Coliseum and were planning their first season, which was to open on 21 August and to end in the

middle of June 1969. They reassured the Covent Garden management that their policy towards works and singers, who would need
to have Commonwealth passports, would not change. It was recognised, however, that 'with the close proximity of the two houses the
greatest care should be taken to avoid near clashes of date'.

While ostensibly seeking to reassure Covent Garden, Arlen's next
suggestion was unlikely to have the desired effect. After Goodall's
success with *The Mastersingers* he informed them that Sadler's
Wells was anxious to produce *The Valkyrie* in English and mentioned the possibility of Sadler's Wells eventually mounting a complete *Ring*. He proposed an arrangement whereby Goodall could do
more work for Sadler's Wells and still coach at Covent Garden.[50]
After some debate, Covent Garden agreed to let *The Valkyrie* go
ahead but insisted that there would have to be further discussion
afterwards.

On 22 April the governors of the Sadler's Wells Foundation and
Sadler's Wells Trust held an extraordinary meeting to make the
momentous decision that the company should move from Sadler's
Wells to the Coliseum. The chairman thanked Arlen for 'his persistence in reaching a satisfactory agreement'.[51]

At a press conference two days later Arlen announced the move.
The Arts Council grant would, as requested, be increased by
£100,000 for 1969/70. The GLC grant would remain at £100,000.
Initially there would be twelve touring weeks instead of twenty,
with the hope that it would rise to thirty. The Sadler's Wells company would also receive a £5,000 grant from Sir Robert and Lady
Mayer. Edward Greenfield of the *Guardian* wrote that Arlen conducted 'a difficult press conference with the operating skill of a
Wilson and Butler combined'.[52] A performance of *Peter Grimes* on
15 June with Gregory Dempsey was to be the last performance of
Sadler's Wells at Rosebery Avenue. Arlen invited the entire 1945
cast of *Peter Grimes* to the last night at Sadler's Wells.

The move to a 2,400-seat theatre at the heart of the West End
immediately set up a rivalry with Covent Garden that was to prove
both stimulating and fraught with difficulties and dangers. In his
memoirs, Lord Goodman recalled his efforts to mellow antago-
nisms and 'inspire feelings of positive affection' between the top
brass of both institutions with good wine and food at three or four

dinner parties. He admitted that these efforts had been to no avail. Lord Drogheda, with whom Goodman enjoyed a close friendship, was not 'an easy man with whom to communicate a view that was not wholly palatable to him'.[53]

The first meeting of the Covent Garden/Sadler's Wells Co-ordinating Committee was held on 22 May, when it was agreed that there should be a four-month separation between performances of the same opera. Sadler's Wells consequently agreed to postpone a production of *Carmen* planned for August 1969 as Covent Garden claimed that it was the only production that they could put on with *Die Frau ohne Schatten*. The rest of the duplications were reasonably well separated. Covent Garden expressed reservations about the intention of Sadler's Wells to 'extend into the later Wagner repertory'. These objections would, Covent Garden warned, become still stronger if Sadler's Wells put on a complete production of *The Ring*. Sadler's Wells replied evasively that 'there was no foreseeable prospect of this'.[54]

On 15 July it was agreed that Koltai should design *The Valkyrie* in the context of a complete *Ring* cycle. Its budget was set at £12,000 for the set and £3,000 for the costumes. Goodall agreed to conduct and Donaldson, when asked about a potential clash with Covent Garden, reiterated that Covent Garden was not doing *The Ring* between 1968 and 1970.

After the May meeting Arlen expressed alarm to Donaldson. The rule of a four-month gap between performances of the same opera at the two houses made the position 'virtually impossible' and seemed too generous for a popular work. He had, he wrote, 'a sort of feeling that if the Garden wanted to do it they should have priority and we should move round, but this is just not possible'. With twice as many performances, Sadler's Wells should have priority on standard works.[55]

*Don Giovanni* was chosen to inaugurate Sadler's Wells at the Coliseum on 21 August 1968. In July preparations for the opening night at the Coliseum were progressing rapidly. An £8,000 sprinkler system, insisted on by the Greater London Council, was being installed. By 19 August rehearsals were reaching a climax. Arlen reported that the orchestral sound seemed to be successful and that three Sadler's Wells sets could be fitted backstage without being broken down. Box-office advance bookings were £45,000 compared with £13,500 at Sadler's Wells. Arlen congratulated the marketing manager on the publicity. He was organising a party after the first night, as it would be sad for the company to go straight home after such an historic event.[56]

Mackerras had been asked to prepare the edition and conduct the first night, although he was still working in Hamburg. He decided to make it less elaborate than his *Figaro*. Gielgud was to direct and Derek Jarman, a painter with no previous opera experience, was to design, despite Mackerras's reservations. Less than a month before the opening Mackerras got severe peritonitis while on holiday on Elba. He spent two weeks in hospital, after which he was out of danger. Bernardi took over and conducted the opening night. Gielgud, neither comfortable nor experienced at working with music, was reported shouting at Bernardi during rehearsals to 'stop that terrible music' so that he could gain the attention of a chorister.[57]

Shawe-Taylor described the 'fizzing sense of occasion' and volleys of applause at the opening night. At the same time he set out his doubts, asking whether the Coliseum would prove too big for Mozart. Sadler's Wells singers, he advised, would need to articulate with the utmost care if they were to delight as they had done in Rosebery Avenue.[58] Rodney Milnes was wholeheartedly behind the move, describing it as the most 'stimulating operatic event for decades'. The company would be able to relegate to the past the limitations imposed on them by the 'deadening acoustic, the unsympathetic ratio of stage to auditorium and the consequent lack of involvement, and the absence of backstage facilities'. While Milnes understood the management's desire to seek out a famous personality as director for so auspicious an occasion, it would, he thought, have been better to use an opera director.[59] Shawe-Taylor was less lenient, finding the combined Jarman/Gielgud effort 'disastrous'.[60]

William Mann also thought the production did not quite live up to the expectations and was alone in praising Leonard Delany's oily, bullying Don Giovanni and Pauline Tinsley's 'passionately demonstrative' Elvira. On the whole, however, it was agreed that the production lacked spice, drama and warmth.[61] Andrew Porter wrote of the lack of feeling, passion and sexual violence ('I wish to tear out his heart' was translated as 'until I break his heart'); nonetheless, he was careful to point out that although the production was not altogether a success and that the company had forfeited the 'swift, certain impact' of Rosebery Avenue, they had been right to move. 'We are going to expect more of them,' Porter warned, and 'they will want that'.[62]

The 'more' was already apparent on the following night, when a revival of *The Mastersingers* looked and sounded better than it had at Rosebery Avenue, and, despite Goodall's exceedingly slow tempi, was 'inspired', in the words of William Mann.

Stormy relations were rapidly developing with Covent Garden. At the meeting of the Covent Garden/Sadler's Wells Co-ordinating Committee on 18 September Arlen said that plans for a Sadler's Wells *Ring* cycle were 'very tentative' but suggested they might culminate in *Götterdämmerung* in February 1972. Covent Garden was firmly against Sadler's Wells putting on large-scale operas such as *The Ring*, *Aida* or *Tristan and Isolde*. It was nonetheless exactly such large-scale works for which the Coliseum was ideally suited and which were to constitute a central element of the company's programming. The stage was therefore set for the pattern of future conflict and controversy from the very first moments of Sadler's Wells' life at the Coliseum.

At the September meeting the Sadler's Wells representatives refused to accept that they should be excluded from any of the repertoire, arguing that not only could they attract a new public for these works in London but also introduce them to the provinces. Solti was on record as saying he welcomed a Sadler's Wells *Ring* as an introduction for people who might then go on to Covent Garden. Donaldson said it would have to be discussed with the Arts Council.[63] Meanwhile, preparations for *The Valkyrie* continued.

Arlen was preparing the offensive for confronting Covent Garden, informing his board on 21 October that whatever Covent Garden said, they were fully aware that there would be no clash with their own *Ring*. The Trust agreed a strategy, which Arlen and new board member Bernard Williams were to take to the Arts Council for a meeting with Covent Garden.[64*]

The meeting took place at the Arts Council on 22 October in the

* Williams, a witty, erudite and brilliant professor of philosophy at Bedford College, London, would remain a wise counsellor and active in the affairs of Sadler's Wells for many years.

presence of Goodman, with Harewood in the chair. Covent Garden, represented by Drogheda, Webster and Tooley, argued forcefully that large-scale works such as *The Ring* should be left to Covent Garden. The proposition would entail 'wasteful competition at a time of acute financial and economic stringency'. Although Covent Garden's last revival of the Solti *Ring* would be in 1970, the new music director would want to bring in his own, starting in 1972.

Sadler's Wells, represented by Arlen, Williams and Tracey, argued that *The Ring* would be a very different proposition in English, with its own singers and a different 'style of interpretation'. It would complement rather than conflict with the Covent Garden version. Furthermore, Goodall should be allowed to express his talent, and the English language would provide audiences with a deeper understanding of the work, both in London and the provinces. Covent Garden dismissed each of Williams's arguments. Goodall's talent was not a sufficiently weighty factor, given the costliness and the risk of public criticism; recordings meant that the public did not need English-language productions in order to understand the meaning of the words; the scope for touring was very limited; the Covent Garden *Ring* was not so oversubscribed as to suggest 'enormous unsatisfied demand'.

The tide was going against Sadler's Wells, with Harewood admitting that the Arts Council was worried about criticism. Goodman urged Sadler's Wells to show that the two houses were able to 'run in harness' and not compete with each other. He felt that Sadler's Wells should 'exercise a measure of self-denial, even of self-sacrifice', should test the tastes of audiences at the new house and avoid giving the appearance of provocation.

Arlen agreed that he might drop *Rhinegold* but said he would still like to do *The Valkyrie*, which had already been agreed to by the Co-ordinating Committee. Then, at the end of the meeting, when the decision had finally gone against Sadler's Wells and Tracey saw Drogheda's 'satisfied smile', he decided to intervene. He told Goodman that Sadler's Wells had already engaged a conductor and producer.[65] At this, Goodman, with his customary wiliness, suggested that when they did *The Valkyrie* in August 1969, 'it could be regarded as an experiment with *The Ring* in English'. If there was a massive public demand, then it might be appropriate to reconsider the general policy.[66] When Arlen reported back to the Sadler's Wells/Covent Garden Co-ordinating Committee on 20 November, he said that while Goodman had 'not absolutely debarred them', they should not go on to *Rhinegold* immediately.[67]

Sadler's Wells were not alone in their efforts to widen the audience for opera. The Arts Council *Report on Opera and Ballet*, published in December 1969, recommended that there should be a substantial increase in the grant to opera, which in 1968/9 amounted altogether to £2,874,910. This included £1,280,000 to Covent Garden and £787,000 to Sadler's Wells, a large percentage of which was tied to touring and some of which had been geared to covering the deficits of the two houses. It recommended that new opera houses should be built as soon as possible in Scotland, Wales and probably in Manchester, depending on the willingness of the local community. Television and radio should be fully utilised. There was no doubt, they concluded, that 'had the British Isles been gifted with real opera houses, both opera and ballet could have advanced in popularity with greater speed'. Supply to a large extent created demand, 'particularly if the supply is regular and of high quality'.[68]

The Arts Council report had stated that the move to the Coliseum would be assessed when the lease came up for renewal in 1978. In the meantime the company were trying to get used to the expanses of the new venue. The second new production, *The Italian Girl in Algiers*, showed that the Coliseum had not yet been fully mastered. Bernardi's conducting was tasteful rather than full-bodied and Toye's production was considered to be disorganised, with the scale of the new theatre misjudged.[69] Patricia Kern's Isabella was a different matter. In Porter's view she sang with delightful Rossinian technical skill and seductive inflexions and colour, smooth and poignant with a dark lustre.[70]

Colin Graham's new production of *The Force of Destiny*, however, two months later on 18 December, showed that Sadler's Wells was beginning to adjust to the scale of its new home. In the Milan version, virtually without cuts, translated by Tom Hammond, the production caught the work's epic breadth. Many critics were so impressed that they felt it necessitated a revision in critical attitudes to the work. Porter compared it to that of *The Mastersingers* in its intelligence and sensitivity, and in the animation and vitality of the ensemble company. Rosenthal thought it was the most dramatically convincing he had seen, and although imperfect, it was a company success with 'everyone singing and playing as if they loved and believed in the piece'. Balkwill sometimes let the tension sag but the combined companies gave the right volume to both chorus and orchestra. Pauline Tinsley was Leonora, and Donald Smith Don Alvaro. If this was the kind of show Sadler's Wells produced over the next few years, Rosenthal commented, it would be able to forge its new destiny.[71]

Arlen was soon preoccupied with the task of forging one flexible company out of the two equal company structures, with one music director. On 18 November he was authorised to approach Mackerras formally to offer him a position, the Trust chairman David McKenna having agreed that the organisation needed a conductor of international status.[72] When approached this time, Mackerras expressed great interest and agreed that he might leave Hamburg early and start at the beginning of the 1969/70 season. The decision had been eased by his having been passed over in favour of Colin Davis to take over from Solti at Covent Garden in December 1967.

By 1968 Mackerras was both a senior and highly experienced opera conductor, never sentimental, always energetic – a master of his art. With all his strengths, after his time in Hamburg he was nonetheless not entirely in harmony with the Sadler's Wells ethos. His outlook had become more international and he was accustomed to international casts.

The impetus to press ahead artistically at the Coliseum – redoubled by the leadership of Mackerras – was accompanied by increasingly serious deficits. The Arts Council was obliged to defend the company vigorously in the face of growing concern at the Department of Education and Science. More capital expenditure was needed for the theatre than had originally been estimated – £180,000 had been spent and £85,000 was still needed. The DES was soon expressing annoyance at the Arts Council's lack of frankness about Sadler's Wells' deficits and budgeting. It was also getting impatient with unanswered letters and the difficulties of 'pinning Sadler's Wells to a firm budget as the basis for a year's work'. Cruft at the Arts Council continued to defend Sadler's Wells, writing to Ian Thom at the DES on 8 November that on a budget of £1 million to March, it had overspent by only £5,000 up to January 1968. The end of the financial year was hard for all clients, he argued.[73]

While the DES grew more restive, Arlen's efforts to reorganise the company on a more rational footing were supported by Cruft. On 15 November Cruft informed the new secretary general, Hugh Willatt, that Arlen was planning to reduce the combined size of the two companies by 12.5 per cent. A note by Willatt on the file reads: 'I have always advocated this,' but he added that this still seemed to leave the S.W. budget in 'their usual fog'. Three days later, Anthony Field, the director of finance at the Arts Council, urged Sadler's Wells to adopt a budget that balanced, in order to strengthen its hand if extra money were needed. Field and the Arts Council were accused of exerting 'dangerously slight controls' by the DES on 20 November. Sadler's Wells decided to postpone *The Damnation of Faust* to the following year and to raise seat prices. The orchestra was also to be reduced by an eighth.[74]

Arlen's annual report at the end of the 1967/8 season stressed the positive. Coliseum attendance had gone up enormously, the company loved working in the theatre and the public seemed to find its atmosphere enjoyable. On 8 January 1969 Rosenthal suggested that the ill-timed applause indicated that there was indeed a new audience for *La traviata*. On the other hand, he pointed out that Desmond Heeley's sets, which had looked handsome in Rosebery Avenue, seemed 'a bit sparse and cheap at the Coliseum'.[75] At the Arts Council Field was both encouraging and supportive. He noted on 22 February 1969 that although the box office was only averaging 55 per cent of 2,351 seats instead of 66 per cent of 1,497, there was a strong case for the success of the move to the Coliseum in that up to mid-February 320,000 people had attended the Coliseum, whereas 144,000 had attended Sadler's Wells in a comparable period.[76]

Teething problems at the Coliseum were exacerbated by the paucity of productions suitable for the new house. One of those that did make the transition successfully was the 1958 Arundell *Flying Dutchman*. When it opened on 29 January, it was apparent that Charles Bristow had managed to reconstruct his ingenious lighting scheme, as well as the appearance of the phantom ship, which even in the Coliseum remained a *coup de théâtre* that drew gasps. Norman Bailey, who had recently stood in for Hubert Hofmann at Covent Garden as Sachs, was an excellent if somewhat genial Dutchman, more than equal to the demands of the Coliseum's expanses. The Newman translation, however, was 'packed with grating archaisms'.[77]

*The Flying Dutchman* was one of the few successful transfers. *La traviata*, *La bohème*, *Hansel and Gretel* and *Rigoletto* did not look good on the Coliseum stage. Two and a half years after the move, Arlen reflected that they should have prepared eight productions especially designed for the Coliseum. 'We did not have enough suitable productions in the blood bank,' he commented.[78]

The initial disappointment of *Don Giovanni* and the lack of suitable productions for the Coliseum stage opened up a debate about the speed with which the relocation had been carried out. Looking back in 1978, Harewood expressed the opinion that the move had not been made too fast. At the time, when he was on the Arts Council Music Panel, it had been clear that they needed someone like Arlen, whom he described as a revolutionary 'who could move mountains'.[79]

Even in these early stages there were compensations and successes, as the company brought in new talent and developed stars of its own. On 5 February Ava June won hearts in a major revival of the Colin Graham *Madam Butterfly*. Josephine Barstow had been developing into a fine artist after her debut in 1967/8 as the Second Lady in the new Frank Hauser *Magic Flute*. Barstow later recalled that the opportunity to take on such roles as Violetta on tour made it possible for her to be in the new production in 1973.[*]

In November Jacobs was delighted with the debut of Anne Evans as Mimì in *La bohème*.[80] She had an appealing tone, which was smoothly produced throughout the range, and an attractively gentle personality. Evans, who had been studying in Geneva, had been auditioned the previous year on the same day as Gwynne Howell, and engaged on a salary of £25 a week. With plans to move to the Coliseum, she recalled, they were 'looking for bigger voices'.

---

[*] Backed by Harewood, Tracey and Edward Renton, Barstow joined Sadler's Wells after training at the London Opera Centre. Her debut was nerve-racking, as Mackerras complained she was out of tune, which was something, she recalled, 'he could not bear' (interview, 26.2.08).

Joining Sadler's Wells at the time was an opportunity both to learn from the experience of the mature members of the company as well as to work on different roles and gain experience on tour. 'You lived cheek by jowl on tour,' she recalled, which instilled feelings of camaraderie and confidence.

Behind the growth of the great ensemble company lay the leadership of Arlen. He was, Evans said, 'a great man of the theatre; there was nothing he did not know about what makes a theatre tick, and he was approachable at all times'. She also greatly admired Mackerras and loved working with him. He was inspirational: 'You never felt anything could go seriously wrong, there was a great musician in the pit.' She also described him as great fun to be with, with a fantastic sense of humour.[81]

*The Valkyrie* was the project that was intended to galvanise every element of the company and further develop its cohesion and confidence in the new house. It was, however, proving a great challenge. On 20 January 1969 Arlen noted that it would have to be postponed because Norman Bailey had been invited to Bayreuth, which 'would mean so much to his career'.[82] Tracey was distressed by the delay, informing Porter on 6 February that the project was not going well, and adding that 'people (not Goodall or I) are muttering about Rita Hunter's unsuitability for Brünnhilde'.[83] Mackerras remained unconvinced about continuing with *The Ring*.[84]

Hunter, born in Cheshire, was thirty-six years old and had joined the Sadler's Wells chorus in the 1954/5 season. She had gone on to sing small parts with Carl Rosa and had been a principal with Sadler's Wells since 1958, singing Frasquita in *Carmen*, Marcellina in *Figaro* and Berta in *The Barber of Seville*. She had studied with Clive Carey and with Eva Turner since 1959. She had what was described as 'a voluminous, rock-steady' soprano, as well as having an 'ample girth' which brought 'emotional as well as physical weight' to her Brünnhilde.[85] She later said that Goodall told her to approach Brünnhilde as she would Verdi. 'He can't stand people who hoot like owls in Wagner.' Goodall's faith in Hunter was well rewarded and she became a favourite of Sadler's Wells, establishing a 'warm two-way relationship' with her audiences.[86]

This developing relationship was enhanced by the immediacy of Andrew Porter's translation of the text. Porter recognised his debt to previous translators such as Frederick Jameson at the end of the nineteenth century, whose work was used by Hans Richter at Covent Garden in 1908 and as late as 1948, when Hans Hotter and Kirsten Flagstadt sang in English there. Porter's contribution was to make *The Ring* accessible to an audience unfamiliar with the work and to make it feel as compelling a theatrical as a musical experience.* In the event of a clash between the needs of the music and the words, Tracey was the arbiter and, according to Porter, always came down on the side of theatrical utterance.[87] Porter was the first to admit that much was lost in translation, but when he heard Rita Hunter singing even a sentence as stilted as 'You who this love in my heart inspired', he had no doubt that the gains far outweighed the losses. Nor did the public, for whom the translation was a revelation.

Preparations continued during the autumn. Tracey later described Goodall's methods. He was constantly saying to singers, 'Please stop making tone, dear, I want to hear the text.' Porter, working closely with Goodall, continued to make changes to ensure that the text could be easily sung and heard. Anne Evans, who graduated from Wellgunde in 1970 to Sieglinde in 1977/8, described how Goodall worked with the singers with the German text open. 'If you could not find the colour in the English,' she said, 'you went back to the German.'[88]

On 25 October Arlen stressed that it was management's duty to try to produce as much of the *Ring* cycle as possible in English while Reginald Goodall was available. Koltai had therefore continued to design *The Valkyrie* with the whole cycle in mind.[89] On 18 November Tracey asked Porter to press on with the translation of *Siegfried*, as Remedios needed to start learning the long role.[90]

Although Mackerras was still commuting to Hamburg, he was already insisting that the changes to the orchestra and chorus be made by the start of the season, not, as Arlen had suggested, the fol-

---

* Porter was also dusting off some cobwebs. At the opening of Brünnhilde's immolation scene, Jameson's 'mighty logs' did not seem to him to be a vast improvement on the previous translation's 'mighty faggots', nor Robb's 'Let great logs be', which 'inflected like the *Great Gatsby*'. His solution was 'Sturdy branches'. He also sought to avoid pitfalls such as Hunding's call 'Woe King Woe King', for fear of provoking a response of 'next stop Basingstoke'. Porter describes his work in the introduction to *The Ring of the Nibelung*, German text with English translation by Andrew Porter (London: Faber, 1976), pp. xvii–cviii.

lowing spring. There were to be two choruses of forty-four plus a permanent 'floating' nucleus of sixteen.[91] It was finally decided in August that there would be one company from the start of the rehearsals for 1970/1. It soon became clear that there were going to be some changes of emphasis once Mackerras was established at the Coliseum. He was suggesting that artists should take curtain calls after each act. The atmosphere was 'ruined by the rule that Sadler's Wells singers do not take calls'. It was a pity not to '"milk" every possible bit of togetherness with the public'.[92]

On 13 August Mackerras conducted Berlioz's *Damnation of Faust*, directed by Michael Geliot. Although critics were divided by the set of Gothic frames surrounding tall glass panels with projections, the excitement generated from stage to pit and back again was universally admired. Just one year after the premiere of *Don Giovanni*, the strides taken by the company were evident. When Mackerras conducted, with electrifying intensity, a revised staging by Blatchley on 22 August, disappointment was transformed into 'triumphant success'.[93] Alan Blyth wrote of Mackerras's 'unerring instinct for the right tempos, for the shape of a Mozartian phrase, for a pulse that keeps the music continuously flowing and above all, in this work, for the dramatic stature of the music'.[94] Blatchley also inspired his cast into quick, pointed reaction to each incident, and underpinned the production with a strong sense of character.[95]

Mackerras's music-making, the development of fine company artists and a stronger group of directors on the staff were all contributing to the company's development. Soon there were also increasingly confident productions. The first classic hit of the new era was John Cox's *Patience*, which opened on 9 October. Porter wrote that Cox recognised that the piece lived in its period and that it was performed with wit, style and spirit. Derek Hammond Stroud was a perfect Bunthorne. In the first cast Heather Begg, and later Anne Collins, played Lady Jane. According to Porter, John Stoddart borrowed visual references from Pre-Raphaelite art, with the colours rich and right and the ladies of the chorus decoratively clad.[96]

The numerous problems that had emerged at the Coliseum were being faced with resourcefulness and determination. The repertory

Technical Committee was endeavouring to improve the working relationship between the technical departments and the producers and designers. The spacing of revivals was too close, which was causing impossible pressures and resulted in overspending and frayed tempers. The committee was to present proposals for much longer-term planning.

By now both the qualities and defects of the theatre were clear. Balkwill was delighted by the warmer sound of the orchestra. Because the players could hear each other, as well as the singers, which they had not been able to do at Sadler's Wells, they were already playing better. Nonetheless, the orchestras were numerically under-strength. On 15 September Mackerras expressed his concern that fifty-seven players was dangerously under-strength for a theatre in a major city. He asked the Trust for £4,000 to bring the orchestra numbers up. McKenna agreed that Mackerras's request was reasonable and should be discussed in the light of future policy.[97]

Another problem was the comprehensibility of words. Mackerras used to listen to performances from various vantage points and never understood why it was easier to hear words in one part of the auditorium than in others.[98] It was a challenge met head-on and overcome at this time. Singers were nagged to pay more attention to projection and diction, as they were much more concerned about a beautiful line. It was suggested that someone should sit in at rehearsals and report on the audibility of the text.[99] This task fell to Tracey, who fulfilled it until the 1980s. 'Edmund sat up front with a little black book,' Anne Evans recalled, 'and if he could not hear the words he would sit you down and say, "It is not good enough."'[100]*

Plans for the reorganisation as well as for future economies were finalised by 15 October. New works were to take priority for rehearsals and the companies were to be amalgamated. They would remain in London and tour between seasons, when they would split into two groups: a larger one suitable for the big cities like Liverpool, and the smaller to do chamber works for towns with smaller theatres.

---

* Mackerras recalled many years later that there were certain singers whose words could always be clearly heard; one was Valerie Masterson, another was Derek Hammond Stroud, who was, in Mackerras's words, 'marvellous as Beckmesser and as Alberich in the *Ring*'. Lesley Garrett in a later era was another. (Interview, 29.4.06.)

Charles Mackerras moved into his office at the Coliseum on 1 January 1970, when he conducted his inaugural performance – *The Magic Flute*. At the end of the month *The Valkyrie* opened. The opening-night audience responded with tumultuous applause to a powerful performance integrated dramatically and musically. Shawe-Taylor described Porter's translation as direct, clear, 'shapely and respectful'. All the critics praised Goodall's long and detailed coaching of the singers, as well as his 'noble, lyrical, and finely proportioned' conducting. They also commented on tempi that added twenty minutes to Richter's initial Bayreuth performances and stretched the singers.[101]

The cast demonstrated the rewards of nurturing the ensemble company and the intense period of rehearsal. Norman Bailey's Wotan 'conveyed sorrow and majesty in tones of unmistakable authority', with 'resonant low tones and imperious declamation'.[102] Rita Hunter's Brünnhilde 'struck fire from the outset with her ringing and confident war cry'. She shaped her phrases with 'a distinction of line and an aptness of tone colour' that lingered in Desmond Shawe-Taylor's memory. Alberto Remedios sang Siegmund with 'natural ease and fervour'. Ava June as Sieglinde, Clifford Grant as Hunding and Ann Howard as Fricka all gave performances that clearly revealed the care of Goodall's coaching. Directors Blatchley and Byam Shaw produced a respectful *Valkyrie* that built to thrilling climaxes. Critics appreciated their approach, which, as Blatchley himself said, was about 'human beings, with human feelings and failings'. They were faithful to the psychology of the drama.

Koltai's abstract set of gleaming rods and metallic spheres was inspired by man's first steps on the moon on 21 July 1969 and was described by William Mann as strange but exciting and practical.[103] It was made up of reflective surfaces, with a mysterious sheen, the floor silvered and encrusted with black PVC waste, everything on stage reflected in the dull gleam of a back mirror made from perforated white film-screen plastic, all of which was lit by Robert Ornbo.

Although negotiations with Covent Garden were not complete, it was clear that *The Valkyrie* was both a work in progress as well as an impressive company achievement. Ronald Crichton wrote that there could be no doubt that this team would produce an English

*Ring*.[104] The die was indeed cast. On 3 February Edmund Tracey expressed his admiration for Porter's translation, and in thanking him urged him to get going with the next instalment of *The Ring*, *Götterdämmerung* or, as Tracey wrote, '*Twilight*, as we must now begin to call it'.[105] A week later, at the Co-ordination Committee meeting, Jack Donaldson said that the 'tremendous critical and public acclaim meant Sadler's Wells should proceed with *The Ring*'. Arlen said he intended to prepare *Twilight of the Gods* next. On 18 March Covent Garden formally withdrew their objection to the Sadler's Wells *Ring* cycle.[106]

As the new decade began, Arlen was faced by the conflicting demands of a powerful music director and an anxious Arts Council, which was watching the deficit building up. During his first week Mackerras suggested original-language performances of early Verdi and Puccini, which the Opera Subcommittee turned down, stressing that the identity of Sadler's Wells rested on a permanent company singing in English. Guest singers should be employed, they said, only where roles could not be filled by resident company members.[107] This discussion was not over.

Then, on 16 January, McKenna told Arlen and the board that the Arts Council was demanding a surplus when there was likely to be a heavy deficit. Drastic measures would have to be taken. The Opera Subcommittee suggested more popular works and the cancellation of all new works, including *Le Prophète* and *War and Peace*. Arlen said he needed an absolute statement of the Trust's policy, as some change in accent was inevitable, both because of the move to the Coliseum and because of Mackerras. The chairman said Sadler's Wells should not attempt to be 'a second Covent Garden'.[108]

The deficit had reached £88,000 by February, when Arlen was forced to prepare a completely new production schedule.[109] Mackerras found the changes of plan disturbing and was annoyed when Arlen told Tooley that Covent Garden was welcome to do *War and Peace*, when it was something he very much wanted to do himself.[110] He was also still determined to press the idea of tackling bel canto works such as those by Bellini, and especially Verdi's *Il trovatore*, in the original language. Some Italian works, he argued, 'sounded rather ludicrous in English' and he was convinced that

1 Lilian Baylis in the 1920s. The creator of and enduring inspiration behind the entire enterprise.
2 Edward J. Dent, c.1902 – the Cambridge Professor of Music, translator, teacher and mentor to Baylis, who contributed so much to the company's founding principles: opera in English and opera as drama.
3 Clive Carey's production of *The Marriage of Figaro*, November 1938. Left to right: Morgan Jones as Don Curzio, Sumner Austin as Count Alamviva, Ruth Naylor as Susanna, Arnold Matters as Figaro, Valetta Iacopi as Marcellina and Harry Brindle as Bartolo.

4 Joan Cross as Elisabeth and Ronald Stear as the Landgrave in Clive Carey's new production of *Tannhäuser*, November 1938.

5 Joan Cross and Lawrance Collingwood standing outside Sadler's Wells before the war. Cross was the company's director during the period of gruelling wartime touring, with Collingwood its music director.

6 A new *Così fan tutte* in August 1944, with John Hargreaves as Guglielmo, Joan Cross as Fiordiligi, Rose Hill as Despina, Owen Brannigan as Don Alfonso, Margaret Ritchie as Dorabella and Peter Pears as Ferrando.

7 Sadler's Wells reopened after the war in June 1945 with Benjamin Britten's *Peter Grimes*. Peter Pears as Grimes, with nieces Minnia Bower and Blanche Turner and members of the chorus.

8 Norman Tucker, Director of Sadler's Wells from 1948, ensured its survival after the war and set firm foundations for its further development. Tucker with Lotte Lenya, who had come to London to advise on the production of Kurt Weill's *The Rise and Fall of the City of Mahagonny* in 1963.

9 After Charles Mackerras introduced Norman Tucker to the work of Janáček, Sadler's Wells championed his work, starting with *Katya Kabanova* in 1947. Amy Shuard (right) as Katya and Marion Studholme as Varvara in the 1951 revival.

10 Patricia Kern as Angelina, Nancy Creighton and Anna Pollak as Clorinda and Thisbe in *Cinderella*, October 1959. Sadler's Wells contributed to the Rossini revival with its witty translations and lively productions.

11 Michel St-Denis's seminal production of Stravinsky's *Oedipus Rex*, January 1960, with David Ward as Tiresias, Ronald Dowd as Oedipus and Monica Sinclair as Jocasta.

12 Michael Geliot's production of Kurt Weill's *The Rise and Fall of the City of Mahagonny*, January 1963, in Ralph Koltai's ingenious set. Inia Te Wiata as Trinity Moses, April Cantelo as Jenny, Patricia Bartlett as Mrs Begbick and John Chorley as Fatty the Bookkeeper.

13 Elizabeth Fretwell, Colin Davis and stage director Frank Hauser discuss the new production of *La traviata* in 1960, the year before Davis became the company's Music Director.

14 Stephen Arlen, Managing Director from 1966 to 1972, was instrumental in taking Sadler's Wells to the London Coliseum and preparing it for its glory years.

15 *The Makropoulos Case* in 1964, directed by John Blatchley and designed by Motley maintained the Sadler's Wells Janáček tradition. Marie Collier as Emilia, Gregory Dempsey as Albert Gregor and Eric Shilling as Doctor Kolenaty.

16 The legendary 1968 *Mastersingers,* directed by Glen Byam Shaw and conducted by Reginald Goodall, launched Sadler's Wells into its great Wagner productions. Front row, left to right: Gregory Dempsey as David, Ann Robson as Magdalene, Norman Bailey as Hans Sachs, Margaret Curphey as Eva, Noel Mangin as Pogner, Stafford Dean as the Nightwatchman, and Alberto Remedios as Walter.

17 In January 1970 *The Valkyrie* was the first instalment of ENO's *Ring* cycle at the Coliseum with Rita Hunter as Brünnhilde and Norman Bailey as Wotan.

18  Charles Mackerras, ENO's Music Director from 1970 to 1977, galvanised the
company and raised its musical ambitions and standards yet further.
19  Edmund Tracey – ENO's guardian of diction, nurturer of singers and general adviser
to both artists and administrators for thirty years – and Reginald Goodall in 1986 during
rehearsals of *Parsifal*.
20  Lord Harewood, ENO's Managing Director from 1972 to 1985 and Chairman from
1986 to 1995, with Josephine Barstow, preparing her role as Natasha in *War and Peace*,
October 1972.

21 Janet Baker as Mary, Don Garrard as the Earl of Shrewsbury and Keith Erwen as the Earl of Leicester in *Mary Stuart*, December 1973. The ensemble grew in the 1970s.
22 Ann Howard as Carmen, May 1970.
23 Lorna Haywood as Katya in 1973.
24 Jonathan Miller's first production for ENO, in November 1978, was *The Marriage of Figaro*. Lillian Watson as Susanna, Valerie Masterson as the Countess and John Tomlinson as Figaro.

performances in Italian would fill the Coliseum. Donaldson, not surprisingly, remained non-committal; the suggestion needed discussion, he said.[111]

Relations between Mackerras and Arlen were rapidly deteriorating. 'After a while', Mackerras recalled in 2006, 'he and I did not get on so well – partly my fault, I now realise.' He admitted that he had become more 'international' in attitude and felt that Arlen did not like his frequent conducting at Covent Garden and walking from one house to the other. Mackerras had accepted a much lower salary than he could have demanded, so that he felt free and less guilty about continuing to take outside engagements.[112]

Above all, the constant need to reschedule repertoire owing to the financial situation, as well as differing taste, caused occasionally fractious debate between the two men. Arlen wanted Offenbach's *Dick Whittington* for Christmas, but Mackerras insisted that the music was not good enough; they should do *Hansel and Gretel* and spend the money on a new *Il trovatore*, *La bohème* or *Seraglio* conducted by himself.[113] On 16 February Mackerras expressed extreme perturbation at the change of programme. He warned that although he was accepting it because of the financial stringency, if such changes occurred every year, it would render his position intolerable.[114] On 5 May the Trust learnt that Mackerras had raised an anonymous donation of £10,000 for guest singers or musicians. He was keen to put on a musical such as *Show Boat*, but the board was horrified at the prospect. It was 'too low brow'.[115]

Despite the friction, Arlen's patient building up of the company style was beginning to pay dividends. The new production of *Carmen* on 6 May introduced to Coliseum audiences the partnership of Stefanos Lazaridis and John Copley, and, together with *Patience*, inaugurated a new era of revivable basic repertoire for the company.

As a student at the Central School of Design, the opera-mad Copley had spent every day at Covent Garden, covering small parts and observing conductors such as Kleiber in rehearsal and performance. He had also been a close friend of Joan Cross, who introduced him to Sadler's Wells, and inspired in him a dedication to clarity of diction. He had worked as a stage manager at Sadler's Wells for two years from 1954 and had then been house producer at Covent Garden 'for his galley years', learning the repertoire. On Tracey's urging, Arlen invited him back to Sadler's Wells for what was to be a highly productive and warm relationship with the company.

Copley brought with him a young designer, Stefanos Lazaridis, who had been born in Ethiopia of Greek parents and educated in Switzerland and London, after which he had taken a technical course at the Central School and had worked at the National Theatre. Lazaridis, who described himself as a 'cynical romantic', had a tempestuous nature, as he explained: 'You see in my youth I was terribly violent. Very aggressive.' For British opera lovers, he said, 'anything passionate is considered unhealthy and therefore if you find a way of expressing your passions, however violent they are, in a civilised way – you are OK'.[116] Lazaridis's work with Sadler's Wells and ENO was to develop an intense, powerful and dominating design aesthetic at the Coliseum over the next decades.

In *Carmen* there was an exciting coherence between stage and pit that was the hallmark of Mackerras's directorship. David Cairns was pleased to see 'a solid tough core of truthfulness' in Copley's production, and the crowd scenes swarming with life. From the ferocious vehemence of the prelude, Mackerras ensured that the familiar score sounded 'unfailingly rich, varied and incisive'. Cairns welcomed the constant presence of the tragic theme in the production, the resolutely unpicturesque and squalid grandeur of Lazaridis's set and the vision of a 'slice of life as it is lived'. At the same time, under Mackerras's direction, 'the big tunes soar as grandly, the Spanish rhythms pulsate as powerfully, the hot, clear colours burn as pungently, and the delicate instrumental inventions strike as astonishingly fresh and radiant as ever'. Ann Howard, who had 'last been seen defending marital sanctity as Fricka', was now an intriguing 'free spirit', singing Carmen with new freedom and intensity. Blyth praised her skill in matching English words to the music and marvelled at her ability to hold her audience in 'the palm of her hands. Her Carmen looked as though she could gobble up her two men for breakfast,' he said.[117] Hugh Beresford was one of them, a plausible, simple, lovestruck dragoon, and Norman Welsby the other.

The production established Copley as a member of the Sadler's Wells team. After the first night, Copley recalled, Arlen said to him: 'After this you will come back every season.' His skill in working with the chorus, and in creating individual characterisations, whether in great or small roles within the big picture, was later commented on by Ann Howard. In particular, Copley found that each member of the chorus was able to give an acting performance, which at that time was not true of the Covent Garden chorus, since their chorus master was not interested in anything other than the sound. At Sadler's Wells the drama was always important. 'I had a wonderful time there,' he later reflected.[118] The production was also a turning point in Ann Howard's career. She later described the growth of her fan club after *Carmen*, and how members would comment on her different roles.[119] In general, audiences were beginning to follow the careers of their favourite singers, whom they observed as they developed within the ensemble framework.

Another such company rising star was Anne Evans, who sang two and acted three of the soprano roles in *The Tales of Hoffmann* in August 1970. Shawe-Taylor found her 'outstanding in Antonia's music, warm in phrasing, creamy and intense in tone'. She mimed Olympia, who was sung by Rhonda Bruce as if through a gramophone. It was the work's first airing by the company since Clive Carey's 1931 production, in a fresh performing version by Tracey, skilfully and imaginatively directed by Colin Graham and with ingenious, tasteful sets by David Collis. It was conducted by Nicholas Braithwaite with spirit and skill.[120]

These new productions set the standard for the Sadler's Wells company as they settled into the Coliseum and forged both an identity and a loyal following. John Higgins defined the house style, as displayed by *Carmen*, as an admirable directness and a 'determination to make the plot and words as clear as possible without any coarse, rib-nudging underlining'. Sadler's Wells was, he thought, determined to bring in a new public.[121]

Both inside and outside the house, Baylis's vision was being fulfilled as new professional staff were introduced in order to improve the standards of the repertory and ensemble for the growing public. It was at this time that the young director David Ritch, who had worked at the Old Vic and in repertory theatre, came to work with Blatchley and Colin Graham, particularly on dialogue, and helped to start the scheme to train young directors. For Ritch the long hours and modest remuneration were more than compensated for by the excitement and thrill of the enterprise and the amazing family feeling in the company.[122] Charles Kraus, the son of the baritone

Otakar Kraus, joined the company shortly afterwards as house manager. He has remained a loyal and devoted member of the company for over thirty-five years, becoming company manager in 1975 and chorus manager in 1993.

On 19 June 1970 Edward Heath became prime minister. He inherited a trade deficit, in real terms worse than at any time since 1951, with a 2 per cent growth rate and unemployment continuing to rise. Harold Wilson had increased taxation by over £300 million between 1964 and 1970, with selective employment tax, corporation tax and capital-gains tax. In the Conservative manifesto, taxation was to be reduced, public expenditure and trade-union power curbed. It was a period of great economic uncertainty.

David Eccles became Paymaster General with responsibility for the arts and was given a Cabinet position on 20 June. Goodman later wrote that Eccles would not have been his choice as Minister for the Arts, since there was a rigidity about him which he found difficult to deal with. Goodman commented, 'Not only did he lack any particular affection for artists but he regarded them as members of the community who could be dealt with on a summary basis.'[123]

Arlen was soon expressing his concern that it might be impossible to sustain the progress so far achieved, with the company overdraft reaching £200,000, which was the bank's limit. The company's purpose – to establish a self-sufficient ensemble that would be able to provide from within the human material required to put on first-class productions – 'was being bent' for lack of funds, he told the Opera Subcommittee. *Valkyrie* was an example of what could be done in the creation of a company style, with their own school of singers and designers, and a small team of resident people.[124]

Backstage, industrial relations were also becoming fraught, as was the case in the country at large. The move to the Coliseum had changed the working environment from regional playhouse to West End theatre at a stroke. The subsidised repertory work at Covent Garden and Sadler's Wells was quite different from a West End show, which had comparatively small crews of stage staff servicing a single production. At the same time sets were becoming bigger, heavier and technically more sophisticated.[125]

The Royal Opera House had managed to negotiate a new agreement with the National Association of Theatre, Television, and Kine Employees (NATTKE) in 1967/8, which came into effect in 1969/70. Covent Garden had the advantage of having been in situ as a repertory company in the West End for far longer than Sadler's Wells. The Covent Garden agreement stipulated an increased basic wage, a six-week, five-day roster pattern and a monthly ceiling on Sunday and all-night working sessions. Management was liable for very high overtime payments if it breached the conditions. The system gave the staff a predictable pattern of work and the higher basic salary gave them greater social security. It was considered a revolutionary system, for no theatre had ever worked that way.[126]

Between May and August 1970 the Sadler's Wells management made two attempts to achieve an agreement similar to that at Covent Garden. On 17 August, however, the agreement reached with the union was rejected by the staff, who had not been consulted, because it included regular night shifts and less advantageous time off. Although it included a higher guaranteed weekly wage, there would be less overtime available.[127] 'Wildcat strikes' were threatened, the board learnt that day.[128]

NATTKE, a fairly weak and disparate union with no 'closed-shop' agreement,* was unable to negotiate a settlement that the staff would support. In the first two weeks of September there were efforts to seek a formula on which all could agree, but on 16 September the Trust decreed that any agreement must not be detrimental to Sadler's Wells, even if that resulted in a strike.[129] The men reorganised with a new steward and committee. The union requested a meeting with Sadler's Wells, which was refused.[130]

As the curtain went up on *Carmen* on 20 September, the stage staff struck after learning that NATTKE had accepted an agreement without consulting them. The agreement would come into effect on 28 September. The board urged management to try to strengthen the union, which was weak, and not to negotiate with the staff until they returned to work. All but one of the strikers refused to come back and were dismissed.

During the strike, management, heads of department and assistants, together with the musical performers, managed to keep the

* An arrangement whereby all employees were members of the same trade union.

theatre open with skeleton sets. At its meeting on 13 October the
board learnt that the stage staff were adamant in their dislike of the
Covent Garden six-week rostering pattern, because one group was
required to work for four consecutive nights. Finally, agreement
had been reached for a return to work based on the Covent Garden
pattern but with adjustments for the Sadler's Wells working pattern.
The men would work two nights a week with one additional night
call per week during the period of the implementation of the agreement. The rate remained unchanged. Arlen thought it was a very
satisfactory agreement and believed that it was 'derivative of the
ROH agreement'.[131] He believed that the fact that they had managed to keep the theatre going had had a profound effect on the
result.[132]

With time, however, the shift roster pattern was found to be
unsatisfactory for the Coliseum, and the staff were unhappy with
reduced earnings, so that the following year it was renegotiated on
the basis of three weekly shifts of fifteen and a half hours, in contrast to the five-day roster at the Royal Opera House.* The Arts
Council later said that this agreement was the crucial element in the
development of poor industrial relations at the Coliseum.[133] It also
soon became apparent that the basic working week was too short.
At the Coliseum the staff were paid double for all overtime and
Sunday working, which was crucial for technical rehearsals of new
productions. Moreover, everyone called in was paid for the full
shift, whether all the hours were worked or not.[134] It was the result
of what was later described by one trade-union official as a 'low-
pay culture supported by overtime'.[135]

When the Arts Council instituted a committee of enquiry after a
longer and more serious strike in 1974, it also reported on the 1970

---

* In the fifteen-and-a-half-hour day there were two one-hour meal breaks and
two unofficial half-hour breaks. Gerard Wood at the Arts Council later said it
was 'an ineffective agreement as no-one can work for fifteen and a half hours
at a stretch, even with breaks, and that in the theatre there was no call for such
long stretches, other than for the purpose of staying to see nothing went wrong
once the stage was set'. During those slack times, it was 'customary' for people
to take the opportunity to go to a 'convenient hostelry next door'. Wood also
reported a story current in the theatre of a cymbals player 'who is seen in the
pub counting, with a pint in one hand, "145, 146, 147", because he has to be
back at bar 149' (ACGB, Minutes of Proceedings of Committee of Enquiry,
13.2.75, ENO Ad 112 Box 121).

strike. It pointed out that Sadler's Wells management had had no previous experience of large operations such as were developing at the Coliseum and little expertise in managing large groups of workers. Their prime interest and expertise was in getting the show on. As a result, concessions, custom and practice grew up almost within a week of the October 1970 agreement being implemented. Within a year the unions were asking for modifications to remove the few remaining 'free' night calls.[136] Later Tom Lever of NATTKE told the Arts Council committee that the 'boys on the Stage Committee or the officer of the union took advantage of weak management. That was nothing unusual.'[137]

Management's hands had also been tied during the negotiations because of doubts about the move to the Coliseum that were now being expressed by the Arts Council. It was believed that Goodman had warned Arlen that if he stood firm and closed the Coliseum, it might never reopen. This, the then finance director John Snape later wrote, 'undoubtedly influenced Stephen in the subsequent negotiations' and had put management in a very weak position whenever there was a fight with the unions.[138]

Anthony Field, the Arts Council assessor, was indeed warning the Sadler's Wells Finance Subcommittee in October that the Arts Council was extremely worried about the whole situation and was under criticism from the Paymaster General's office because of the deficit which had been incurred since 1969/70. He warned them that there was no chance of their receiving the kind of grant they were requesting for 1971/2.[139] Willatt was under pressure from the Public Accounts Committee, not only because of Sadler's Wells' problems but also because of the deficits of Welsh National Opera and increased demands for housing the arts.[140]

On 10 October Arlen wrote to Arnold Goodman directly to ask for support: 'I beg of you to bring the Minister with you to see us and our work as soon as possible,' he wrote, adding, 'We can find no occasion on which he visited this theatre unless he has done so in a false beard.' For 1971/2 he asked for £1,004,000, which he reckoned was an increase of just 6.6 per cent per year over the last three years.[141] Sadler's Wells also asked the Arts Council to cover their accumulated deficit of £205,718, as well as the estimated loss of £93,000. The union negotiations had cost £80,000 in increased wages.

The Arts Council decided to investigate the financial situation at Sadler's Wells and appointed a subcommittee chaired by Sir Joseph Lockwood, chairman of EMI. Nicholas Payne, then an Arts Council finance officer and secretary to the Arts Council Enquiry, wrote the minutes and much of the report. George Harewood, the enquiry's vice-chairman, its secretary general Hugh Willatt and Arts Council music director John Cruft also attended. Amongst the options discussed were a return to Rosebery Avenue, Covent Garden taking over Sadler's Wells, and the Royal Ballet sharing the Coliseum. In Harewood's view, the hopes for the Coliseum had not been borne out – 'the building was destroying what the company did best – small-scale operas, operetta, inexpensive productions'.[142]

During the discussions the two positions in the Sadler's Wells/Coliseum debate were defined. On the one hand there were those who saw a second large-scale operatic organisation in London as an unnecessary extravagance, and on the other were those who saw Sadler's Wells as not only a worthwhile institution but also one whose momentum, like that of all arts institutions, would always be towards improvement and excellence. At the same time it also became apparent that the move to the Coliseum had been made without the question of adequate funding in the future having been tackled by either Arlen, his board or the funders themselves.

On 29 October Willatt asked if the deficit was due to bad management control, union negotiations or the failure of receipts. Cruft explained that the year after Sadler's Wells moved to the Coliseum, 1969/70, had been crucial for the company's finances and acknowledged that Sadler's Wells had 'been under-subsidised partly because they had under-budgeted in order to seem financially viable'. Lockwood suggested that Arlen was making all the decisions and his board probably did not interfere enough. Perhaps David McKenna, who was on the board of British Railways, 'was used to large deficits', he suggested.[143]

James McRobert, the Arts Council deputy secretary general, represented the views of those who saw the move to the Coliseum as a dangerous development. It had always been accepted that Covent Garden needed a lot of money, he said, but the location of Sadler's Wells now impelled a new kind of ambition and aspirations that were contrary to Arts Council policy. McRobert saw no case for two opera companies on the same footing. Sadler's Wells should work as a folk opera house on a shoestring and be geared to slot into a provincial centre one day when needed. Defending Sadler's Wells, Cruft responded that it was the company's ambition at Rosebery Avenue that had been 'a contributory cause of the move'. Willatt argued that if Sadler's Wells lacked ambition it would sink into mediocrity. Lockwood claimed that ticket prices were not high enough – too high a proportion of Sadler's Wells' income was from subsidy. Cruft responded that Sadler's Wells had prepared a careful study and made adjustments according to the market.[144] For the 1970/1 season, Arlen had brought down the top price from £2 5s to £2, but raised the lowest from 5s to 6s.

For the next two years the threat of insolvency and closure lurked in the background. The Arts Council had written to Sadler's Wells warning of possible closure, and on 10 November McKenna asked Cruft if the warning still stood and whether the Arts Council would pay off the company's debts if it closed at the end of the following summer. Cruft was sure that the Arts Council would honour such an agreement, but that the increase in subsidy would not be more than £65,000, while the deficit in the budget was still £189,573 for 1970/71.[145] The pressure from the DES on the Arts Council was constant. The next day Willatt had to reassure them that they were chasing Sadler's Wells and Welsh National Opera about their deficits.[146]

The gulf between the need to plan ahead, as demanded by Mackerras, and the need to stay solvent, as being pressed by the Arts Council, was seemingly unbridgeable. Nonetheless, Arlen exerted all his efforts to reduce the deficit in the 1971/2 budget. On 16 November the board discussed his suggestions for cutting the orchestra from ninety-three to eighty and the chorus from eighty to seventy-five, which would save £6,000. The chairman was to write to the Arts Council suggesting either they should close down completely or continue to operate with a popular programme which would require an adequate grant.[147]

On 23 November the Arts Council's report, drafted by Nicholas Payne, noted the financial needs of the company and its efforts to balance the budget. There was to be an increase in seat prices of 20 per cent (£40,000) There would be fifteen extra performances of *Kiss Me, Kate!*, and *The Coronation of Poppea* was to be cancelled

(£17,000). It was suggested that an enquiry to be undertaken by the management consultancy Peat Marwick might suggest further savings.[148] In December the Arts Council offered a grant of £815,000, which would also cover the £82,000 deficit.[149]*

With Mackerras as music director, the advocates of retrenchment were to find themselves fighting a losing battle. For Handel's *Semele* on 21 October Mackerras brought in the Italian director Filippo Sanjust, with whom he had worked in Hamburg and whom he described as 'the type of cultivated producer who had historical awareness'. Sanjust, who designed and directed, placed the work with wit and perception in Georgian England, with gardens and palaces in subtle colours and with airy spaciousness. Clouds and walls were painted on flats rising as if on old-fashioned pulleys.[150] Athamas was sung by counter-tenor James Bowman, in his first appearance on the Coliseum stage, with a startling and powerful impact. Alexander Young gave a very witty performance as Jupiter.

It was at this time that sets started to become a major problem for those attempting to work within a budget. On 17 December it was noted that Koltai, despite all attempts at rigid control, was going seriously over the limit with *Twilight of the Gods*. Final designs were late and a major crisis loomed as a result.[151] Lazaridis's design for a new *Seraglio* was also well over budget. This was the beginning of what became a long-standing propensity for set designs to undermine ENO's budgeting.

As the financial pressures mounted, so did the friction between Arlen and Mackerras. Mackerras was discussing possible roles with Janet Baker, who expressed keenness to sing in *Coronation of Poppea* and Berlioz's *Damnation of Faust*, starting rehearsals in November 1971 and ending in January 1972. He believed it was crucial to get in bigger-voiced singers as guests, who could fill the theatre and bring in the audiences. Janet Baker was then at the height of her fame, and an anonymous friend of Mackerras sub-

---

* The figures of the subsidies of European houses at the time were provided for the subcommittee. Milan received £1.5 million for a six-month season (1969); Paris £3.1 million for its two houses, the Opéra and the Opéra Comique, with one administration; Berlin £2.05 million (1968); Munich £1.6 million (1968); Hamburg £1.65 million (1968). Covent Garden's subsidy was £1.25 million in 1969 (ACGB 13/229).

sidised her fee, which was out of the range of usual ENO payments.[152] Mackerras instructed management to plan the repertoire
around her dates and to confirm her engagement with her agent.[153]

The possibility that Arlen might find it necessary to cancel
*Coronation of Poppea* for financial reasons was therefore alarming
for Mackerras. On 1 December he told the Opera Subcommittee
that 'if Poppea were cancelled or postponed he would resign from
the company'. He suggested a fund-raising evening with Joan
Sutherland, Noël Coward and Sadler's Wells singers.[154] He repeated
his warning on 22 December, when the administration agreed that
they too were worried that the repertoire was becoming too 'popular'. Arlen agreed that *Coronation of Poppea* would stay and
*Rhinegold* would be taken out of the spring repertoire and replaced
by *Il trovatore*. *Siegfried* would move to the autumn of 1972.

*Kiss Me, Kate!* – the first Sadler's Wells American musical –
opened on 24 December 1970 and was not as successful, either critically or at the box office, as had been hoped. It was considered a
stylistically impossible task for the company; an 'artistic indiscre-
tion', according to the *Observer*.[155] This unsuccessful first foray
into the unfamiliar territory of American musicals did nothing,
however, to undermine the steady realisation of Arlen's and Tracey's
vision for the company. When *Twilight of the Gods* was premiered
on 29 January, Shawe-Taylor thought that it surpassed even *The
Valkyrie* in its 'density of interest and continuity of inspiration'.
Despite occasional slips, the orchestra played as though they loved
and understood the meaning of every phrase, and they gave their
all. Remedios, singing with 'freshness, ring and vivacity' and displaying evidence of long coaching, was 'so overflowing with good
humour and good nature as to banish all notion of the bullying
proto-Nazi superman'. Shawe-Taylor was delighted that the
provinces were going to have the opportunity to see *The Ring*.[156]*

*Seraglio* in March, with new prose dialogue by Tracey, was
praised as 'a new and true experience of the opera'. Lazaridis's over-

---

* Tracey recalled that Goodall could be very variable. On a good night he
would knock you for a six, but sometimes he was too slow. One night Tracey
went in at the interval and said, 'It's terribly slow tonight.' Goodall responded:
'I'm glad you told me. I'll speed it up . . .' Act II was even slower, but Tracey
'did not have the heart to tell him' (unpublished interview with John Lucas,
1991).

budget sets were deemed 'sumptuous and glittering' in gold and blue, rich not gaudy, with a detailed yet spacious effect. Porter pointed out that even though the Sadler's Wells *Seraglio* lacked great voices, it was 'so well-rehearsed, produced and conducted, designed and thought' that he was able to apply to it standards appropriate to Glyndebourne or Salzburg, even though the tickets were about a quarter of the price. Lois McDonall had presence and dignity and sang with poignancy. Alexander Young phrased the role of Belmonte with 'uncommon sensitivity and grace'.[157]

Mackerras was still determined to see Italian-language productions, starting with *Il trovatore*. The situation was further complicated by the fact that the new team at Covent Garden, Colin Davis and Peter Hall, were engaged in a battle with their board to perform *Figaro* in English. Donaldson, the chairman of the Opera Subcommittee, was strongly opposed to such an experiment, explaining on 5 January 1971 that 'it was an extremely dangerous precedent' and it seemed to him to 'undermine the identities of the two houses which had always complemented each other so well'. For the company it was a matter of survival. Arlen also feared that if the chorus sang in Italian they would want Covent Garden rates. When Mackerras insisted that the original language would only be used for operas 'not noted for dramatic complexity or literary distinction', the Opera Subcommittee decided to advise the Trust to accept the experiment if Covent Garden did an English *Figaro*.[158]

When the discussion reached the board, however, it was against the idea, particularly as Mackerras was now thinking of extending the experiment to *La traviata*.[159] Tracey pointed out that there had been much opposition to *Orfeo* in Italian and that it would weaken Donaldson in negotiations with Covent Garden. The chairman undertook to tell Mackerras that it was not the right moment for experiment because of the financial situation and possible adverse comment. Luckily for Sadler's Wells, Davis and Hall had to drop the idea when members of the Covent Garden cast refused to learn their roles in English. On 2 February it was noted that both houses would have to stick to their policies.[160]

Survival remained the main concern into 1971. In February the controller and auditor general conveyed their concern about the Sadler's Wells deficit of £156,000 to Parliament and were considering whether the company should remain at the Coliseum. A month later McKenna said that he should draw the attention of the Finance Committee to the fact that the organisation was at the moment bankrupt and, as the directors had permitted it to go on trading, they were liable under company law not only to a heavy fine but also to a term of imprisonment. The chairman asked again if the Arts Council – in the case of insolvency – would allow the remains of the grant to pay off the debts. Abernethy was not re-assuring. 'If the organisation was declared bankrupt there was no question of honouring contracts forward of the date of the declared bankruptcy,' he warned.[161]

Not unnaturally some members of the board were perturbed, but Donaldson was standing firm. At the Trust meeting on 15 March, when McKenna drew attention to the directors' liability, Donaldson said it was a grave mistake to discuss closure when the organisation had never been more successful and was well established at the Coliseum. The Arts Council, he rightly judged, would find it very difficult to justify closure. Board member Kenneth Robinson supported him. Arlen pointed out that the inflationary trends were continuing at such a speed that budgeting was extremely hard.[162] On 31 March the Arts Council deficiency grant was agreed. Two and a half months later the Arts Council made an advance of £200,000 to pay off the accumulated deficit. It was a critical moment for Sadler's Wells at the Coliseum. Good work had ensured that despite the deficit, the company was worth saving.

A spirit of adventure was in the air and more traditions were being created. On 29 September 1971 the John Blatchley/Annena Stubbs modern-dress *Cavalleria rusticana* and *Pagliacci* located the protagonists in a contemporary Italian village. It proved to be the company's first 'scandal'. Literalist critics were irritated by details, such as a horse-drawn cart being represented by a car trailer.[163] Porter was also unenamoured, despite what he described as the fine opening when Rita Hunter exerted a powerful presence on a bare stage, soprano and tenor being held in pools of light. Mackerras, too, was critical of the production, writing to Blatchley to ask if anything could be done to make it look more like an Italian village. The singers and chorus were 'terribly pale' with 'too many blondes', he wrote, and it all looked as though it took place in Scandinavia.[164]

On 24 November the rescued *Coronation of Poppea* opened, with

Janet Baker singing the title role. Shawe-Taylor thought she sang and inflected her phrases so as to bring life to every scene in which she appeared.[165] Porter thought her Poppea was seldom playful and always hard-headed, her singing throughout 'trenchant, passionate, thrilling to hear'. Above all, she alone of the cast conveyed the meaning of the words.[166] For Stanley Sadie, however, Baker lacked 'tenderness', and emerged cool and unsensuous.

Shawe-Taylor pointed out that the familiarity with Monteverdi's idiom – to which Leppard had contributed so much since the time of the Glyndebourne production – had made the critical fraternity more censorious of his 'elaborate scoring, recomposition and cutting and transposition of material'. Transfer to the Coliseum had 'further blurred the impact of the vocal line and submerged the formal shapes in a rich sauce of string, harp and organ sonorities'.[167] The time had come, Sadie wrote, when it was no longer necessary to dress up baroque opera to make it acceptable to modern audiences.[168]

The board later regretted not having ensured more publicity for Baker, as houses were disappointing.[169] Nonetheless, Baker's association with Sadler's Wells, despite its slightly disappointing start, developed into an exciting and creative partnership. When she sang three performances of Marguerite in Berlioz's *Faust* in December 1971, Porter wrote of her 'combination of affecting presence, musical penetration, poignant utterance of the words, intensity of phrasing – as well as timbre, which was so eloquent, so passionate, and in all but the highest range so full and beautiful'. The orchestra under Mackerras went from strength to strength, and his reading gathered momentum, until it 'plunged into Pandoemonium with shattering effect'.[170] When Baker expressed her desire to continue working with the company, and Mackerras his wish to conduct more bel canto, the idea of *Maria Stuarda* emerged.[171] On 21 February Baker agreed to sing the role.

In December another new Sadler's Wells star made an impact in a revival of Wendy Toye's *Orpheus in the Underworld* – still fresh and inventive, if tending to vulgarity. Valerie Masterson was, in Milnes's words, an 'irresistible little blonde trollop of a Eurydice'.[172] It was Tracey who had spotted Masterson's talent and suggested she be brought on contract in March 1971, when she stood in for Lois McDonall in *Seraglio* rehearsals.

Reflecting on the hits and misses of the programme, Tracey wrote to Tom Hammond in December: 'Sometimes the whole team fits together beautifully and the end production is a delight; on other occasions it is all blood, toil, sweat and tears from start to finish and the result can be either triumph or disaster . . . the theatre is like that.'[173]

On 6 December Arlen was ill and could not attend the Arts Council meeting to discuss the problems of Sadler's Wells Opera.[174] After the meeting, Field informed Arlen that he had been appalled to hear David McKenna and the committee, after learning of an intimated increase of £70,000 from the Arts Council and £30,000 from the Greater London Council in 1972/3, once again 'express their old hopeless reaction and debate whether they should close down or not'. They had been, he wrote, adamant they could not cut costs, that they 'would not reduce the size of the company or orchestra and were reluctant to increase ticket prices'.[175]

In the midst of these battles, Stephen Arlen suddenly died of cancer, aged fifty-eight, on 19 January 1972. Tracey recalled the shock of his death. He was a 'big robust person – never been ill in his life – got cancer of the sarcophagus and just wasted away'. Harewood reflected that he probably worked himself to death getting Sadler's Wells to the Coliseum.[176]

It was a great sadness for the company. Arlen's contribution had been enormous, as had been his support for the artists. By the end of 1971, however, Mackerras had been seriously thinking of resigning. He recalled many years later that he and Arlen had 'disagreed on a number of things to do with repertory, and the way things were done, and of course he was the actual boss and the board sided with him most of the time – and then he tragically died. It was a fairly short illness and everybody was plunged into confusion.' Harewood recalled that Mackerras had actually asked him to take over from Arlen, as he could not 'get on with him at all'. Mackerras believed that Harewood was the right person to run Sadler's Wells. He had never met anybody who knew so much about opera and also had such impeccable credentials – something that he felt mattered in those days.[177] Harewood had responded that he would not try to depose Stephen Arlen. At the same time Arlen, according to Harewood, had been trying to remove Mackerras. Jack Donaldson, who was close to Arlen, had said to Harewood: 'You know if Stephen had lived we would probably have had to get rid of Charlie.' This would, Harewood said, 'have been wrong – not a matter of opinion – wrong'.[178]

Goodall was so distressed by Arlen's death that he was put under doctor's order to rest for three months and could not conduct the first night of *Rhinegold* on 1 March 1972. Mackerras gave up all his other commitments in order to take over. The production was a revelation to audiences and critics, who could understand every word and nuance of the work for the first time. Of the direction Peter Heyworth wrote: 'A clear-minded dramatic intelligence illuminates every crevice of this conversational saga and the characters in it are real, not merely because they are well thought-out and performed, but because they are part of an ensemble in which each is inextricably implicated in the actions of others, as are the themes in Wagner's score.'[179] Koltai's set with gleaming ribbons symbolised the Rhine and the reflecting oval shield hovered above the scene. Emile Belcourt's Loge and Derek Hammond Stroud's Alberich were singled out for praise for their diction and characterisation.

*Rhinegold* was a fitting memorial for Arlen, who had helped Sadler's Wells to develop into a major English ensemble company capable of casting a significant *Ring* cycle. However difficult the relationship between Arlen and Mackerras had been, between them they had ensured that the company was well prepared for what was to be the golden age of Sadler's Wells/ENO. The company included some remarkable singers, whose talents had been nurtured with an investment of time and opportunity – Hunter and Remedios in particular were singing better than ever before and in roles that might never have come their way in a different context. *The Ring*, when completed with *Siegfried* in 1973, would be ready for complete cycles; the limitations of Sadler's Wells were relegated to history; the teething problems of the Coliseum had been largely overcome; and for the time being the Arts Council and the Treasury had accepted that they were there to stay.

As the 1971/2 season drew to its close, audience attendance figures were averaging 75 per cent. They would have been 80 per cent but for *The Makropoulos Case* and *Kiss Me, Kate!*. *Rhinegold* had reached 97 per cent. At the same time, the Arts Council was being more helpful, promising a £253,153 supplementary grant to the existing grant of £865,000, provided it was furnished with detailed monthly statements and prior warnings of wage claims.[180]

Mackerras conducted *The Makropoulos Case* on 7 February. Alan Blyth wrote enthusiastically of the orchestra – 'the strings gleaming and the woodwind subtle and sensitive' – and, he added, 'the house was almost full and enthusiasm ran high'. Josephine Barstow perhaps suggested Emilia Marty's vulnerability even more than had Collier. Her voice was 'steady, cleanly tuned' and responded easily to the often severe demands the composer placed on it.[181] Blatchley's 1964 production stood up well to the test of time, he noted.

As Arlen would have wished, instead of a sombre memorial service there was a celebration of his life at the Coliseum in March 1972. Olivier sang merry songs in music-hall fashion and related anecdotes that had amused his dear friend, breaking down at the end with the words, 'Stevie, I loved him very much. He was a marvellous man, a wonderful partner, I shall miss him very much.'[182] Tracey wrote that Arlen had been known for his toughness and skill at administration but that he also had a visionary quality, which made him, in his opinion, an artist. For Tracey, Arlen was a man of unending ideas and not in the least interested in status symbols. 'He was one of the most intensely real and life-affirming human beings I have ever known.'[183]

# 8

# 1972–1975: English National Opera, 'A Genuine Music Theatre'

The sad and untimely death of Stephen Arlen resulted in the appointment as managing director of George Harewood, with whom Charles Mackerras enjoyed a closer and more constructive working relationship and under whom he was happy to remain as music director. At a meeting of the Trust on 10 April 1972, Harewood was unanimously thought to be by far the strongest candidate and it was decided that his appointment should be announced on 1 May. On his appointment to Sadler's Wells, Harewood immediately resigned from the Covent Garden Board. Ironically, although both Harewood and Charles Mackerras were more suited to, and might well have preferred, Covent Garden, their dedication and the compatibility of their outlooks resulted in a golden age for the company, as well as providing a distinct and worrying challenge to Covent Garden's supremacy.

Born in 1923, George Lascelles, 7th Earl of Harewood was a grandson of George V and son of Princess Mary and Henry Viscount Lascelles, 6th Earl of Harewood and a first cousin of the Queen. Opera had been his passion since his youth. A performance of *The Magic Flute* in English at Sadler's Wells in June 1940, with Joan Cross and David Lloyd, had left him, he recalled, 'in a state of pure delight at the grandeur of the performance and the glory of the work'. Harewood never forgot Cross bringing the reduced *Marriage of Figaro* to the hospital at Harewood House just before he joined the army in 1942, and she became a lifelong friend. His operatic experiences gave Harewood more excitement and pleasure than anything else, and from 1938 he knew that he wanted to work in an opera house, as he said, 'in *any* capacity'. During his time as director he never lost the feeling of magic for the theatre, and while at the Coliseum he continued to tremble 'with excitement and fear before any first night' with which he was concerned.[1]

During the war Harewood had served in Italy, where he went to

the San Carlo opera in Naples, before he was wounded and captured in June 1944. He was kept by the German army as a
*Prominente* prisoner of war – one with 'illustrious connections'.
From November of that year he was incarcerated in Colditz. After
being moved to various prisons, he was released in May 1945 and
brought back to England, where he went to Cambridge to read
English. He succeeded to the earldom in 1947. Three years later he
founded, with Richard Buckle, *Opera and Ballet* magazine, leaving
it – renamed as *Opera* – in the care of Harold Rosenthal when he
joined the staff of Covent Garden in 1953 as assistant manager. At
Covent Garden he was given the title of Controller of Opera
Planning by David Webster in 1959. From 1961 to 1965 he was the
Artistic Director at the Edinburgh Festival, launching his themed
programmes with a Schönberg festival.

Harewood believed that opera 'should partake of myth, truths
which concern us all and which we all understand – instincts and
emotions which belong to whole generations or nations'. In the
1970s opera houses were being derided as museums but, as far as he
was concerned, this was only true in the sense that they were 'full of
masterpieces which are worth interpreting for to-day and made real
in terms of contemporary anxieties, taboos and shibboleths'.[2]

Harewood's belief in the ensemble system was ideally suited to
Sadler's Wells. From 1953 to 1960, at Covent Garden, he had been
strongly in favour of the effort to build up both the ensemble and
the audience. His work at Sadler's Wells was to be aided and supported by Edmund Tracey, who became, as Harewood recalled, his
closest friend and colleague as well as an inspiration and sounding
board for his ideas. Tracey continued to work on repertoire and,
together with Harewood, ensured the sanctity of their maxim that
they absolutely must not lose 'the public for *Faust*'.[3]

Tracey continued to nurture and encourage singers and attend
rehearsals in order to ensure that their words were clearly audible.
Together, he and Harewood further developed the cohesion of the
ensemble, while at the same time developing the talents of individual members of the company. Home-grown stars, Harewood
believed, should be encouraged 'to move around the world a bit' as
it was neither possible nor advisable in the modern world of travel
and greater opportunities to keep all singers in permanent tow.
Although some of his singers sang only fifteen or so performances a

year, they still regarded themselves as members of a flourishing company that employed mainly British singers. What Harewood found 'completely and revoltingly unacceptable' was Herbert von Karajan's contention that the only possible future for opera would be festival opera that would transport great casts from one job to another. In a world of festival opera alone, Harewood asked, where were 'the poor devils going to learn their jobs in the future'?[4]

Mackerras and Harewood shared many operatic tastes, enjoyed working out programmes together and were determined to raise standards in the house, somewhat regardless of financial restraints. At the same time, Mackerras had now moderated his international Hamburg tastes and was more prepared to maintain Sadler's Wells traditions, especially that of the English language. The two men had great respect and affection for each other. Jeremy Caulton, Harewood's new assistant, later recalled Harewood's infectious pleasure as he observed Mackerras rehearsing *Gloriana* in August. Beaming, he told Caulton that he thought they had 'the best music director in the world – a man unique in his range and brilliance'.[5]

When Harewood arrived at the Sadler's Wells company, now installed at the Coliseum, plans were already well advanced for Janet Baker to sing Donizetti's *Mary Stuart*, as were two complete *Ring* cycles, *Katya Kabanova* and *Manon* and Hans Werner Henze's *The Bassarids*. On 24 May Harewood received a long letter from Henze, who expressed his delight that his 'favourite audience' would come to know his work, and to suggest that he direct *The Bassarids* himself.[6] After *The Ring*, Mackerras was determined that the company should tackle another large project and was considering an uncut version of *Don Carlos* translated by Andrew Porter. The Covent Garden production, he pointed out, was very old and, except with the 'common property' works like *Traviata*, there had as yet been very few clashes of repertoire.[7]

The previously unconvinced Opera Subcommittee was soon persuaded by Harewood and Mackerras that more contemporary work should be produced by the company. Their joint impact was immediately felt when Harewood told the Opera Subcommittee on 15 May that contrary to previous policy, he believed it was an ideal opportunity to do 'a really modern work'. He suggested Penderecki's *The Devils*, Zimmermann's *Soldiers* or *Bomarzo* by Ginastera. When committee members argued that they were already committed to doing *The Bassarids*, Harewood replied that the casting of *Bassarids* could not be hurried and that 'certain modern works should be done while their impact is still fresh'.[8]

Mackerras later recalled that the Opera Subcommittee was not particularly interested in contemporary works, although he conceded that he and Harewood had not always made the right choices, citing *Bomarzo* as one that had not been a great success.[9] Harewood, on the other hand, thought the committee was more open to suggestion, since its members were 'very bright' and its chairman, Professor Bernard Williams, was 'one of the most intelligent men in England and a fine guide who loved opera'. Also on the Opera Subcommittee was the principal of the Royal Academy of Music, Anthony Lewis, who, although he was liable to fall asleep during meetings, was also a wise adviser. The discussion, Harewood explained, if not quite amongst equals, was amongst knowledgeable people. When asked if his Trust or committee was a terrible nuisance, Harewood would say: 'If I can't persuade people who are on our side that something is a good idea, maybe it isn't.'[10]

Harewood strongly supported Mackerras's plan of September 1971 to produce *Der Rosenkavalier*, which had not been sung in English since the 1957/8 season. It would, he believed, be a tremendous encouragement to both singers and orchestra. Moreover, it would provide a significant new challenge for the orchestra after the great success of *The Mastersingers* and *The Ring*. When the Opera Subcommittee demurred at the prospect of potential opposition from Covent Garden, Mackerras tried to reassure them that there was room for more than one production of the main repertory pieces, and agreed to visit John Tooley to discuss the problem.[11]

At the same time Harewood enlisted the help of Jack Donaldson, a member of both the Sadler's Wells and Covent Garden boards whom Harewood considered a helpful and highly intelligent colleague, to overcome potential opposition from Covent Garden.[12] Since Harewood felt that Covent Garden always objected to anything that Sadler's Wells suggested, he persuaded Donaldson that they should confront John Tooley together in the Covent Garden crush bar during a performance. This they did, Donaldson remarking to Tooley: 'John – they would like to do *Der Rosenkavalier* at the Coliseum – I don't think we would have the faintest objection at Covent Garden,' adding: 'It would be in English, it would be totally different. You would agree, wouldn't you?' To Harewood's amusement, the tactic worked: Tooley at first prevaricated and then agreed, he later recalled.[13] On 24 July 1972 the Opera Sub-committee learnt that *Der Rosenkavalier* could go ahead in the 1974/5 season as Covent Garden had dropped it.[14]

Harewood's amusement at Tooley's discomfiture was not only the consequence of his having been passed over in favour of Tooley for the position of general director at Covent Garden in 1970, it also reflected the growing rivalry between the houses, exacerbated by Lord Drogheda's innate antipathy to Sadler's Wells. It had been a different matter when the company had been at Rosebery Avenue, Mackerras recalled, but Tooley and the Covent Garden Board did not take kindly to the fact that just down the road there was now competition that was getting keener all the time. Mackerras, who was also conducting regularly at Covent Garden, sensed that they felt threatened. *Der Rosenkavalier* was, he said, 'a big, big opera, and John got very jealous of the fact that we were doing these big operas'.[15]

The peripatetic nature of Mackerras's career was the one disadvantage in his directorship. Harewood tried to persuade him to spend more time at the Coliseum, offering him a higher salary and even seeking his wife Judy's help, but he continued to conduct regularly both abroad and at Covent Garden, including *Aida* with Leontyne Price in March 1973 and, in 1974, *A Midsummer Night's Dream* and *Otello* with Kiri te Kanawa.[16] At least once a year he conducted in Paris and also at the Met, Chicago and Houston. Many years later, Mackerras recalled with a smile, 'there was one famous week [in June 1973] when I conducted *Il trovatore* at three different places in the same week: Covent Garden, on tour in Liverpool and then in Paris' – Riccardo Muti having walked out on the Paris production at the last minute.[17] Despite his absences, Mackerras's work with and ambition for the company formed the cornerstone of its improvement at this time.

Harewood's first season, 1972/3, included four extraordinary new ensemble productions. The first was *Il trovatore* in August 1972, conducted by Mackerras, who gave a revelatory and 'vivid account of the score', according to Andrew Porter.[18] It was directed by John Copley and translated by Tom Hammond, with Rita Hunter as Leonora and Norman Bailey as Luna. Hunter was the star of the evening, her devoted followers in the house greeting her performance with clamorous enthusiasm. Porter was also enraptured by Hunter, commenting on her 'heroic voice' – used with 'fleetness, lightness and delicacy' and yet with the requisite 'touch of metal', which he found very affecting. He also admired her 'facility in passages, turns, and *gruppetti*, and the gentle, delicate emission of the floating phrases of the last act', as well as her 'instinctive feeling for the musical line and dramatic expression'. It was Hunter's unaffected dignity, directness and sincerity that had made her a favourite of the Sadler's Wells audience. Harewood himself was quite carried away, years afterwards recalling Hunter's early performances: 'She did it better than I have ever heard it sung by anyone, including Leontyne Price.'[19]

In addition to its musical qualities, good design and direction lay behind the production's success. William Mann described Lazaridis's 'imposing monumental sets, smoky clouds, falling snow, extempore gypsy tents' and its 'massive stone walls, gold-glinting costumes, a strong sensation of Velásquez, with spectacle built in'.[20] Porter found Copley's production 'sensible, vigorous and free from nonsense'.[21]

In the era before the German-inspired *Konzeptregie*, or concept-based direction, came to dominate in opera, and at a time when convincing acting by singers was not a reliable commodity, Copley was greatly appreciated by the artists with whom he worked, as well as by his audiences. Colin Davis appreciated how thoroughly Copley knew the operas,[22] and Mackerras later described him as a marvellous director who followed in the tradition of Tyrone Guthrie at Sadler's Wells, and to some extent Dennis Arundell, and 'made these talented *singers* but less talented *actors, act*'.[23] Copley, who was extremely busy during 1972 at Covent Garden, where he was associate resident producer after Peter Hall's abrupt departure, was the first to admit that he approached direction with a ground plan rather than a concept.[24] He approached *Il trovatore* in an unsophisticated way, telling John Higgins in *The Times* that the music demanded 'the wild, swashbuckling energy of an Errol Flynn picture of the forties'. There were certain Verdi operas that 'simply had to be done' and could not be 'interpreted'.[25] It was another triumph for Sadler's Wells, and Trust chairman David McKenna congratulated Harewood on the excellent start to the 1972/3 season.[26]

\*

Although the 1970s were a time of great artistic development at the Coliseum, it was also a period of increasingly serious inflation and widespread industrial unrest, to both of which the company was highly vulnerable. Union disputes were to bedevil Harewood's time and cause as much disruption to the company as they did throughout the country. The Heath government introduced value added tax in the 1973 budget, as a prelude to joining the EEC, and made an undertaking not to allow the prices of nationalised industries' products to rise by more than 5 per cent. On 17 October the European Communities Act, after being passed in Parliament by eight votes, received royal assent.

At the end of the 1971 Parliament, the government had tabled a trade-union reform bill repealing all previous legislation, some of it going back a hundred years. It aimed at the registration of the unions, reducing the power of the national executives and transferring it to the rank and file. Based on the belief that individual workers did not want to strike, the bill gave workers the right not to join a trade union, as well as the right to appeal against unfair dismissal should their opposition to the union result in their losing their job. There was also to be a ninety-day cooling-off period before strikes. The TUC opposed the legislation and many unions refused to register. On 18 February 1972 the government met the miners' full claim of a 22 per cent wage increase while inflation was at 10 per cent, which led to similar demands from other unions. By the autumn inflation had reached 20 per cent. On 26 September the government brought in an anti-inflation programme comprising a pay and price freeze.

Such was the background to the worsening industrial relations at the Coliseum in the early 1970s. The introduction in 1971 of a working week of three fifteen-and-a-half-hour shifts had resulted in vastly increased overtime, and costs were rapidly escalating. Wage negotiations for the tour were proving particularly problematic. John Snape, the new finance director, had been in charge of the union negotiations since January 1972. From January to March he had tried to negotiate all-inclusive weekly salaries of £85 to £110 for the tour. When the union refused, McKenna, interceding at the eleventh hour, gave in, with the result that salaries averaged £150 a week.[27]

In May the cancellation of the Bolshoi/Kirov season was seen by management as an opportunity to terminate the employment of twenty-two members of staff, some of whom were described as militants. After objection from the union, the notices of the men were suspended for two weeks while the union prepared suggestions for savings.[28] At a meeting on 8 June Harewood met the NATTKE national officer, James Lascelles. Mackerras remembered the meeting: 'George said quite jovially: "I believe we have a name in common," to which Lascelles had replied, "Yes. I think it's the only thing we have in common."' The union regarded Lord Harewood as a 'toff', Mackerras commented.[29] The men agreed to short-term efforts to make savings and agreed to try to make a long-term agreement if the twenty-two employees were not made redundant. The board decided that it was essential to maintain good relations and agreed to reinstate them on condition that negotiations would be concluded as soon as possible.[30]

While the negotiations dragged on, Harewood commissioned an independent survey from the management consultants Urwick and Orr in August. Gerard Wood, who prepared the report, did not recommend a major change. The stage staff wanted to keep the existing roster, he pointed out, and 'were not going to let it go without a fight'. It was known that there was 'moonlighting down the road'. He commented that the negotiations were being hampered by mistrust between the stage staff and the union, which dated back to 1970, but that his own meetings had been conducted in a friendly atmosphere, and that the situation could be kept in check by pursuing a joint policy with the other grant-aided companies.[31]

One positive result of the exercise was that Wood was taken on by the company as a part-time adviser on personnel matters. The new Trust chairman Kenneth Robinson – whom Harewood described as a 'wonderful' and extremely nice man who liked opera but did not interfere – admitted to the Arts Council that Sadler's Wells had appreciated, rather belatedly, that personnel matters were regarded as almost a part-time activity by members of senior management, who were very overburdened with their normal jobs.[32] Thereafter Wood and Rupert Rhymes, the director of administration, conducted all the union negotiations together. Unfortunately for Sadler's Wells' industrial relations, Rhymes was a stickler for protocol and, as Harewood's new assistant Jeremy Caulton recalled, 'mutual antagonism seemed to be the norm between Rhymes and NATTKE'.[33]

Inflation was hitting the company hard. Harewood was concerned about the inadequate salaries of some staff members, but when the 1973/4 budget was being discussed in the autumn of 1972, it became clear that it was going to be extremely difficult to meet any increases. He remained insistent, however, that money would have to be found. The chorus was also asking for a review because of the exceptional increase in the cost of living during 1971/2.[34]

Negotiations with NATTKE continued, and in October the Trust realised that if the current union demands were met in full they would cost £36,000 a year. Harewood persuaded the stage staff to work on *War and Peace* without prejudice to the negotiations after the Trust decided not to take a firm stand on Sunday working. The English premiere of the work thus took place as planned on 11 October.[35]

*War and Peace* was one of the outstanding successes of the era. Virtually unknown in Britain, where it was considered to be late Prokofiev and therefore 'Soviet', it had been critically out of favour. The Sadler's Wells production directed by Colin Graham and conducted by David Lloyd-Jones resulted in a major reassessment of the work. During a visit to Russia in 1965, Graham had fallen in love with it and persuaded Arlen to stage it. In the programme notes Graham described his and Margaret Harris's non-realistic approach to the design, which consisted of a central raked platform, back-projections with tiered trolleys for the chorus and a front-drop screen on which projected inscriptions announced the next scene.

*War and Peace* was universally acclaimed by the critics, who were surprised by the dramatic power of the work and impressed by the company's boldness and skill in putting on such an epic production. Lloyd-Jones was especially praised for a remarkable achievement in preparing singers, chorus and orchestra. The cast of ninety named characters was covered by the company, with many doubling or trebling roles and with only four extra artists engaged. Both the ballroom and battle scenes, with more than 150 people on stage, were handled with great dexterity by Graham. So too were the characterisations of the individuals in the intimate moments, using minimal props, combined with realistic movement.

*War and Peace* was a remarkable ensemble effort. The cast included Josephine Barstow, perfect as Natasha, as was Kenneth Woollam as Pierre; Tom McDonnell – an Australian baritone – was a handsome Andrei and John Brecknock, Anatole. Norman Bailey, upon whose involvement Harewood had insisted, dominated the performance as Kutuzov. The first chorus, with everyone lined up on the apron, 'knocked you back in your seat', Anne Evans recalled.[36]

There were also successful revivals at the start of the season. David Ward returned to the company that had launched his career to sing Bluebeard in a distinguished performance of the Byam Shaw *Duke Bluebeard's Castle* and the St-Denis *Oedipus Rex* under Mackerras's direction on 20 September.[37] Although the double bill had been critically welcomed, the theatre was depressingly empty. Nevertheless, average attendance was 82 per cent capacity when *The Ring* and Copley's *Carmen* were included. On 16 October Professor Bernard Williams felt that the company could be justly proud of its achievements. He also commented, as had many critics, on how far the company had come since they had left Rosebery Avenue.[38]

Management was considering the further development of operetta as a way of easing the pressure on the company and giving the public some more popular repertoire.[39] In December *The Merry Widow*, with lyrics by Christopher Hassall and dialogue by John Cox, was added to the repertory. Once again, most of the critics enjoyed the production and praised Cox's faithfulness to Lehár, as well as a cast that included Lorna Haywood's beautifully sung Hanna Glawari and John Wakefield's charismatic Danilo. Although it did well at the box office, Tracey thought it unattractive and asked Cox to improve it.[40] Milnes later recalled that budget cuts had meant there was no staircase down which the Widow could make an impressive entry.

Arthur Jacobs welcomed the revival of the more successful 1966 Byam Shaw *Die Fledermaus* on 20 December, when Valerie Masterson was a 'wholly charming Adele, at once pert and sympathetic'.[41] Having been brought up on Gilbert and Sullivan at the D'Oyly Carte, she was another precious asset for Sadler's Wells. 'You could always hear what Valerie sang,' Mackerras said, 'even when she was singing coloratura as Constanze in *Entführung*.'[42]

The search for an operetta production that would consistently fill the 2,354-seat Coliseum proved much more elusive than it had at the 1,499-seat Sadler's Wells, where such shows as *Iolanthe* and the 1958 *Merry Widow* had rarely disappointed. Over the next twenty years, the only operetta that could be revived on a regular basis was the Byam Shaw *Fledermaus*. It was also some time before the company struck gold again, with Jonathan Miller's *Mikado* in 1986. In the mid-1970s, there was still wholehearted opposition from Donaldson and Williams on the board to the company doing more Gilbert and Sullivan. However, in June 1975 the Opera Committee learnt that Mackerras was a keen advocate of Gilbert and Sullivan, not least because of the current successful tour to Vienna of Cox's 1969 *Patience*. 'It exports well', he argued, 'and we do it well.' The committee was still not convinced, however, discussing with varying degrees of gloom *Ruddigore, Yeomen, Pirates, Pinafore, Mikado* and *Princess Ida*. Byam Shaw pointed out that the continental audiences particularly liked the Gilbert and Sullivan pieces 'where the British made fun of their own traditions and idiosyncrasies'.[43]

The third great new production of the season was *Siegfried*, which completed the *Ring* cycle on 8 February 1973. The company members had grown impressively into their Wagnerian roles: Anne Collins's Erda, Gregory Dempsey's Mime and Derek Hammond Stroud's Alberich. Remedios acknowledged Goodall's responsibility for his emergence as a fine Wagner tenor and spoke of his meticulousness in rehearsal as well as his gift for making performers give totally committed performances: 'He makes you want to scrub the floor if you sing badly in rehearsal – when you sing on stage you are utterly confident. Without him I would never have sung Wagner; nobody had any confidence in me being a Wagner tenor until he chose me for Walter in *Meistersinger*. He gives me the confidence of a colossus.'[44]

The writer and broadcaster Bryan Magee was almost wordless with admiration for Remedios and Hunter, who had, he wrote, during their fifteen years with the Sadler's Wells company worked their way up 'from the mediocrities of Rosebery Avenue at its greyest to the peaks of international acclaim'. It had been done, he pointed out, by 'sustained, unglamorous application to professional tasks – fifteen years' hard slog'. With its *Ring* and other productions reaching a standard of which no opera house in the world would feel ashamed, the company, he declared, had come of age and should no longer be judged in the light of its less illustrious past but by the standards of its present maturity.[45]

There was a great sense of progress within the company. While preparing the new version of *Don Carlos*, Porter was in correspondence with Tracey. On 5 January he wrote some 'loving and grateful words' about the plans and achievements of Sadler's Wells 'and all the joy and excitement it provides' for all who cared about opera. Tracey responded that it had indeed been a 'very exciting period', with 'a marvellous feeling in the company of artistic unity and purpose'.[46]

Artistic achievement was built on a system of ambitious planning followed by a somewhat optimistic counting of cost. It was not, however, a system that was to last indefinitely, as governments were increasingly forced to find ways to counter inflation. The price-restraint policy instituted by Heath's Chancellor of the Exchequer, Anthony Barber, had been giving cause for concern to Sadler's Wells as it entailed a freeze on ticket prices. Harewood told the Finance and General Purposes Committee of 26 October 1972 that in order to compensate for the loss of revenue, management would have to look into reducing production expenditure. Mackerras, however, continued to press for further expansion, arguing that the policy of sacrificing tight control over expenditure rather than reducing the number of new productions had paid dividends.[47]

Inflation hit not only wages and labour costs but also the production side of the company very hard indeed, as Tracey pointed out on 22 November. If the previous year's *Lohengrin* set had cost £14,000, it would cost £28,000 in the current year. The designer of *La traviata*, David Walker, was prepared to dispense with a solid construction and make do with painted sets, but even these came in at £7,000 more than the budget. *Traviata* must have four sets, Tracey insisted, was a period piece and must look pretty.[48]

Despite the economies, *La traviata*, the final new production of Harewood's first season, was warmly received when it opened on 14 March 1973. It was translated by Edmund Tracey and directed by Copley with Charles Bristow's lighting. Critics commented on the clarity and truthfulness of the direction and the setting in *demi-monde* Paris, and on the naturalness of the acting of the entire ensemble. Stanley Sadie, unaware of Walker's efforts to economise on the sets and costumes, reported the curtain rising on a 'breath-taking ensemble of browns, russets, blacks and golds'.[49] The contrast with Violetta's elegant but lived-in country retreat was also noted. Copley's penchant for 'photographic realism'[50] was not yet held against him, and the authenticity of the whole was appreciated and enjoyed.

Nicholas Braithwaite conducted with empathy and consideration for his singers. Josephine Barstow won her audience over with her beauty and with the intensity and conviction of her acting. Copley, she later recalled, enabled her to understand every thought of Violetta from beginning to end.[51] For his part, Copley was inspired by the 'terribly high' standards he found at the Coliseum with such artists as Barstow, Baker, Bailey and Brecknock, and above all Mackerras himself. For fourteen years he prepared a new production at both houses each season, but it was his work at Sadler's Wells that he enjoyed most.[52]

The Harewood/Mackerras team was giving Covent Garden a good run for its money at a time when their music director, Colin Davis, had not yet established his authority and reputation, and when vehicles for star singers did not always live up to expectations. The abrupt departure of Peter Hall, who was to have been Covent Garden's artistic director, had not only left Davis anxious and unhappy but had also delayed Covent Garden's new *Ring* while negotiations with Hall's replacement Götz Friedrich were being pursued. Sadler's Wells, however, was ready to present a complete cycle from 31 July to 4 August 1973. Tracey, in the illustrated accompanying booklet, wrote: 'These were the founder-members of a closely knit group of artists, most of them resident, who gradually learnt to develop a coherent and flexible house-style; singing in English to an English speaking audience and giving Wagner the dramatist equal due with Wagner the composer.'

William Mann watched fascinated as Koltai's settings evolved through the cycle. He felt they conveyed the magic of *The Ring*'s events, 'the omnipresent mystery of the gold on the bed of the river, the intangible grandeur of Valhalla, the repressive descent of the Nibelheim ceiling as the orchestra thunders forth the theme of sub-jugation, even the flashes of light reflected into thin air from the per-spex horns on Wotan's helmet'. He also praised the steady improvement of the orchestral playing since *The Ring* had been launched in 1970.[53] Words were audible, and the exchanges between characters endlessly absorbing for an attentive and thunderously appreciative audience. Philip Hope-Wallace thought Bailey's farewell to Brünnhilde 'crowned a noble interpretation with a warmth of voice and glow of feeling recalling the greatest Wotans'.[54]

*Siegfried* was performed on 8 August, and three days later *Twilight of the Gods*. On 14 August Mackerras conducted an inter-cycle performance of *The Valkyrie*, giving the music dramatic tension and a natural, sensuously lyrical flow.[55] For four years *The Ring* had occupied the minds and feelings of the company, John Blatchley said in an interview. It was their 'corporate achievement'.[56]

When Mackerras's new edition of *Katya Kabanova* received its first performance on 12 September, William Mann pointed out that the Sadler's Wells orchestra had played more Janáček than 'any band outside Brno' and could claim to have developed 'an English-speaking Janáček style'. Mackerras had based his edition on the composer's own scarcely decipherable autographs, which had a 'keener, more telling edge' as well as two unfamiliar interludes, Porter noted.[57]

Lazaridis's permanent set for *Katya* was a sharply raked stage of duckboards with light projections. Within it, Blatchley directed with the right sense of urgency and a scrupulous attention to character detail and balance. He elicited fine performances from his artists, Lorna Haywood's Katya displaying vocal accomplishment as well as dramatic physical intensity. Mann described Kenneth Woollam's Boris as 'a possible object of passion' and wrote that Kabanicha provided an 'imposing and villainous vehicle' for Sylvia Fisher's prowess as a singing actress.

Porter saw *Katya* as one of the great achievements of Sadler's Wells. It was a measure of the company's growth in its ampler home. Mackerras's conducting was a 'miracle of eloquence and beauty, with spellbinding judgement of accent, colour, and speed'. Morale was high and Sadler's Wells gave an impression of a company 'sure of its director, buoyant in heart, and confident in all it does'.

While the Sadler's Wells company was reaching increasingly high standards, economic and social upheaval in the country had been growing ever more threatening. In 1973 the miners had gone on strike for more money and improved working conditions, with their leader Arthur Scargill determined to bring down the Heath government. After the October 1973 war in the Middle East, the price of oil went from $15 to $56 a barrel, later touching $100. On 1 January 1974 Edward Heath reverted to the Emergency Powers Act of 1920, under which he announced a three-day working week. On 7 February Parliament was dissolved, and Labour won the general election by a narrow margin on 4 March. Harold Wilson, in his second premiership, which lasted until April 1976, could only react to events as they piled up against him. The miners' strike was settled by giving in to their demands. Michael Foot, who was Secretary of State for Employment, gave what amounted to carte blanche to the trade-union movement, and annual inflation rapidly approached 20 per cent. Spending continued to rise and the economy was in free fall.

To add to Sadler's Wells' own problems there had been a fire at its Dalgleish Street storage facility on 12 April 1973, which destroyed 3,000 costumes from thirty productions. The cost of the fire was estimated at £200,000, of which only £70,000 was covered by insurance. Although Tooley offered Covent Garden's *Masked Ball* costumes, by the autumn the company was feeling the effects of the loss and was forced to buy some old costumes from the RSC in November.

Bravely the company pressed on with its policy of presenting new work in serious productions. *The Devils of Loudun* by Krzysztof Penderecki, adapted from John Whiting's play, was premiered on 1 November 1973. It was directed by John Dexter and conducted by its strong advocate, Nicholas Braithwaite, who described it both as 'an emotional thumb screw' and as 'effect music'.[58] William Mann applauded Sadler's Wells for its progressive policy in bringing foreign works to London. *The Devils of Loudun* was, he suggested, to be approached as 'a modern music drama of inexorable fate, not as an opera of vocal display', although Barstow's Jeanne had two extended arias of 'great lyrical beauty and expressive power'.[59] Porter, however, described the music as 'sonic décor' which had lost much of the coherence of Whiting's play without adding musical elucidation.[60] The box office was disappointing, as was that of a revival of Richard Rodney Bennett's *The Mines of Sulphur*.

In December Mackerras was back in London, after a tour in Australia, for the long-planned production of Donizetti's *Mary Stuart* directed by John Copley, with Janet Baker as Mary and Pauline Tinsley as Elizabeth. Tracey and Harewood had both believed for some time that *Mary Stuart* would be a suitable vehicle for Baker both vocally and dramatically.[61] Their faith was rewarded, although a few critics expressed ambivalence about both the merits of the music and Baker's vocal suitability for the role. There was a generally positive reaction to Sadler's Wells once again staging a little-known work, Hope-Wallace deeming it 'another smash hit for Sadler's Wells opera'.[62] Andrew Porter's four long columns in the *Financial Times* on 17 December analysed both the proliferation of Donizetti productions as well as the downward transposition of some of the music for Baker. He pointed out that what could look thin and dull on the page could prove thrilling in the theatre and, while he felt that Baker was not a natural for this 'far-flung kind of vocal writing', he was nonetheless overwhelmed by 'the intensity of her delivery and acting, the rich emotional identification with the character, the quick phrase-by-phrase sentience, the individual and affecting beauty of the timbre and the beauty of appearance and demeanour'. Baker's ability to create a feeling of unity between stage and audience affected even the most seasoned critics and delighted and moved all those who heard her. Copley was praised for his skill in creating a real interplay between the characters: Tinsley's awe-inspiring Elizabeth, Keith Erwen's ardent Leicester and Don Garrard's sonorous Talbot, Earl of Shrewsbury.[63]

Graham's *Madam Butterfly* on 28 February 1974 was a convincing addition to the repertoire and continued to be performed for many years with different casts. Graham had made a study of Japanese theatre and used the Japanese adviser Michiko Aoki together with designer John Fraser to present a production authentic in its visual details and reduced to its essence. David Lloyd-Jones conducted with splendid energy and Ava June was a touching Butterfly.[64]

In early 1974 Mackerras gave notice of his intention to resign from Sadler's Wells at the end of 1976 and thereafter to be its principal guest conductor. He intended to take up a completely international freelance career, conducting in Berlin, Vienna, New York and San

Francisco, as well as his native Australia. Mackerras's new contract stipulated that after 30 June 1975 he would be available to Sadler's Wells for a minimum of thirty-five and a maximum of forty-five performances.[65]

There were those who believed that there was a possibility that Mackerras might take over Covent Garden's music directorship. Although he later said that he was never actually offered the position, Covent Garden's board had indeed been considering the idea of replacing their own music director, Colin Davis, since relations between Davis and the board had become severely strained. Davis was also getting a poor press at the time. In April he complained to his chairman, Lord Drogheda, that in the eyes of the critics 'Sadler's Wells can do no wrong, and we no right'. Certainly this marked the beginning of a trend whereby if one house was seen to be successful, the other was more heavily criticised in the press. In October 1974, however, the Covent Garden Board decided to renew Davis's contract. Mackerras told the journalist Michael White in 2005 that he nearly got the job at Covent Garden twice. The first, he recalled, was after Solti, when Drogheda had been keen on his appointment, but at that time he had only just been made music director at the Wells, and it would have been awkward for him to leave. He wondered if other factors had influenced the board. 'Maybe I am wrong,' he mused, 'but I suspect that in those days I wasn't thought to be enough of a gentleman for Covent Garden.' Many years later it was clear that Mackerras, despite his success at both English National Opera and Welsh National Opera, regretted this lacuna in his career, telling the author: 'I repeat that I still would have preferred to have been at Covent Garden.' The best thing of all, he added, 'would have been to have George in charge at Covent Garden'.

Having failed to dissuade Mackerras from retiring in the new year, Harewood approached Charles Groves to take over.* Groves had greatly impressed Harewood and Tracey with his sangfroid during rehearsals for *The Story of Vasco* in the bitter late winter just

---

* Groves had accompanied choral rehearsals under Toscanini for Brahms's *German Requiem* in 1937. He had played the piano for opera before the war, including the Maggie Teyte *Manon* for the BBC. In 1944 he became the conductor of the BBC Northern Orchestra until 1951, when he left to become the music director of the Bournemouth Municipal (later Symphony) Orchestra.

after the three-day week, when rehearsing was 'sheer misery' because there was no heating and light. Groves, Harewood recalled, had managed the situation beautifully, keeping the orchestra in good temper and everybody on an even keel with extra breaks. This was a man, they thought, who could deal with a crisis. When they approached him, Harewood recalled, 'he was frightfully pleased; longed to do it and he came'.[66] Groves was to start in January 1977.

*The Story of Vasco* was not more warmly received on 13 March 1974 than *The Devils of Loudun* had been. It was composed by Gordon Crosse with a libretto based on Ted Hughes's English version of *L'Histoire de Vasco* by Georges Schehadé. It was produced by Michael Elliott and Richard Negri, who also designed it. Some critics felt that the theme of the futility of war was not so relevant or controversial in 1974 as it had been when the Vietnam War was raging in 1965, at which time the commission had been supported by a Gulbenkian grant. The libretto was criticised as 'weak and ineffective', although much of the music was individual and powerful.[67] It was a constant challenge for Sadler's Wells to commission and produce new work of high musical quality with good libretti. Donaldson told the Opera Subcommittee on 12 March that Sadler's Wells should restrain, if necessary, composers from embarking on unsuitable subjects.[68]

Although he was planning to give up the music directorship, Mackerras's rigorous musical standards, together with the discovery, nurturing and keeping together of singers of differing talents and skills, lay behind the fine work of Sadler's Wells in the early 1970s. In March 1974 a *Katya* revival was received with enormous enthusiasm by critics and public alike. The orchestral playing, Blyth wrote, was of a 'gleaming, sumptuous nature exceptional even from this much-improved pit, seconding the tale of personal anguish and bliss on stage in a heart-rending manner'. Lorna Haywood was 'the complete Katya by virtue of her better focused, warmer vocal line'. Blyth delighted in what he described as the growing confidence of the singers and players under Mackerras's enthusiastic and urgent lead.[69]

Anne Evans was yet another outstanding singer to become a star from within the company set-up. On 4 September 1973 she had taken on the role of Violetta under Mackerras. He later recalled that Evans had started as a semi-light soprano, who grew into a great dramatic soprano. She never had the huge, loud voice that Birgit Nilsson had, but she became a 'truly great Isolde and Brünnhilde'.[70] Hope-Wallace thought she sang Violetta 'most affectingly, with much feeling for the big phrases, which she fills out nobly'.[71] She was also a ravishing Rosalinda in November 1973 in *Die Fledermaus* with Valerie Masterson, who was a pert Adele with impeccable diction.[72] One of Evans's finest achievements was the Marschallin in 1975.

The baritone Derek Hammond Stroud's career was also developing in a wide repertoire. In March 1975 he ranged from a 'cringing, hectoring, malevolent, ultimately sympathetic Alberich' in *Rhinegold* to a 'mincing poseur of a Bunthorne' in *Patience*.[73] Not only could Sadler's Wells employ the right singers for the roles but its stars were gaining international reputations. Rita Hunter was reaching a pitch of international success and it was felt that she should be given vehicles suitable for her status.[74] The company principals were 'being watched and nurtured', recalled Barstow, who loved Harewood and felt she owed a huge debt of gratitude to him.[75]

The box office reflected the company's strength, with an average of 80 per cent attendance, despite *Katya*'s 67 per cent, *Sulphur*'s 55 per cent and *The Devils*' 54 per cent.[76] The Trust recorded a very satisfactory state of affairs, with performances often playing to capacity.[77] Rhymes felt that the company's image had been established since the move, due to both the high quality of its product and the hard and careful work of everyone concerned.[78]

The achievements of the box office did not improve the company's financial situation and in late March there were serious problems of liquidity. On 22 March John Snape asked Anthony Field, finance director of the Arts Council, for £100,000 on account, which was accepted.[79] It was a hand-to-mouth existence. In a letter of 5 April Harewood informed Field that the company would reach a £36,000 deficit if the 12.2 per cent increase in subsidy in the 1974/5 budget were adhered to. It was, he said, totally unrealistic. The answer – that it was a difficult year for everyone – did nothing to allay his concern. The Arts Council itself was only receiving an 8.3 per cent increase, when the increase in the cost-of-living index was 13.6 per cent.

In order to pay the summer salaries, Nicholas Payne sent Snape a further £100,000 advance on 30 May.[80] Harewood's hopes of taking *La Belle Hélène* to the Edinburgh Festival were dashed and in June he wrote to the festival director, Peter Diamand, to say how disappointed they were not to be able to go to Edinburgh. In reply, Diamand pointed out the irony of foreign companies being subsidised to visit Edinburgh while Sadler's Wells could not afford the journey from London.[81]

On 13 August the proposed Goodall *Tristan* had to be shelved as it was too expensive and it was also too soon after the Covent Garden revival of the Peter Hall production. It was also thought that Remedios and Hunter might not be able to carry it off.

Ever since the move to the Coliseum in 1968, a decision about the company's new title had been thwarted, largely due to Covent Garden's opposition. The Trust thought that the most suitable title would be the National Opera Company, as Sadler's Wells had identical aims in opera as the National Theatre – encouraging British playwrights, composers and artists, and presenting a broad repertory based on the classics. The National Opera remained the preferred title during discussions in May and June 1971, although 'British National Opera' was also considered acceptable by the Trust.[82] Arlen was ill and had not attended the meeting on 17 May at which the Opera Committee learnt that Covent Garden was opposed to the British National Opera title.[83]

The battle was long drawn-out. The Trust could see no reason for any objection to the 'National Opera', arguing that Sadler's Wells was the oldest established opera company in the country and that it forswore the use of any singers other than those who were British or Commonwealth. It performed its work in English, with 40 per cent of its performances outside London. Covent Garden's name was such, they argued, that it could not but be read 'as the senior establishment'.[84] When consulted, neither Scottish Opera nor Welsh National Opera objected to the title, but Drogheda continued to be obstructive.[85] Then, on 15 November, the Trust learnt that the Arts Council themselves had expressed opposition to the word 'National' appearing in the name.[86] So few people had responded to a Sadler's Wells audience survey that although the consensus had been for a title including 'British' or 'National', the board felt that it did not help their cause.[87]

After Arlen's death, on 6 March 1972 the Trust had passed a

formal resolution to change the name to National Opera, despite the obdurate opposition from Covent Garden and the Arts Council. McKenna, however, was instructed by the Arts Council to take the matter up directly with the Department of Trade and Industry.[88] In September Tracey provided further ammunition in defence of the word 'National'. Sadler's Wells collected 'a wide spectrum of the population: young, middle aged, old; novices and experienced veterans; students in jeans and "top people" in dinner jackets – sometimes, indeed, "top people" in jeans and students in dinner jackets'. As a result audiences were growing all the time, especially the young.[89] The Minister for the Arts, Lord Eccles, and John Davies, the Minister for Trade and Industry, however, were against anything with the word 'National' in it.* Although they argued that they were concerned that there had not been sufficient consultation, it was clear that the pressure was coming from the Covent Garden Board.[90]

Covent Garden had powerful allies, including a battalion of past and present ministers. On 29 December 1972 Snape was informed that Geoffrey Howe, the new Secretary of State for Trade and Consumer Affairs, had decided that the proposed change of name to the National Opera Company could not be approved since the word 'National' would be likely to cause confusion with the Royal Opera Company at Covent Garden and might also imply an unintended slight on any provincial opera company that may be established in the future.[91]

The National Opera title was finally laid to rest by a letter from Peter Walker, the new Minister for Trade and Industry, on 5 February 1973, which added insult to injury by explaining that it would 'give the unjustified impression that the organisation was pre-eminent in its particular field of activity'. He was sure Sadler's Wells would not like to suggest that it had no rivals. There was also, he wrote, a 'strong risk of confusion with the Royal Opera House', although Walker was quick to point out that he had had no 'formal'

---

* Lord Eccles returned to the government in 1970, when Heath appointed him Paymaster General and Minister for the Arts, a post he held until 1973. As Minister for the Arts he clashed with the chairman of the Arts Council of Great Britain, Arnold Goodman, over the funding of controversial plays and exhibitions and introduced mandatory admission charges at public museums and galleries.

expression of view from Covent Garden. Furthermore, no title should include 'National', 'British' or 'English'.[92] The minister favoured the Coliseum Opera Company, despite the fact that apart from any other considerations, the company did not own the free-hold.[93]

The Trust was going round in circles again looking for alternative names, but another effort was to be made to see if the minister could be persuaded to accept a title with 'English' in it.[94] At a meeting with Sir Geoffrey Howe, to whose ministry the name issue had been transferred, on 11 September Harewood argued that it was logically impossible to refuse an application for a title including the word 'English'.[95] 'We argued till we were blue in the face,' Harewood told *The Times* on 2 July 1978, and he added that he and Robinson, an honourable and charming man, had been so rude that they thought that they had 'lost the day'.* The battle had been a long one, and, Harewood recalled, they thought they were never going to win it.[96] Finally, Howe agreed the way out of the 'impasse' was the title English National Opera, as discussed at his meeting with Harewood and Robinson.[97] On 5 November the Trust unanimously agreed to the title, and Robinson accepted on their behalf.[98] The Trust was to be known as the ENO Board after the change of name.

On 3 August 1974 the company celebrated their first performance as English National Opera with a revival of *La traviata* conducted by Mackerras and sung by another fine Violetta, Valerie Masterson, with Keith Erwen and Norman Bailey.† Two days later Harewood wrote to Lincoln Kirsten, the American arts guru: 'We started off quite well with *Traviata* on Saturday night and Norman Bailey was the most completely authoritative and at the same time sympathetic Father Germont that I have ever seen – one positively sympathised with the odious task that fell to him.'

The same evening saw the inauguration of a bursary fund in

---

* The department that the issue fell under was the Registry of Business Names, which Harewood referred to as the 'Department of Sensitive Names' and which reminded him of the Department of Silly Walks in *Monty Python* (*The Times*, 2.7.78).
† There were still doubts about the new title. Hope-Wallace wondered whether the word 'ENO' would conjure up visions of 'morning fruit salts' or 'ENOC' one of 'Powellite scorpions' (*Guardian*, 5.8.74).

Arlen's memory, and the publication of an illustrated history of the company, whose members were proud to acknowledge those who had contributed to its past achievements, including Joan Cross, Edith Coates, Arnold Matters and many more.

It was a moment for reflection on the achievements of the company. On 21 June 1974 Sir Robert Mayer had written to tell Harewood of a donation that he and his wife Dorothy had made to enable the company to take on Kenneth Woollam.* The money had come out of funds – now exhausted – that they had used over fifty years to help build up the 'new musical Britain'. It was part of their dream that 'the gap in our musical structure – opera – would be filled one day'. Harewood had made their dream come true. In his reply to Mayer on 10 September Harewood wrote:

My own musical dreams centre around the establishment of a genuine 'music theatre' in this country. I think at our best at the Coliseum we some-times get near it – 'Katya' or 'War and Peace' or 'Traviata' with Josephine Barstow – and I should like us to do more on this level. I believe so strongly that the combination of music and theatre add up to so much more than simply the sum of its parts, which stop people wondering if opera is on the way out. I am convinced it isn't but I would like more people to agree with me.[99]

\*

The great progress being made by ENO towards the realisation of a 'genuine music theatre' was threatened by the inflation and instability that dominated British politics and society in the mid-1970s. The Labour Party, which had been in power since March 1974, was divided both in its policy of repealing Conservative trade-union legislation and on holding a referendum on EEC membership. The opposition was also far from united, Margaret Thatcher, its new leader, not yet having gained complete authority over her party. The settlement with the miners in 1974 involved a 26 per cent wage increase that was 6 per cent above inflation. Average wage settle-

---

* For many years Sir Robert Mayer had been introducing young people to classical-music concerts and to opera at Sadler's Wells and the Coliseum through his organisation Youth and Music. One such event was a performance of *The Marriage of Figaro* on 22 February 1973 that had elicited 'spontaneous laughter and other signs of positive enjoyment from the upper parts of the house, which on this occasion was largely peopled by his "Youth and Music" young people' (Rosenthal in *Opera*, April 1973, p. 370).

ments for industrial workers were 29 per cent, costs were escalating and productivity was falling.

The task of producing first-rate art at the same time as maintaining good industrial relations, and endeavouring to cope with inflation and underfunding, created a challenging dilemma for the managements of the state-funded institutions. ENO was in a particularly vulnerable position as it had only recently moved from a small, intimate, local theatre into a vast, unmodernised West End music hall and was rapidly adapting its style to one more suited to the size and grandeur of its new venue. The productions were growing to meet the capacity of the new location, and the stage crew were working long hours and earning substantial overtime.

Pressure had continued to build up from the unions, ever since industrial action by NATTKE had been averted for the premiere of *War and Peace* in October 1972. Harewood's efforts to set up a joint negotiating body with Covent Garden had failed as Covent Garden were satisfied with their current agreement, which included a certain amount of overtime that was obligatory within the basic weekly wage.

The price freeze had given management breathing space to continue to try to negotiate a new house agreement, but on 22 November 1972 Snape had told the directors that all the negotiations were in abeyance after the stage staff demanded extra pay for the Christmas show *Peter Pan* because of the greater volume of work resulting from the increased number of productions. This management declared to be unjustified and illegal because of the pay and price freeze, and threatened that if they did not handle the scenery they would be liable to dismissal.[100]

On 21 December NATTKE agreed to arbitration, which resulted, in February 1973, in an agreement signed by John Keenan of NATTKE and Snape that included a supplementary disputes procedure, with an ultimate referral to an independent arbitrator in the event of failure to reach a settlement. It was hoped that this procedure would obviate situations of last-minute demands in the future. It included the sentence: 'Under no circumstances shall the employer or the member of the Union indulge in any action, such as lock-out or a stoppage of work or interference of the pattern of work, of any kind until the foregoing procedure has been followed through.'[101] This clause was to prove costly to management in the 1974 dispute.

The problems did not abate and in April 1973 performances were lost to industrial action in Leeds on the tour. There was no progress in the negotiations during the year, and in November management put forward proposals for the development of higher and more stable rates of earnings, together with the elimination of the three-day rota system and standard minimum calls. These 'minimum calls' consisted of a fixed period with a fixed crew regardless of the show, which left a great deal of 'dead' time, paid for but not worked, because there was sometimes no work to do.[102]* On 11 December all management's suggestions were rejected. The stage staff's House Committee had then been asked to put forward their own proposals but had not done so. The question of a house agreement then remained in abeyance until 19 June 1974, when management proposed a pool of £15,000 for salary increases for the lowest paid, the running wardrobe and wigs. Management again proposed a gradual increase in the overtime hourly rate in return for the removal of restrictive practices and the modification of minimum calls.

There continued to be regular confrontations between management and stage staff on several issues, especially over arrangements for touring, the rates for which were being negotiated later and later because of the increased complexity of the sets. There was trouble throughout the spring and summer of 1974. In August *Siegfried* could not be telerecorded as the stage crew would not agree to the fees.[103] By September the wardrobe was getting more militant and by October negotiations had broken down over the amount of overtime and payments for 'get-outs' – payments made by visiting companies for work in getting the shows in and out of the theatre – which led to the cancellation of ENO's participation in the Europalia Festival. Lord Goodman suggested that, in future, union agreements should be finalised before such arrangements were made since it was bad for ENO's reputation abroad.[104]†

---

* Stage-staff wages for the tax year 1973/4 varied between £2,433 and £5,540, depending on the amount of overtime worked.
† After he left the Arts Council Goodman had been a director of the Royal Opera House since 1972, and, as was traditional, acted as liaison between Covent Garden and ENO, to whose board he had also returned. With his skill in negotiation and his wide-ranging connections he was later a much respected and well-liked chairman of the ENO Board from 1977 to 1986.

Management were increasingly aware that they needed to improve communication in all areas with their employees. On 17 September 1974 Harewood wrote to all departments announcing the formation of a Company Liaison Committee, the aim of which was to achieve a two-way flow of information.[105] The Liaison Committee, although it represented an attempt to move towards less fragmented relations within the organisation, was not an official body and was not intended to cut across union negotiations.

It was the union negotiations, however, that were about to reach a crisis. Fourteen meetings had been conducted in July with an increasing sense of urgency until, on 9 August, unofficial industrial action by the running wardrobe prevented the old and tatty costumes of the Byam Shaw production of *Così fan tutte* from reaching the stage. On 20 August a new shift arrangement and higher rates of pay for the wardrobe and wigs ended the strike.

During the strike, management had succeeded in keeping the theatre open. Mackerras observed admiringly that both Harewood and Tracey were there in open-necked shirts, actually working as stagehands. On 28 August Harewood reported to Lincoln Kirsten about the 'unofficial strike'. The wardrobe, he explained, had indeed been underpaid, but they had been guaranteed a 50 per cent increase by management under certain conditions. The strike had resulted in 'ten performances without costumes, three of which were without scenery as well!' It was, he said, 'pretty good hell and we had to give quite a lot of money back in addition to cancelling two further performances'. It had also 'very much interfered with preparations for *Don Carlos*'.

*Don Carlos* did manage to reach the stage on 21 August. It was intended to be a major musical event. The edition prepared by Mackerras and Andrew Porter included unpublished passages that Porter had found in the Paris Opéra archives and reconstructed from the original Paris material, including the introductory chorus of Act I, in which Elisabeth sees the suffering of her people and so agrees to marry Philip.[106] Porter also translated from the French. According to Peter Heyworth, Mackerras conducted a spacious and finely proportioned performance that did 'full justice to the opera's epic scale'.[107]

The effects of the strike on the rehearsals and the resulting lack of preparedness did not, however, pass unnoticed by the critics.

Graham was also censured for his handling of the chorus and crowds, especially in the *auto-da-fé* scene, which Heyworth thought more Ken Russell than Verdi. Tracey told Harewood that he thought the torture at the beginning of the scene was 'ludicrously inappropriate and altogether tiresome', and the burning at the end 'unbearably maddening'.[108] Although perceptive about the psychology of the personal relationships within Philip II's unhappy court, Graham was taken to task for the ultimate coldness of the effect. Neither Christopher Morley's designs nor the costumes of Ann Curtis did much to lighten the disappointment or lessen nostalgia for the Giulini–Visconti Covent Garden production of 1958.* Graham was distraught by the critical response to the production, pointing to the lack of time for lighting rehearsals due to the financial cutbacks. It was agreed that there should be a stronger cast and a new lighting designer at the revival.[109]

The cast was also not up to the vocal or dramatic demands of the epic work. A South African tenor, Joseph Gabriels, had been chosen to sing Don Carlos after a disagreement between Mackerras and Harewood, who wanted Tom Swift, a company member. Gabriels turned out to be a poor actor and Swift took over after five performances, although he too proved to be less than heroic. Benjamin Luxon's Posa was the truly outstanding performance. It was his first Verdi role, and was distinguished by 'musical phrasing, a beautiful legato line, and a feeling for words'.[110]

Despite the summer's industrial disruptions, another extremely complicated production, Hans Werner Henze's *The Bassarids*, was prepared by the artists in good spirit, reaching the stage on 10 October. It was as assistant to Henze on this production that the twenty-seven-year-old Mark Elder was introduced to the company as a staff conductor shortly after his return from two years under Edward Downes in Australia. Elder, who was to make such a great contribution to ENO for twenty years, later described *The Bassarids* as a 'real beginning' for him since the work was on such a big scale; it was, like Richard Strauss, late Romantic and full of drama and colour.

The libretto of *The Bassarids*, based on the *Bacchae* by Euripides,

---

* It was later pointed out by Jeremy Caulton that although the budget had been a large one for ENO at the time, it was hardly comparable to that of Covent Garden for Visconti (interview, 26.7.08).

was by W. H. Auden and Chester Kallman. The composer, Henze, produced and conducted, with designs by Timothy O'Brien and Tazeena Firth. It was a major musical event in London, coming eight years after the opera's premiere in Salzburg, and one to which the critics on the whole responded with enthusiasm and admiration. Heyworth called it 'one of the most compelling performances of a major new opera'. Although there were hints that not every detail in the Christian, political and psychoanalytical elements contained in the work were entirely comprehensible, critics were impressed by what Heyworth described as the composer's 'range of invention and technical virtuosity'.[111] Above all, ENO – company and orchestra – was praised for responding to the demands of the piece with skill, assurance and commitment. Katherine Pring's Agave was a brilliant performance in sanity and in madness, and Josephine Barstow sang Autonoe beautifully. Both Norman Welsby's Pentheus and Gregory Dempsey's Dionysus were strongly portrayed.

Henze was happy to find *The Bassarids* playing to full houses, the result, he said, of 'those lovely weeks in Camperdown House in the East End where singers, mimes, conductors and producers and assistants sorted things out in happy togetherness, with clarity always the greatest aim'.[112]

*The Bassarids'* success at the box office and in the press was soon eclipsed by a major crisis in industrial relations. Between August and October there had been no further meetings between the stage staff and management, who said they were waiting for the negotiating committee to put forward their proposals for making economies. In October the stage staff elected new representatives, who immediately raised the question of 'threshold payments' – payments related to the cost of living – which, according to the government's pay code, could be negotiated separately outside the pay limit, subject to the conditions of the code. Rupert Rhymes, the director of administration, was first approached by the new national West End officer of NATTKE, Roger Wraight, on behalf of the newly elected House Committee with this issue on 14 October.

The new House Committee was to prove far more active than its predecessor. The new chief steward was an electrician who had been persuaded to take on the role by the technical crew, some of whom, according to Ted Murphy, head fly man and later a technical manager, were somewhat 'hot-headed'. They felt that since he was well educated and intelligent, he would be the right person to represent their interests.[113] The stage staff had also, according to a representative, lost faith in the officers of the union, who were being used, he later said, 'rather like a squash court wall'.[114] After Wraight and Rhymes eventually met on 29 October, Rhymes wrote to Wraight, with a copy to the chief steward, that he still required proposals for changes in working practices before meeting the new committee to discuss threshold payments.[115] The letter, which was delivered by hand, crossed with a memorandum from the House Committee which expressed their need to discuss several issues with urgency.

On 30 October the stage staff held a meeting to discuss the previous day's events and decided to work to rule on *The Bassarids*, an opera particularly vulnerable to industrial action as instead of an interval it had an intermezzo during which the stage staff changed the scenery in costume without a curtain. This sort of activity was considered to be 'special' work, and a work to rule meant that the stage staff would not fulfil such 'special duties'.

Neither the union nor management received warning of the work to rule until 6 p.m. – just an hour and a half before the performance was due to begin – when the chief steward dropped a note into Wraight's office near the theatre informing him that a selective work to rule 'could commence this evening'. Although Wraight was in his office, no attempt was made to speak to him and he did not notice the letter till 9 p.m., by which time he thought it was too late to do anything and went home. Indeed, at 7 p.m. a meeting of the stage staff had decided to start to work to rule.

At 7.29 p.m. the stage controller, Peter Bentley-Stephens, was telephoned by the duty stage manager to inform him that some members of the committee were asking for a meeting with him.[116] According to Bentley-Stephens, he had said that as the performance was about to begin, a meeting should be arranged as soon as possible after curtain up. At 7.31 p.m. Bentley-Stephens discovered that the performance had not started and went to the front-of-house lighting-control box to see what was happening. He found the duty officer putting on his coat and leaving, but was informed of the work to rule only when he reached the prompt corner.

The union later said that Rhymes had cancelled two meetings, and the chief steward claimed that if he had received a promise of a meeting with management, he was 'sure that the show would have been performed as per normal'.[117] Rhymes responded that he had not cancelled meetings as no meetings had been arranged. He told the Committee of Enquiry that his brief from the board was to negotiate 'on a formal basis', according to procedure, and that he could not therefore meet the House Committee 'when there was unofficial action going on'.[118] Rhymes became, in Mackerras's words, 'the object of the strikers' wrath'. He believed in sticking by the rules, 'the kind of person who would really infuriate union stewards'.

After discovering the work to rule, Bentley-Stephens immediately called a meeting with Rhymes, heads of departments and their assistants, stage management and Hans Werner Henze. Management decided to put on an amended form of the performance, with a curtain at the intermezzo and volunteers to carry out the scene changes. During the meeting Edmund Tracey tried to pacify the composer, who was extremely agitated and was threatening to withdraw altogether, claiming he could not understand 'how a fairly elaborately planned production could go on in this improvised way'.[119]

The performance then started forty minutes late. Bentley-Stephens recalled that while he was operating the lighting board during the intermezzo, the chief steward came in and asked him if he was a member of NATTKE. Bentley-Stephens said he was and agreed to show the union representatives his card after the performance. It later emerged that Bentley-Stephens had 'lapsed member' status with NATTKE, having joined Equity on becoming a stage manager. This incident, as Mackerras later put it, 'really caused the "General Strike"'.[120]

When, at 9.45 p.m., at the end of the intermezzo, the stage staff were called over the tannoy system to strike the set, there was no response. The performance ground to a halt and the curtain was lowered. The stage staff were holding an emergency union meeting to discuss Bentley-Stephens manning the lighting-control box. Holding a union meeting during working hours was against agreed procedure.

There was later a conflict of evidence about what ensued. Management said that Bentley-Stephens went to find out what was happening, only to be told by the heads of departments that the stage staff had walked out. This report was confirmed at the stage

door. After these checks it was decided to cancel the rest of the performance. The stage staff had a different version of events. They
said that they saw the cast leaving when they came out of their
meeting and that the management abandoned the performance
when all the stage staff were still in the theatre. They accused management, and especially Rhymes, of provocation by saying at the
management meeting that he would not speak to the committee.

When the Arts Council held an enquiry into the events of that
evening in November 1975, they reported that the performance
could not have been continued without Bentley-Stephens manning
the lighting-control box in any case.[121] Furthermore, although the
stage staff maintained that the performance could have continued,
the Arts Council agreed with management that irreparable damage
had been done by then.

At its 4 November meeting the board was unanimous that management had no option but to issue summary block dismissal
notices to those who had attended an unscheduled and unautho-
rised meeting during the performance on 31 October, even though
this might close the theatre for some considerable period.[122]
Robinson later told the enquiry that the board could not let the
action go unpunished and that it had been thought preferable not to
select individuals as this might have led to accusations of victimisa-
tion. 'We came to the conclusion that the whole enterprise of ENO
was losing credibility with the public.'

When NATTKE later pointed out to the enquiry that they could
have suspended the men on full pay and then heard the evidence
before dismissal, Robinson agreed 'in hindsight' that that might
have been a better course of action.[123] It also later emerged that
some of those dismissed had actually been off duty. One of them,
Ted Murphy, later recalled that he had returned from time off to
discover his own dismissal notice. Records, he recalled, were so
badly kept that management did not know who was on duty, and
relations were 'awful'. Murphy added: 'We were not going to give
up our money, we did not believe them.'[124]

The dismissal of the forty-six members of the stage staff brought
the remainder of the stage staff, including wardrobe, wigs, stage,
electrics and props, out on strike on 4 November. All performances
were cancelled from 5 November and did not resume until 14
December. Harewood wrote to the company on 8 November to

explain that the disruption of half a dozen performances together with *The Bassarids* debacle had seriously shaken public confidence in ENO's ability to deliver the goods, and there was a serious risk of alienating their new Coliseum audience.[125]

When NATTKE met on 25 November, the strike was declared official, although there was a dispute as to whether the strike had or had not indeed been so after 5 November. The Arts Council thought the strike unofficial, Cruft noting on 19 November that it was 'not an official strike'. He also reported that both Equity and the Musicians Union had indignantly removed their notices about crossing the picket lines the previous day as they had been 'duped' into believing it was an official strike.[126]

After strenuous efforts to find a formula for resuming negotiations, on 2 December an agreement was reached on the basis that the forty-six dismissals would be suspended, the staff be reinstated to the pay roll with effect from 4 November, and that a conciliation board consisting of members of NATTKE and SWETM (the Society of West End Theatre Managers) would determine whether the forty-six had been dismissed within the 'agreed ENO/NATTKE disciplinary procedure'.[127] It was agreed that the basic wages of the dismissed staff should be paid while the conciliation procedure was under way.[128]

The conciliation board reported on 11 December. It severely censured management for what it called 'this shameful culmination of events'. Labour relations and discipline at the Coliseum had been 'deplorable for some time', timekeeping so lax that management did not know who was in the building at any one time or who was on duty that particular evening. Gerard Wood, ENO's part-time adviser on personnel matters, later told the enquiry that 'when the company moved from Rosebery Avenue to the Coliseum, for some reason or other all time recording systems got lost on the journey . . . for six years nobody had ever checked in or out'. The conciliation board also declared that the summary dismissal of all forty-six workers, rather than identifying and punishing only those responsible for the disruption, was contrary to the rules of 'natural justice'. They recommended that the forty-six be reinstated and that investigations as to individual responsibility should be conducted. NATTKE should arrange the election of a new House Committee and a new NATTKE/ENO agreement be negotiated as soon as possible.

The conciliation board's findings were discussed on 11 December at an extraordinary meeting of the directors. Arnold Goodman in the chair expressed strong doubts as to the validity of the conciliation board and its procedure. They had not called for sufficient evidence from management, who had not been kept informed of the evidence produced by the union, and only eleven of the forty-six dismissed had given evidence. He felt that the report might have been influenced by the need to maintain the position of the general secretary of NATTKE against militant elements, as well as SWETM's efforts to keep the peace with NATTKE in order 'to preserve their profits'.

What action should be taken, Goodman asked, given that their primary responsibilities were to the 'great institution' they represented and 'secondly to the staff it employed'? Mackerras, supported by Rhymes, felt very strongly that there was a matter of principle involved and that ENO should continue to stand up to militant and anarchic elements amongst its employees on the stage staff, even if rejection of the conciliation board's findings might result in a long closure. Harewood said he might have to resign if the report was accepted, given his position during the negotiations.[129]

Goodman sought to calm the directors, reminding them that their first duty was to get performances back at the Coliseum. He advised that they accept the recommendations and proceed with investigations into the responsibility of individuals. At the same time they should express their 'dismay at the procedure of the conciliation board and its findings'. In addition, the Arts Council should be asked to set up a board of enquiry. If these measures did not get the company back to work permanently, Goodman felt that 'that would be the best moment for members of the directorate to express opinions by tendering their resignations'. Willatt warned them that the Arts Council would not continue to provide funds if they did not accept the findings. That rather settled the matter.

Both Goodman and board member Sir Leslie Scarman thought that although it might be hard to prove in law, management had been right in their action on the night of 31 October. Goodman advised that a procedure should be worked out with NATTKE for disciplining the strikers, 'in view of the fact that specific evidence existed against various individuals'. They should be sent the evidence and asked to defend themselves. If their guilt was established, NATTKE should be consulted about the action to be taken.

Harewood told *The Times* on 13 December that he considered it startling that management had not been asked to comment on the criticisms made against them by the conciliation board. It was also made clear that Mackerras would resign if there were no enquiry into individual responsibility. The results of the industrial action were extremely serious. Thirty-two performances had been lost by the time that work resumed on 17 December. The strike had resulted in a net loss of £93,000, leaving an estimated deficit for the year of £247,000.

The future looked bleak. There was an increase in the cost of new productions, due partly to the increasing size and complexity of the productions themselves and partly to considerable increases in overheads. There had, for instance, been a 100 per cent increase in the cost of timber.[130] During the 1974/5 season the top ticket price more than doubled to £5.20, although the cheapest seats were kept at 50p. In November 1974 Nicholas Payne at the Arts Council indicated that the grant would be £1 million, which, with the GLC grant of £275,000, would leave Sadler's Wells £245,000 short even without taking into account the new singers' pension scheme and the need for repairs to the Coliseum.[131]*

The sole advantage of the strike had been, in Mackerras's words, twenty weeks of uninterrupted rehearsal for *Der Rosenkavalier*, which opened on 29 January 1975. Mackerras had so much time that he was even able to rehearse the alternative principals. By the opening, he recalled, 'the orchestra knew it just as well as if they had been playing it all their lives. They could have played it from memory. Wonderful.'[132]

*Der Rosenkavalier* was greeted warmly. Mackerras was praised by Ronald Crichton for his 'complete control of a score that sometimes carries conductors away with it'. The orchestral sound was 'by turns sonorous, delicate or stinging'. The introductions had 'a hectic brilliance'.[133] Both first and second young casts had benefited

---

* The Arts Council set up a chorus Equity pension scheme in 1974, which applied to all the opera companies but to which ENO was a main contributor. The remuneration was 14 per cent of salary and contributions were 8.5 per cent of salary from the company and 5 per cent from the employee.

from their musical preparation; the first included Anne Evans's poignant Marschallin, spinning long, soft-grained lines, Valerie Masterson's Sophie, Josephine Barstow's Octavian, and the Ochs, Neil Warren-Smith, was described by Milnes as a 'quietly dignified, eager to please outsider who managed to be extremely funny without being vulgar'.[134] The equally impressive second cast appearing just four weeks later caused Shawe-Taylor to comment on the skill of Harewood and his colleagues in detecting vocal and histrionic talent.[135] Lois McDonall was the Marschallin, Lyn Vernon Octavian and Norma Burrowes Sophie.

John Copley's conventional production delighted with its liveliness and a sensitive and musical attention to detail that illuminated both characters and plot. Together with his designer, David Walker, Copley succeeded in making the work emerge fresh while firmly placing each act in its social milieu. The production, Crichton observed, excelled in 'placing, timing and expressive movements'.[136]

Although performances had been restored, 'shotgun bargaining' – as the Arts Council called it – resumed as early as January 1975 when the premiere of *The Magic Flute* was threatened by a strike of the stage staff, who were demanding extra payments. It did, however, open on the following day. The Anthony Besch/John Stoddart *Flute* was translated by Michael Geliot, with dialogue by Besch. The critics welcomed the clarity of the dialogue, faithfulness to the score and the skilful blend of magic, humour, naivety and solemnity that Besch and his designer achieved. The critics were impressed by the company's ability to rally after the industrial upheavals. Heyworth contended that the music director was 'one of the finest Mozart conductors of his generation' and showed 'an uncanny sense of the music's movement, so that his tempi seem a natural expression of what is happening on the stage'. Heyworth captured the essence of Mackerras's conducting: 'Sanctimoniousness never invades the more "solemn" sections of the opera. From the first to the last there is a sense of naturalness that is the final hallmark of musical authority, and a total absence of mannerism or self-love.'[137]

Noel Davies took over from Mackerras on 22 January for the remaining seven performances. Davies was resident conductor, a true company man, respected and held in affection by all those who knew him for thirty years. After studying at the Royal College of Music he had won the Michael Mudie award for opera-conducting and first joined the Sadler's Wells music staff in 1967. He remained at ENO from 1975, where he coached singers, brought co-ordination to the various departments in the house and conducted a wide repertoire, particularly excelling in Puccini.

The Arts Council's Committee of Enquiry into the events of 31 October 1974 began its meetings on 13 February 1975. Before the committee began its deliberations, the ENO board was told that Sir Hugh Willatt and the Arts Council viewed the success of ENO as 'one of the major contributions to the Arts for a decade and had been most unhappy to see the recent industrial troubles arise'. Goodman urged the board's representatives, Bernard Williams and Joanna Smith, to present the case 'in the most vigorous form'. Goodman also stressed that the company should seek the overt support of the union through its disciplinary procedure.[138]

The new House Committee whose election had been suggested by the conciliation board was still not in place by 17 February. In his notes of 4 February the Arts Council music director, John Cruft, said he had continued to 'needle the board about the House Committee about which nothing had been done' and suggested a telegram to the indisposed Keenan at NATTKE.[139] Overtime was also continuing to escalate. These problems persisted despite the appointment of a full-time personnel manager, Leon Fontaine, in February and a technical administrator.[140] Fontaine, an accommo-dating and conciliatory personality, was only the second full-time personnel manager in a theatre in London, Covent Garden having employed the first in 1970.

Following individual interviews with the six stage-staff commit-tee members who had been present at the disrupted performance, management concluded that they had been guilty of 'gross indus-trial misconduct' and sent a formal complaint to NATTKE with a request to 'process the matter as quickly as possible'. NATTKE replied that the issue could not be considered until their 23 March meeting. They pointed out that they had received no specific charges from ENO, a fact which the Arts Council Enquiry later found sur-prising.

On 22 March Mackerras wrote to the ENO directorate to defend himself against the accusation by some Equity members that he had made 'inflammatory and ill-informed public speeches to the company' during the strike. Mackerras's own view of these events, recalled years later, was that 'the chorus and orchestra were not on strike and I made a speech twice on one day to the chorus and orchestra saying: "Do you want this to go on? I know you are all union members – ought we not to call a halt to all this and tell the stage staff to behave themselves?" I did not clear it with anybody else – I just did it.'[141]

At the time he had in the main been 'congratulated and applauded'. He had 'tried to speak the truth' and felt that it had been welcomed as coming from 'an individual artist who cared very much about the issues involved'.[142]

In his letter Mackerras analysed the dispute in the context of the move to the Coliseum, when plans for the larger amalgamated companies became far more ambitious and the atmosphere less friendly and intimate. The aspiration for a more international standard of performance had, he admitted, changed the nature of the company, and 'to some extent changed the nature of the participation of the chorus'. Chorus members had to learn fewer parts and no longer took so many principal roles on tour. From the artistic point of view this was a great improvement, and one that was vital to the company's survival after the controversial move to the Coliseum. Management had been 'so successful in raising standards that some people in the world of opera now considered the orchestra and chorus of ENO to have greater achievements than the Royal Opera House'. At the same time, Mackerras conceded, the effort had involved a 'certain amount of driving and overwork', and it was now accepted that this was becoming 'counter-productive'.

Mackerras did indeed have substantial support. A 'round robin' signed by a large number of singers was sent around pressing for the enquiry to go ahead as soon as possible and 'regretting any possibility that Mr Mackerras might not feel that he could remain on in the present situation'.[143]

The return to work had not brought a solution to either the financial or the industrial situation. Snape told the board on 7 April that although the tour payments were higher, the increase was only keeping pace with inflation. In the meantime Keenan had died and

Leon Fontaine was pressing for a fresh house agreement with the new head of NATTKE, Tom Lever. On 5 May the directors discussed the cancellation of the Royal Ballet season, which had resulted from the stage staff's demands for 'get-out' payments too high for the Royal Ballet to pay. The cancellation incurred a loss of revenue of £32,000.[144]

There would have to be cuts in the plans. After much heart searching, and to the consternation of his widow, the board decided to cancel Ben Frankel's *Marching Song* in an effort to reduce the deficit. It was a hard decision, for not only was it a rare new English work but it was also a cheap production at £15,000 with no chorus. Once lost to the schedule, it would never be put back in because of the queue of other new works.[145]

There was at last some good news for management when the Arts Council's report on the strike rejected the conciliation board's contention that management was 'solely to blame for the bad industrial relations'. The only example of management's 'intransigent and unsympathetic' behaviour, they decided, had been that of the night of 31 October. At the same time the report did criticise management for 'recurrent infirmity of purpose in pursuing courses that they considered to be right'. The company had also failed to record overtime thoroughly and had not planned the tour programmes in good time, although this was admittedly sometimes unavoidable, not least because of the lateness in the Arts Council tour payments. Above all, the Arts Council recognised that management was always hamstrung in its efforts to control the staff by the fear of having to cancel their programme. They recognised the 'unremitting strain on theatre managements of having to balance pride of artistic achievement against the stretching of available resources'. On the other hand, the stage staff were anxious about inflation. Both were rival claimants for the same money.

The Arts Council placed much of the blame for bad relations at the door of the stage staff and the weakness and ineffectiveness of the union. NATTKE itself had admitted that the 'boys had got the bit between their teeth'. The staff's action, the report concluded, 'was not only indefensible in itself, but quite senseless as a negotiating move'. It was simply a show of power. The disruption of the opera was, as ENO had claimed, 'an enormity', and an ordeal for the cast, the orchestra and the audience. The report endorsed the view of the ENO management that the basic cause of the difficulties was the unsatisfactory three-day-week working arrangement entered into by their predecessors, pointing out that the staff, for whom the agreement had obvious advantages, were naturally reluctant to depart from it and had consequently adopted a militant attitude. They suggested the main principles on which to concentrate in the formulation of the new agreement.

In the end, as the Arts Council pointed out, no action at all had been taken in respect of the six committee members who had been considered to be guilty of gross industrial misconduct. ENO claimed that Keenan's illness and death had been responsible for the confusion. Before his illness, Keenan had made it clear to Goodman and Harewood that he fully understood the position, but he had not communicated with his colleagues and his death had left them in ignorance of what had been understood.[146] The Arts Council commented that the lack of action must have 'come as an agreeable surprise to the stage staff and increased their confidence in any future action they might decide to take'. Finally, the Arts Council advised ENO not to make specific charges but to lodge a formal complaint to NATTKE for the union to take appropriate disciplinary measures.[147]

The board was relieved by the conclusions of the report and on 23 July noted 'with satisfaction' that the enquiry had in effect repudiated the strictures on management made by the SWETM/NATTKE conciliation board.[148]

On 4 August Fontaine reported that the NATTKE negotiations were making progress on the basis of SWETM rates, plus a 15 per cent differential for repertory working, threshold payments and cost of living. The contract would work satisfactorily for ENO if overtime was successfully contained, and would, Fontaine hoped, form the basis of a trouble-free season.[149] On 18 September 1975 the agreement was signed. Some restrictive practices were bought out, including demarcation between stage, flys and props. 'Get-out' payments were to be made by ENO and added to the gross pay of staff with income tax deducted.[150]

The bad industrial relations at ENO reflected a period of general industrial unrest in the country, but they had also been the result of inexperience and inflexibility on the part of some members of ENO management and the difficulties of working a repertory system in a large West End theatre not designed for opera or a quick turnover of productions. Although the problems of repertory work in the Coliseum were never fully resolved, relations between unions and management improved greatly under Fontaine and, from 1985, Richard Elder. Had Harewood had more experience in industrial relations when he arrived at Sadler's Wells, Jeremy Caulton believed, the strike might well have been avoided.[151] As Mackerras later recalled: 'George did not join an opera company on a not very good salary just to deal with strikers,' and he added with acquired English understatement, 'It was a great pity for him that it struck just at that time.'[152] It was ironic that at a time when artistic standards had reached unprecedented heights at Sadler's Wells, industrial upheaval was at its worst in England and had affected ENO so harshly.

# 9

# 1975–1978: 'Sure of Its Mission' – the Last Mackerras Years

ENO had always been underfunded for its task, and as the 1970s evolved it was becoming increasingly clear that even if the box office was performing well, the subsidy would have to be supplemented by other forms of income. There had been great reluctance within the Board to face the new economic imperatives since the subject of fundraising had first been mooted in August 1972. Sadler's Wells/ENO had been traditionally and spiritually dependent on, as well ideological believers in, subsidy as the sole basis for post-war arts funding. On 15 August 1972 Harewood had told his then chairman, David McKenna, that he had been 'very taken aback' at the Trust's negative response to the suggestion of establishing a Fundraising Committee for an exhibition to celebrate the company's change of name and to invite Arnold Goodman to chair it. He doubted that the existing Trust was geared to raising substantial sums of money, but believed that in the present mixed economy, it was essential that they were occasionally able to do so.[1]

Covent Garden itself had, under its new chairman Claus Moser, been so concerned about the company's deficits that a trust had been created in January 1975 to co-ordinate fundraising and sponsorship activities.* Just before the strike, on 14 October 1974, Harewood had written to his chairman, Kenneth Robinson, that the time had come to think seriously about fundraising. Covent Garden was doing it successfully, he pointed out, and was paying for its expensive Friedrich *Ring* from private sources. Harewood warned that if the Arts Council grant continued at its present level, by 1975/6 ENO would be £500,000 in deficit. This would mean no new productions or touring. 'I do not personally know how to raise

* Moser, an academic statistician and gifted amateur pianist, had been head of the Government Statistical Service from 1967 to 1978, directly responsible to the prime minister. He not only had important connections but also an acute financial mind and experience.

money,' Harewood added, 'and would probably be a failure at handing the bag around the church but there are others who can.' Robinson replied that not only were his instincts 'strongly against professional fundraising', he was also concerned that if word got to the Arts Council, they might write ENO 'off their crisis list'. He realised, however, that the situation was such that they must not ignore any possibilities, while hoping that as all the major arts organisations were in dire straits, the government would have to do something.[2]

Distasteful as the need for fundraising was, on 19 February Harewood told the Marketing Committee that he was discussing the possibilities of sponsorship with Arnold Goodman.[3] Goodman informed Robinson four days later that he was going to make an onslaught on the merchant banks in order to raise £100,000. He was quite certain, he wrote, that ENO was going to need the money, 'repugnant although the necessity' was. Harewood later recalled: 'Kenneth wasn't interested, he was an ex-Labour minister who said, "We don't do that, we get it from the government." And I agreed with that. Arnold said, "My dears, I think we must emulate some of the others, much as it goes against the grain – I will look for it."'[4]

Goodman and Harewood had judged the situation correctly. On 25 April ENO was warned that there would be no growth in aid from the Arts Council for 1976/7, and on 30 May it was notified that the Arts Council grant for 1975/6 was £1.5 million.[5] This was despite Anthony Field's recognition of the fact that there was little scope left for cuts and also that wage settlements still remained an unquantifiable factor.[6]

In June 1976 the new Appeals Committee was set up under the chairmanship of Lord Barneston. Within three months the committee had raised £18,630 in donations and £100,130 in covenants.[7]

The shift towards more private arts funding was gaining political acceptance. In the summer of 1977 the Labour Minister for the Arts, Lord Donaldson, told the Arts Club in London that the arts would not be able to grow in the current economic climate without the support of business.[8] It would also be necessary to invite people with fundraising credentials onto the boards. In June 1977 Nicholas Goodison, the chairman of the Stock Exchange and a new member of the ENO board, suggested the patronage of individual productions.[9]

*

While fundraising had become a disappointing necessity for Harewood and his board, another solution to the company's incessantly dire financial straits was more creative, resulting in the establishment of the first permanent company in the north of England. The financial and technical strain of the tour, with a commitment of up to twenty weeks – achieved in a ten-week 'double tour' – was growing and involved endless discussions about the possible combinations and permutations. In 1970 Jack Phipps and a small staff had been appointed by the Arts Council to run a scheme to organise the touring of opera, ballet and drama, known as DALTA (Dramatic and Lyric Theatres Association). One of the projects they helped to organise and fund was a set with which *The Ring* could tour to the larger provincial theatres from 1974 to 1977. The tours were, however, increasingly burdensome for ENO. Harewood, horrified by the poor receipts of the June 1974 tour, asked the Arts Council to separate the touring budget from the general budget. This they agreed to on 2 October, but they remained critical that ENO had still failed to make a commitment to guarantee in full all the towns that DALTA wished ENO to visit.[10]

Harewood had warned the Arts Council on 19 June 1974 that the two simultaneous tours were causing 'intolerable strain'.[11] By November the Arts Council, however, were getting tough and suggested that they might call Harewood's bluff by letting him cancel the tour and then face the consequence of losing the saving of £200,000 from the proposed subsidy. Cruft cautioned Harewood that the Arts Council might have to close the Coliseum and company before the end of 1975 if there were not enough funds for touring.[12]

In April 1975 the board learnt of exceptionally poor attendances in the first week at Newcastle. Goodman felt that the time had come for the Arts Council to re-examine its touring policy and spend more money in supporting local operations and less on sending out national companies on expensive regional tours. Harewood pointed out that none of the regional theatres could now stage *The Mastersingers* or *The Bassarids* and that the audiences would not go to *Gloriana* or *Mary Stuart* and had had a surfeit of *Bohèmes*.[13] By June the Arts Council had to acknowledge that the touring pattern was outdated: subsistence for the stage staff and singers was too expensive and in many cases the small audiences did not justify the amount of money spent.

Touring as it had been known ever since opera was first heard in the provinces was coming to an end. The need for a long-term solution was increasingly clear, and in September 1975 the Arts Council set up a working group to examine the demand for touring opera and the resources available to meet it. In August Brian McMaster, then controller of opera planning at ENO, had prepared an early draft plan, including a work schedule and funding ideas, for a provincial company. Nicholas Payne, subsidy officer at the Arts Council, had responded in November with details of how much each authority spent on the arts. Yorkshire, he wrote, were doing comparatively little for the performing arts and would 'be getting an opera company on the cheap'.[14]

On 17 December Harewood's proposal for a regional base for ENO was accepted by the Arts Council. The company was increasingly stretched by the double tour, he explained, and at the same time an 'explosion of talent' would make it possible to contemplate basing some of its artists in Leeds, where they could take on much of ENO's responsibility for touring the north, with an eighteen-week tour of the larger theatres and eight in middle-scale theatres. A section of the company could be based at the Grand Theatre, with a nucleus of twelve contract singers, a chorus of forty and a technical staff of fourteen.[15]

The proposal for a possible Yorkshire base for ENO was welcomed by the *Yorkshire Post* music critic Ernest Bradbury when it was announced on 19 December. He called it an 'unexpected Christmas present – inevitable – especially remembering the triumphant *Ring* tour of last Spring'.[16]

In its early stages the plan had modest pretensions. On 30 January 1976 Rhymes wrote to Harewood to explain that at the moment it was simply an extension of ENO's pattern of weekly touring and it was not intended to make radical alterations to the Grand Theatre in Leeds.[17] On 1 March Rhymes prepared a paper for a meeting to be held on 5 March at Harewood House in which he described the Leeds scheme as a natural development of the move from Sadler's Wells theatre to the Coliseum. It hoped to meet the demand for ENO performances outside London on a regular and more evenly spaced plan. In addition to its appearances at the

Coliseum, ENO would play eight weeks in Leeds and thirty-four weeks in about twenty-nine centres going up to forty-two weeks in 1977/8. The great increase in touring activity outside London would justify the cost of the scheme, which was assessed at £800,000. The Arts Council was enthusiastic, and would be asked to find £400,000. A hundred company members would live and work in Yorkshire. The scheme would, they concluded, offer an enormous stimulus and challenge to everyone and was a unique opportunity.[18]*

Harewood saw local involvement as the crucial ingredient for success, writing a note on a memorandum about the likely cost of the project: 'No! Build on local support, which is already very good.' Harewood was the ideal person to rally such support and transform the idea of a local opera company into a reality. On 5 March he held a splendid meeting at Harewood House for potential supporters at which ENO members sang extracts from *The Ring*, *The Magic Flute* and *Tosca*, before Harewood told his guests that the estimated subsidy required was £500,000, most of which would be met by the Arts Council, with Leeds and the surrounding areas hopefully providing £125,000. There would be a chorus of thirty-two and an orchestra of forty. The director of Humberside leisure services later wrote to Harewood that the discussion had been 'lively and fully in support of bringing the best to Northern counties'. New motorways would mean that a visit to the opera could be an evening's outing.[19]

Rhymes was working out the strategic planning. On 8 March he informed Harewood that he was concerned that a long list of proposed alterations to the theatre might put off the Leeds councillors. He thought it would be best to move into the Grand Theatre and 'prove the venture such a success that everybody felt it should become a permanent feature'. Then, he suggested, would be the appropriate time to say what improvements 'they would like'.[20] Great though the enthusiasm was, it was not generating much local

---

* Mackerras later recalled the work of the regional committees and their reluctance to have anything at all modern on the tours, with even Janáček and Britten regarded as modern. Mackerras said: 'I always remember Brigadier Hargreaves – an army officer type – saying, "Why do we have to fill up the touring rep with things like *Odious Rex* and the *Mackerras Case*?"' (interview, 27.4.06).

cash. Rhymes informed Harewood in April that the enthusiastic correspondence revealed that the local authorities wanted to know what ENO could do for them in terms of touring and also wanted more details of possible budgets. Local cultural groups and arts associations were very keen but could 'obviously only offer practical help'. Rhymes's meeting with Leeds representatives on 24 May proved difficult, as none of the parties present felt they had any mandate to offer any specific sums of money.[21] On the plus side, there was already talk of a Friends of ENO to raise money. It would be, wrote Richard Phillips, the music officer of the Yorkshire Arts Association, a good basis for a subscription scheme and 'the best propaganda weapon available'.[22]

The 1975/6 season's *La Belle Hélène* by Offenbach was mainly viewed as a sure-fire hit needed by ENO to 'fill the kitty' in such hard times when it opened on 4 September.[23] Some critics were shocked by what Rodney Milnes referred to as 'some splendidly dirty lines' in the lyrics of Geoffrey Dunn and the dialogue of Edmund Tracey, and were also disapproving of the earthiness of Copley's direction and Bruno Santini's designs. Even the most censorious, however, were won over by the sparkle, care and felicity of Mackerras's conducting, and the beauty, humour and wit of the Hélène of Anne Howells: 'She has mobile, constantly expressive features, and the ability to turn herself into a shameless hoyden and then in a twinkling to reassert the regal image.' Brecknock's Paris and Shilling's Calchas were also praised.[24]

On 5 November ENO announced the appointment of Sir Charles Groves as music director, to take effect from 31 December 1977. Mackerras would remain as principal guest conductor until the summer of 1980. Mackerras told the *Evening Standard* two days after the announcement that he would have been at ENO for eight years, and believed that quite a lot had improved in this time, especially the orchestra. He would be celebrating his fiftieth birthday in November both in Vienna and at the Coliseum. When questioned about the rumours about the Royal Opera House, he replied, 'I don't know the length of the present music director's contract.'

In January 1976 Mackerras conducted his first complete *Ring* cycle. Alan Blyth was pleased to see a young crowd in the audience. Mackerras, he wrote, 'discharged his duties admirably, eliciting from the orchestra playing that never flagged and would be an adornment to any repertory house in the world'.[25]

The inflation of the 1970s was wreaking havoc with all the arts companies' finances. In October 1975 Payne had informed the secretary general that although all Arts Council clients were having problems with costs, ENO had the worst financial controls of all the major institutions, their estimated deficit having reached £267,500, with production costs £21,500 over budget. Snape, who had always been over-optimistic, had left and his replacement as finance director, Caroline Phillips, who was more realistic, was only just finding her feet. The directors were not 'financially minded' and there was an attitude that since things were so bad, it did not matter if they got slightly worse.[26]

Harewood was not going to let financial restraints diminish his plans and artistic goals. In April 1975 he had persuaded the Opera Subcommittee that the East German Joachim Herz should direct *Salome*. When questioned by board member Leo de Rothschild as to whether foreign directors should be used at ENO, Harewood said Herz was a 'most distinguished pupil of Felsenstein and likely to produce work that would suit the Coliseum company'. Tracey and Byam Shaw both argued that it was 'always valuable to inject new talent into the regular team of producers'.[27]

Herz's *Salome* was ENO's first production of the work. It had been a dearly held project of Harewood, who had invited both John Dexter and Ingmar Bergman to direct Josephine Barstow as Salome. When both declined, it was Brian McMaster, who had spent time in East Germany when working for EMI and who had been riveted by the work of the Komische Oper, who suggested Herz.

It opened on 11 December, translated by Tom Hammond. Sets and costumes were by Rudolf Heinrich, who had designed at the Komische Oper for Felsenstein, including his famous *Cunning Little Vixen*. Heinrich, who had died during rehearsals, and Herz set the action in a semi-circle of stone arches, brickwork and multiple galleries on which various shadowy figures observed the proceedings, at once both 'fussy and drab', according to William Mann.[28] Crichton was impressed how the early greyness – 'in the old German way' – built up 'to garish splendour' with the arrival of Herodias and Herod.[29] Some critics commented on the restless activity on stage and questioned such directorial licence as Salome's expiring 'having attained her fulfilment', according to Herz's programme notes, rather than being killed on Herod's orders. Milnes thought the socialist-realist production had dishonestly adjusted the synopsis, transforming Wilde's and Strauss's religious fanatic John the Baptist into a symbol of socialist progress, Herod's guests into figures from the socialist demonology, and his decadent court into a Hollywood 'Decline of the Roman Empire' epic.[30]

There was, however, a general recognition of a major event, and of the energy, intensity, discipline and involvement of the production, as well as of Barstow's thrilling portrayal of the 'imperious slender child'.[31] Strongly encouraged by Harewood to tackle the role, Barstow's *Salome* was another milestone in her career.[32] Herz's rehearsal period for the one-act *Salome* had been five weeks before reaching the stage, with a week and two weekends, crucial for technical rehearsals, on stage. As most new productions and major revivals received four weeks' rehearsal, Milnes pointed out that Herz's working conditions 'would have been the envy of those native producers who have had to make do with the management's admirably stringent policy on costs'. According to Harold Rosenthal in *Opera*, this had led to 'mumblings that ENO was employing foreign directors'. He also pointed out that London now had the opportunity to compare the two disciples of Felsenstein: Friedrich, who was producing *The Ring* at Covent Garden, and Herz with *Salome* at ENO.[33]*

Harewood remembered the production with pride. It was, he believed, 'one of the biggest successes we ever had, a wonderful production'.[34] Delighted by *Salome*, he suggested on the day of its opening that Herz should direct a new *Fidelio*. A new production was needed since the *Fidelio* costumes had been burnt in the Dalgleish Street fire of 1973. Harewood had hoped that Felsenstein would direct it, but he had died on 8 October 1975.[35]

Mackerras was initially to have conducted *Salome*, but when it

---

* Barstow later recalled Harewood's encouragement to tackle the role when she expressed her uncertainty and the importance of the experience despite her boredom during the militaristic and repetitive rehearsal period. She also expressed her appreciation of the choreographer Terry Gilbert, who had helped her overcome her dislike of dancing (interview, 26.2.08). Barstow stripped naked in the Dance of the Seven Veils, which caused much comment.

was discovered that he was not available, Harewood decided that Mark Elder would replace him. It was, Elder recalled, a great responsibility – a piece the company had never done before. Heyworth wrote of an 'impressive achievement from a singularly promising young conductor, who drew rich and lucid playing from his orchestra'.[36] At the first revival Stanley Sadie wrote that he conducted it with great precision, 'with taut rhythms, sharp and nervously alive textures and a strong sense of the shape and climax'.[37]

Elder had been making a growing impression at ENO. Harewood described him as 'the brightest conducting prospect for some time'.[38] Elder had studied music as a boy chorister at Canterbury Cathedral, and won a music scholarship to Cambridge. He had been on the music staff of both Covent Garden and Glyndebourne, before joining Harewood's old friend Edward Downes as assistant in Australia. It was there that Harewood had met him in 1973, at the opening of the Sydney Opera House. It was Elder's first conducting job, and Downes had advised Harewood: 'This is a good conductor, come and hear him.' Harewood and Elder had found an easy communication in their mutual passion for opera, and despite a twenty-year age gap they became close friends.[39] The young conductor had many opportunities during Mackerras's absences from ENO, early on conducting some performances of *Der Rosenkavalier*, which he had learnt under Downes in Australia.

Working with Herz on *Salome* made an indelible impression on Elder, who felt on his return from Australia that ENO was unaware of the forms of design current in Germany and Austria and in the straight theatre. He found the prevailing aesthetic – such as that of Copley's *Rosenkavalier* – to be 'incredibly decorative' and dreamt that the company might one day be more on the cutting edge of theatrical style. During *Salome* rehearsals Elder was in awe of Herz's physical stature, his intellectual command, his precision and his 'powerful dictatorial rehearsal style'. He recalled how Herz shouted and screamed and complained to management all the time, and how there was pandemonium if someone did not turn up for a rehearsal. Elder found the tension resulting from Herz's short temper and his criticisms quite inspiring. At last, Elder felt, they were going to get something where the music and staging were on a high level of intensity.[40]

Many years later, in an interview with Max Loppert, Elder admitted that his first five years at ENO had been very frustrating as he felt that the productions were not often vivid, acute and involving enough, that ENO needed more of the kind of concentration and organisation that Herz employed.[41] Frustration was a general condition of the impatient Elder's early years. 'They believed in me', he recalled in 2007, 'and were extremely supportive but I was pressing all the time to get better work.' He was ambitious and hungry to develop, and ENO was a company in which he could move forward. Harewood helped his growth by showing he had trust and belief in him. Being asked to conduct *Don Carlos* in September 1975 and March 1976 was, he said, 'a massive thrill', but not being given the February 1976 premiere of *Tosca*, which he believed he had been promised, was equally disappointing for him.[42]

The new John Blatchley *Tosca*, translated by Tracey and designed by Harris, was conducted, in the event, without much intensity by Roderick Brydon. The production inspired Blyth to describe the house style as 'sets in dull colours',[43] and Rosenthal asked why *Tosca* needed to look 'so drab and utilitarian'. Rosenthal noted that the rethought lighting by Robert Ornbo had somewhat reduced *Tosca*'s drabness on 30 July.[44] The Marketing Committee, however, was concerned that the poor press had affected its box office. It was unclear why *Salome* and *La Belle Hélène* had also not done well.[45]

Management were fully aware of the need for a change in design style. In late 1975 they had decided to invite Stefanos Lazaridis to join the company as resident designer, on a full-time basis with a three-year contract. In discussing terms with Lazaridis, Tracey agreed that he would design new productions, consult and advise on revivals and refurbishments, and help make touring versions. He would be provided with an office workroom in the Coliseum and a full-time assistant.[46] In the end the title chosen was 'design consultant'.

While Lazaridis's appointment was destined to bring an exciting visual aesthetic to ENO, it was not part of a plan to ensure economy. The programme for 1979/80 looked too ambitious to Professor Williams, at a time when ENO was trying to economise. Harewood, however, said they had been carefully budgeted and that Tracey was endeavouring to contain the scale of productions by asking designers 'to offer shows that were light and easily managed and conformed to relatively low budget costs'.[47] On 10

February 1976 Tracey asked for the board's support in case there were 'difficult confrontations with producers or designers'.[48]

Harewood himself was thinking creatively about some economical ways of designing. His idea was for a possible basic set for Smetana's *Dalibor*, Weber's *Euryanthe* and Verdi's *I due Foscari*, which were, he explained to Robinson on 5 January 1976, operas with only a generalised sense of place. He reported that Blatchley had fallen on the project enthusiastically.[49]

It was also agreed in January 1976, after eighteen months of difficult negotiations, that Covent Garden and ENO would borrow productions from each other. ENO's set and costumes for *Mary Stuart* would be used at Covent Garden for original-language performances with Joan Sutherland in December 1977. In March it was decided to share the production costs of *Werther*, and in December Tooley was offering *Entführung*.[50]

While searching for economies, ENO was let off the financial hook on 25 March when the Arts Council informed Robinson that they were offering £1.79 million plus a £50,000 guarantee against loss. This would enable ENO to start the next financial year without an accumulated deficit. Time was running out, however, for such bailing-out operations, and the latter half of the decade witnessed the gradual widening of the gap between ENO's income and expenditure.

In July 1975 the government had decided that wages could not rise by more than £6 a week. By August the retail price index was up by 26.9 per cent, and in November cash limits were placed on all public expenditure. On 19 February 1976, after a year of unprecedented inflation, the Chancellor of the Exchequer, Denis Healey, issued a White Paper on public expenditure that promised billions of pounds of cuts in the current and following financial years. On 5 April James Callaghan took over as prime minister from Wilson and Lord Donaldson became Minister of State (Arts), with the result that he had to resign from the ENO Opera Committee. In August 1976 the Arts Council warned ENO that not only was the government not going to provide any growth in aid in 1978/9, but that there would also be a reduction in real terms for 1977/8.[51]

There was an immediate if temporary casualty of the government's stringency measures: on 19 July 1976 Harewood learnt that the Arts Council was insisting that late 1978 would be the earliest moment for the inauguration of ENO North because of the depressingly negative atmosphere created by the government restrictions on local-authority expenditure and the local-government elections in May 1977. Harewood had warned the Opera Committee of this development on 13 July, when all were agreed that it would be 'very dangerous to postpone it longer than one year because, having gained the enthusiastic support of the company, we don't want to risk their disappointment'.[52]

Undeterred, on 9 September Harewood urged Robinson to push the Arts Council to commit itself, and to get Equity and the Musicians Union strongly to advocate the scheme. They should stress the underprivileged nature of the north and the desire of the unions to provide more places for their members. Harewood added that 'mature thought' suggested that they would need every kind of help if the scheme were to get off the ground.[53]

While pressing for ENON, the box office at the Coliseum was causing concern in the autumn, and the two new productions did not reverse the trend. Even though Smetana's *Dalibor* had had to wait a century for its first professional staging by a British company, and was described by Mann as 'the most unjustly neglected of the world's great operas',[54] ENO's audience was generally unwilling to try such new repertoire, however worthwhile. Mackerras conducted *Dalibor*, which opened on 29 September in an English version by Tom Hammond. Produced by Blatchley, it was the first production to employ Harewood's proposed multiple-use basic set designed by Lazaridis, on a two-tier adjustable set of planks. Lazaridis also used a black backcloth and back-lighting in the Svoboda style, together with handsome and striking costumes.*

Porter described *Dalibor* as a 'beautiful and stirring opera' which was presented in a 'strong and moving performance'. *Dalibor* was part of the Czech national heroic tradition, 'a kind of Czech *Fidelio*

---

* Josef Svoboda, the influential Czech architect and stage designer, who was director of design of the Prague Grand Opera (the Smetana Opera from 1948) and of the National Theatre from 1951. Influenced by Appia and Craig, Svoboda developed the concept of 'psycho-plastic stage' – assimilating cubo-futurism, constructivism and the Bauhaus in a symbolist way. His designs focused on the inner psychological meaning of the works, and employed lighting techniques such as laser beams, low-voltage light walls, holograms and projections.

– a rescue opera with a tragic ending'. Although its weaknesses were evident, with its 'uncomfortably large amount of tonic-and-dominant processional music' in the first act, Porter delighted in its 'copious stream of lyrical music, spontaneous yet finely organised'. Its 'strains of such warmth and eloquence' transfigured the weak libretto and gave a 'shining, symbolic quality' to its themes of friendship, freedom and heroic self-sacrifice. John Mitchinson sang the title role with a 'variety of tone colour and dynamic' and a 'sensuousness of phrasing',[55] while Milnes thought that Anne Evans's Milada was 'alive in every utterance – in tone, phrasing and acting'.[56]* Mackerras conducted with what was evidently a 'passionate (and well-founded) belief in the beauty and power of the score'.[57]

*Dalibor* did not reach even its low budget figure.[58] Nor did Johann Strauss's *Night in Venice*, which premiered on 8 December, conducted by Henry Krips, produced by Murray Dickie and designed by Walter von Hoesslin, and drew in a disappointing 53 per cent instead of its budgeted 70 per cent.

The four performances at the Coliseum of Ginastera's *Bomarzo*, on the other hand, were a pleasant surprise at the box office. It opened on 3 November in a New Opera Company/ENO production, after Harewood's and Caulton's successful efforts to revive links with the New Opera Company four years earlier. In consultation with the Arts Council, Harewood had made Caulton general manager of the New Opera Company in 1972 in order to rebuild and repair it after a period of neglect. Amongst its British premieres was Alexander Goehr's *Arden Must Die*, which marked Jonathan Miller's operatic debut as director and took place at Sadler's Wells, Rosebery Avenue, in April 1974.

In order to save money, it had been decided in September 1975 that henceforth the New Opera Company would once again mount its large-scale productions at the ENO venue; the NOC's Arts Council grant would cover certain fees and production costs and make it possible to put on unfamiliar repertory, while ENO would provide the personnel and, of course, the theatre. *Bomarzo* had

---

* Evans left ENO in 1979 because she felt that Harewood was not giving her the parts she deserved and insisted she cover Leonore rather than be in the first cast in the new Herz *Fidelio*. Meanwhile, Brian McMaster asked her to sing Chrysothemis in *Elektra*, directed by Harry Kupfer, at Welsh National Opera (interview, 3.5.07).

been the first choice under this new arrangement. The handsome and imaginative production by Besch, with designs by John Stoddart and costumes by Jane Bond, was much admired, as was Graham Clark's performance in the leading role, but the work itself was generally regarded as meretricious, flashy and tedious, without much musical or dramatic substance.

The second NOC choice of a work unfamiliar to British audiences was a happier one: the British premiere of Martinu's *Julietta* on 5 April 1978, directed by Besch and conducted by Mackerras with Joy Roberts and Stuart Kale in the leading roles. Apart from these two new productions there were also transfers to the Coliseum of earlier NOC productions from Sadler's Wells, including Szymanowski's *King Roger* on 16 March 1976, again conducted by Mackerras and with an ENO cast including Felicity Lott, Gregory Dempsey and Geoffrey Chard. Finally, on 2 June 1979, the Besch/Stoddart production of Shostakovich's *The Nose* was transferred, Alan Opie repeating his performance of Kovalyov. This time, the opera was conducted by the composer's son, Maxim Shostakovich.

Although in the 1975/6 season both *Bomarzo* and *Der Rosenkavalier* had come in above their box-office budgets, Harewood was somewhat perplexed by the generally falling receipts, suggesting that the box office had never really recovered from the exceptionally hot weather at the end of the season. With the box office declining, expenses rising and the grant static in real terms, the board faced impending disaster. Harewood again turned to the reduction of touring as the solution, telling the Finance Committee that the only way to balance the coming year's budget without a higher grant would be to exclude touring for one year. Robinson reported that although the Arts Council was sympathetic, it was nonetheless insistent that the company had to find more economies, and suggested that their officers would examine the budget with the ENO finance director. Harewood saw no way of bridging the gap of £250,000 by pruning the company's expenditure, and was not altogether focused on such action.[59] As Mackerras later said: 'He was interested in opera, he wasn't interested in budgets and those sorts of things at all.'[60]

Lazaridis's appointment, while making a distinct contribution to ENO's house style and solving the problem of drabness over the next decade, was already proving to be an expensive departure. It soon emerged that even his plans for his new office were beyond ENO's slender means. On 23 December Tracey told Rhymes that Lazaridis was thinking of his office as 'a duplicate of his home studio rather than a room equipped to the normal ENO economy standards'. Lazaridis wrote to Edmund Tracey on 7 January 1977: 'Just to inform you that I visited my "office" last Tuesday only to find that, apart from the fact that absolutely nothing has been done to it, it has been divested of the 2 rickety chairs that adorned it,' and he added: 'Bizarre! But not funny.'[61]

The increasingly elaborate sets were proving costly in terms of time as well as construction. On 21 February 1977 Caroline Phillips, the new finance director, noted that the growing deficit for the current financial year, even with the Arts Council supplementary grant, was partially explained by the weight and size of the repertory of the current season. The technical director, James Sargent, said that the budget had been drawn up before the designs for certain productions had been known, and difficulties had arisen from the difficult juxtaposition of complex productions in the house. Seven additional Sundays had been needed for technical rehearsals and overtime in some departments.[62]

The pressures were too great and, reluctant though he was, Harewood had to agree to delay The Adventures of Mr Brouček, which, by its very nature, Harewood believed, could not be produced cheaply.[63] A greatly disappointed Mackerras agreed to the postponement, provided he could conduct a revival of From the House of the Dead as his last production as music director. Even this compromise, Tracey explained, was not going to improve the situation much, as although From the House of the Dead was a revival of the 1965 production, all the costumes had been burnt in the fire and the set had to be adapted for the Coliseum. At the same time it was decided not to give up Aida, as it was a long-term investment which Copley apparently conceived more as a 'fast-moving dramatic work than as a vast production with lavish spectacle'.[64]

After discussions with Arts Council officers, a deficit of £6,700 in the 1977/8 budget was accepted as a basis for continuing to plan. The Arts Council warned, however, that even though they had not yet allocated specific sums for touring, if the tour were to be cancelled the grant would be reduced. It was suggested that the budget be drawn up with repertory changes to make it look more balanced.

It was a tricky business, for, as Harewood pointed out, while the calculation of the touring allowances was one of the main features that 'allowed the budget to work', it was not certain that those involved would necessarily accept them. Despite the uncertainties, the budget was accepted by the board, although it 'involved a number of risks and painful cut-backs for the Company'.[65]

Iain Hamilton's *The Royal Hunt of the Sun*, premiered on 2 February 1977, was one of the few commissioned works that reached the stage. It was also one of the 'complex productions' to which Phillips had referred. The opera had faced a long history of near abandonment. On 16 September 1975 a new commissioning policy had been forced on ENO after the Gulbenkian Foundation chose to support small-scale regional activities, and ENO had decided to commission new operas themselves and to seek sponsorship for the production costs. So steeply had production costs risen, however, that by December Santa Fe Opera had pulled out of the co-production.[66] A new designer, David Collis, was then brought in to prepare cheaper designs.

Hamilton was interested in the 'opportunity for space and spectacle' and the subject of 'the collision of two great empires and civilisations'.* The role of the Inca King was written for a high baritone and that of Pizarro for a bass or baritone. Hamilton's music provided a 'more exotic and colourful means of expression'. It did not have a serial structure but had 'definite tonal characteristics'.[67]

*The Royal Hunt of the Sun* was masterfully conducted by David Lloyd-Jones and produced by Colin Graham, whose cast were 'admirable in diction and histrionic gifts'. Geoffrey Chard was Pizarro, and Tom McDonnell as Atahuallpa performed 'movements of acrobatic intricacy'.[68] David Collis's magnificent costumes and banners and John B. Read's evocative lighting made up for the lack of scenic splendour provided by the backcloths and painted sets, according to Rosenthal.[69]

Critics were unanimous that the music did not illuminate

---

* Hamilton wrote his own libretto from Peter Shaffer's play, which had first been performed in 1964 at the Chichester Festival with Robert Stephens as Atahuallpa and Colin Blakeley as Pizarro. Shaffer supported the project. The main composition was done by 1968, but had been put aside when Santa Fe decided not to participate. He went back to it after Scottish Opera's production of *The Catiline Conspiracy*.

Hamilton's theme and did little to enhance the text, which, according to Rosenthal, was monotonous, with 'long stretches of arioso-
type vocalism'. Shawe-Taylor was irritated and depressed by all the
effort put into new work for such paltry returns. It was, he thought,
merely another play with incidental music.[70] The public, however,
were more curious than they were about most new work. Budgeted
at 40 per cent, it did a very satisfactory 56 per cent.

Despite the disappointments of most of the commissioned new
work, the Opera Committee had decided in 1976 that David
Pountney should direct David Blake's *Black Napoleon* early in the
next season. The opera was retitled *Toussaint* in December. When
its future was threatened for the 1977/8 season, its designer, Maria
Bjørnson, and Pountney managed to reduce its budget and it was
premiered on 28 September 1977.[71]

Hamilton and Blake, Harewood observed, were composers
attracted by large-scale work, having been fired up by seeing
Prokofiev's *War and Peace*.[72] It was a clever production of an ambitious and impressive political piece in twenty-two scenes about the
struggle of Haiti for independence from the French in 1801. Neil
Howlett played the title role of the house slave who became the
commander of the island but who was betrayed by Napoleon and
died in prison. In Rosenthal's view, it was an evening of Wagnerian
length without Wagnerian grandeur or dramatic unity, but con-
densed might constitute a powerful and absorbing piece. Willard
White made a most moving debut as Toussaint's nephew Moise.[73]

Opera Committee member Professor Anthony Lewis was enthusiastic about the piece and considered it the best of the commissions. Other members of the committee, however, thought it should
be cut for the revival.[74] Before the cuts it was too didactic, like a
'history lesson', but after the cuts it lost some of its meaning and the
clear elucidation of the plot. Harewood felt that the massive production had been a 'cardinal error', even though it had, overall,
been a great achievement. A performing work, he explained, 'can
only be judged on the stage, and very often, as with *Toussaint*, the
whole opera was first experienced at the dress rehearsal'.[75]

The gala premiere of the new production of *Werther* on 16 March
1977, in aid of the ENO's benevolent fund, had been attended by
Princess Margaret. William Mann, who loved the opera, was not

disappointed, writing that Janet Baker brought 'all the touching eloquence, the pride, the nobility of soul, and the sense of fun to the act that blends them so cogently'. Mackerras 'drew out sustained euphony and drama from Massenet's brimming score, plentiful diversity and particularity of mood in exemplary style: a newcomer might suppose him to be a specialist in French music of the 1890s'. Brecknock's Werther was also a 'brilliant achievement', with Copley's direction 'gently but firmly' individualising every character.[76] Lazaridis's handsome designs seemed to Higgins to be a veritable 'gallery of eighteenth century paintings', with references especially to Fragonard and Romney.[77] This, together with Charlotte's grand, flowing, creamy-white dress, somewhat obscured the small-town provincial background of the drama.

Whether it was a traditional English suspicion of Massenet or part of a steady yet puzzling decline in the public's interest in the company's work, it became clear that Baker's participation had not helped the box office. The Marketing Committee remained perplexed, wondering if Baker's role had been stressed enough in the publicity, and some suggesting that it was a test case for stars.[78] Cruft pointed out the public had not been made fully aware that she was singing, as she immediately sold out in recitals.[79]

As he had warned, Field informed Harewood on 1 June that the 1977/8 grant was to be £2,340,000, which represented – alas – no increase over the previous year's grant. Field was aware how 'precarious' ENO's position was, but the Arts Council's own grant-in-aid left them with no reserves for clients getting into trouble. There would, he warned, be no chance for a supplementary subsidy.

In the summer of 1977 the main concern of the board was that if the government agreed to an immediate rather than phased return to free collective bargaining with the unions, the enormous pay claims that might ensue would cost the company as much as £500,000 over the current budget and could not be afforded. At the same time they were concerned that if the Arts Council continued to insist on only a 5 per cent increase, there might well be a strike. On 13 July ENO wrote to Cruft to warn that there would be serious trouble if phase two of the government's pay policy was to be rigidly enforced by the grant-aided theatres but not imposed nationally.[80]

Two days later the Callaghan government posited a return to

orderly and phased collective bargaining within the social contract. Its aim was to give working people confidence that their living standards could be maintained with moderate settlements concentrating on tax relief for families. In October the TUC supported a policy of restraint on incomes.

On 1 August NATTKE expressed its willingness to accept a 5 per cent pay increase, but by November Fontaine was describing the industrial situation as once again very depressing. The Equity agreement was complicated by the joint negotiations with the Royal Opera House, as they were at a different stage of the government's phased wages policy. The chorus was aggrieved that their £12 agreement had been reduced to £9 after the Royal Opera House referred the matter to the Department of Employment.[81]

There was an extraordinary board meeting presided over by the new chairman, Lord Goodman, on 21 November. It was called to discuss the chorus's threatened work to rule unless they received their full £12 increase. Harewood considered that they were underpaid and had a genuine claim. He reported their unanimous feeling that they were overworked, with 'too many operas and production rehearsals and insufficient time to learn the operas themselves'. Their general mood had been very civilised, but their claim, however legitimate, was one that management could not meet. In any case, to meet the pay rise being demanded would be illegal, and ENO had been warned by the Arts Council that to do so would 'jeopardise their grant'. The board told Harewood that he could close the theatre if he 'deemed it to be necessary'.[82]

There had been numerous industrial interruptions to the rehearsals of Weber's *Euryanthe*, which opened on 2 November, conducted by Charles Groves and translated by John Warrack. Harewood felt in retrospect that it should have been cancelled. It had, he said, been a 'low point for him'.[83] Milnes also felt that 'with the enormous benefit of hindsight', it had been the wrong decision not to cancel. The effort to 'rehabilitate an unjustly neglected work' had been put back fifty years by Groves's 'cautious conducting, the flabby orchestral playing, and the horribly ill-tuned singing of the chorus (and their near total inactivity on the stage)'.[84]

Groves complained to the Opera Committee on 13 December that the workload was so heavy that he had no time to do detailed work with the chorus and that they barely knew the music before they went into production, and that their morale was consequently low. Tracey agreed that the production workload was too heavy.[85]

These were no longer the concerns of Mackerras, who was about to cease being music director. Before he left he received the Society of West End Theatres (SWET) award for 'outstanding achievement in opera' for *Toussaint* and *Werther* on 4 December. A revival of Graham's 1965 *From the House of the Dead* by Janáček was fittingly his last production as music director. When it opened on 30 December, he was warmly greeted by the audience, who enjoyed Graham's 'sensitive and entirely convincing recreation of life in the Siberian prison'. There were four surviving members of the 1960s cast: Emile Belcourt, Gregory Dempsey, John Kitchener and Denis Dowling.[86]

After the performance Harewood spoke from the stage, describing Mackerras as not only the greatest conductor of Janáček in the world but one whose repertory ranged from *The House of the Dead* to *Patience*. He went on to pay tribute to his much-loved friend in the 1976–8 biennial review:

He brought resourcefulness and enthusiasm to a very wide repertory – there was hardly a work he did not like, even love, and was not keen to conduct. To this he added a wide background of knowledge, so that on every score under discussion he knew where and why famous (or infamous) conductors had made cuts. And his performances, after however long or short a rehearsal period, had a fizz and bounce that made them exciting.

Mackerras's time at ENO, although bedevilled by industrial unrest and national financial crises, was one of rigorous musical preparation, ensemble, singing talent, and high orchestral and choral standards. At that time ENO was, Brian McMaster recalled, 'fantastic in all sorts of ways. The morale was quite extraordinary, the audiences were passionate and it was a great place to work.' There was 'a huge pride and celebration in being there. It knew what it was doing and why, sure of its mission.'[87]

# 1978–1982: 'The Most Critical Battle to Survive'

The Arts Council was struggling by 1978 to maintain the growth of the arts in the previous decades, as well as its 'bailing-out' system, whereby deficits were covered by supplementary grants. ENO caused particular concern, continuing to spend more than could be sustained within its grant. Nicholas Goodison, who was worried that Harewood was not sufficiently focused on the precariousness of ENO's situation, pointed out in January that there was still no contingency planning for pruning expenditure in the likely event of the Arts Council and the Greater London Council deciding to 'turn off the tap' and refusing to make up the deficit.[1]

The new secretary general, Roy Shaw, warned Lord Goodman on 23 January that he had found it hard to convince his colleagues to give ENO a guarantee against a loss of £300,000 when the company was not making plans to work within its resources. The previous autumn Cruft had defended ENO from suggestions within the Arts Council that management should be condemned for poor financial controls. By the spring, however, even Cruft was warning that ENO's production costs were getting close to those of the Royal Opera House, which had the benefit of sponsorship. He and Jack Phipps told the secretary general that ENO was incapable of planning repertory in a 'practical' way.[2]

Only after Goodman attended a meeting at the Arts Council in March to discuss ways of making internal economies of £150,000 was a grant of £2.6 million secured for the 1978/9 season. *The Adventures of Mr Brouček* escaped the knife again only because so many promises had been made to Charles Mackerras.[3]

Mackerras's departure, and the constant, grinding deficits, provoked an identity crisis at ENO, after ten years of uninterrupted growth. Harewood, although he was aware of the dangers of pursuing too ambitious a programme, was unwilling to curtail his aspirations for the company. When, on 10 January 1978, he told the

Marketing Committee how difficult it was both to schedule operas with large sets and to provide enough time for the chorus to learn so much new work, Bernard Williams felt compelled to warn him that it was impossible to compete with the 'prestige that the Royal Opera House enjoys'. Covent Garden was associated with great international artists, Williams argued, and ENO thus needed to have other qualities to attract the public. It was, Harewood admitted, a challenge to assess what would and would not sell.[4]

The language question also re-emerged. On 5 June Harewood and Tracey suggested to the board that a limited venture into original-language productions, such as an Italian *Il trovatore*, might attract singers with international reputations, as might Verdi's Shakespeare operas. They pointed out that they had encouraged David Lloyd-Jones to start the new venture of ENO North with *Samson et Dalila* in French, so that the infant company would not find itself in a 'straightjacket' similar to that of the parent.[5] In a paper prepared for the Marketing Committee, Tracey suggested that there would not be any conflict with ENO's policy if they employed 'rather looser and more flexible terms of reference' for some specific works. The artistic directors remained committed to opera as drama, to an understanding of the text, proper rehearsal time and a regular team of designers and directors. 'The level of intensity in a performance could only be heightened by helping the audience to understand the words as well as the music.' Never in his thirteen years at ENO, Tracey claimed, had there been a case of a singer turning up with his own costume and 'gestures learnt in a previous production'.[6]

The board and the Opera Committee were composed of people with a resolute sense of purpose and sound judgement. Goodman in particular was the wise counsellor on whom Harewood came to rely, particularly in relation to the unions and fundraising.* Together with Williams he stressed the need to retain clear differences to the Royal Opera House, particularly on the language question, where a change of policy could have dangerous repercussions.[7] Harewood persisted, however, and on 12 September he presented the Opera Committee with a 'very short' list of potential operas to be sung in the original

---

* Harewood recalled in an interview that he respected Arnold Goodman's opinion 'on almost everything, because he was so clever and able to balance things'. He was, Harewood said, 'a wonderful chairman'.

language: *The Barber of Seville, Il trovatore, Tristan and Isolde, Tosca, Madam Butterfly* and *Turandot*, all for casting reasons. ENO would provide an opportunity for those who could not afford to see these operas in the original language at Covent Garden.[8] On 2 October he informed the board that the Opera Committee had agreed to some relaxation of the English policy, but not without their careful consideration.[9]

Sir Charles Groves's leadership of the company and orchestra was proving to be patchy. His conducting of *The Force of Destiny* in March 1978 was favourably reviewed by David Cairns as 'grand and unhurried, slow enough to let the words tell . . . eschewing easy excitement, yet never slack'. Barstow immediately established the 'authentic mood of tragic obsession and souls laid bare to the lacerations of fate'.[10] A revival on 17 May of *Euryanthe* was, however, less accomplished. According to Max Loppert, it was 'under-produced (though grossly over designed), mostly undersung and distressingly under-conducted'. It was 'dull, plodding, untheatrical', and the choral singing 'of an atonal paltriness, a half-heartedness simply not to be believed by those with memories of *Gloriana* and *War and Peace*'.[11]

One of Groves's more successful performances was *The Two Foscari*, translated by Rex Lawson, in a Lazaridis set, directed by John Blatchley also in May. It was the third production in Harewood's multi-purpose set that won Milnes's praise for economy. The production satisfied Harewood's belief that an opera house must have a strong Verdi component in its repertoire and that some of the lesser-known works deserved an airing, but did not win critics over to the work itself.

The chorus had continued to be dissatisfied with their pay and conditions. At the 8 May board meeting, Groves unhappily reported 'dispiriting unrest', but Harewood and the board insisted that the government's 10 per cent limit must be adhered to.[12] On 24 July Harewood reported that the Musicians Union, Equity and NATTKE had settled within the government guidelines but that the chorus was refusing to rehearse. Again Goodman warned that it would be dangerous for ENO to close, and management therefore decided to replace *Carmen* with a non-choral work, Menotti's *The Consul*.[13] This opened on 12 August, with David Ritch directing. It was not a hit, with 76 per cent of the audience asking for their money back.

In September the chorus was still refusing to rehearse outside the Coliseum. They were demanding parity with the Covent Garden chorus, as well as increased travel allowances, both of which were unacceptable to management.[14] By November, however, Leon Fontaine was able to report a better atmosphere in the house, the chorus having decided not to strike in case the Department of Employment looked into the current agreements. They accepted 10 per cent with a productivity deal and a lighter workload. Harewood pointed out that there had been a real effort to decrease the gap between the rank and file of the orchestra and chorus.[15]

There were leadership issues, too. At the end of May the board had been told that Groves was unwell and had been ordered to rest. Although he was back in July rehearsing *The Ring*, a vacuum was forming at the head of ENO which Mark Elder was rapidly filling as a rising star in the company. Elder had received critical praise for his conducting of the improved 1974 production of *Don Carlos* in March 1976, and also for a revival of *Tosca* with Barstow in July. In January 1977 he had conducted a fine revival of *Il trovatore* to a packed and enthusiastic ENO Saturday-night audience. Arthur Jacobs described the young conductor as 'persuasive' and 'not afraid of the dramatic pause of silence between sections'.* At this revival, the South African mezzo Elizabeth Connell offered an Azucena of international quality.[16]

On 8 February 1978 Elder conducted Byam Shaw's 1972 production of *Duke Bluebeard's Castle* and a new Colin Graham production of *Gianni Schicchi*, which David Collis set in late-nineteenth-century Florence rather than in 1299. So new was this practice to English audiences that Graham and Elder felt it necessary to explain their reasons in a statement to the critics:

---

* Jacobs praised Hammond's translation. Hammond died in October 1981. In his memory Mackerras conducted a memorial concert of the Mozart Requiem with three different quartets of soloists that he had helped, nurtured and trained, Mackerras recalled, plus Elizabeth Harwood, who sang the beginning and the end solo. Then, much to his surprise, 'a whole lot of soloists in the company came and sang in the chorus' (interview, 27.4.06). Hammond left the royalties of his translations to the Sadler's Wells Benevolent Fund.

It allows an actor greater freedom of movement and expression without any need for period stylisation; then, more important, he is able to project a character and situation with which a contemporary audience is much more easily able to identify – the clothes, the manners, and behaviour patterns are much nearer home than the fancy dress of 1400.

According to the team, the setting also made the wit of the comedy even more palatable to the audience as it 'spiced the work with a more apparent social irony'. Rosenthal was indignant not only about the relocation but about their referring to 1400 rather than Puccini's intended 1299, describing their arguments as 'arrant nonesense', even arrogance.[17]

While cultivating Elder, Harewood also endeavoured to overcome failings in the stage departments and revivals by appointing Colin Graham director of productions in February. Graham, Harewood recalled, was an excellent producer, 'one of those unshakeable Englishmen who have a stiff upper lip and very talented. We always used to say that he was the one for difficult classical pieces.'[18]

Harewood was also bringing new young directorial talent to ENO, including Nicholas Hytner, Elijah Moshinsky and Steven Pimlott, who directed *Seraglio* at ENON in September 1978, with Ariane Gastambied designs and a cast that included Anthony Rolfe Johnson and Valerie Masterson. One of the new directors Harewood welcomed to ENO was Jonathan Miller, who also became a friend. Harewood greatly appreciated his work, made him feel at home at ENO and, while he was in charge, ensured that Miller did regular productions. Harewood was brave enough to defy the warning he had received that Miller might 'set the production in Marks and Spencer' and was rewarded for his courage with a fine series of very successful Miller productions that were to prove financial mainstays for ENO long after Harewood had left.[19]

Miller's first production for ENO was *The Marriage of Figaro*, which opened in November 1978. Critics anticipated the possibility of 'prima donna' or 'director's' opera with varying degrees of anxiety. Most, however, were pleasantly surprised by Miller's light touch, his acute observations on the conventions of eighteenth-century theatre and his understanding of the historical and social context of the opera. He presented individual characters rather than caricatures, with a 'detailed yet unobtrusive harmony of production'.[20]

The final setting bore no relation to Marks and Spencer. Designed by Patrick Robertson and his wife Rosemary Vercoe, *Figaro* was set in Robertson's grey-green panelling with windows opening onto parkland vistas – Loire château, not Marbella Spanish villa or Salzburg rococo, according to Miller.[21] Vercoe's costumes were in buffs, terracottas, yellow-greens and pale blues. Arthur Jacobs found it a 'smooth, articulate and well-judged staging, blessedly free from the current brand of pretentious "re-thinking"'. Masterson sang the Countess with 'freedom and freshness'. In general the singers were roundly praised: John Tomlinson was a 'charming apple-cheeked juvenile' Figaro, who 'radiated a quiet contentment' and whose 'rich burr' reminded David Cairns of the young Norman Bailey. Cairns thought him a bass rather than a baritone, who would one day sing a fine Sachs. Lillian Watson was a 'pert and nimble' Susanna, Eric Shilling a 'wizened, bemused Antonio' and Sally Burgess a convincing Cherubino 'in ardent voice and gawky gesture'.[22] Harewood believed Miller's *Figaro* was the best ENO ever did – full of revealing little inventions.[23]

Groves, however, disappointed. Bryan Northcott wrote of his lack of incisiveness and of sour woodwind and lapses of ensemble. Miller later said that he was coming new to the work and that he had received no feedback from Groves. Miller was upset by some of the reviews, but his *Figaro* became a standard production with ENO until 1990. It also averaged 90 per cent at the box office until mid-January. Harewood invited Miller and David Collis to become associate artists of ENO. He also asked Miller to prepare a modest *Arabella* rather than buying in an expensive adaptation from Covent Garden.[24]

After all the delays, Janáček's *The Adventures of Mr Brouček* had finally reached the stage on 28 December. Other than two perform-ances by the Czech opera company at Edinburgh in 1970, it was the first production in Britain. Loppert called it a magically 'unpre-dictable voyage' through comedy, satire, fantasy and historical epic. Peter Docherty's set represented the locations for the moon act and the 1420 location of the second act with projections of a distorted Prague together with the steps of the castle. In the sure hands of Graham and Mackerras, it astonished Desmond Shawe-Taylor 'with its freshness and vitality'. Mackerras brought out the work's lyricism, luscious orchestral interludes and stirring patriotic music.

He inspired the chorus to 'amazingly stout-toned singing' and the orchestra and soloists to brilliant playing and singing. Gregory Dempsey's Mr Brouček, the 'strangely lovable monster', was a 'tour de force'.[25] Lorna Haywood heroically and uninhibitedly retained her beauty of tone, even when flying, while singing top 'C'. *Brouček* did surprisingly well for an unfamiliar work, averaging 80 per cent, and the last performance completely sold out.

Mackerras received a knighthood in the 1979 New Year Honours List. He was to maintain his close ties to the company so long as Harewood was at the helm. On 20 August 1980 Harewood wrote to ask him if he would be an associate artist: 'That your period as Principal Guest conductor is coming to an end', Harewood wrote, 'is a matter of sadness, just as the period of frenzied ENO activity on which you are embarking is a source of pleasure.' Mackerras replied that he was 'most honoured' to accept.[26]

The translation of *Brouček* was that of Norman Tucker, who had died on 4 September 1978 at the age of sixty-eight. The first night was dedicated to his memory. Shawe-Taylor wrote: 'The large audience of to-day's ENO should pause, every now and again, to salute the memory of this dedicated pioneer.'[27]

Although delayed, the plans for the establishment of ENO North had been moving ahead. In January 1977 the Arts Council regional director, Jack Phipps – described as the midwife of ENON by Harewood[28] – had told Covent Garden and ENO that there could probably be no worse time economically in which to try to map out a long-term scheme for the development of opera touring. He nonetheless agreed that the establishment of a regional association for ENO North and efforts to obtain a response from the local authorities should be vigorously pursued. It was clear that ENO could not continue touring, as standards of performance were seriously impaired and the artists were unlikely to continue to agree to tour for much longer.[29] Furthermore, ENON offered the local authority an opportunity to make a mark in the community-service area, since it did not handle health or education. He noticed a growing 'local groundswell of opinion' in favour of a project that would be of great prestige value. Harewood, who had virtually written the scheme off, was willing to start planning afresh.[30]

On 10 February Harewood informed Robinson that the representatives of West Yorkshire County Council had been very excited by the ENON scheme, and that he had asked David Lloyd-Jones to be its music director.*

Harewood told Angus Sterling at the Arts Council that they had to make a formidable commitment by guaranteeing three seasons in order to enable the ENON scheme to get going, as the local authorities would have to see it working before they committed themselves.[31] By May the Arts Council was prepared to give the go-ahead for ENON from the autumn of 1978, once the local-government elections were over.[32]

The tour results had continued to be disappointing. In June 1977 it was suggested that the local authorities should be asked in future to guarantee the tour against loss. ENO asked the Arts Council to agree that there would be no major tour in 1978 and only a small tour in 1979.[33] In August the Arts Council agreed to a mini-tour of five weeks for the next season.

In July Leeds City Council promised ENON its full backing, and the following month David Lloyd-Jones started working on the project and meeting with the chief executive of the council. It was decided that ENON would open in November 1978. Work progressed during the summer, with a repertory drawn up and a number of singers pencilled in.[34] Applications for chorus master and orchestral manager were studied by the management. On 26 October Phipps said that he believed that once it was up and running, the local money would come through.[35] It was decided to set up a Leeds Committee before Christmas, and in November the Arts Council gave ENON its two-season guarantee.[36] The opening in mid-November 1978 of ENO North at the Grand Theatre Leeds was announced in January 1978.

Harewood's first priority had been to elect a strong steering committee and chairman who would make themselves financially independent of ENO as soon as possible. Since Cruft was warning that there would be no further money from the Arts Council, Goodman approached such firms as Marks and Spencer for sponsorship. Leeds City Council decided to give £200,000 for the 1979/80 season.[37]

* On 4 April Robinson, who was about to become chairman of the Arts Council, attended his last meeting of the ENO Board. Lord Goodman took over on 7 April.

The Northern Steering Committee met for the first time on 24 February 1978. Its chairman, Lord Scarman, encountered remarkable goodwill and enthusiasm and believed that it was an event of national importance for the arts in Britain. The first Friends of ENON meeting was held three weeks later, its membership having reached 1,800. When the Executive Committee, ENON's equivalent of the ENO board, met for the first time on 8 June, they learnt that the standard of the orchestra and chorus was high, and that there were £21,000 worth of bookings. Harewood was to be managing director of both companies, and ENO would give ENON some of their touring productions.[38]

The opening of English National Opera North at the Grand Theatre Leeds on 15 November 1978 with *Samson et Dalila*, under its music director David Lloyd-Jones, was auspicious. Alan Blyth wrote that 'players and singers alike looked young and eager and they performed as if their hearts were wholly in their work'. The musical establishment was present at the birth of the first-ever regular company in the north of England.[39]

Milnes praised *Dido and Aeneas* in November for its production, design and lighting, as well as for the cast. Ann Murray, he wrote, was 'almost unbearably moving', and the chorus magnificent. Clive Timms conducted.[40] Lloyd-Jones had told *Opera* in November that ENON aimed to provide the region in which it operated, and from which it drew its audience, with its own opera company, 'possessing its own policy and inspirations and its own style'.[41]

ENON became an independent company, as Opera North, in late 1981. Nicholas Payne was appointed the company's first general administrator in November 1982. ENO's touring days had drawn to an end. Its commitment soon fell to four weeks, and from 1981 ENO only visited one venue each year. The company ceased touring completely in 1983, except for two major tours: to the United States in 1984 and to Russia in 1990.

The birth and survival of ENON was a near miracle. On 20 November 1978 ENO acknowledged that its deficit for 1979/80 was going to be £500,000, which included the cost of major repairs to the stage. The box office was worsening, with even *La bohème* faring worse than predicted because its assessed percentage had been fixed too high the previous year in an effort to present a balanced budget.[42] The board decided that in informing the Minister for the Arts about the situation, it should be pointed out that the grave position of the national companies was the result of the Arts Council's inability to match the pace of inflation. With Field suggesting that the grant for 1979/80 would be £3.8 million, the company was, Harewood wrote, 'undersubsidised for its task'.[43] This was increasingly the case as the task became more ambitious.

Underfunded as it was, ENO was also failing to improve its budgetary controls. The new technical director, Noel Staunton, warned Lazaridis on 6 November that it was vital that the £70,000 budget for the sets and costumes of *Aida* should not be exceeded.[44] The production had already been delayed to the 1978/9 season, partly because the original designs that Lazaridis had presented had been £20,000 over budget.[45] Just two months later, in January 1979, Staunton was warning Lazaridis that *Aida*'s set alone was going to cost £65,000.[46] It also took two complete days to build, which made it impossible to schedule the post-tour London period.[47] Harewood decided that the new touring version, prepared by Nicholas Hytner because Copley was busy, would be used at the Coliseum after the tour in April. The original set, he explained to the Opera Committee, would not fit into the theatre with *Fidelio*.[48] By March it was apparent that there was an overspend of £128,000 on productions – most of which were exceeding their budgets – and the board was told that internal investigations were proceeding. It was also suggested that budgets should be more realistic.[49]

The crisis that Nicholas Goodison had feared arrived, though less as a result of overspending than of a political revolution. The cultural consensus, together with the bailing-out system that had maintained the growth of Sadler's Wells and ENO, as well as the National Theatre, Royal Shakespeare Company and Royal Opera House, was about to be challenged. After 'the winter of discontent' of 1978–9, although inflation had fallen below 10 per cent that year, the non-industrial unions had continued to disregard the TUC and there was a series of strikes, especially in the service industries. Prime Minister James Callaghan's decision to delay the election was disastrous for him, and on 28 March 1979, after a vote of censure brought by Margaret Thatcher, the Labour government fell.

Thatcher became prime minister on 4 May 1979 with a majority of forty-three seats.

Thatcher's position was not yet secure and she decided to pursue trade-union reform cautiously. She was, however, determined to institute a severe anti-inflationary policy. Her Chancellor of the Exchequer, Geoffrey Howe, had suggested cuts in public spending amounting to £500 million but, despite fast-rising unemployment, she demanded cuts of £3.5 million that were instituted in the budget of June 1970. A policy of privatisation was also initiated with the selling off of council housing.

The artistic institutions belonging to the nation would inevitably be affected by the strict monetarist policy. If they were not actually privatised or closed, they would have to show greater self-sufficiency by acquiring funding from private sources. Nicholas de Jongh of the *Guardian* charted the developments in articles over the next weeks. On 25 July he reported that the new Minister for the Arts, Norman St John Stevas, had lost the battle to get the arts exempted from the government cuts and that his pleas to zero-rate the arts for VAT had fallen on deaf ears. De Jongh warned that the Arts Council might have to consider dropping one of its major national companies, mentioning ENO by name. It was known, he explained, that both Geoffrey Howe and Thatcher believed that monetarism would facilitate major private investment in the arts and that the higher prices caused by VAT would be paid by a public able to pay more, 'thanks to diminished income tax and more pounds in the national pocket'. It was a policy that implied that the better-off would make up the audiences of the future. During the Thatcher era ENO's top prices increased more than sixfold, from £6.20 in 1978/9 to £49.50 in 1988/9. Bottom prices went from 90p in 1978/9 to £2.50 in 1988/9.

John Tooley, at Covent Garden, while acknowledging that change was inevitable, warned that if they were forced into mixed economy patronage too fast, 'companies would go under and there would be nothing left to support'. The arts world realised, de Jongh wrote, that they were facing their most 'critical battle to survive since the founding of the Arts Council'.[50]

ENO was extremely vulnerable to too rapid a shift in the balance between government and private funding as it still received 71 per cent of its income from grants. On 2 August Harewood talked to the assembled company about the crisis. For years, he explained, the Arts Council's policy had been that government-funded organisations should not hold capital reserves. Tony Field had reassured his clients that 'if disaster overcame them the Arts Council would bail them out'. This policy had gradually been eroded, and in June 1979 the change in government policy was made explicit both publicly and privately. ENO's budget for 1979/80, already allocated, had to be reduced by 2 per cent to £2 million. Harewood encouraged the company to make even greater efforts and sacrifices. The running of the company demanded a certain tolerance and acceptance of other people's views and 'the subordinating of personal and individual wishes for the overall good'. Harewood concluded his appeal: 'If we stand together we shall succeed in keeping this the essential organisation and musical powerhouse it has always been.'[51]

ENO was, however, not quite the 'powerhouse' it had been. Groves's *Ring* cycle in August 1979 not only compared sadly with those of Goodall and Mackerras but also revealed the decline in orchestral standards since Mackerras's departure. Rodney Milnes wondered whether it was possible that 'musical fastidiousness' prevented Groves from 'realising some of the more visceral climaxes in *Rhinegold* and *Valkyrie*', and wrote of a 'lack of grandeur and dramatic excitement in *Twilight*'. Some of the brass playing 'was impossibly coarse and the fluffs were by no means towards the end of the performances where we know the ENO cannot afford the luxury of extra players'. The woodwind was not always in tune, and there were 'some particularly nasty noises all round in Loge's music in *Rhinegold* and too many domino entries'.[52]

One of Groves's unqualified successes had been *Manon* in April, directed by John Copley in a more orthodox staging than that of Colin Graham in 1974. The naturalistic sets were designed by Henry Bardon and the libretto was translated by Edmund Tracey. Alan Blyth described Groves's conducting as 'well-paced, involved and responsive' to a work that he obviously loved. Blyth was pleased with its qualities, after the previous night's disastrous Terry Hands *Parsifal* at Covent Garden, at what was a 'rather barren time in London opera houses'. He praised Valerie Masterson's 'almost ideal Manon' and John Brecknock in 'free and fresh voice'.[53]

Milnes later described Groves as a sound conductor and an

'achingly nice' man, kindly and conscientious, but did not feel that he was the right person to run an opera house. Groves had always been immensely encouraging and supportive of Mark Elder, who later spoke of him as an extremely good and generous man, but Elder observed that Groves began to feel like a fish out of water – that his great enthusiasm for the pieces was being undermined by his lack of confidence and his inability to keep the energy of backstage, stage and pit centred.[54] Harewood came to realise that Groves himself did not actually believe that he could run an opera company.

It was decided that Groves's contract would not be renewed and that Elder would take over in 1981. Elder recalled that Harewood spoke to him the weekend that Margaret Thatcher came to power – 4 May 1979. It was agreed that he would take two years off from the company to spread his wings, gain wider experience and come back with fresh energy. Meanwhile, he attended planning meetings for the years after he was to become director.

Groves prepared and conducted the new *Aida* on 26 September 1979. Milnes described the first night as 'musically a gentle evening, smooth and homogeneous', but lacking 'the Verdian snap'.[55] Heyworth thought Groves's deficiency had communicated itself to the cast, especially Barstow, usually sure in her dramatic instincts, but here seemingly ill at ease.[56] Robert Henderson pointed out the clash between the flamboyant ostentation of the setting and the modesty of the singing, and the solidity rather than splendour of the conducting. For him it was a performance biased 'firmly in favour of the eye rather than the ear'.[57] The massive and colourful Lazaridis set, dripping with gold, with its huge metal masks, gateways, statues and hieroglyphics, was described as a traditional *Aida* that substituted spectacle for drama. The public spectacles, especially the sadomasochistic ballet, fared less well than the intimate scenes, which were placed on a central raised platform. Milnes criticised some of Copley's details, such as placing the trial of Radames in full view so as to upstage Amneris in her great scene. Barstow's 'luxuriant fuzzy-wuzzy wig', he wrote, got up the nose of Tom Swift's underrated Radames.[58] On 25 October Elder successfully took over *Aida*, which had already been rethought and had lost its universally disliked ballet, although critics were still suggesting that even further rethinking was required.

The Groves 'debacle', as Harewood later described it, occurred during rehearsals for Miller's production of Britten's *The Turn of the Screw* in the autumn of 1979. Although the work is a chamber opera involving only four adults and two children, Groves, in Harewood's words, 'began to lose his grip'; Harewood told Groves that he thought he should resign from *The Turn of the Screw* and let someone else conduct it.[59] In the event Lionel Friend lucidly conducted the opening performances with the thirteen-piece chamber orchestra.

Loppert described *The Turn of the Screw* as a 'cogent production unified in visual style and dramatic direction'.[60] Miller and his usual designers, Patrick Robertson and Rosemary Vercoe and the lighting designer David Hersey, skilfully used back projections of great trees and Gothic architecture, some of which played onto the shining surfaces of two walls and a floor raked steeply to a point over the pit, others onto the vast Coliseum stage. Together with minimal props, they suggested the variety of locations for each episode, some representing long rambling corridors, a labyrinth both physical and mental. Stephen Walsh, describing Miller as a 'connoisseur of Victorian neurosis', pointed out his certainty about the sexual connotations in contrast to Britten's own equivocation.[61] Loppert praised Miller for 'introducing economy of gesture' to the lyric stage and in so doing eliciting fine performances from Eilene Hannan as the young, vulnerable Governess, Michael Ginn as the very knowing Miles, Ava June as a young Mrs Grose, Rosalind Plowright as a sensuous Miss Jessel and Graham Clark as a seedy, fiendish Peter Quint.

Shortly after *The Turn of the Screw*, Groves resigned from the directorship, ENO agreeing to pay him for the rest of the season. Harewood later recalled how Groves behaved 'as a true gent', with no recriminations on either side, or against Harewood himself, which there easily could have been.

When Groves, in Harewood's words, 'faltered', Harewood sent for Elder and told him that his two years' break was not to be. Harewood remembered the ensuing conversation:

'Now look, this is going to come your way.'

'Oh no,' said Mark, 'much too early', and he prevaricated very much.

A week or two later I said, 'Come on, Mark, it has come your way. I am inviting you to do it.'

'Well I am not accepting it. Not yet. I must think about it.'

He thought about it and he did it.

Harewood added, with a smile: 'He was always going to do it.'[62]

It was announced in November 1979 that Elder's first performance as music director would be *The Force of Destiny* on 4 January 1980. At the time of the announcement Elder gave an interview to *Opera*. He told Rosenthal that for him opera was primarily a visual art, an opinion that might be considered heretical. It was certainly not 'a sort of aural duvet'. Elder fully intended to have a role in the choice of directors in order to formulate the style, the shape and the image of the company. Perhaps, Elder added, 'we can afford to be more risky in our choices'.[63]

There were going to be changes in emphasis at ENO. Gillian Widdicombe reported that Elder had made conditions to Harewood that he would bring his close university friend, David Pountney, the thirty-three-year-old director of productions at Scottish Opera, with him.[64] Elder recalled that he and Pountney 'had grown up dreaming of doing opera together and here it was happening, a dream come true'. He admired Pountney as an excellent musician whose visual and intellectual horizons were broader than his own. 'He's much cleverer than me,' he added. 'Razor sharp.'[65]

They would be a powerful team. Elder was found by journalist Geoffrey Wheatcroft to be a mixture of 'intelligence, charm, ambition and ruthlessness'.[66] Widdicombe described him as a 'sharp-witted, articulate, clever young man', but was concerned that the 'arrogance or exuberance natural to fledglings' might cause the collapse of the already battered nest.[67] Together, Elder and Pountney were outspoken in their irreverence and reaction to the atmosphere of Thatcherite materialism. Pountney in an interview in December 1976 had said: 'I don't think any producer of respectable standing has ever said that one should just do something that the middle-aged members of the audience are going to find easy to understand,' and he added, 'I think annoyance is a very useful emotion.' He was rebelling against what he called 'hairdresser's opera'. Opera production should not be a version of a Fortnum and Mason window with a Thatcherite taste for rich things, but should have a 'healthy vulgarity and terrifically wide range of appeal'.[68]

Elder, who after *Salome* had worked with Herz in January 1978 in Berlin on a famous production of *Madam Butterfly*, had been much affected by Herz's work. Elder was also in close contact with David Pountney, and for some time both had been impatient with

ENO's aesthetic. By the beginning of the 1980/1 season Copley had provided twelve productions going back to the 1970 *Carmen*, all of which were still in the repertoire. Graham had directed twenty-five shows, of which thirteen were still extant, the oldest being the 1966 *Gloriana*. Elder and Pountney considered Colin Graham's productions to be even more outmoded than those of Copley. Together the two directors' work had defined the aesthetic and Elder wanted something much more 'groundbreaking, risky, probing and theatrically inventive'. They did not want to go on with 'Copley's pretty flowers', he later recalled.[69] While respecting their skill, he felt a need to reject the 'cosy old opera' of the past, in the pursuit of making the Coliseum an important place of debate and controversy, which would draw the public in.[70]

Harewood wanted to wait until Graham's contract came to an end before Pountney became director of productions since he had been in the position for only one year. It was a hard decision for Harewood, who had, as Elder later said, 'incredible standards of loyalty and integrity'.[71] Jeremy Caulton recalled that Elder had told Harewood that he wanted Pountney at the planning table immediately.[72] He believed that he and Pountney would be able to give what he felt was a long overdue sense of purpose for a new direction. Pountney wrote to Harewood in July to express his excitement at being able to work in his theatre and collaborate with Elder to create rigorous standards of production equal to those of Herz.[73] He was asking that there should be no major repertoire or casting decisions without his being consulted.[74] Pountney's appointment as director of productions was announced on 12 February 1980, to start from July 1982.

Elder's first show as music director was *The Force of Destiny* on 1 January 1980. It was warmly welcomed as 'a stirring Verdi performance of rare power'.[75] Rosenthal noticed that in the programme it was announced that he was starting his directorship earlier than had been planned, but as far as he and the audience were concerned, it was not a moment too soon. The performance showed him to be a good leader and accompanist, with admirable pacing and 'perfectly judged long musical paragraphs'. His conducting of Verdi, Strauss and the modern repertoire at ENO had revealed him to be a rare talent.[76]

His was indeed a rare talent, but Elder was the first to admit that

Harewood's support and encouragement were crucial in his development both as a conductor and as music director. They would regularly meet together to discuss company matters away from the hurly-burly of the daily grind. Harewood, Elder later said, was an amazing man, who gave him 'so much confidence to develop and grow within his umbrella of experience, concern, protection and judgement'. He added: 'In a way he is a second father to me because he allowed me to find and develop myself in a very careful and gentle way, never dogmatically.'[77]

In December Handel's *Julius Caesar*, conducted by Mackerras, was another groundbreaking musical event for ENO, one that Milnes described as 'an occasion for great rejoicing'. The opera's last staging in England had been in 1963, at Sadler's Wells by the Handel Opera Society. Indeed, the two London houses had staged only four Handel operas since the war. The Opera Committee had been looking for a suitable Handel work, and it had been Anthony Lewis who, on 10 February 1976, had suggested *Julius Caesar* and *Xerxes*. Janet Baker, he said, must be in the cast and Mackerras must conduct. Mackerras had adapted the role for Janet Baker, whose voice was higher than the original castrato. 'Tailoring roles for singers', Baker told *The Times*, 'was an accepted eighteenth-century practice', and she fully appreciated Mackerras's adaptation of roles to suit her gifts.[78] Mackerras also added decorations and, with the assistance of Noel Davies, edited the opera.

Mackerras, who disliked the sending up of the baroque style that was popular in Germany, had wanted Copley to direct, believing him the right person to provide a production free of such caricature. Copley duly gave the singers time to stand and deliver and allowed processions to move in stately and grand style. John Pascoe designed an emblematic set and Michael Stennett colourful costumes.[79] The English translation was by Brian Trowell.

*Julius Caesar* was a musical triumph – Mackerras's conducting 'virile and expressive', with rhythms crisp and 'tempi sensitively chosen'.[80] The orchestral playing was full-bodied, the singing exemplary. Baker's masterly portrayal of the 'grey-templed conquering hero' was for Milnes 'sublime'. She led a cast that included Della Jones's bright Sextus, Valerie Masterson's glorious and graceful Cleopatra and Sarah Walker as a 'noble and tragic' Cornelia. The vocal wizardry that negotiated embellishments and cadenzas, while causing raised eyebrows amongst some zealous Handelians, generated, Milnes wrote, 'a sense of growing exhilaration so essential in opera seria'.[81] Alan Blyth judged that Baker's arias were as they should be, 'the true expression of the sensations of the moment', and added that 'the total conviction she brought to Caesar's moods of anger, love, and determination was as uncannily right as her dispatch of the fearsome divisions was accurate and pointed'.[82*]

In February 1980 the Opera Committee was told that *Julius Caesar* had been fraught with design problems but had been a resounding success owing to its musical strength under Mackerras. A basic set had been made for eight to ten new productions over the following two years. These were to be in a white, brown or black box. *Julius Caesar* was the brown one.[83] Copley later recalled that there had been absolutely no money for the set and he had chosen the brown one as it seemed to have some connection with Egypt.[84]

Elder's first new production as music director was *Fidelio* on 10 May. Herz's production proved a disappointment after his *Salome*, partially because of Reinhart Zimmermann's dispiriting, ugly grey sets composed of noisy metal grilles, and partially by Herz's didactic presentation of a favourite work. Herz believed that *Fidelio* is 'not a celebration of liberty, but an opera about how difficult it is to achieve freedom': hope and belief are not enough but must be accompanied with a gun.[85] At the end of the opera, he left an additional, still-chained chorus behind the freed prisoners as a warning of the continuing struggle. There were elements of the production that were more appreciated, such as the restoration of Rocco's dialogue after Florestan's liberation, which contributed to a deeper portrait of what Heyworth described as the '*Mitlaufer*, the man who instinctively knows when it is time to change uniform'.[86] This, and all the spoken dialogue, was excellently translated by Rodney Blumer [aka Rodney Milnes].

---

* It was the revival of this production that caused Winton Dean, a musicologist who had published several books about Handel and his works, to launch a furious attack on Mackerras, accusing him of indulging in the 'tasteless treatment of *da capos*' and advising him to leave such arrangements to someone with 'more sense of Handel style' (*Opera*, June 1981, p. 644). Mackerras replied that Dean's edition was not suitable for ENO's singers (*Opera*, December 1981).

Elder recognised that Zimmermann's set did not help the production with its noisy, metallic quality. He also pointed out that *Fidelio*, a less brilliantly theatrical piece than *Salome*, depended on its cast and Herz did not work well with Remedios, who was, in Elder's words, a poet and instinctive performer and in no way a disciplined intellectual. Barstow, on the other hand, was a dramatically convincing Leonore and Dennis Wicks a masterly opportunist Rocco, according to Rosenthal.[87]

Elder was thrilled that Herz had given ENO another distinctive and controversial production. He also loved the ambiguity in Beethoven's signature on the final scrim, the reason for which Herz never divulged even to him, and which was the cause of some booing at the end as it seemed to some critics to be a presumptuous suggestion of Beethoven's imprimatur.[88] While Milnes thought the use of a full version of the dialogue added considerable depth to the equivocal character of Rocco, he thought it a 'repulsive' production, echoing Jonathan Miller's distaste at being lectured on freedom by an East German.[89]

Milnes preferred the first English *Arabella*, which opened on 16 October, translated by Robert Gutman. He was delighted that Elder should 'pace so well and coax such fine playing from the orchestra'.[90] In his generally well-received production, Miller sought to allow the audience to decide whether the characters were funny or pathetic in their pretensions, believing the composer and librettist had withheld their own judgement. He spoke about a 'certain irony that *Arabella* was written at a time when the sound of the goosestep was just beginning to be heard'. Since he believed that Strauss and Hofmannsthal were looking back to the Vienna of their grandparents, he set the work, as prescribed, in 1860s Vienna.[91]

Although Miller's brief had been to prepare an economical production, only Milnes thought it looked cheap and most critics commented on the handsomeness of the production, with its clever use of mirrors and its spectacular double staircase. Norma Burrowes was an irresistible Zdenka and Josephine Barstow an exquisitely musical Arabella, distinguished in crinolines with parted hair. Peter Glossop's Mandryka was 'strong and decent'. Graham Clark was an incisive, red-hot tenor Matteo.[92]

Unlike *Arabella*, the £25,000 shaved off the production costs of Mussorgsky's *Boris Godunov* did not entirely escape the critics' attention when it opened on 26 November. It lacked magnificence, they thought, and Jacobs criticised David Collis's merely emblematic scenery, which left the 'sides of the stage ragged and prevented the necessary realism of action'. On the plus side, Graham as usual handled the historical panorama with aplomb, as he did the chorus, who were in fine fettle.

ENO was considered fortunate to have two scholars at its command – Mackerras for Janáček and Mozart and David Lloyd-Jones for Mussorgsky. Lloyd-Jones was praised for restoring the composer's *Boris* to London, with its 'startlingly bold original coloration'.[93] Against the trend at the time, both *Boris* and *Bohème* did well at the box office.

One of Elder's most urgent and demanding tasks was to improve the orchestra. Since the move to the Coliseum, when the two orchestras had been amalgamated, there had been little change of players. Caulton recalled that the system of rotation was universal and that Mackerras had, as was usual with music directors, taken the best members of the orchestra for his own shows. When Elder came, he insisted on refashioning the orchestra. In December 1979 he sent nine warning letters to orchestral players that they might not be granted contracts for 1980/1: three for disciplinary and six for musical reasons.

Harewood later recalled that ENO had to give a long notice – up to six months – to make members of the orchestra reaudition. Their colleagues would be present. If the players did not pass muster at that point, they received a warning that in a year's time their contract would not be renewed. 'Mark started this off with some players that he didn't think were up to it,' said Harewood, but the warnings, which had to be given by the end of the year, were delayed in the Christmas post. The letters did not arrive until 2 January, at which point they said 'This doesn't count' and threatened to strike, which could have resulted in the cancellation of the tour. On 16 February 1980 there was a meeting at Goodman's flat.[94] Elder agreed to rescind the notices, and Harewood recalled him telling the full orchestra in rehearsal: 'It doesn't count, it's entirely withdrawn, it has to be.' Elder nonetheless made it clear that his view had not changed, which Harewood thought was very brave.

Elder did not regret his decision to move decisively on the nine players, despite the pain and resistance. A 'live and let live' approach would have taken much longer, he later said. It nonetheless created 'flak' and bad feeling, and for his first three seasons relations between Elder and his orchestra were tense, as similar letters and painful confrontations resulted in the replacement of the weaker players. 'It showed Mark's strength and toughness,' thought Caulton.[95]

The players gradually realised that Elder was in 'for the long haul' and, as time went by, the bitterness declined. Elder recalled how the sound quality and precision of the orchestra continued to develop. His conducting of a broad repertory helped it to become more refined and expressive. Four and a half years later, during the American tour, Elder felt that the pendulum had swung the other way, with certain players speaking up for quality. The freelance world was changing and ENO secured some very senior players, especially in the string section. A most important moment for the orchestra was when Barry Griffiths, a highly experienced leader, came from the Royal Philharmonic in 1988. It was an enormous fillip to the orchestra's inner confidence and morale. He brought with him seniority, experience, technique and organisation, and gave the orchestra solidarity and consistency. His first show was *Hansel and Gretel* on 16 December 1988. In Elder's view, the arrival of Griffiths was 'absolutely seminal in putting the orchestra a whole level higher in terms of their feelings about themselves. He was brilliant.'[96]

As Elder gained control on the musical side, Harewood was failing to do the same with production costs. On 31 March 1979 he had had to admit to the board that there was an over-expenditure of £128,000 on productions.[97] A year later it was apparent that last-minute changes to the designs of *Julius Caesar* and the ongoing complexities of *Aida* had increased the deficit to £89,000. The Arts Council was increasingly frustrated by ENO's constant deficits. The finance director, Anthony Blackstock, wrote in March that the malaise at ENO was deep, the legacy of supplementary subsidies in the past having created a false sense of security. Finance was not considered very important and had to follow what the other departments did and decided. He could see little evidence that the company was unduly alarmed by its predicament and it must be told to put its house in order, even if this meant being in a smaller theatre performing for less time.[98]

On 30 September the accountants Peat Marwick found the cost-control situation extremely serious and recommended the imposition of strict cash limits, supplemented by stringent financial discipline and self-regulation.[99] ENO's bank manager 'read the Riot Act' to the finance director, warning him that a request for a loan of £1 million by the end of March 1981 would not be viewed with sympathy if the overspending continued.[100] The Arts Council strongly supported the Peat Marwick report's conclusion that ENO must introduce 'stringent controls over expenditure', warning of a possible Public Accounts Committee Enquiry.[101]

In order to protect the new productions, other solutions had to be found. At Goodman's suggestion, ticket prices were increased by 30 per cent. Top price went up to £10.30 and bottom from £1.50 to £1.80 for the 1980/1 season. At Harewood's instigation a subscription system was introduced in an effort to fill the 30 per cent spare capacity.[102] The subscription, although disappointing at first, was achieving a 70 per cent renewal rate by its fourth year. Negotiations also began with the unions for cuts in staff, including the recently increased chorus.[103] Harewood had to recognise that the old Arts Council attitude, that artistic ends sometimes justified overspending, was wholly at odds with the current climate.[104]

In November 1980 Tracey urged that ENO should regard the ten-year series of Coliseum spectaculars as having come to an end, and should copy the RSC in putting on very cheap productions to last one or two years, staged in a very vigorous fashion.[105] Director Harry Kupfer had to agree to a lower budget for Debussy's *Pelleas and Melisande*, and it was decided that Pountney would direct a one-act *Flying Dutchman* on a low budget instead of *The Queen of Spades*. But a year later, in September 1981, *The Flying Dutchman* had gone seriously over budget and the board had to choose between sanctioning the overspend of £20,000 or cancelling the show.[106] The show went ahead.

Harewood tried to convey to the Minister for the Arts, Norman St John Stevas, in a letter on 14 November, that cutting new productions would be counter-productive, and that the increase in ticket prices had met with considerable audience resistance and a falling-off of interest in revivals. The prospects for the company, he wrote, were gloomy.[107]

For Thatcher's government, however, sponsorship was the main method of increasing revenue, and its role was being debated throughout the arts community. In February 1981 Alan Blyth in *Opera* magazine quoted Milnes's passionate denunciation of the decline in government responsibility for the arts on Radio 3, and John Tooley wrote: 'In an ideal world, the government would be the sole provider'; reality, however, had to be faced, and 'with a government holding other views about mixed patronage it would be foolish not to seek private sponsorship to supplement our inadequate government subsidy'.[108] Arnold Goodman was quoted as saying that 'governments in their infinite folly, might remain tight fisted, but city gents could make up the rest'. Investment in the arts, he declared, was not only virtuous, but wise.[109]

A corporate membership scheme had been introduced at ENO in October 1978. For the sum of £2,500 it bought four first-night complimentary tickets and free advertising. The following year it was decided to set up a trust, as Covent Garden had in 1975, and to start to entertain corporate members. In January 1981 the ENO Trust gave £30,000 towards *Tristan and Isolde* and *The Flying Dutchman* and the Friends £30,000 towards another production.[110]

The prime minister enjoyed her visit to *Tosca* on 7 January 1981. It was timely, for it coincided with the dominance of her views on state funding of the arts. This change resulted in an inexorable development of corporate marketing and sponsorship-hunting, which eventually became not a mere adjunct to the company's artistic work but central to its way of thinking.

It was now fifty years since the opening of Sadler's Wells, and a jubilee appeal was launched on 14 January, after the first night of Gounod's *Romeo and Juliet*, to raise funds for all aspects of ENO's work. At the end of the 1982 season it was replaced by a continuous development campaign. In March the new appeals director, John Guy, outlined the degree of fundraising abilities and donations that should be required of people who were invited to sit on the board. His stated aim was to sell the 'product' and promote ENO's image, so that its supporters would realise that ENO was an organisation worth supporting.[111] On 9 July the Society of West End Theatre Management's audience survey report, 'Ready for the 80s', advocated modern marketing techniques and a 'collective marketing role for the industry as a whole'. One of its results was the ticket booth in Leicester Square selling half-price tickets for the current day's performances.

In July 1981 ENO embarked seriously on the process of improved marketing when it employed the J. Walter Thompson corporate communication company to advise and to prepare its first audience survey. As with the majority of ENO and Royal Opera House official and private reports over the next twenty years – and often to the chagrin of the government – it confirmed that ENO was underfunded for the task it was trying to do. This was especially true of ENO in relation to Covent Garden. Not surprisingly, JWT supported most of management's policies, especially that of maintaining a stream of new productions, recognising that variety and freshness were the essential ingredients of ENO's work. Average attendance at a new production was thirteen percentage points above that of revivals. 'Excitement', in JWT's opinion, 'relies on an eye for fashion and special talent in whatever field,' and Harewood was fully aware of the need to distinguish trends. Directors that ENO punters referred to with enthusiasm were Herz, Moshinsky, Hytner, Miller and Pountney. It surely came as no surprise to ENO that, as J. Walter Thompson suggested, they needed £1 million extra a year for productions, refurbishment, education and enhanced marketing and promotion – a sum which would have to come from the box office and private donations. JWT pointed out that ENO must stop being preoccupied with percentage of capacity and start thinking of revenue. Seat prices should therefore be brought up to the maximum. John Guy, the newly appointed appeals director, should have a young sponsorship executive, and ENO should also appoint a marketing director and make marketing 'a continuous, daily effort at the very heart of the organisation'.[112] It was not in ENO's interest to rely on skills donated charitably.[113]

Arts sponsorship had reached £5 million a year. Paul Channon, the Minister for the Arts, wanted the figure increased to £8–10 million by 1982, and he promised, without much foundation as it turned out, that organisations successful at fundraising would not be penalised by a corresponding reduction in their grant. The board was, J. Walter Thompson advised, 'the crucial element in achieving sponsorship', and they added: 'As our American advisers say: "The key to corporate money is the board of Directors."' The most highly regarded attribute when board members were chosen was their 'ability to secure external finance'. They would also be expected to give generously themselves – a development that would change the nature of public boards over the next twenty years.

In December Guy told Harewood that new board members would be part of the planning group for the ENO Development Trust that was to be set up in the summer of 1984, and in June 1983 a planning group was formed to launch a major gifts campaign.[114]

On the weekend of 25–27 September 1981 ENO held a music marathon to raise money. It was a splendid and delightful event with a variety of entertainments and fifty hours of continuous refreshment. Alex Ingram endured a twenty-eight-hour non-stop relay piano solo, during which he was fed sandwiches by his wife. There was intimate musical entertainment and a midnight cabaret performed by such personalities as Elder, Miller, Ann Howard, Eric Shilling and Terry Jenkins, together with the orchestra and chorus.

The marathon was an event reflecting the kind of company solidarity that had been built up over nearly a century. For those who worked at ENO in the 1970s and 1980s, many of whom remained with the company for twenty or thirty years, the word that personified the company was 'family'. Philip Turner, who started as an assistant stage manager in 1978 and was still with ENO in 2009, recalled not only the welcoming feel of the place but also the nurturing and training given by the superb and experienced technical people who had themselves been in the business for years.[115]

As the free-market ideology took hold over the next decades, marketing, sponsorship and ever-increasing ticket prices came to dominate the concerns of management, while its responsibilities towards the welfare of the individual members of the company were slowly but inexorably eroded. J. Walter Thompson said that while it was important for ENO to remember its history, the Baylis tradition must not be allowed to become 'stifling'. It was, however, that late-nineteenth-century belief in the civilising power of culture and its accompanying ideology of endeavouring to make it available to an ever-widening audience that lay at the heart of ENO. However didactic or patronising it may have appeared to later generations, it had inspired commitment from audiences and company members alike for nearly a century.

The new system was ultimately to prove both perilous and demoralising. Harewood was already aware of its wastefulness. On 29 June he told the Education, Science and Arts Committee of the House of Commons that ENO was now spending time 'on raising money which would be better employed in running the opera house'.[116]

ENO management endeavoured to cling on to its traditional mission. In discussing the J. Walter Thompson report it was pointed out that however many public statements they made, nothing could promote ENO's image so successfully as high-quality performances. Underfunding meant that ENO employees were paid much less than those in comparable jobs at Covent Garden and there was a 'grave danger' of exploiting their loyalty and job satisfaction.[117] At the 12 July board meeting, Colin Willis, chairman of the Marketing Committee, emphasised the importance of the Coliseum remaining a house 'which people could afford'.[118]

Economies had to be made, however. The first major reduction in the company was made in January 1982, when it was decided that drawing from the Movement Group was no longer the best way to fill incidental roles.* Their quality was not good enough and it was not a flexible enough system.[119] They were given six months' notice for the termination of their contracts. In response, they claimed that they were not well used and that their dismissal would further weaken the fabric of the repertory system.[120]

There was also concern, expressed by Colin Graham, that technical rehearsal time was being squeezed for reasons of economy and that too many corners were being cut. Rehearsals for *Anna Karenina* in particular had been a nightmare and the time being allowed for Gustave Charpentier's *Louise*, *Katya Kabanova* and the revival of *Gloriana* was, he said, ridiculous.[121]

The opening of Iain Hamilton's *Anna Karenina* on 7 May 1981 was nonetheless a triumph of professionalism, the critics unreservedly praising the fluidity and effectiveness of the splendid staging and production of the cast of 102 in Koltai's set, using a revolve at the Coliseum for the first time in more than twenty years. They even liked the often tonal, Straussian quality of Hamilton's creation. Equally well received by both critics and

---

* The Movement Group was a group of around twenty actor/dancers on permanent contract with the company who were called upon as required.

audiences was David Freeman's Opera Factory production of Monteverdi's *Orfeo*, conducted by John Eliot Gardiner on 20 August. Orpheus was sung by Anthony Rolfe Johnson and Charon by John Tomlinson.

On 8 August *Tristan and Isolde*, conducted by Goodall and translated by Porter, was musically a triumph, but Hayden Griffin's dated set was visually a near disaster. Restrictively confined to an omnipresent narrow ship's prow, and with Carol Lawrence's garish, ugly dappled costumes, Robert Henderson in the *Telegraph* found it a disappointingly dull production by Glen Byam Shaw and John Blatchley.[122] All the critics, however, wrote rapturously of the burnished tone, the fine balance between singers and orchestra, and the classical measure and 'awesome pitch of intensity' of Goodall's conducting.[123] The singing was also fine, Linda Esther Gray singing Isolde with 'lyrical radiance' and fearless beauty of tone.[124] Remedios brought strength and command to the role of Tristan as well as lyrical beauty when required.[125] The Opera Committee concluded that a failure of communication between the producers and the designer caused a 'lack of success of the sets'.

Six weeks later the Miller *Otello* was well received. Loppert wrote of the 'vital alliance, sinewy, urgent, admirably strong on purely musical considerations between stage and pit'. The director not only provided an unobtrusively intelligent and penetrating framework for his artists but also elicited fine performances, tailor-made to their own characters and histrionic skills. Charles Craig's 'natural dignity and probity' defined his characterisation of Otello and Neil Howlett's Iago was chillingly convincing. Critics revelled in the grace, pliancy and aptness of Rosalind Plowright's characterisation of Desdemona, her soft-spun delicate legato and the beauty, fullness, richness and evenness of her tone. Following her Miss Jessel, Plowright was revealed as another valuable ENO star, shortly after Linda Esther Gray's Isolde. Elder's Verdi once more thrilled with its 'mercurial and theatrical response to the music'.[126]

The chorus had appeared in their everyday clothes for Act I of *Otello* on 3 October, while negotiating payment for the half-hour they were expected to spend, but were not paid for, in preparation for the performance. They were feeling the effects of the recession.

November was the worst box-office month on record, not a single revival reaching 60 per cent except *Così fan tutte.*[127*]

The working methods of Miller and Elder's next collaborator, Harry Kupfer, epitomised the difference between the German and British styles. Miller disliked the detailed German preconception and sought inspiration and initiative from the personalities and instincts of his cast. For Kupfer, rehearsals were like 'organising battalions for battle'. As Elder commented, although *Pelleas* is a quiet opera, the rehearsals were dominated by Kupfer sitting on a table, smoking his pipe and screaming encouragement or criticism. Elder was excited to be working with both Miller and Kupfer: it was absolutely what he thought the company should be doing.[128†]

Harry Kupfer's production of *Pelleas and Melisande* on 2 December 1981 was the first-ever performance of the opera in English. For William Mann, in translation it had an immediacy similar to that of the ENO *Ring*.[129] For Milnes, however, Hugh Macdonald's translation straight from Maeterlink's play had radically and unacceptably adjusted Debussy's notes to fit.[130]

*Pelleas* was set by Kupfer and his designer Richard Heinrich in a pre-First World War Europe in morbid condition, 'standing at the turning point between the rarefied neo-medievalism of art nouveau and the modular geometry of modernism'.[131] The set consisted of 'two mobile, self-propelled greenhouses with flat practicable roofs reached by staircases'. They were lit from the inside, forming spaces for the acting, with the hothouse plants inside and withered blackened creepers outside.[132] Milnes heartily disliked Kupfer's 'ruthless' reduction of the work, which 'robbed it of its status as a universal myth' and rendered everything commonplace and pointless. For many critics, however, Kupfer's production was serious and intelligent, despite a surfeit of expressionist rolling about and heavy-handed symbolism, especially that of a brooding, hovering, tattered

* In an attempt to reduce its overheads, on 5 October 1981 ENO decided to leave Camperdown House, used for rehearsals and wardrobe, and buy the old Decca studio in West Hampstead. It would cost about £850,000, of which £350,000 could be raised by a government grant and bank loans, as well as the saving on rental. The building was renamed Lilian Baylis House (aka LBH).
† Herz, another of Elder's admired collaborators, would give stage management the exact moves of the day before he had even seen the singers (interview with Philip Turner, 12.12.07).

moth. Elder was very influenced by Kupfer's remark that 'if the stage is harsher the beauty of the music will well up and make itself seem more beautiful'.[133]

Porter concluded that with all its idiosyncrasies, ultimately the production impressed because of its musical quality. With commitment and cohesion, Elder held together a cast headed by an expressive Eilene Hannan as Melisande, with Robert Dean (standing in for Russell Smythe) as Pelleas. The young couple were near ideal, both natural and straightforward. Porter found it so well sung, so well played and so well acted that the work emerged 'natural, direct and true'. John Tomlinson beautifully and gravely sang a shabby little Arkel in dark glasses.[134] There was only half-hearted booing on opening night. Elder had told Tom Sutcliffe just before the opening: 'I want people to come and shake us up.'[135]

The shaking-up process began gently. In February 1982 *The Flying Dutchman*, given in one act, was the first Pountney–Elder collaboration since the announcement of the former's appointment as director of productions to start in the summer. Pountney translated *Dutchman* as well as directing it. Milnes wrote of the 'quite extraordinary vigour and energy' of the performance, which was musically and dramatically 'hell bent, viscerally exciting, occasionally untidy'. There were, however, 'too many ideas, not all of which were clarified'.[136]

Nick Chelton, who was to make a substantial and very effective contribution to the powerful visual aesthetic of the next decade, used modern lighting techniques and projections, around Lazaridis's revolving stage. Peter Heyworth complained that the set 'was awash with so many flashing lights, revolving platforms, and shifting projections that any clarity of conception was lost in the melee'.[137] The director nonetheless obtained fine performances from his gifted team. Barstow's crimson-robed portrayal of a girlish, obsessive Senta impressed Heyworth. Norman Bailey's Dutchman was resplendent with his warm, burnished sound, John Treleaven an impressive Eric. If the *Dutchman* was anything to go by, Milnes wrote, life was 'not going to be dull'.[138] The Opera Committee later asked Pountney to rethink the bodies flown in and out during the last act.[139]

Harewood's later years were a period of dramatic excitement as his shrewdly identified young talents made their marks. In

September 1982 Jonathan Miller's *Rigoletto* was one of ENO's most successful productions ever. Miller had been inspired by the films *The Godfather* and *Some Like it Hot*, in which George Raft, when being interrogated, claims as his alibi at the time of the St Valentine's Day Massacre, 'I was at *Rigoletto*.' He had discussed his ideas with Harewood, who, after swallowing hard, said, 'Yes, I think it will work,'[140] and Miller consequently set the opera in Mafia-controlled Little Italy in New York of the 1950s, with the 'Duke' as a Mafia boss and Rigoletto as the barman and joker. The rethought historical references brought their own effective resonances, and the Vercoe/Robertson team again produced perfectly observed period designs. Andrew Clements found the 'juxtaposition of fierce primitive passions with a near contemporary setting infinitely more involving than many a more glamorous and international setting'. He also felt, however, that it 'exchanged one kind of historical naturalism for another' and entailed a certain loss of the social stratification inherent in Verdi's work. What he described as a 'sharpening of visceral impact', however, appealed to audiences in 1982 and for at least a further twenty years. Miller was wounded by the few dissenting critical voices, Peter Stadlen in the *Daily Telegraph* and Loppert in the *Financial Times*, who was concerned by a lack of consistency, although he too was impressed by the fresh urgency imparted to the relationships.[141]

Miller himself recalled that the production also showed what an extraordinarily high level of ensemble ENO had achieved and what a vigorous company it was. John Rawnsley was a deeply affecting, bitter, agonised Rigoletto, with a 'huge, house-filling personality'. Marie McLaughlin's Gilda was 'a *West Side Story* waif with a voice of full-bodied lyrical beauty and firmness . . . never more touching'.[142] Arthur Davies was a 'macho' Duke and John Tomlinson a sinister Sparafucile. James Fenton's new translation avoided specific problems of location with phrases such as 'not from these parts'.[143]

The music was as exciting as the production. Loppert wrote of the characteristic ingredients of Elder's reading of his much-loved Verdi: 'a base of authentically Verdian musical values – care for colourful accent, a feeling for tempos in which melodies can breathe, an ability to combine dramatic momentum and lyricism'.

In March 1983 *Rigoletto* received the *Evening Standard* award for outstanding achievement in opera. Harewood hailed it as ENO's greatest-ever success – no seat was empty in its first season.[144] Hugh Canning bade a fond farewell to the production at its revival in November 1988, having seen all the Gildas – Marie McLaughlin, Helen Field, Valerie Masterson, Joan Rodgers and Joan Dawson[145] – but it remained in the repertoire and was still drawing large audiences in 2006, and was to be revived again in September 2009.

The success of *Rigoletto* was based very firmly on Miller's grasp of history, philosophy and social anthropology, which, he believed, were the 'essential equipment to bring to theatrical interpretation'. Miller explained:

Transposition should depend on a concept of isomorphism, the ability to see that the period in which you are setting it has social structures that are apparently represented in the original text. There is something comparable between the power of the Renaissance ducal court to the structure of the Italian mafia, where there is a boss with power and sponsorship and a clientish relationship with his followers. The one does map onto the other . . . I do not do it because it is relevant, I do it because it allows you to see round the corners of the structure.

'The audience', he explained, always instinctively 'detect the mappability. They feel "Good heavens I had not thought of that!" There is correspondence.'[146]

After *Rigoletto*, Miller went back to his medical research, and in July 1983 Caulton found him happily ensconced at McMaster University's Department of Medicine in Hamilton, Ontario, contemplating only the occasional foray into the theatre for special productions, including *Don Giovanni* at ENO in 1985. Caulton noted that during conversations Miller had referred to '*our* company' and said that it was unlikely that he would work anywhere else, explaining some of the obstructions, which included Peter Hall at Glyndebourne and Kent Opera's recent poor casting. Miller added that as far as Welsh National Opera was concerned, he did not intend to take up Bulgarian nationality, which he reckoned was 'a must before Brian [McMaster, by then at Welsh National Opera] pays any attention to him'.[147]

Elijah Moshinsky was also making his mark on the company. On 2 December 1982, when György Ligeti's *Le Grand Macabre* opened, it was, as Milnes put it, already trailing 'a heady whiff of scandal', and billed in the press as 'Porno-opera'. Moshinsky and O'Brien set the work on a debris-strewn slip road of the M4 motorway, complete with hearse in which the young couple made love throughout the opera. The urban landscape was intended to enhance the sense of menace and fear in Ligeti's opera about the end of the world, first produced in Stockholm in 1978. Designer and director had as their points of reference *Waiting for Godot* and *Entertaining Mr Sloane* – both of which O'Brien had designed – rather than the composer's imagined fairy-tale 'Breughelland' setting with its middle-European symbolism. Punters and critics were divided, some responding favourably to the production as 'opera of the absurd', a late offspring of the school of English drama of the Royal Court of the 1960s and the mixture of belly laughter and dark thoughts it engendered. The humour, and even the slapstick comedy, won over William Mann, who enjoyed its laid-back frame of mind.[148] Milnes found it witty and aware, with genuine musical substance and with, 'like all good comedy, a worrying undertow of unease'.[149]

The composer was content with the musical side but thought the production lacked 'fantasy'. It had, however, a successful opening, and although it was budgeted low as a modern work, it improved on its budgeted 50 per cent by 1 per cent.[150]

As the forward movement of the company was gathering momentum, there was a brief moment of nostalgia in April 1982 when Janet Baker sang the first of her farewell performances at ENO in *Mary Stuart*. She wrote in her journal of the joy of working with Mackerras and John Copley at the Coliseum. 'We have', she wrote, 'done some exciting productions in this house. The atmosphere is different from Covent Garden, altogether more homely, somehow, and less intimidating in a way.' In March she described working with Mackerras during rehearsals: 'My delight in the clearly defined and contrasting rhythms of the Donizetti score immediately transferred itself to him across the pit. I could see his body and shoulders react to my voice as he caught my mood and reacted to it in his own inimitable way. I owe so much to this man, who has encouraged me to explore an ever-wider range of styles and roles.'[151] Their last ENO collaboration marked the end of an era.

# 1982–1985: 'A "European" View of Production'

David Pountney lost no time in making his strong opinions felt at ENO after he officially became director of productions in the summer of 1982. It soon became clear that he had very distinctive tastes and decided views. While his interests lay very much with the Czech and Russian repertory, he told Rodney Milnes in March 1983, he displayed a distinct distaste for 'droopy French stuff' and suspicion towards nineteenth-century 'number' operas, whose style made it difficult to justify the musical formalities in terms of what the characters were actually doing. He was impatient with text freaks who held that operas should be treated with 'a quasi-religious respect never accorded to Shakespeare nowadays'. He was determined to shake up opera audiences.[1]

Pountney came from a musical rather than a theatre background, having played trumpet in the National Youth Orchestra – where he met Mark Elder, a bassoon player – and sung in school choirs. After leaving Cambridge he had spent time in the German Democratic Republic, where he had been struck by the highly professional level of directing he witnessed at the Komische Oper and at the Berliner Ensemble, which he felt contrasted with the 'decorative, genteel, dilettante' method of English direction. He learnt lessons from what he called the detailed, faithful and beautifully crafted work of Felsenstein, but was even more impressed by Herz and by Ruth Berghaus, whose abstract, surrealist work exploded the boundaries and revealed what might be possible.[2]

When asked how Harewood responded to Pountney's arrival, Mark Elder later said: 'George was always alive to the need for a new direction in the knowledge that it might take the company into stylistic areas he might find tricky.'[3] Harewood had indeed been employing exciting new directorial and design talents well before Pountney joined the team, but at the same time, as Jeremy Caulton pointed out, he was a believer that there was a 'boss'. The final decision, Harewood believed, must be made by the chief executive.[4]

It was to prove a lively period. 'We were a feisty group of people,' Elder recalled. 'We all had very different attitudes, particularly David; both of us and Jeremy very often did not agree with George.' Harewood could be 'incredibly Hanoverian', with his favourite expression: 'No! No! I am going to lie down in the road over this one!' Elder's and Pountney's choices came from a very 'different aesthetic horizon'. They were seeking something with more edge.[5] And they were not going to wait. Elder later explained, 'We wanted to change the focus of the company very quickly and it was a big liner to spin round.'[6]

Pountney believed that opera productions should be ephemeral and in an ideal world there would be no revivals. The burden of each new production, he told Alan Blyth, lay 'in its artistic vitality and not in its status as a crucial investment in the company's future'.[7] Pountney was not so interested in long-lasting productions with a more general or universal appeal. In his paper of 22 March 1991, 'What the Programme Is For', he emphasised that a vital part of ENO's artistic identity depended on each production presenting a unique challenge to the audience's susceptibilities. The programme, like the production, reflected a conscious act of interpretation, which was by definition 'partial and temporary and possibly tendentious'.[8]

Another area of disagreement was the large ensemble. Pountney felt that it could become 'a repository for carelessness and cosiness' and that there was a danger of employing people because they were part of the ensemble rather than because they were the best.[9] According to Harewood, there were four company singers whom Pountney would not use and whom he had been forced to drop, 'which rather went against the grain'. Neil Howlett in particular Harewood thought a most versatile singer and a fine musician, who could learn any role in a week. The benefit of the ensemble company, in Harewood's opinion, was both technical and artistic. If necessary it was possible to change plans at the last moment without any extra cost. More important, he explained, 'people grow together like a football team – they play better together when they have played together a lot than when they don't'. Harewood had been able to double-cast The Ring, and in the mid-1970s, when there were still two tours going round the country, there were between forty-five and fifty-five company principals. In July 1981 there were thirty-nine company principals and by the end of Harewood's time there were thirty-one. By 1992 there were twenty. Harewood later recalled that Pountney allowed it 'to run down a bit'.[10]

'Director of productions' was a role defined by the personality and beliefs of its incumbent. While Colin Graham had been in the position it had not involved a clash of policy with Harewood, who was a managing director with his own clear ideas about artistic planning. For Elder and Pountney, however, planning would also reflect the tastes of the director of productions and his enthusiasm for certain directors. They shared a vision whereby the Coliseum would be a ground-breaking forum for the best, most dangerous work, said Elder. 'We dreamt of excitement, of challenging and inspiring people to hear familiar music with new ears because their eyes were being led in a different direction. We dreamt of making it a talking point, of making everybody fascinated by the company's work rather than turning up because it was the thing to do . . . The David and George relationship was not easy.'[11]

The first hints of a clash of authority came at a planning meeting on 10 August 1982, when Pountney suggested that David Alden, whose assistant he had been at Houston Grand Opera in 1976, should direct *Simon Boccanegra*, explaining that he was owed a production. When Tracey and Caulton pointed out that Herz was expecting to direct it, Pountney again pressed for Alden to direct the Italian repertoire and suggested Herz direct *Tannhäuser*.[12] Caulton later recalled that when Pountney said he had asked Alden to produce *Boccanegra*, Harewood went white – no one had ever chosen a director 'without securing George's agreement'. According to Caulton, Harewood was collegial, but he had the final decision.[13]

It was nonetheless still Harewood's guiding influence that dominated policy at this time. At the same 10 August planning meeting it was decided to go ahead with his concept of a semi-staged, cheaply produced opera series, which was intended to keep interest going in unusual works and to achieve a balance with the more popular operas. In September Harewood described his idea of the 'connoisseur series' to the Opera Committee, 'succinctly if revolt-ingly' as 'disposable opera'.[14] It was to consist of the non-repertoire works of the great composers, on a slender budget, with less durable sets, costumes and most of the scenery from stock, and the chorus reading their music. They were to be produced 'without apology' and, he hoped, 'always excitingly'.

Wagner's *Rienzi* was to be the first and Pountney suggested Tchaikovsky's *Mazeppa* to follow. Harewood, Tracey and Caulton agreed that Nicholas Hytner should direct *Rienzi*.[15] When, in January 1983, the construction company Norwest Holst agreed to sponsor the series, the title was changed from 'Connoisseur' to Norwest Holst.

On the stage, Pountney was setting his own seal firmly and fast on ENO's house style. On 26 January 1983 his production of Tchaikovsky's *The Queen of Spades* was greeted by vociferous boos as well as applause. Pountney shocked the critics with what they saw as his impertinence in rewriting Tchaikovsky's scenario, relat-ing the opera as a dream wrapped in Maria Bjørnson's white gauze, each scene running into the next, which, they complained, caused confusion.* Milnes wrote at the 1993 revival: 'If everything is fan-tasy, then even such scenes as the Countess's death and her appear-ance in the barrack room (there is of course no barrack room) fall flat.' There was dismay at Lisa being portrayed as a 'loonie nympho' with much sexual writhing on the floor, murdered by Herman rather than committing suicide as in the text. Milnes thought Pountney considered the chorus to be an encumbrance that interrupted his scenario, as he presented them as regimented nurses and orderlies in drab khaki.[16] Max Loppert was even more enraged, writing that 'Mr Pountney's sympathies are not natural to Romantic figures' and that he breached the forms of Tchaikovsky's quintessentially romantic opera by failing to strike up a relationship with the sense and colour of the music.[17] In the annual report Milnes wrote that Pountney's 'nightmarish approach' to the opera had been 'wrong-headed in spades'. It did not fare well at the box office.

---

* Bjørnson had been a pupil of Ralph Koltai and was in the same class as Sue Blane and David Fielding at the Central School of Design. Equally inspired in the romantic and the conceptual idioms, she was a perfectionist and a commit-ted and generous colleague. She died suddenly in 2002.

Pountney and Elder's next collaboration, Dvořák's *Rusalka*, which opened on 16 March 1983, was an iconic production of the Elder/Pountney/Harewood era. It had been planned by Harewood and made possible by Mackerras, who had found an anonymous donor in 1980, originally on the condition that Mackerras would conduct. The donor had insisted on *Rusalka*, despite Elder's suggestion that he should be asked to donate to a more popular Czech opera.[18] The donor had given £40,000, but Lazaridis's sets cost £20,000 more than budgeted.*

Pountney's *Rusalka* stimulated ENO's apparently complacent audience in the right way. They were jolted out of their 'ritual gaze', according to David Cairns. There was once again some booing on the opening night, but critics and audiences were quick to recognise the style, panache and coherence with which Pountney expounded his concept.

Pountney usually worked with Maria Bjørnson and had associated the work of Lazaridis with John Copley. It was Noel Staunton, the technical director, who persuaded him that Lazaridis was 'just waiting to do a different kind of work'.[19]† *Rusalka* was the beginning of an intense and productive collaboration. Together, Pountney and Lazaridis transformed Dvořák's woodland glade into a Victorian nursery, in a gleaming white box with Nick Chelton's luminous lighting on shimmering water. It was the setting for the teenage heroine's sexual awakening. 'The Freudian subtext implicit in every myth or fairy tale', wrote Loppert, was 'extrapolated to serve as the main text'. Helped by Rodney Blumer's fluent translation, the 'taut propositions were followed through to the end', when the fantasy death of Rusalka's beloved enabled the heroine 'to shed her father-fixation to become a woman'. Elder's conducting was universally praised for its conviction and passion and the glowing, lyrical ensemble he achieved.

---

* Ted Murphy recalled that to the stage staff Lazaridis was known as the bank manager, as no one said 'No' to him and they could count on plenty of overtime with his sets (interview, 17.12.07).

† Copley looked back with unhappiness to his exclusion during the Pountney regime: 'Life went very sour for me when Pountney took over,' he recalled. He was particularly angered when his beloved *Rosenkavalier* in April 1983 was given to a staff director who, he believed, had not done the production justice, thus ensuring that his work looked inadequate in the new era (interview, 15.10.07).

John Treleaven was the prince and Eilene Hannan a youthful-sounding, touching Rusalka.*

Prokofiev's *The Gambler* on 28 April had, according to Robert Henderson, 'all the grotesque realism of a Pountney production'. Maria Bjørnson's use of mirrors contributed to the 'exact, brilliantly incisive theatrical fidelity, not only to those precise qualities of excitement, freedom, flexibility and verbal immediacy that Prokofiev himself held in such high esteem but also the gradual transformation of the characters from at least a semblance of naturalism into a group of obsessed and posturing caricatures'.[20] *The Gambler* was translated by Pountney and Rita McAllister.

In the 1982/3 annual review Milnes wrote that Pountney and Elder had 'stamped their image indelibly on the company's work'. The series of new productions, whose stimulating qualities 'occasionally crossed the borderline into the realm of the controversial', had certainly created a new excitement. At the same time, Elder and the orchestra had become 'as one'.

The previous year had seen a sea change in the Arts Council leadership when Kenneth Robinson was succeeded as chairman in May 1982 by William Rees-Mogg, a staunch ally of Thatcher who was to prove a less than rigorous defender of the Council's clients. Basil Deane, a much respected musician and musicologist who was head of music, soon left, attending his last ENO board meeting as Arts Council assessor on 31 March 1983, when he was replaced by Richard Lawrence.

The general election of June 1983 gave Margaret Thatcher a majority of 144 over all parties and 188 over Labour, which, under Michael Foot, had fought on a left-wing programme. Labour also lost votes to the Liberal/SDP Alliance – formed in March 1982. The fierce and successful execution of the Falklands War in May not only increased Thatcher's popularity but reinforced her inclination to govern with the support of close colleagues rather than her entire Cabinet. The War Cabinet had showed her the advantages of ruling through small groups of politicians who supported her policies. It was a period of centralised and determined power, and

---

* It was explained by Pountney to the puzzled Ann Howard, who played the witch Ježibaba in the 1984/5 revival, in one of her actions that she was looking for blood on the sheets as a sign of Rusalka's reaching the age of menstruation.

deflationary economic policies, which were vigorously pursued.

In August 1983 the Arts Council made an unprecedented cut in funding to ENO of 1 per cent after the government had reduced their grant-in-aid. According to some warning voices on the board and the finance director, ENO appeared to be a 'company in decline' from the financial point of view, as the deficit reached £150,000. Sponsorship – the foundation stone of the new funding policy – was becoming more elusive because of the general economic situation in the country. Donations were not reaching their targets; salaries, particularly those of senior management, were far too low, and Noel Staunton, the technical director, was warning that the density of new productions in the future programme was causing unsustainable pressures on the technical side. In the autumn the board considered cancelling a new production of *The Mastersingers*, but decided that it would cause problems with sponsors in the future and that it was needed for marketing the second part of the season. Instead, seat prices were increased in January 1984 by 20p in the stalls and 10p in the upper circle.* Harewood remained concerned that if new productions were cancelled, the public would lose interest in the company, and pressed ahead with his innovations.[21]

On 29 September the first of the Norwest Holst series opened with the twenty-seven-year-old Nicholas Hytner's production of *Rienzi*. The *Guardian*'s drama critic, Michael Billington, was delighted to see young producers 'with a strong theatrical flair' being given the run of the Coliseum. Updated by six centuries, David Fielding's set evoked Mussolini's Rome with 'vast expanses of black marble, chromium plated doors, and intimidatingly enormous statues of muscle-bound warriors', Billington wrote. Hytner believed that for contemporary audiences the nationalist fervour of 1840s Germany, from which *Rienzi* emerged, held the wrong resonances. He sought to show 'a modern charismatic super-leader'.[22] Michael Tanner in the *TLS*, however, was not convinced that the drama, the music nor Kenneth Woollam's comfortable portrayal of a well-meaning figure in his early sixties corresponded to the 'apparatus of repression' in the production.[23] Revolvers, searchlights,

---

* Seat prices ranged from £3.50 to £15.50, while those of the Royal Opera House were £1 in the upper slips to £42 (Financial information, 17.2.84, B36 Box 72).

archive film clips and tanks did, however, add excitement to the visual impact. The chorus, who, in accordance with Harewood's brief, had not learnt the score by heart, were placed above the stage, seated in Mao caps with their scores on stands before them. David Murray described the production as 'loaded, exultant music theatre'.[24] Heribert Esser conducted with an ebullience equal to that of the production.

Norwest Holst were pleased with *Rienzi*, despite some additional costs incurred by contracts to singers and to the dancers hired after the demise of the Movement Group the previous year. The box office, however, was declining and there was an £8,000 variance on the *Rienzi* budget, even though as planned it had 'not been an extravagant production'.[25] *Rienzi* received the Society of West End Theatres' outstanding new opera production award for 1983.

The preparation of the new *Ring* cycle revealed strains within the administration when, in order to maintain the scheduled first night of *Valkyrie* on 22 October 1983, two performances – one each of *Orfeo* and *Rienzi* – had to be cancelled. Working closely with Pountney, Maria Bjørnson had designed a large and complex set, crucial elements of which had not been delivered in time for the technical crew to familiarise themselves with the complicated act changes. It was agreed that it would have been dangerous not to extend the stage time and therefore it was necessary to cancel the two performances.[26] Their loss was regarded by Elder as 'appalling and shaming'.[27]

The history of the *Valkyrie* set had been fraught with difficulties. The original design had been rejected by the technical director, Noel Staunton, on grounds of cost and size, and even when it was finally accepted on 28 April some revision was needed. In mid-July the board had accepted that the £75,000 budget had to be increased by £25,000 rather than cancel the production. The period up to the beginning of rehearsals on 12 September was devoted to building the floors, including the complex rings, and the other scenery was shelved until rehearsals had begun. In August and September Pountney and Bjørnson were also working on the revival of *Toussaint*. Because of the late start in building the rest of the scenery, the stage crew had no time to get used to building the complete set.[28]

When *Valkyrie* opened in October, its ambition appeared to be somewhat greater than its achievement. Elder's and Pountney's admiration for Patrice Chéreau's 1976 Bayreuth *Ring*, not shared by Harewood, encouraged them to set their *Ring* in a notional nineteenth century. The Jacobean baronial hall of Bjørnson's Act I had a leafless ash tree growing out of a central staircase, and a magnificent library circled a swimming pool in Act II. Both provided strong visual images, while presenting obscure symbolism, reflecting Pountney's and Elder's interest 'in creating a visual space for ambiguity, for the audience to ponder'.[29] The striking war memorial of Act III was telling as well as being visually impressive. Tom Sutcliffe described the floor, which was occupied with concentric circles 'moving in contrary motion on a steep rake', creating constantly changing perspectives.[30]

Elder's conducting, according to David Cairns, seemed, like the set, to be striving for a 'monumentality beyond its power to sustain' and somewhat at odds with the music's 'passionate exuberance'.[31] By the third act, however, Loppert felt that he found the necessary resources of colour, warmth and fluency.[32] The cast was mixed. Linda Esther Gray did not sing on the first night, but returned for two of the subsequent eight performances. Marie Hayward-Segal valiantly stood in for her, while being asked to portray an unprepossessingly clad Brünnhilde. Remedios returned for his well-liked and ardent Siegmund. Anthony Raffell as Wotan, however, while revealing strength and stamina, disappointed with his lack of vocal or dramatic characterisation. Sarah Walker's Fricka and Willard White's Hunding were the strongest performances. Pountney's Ride of the Valkyries was dazzling and his direction of Wotan and Fricka penetrating.[33] Barstow was directed as a hysterical Sieglinde, and the consummation of the relationship at home rather than after escaping to the forest annoyed some critics. *Valkyrie* seemed to be very much a work in progress.[34]

Harewood was concerned about the *Valkyrie* situation. He considered the cancellation of any performance to be a 'disaster' and felt it necessary that the board be given a full account of events. On 7 November Pountney explained to the board that the designer had been working on three operas and that a crisis had been reached in April, when the original design concept had had to be accepted for lack of time to rethink it. Board members expressed concern about the financial situation this had created, and Nicholas Goodison sought greater information about the planning and budgeting process. Board member Edmund Dell pointed out that both the cancelled performances and the contractors' overtime had added to the deficit. Lord Goodman again sought to soothe. The company had a good reputation and should admit error and be candid about the reasons for cancellation. He urged that they should all learn from the mistake.[35]

The design had proved costly not only in terms of construction and material but also in technical time on the stage. It was also becoming apparent by November 1983 that it would be impossible to fit anything but two light productions in the theatre at the same time as *Siegfried*. Finance director David Fletcher warned Harewood that although a large part of the expense related to elements common to the whole cycle, the design of the remainder would still have to be completely rethought as the kind of set required to cover the *Valkyrie* revolves was too expensive.[36]

The *Valkyrie* situation was discussed at the Oxford board conference on 11–12 November. According to Caulton, it was a terribly difficult meeting, which left even the buoyant Goodman downhearted. Caulton recalled that there was a lengthy discussion and strong complaints, particularly from Edmund Dell, about *The Ring*. There was even a suggestion that the project be abandoned altogether. In general the board concluded that ENO was striving for excellence without the ability to pay for it.[37]

On 5 December the Finance and General Purposes Committee learnt that the expenditure for *Valkyrie* was nearer to £200,000, as against the £150,000 reported at the previous meeting and against the revised authorised budget of £100,000. The committee expressed concern at management's report and the omission of certain items from the budget. It was suggested that the future of the *Ring* cycle should be debated by the board.[38] To make matters worse, the *Valkyrie* achieved only 69 per cent at the box office, having been budgeted at 85 per cent.

The *Valkyrie* imbroglio continued into the new year. Casting had been causing concern since November, since it was thought that there was no point in mounting *Siegfried* with Hayward-Segal and Woollam as the first cast in the likely event of Linda Esther Gray being unable to continue.[39] On 9 January 1984 the board learnt that Gray had withdrawn from the role of Brünnhilde. It was decided that there should be a new schedule, with *Rhinegold* to be performed in September 1986, *Siegfried* in November 1986 and *Twilight* in 1987; there would be a full cycle in autumn 1987.[40] Elder was disappointed by Gray's withdrawal; he 'admired and adored' her as a colleague and believed she had the right epic scale of generosity and warmth for Brünnhilde. The rehearsals were thrilling, he recalled in 2007, but sadly in the end the 'technical difficulties of achieving the role proved too great'.[*]

The future of the cycle was in doubt and the indecision continued for a year. For several weeks there were discussions about rescheduling to fit in with Anne Evans, who was committed to *Götterdämmerung* in Wales. There was much correspondence with Bjørnson, who felt that she was being asked to make model after model until one fitted a notional budget.[41] In the end the cost proved insurmountable and the decision to cancel the cycle was finally accepted by the board on 5 November 1984, by which time the company's finances were in an even more parlous state after its tour of America.[42]

The November 1983 *Valkyrie* cancellations had been a blow for Harewood, and he was occasionally losing arguments in the face of the forceful opinions of Pountney at planning meetings. He was unsuccessfully pressing for Opera Factory's David Freeman to be given a production every year, believing him to be 'one of the strongest production voices we have heard or seen in the last few years'.[43] Harewood was also having a battle trying to persuade his colleagues to expand the French repertoire. Masterson, he told *Opera News* in June 1984, was the best Marguerite (in *Faust*) around but, he added ruefully, 'only to set out to please the public is a rather dull thing but not to please the public is a failure'. Caulton later recalled that when Harewood felt that he could do no more to change matters, he became deflated.[44] According to an interview that Harewood gave to the *Sunday Times* in 1985, he told his wife during Christmas 1983 that he had decided that rather than reassert his authority, which he felt had been eroded, he would announce his resignation the following year.[45]

At the end of 1983 Harewood was being harried on all sides.

* Elder, although 'courted' for at least four *Ring* cycles, had still not conducted one at the time of writing.

Despite the unfavourable economic climate, Rees-Mogg's Arts Council was continuing to press its clients rapidly to increase their fundraising. Luke Rittner had taken over from Roy Shaw as the Arts Council secretary general in what Shaw described as a symbolic moment, since Rittner had been a Conservative councillor who had directed the Association of Business Sponsorship of the Arts. Before he took up his office Rittner had announced that 'lack of Arts Council funds is not the end of the road but the beginning of a different road'.[46] In November 1983 he proposed an exercise to Harewood, who was asked to assess the likely result of both a cut of 25 per cent in the Arts Council grant and an increase of the same amount. He wanted a response by 30 December and a decision would be made by 1 April 1984 as to whether to increase, decrease or terminate the funding of various clients.[47] On 21 December the Arts Council wrote to Harewood formally asking ENO and Covent Garden to enter into discussions about sharing a theatre.[48]

Harewood's response was immediate. The suggestion was, he later said, 'preposterous'.[49] A 25 per cent cut in funding would result in ENO ceasing to exist, and amalgamation would not help. The logistics of two different companies sharing their activities in one building (as opposed to merging into a new third entity) was 'mind-boggling'. They would have only a few months in which to perform and would have nowhere to rehearse. Harewood reminded the Arts Council that ENO presented an ensemble with a closely knit company of singers, rehearsing in depth and playing over forty weeks a year. That was not a body to be moved easily.[50]

ENO was indeed still very much a close-knit ensemble. In 1983 Zeb Lalljee started working in the costume-making department, where she was trained as a costume supervisor by Bill Strowbridge, the hands-on and much respected wardrobe manager at Lilian Baylis House. Lalljee recalled the sense of community within the costume-making rooms in the 1980s and in the wider company at Lilian Baylis House as well as at the Coliseum. The canteen was a meeting place for different branches of the company as well as for the directors and designers. In the era before health and safety regulations, and regardless of overtime costs, work would sometimes go on late into the night after a short break in the pub and fish and chips in the cutting rooms, and even on Sundays, in the effort to get the show on.

Salaries were low – Lalljee's was £92 a week – and working hours long, but the combination of Strowbridge's consideration, the camaraderie of the company and the excitement of seeing the final product on stage was exhilarating. 'It was about the show, nobody grudged the hours. We loved being here, it was a big part of our lives,' recalled Lalljee. Josephine Barstow remembered Strowbridge as the human core of the company whom everyone loved.[51]

The process was costly in overtime and the budgets somewhat open-ended. Such methods of work, which were symptomatic of the whole enterprise, were going to be hard to sustain in the new political climate. Furthermore, by December 1983 it was clear that raised ticket prices were affecting the box office. Maggie Sedwards, head of press and publicity, at the same time as studying the steady decline was looking at the composition of ENO audiences in an effort to decide how to balance ticket prices and get the most out of the box office. Sedwards pointed out that the controversial new shows were contributing to the box-office deterioration, which had been cushioned by the success of *Rigoletto* the previous year. While middle-of-the-road patrons were booking for the safe repertoire, they could no longer afford top price. Newer patrons were attracted by the new work but were not prepared to come regularly for what appeared to be experimental offerings. There had been a steady box-office decline since 1980/81, but the sharpest decline had been in 1983, when bookings for all the new productions had been disappointing.[52] This was true of most classical-music audiences and even the National Theatre. Another research paper by the Society of West End Theatre Managers had concluded that seat prices had 'risen faster than the market would bear'. There was a pool of about 500,000 operagoers, who were very sensitive to prices. Other members of the management team shared Sedwards's concern that ENO might be trying to lead the London opera public too quickly in a new direction.

Sedwards offered suggestions for increasing box-office returns. It was clear that the cheaper seats sold, and that the best stalls and dress circle also sold well but often at discounts. The rear dress circle and upper circle were overpriced and bad value. Her most radical suggestion, and that favoured by management, was for all seats to be sold at £10 or £5 with massive publicity. Another was a return to the prices of three years earlier.[53] Rupert Rhymes was particularly keen on drastically reduced prices but felt that the Arts

Council reaction was 'bound to be coloured by government think-ing'. He was sure that they would not look kindly on anything that was not in line with inflation.[54] In the end the only solution that could be decided upon without increasing the risk of insolvency was a price freeze, combined with increased marketing.[55]

At this difficult time, City University conducted an audience sur-vey for *The Rape of Lucretia*. Although its information was a snap-shot of a particular work at a particular moment, and the opera surveyed was not a core repertory piece, it was still revealing. It showed an audience largely over thirty years old, mainly from London or within a radius of forty miles, 52 per cent of whom were male. This sort of opera drew mainly dedicated operagoers and peo-ple who subscribed to the mailing lists of most of the subsidised companies. The overall picture was of a serious audience, well informed about the works they wished to see.[56]

Early in the new year it was estimated that the budget deficit for 1983/4 was liable to reach £500,000.[57] Thatcher's suggestion that more pounds in the pockets of those paying less tax would result in higher seat prices being manageable for the public, and sponsorship readily available, was proving to be fantasy. While the recession bit deeper, the very survival of ENO was yet again in question. On 4 January Goodman wrote directly to the Arts Minister, Lord Gowrie, asking for an urgent meeting to defend ENO from the threatened axe. Although ENO's financial situation was 'little short of disastrous', he argued that ENO was 'the main nursery of opera' in the UK. ENO, he wrote, 'not only breeds, trains and raises to a very high standard a host of young singers and musicians but also creates an ever widening circle of people who become interested in and support opera and the cultural and social satisfaction which it can give'. If it did not exist, he said, 'there would be a devastating gap'. ENO was 'reforming' itself. The board had been strengthened, and a major firm of accountants was now giving it a clean bill of health financially. Salaries, however, were far too low and there were no pension arrangements.* No fund-ing was available for the urgently needed improvements to the build-ing since ENO only leased rather than owned it.[58]

---

* Even by 1991 the only pension arrangements at ENO were the Equity chorus pension scheme of 1974 and the orchestra and music staff scheme whereby they received £675 a year towards their personal pension plans (B83 169, April 1991).

Although the Arts Council informed Harewood that the 1984/5 subsidy would be higher than expected, with a 12.5 per cent increase (to £5,918,250), that sum included £200,000 for capital expenditure and there would be no supplementary subsidies.[59] This was worrying since the decision to freeze ticket prices meant that a deficit of £320,000 was forecast.[60]

The previous September Covent Garden, which had also been suffering from severe deficits, had undergone an enquiry led by Clive Priestley of the government's Management and Efficiency Group, resulting in a recommendation that Covent Garden's grant be raised to £12.5 million to cover the deficit, together with a three-year commitment based on index-linked 'targeted funding'. Harewood later said that at the time of Priestley and after, he had thought it better to 'behave nicely' and work behind the scenes, but he later regretted it and wished that he had 'shrieked with the rest of them', having seen them rewarded.[61] Harewood's annoyance was somewhat misplaced, as it was only eighteen months later that Gowrie went back on the three-year commitment to Covent Garden. In the battle between monetarism and the arts, monetarism was the winner and none of the great institutions were safe.

Harewood's planning, however, was still bearing artistic fruit. In February 1984 Moshinsky's *The Mastersingers* opened. It was one of the battles that Tracey and Harewood had won. Harewood later recalled how Tracey had saved Moshinsky's production on 5 March 1981, when Elder, after having tea with 'Reggie' Goodall – as he was affectionately known – had tried to replace it with *Parsifal*, conducted by Goodall. Tracey, however, gave the idea short shrift and insisted that ENO needed *The Mastersingers*, both for itself and for the box office.[62] *Parsifal* was the only opera that Harewood would not countenance; he admitted that although he recognised it as a masterpiece, he rather hated it. He thought it 'a boring tiresome old story'. It was just 'endless discussions by basses'.[63]

Moshinsky's inspiration for *The Mastersingers* was drawn directly from the music, with what Cairns called 'a fresh eye and mind', while Elder, in the pit, gave coherence, shape and zest. The uncluttered space, Cairns thought, was created in order to people it with 'living individuals and their constantly developing relationships'.[64] According to Paul Griffiths, by updating the setting to the seventeenth century O'Brien and Moshinsky were able to borrow from the Dutch art of the period to create 'an atmosphere of cool, calm luminosity'.[65] The private action was played downstage on an apron stage over the orchestra, enabling Moshinsky 'to exercise his talent for gestural understatement and significant grouping with the utmost intensity'.[66] All the critics pointed to the inspired performances that the director elicited from the singers, 'every gesture making sense and every movement serving its purpose'.[67] Jean Rigby was Magdalene, Graham Clark David, and Janice Cairns Eva. Above all, Gwynne Howell, as well as singing fully and beautifully throughout the range, revealed acting skills that could not have been guessed from the 'static nobility' of such roles as King Mark. His inner turmoil was movingly conveyed, and his moment of loss was 'almost shocking in its bitterness'.[68] Griffiths found the new *Mastersingers* 'every bit as joyful, humane and mischievous' as its legendary 1968 Rosebery Avenue predecessor. 'One can only feel grateful', Cairns wrote, 'when a classic is reinterpreted in the light of a keen and sympathetic intelligence.'

The balance of power and planning, however, was shifting, and this was revealed in an interview between Nicholas Kenyon and Pountney, Elder and Harewood on 11 March 1984. Kenyon asked if ENO was neglecting the mainstream in favour of controversial successes. Pountney responded: 'It has been our vaunted aim to put on opera in an imaginative performance style that's stimulating.' The result was bound, he said, to make 'the older productions seem . . . different'. Harewood added, '. . . seem slacker, perhaps'. Elder pointed out that an evening at the Coliseum was not necessarily 'as safe' as it had been five years previously. He gave *Patience*, which he had recently seen with Pountney, as an example of the progress of the company. 'It works quite well,' he said, 'if you want a simple pretty approach.' But it was 'the sort of also-rans' that they intended to get rid of. What happens in the theatre, in his view, was 'eminently discardable'. Pountney went so far as to say that he would prefer to have no revivals at all, and Harewood admitted that Pountney's view had had an influence. Next season there would be nine new productions and thirteen revivals. Harewood concluded: 'We will have to gamble that we will catch the public's imagination and sell the tickets.'[69]

The Opera Committee, however, were doubtful that they could raise funds for the six new productions planned for the 1985/6 season, which included Alden's *Simon Boccanegra*, Miller's *Don Giovanni*, Copley's *Pearl Fishers* and Freeman's *Mask of Orpheus*.[70] On 11 April the finance director, David Fletcher, warned that the nature of the new productions was not yet accepted by the audience and advised cutting one or two of them and renewing the popular repertory so that ENO had some good revivals on the stocks.[71] On 14 May the board accepted the budget for 1984/5 without losing any new productions, as it was not felt that cancelling *Xerxes* would bring any financial advantage. The budget was balanced by basing it on a box office of 70 per cent rather than 67 per cent.[72]

On 2 April Harewood announced his retirement from the end of the 1984/5 season. The news buzzed around the bars of the opera houses. He had said that he was going to look after his estates in Yorkshire, but he was described as 'a man of rapid and fairly overpowering intensity' and it was pointed out how very *un*frail he looked at sixty-one.[73]

Harewood's last year was a combination of extraordinary artistic success, radical new productions and financial disaster. In July 1981 a group of Texan businessmen had suggested to Harewood that ENO visit Houston, and when Anthony Bliss – the Met's director – extended an invitation to New York, the idea of a USA tour in 1984 became a serious possibility. New Orleans was planning its World's Fair, San Antonio its second arts festival, and Austin University in Texas was also a possible venue. In 1982 Harewood had visited the US to discuss fundraising for the proposed tour. The fundraising consultant, Princess Obolensky and Associates, reported in June 1982 that although they had not identified any guaranteed funds, they had made considerable progress in establishing discounts on transport and accommodation and finding solid support for benefit events. Obolensky advised that another firm should be employed to source $1 million from corporate sponsorship.[74] Repertory planning began in November, with Valerie Masterson to sing Gilda.[75]

The first warning voice on the board was that of Nicholas Goodison on 10 January 1983, who stressed that it was essential to assess the potential costs involved. ENO was technically being invited by the American Friends, but although they were personally very wealthy, the organisation itself still possessed very limited resources.[76] In July 1983 the final decision about the American tour was delayed for six months. The board was informed by the development director, John Guy, on 16 January 1984 that the tour was estimated to cost $4 million and that although corporate approaches had been unsuccessful, Princess Obolensky had raised nearly $230,000, of which $37,000 was guaranteed. Governor White of Texas had indicated his willingness to raise $750,000. Guy estimated that with the guaranteed income, the planned activities and Governor White's funding, ENO could cover the budget total.

The board was less convinced and expressed doubts about Governor White's fundraising abilities. The new Arts Council music director, Richard Lawrence, said the Arts Council could not countenance such a potential loss. It was felt that the risk of going ahead was greater than that of cancelling. Goodman, as usual a positive and energetic force, asked other members of the board to try to secure some guarantees as he had already done, while Elder stressed 'the effect the ensemble nature of the company would have in the US' and emphasised the importance of the tour to the morale of the company. The cost of aborting it would already be $376,000.[77]

The final decision was again postponed, this time to 2 February, when Harewood told the board that he had personally met Governor White and had 'considerable confidence in his ability to raise the target set'. The board was again less impressed and pointed out that White's telegram had indicated no more than his willingness to approach certain interested organisations with a view to sponsorship of $100,000 each. There was also concern about the lack of response from the American corporate sector, even though there was an overall improvement in committed funds of $196,000. Dell thought that the deficiency on the tour could reach $1 million. Some board members were convinced that the risk was too great; others that the tour would greatly enhance the morale and the international reputation of the company.[78] The decision was delayed yet again, until Harewood received an encouraging letter at the end of the month from Governor White, who was making progress with such corporations as Texaco and Exxon. 'The US tour is important to Texans', he wrote, because it would 'show the vitality of Texas as a place to be'.[79] After reading this letter on 29 February the board decided to go ahead with the tour.

There was further unease, however, in the Tour Subcommittee on 9 April following Fletcher's confirmation that the company 'might experience a $1 million shortfall'. On 11 April Goodman reported his meeting with Grey Gowrie, the Arts Minister, who had agreed to present the financial situation to the Treasury and had emphasised the government's desire for the tour to proceed.[80] On 14 May Goodman told the board that he believed he could make up from individuals the amount promised by White if necessary, and reported Gowrie's support. Although the board felt the overall position was unsatisfactory, the risk was sufficiently reduced for the tour to go ahead.[81]

With the minister's encouragement, and Goodman's assurance, the tour began as planned on 24 May in Houston and ended on 29 June at the Metropolitan Opera in New York. ENO was the first British company to play in Texas and at the Met. The travelling company consisted of 360 people, plus seventeen containers of scenery and a full orchestra. They performed *Gloriana*, *Patience*, *War and Peace*, *The Turn of the Screw* and *Rigoletto*. A member of faculty at Austin University told Elder, 'You're not just an opera company, you're missionaries.'[82]

The 9 June performance of *The Turn of the Screw* at San Antonio was poorly organised with minimal promotion and played to empty houses. The Louisiana World Exposition was in deep financial trouble, and the theatre could not be opened for weekend rehearsals, so that the first night of *Rigoletto* on 11 June had to be cancelled. Once word of mouth spread, however, *Rigoletto* became full and wildly popular.

Elder conducted a gala performance of *Gloriana* in New York on 23 June attended by Princess Alexandra. *Patience*, with Anne Collins, Eric Shilling and Derek Hammond Stroud, got a standing ovation at the Met on 21 June. *Rigoletto* was also enthusiastically received on 20 June at the Met, with just a few boos from some of the house's more conservative audience. Masterson could not sing Gilda at the first performance because of a sore throat and Helen Field took over in an admirable Met debut. Masterson returned later to wild acclaim. Ronald Gellat wrote in *Opera News* in June 1984: 'At its best, the ENO performs with a zestful panache and precision more typical of a Broadway musical than an ordinary opera company', adding that 'the singers are used to collaborating as a team and it shows in their work together'.

Management felt that the tour was another landmark in the development of the company's reputation and self-esteem, which, like the Goodall *Ring*, enabled the company to move on to the next stage of its artistic achievement. There was, however, a deficit of $944,000. It was clear that the minister would have to be reminded of the 'strong hint' that he had given about finding additional funds before the tour began. In August Harewood reported to the board that the tour had been a tremendous success and morale had been very high. In New York they had been received with rapture. Most of the fundraising events had met their targets and the theatre guarantees had been provided, but there was still no news from Governor White.[83]

To add to the company's woes, *Orpheus in the Underworld* had to be postponed as Gerald Scarfe had been too late with his designs owing to his inexperience with opera. Pountney had chosen Scarfe because he had so liked a cartoon he had drawn of *Valkyrie*. It was decided that a revival of *Arabella* with Barstow and conducted by Elder would take its place. On 10 September the board insisted on a balanced budget for the 1985/6 financial year. Savings of £1,065,000 were to be made. After long discussions it was decided that both *Simon Boccanegra* and *The Pearl Fishers* would have to be delayed and replaced by *Don Carlos* and *La bohème*.[84]

Harewood wrote to Governor White two days later, asking for a clear statement one way or the other. The situation at ENO, he wrote, was a grim one. Arnold Goodman finally heard from Governor White that he felt that he had fulfilled his undertaking. Goodman immediately set about forming a Fundraising Committee to cover the tour deficit. By end of the 1984/5 season $622,899 had been raised towards the debt. Bernard Williams summed up the results of the tour in a letter to Goodman: 'The financial result is terrible' and without Goodman's efforts would have been even worse. Equally important, however, was the tour's 'immense success, beyond anyone's expectations', which might 'prove one of the best things we have done'.[85]

*The Ring* was finally cancelled in the autumn. On 20 September it was decided by the planners that other roles were to be found for the singers.[86] Elder was bitterly disappointed. He had grown up with Wagner's music, having been the prompter during Solti's last *Walküre* at Covent Garden. The company had a Wagner tradition, the Coliseum had the right acoustic for it and the orchestra was fit and ready.[87] At the meeting Harewood expressed his concern that there were fewer and fewer small and simple productions to fit into the repertoire. Designers, Harewood also said, must be told that ENO needed repertory not festival productions.[88]

The first new production of the autumn season was Janáček's *Osud*, partnered with Weill's *Mahagonny*, on 8 September. Rodney Blumer translated *Osud*, suffusing this previously neglected small master-piece with his admiration and understanding. Blumer and Pountney succeeded in giving coherence and meaning to what had previously been considered a diffuse and amateurish libretto by the best friend of Janáček's dead daughter, the young Fedora Bartošová. Milnes wrote of the libretto's 'Strindberg, dream-like, proto cinematic con-struction, the motivic recurrence of words and phrases as complex as Janáček's score'.[89] Cairns believed that by treating it sympathet-ically with the techniques of the cinema, Pountney and Lazaridis enabled it to spring to life and take on 'meaning, shape, coher-ence'.[90] Philip Langridge as the composer, Živný, gave a perform-ance 'as psychologically acute' as it was musically fine.[91] Eilene Hannan's Mila also presented 'compassion on a truly tragic scale'.[92]

In September Graham Vick's new production of *Madam Butterfly* stripped away all vestiges of sentimentality, presenting a harsh pic-ture of 'occidental callousness and oriental suffering'. John Mauceri paced and shaped the music thrillingly, drawing 'sublime playing' from the orchestra and strongly underlining the cruelty and pain emphasised in the production.[93] Janice Cairns had taken over when Linda Esther Gray withdrew, singing Butterfly with occasional vocal harshness but full dramatic power and conviction. Vick focused on Butterfly's self-delusion, and on the shabby callousness of David Rendall's Pinkerton. Norman Bailey gave a shattering depiction of the world-weary Sharpless. Lazaridis's monochrome set on two levels, beautifully lit by Mathew Richardson, placed the opera in a cluttered shanty approached by a muddy path. Together with Mauceri's superb musical direction, Vick, although occasion-ally underlining his concept too insistently, brought a fresh eye and ear to an overfamiliar work. Milnes alone felt that the emphasis on

Butterfly's self-delusion suggested a pathological condition that diminished her stature and lessened the tragedy.[94] Within the house Vick's *Butterfly* assumed the status of an iconic and greatly admired show that was not replaced for twenty years.

Harewood's day was nearly over and ENO's planning was about to enter a new era. On 9 July 1984 the board was asked by the sub-committee to ratify the appointment of the thirty-seven-year-old Peter Jonas as the next managing director, after advertisements in the press had resulted in over thirty applications and interviews with several serious candidates.[95]

Jonas, who had spent most of his adult life in the United States, had first met Elder through a mutual friend in the late 1960s while he had been studying English at Sussex University. They had all three then worked at Glyndebourne as 'supers' – walk-on extras. With a Jewish father – a refugee from Hamburg before the war – and a mother of Lebanese extraction born in Jamaica, Jonas himself had been educated at a Roman Catholic English boarding school. He was an admirer of German cultural life and, with time, a fluent German speaker. After university Jonas had studied musicology at the Royal College of Music, where the principal, Sir Keith Faulkner, had introduced him to an encouraging John Tooley at Covent Garden. Tooley, in turn, had introduced him to Georg Solti, who urgently needed a temporary assistant at the Chicago Symphony Orchestra for three months. As a result of this, Jonas worked at Chicago for eleven years, from 1974, first as Solti's assistant and then as director of artistic administration. It was a post that had given him not only an understanding of daily arts administration but also of marketing, fundraising and advertising.

Jonas had invited Elder in the spring of 1983 to conduct the Chicago Symphony Orchestra. It was on the return journey from Chicago that Elder's wife Amanda suggested that Jonas would be the right person for ENO. ENO held a 'huge fascination' for Jonas, who had learnt about opera from Sadler's Wells and ENO – especially the Goodall *Mastersingers*. Encouraged by Elder, Harewood met Jonas in New York, where they had a long conversation about opera and life. Harewood was impressed, later describing Jonas as 'unputdownable', although some members of Goodman's selection committee were concerned about his budgetary skills and the fact that he did not come from a business background.[96] Although Jonas stressed during the interview that his task was to promote and drive forward the artistic aspirations of the company, he also impressed upon them that he had handled a budget of $17.8 million at Chicago. This helped the case of his supporters, Harewood and Goodman. From September 1984 Jonas was involved in planning.

The end of Harewood's era at ENO marked a sharp deterioration in relations with the Arts Council. Rees-Mogg was widely considered by the arts community to be a cuckoo in the nest of the Arts Council. Sir Roy Shaw later argued that Rees-Mogg was appointed chairman to undermine the independence of the Arts Council and weaken the arm's-length principle. The previous three chairmen – Lord Goodman, Lord Gibson, a Tory, and Kenneth Robinson, Labour, later SDP – had all kept their political allegiance firmly out of the way, Shaw wrote, whereas Rees-Mogg had 'worn Mrs Thatcher's favour on his cockade'.[97] From this time the Arts Council changed from being the defender of the arts to being the policeman.

Rees-Mogg gave a speech on 11 March 1985 in which he stated:

The great drawback to subsidy is that it can weaken the sinews of self-help. Too often subsidy has created dependence and dependence has led to the demand for higher subsidy. I am shocked by the number of performing companies who congratulate themselves on having built their taxpayers' subsidy levels to more than half their total revenue.

He was depressed by the way artists were trapped 'in the post-Fabian *Guardian* consciousness of genteel and academic English collectivism' and was determined to 'liberate' the national companies from such insecure reliance on the state, at the same time as shifting the balance of subsidy towards the provinces.[98]

The Arts Council document 'The Glory of the Garden' of March 1984 had stressed the need to decentralise the artistic life of the country. In it Rees-Mogg had waxed metaphorical: 'We can dung and we can water but we cannot create a single flower. The British garden of the arts has great beauties throughout, and a magnificent display at the centre, but there are empty beds and neglected shrubberies.' The policy of the next few years managed to distribute the neglect more widely.

The message was clear. In August the chairman of the Finance and General Purposes Committee, Edmund Dell, warned that he believed that a different attitude was being adopted by the Arts Council and the government towards opera and that deficits were not going to be so easily cancelled by special grants in the future. It was agreed that the company was underfunded, but they still had to pay their bills.[99]

Dell's suspicions were justified. Jonas, on one of his visits to London before he took over, went with Harewood to see Luke Rittner, the new Arts Council director general. Jonas recalled how Rittner voiced the Arts Council's concerns about ENO's expenditure, the loss on the American tour and the unsolved problem of the Coliseum lease. London received too much money and there would in future be no guarantee against loss. There was, Jonas recalled, an antagonistic atmosphere. Harewood was reported as saying, 'Once the Arts Council was on the side of the performers. Now it has changed sides.'[100]

Confrontation was indeed becoming the main system of interaction in politics and society. In the spring of 1984 Thatcher took on the miners' union, after three years of building up stocks of coal so that it would be possible to withstand the reaction that would ensue from the closure of pits. The general secretary of the National Union of Mineworkers, Arthur Scargill, was as determined to bring down Thatcher as she was to defeat him. The government's offer to the NUM provided compensation for those losing their jobs and that there would be only voluntary redundancies. The general public, who had always been sympathetic to the miners, felt this to be a fair offer and as the strike continued, public support for the miners waned. There were violent confrontations between police and strikers. Thatcher's language was confrontational: 'We had to face an enemy without in the Falklands,' she told the 1922 Committee on 19 July, and 'we have always to be aware of the enemy within . . . tyranny may always enter'.[101]

At the start of Harewood's last season there was an element of dissatisfaction within the company as productions grew in size and expense, while ENO's efforts to match salaries in comparable institutions were always being put on hold. Low wages were constantly being mentioned and had begun to cause trouble with the Musicians Union. Kenyon in the *Sunday Times* reported that the chorus were also disgruntled, feeling that ENO did too many productions and could spend some of the money on them. He wrote of the ninety-one musicians of the orchestra, whose 'enthusiasm survives the rain and smell of drains that assails them after a storm'.[102*]

In late November 1984 the board and management met at University College Oxford for the weekend to discuss in depth the financial problems and serious concerns about the box office. There was a projected deficit, not including the American tour, of £118,000.[103] During the conference there were criticisms of the fundraising set-up, and discussions about the need for a development trust to be created as soon as possible. Significant sums had been raised by Arnold Goodman to cover the US deficit, but it was made clear that other members of the board would have to be more active in finding sponsorship.[104]

As well as agreeing to make efforts to bring in more private revenue, the board attempted at the conference to lay down the law to management by demanding that experimental or unconventional activity must be 'contained within the company's financial capability'. The Finance Committee did not receive information early enough, and the Opera Committee wanted more reporting about general artistic policy. There needed to be sophisticated controls to monitor the financial implications of all planning decisions.[105] In response to questions at the Opera Committee two weeks later as to the balance between what the consumer wanted and what ENO thought they should want, Tracey explained that Pountney was trying to do something quite different from the popular big-house style developed under Arlen and Harewood. The public might begin by being suspicious of the 'new look', Pountney admitted, but the enthusiasm for *Butterfly* was very encouraging.[106]

The board was not going to halt developments. The next new production, the Norwest Holst *Mazeppa*, set the seal on the new era. Harewood had not been informed of the concept of its director, David Alden, before the work was complete. Alden told Hugh Canning on 20 December, the day of its premiere, that he thought it 'thoroughly appropriate to take an openly aggressive, anti-traditional and angry stance'. His guru was Ruth Berghaus, with whom Alden shared a love of everyday objects as well as a desire 'to rouse

---

* Elder pointed out that the drains occasionally still stank backstage in 2007.

conflicting responses in audiences' and 'to set music and action against each other'.* His and his designer David Fielding's production of *Mazeppa* was, he explained, an attempt to find 'some scrappy modern metaphor for the Cossack world in modern clothing, with only occasional references to Russian History and with echoes in the world of Stalin and Solzhenitsyn'. By setting *Mazeppa* in an unappealing Communist municipal building, they were creating a frame for what they called a 'tortured-up' view of love and presenting the story with brutal realism and simplicity. Alden said he would be very disappointed if there was not 'some kind of anti-reaction', and he added: 'Our style is essentially provocative.'[107]

In the *Mazeppa* programme, Alden elucidated his theme further:

Ideally, every theatrical event should draw a fine line between something extremely clear and immediate to the audience and something which speaks to the unconscious and may seem random and unfathomable at other levels. Music itself is very unclear about what it is describing. To spell it out on stage is to dictate a meaning; it's better to open up something inside people and let the music speak to them in their own way. As a director, my greatest wish is to rid myself of hideous and uninteresting theatrical tradition.

The production indeed provoked. Both audience and critics reacted as strongly as Alden had hoped they would. At the first night there was booing after the ballet and for the choreographer – possibly mistaken for Alden, who was not present during the curtain call. Audiences were not yet familiar with the future clichés of deconstructionist and conceptual production: white-walled utility rooms, naked light bulbs, the hospital-waiting-room set with its

---

* Berghaus (1927–96) had been the Intendant of the Berliner Ensemble from 1971 to 1977 and staged many radical ideological productions at Frankfurt in the 1980s. Although a member of the Communist Party, and privileged to travel abroad, some of her productions were too radical for the East German authorities. For Berghaus the visual was an ironical intellectual comment on a dead art form. Her famous November 1974 Munich *Barber of Seville* took place on a sculpture of a huge naked female torso designed by Andreas Reinhardt. Rosina was incarcerated in this torso, Almaviva climbed over its pubic hair and Rosina emerged through a bosom-balcony (*Opera*, June 1975, p. 575). Berghaus's series of productions at Frankfurt for music director Michael Gielen from 1980 to 1986 continued to focus on a subtext, using an obscure language of gestures and movement whereby the scenery and blocking rather than the music suggested the story.

blinding fluorescent lights, washbasin, Ascot water heater, serried rows of chairs for patients and the tea trolley, or the trilby-hatted henchman 'entirely swathed in bandages and all crawling along with suitcases'.[108]

The level of violence in the production – murder by chainsaw, torture and blood liberally spattered on the walls – shocked, despite its inherent place in the story and text. Milnes was provoked into one of his wittiest reviews. Having been told by a 'bright young opera producer' that this one was going 'to give all you opera critics hernias', he had laced himself up in his sturdiest stays, armed himself with a hip flask and proceeded to the Coliseum. Milnes continued:

We all, as Orwell knew so well, have little things we can't take, and amongst mine are anything to do with arms and wrists. When an orgy of slashing closed the first act, I damned nearly threw up over the chap sitting in front of me, and the fact that he happened to be ENO's director of productions suggests that there may be some justice in the world after all.[109]

All the critics recognised the value of staging *Mazeppa* in a cheap and modern-dress production, and accepted the moral truth in Alden's reading of 'political power violently abused'.[110] They also recognised his technical skills. What they objected to, and what remained one of the main areas for conflict in the debate, was the intentional pitching of music against the staging. Norris asked how Mazeppa could pop up through the floor surrounded by deformed corpses in the hospital waiting room and sing of the 'sweetness of the Ukrainian air and the stars twinkling in the sky'.[111]

While the dislocation disturbed, there were no complaints about the actual music-making. The sound Elder drew from the orchestra was 'unmistakably Russian, big, fat, hotly energetic' and the orchestra's playing 'stunning', wrote Milnes. The entire ensemble of singers was also highly praised, especially the strong and steady spinto singing of Janice Cairns and Malcolm Donnelly's firmly focused Mazeppa.

Elder later recalled the excitement of the first vociferous expressions of anger and support within the audience. There were many letters of enraged and offended complaint to Harewood and Tracey, most from regular visitors to ENO, many of whom had left at the interval. They were particularly upset by the torture, sharing Milnes's reaction that it was 'too revolting to watch' and complaining that there should have been a warning about the violence. Correspondents were anxious to prove their open-minded credentials by pointing out that they had enjoyed *Rigoletto*, *Rienzi*, *Butterfly* and *Osud*, but they stressed that far from having their emotions 'opened up', they had not been aware of any idea at all emerging from *Mazeppa*. Many were particularly distressed because *Mazeppa* was an opera that they would probably never have the chance to see again.[112]

Harewood wrote a very thoughtful reply to one correspondent on 15 February 1985. He had not agreed with Alden's treatment of the second-act monologue, which was supposed to show 'the good and poetic side of an anti hero – Mazeppa'. There, he thought ENO 'did less than justice' to Tchaikovsky. He defended, however, what he called 'the bloody stuff' as not lacking in logic. *Mazeppa* was an opera that could take such treatment, whereas *Bohème* or *Traviata* would not be treated in such a manner by ENO, as they were in Europe. He was sorry for any offence as the main purpose of operatic performance was 'to give pleasure', even when it was hoped to make the audience 'sit up and take a bit more notice' than usual.[113] Pountney was less conciliatory with another correspondent, revealing a different emphasis to that of the outgoing managing director. Tchaikovsky himself had not wanted his work to appear 'like some rarefied piece of furniture in an exhibition being examined for the neatness of its curves and the originality of its carving'. His correspondent seemed, he told him, to be expecting a 'kind of museum exhibit'.[114]

Harewood's idea of the Norwest series proved to be highly influential on ENO style over the next decade. It made it possible, Pountney later explained, for directors to do 'essentially big grand operas on no money', in a minimal or ironic way, with the 'rather Brechtian device of the chorus not learning their parts'. Pountney added, 'It was a bit of a Trojan horse, really, and I am not sure that George or any of us quite realised what we had set in motion.'[115]

Harewood made a last plea to his young colleagues for planning variety and good sense, writing to Elder, Pountney and Jonas on 27 January 1985, urging them to countenance an 'elegant' *Faust*, to which he believed the audience would still come. It could have a fine cast with Joan Rogers, Arthur Davies and John Tomlinson. He favoured 'a mid-nineteenth century concept' but would preclude 'making the soldiers' chorus into an anti-war hymn (limping veterans, bloody bandages, sorrowing population)'. It was not, he insisted, 'that kind of affair'. Even Mephistopheles was more a 'boulevardier blagueur' than a sinister character. He asked them to find a producer who would respect the music's elegance.

Harewood was worried that Alden was refusing to discuss his concept for *Boccanegra*, even though he excused Alden's earlier reticence about revealing his plans for *Mazeppa*. 'One could easily argue', he wrote, 'that it was a one-off affair, which demanded a single simple direct idea which he had not really got when he discussed it with Mark.' *Boccanegra*, however, was quite different. It was 'a dark masterpiece' and it belonged in its period and in its setting, 'which must be Genoa'. To do it another way, Harewood believed, would be 'to plan for failure and to waste money'. He believed in Alden's talent and thought he could do it 'marvellously', but 'his ideas must fit the music'. Otherwise ENO was heading for 'a deserved failure with Public and Press alike'.[116] On 8 February Ian Judge was chosen for *Faust*. Although he had little experience in opera, he loved the piece.[117]

*Mazeppa* was a shot across the bows for ENO's wary audience. The remainder of the season saw some exciting yet easily acceptable productions new to ENO. The first was *Tristan and Isolde*, on 26 January. It was Friedrich's 1974 production for Netherlands Opera, which he prepared himself, working for the first time at ENO. Michael Tanner judged the production to be both 'very Seventies and utterly timeless'. A flattened spiral provided 'confined brightly lit acting areas amidst the encircling gloom'. Friedrich's direction was 'fresh, purposeful and technically impeccable', with an extraordinary *coup de théâtre* when the couple are discovered and the sky falls in: the glowing stars glowing ever brighter in the love duet were replaced by a bank of harsh footlights, the lovers ringed by soldiers. Remedios was 'quite extraordinarily convincing in Act III, transformed out of recognition from 1981 . . . supported and led at every moment by Goodall, he projects an anguish that seems to come entirely from within'. Goodall built up the tension slowly so that the last act was extraordinarily powerful, 'with both singers apparently possessed, and the orchestra pouring out tone beyond imagining'.[118] Linda Esther Gray could still not manage to return for a role in which she had been outstanding, and Johanna Meier, an experienced Isolde, learnt the role in English. She was a fine actress and very musical, her voice 'glorious at the top and always mellow and round'.[119]

Nicholas Hytner's production of *Xerxes*, edited by Mackerras and Noel Davies, and translated by Hytner, was premiered on 23 February 1985, the tercentenary of Handel's birth. The production was hugely appreciated by audience and critics alike and proved to be one of ENO's most loved and admired productions for over two decades. Milnes later commented that *Xerxes* was a breakthrough in Handel production. Hytner, having read English literature at Cambridge, specialising in the eighteenth century, understood the piece in depth. 'He was so inventive – even including the unities with dawn to dusk lighting.'*

The action was presented 'in eighteenth-century terms through twentieth-century minds, perfectly attuned and sympathetic to those terms'. Fielding, responding to Hytner's vision, presented a witty and elegant set, not in Persia, but in a fantasy Vauxhall Gardens, 'in the throes of a near eastern fad', wrote Stephen Walsh.[120] Grey silk-clad tourists wandered through the gardens examining the engineering and natural-history exhibits, or sat reading newspapers in deck chairs. Bald valets moved huge topiary sphinxes on and off. Persepolis was a mere model village, set in the desert at the back of the stage 'below a ravishingly varied sky'.[121] The Hellespont bridge was as 'fragile an exhibit as an ostrich egg'.[122] Kenyon was also delighted. The designs were realised with 'such exquisite visual sense' and were so beautifully lit and the production itself 'so responsive to the music, so witty and perceptive that it was an unqualified triumph'. In this production it was generally agreed that the acute artificiality of the setting pointed up the 'contrast with the real passions unleashed', that the laughs and slightly distancing framework only enhanced the depth of emotion felt within it.

Hytner's production rightly relished 'the exaggeration of

---

* Pountney later recalled that he had wanted to direct *Xerxes* but that when Hytner had expressed his desire to do it, he had agreed, in what turned out to be 'an inspired move' (email to author, 10.8.08).

emotions both comic and tragic, in which Handel indulges so glori-ously', Kenyon wrote. Hytner explained that Handel requires singing actors capable of sustaining great arcs of emotions, actors of poise and concentration. In a Handel aria it was necessary to expand one feeling and make it last ten minutes. 'You can save Stanislavsky for the recitatives,' he said, 'but you must work to make your world special enough, odd enough, to make your appar-ently odd way of behaving seem natural.'[123] Milnes was won over. The whole staging was sophisticated, knowing, sharp and 'enor-mously *educated*'.[124]

The evening also set new vocal and orchestral standards for Handel under Mackerras's direction. The playing was precise and lively, beautiful and full of dramatic point. As with the production, twentieth-century know-how was 'put to the service of eighteenth-century sensibility'.[125] There was highly distinguished singing as well as characterisation from Ann Murray as Xerxes and Chris-topher Robson as Arsamenes, Valerie Masterson as Romilda and Lesley Garrett as her wickedly flirtatious sister Atalanta. Jean Rigby's Amastris showed depth of emotion, while looking gor-geous, disguised as an abbé or an officer. Mackerras thought it the most successful Handel production that he had worked on. Word of mouth soon improved a disappointing early box office until the Coliseum was 95 per cent full by the end of the run. It won both the Laurence Olivier Award for best opera production and the London *Evening Standard* opera award. As with Miller's best productions, *Xerxes* was still appealing to audiences in 2006.

Another ensemble production that delighted public and critics alike was *The Bartered Bride*, directed by Moshinsky and designed by one of the greatest designers of the era, John Bury. It opened on 4 April. Bury's grassy paddock surrounded by giant sunflowers stood in front of flats displaying a rolling Czech landscape, like a primitive Monet or Bonnard. Across the proscenium stretched a candy-striped canvas in front of which the more intimate scenes were enacted. Sutcliffe described how Nick Chelton's lighting cap-tured an early summer morning with the 'threat of thunder and headaches', bright at ground level, ominously shady in the sky, and how it perfectly caught the emotional tone. Moshinsky, with the same sensibilities as Miller, found a telling social setting for the work, a slightly post-First World War one, with bikes, cameras, Fair

Isle jumpers and loads of beer drinking. Rustic glamour and pretti-
fication were out; each inhabitant of the village was brought 'pul-
satingly to life'. During the exciting, 'tacky and lively' last-act
circus, Rosemary Ashe's Esmeralda did manage a few steps on the
high wire despite the financial restrictions placed on the rehearsal.
Eleanor Fazan's choreography contributed to the individualisation
of the chorus, dancers and actors. David Murray wrote how youth
cavorted, seniors proved they could still remember the steps, infants
insisted on being included, children were everywhere. The result of
all this intelligent detail was a 'plausible, endearing and funny' production.[126]

The last production and another success of the late Harewood
era was the British premiere of Philip Glass's *Akhnaten*, on 17 June
1985. Harewood had supported Houston Grand Opera's suggestion of a proposed collaboration in July 1982 because he realised
that Glass had a tremendous following amongst young people and
that he was looked upon with something like reverence.[127]

Conducted by Paul Daniel, the show made 82 per cent capacity
on a schedule of greatly reduced prices and brought a substantially
new audience into the Coliseum, much to management's delight. In
the company's review of the season it was noted that *Akhnaten* had
been mesmerically produced by David Freeman and had had the
delightful effect of 'non-plussing the musical establishment'.[128]

Harewood had prepared for a new era of opera production with the
original yet popular work of Miller, Moshinsky, Freeman and
Hytner. The new regime, however, was to find its own and very distinct style of production. Of the new management, Harewood
reflected many years later that 'they purported not to use personal
likes and dislikes'. Nonetheless, they succeeded in not using Miller,
he said, 'and Jonathan knew it. They thought it was going back.
They were quite wrong. He was a forward-looking producer in a
different way to them. He didn't want to splash paint in the face of
the public.'[129]

Pountney had given his promised planning statement to the
Opera Committee on 11 February. Any successful period in the
management of a theatre, he argued, should be regarded as 'an
artistic tyranny in which the passionately held views of those running the theatre dominated the artistic criteria governing the many

decisions which formulate the company's plans'. What was important was the 'tilt', which he was steering 'towards the unusual'. As far as he was concerned this was the justification for the existence of a second opera house in London, as ENO could not compete in the mainstream repertoire. Theatre was not 'passive' but spoke 'passionately to its age', and the demands made of the audience should be equal to the pleasure. ENO was moving towards a '"European" view of production'. Such a 'radical, enquiring and sometimes provocative style', he admitted, would not appeal to all ENO's present audience, but more could be gained from a new generation of operagoers than would ultimately be lost.

Board member Ronald Swayne thanked Pountney for his fascinating precis but wondered if a radical policy that could only pay off later could be afforded at present. Jonas responded that they could not afford *not* to choose such a way forward. He argued that England was not very advanced compared with Germany, and added a little aside about the *Mazeppa* violence, wondering whether the 'social and political preoccupation of the arts in Germany was the result of their violent history', especially in the first part of the twentieth century.[130]

While Pountney was preparing to jolt the audience, Harewood had warned on 4 March that the next few weeks were critical for the company and expenditure was being monitored on a weekly basis to ensure that the company's overdraft was not exceeded.[131] At Harewood's last board meeting on 13 May it was noted that although the 1985/6 budget had been accepted, it was based on a forecast of 72 per cent box office, which had depended on an advertising budget that had now been cut. The future indeed looked perilous.

Jonas had told the 11 April Opera Committee that his aim was to broaden the public's attitude to opera. There were, he felt, no easy solutions to attracting the public. He pointed out that the *Count Ory* revival in March had been enjoyed by the press and the public and exceeded its budget at the box office, although it was not good musically or visually and management's aim was to get away from this style of production.[132]*

* An audience survey carried out by Caroline Gardner of City University from February to June 1985 confirmed that most visitors were attracted by the company's reputation as exciting and innovative, but at the same time most nega-

Harewood had known very well how to attract audiences. *Tristan* and *Rigoletto* had both achieved 97 per cent, a revival of *Tosca* 90 per cent. *The Bartered Bride* had started at 75 per cent but after word of mouth reached 91 per cent at the last performance. *Figaro* had played to packed houses throughout its run. An educated and discriminating audience, built up over many years by such directors as Guthrie, St-Denis and Byam Shaw, which was enjoying the work of Miller, Moshinsky and Hytner, was either to be educated into accepting a post-Felsenstein, post-Strehler, European way of thinking or to be replaced by a younger, more modern audience. Harewood was of an older and gentler world view than his young colleagues. On 23 March 1985 he wrote ruefully: 'I suppose the middle-aged followers of Felsenstein would all be thought rather behind the times by those who want novelty at any price.'[133]

---

tive comments had been directed against the extremes of 'producer's opera', especially of *Mazeppa*, as well as poor diction. Up to 42 per cent of visitors came from within the Greater London, but not central London, area. Two thirds of the audience were between twenty-five and fifty-four, thirty-five- to forty-four-year-olds making up the most significant group. Average *Akhnaten* audiences were younger at between twenty-five and thirty-four. The core audience made between three and ten visits a year. The most important sources of information were the mailing list and word of mouth. *The Times* was the most important paper; *Opera* the most important magazine.

# 1985–1987: 'The Shock of the New'

The mid-1980s was an era of confrontation in British politics, the culmination of which was the miners' strike of 1984–5. ENO mirrored the political battles in its engagement with the Arts Council and even with its audience. As Prime Minister Thatcher fought the unions, reduced the size of the welfare state and 'educated' the British people to be more self-reliant, so the ENO management, responding to the zeitgeist of an increasingly materialistic era, battled with the politicians and Rees-Mogg's Arts Council, and confronted their audience with radical productions in order to shake them from complacency and to create lively debate.

The embattled were characters of strong personalities and convictions. Peter Jonas, two years before he left ENO, advised Harewood on what qualities to look for in a new general director. The 'Intendant' must not only have a clear artistic point of view, he wrote, but also 'charisma, leadership quality, and "civil courage"'. *Zivilcourage* – a German concept meaning the courage to defend one's beliefs – was defined by Jonas as 'the strength to stand up and disagree with the community, the government, the Arts Council, Unions, colleagues, even the Board if necessary'. It was, he said, 'fatal to cowtow [*sic*] or bow to the pressure of criticism if after due thought and consideration, one is still of the opposing view'.[1] According to Elder, Jonas relished the battle; he was 'quite fearless and loved confrontation'.[2]* In contrast to Harewood, who did not believe in the cult of personality, Jonas was also keen to maintain a high public profile. There was also a rare unity of vision, mutual

---

* Elder recalled how Jonas would conduct difficult negotiations in his small office with the windows and door closed and the heating turned up full blast, whatever the time of the year, and let them 'stew until they agreed to his demands in order to get out of the room' (interview, 9.4.07). It was a technique, Jonas recalled, he had learnt from the president of the Chicago Symphony Orchestra (interview, 9.5.08).

respect and lack of infighting in the triumvirate – Elder, Pountney, Jonas – that created a technically effective and highly creative and enjoyable workplace for those employed there.

The battle was not just one between strong personalities; it also had powerful political undertones. As Jonas later put it, they were producing their work at a time when there was a 'right-wing, vivid prime minister' who was alive to the way society was being formed, and they were being told to 'sink or swim by virtue of the market'. They saw the dream built up in England after the war of a benevolent Arts Council and national companies – in which there was a great deal of pride – as being threatened and were reacting to the status quo. Furthermore, being young and influenced by Middle European dramaturgy, they would 'wield a hammer' to do it.[3]

The Arts Council's unhelpful attitude remained a source of friction throughout Rees-Mogg's chairmanship, and Jonas's relations with him proved to be very stormy. He later recalled to Harewood how the years that Rees-Mogg had spent at the Arts Council had been 'a solemn purgatory from which we hardly recover'.[4] One of Jonas's early tasks was to respond to the report of the Arts Council's Opera Study Group, which proposed greater regional activity at the expense of the London companies. A cut of £550,000 to support the regional companies, he told the secretary general Luke Rittner, would mean that ENO would not be able to sustain its 600 employees. The implications of the report, he said, 'could be severely damaging to opera in this country'.[5] Rees-Mogg had told Jonas that although the party was not over, 'the limits of the hospitality' had been reached.[6]

ENO's immediate survival depended on its ability to prove to the Arts Council that it could raise £400,000 towards the US tour deficit. Without this assurance the Arts Council was refusing to forward even the cash it was late in paying over and without which the bank would not extend ENO's overdraft facility in order to pay the immediate bills. By July 1985 there was a serious cash-flow problem. The delay in the Arts Council payment alone incurred £15,195 interest.[7]

David Elliott, who took over from David Fletcher as finance director in June, later recalled that two weeks after his arrival it seemed as though it would be impossible to pay the wages, Coutts having indicated that they were not willing to continue with the overdraft, at which point the Arts Council withheld the monthly grant on the basis that if ENO was about to become insolvent, 'it would be irresponsible of them to disburse public funds'. Elliott recalled that Lord Hoffman urged the Arts Council not to precipitate insolvency, while he persuaded Coutts to extend the overdraft so that he and Jonas could come up with proposals to fund the tour deficit as well as prepare a business plan to put the company on sounder footing.[8]

Insolvency was finally averted when the government stepped into the tour-deficit breach in September. Richard Luce, who had taken over from Grey Gowrie as Minister for the Arts, told Jonas that he would honour his predecessor's commitment to provide £200,000 towards the US tour deficit if ENO could raise £400,000.[9] Arnold Goodman, Harewood and Jonas managed to raise the funds from American and local donors, and on 6 December the minister announced the government contribution of £200,000.

Although the immediate crisis was resolved, the longer-term pressures were still apparent. According to the Arts Council, it was up to ENO to make up for the fall in real terms of the subsidy from the box office and private funds. Higher ticket prices, however, were continuing to affect audiences. Maggie Sedwards suggested lower basic prices, pointing out on 27 September 1985 that ENO seemed to be pricing itself out of the market. There was now a substantial differential between the average seat price on offer and the average price paid, with a high level of discounting to maintain occupancy, even for *Rigoletto*. Jonas was concerned about the uncertainty of the box office, and board member Lord Carr was warning that the company had to consider plans for a 'disaster scenario'.[10*]

Given the pressures and the political background, it was natural, Jonas later said, for the prime minister to feature in the first new production of the Jonas era in September 1985 – the delayed Pountney/Scarfe *Orpheus in the Underworld*, which had been completed with the aid of £100,000 additional private support. Sally Burgess as Public Opinion presented a Thatcher clone, a 'proper moral tyrant' in a production that was greeted as a tirelessly exuber-

---

* Robert Carr had been a Conservative MP since 1950 and Secretary of State for Employment and Home Secretary in Edward Heath's Cabinet. He was created a life peer in 1976.

THE SHOCK OF THE NEW

ant, jokey romp in the style of Toye and Copley. The jokes in the Snoo Wilson/David Pountney English text depended not on a straight translation of the French satire but on Scarfe's loopy cartoon jokes. Elder gave a nice edge to the score, according to David Murray.[11] *Orpheus* achieved a high paid attendance, with gross receipts of 87 per cent, which was 12 per cent ahead of budget.

The legacy of the past was still evident in Jonas's early years in the ensemble, so carefully nurtured by Harewood, and in some of his later planning. On 24 October *Faust*, directed by Ian Judge, included Arthur Davies as Faust and John Tomlinson, whose Mephistopheles delivered the sardonic one-liners of Edmund Tracey with relish. Helen Field was an enigmatic and intense Marguerite. Milnes liked the new performing version of Judge and Tracey, with its quicksilver changes of mood in *opéra comique* genre. He found it a 'refreshingly non-naturalistic staging' and thought that Judge caught the right prurient leer of nineteenth-century attitudes to sexuality. The conductor, Jacques Delacôte, a specialist in nineteenth-century French music, found the right 'silky suave tone colour'.[12]

The Harewood ensemble was also in evidence in the 14 November restaging by Pountney of John Blatchley's 1973 *Katya Kabanova*. Eilene Hannan was vocally and expressively right for Katya, both John Treleaven and Kenneth Woollam convincingly weak as Boris and Tichon. Simon Rattle's house debut blazed with emotion and beauty, according to Paul Griffiths in *The Times*.[13] The large ensemble was, however, further reduced in the new era. When Jonas took over ENO there were thirty company members, and by 1992 there were twenty. Not only did the triumvirate enjoy the freedom of choice when there were fewer singers on the books, but times were different and artists themselves less willing to take on full-time contracts.

Another bequest from Harewood that was to prove a repertory mainstay for ENO over the next few years was Jonathan Miller's *Don Giovanni*, translated by Amanda and Anthony Holden. Philip Prowse designed Goya-inspired grey-brick moving towers that were capable of splitting into three elegant and swiftly variable segments. When it opened on 4 December, Andrew Clements found the production to be a fitting framework for an intense, almost psychotic Don Giovanni, who 'abandoned charm for animal intensity and cruelty and was finally delivered up to the shades of the women he has systematically exploited and betrayed'. With William Shimmel's uncharismatic Giovanni, he nonetheless found the effect 'strangely bloodless'.[14] This was perhaps the result of Elder's as yet undefined conducting, which, according to many critics, lacked tension and urgency. Loppert enjoyed the production's 'lively imaginative, serious minded and light-fingered' vision of 'an airlessly constricted society through which a young handsome libertine can flash like a bolt of lightning'. He wrote admiringly of Barstow's Donna Anna, who was 'raddled by unresolved grieving'.[15] Some of the greatest praise was devoted to the brilliantly realised seduction scene of the Zerlina of Lesley Garrett, who was becoming a leading attraction at ENO, with management carefully developing her career. By 11 March 1986 Don Giovanni was enjoying 99 per cent houses, 7 per cent ahead of budget, and was the basis of the improved box office, after the serious concerns of November 1985.

The good box-office results of Don Giovanni were set against a marked deterioration in the financial situation in the new year, due to expenditure being £80,000 above budget each month. Fees of designers and producers had risen by 50 per cent in three years and rehearsal overtime for chorus and orchestra was up by 40 per cent.[16] It was agreed that all the production budgets and expenditure should be reviewed fortnightly and that all Sunday technical work would be banned in the spring, although it was feared that such cuts would affect the quality of the artistic output and could begin a process that would threaten ENO's claim to national company status and to public subsidy.[17]

Luke Rittner at the Arts Council was fully aware of this danger, writing that cumulative shortfalls would sooner or later result in severe and damaging reductions in quality or activity. He warned Jonas on 6 January 1986 that the government's uplift was meagre and that some of it had to be channelled to the regions on the government's orders. ENO would have to conduct a rigorous and detailed scrutiny as the other national companies already had, even though Clive Priestley's rational recommendation of index-linking and optimal investment levels had been rejected by the government as inflationary.[18]

Jonas explained to Rittner a week later that although ENO was eager to do a study on the Priestley model, they had 'no limbs to amputate'. Not only were they an adventurous ensemble, but they were highly productive. Audiences could experience at moderate prices over a three-year span some fifty different operas 'produced by a clear sense of artistic mission'. The company was the sixth busiest in the world, but seventy-eighth in terms of subsidy. Thatcher's sudden abolition of the Greater London Council that year meant that despite the offer of £1.1 million from Lady Porter's Westminster City Council, there still remained a gap of £650,000 in the following year's budget, which it was hoped the Arts Council would supply from its abolition funding.[19]

When the Arts Council grant for 1986/7 was finally announced on 7 March, it was £7,700,550 – 5 per cent short of the total requested. It was decided that the new production of Prokofiev's *The Fiery Angel* should be replaced by *Tosca*, the nine new productions planned would be reduced to six, and *Simon Boccanegra* postponed. There would be a major appeal, including a gala.[20] The board finally agreed to a budget with a built-in deficit of £160,000 for 1986/7.[21]

The end-of-year box office was again a cause for concern. The Keith Warner production of Rossini's *Moses*, the last of the Norwest Holst series, after receiving dire reviews had done disappointing business. The ban on Sunday working had severely affected the technical standard on stage for the *Mastersingers* revival, which had consequently also received bad notices. It was clear that the money saved by banning Sunday working was being lost at the box office.

The production overspends and treacherous subsidy situation were camouflaged from 1986/7 by the 'Lawson boom', which saw an explosive increase in personal wealth under the chancellorship of Nigel Lawson and enabled ENO to focus on a rapid development of corporate and individual donations. The new director of development, Russell Willis Barnes, was to prepare a long-term development programme incorporating all aspects of the company's work – artistic, financial and marketing. She was an American with management training and experience of private-sector fundraising, especially at the Chicago Contemporary Art Museum, who had been enticed to ENO, inspired by the enthusiasm of those backstage as much as by the work on stage.[22]

In March Willis Barnes presented her proposals on how to meet the remaining £300,000 income gap for the following season. She proposed an 'opera circle', a select club whose members would give donations of £500 per year and at the same time introduce management to other potential supporters. It was crucial to create a list of 'new achievers' in London who might be seeking rapid entrenchment into the English social and cultural scene, amongst whom there were wealthy members of the Arab community, newly successful City entrepreneurs, and American and Japanese businessmen. They should be entertained with interval dinners attended by a 'celebrity' such as Jonathan Miller, followed by a direct appeal for money. There should also be public appeals by management after performances.

While Willis Barnes was to give a more focused and modern approach to ENO's development programme, Jonas gave head of personnel Richard Elder even greater responsibility for bringing his industrial-relations skills to ENO's complicated union relations. Both Elder and David Elliott, the new finance director, brought their expertise and experience from the private sector, Elder at the Metal Box Company and Elliott at Baring Brothers. Supported by and working closely with Jonas, Elder brought a more conciliatory and consultative approach from industry which gradually reduced the distrust of management that had led to combative disputes with the unions and technical departments. He was witness to the development of an increasing collegiality and integrity of purpose in the company backstage.[23]

The third and crucial element in the new management regime was Elliott, who instituted more rigorous financial controls, with regular monthly reporting and monitoring of the cash flow so that middle management were able to participate both in setting and holding to their budgets. He also introduced an analysis of the marginal financial contribution of each opera and each extra performance – hitherto not accounted for – to help the fine-tuning of the repertory planning process.[24]

The three ambitious new productions of the last quarter of the season were *Parsifal*, Busoni's *Dr Faust* and Birtwistle's *The Mask of Orpheus*. On 16 March *Parsifal*, directed by Joachim Herz, designed by Wolf Münzler, proved to be an expensive disappointment and one that on reflection management admitted might have been avoided. Harewood had deliberately kept *Parsifal* out of the repertoire. Jonas, however, had been determined to do *Parsifal* as soon as he became involved in planning. 'I am going to be the boss and the boss wants it,' he had told the *Sunday Times* on 14 April 1985.

Not long after Jonas took over it had became clear that Herz's concept was going to be a challenging proposition in every way. By 8 October it was apparent that the production was going to cost £50,000 more than its £80,000 budget. After Jonas told Herz that the extra money could not be found, he agreed to find a new conception and to produce a new model.[25] By February 1986 production costs had again climbed £31,000 above budget, but Jonas warned the board that changing directors might also result in the loss of Goodall. All the board could do was urge more realistic budgets in the future and that designs be submitted in good time.[26] Jonas decided that borrowing a production from Bonn was the 'soft option' and that he should take the risk of continuing with Herz.

When the production was launched in March, the combination of irony and social realistic literalism did not go down well with the critics. According to Rupert Christiansen, the production slipped from the sublime to *Monty Python* in a trice. Milnes, who heartily disliked most of Herz's work, was not surprised by the 'prosaic, would-be analytical, anti-musical' staging, but even he was surprised by what he described as the 'virulent hideousness' of Wolf Münzler's designs. The first scene, he wrote, appeared to be set 'somewhere in the lower abdomen, with yards of livid green intestine draped across the back of the stage and more bits dumped in front of the stage like faeces'. There was general bemusement at the Batman-style Klingsor and his risible flying tricycle, as well as the swan's thumping descent to a Cheddar-cheese slope and the Arthurian knights. The Flower Maidens seemed to Milnes to be 'art-deco Deauville lovelies' in an 'outsize children's paddling pool in shocking pink'.[27] Goodall rescued what he could from the production, the orchestra playing with beauty and nobility for him, especially in the seamless link between the glowing Good Friday music and the final benediction. So too did the cast. Anne Evans as Kundry gave a riveting performance of remarkable dramatic intelligence and sang with unfailing beauty. Gwynne Howell, despite an unfortunate wig, was a compelling Gurnemanz, and when the ailing Warren Ellsworth returned to the cast as Parsifal he proved to be an absorbing stage presence. All three brought, according to Andrew Clements, a measure of sense to the proceedings.[28]

On 5 June Jonas admitted to the Opera Committee that the risk had not paid off. He was more disappointed by the direction of the singers than the actual production but argued that *Parsifal* had received good reviews in the German press.[29] There had been strong advance sales, but the poor critical reception and early performance time had resulted in weak box-office sales.[30]

The critics shared Mark Elder's view that the British stage premiere of Ferruccio Busoni's *Doctor Faust* on 25 April was a most important, rewarding and brave undertaking for ENO.* Milnes admired the work's sometimes Mahler-like, beautiful music with its strong sense of melody and its intellectual quest for knowledge.[31] Elder drew fine performances from the orchestra, chorus and cast with conducting of eloquence and conviction. Thomas Allen gave an impressive, intelligent performance, in a most demanding role of nearly four hours of singing. He was well partnered by Graham Clark as Mephistopheles. The expressionist production and design of Pountney and Lazaridis, including goose-stepping students in the tavern and banks of menacingly tilted filing cabinets, were compatible with the composer's intentions, according to Barry Millington.[32]

Another exciting premiere was that of Harrison Birtwistle's *Mask of Orpheus* on 21 May, eleven years after Harewood had taken on the work believing that it would prove to be the most important premiere since *Peter Grimes*.† He had remained committed to it both during its protracted composition and when it became apparent that extra funds would be needed to ensure the production went

---

* *Doctor Faust* was composed by Busoni between 1916 and 1924, and completed after the composer's death by Philipp Jarnac in 1925. Antony Beaumont rewrote the ending, based more faithfully on Busoni's intentions, in 1984.
† Having originally been commissioned by Covent Garden, Birtwistle's opera was taken from there to Glyndebourne by Peter Hall. When he left, Glyndebourne found it hard to mount and, when they demanded an Arts Council grant to cover production costs and rehearsal time, Birtwistle offered it to Harewood in July 1975. From that moment on, Harewood was its staunchest advocate.

ahead. The technical, electronic aspect of the work was very complex, with both extra players and special instruments required. The marketing manager, Don Keller, supervised an extensive advertising campaign, as it was felt that the *Mask* should appeal to non-opera audiences.

Peter Heyworth sensed a certain amount of perplexity at its reception, even from the musical establishment. The first act was greeted with near silence, although the audience warmed up afterwards, and the final curtain was greeted by prolonged applause. It was indeed a new genre. Birtwistle explained that it was not an opera and not theatre but that it had music. It was, he said, 'full of episodes like a *Beano* strip cartoon, going back and forth in time, in what I call simultaneous contrast'.[33] Dominic Gill described *Mask* as a gigantic symphony for wind instruments, percussion, electronics, with vocal obligato, mime and scenic accompaniments. It was formidably complex and exhilarating but also very hard to understand. The words of Peter Zinovieff's 'archly self-conscious libretto' were almost inaudible, he wrote, and in any case did not tell the story directly. Birtwistle used them as a springboard for his 'powerful, insistent, unyielding' musical inspiration.

The first act described the birth of language and music, the third the birth of lyricism. There was a colossal electronic instrument for the voice of Apollo, electronic instruments for every member of the cast and two invented instruments – a Noh harp and a box with a string stretched across it, with a horn sticking out at the top. The work necessitated two conductors, Elgar Howarth and Paul Daniel, who gained the respect and admiration of the company for their mastery of the extraordinarily complex score. It was not a singers' opera, as much of the singing was amplified offstage. The cast wore masks and more than one singer sang each role: Langridge was the chief Orpheus and Rigby the Woman Eurydice. Director David Freeman was sympathetic to the 'austere, enigmatic, static quality of the music', and Jocelyn Herbert's designs and costumes were sumptuous in black, grey and pastel colours.[34]

Milnes admitted that he had had difficulty understanding what was going on or even knowing which character should be commanding attention, let alone hearing their words because of the masks, the amplification and some invented language. He was not too shy to ask: 'Is not some immediacy of communication at however basic a level (like verbal) desirable if not essential?' He missed Tony Harrison's disciplined text for the National Theatre's *Oresteia*, for which Birtwistle had composed the music. Nonetheless, he agreed that it was a 'reform opera', a challenge to literary opera in the same way as Gluck had challenged singers' opera. It was a musical experience which perhaps should not be in an opera house – 'a mystical rather than a dramatic event'.[35]

Despite massive publicity and supportive notices, *Mask* managed gross receipts of 57 per cent against its budget of 75 per cent, even with a reduced price schedule.[36] At a meeting on 10 June the finance director, David Elliott, again noted the disturbing decline in the box office, but Pountney was determined to brook no compromise.[37] At a planning meeting on the same day he insisted that they should be harsher with themselves about what they were prepared to put on. The money-makers, Pountney said, should be things they could do with 'real passion', like Sondheim's *Pacific Overtures*, and they should be done well and not done to death. Elder and Caulton said this was impossible to achieve, however attractive it sounded, as ENO paid for the esoterics by doing the popular works. There was nothing wrong with *Die Fledermaus*, they argued, but they must 'look to alter' the way such work was done. Pountney insisted that the company's style no longer had room for such productions as *Die Fledermaus*, which at its December 1986 revival played to excellent houses but which Jonas authorised to be disposed of in February 1987.[38]

Arnold Goodman had told the board on 21 April that the company was entering a difficult period during which it should do everything necessary to survive in the belief that its essential role for London would eventually be recognised.[39] By the end of the season twenty-two redundancies had been made, including four choristers. The company mission was being uncompromisingly pursued and Jonas paid tribute to Richard Elder for maintaining good company morale despite the pressures.[40] He told Alan Blyth that the aim of the team was to make 'understandable, enjoyable, thrilling, entertaining, provocative opera, which is in the reach of everybody'.[41]

The tradition of Lilian Baylis remained within the spirit and conscience of the company members. Around this time ENO became the first of the national companies to take a radical and participatory approach to education and outreach, whereby the young people would not only sing but also create. They would be given the tools to understand composition and debate the issues that arose from the works. The scheme was the brainchild of two staff directors at ENO, David Sulkin and Rebecca Meitlis, who were also arts-education specialists. Sulkin had worked at the Royal Court and had been director of their Young Writers Festival, and Meitlis had worked as a trainee staff director at Scottish Opera, where there was a developed education department, 'Opera for Youth', run by Graham Vick. In 1985 they had put their ideas to Pountney, whom they found to be both open-minded and a great facilitator. Out of their initiative and with just one part-time administrator to assist them, the Baylis Programme was developed after their appointment was ratified by the board in October 1985. It would cost £9,000 above the salaries of those involved and the whole programme would cost £50,000, subject to sponsorship.[42]

Sulkin was a great admirer of Lilian Baylis, and together with Meitlis based the programme on the belief that all people are inherently creative and respond to musical and dramatic stimuli, and that ENO could and should work with the educational authorities and local communities to bring music and opera to the young, the old and the sick – for example, Alzheimer's sufferers – in stimulating and unusual ways. Their participatory approach anticipated the spirit of the National Curriculum for Music, which was introduced in 1991. In 1987 Sulkin sought to make closer links with the City of Westminster and the new Inner London Education Authority, introduced following the dissolution of the GLC in 1986.

The pair's strength lay in the fact that they both remained as staff directors, so they not only understood the workings of the theatre from the inside but could base their work on the artistic ideas and impulses of the production teams from the earliest stages of production. They brought into their projects chorus members, designers, conductors, music staff, directors and singers who were good communicators acceptable to young people. Amongst those who became involved were Mary King and Vivian Tierney, singers who were soon to be in the company. Janice Kelly, Nicholas Kok and Willard White, who were already company members, also participated. When children and young people came to the performances,

Meitlis and Sulkin, supported by Pountney and Richard Elder, insisted on acquiring for them the best seats in the house.

The three main areas of activity of the Baylis Programme were participatory experimental projects, commissions and projects to bring the young and those not familiar with opera into the Coliseum with programmes of family days, study weekends and pre-performance talks. The 'Live Wires' and 'Live Culture' programmes developed 'companies' of children and teenagers who participated in specially commissioned works created both in connection with the repertoire and experimentally. *Gretel and Hansel* was a commission from Alec Roth in 1988 which had three performances in January 1988 in Hoxton Hall. Works linked to the 'Opera in Context' repertoire included versions of *Billy Budd* given aboard the *Cutty Sark* in 1988 and *Falstaff*, written for Hackney primary-school children, given in Sutton House, a Tudor mansion.

Meitlis, keen to introduce young people to twentieth-century and contemporary opera, worked during the first year with Harrison Birtwistle. Compositions based on his *Mask of Orpheus* were written by students and facilitated by three composers, Judith Weir, John Woolrich and David Sawyer, who had residencies in three schools. *The Cunning Little Vixen* and *The Adventures of Mr Brouček* were worked on in a similar way. The results were performed at Lilian Baylis House and were attended by everyone involved. Three schools in Hackney participated in another project, with groups writing operas based on Philip Glass's *Akhnaten* in June 1985 and using, as Glass had, a historical idea and minimalism as their starting points. A highlight for the young composers was meeting Glass on the first night.

Another high point was a project on *Pelleas and Melisande* called 'Inner Landscapes' in the autumn of 1991 at Feltham Institute for Young Offenders, with twenty-one volunteers who worked with a painter and a composer and did drama improvisation with Meitlis, looking at the themes of the opera. The young people, she recalled, gave her reams of poems during the period she worked there. Meitlis took Willard White to talk to them about himself, his work and the opera. White gained the respect of the teenagers by taking them through his vigorous daily workout regime. He told them why he was passionate about singing, recalling how he had grown to love music as a small child from hearing his grandmother singing

Jamaican lullabies, some of which he then sang. Twelve of the group attended a performance at the Coliseum. Five of them asked to write an opera, which they did with the director John Abulafia and composer Sean Gregory. The lead characters were two teenagers going to fight in the Gulf War. It was performed in the Terrace Bar by two professional singers accompanied by the boys on keyboard, guitar and percussion. Work in prisons continued with a production based on Kurt Weill's *Street Scene* in Brixton, with a set designed and painted by the inmates.

Experimental work and commissions emerged from a programme entitled 'New Visions, New Voices', which searched for pieces from young composers aged between fourteen and twenty-five, eight of which were developed and four produced and performed. New work included a piece commissioned by Sulkin from Fay Weldon and Ilona Sekacz called *A Small Green Space*, which was performed in six towns with a leading professional cast of opera, rock and pop singers and a different youth chorus – 100-strong – in each location in May 1989. There was a writing-opera workshop performance by Bengali schoolchildren and nine professional singers at the Riverside Studios in June 1986.

Drawing together all the strands of Meitlis's work over ten years was *Orion and the Dolphin* in 1994, an enormous project involving 600 performers, commissioned from Alec Roth and Vikram Seth – just before Seth's novel *A Suitable Boy* was published. The work was developed with a residency in Plymouth in partnership with the Royal Navy, Marks and Spencer, South West Arts, the Bournemouth Sinfonietta and Theatre Royal Plymouth, with a professional orchestra, professional singers and a massive chorus of children from local primary schools who also composed various scenes in which they performed.

The Baylis team also arranged seminars for political and educational figures, MPs and policy-makers to stress the strands of work that they believed to be important. Sulkin, particularly concerned about racial equality in the company, worked on equal-opportunity training and consulted on the casting of black singers and finding black performers for the Brixton prison *Street Scene*.

Known to Pountney and in the organisation as the Marxist Lentilists, Sulkin and Meitlis made the Baylis scheme a leader in developing creative programmes. By 1992/3 the co-directors were full-time, assisted by a full-time co-ordinator and a part-time secretary; freelance staff included a music adviser and directors for the main projects. Every branch of ENO, from marketing to technical, was involved and gave help. By 1995 Baylis had initiated over eighty-six projects, large and small, involving 16,000 people.

In an effort to improve the box office, the 1986/7 season began with a more popular programme. Copley's 1972 *Il trovatore* opened on 27 August to poor reviews but packed houses and *Figaro* was also at near capacity. The first new production, *The Mikado* on 27 September 1986, was one of the most successful productions at the box office of all time. It was directed by Jonathan Miller, who returned triumphantly to the Coliseum. The project was initially conceived with Harewood at a poolside in Houston during the US tour. Miller explained that he was thinking along the lines of an English Marx brothers/Busby Berkeley show, with lots of dancers and a good choreographer, telling the *Sunday Telegraph* that he was envisaging a 'silly Utopia, as in *Duck Soup*'.[43] Much depended on *The Mikado*'s success. Pountney supported the production as the only show that should not be restricted to a low budget, as it was intended to bring in £1 million from twenty-four performances.

The Miller/Lazaridis partnership was inspired. The setting was what Miller described as an Eastbourne-inspired Edwardian spa in grey, black and white. It was full of nostalgia but also, with Lazaridis's slightly unsettling and surrealist perspectives, disconcerting while not deconstructed. The idea, Miller explained, was to 'preserve the strange naïve charm of the work, not to savage it'. With Anthony van Laast's wonderfully camp choreography, Miller hoped to convey a sense of the professional English middle classes 'saucily letting their hair down'.[44]

Sue Blane's zany costumes included the long, long shorts and tennis racket of ex-Python Eric Idle's guest Ko-Ko. Richard Angas was an elephantine white Mikado, Bonaventura Bottone a small, anxious Nanki-Poo, Lesley Garrett Yum-Yum, and Jean Rigby and Susan Bullock sexy St Trinians-style Pitti-Sing and Peep-Bo. Richard Van Allan was a reptilian Pooh-Bah, Felicity Palmer a splendidly monstrous Katisha. The scene was completed with rouged bellboys and pert maids.[45]

Audiences were delighted and *Mikado* played to sold-out houses.

With *Tosca* also well ahead of its budget and a revival of *Don Giovanni* playing to capacity audiences, the box office was looking healthy by October. Caulton told the board that the deliberately popular repertory at the beginning of season, combined with a revised advertising strategy, had paid dividends. He nonetheless stressed that the critical press now looked to ENO to produce interesting productions such as *Dr Faustus* and *Mask of Orpheus* rather than the more traditional shows. After the popular start to the season he hoped audiences would be more prepared to experiment with lesser-known pieces.[46] Despite some earlier reservations amongst the board about Gilbert and Sullivan, there was general delight at *The Mikado*, which had been a 'tremendous success' at the box office and had given immense pleasure to a great number of people. Mark Elder pointed out that whereas it was difficult for an English company to do Verdi, it should be able to do Gilbert and Sullivan very well.[47]

In October 1986 Lord Harewood took over the chairmanship of the board from Arnold Goodman.* Harewood had been uncertain about his suitability for the role as he felt that he was 'too close', and consequently promised Jonas that he would try not to interfere with artistic judgements.[48] During his time as chairman he would occasionally express his belief that certain choices would prove to be unwise, but was reluctant to press harder.

With the Arts Council keeping grant increases below inflation, administrative economies and fundraising as well as box-office receipts were crucial in maintaining balanced budgets. In the summer of 1986, despite the improved box office and booming economy, it was obvious that cuts would have to be made in the long term.

In June 1986 Ian Beesley, successor to Clive Priestley at the government's Management and Efficiency Group and now with the management consultancy arm of Price Waterhouse, had been chosen to prepare ENO's report for the Arts Council. By October

---

* On 17 November 1986 Rhymes left to become chief executive of the Society of West End Theatre and Theatrical Management Association, and on 22 January 1987 Brian Unwin replaced him as honorary secretary to the board of directors. Unwin was chairman of HM Customs and Excise from 1987 to 1993 and was the first British president of the European Investment Bank from 1993 to 2000, when he rejoined the ENO Board after a gap of six years.

Beesley, with much input from Richard Elder, had identified three main areas for attention: savings in the technical department by adopting an industrial-relations approach; better links between planning the repertoire and running the theatre; and more accurate assessment of the likely level of external funding in line with management's objectives. Elder's suggestion that heads of department should become managers in the technical department was adopted in order to emphasise their management responsibilities and to ensure that artistic decisions would be taken with better knowledge of the financial consequences.[49]

As well as clarifying management structures, Beesley provided a view of ENO's long-term future. He was, according to Jonas, a management consultant with a difference, after his experience in Thatcher's Efficiency Group, and was more a 'quick thinking mandarin' who posed questions that needed to be answered by government and covered all the possible negative answers.[50] Beesley proposed that a public debate should be provoked to ensure that 'management changes might be rewarded with further public investment'.[51]

Harewood received the final draft of the Price Waterhouse report on 23 February 1987. During the next three years Richard Elder was busy renegotiating working practices and contracts in the technical departments in the light of Price Waterhouse, as a result of which industrial relations gradually improved within the house. After long negotiations, a working agreement was signed with the Broadcasting, Entertainment, Cinematograph and Theatre Union on 21 May 1990 by its full-time theatre officer, Gerry Morrissey.* It removed many restrictive practices, including minimum crewing levels and hours of work. Such demarcations as those between stage and flies were also removed. Crews would be employed according to need, together with a guaranteed number of hours to be worked in the year, in order to maintain the earnings of the staff. Ten posts were made redundant. Much effort was put into explaining the agreement and training heads of department to be managers, including the involvement of an occupational psychologist.[52] The increased time that managers spent on

---

* BECTU had emerged from the merger of NATTKE and the Association of Broadcasting Staff in 1984, and their consequent amalgamation with the Association of Cinematograph, Television and Allied Technicians.

advance planning was intended to facilitate a faster financial response to repertory questions. This was an industry-leading advance in industrial relations, and labour costs were estimated to have fallen by over 13 per cent by November 1992, with savings of £4–500,000.[53]

Richard Elder was instrumental in ensuring that not only would certain technicians become managers, but that their links with the unions should not be broken, thus ensuring that industrial relations would be improved as well as efficiency. One of the technicians who became a manager responsible for budgets was Ted Murphy, head of stage. Murphy later recalled that he maintained his membership of BECTU despite becoming a manager. It was hoped that by involving the technicians, who actually knew how much things cost, at an early stage, it would be possible to prepare and control budgets more accurately and prevent mishaps. Murphy started to attend planning meetings and was given advance information. Although some directors and designers continued to push beyond their budgets, there was a greater control and scrutiny of costs.[54]

ENO was also responding with its usual energy to the Arts Council's demand for more self-generated income from fundraising. The development director, Russell Willis Barnes, was dividing the activities of her development department into 'cultivation and solicitation', with donations to be sought from corporations, individuals and trusts. With the help of consultants Creative Business, ENO would begin the process of establishing the company's corporate identity and create a 'climate for giving'. By October 1986 there were five new corporate members, and a premium seat holder.

The current year's goal from all sources was £700,000, whereas the previous year's had been £450,000. By November all but £82,513 had been raised. In order to make up the shortfall it was decided that Jonas would make appeals from the stage, which would, he hoped, demonstrate to all the company his willingness to be part of the plural funding economy. His first appeal brought in £2,500.[55] The Goodman gala on 21 December made a profit of £75,000. By the end of January 1987 the special appeal campaign had reached £60,244. The total amount raised by the development department for the season was £720,000, although Willis Barnes warned that such successful campaigning was not likely to be sustainable indefinitely.[56]

While ENO sought to increase its self-generated income, the Arts Council remained implacably unhelpful towards all the national companies, but especially towards the opera companies. A new and menacing attitude was apparent when Jonas went to the Arts Council on 7 November 1986. At the meeting Rittner made it clear there were many in the Arts Council who felt that there might be too much opera available in Britain, given the available funding, and that there should be cuts in specific areas rather than 'equal misery for all'. Opera companies would have to help themselves, as it was obvious that the below-inflation grants were insufficient. A team of Arts Council advisers would monitor ENO performances and review them annually with the company. Jonas was adamant that he intended to renew the repertory in line with the artistic thrust of the company.[57]

The Arts Council announced at the end of November that with grant increases remaining below inflation for a third year, and with all clients expected to trade solvently, there would be some institutions that would cease to exist. Willis Barnes pointed out that such warnings did nothing to reassure potential sponsors. In mid-December Jonas spoke to *The Times* about the growing anti-opera bias at the Arts Council.[58]

The conservative start to the season very soon gave way to a more adventurous and provocative continuation. On 29 October the Ian Judge *Cavalleria* and *Pagliacci* opened to a certain amount of bewilderment. To a letter of complaint, Jonas explained that the Gerard Howland set was supposed to represent industrial Italy east of Salerno at the time of composition but had come out a 'bit Lowryesque' because they were very short of money.[59] The critics did not think it looked cheap but were far from recognising Salerno. There was a general consensus that the setting was Lawrentian Nottinghamshire, which, Max Loppert pointed out – as had Tyrone Guthrie all those years before – was a more comfortable location for both the principals and the chorus than was the Mediterranean. Jane Eaglen's spectacled schoolmarm of a Santuzza impressed, but on the whole Loppert missed the 'full throated Italianate vocalism on which these pieces really thrive'. With its bare city piazza tipped at a surrealistic angle, its puzzling stage business and use of the 'full gamut of alienation effects', including sudden changes of lighting and ostentatiously formal groupings, and the gusto with which it was delivered, it was very much an ENO house-style piece.[60] At 87 per cent capacity it exceeded its budget by 10 per cent.

While the Mediterranean remained elusive, Jonas was full of enthusiasm as he told the board that he believed that Pountney's completely radical approach to his new production of *Carmen*, with designs by Maria Bjørnson, would provoke interesting comment and be an example of exciting work by the company. Like *Cavalleria* and *Pagliacci*, it was a new production on a much-reduced budget.[61*] It was translated by *Clockwork Orange* author Anthony Burgess with a good supply of swear words and jokes. Pountney in interview said: 'There is a connection in my mind between anarchy and a man's response to a woman's sexual power.'[62]

*Carmen* opened on 27 November. Milnes found Sally Burgess vivid and agile and 'unsettlingly, blazingly sexy', and felt that the production had done something to rekindle the shock of *Carmen*'s first performance in 1875. Bjørnson's setting of the 'graveyard for wrecked cars, inhabited by the poorest of the poor', he believed, 'might have made Brecht blanch'. Nor was he fazed by the 'shocking foreplay' and murderous urban smugglers, rather relishing the constant air of lawlessness, intolerable heat, sleaziness and the sense of real danger and anarchy of every kind, not least from the soldiery. Milnes also praised Mark Elder's thoroughly convincing 'big house sound', with brisk, clear textures and constant forward momentum.[63] Other critics were less enthusiastic. Nicholas Kenyon, in describing a scrapyard filled with soldiers in berets and crumpled fatigues, and scantily clad girls, derided what he described as the destruction of atmosphere, context, libretto and characters due to 'total unfocused chaos'. He thought that Sally Burgess was miscast as a girlish Carmen and John Treleaven as a 'withdrawn

---

* Zeb Lalljee, the costume supervisor, recalled scrabbling around in a warehouse containing enormous bales of less than hygienic old clothes for recycling in her search for costumes for *Carmen*. This was in contrast to the costumes for *La traviata* in 1988, when Lazaridis refused the suggestion of cheap cloth for his suits with the words: 'What is this shit?' The excellent new wool used was expensive at the time but the costumes were rented to other companies and were back in ENO for use twenty years later. 'He knew his fabrics,' Lalljee commented (interview, 15.11.07).

wooden-toppish Don José', resulting in an 'infantile sense of the sensuality which underpins the story'. Altogether he believed that there was a 'flailing around with ideas to mask the lack of a central soul'.[64] Elder himself thought it one of Pountney's less successful productions, that he had not been able to provide a sound that was 'visceral, and blowsy enough' for the production, which felt as though it needed a score written by a South American composer or Leonard Bernstein.[65]

*Carmen*'s early houses were very varied but, with extra advertising, improved later to near capacity at 94 per cent over sixteen performances. Jonas told *The Times* that his attitude had become more belligerent since his meetings at the Arts Council. Radical productions like *Carmen* were needed in times of financial stringency for survival. He believed that the public was an impatient animal that looked for speed, lapped things up and then tired. He hoped that the forthcoming *Simon Boccanegra*, on the other hand, would endure.[66]

Jonathan Miller's *Tosca* opened on 28 January 1987. Lazaridis had been chosen in early 1986 to design the production, as he had been contracted for the cancelled *Fiery Angel* by Prokofiev. It was to be a co-production, premiered in Florence and costing ENO £40,000. It was hoped that if Lazaridis was approached early enough, he would incorporate the needs of the Coliseum into the designs. It was to prove a tricky assignment for the new technical director, Jakob Sakiv.

In August 1986 Caulton and Tracey were very impressed, as was the Florentine audience, when they attended the premiere. Miller translated the work to Fascist Italy in the 1940s, in a set of skewed angles, with an unattached Renaissance church wall on the verge of collapse, an angled platform and gloomy but clear background lighting by Nick Chelton. The production and its international cast, including Eva Marton, were cheered to the rafters.[67] Some members of the Italian audience besieged Miller after the performance with names of relations killed during the war.

The problems of the *Tosca* production started when the set reached the Coliseum and it emerged that two side walls did not fit and were too heavy to move, so the set had to be adapted at a cost of £25,000. At the eleventh hour Ted Murphy and Freddie Marshall, the in-house carpenter, had to make two false walls. To add to the stress, a week before opening night the tenor Eduardo Alvarez suffered facial injuries during a fall.

These events and the slack conducting of Jan Latham-Koenig reduced the immediate impact of the production. Milnes did not like the setting in Fascist Italy of Puccini's 'little human drama', feeling that it did justice neither to *Tosca* nor to fascism, and that the piece was physically overwhelmed by the grey set. Edward Greenfield, on the other hand, found the production 'sharply specific', with a strong atmosphere of fear and uncertainty. Lazaridis's tilting set reminded him of Carol Reed's camerawork for *The Third Man*. Barstow was beautiful, vibrant and intense, with hysteria barely suppressed. She impressed both Greenfield and Milnes.[68] Despite what the board noted as a mixed reception, *Tosca* did very well at the box office and there was a thrilling revival by Karen Stone under Paul Daniel's baton in August 1988.[69] Sutcliffe noted that the production had recovered some of the power it had had in Florence, as Lazaridis had restored the vertiginous neoclassical Florence set by the simple expedient of hanging three decaying red drapes. Janice Cairns was a totally committed Tosca and Edmund Barham an excellent, heroic Cavaradossi.[70]

When *Akhnaten* was revived on 26 February, Hugh Canning wrote: 'The days when ENO was recognisably an ensemble company on more or less permanent contract playing to audiences in sensible shoes is long since past. Controversy and pop repertoire are the order of the day.' The policy was 'packing them in'. One hundred per cent for *Akhnaten* was, he wrote, 'an astonishing achievement for a revival of so innocuous a piece'.[71] It was apparent that non-opera audiences were being attracted by the Glass work. Miller's *Don Giovanni*, revived by Karen Stone on 11 April, also played to capacity houses, exceeding its budget by 9 per cent. The idea of casting Jane Eaglen and Rita Cullis paid off handsomely.[72]

The revival of the box office was juxtaposed with continued Arts Council stringency. Jonas's hope that the Arts Council would make additional project funding available in the light of the Price Waterhouse recommendations was disappointed when the Arts Council assessor, Anthony Blackstock, who understood ENO's predicament, intimated to the board on 13 January 1987 that there would be only a 2.6 per cent grant uplift, which would leave a shortfall of half a million pounds in the budget. He warned yet again that any company without a balanced budget would be requested to reorganise or go into voluntary liquidation. Sir Leonard Hoffman pointed out that if a company went into liquidation without the necessary funds to meet its obligations, it would have an adverse effect on the Arts Council, which would be obliged to pick up the debts.[73]

Blackstock reported that all the national companies had produced projected deficit budgets for 1987/8 and that, surprisingly, ENO's deficit was the lowest and their position less critical than that of some of the others. ENO was facing fewer redundancies than the National Theatre and the subscription scheme was coming into its own and helping the cash-flow situation. After savings, including the cancellation of *Boris Godunov* and a revival of *Valkyrie*, in March the board accepted a budget with a deficit of £160,000 for 1987/8.[74]

When the Arts Council's formal offer of £6,748,000 was announced in late March, Jonas complained that although the Arts Council had accepted the Price Waterhouse recommendations, it was not willing to 'respond tangibly' by providing further limited sums over a finite period to provide the headroom within which ENO management could implement the recommended changes. All but seven of the recommendations were already subject to programmes, especially in planning procedures, and discussions were going on with the unions, who were ready to negotiate more flexible working practices.[75] In June 1987 management concluded a two-year deal with the chorus which included a basic better rate for their very heavy workload – a 7.75 per cent increase over two years. They could now be divided into two smaller work groups and relations with them were improving.[76]

In March the Arts Council announced that Covent Garden was to receive an increase in its 1987/8 grant of £131,000 (to £13,226,960) and three-year funding. Jonas decided to go straight to the minister, Richard Luce, after experiencing great difficulty getting to see Rittner. But the direct approach to the minister in May availed him little. Luce made it clear that the Arts Council had stressed that 'incentive funding' was to be the reward for increased fundraising and it was not for implementing such changes as were recommended by Price Waterhouse. Jonas had suggested that such an attitude might create cynicism in the arts world.[77]

Incentive funding caused deep concern in the arts world. It put additional pressure on the organisations to woo even more business support. Roy Shaw, Arts Council secretary general from 1978 to 1983, later recalled that when one client at a meeting at the Arts Council said he was unhappy about the development, a senior Council official had told him sharply: 'The arm's-length principle is dead and you know it.' Although Shaw – who believed the principle to be vital for the 'freedom of the arts' – thought it sick rather than dead, the incentive scheme marked the end of forty years of consensus in arts funding. Luce had warned in 1987 that the arts had to abandon the 'welfare state mentality', which he defined as 'believing that the taxpayer owed it a living', Shaw recalled.[78] The new sponsorship would prove fickle and unreliable and would focus on the needs of the sponsors as much as on the needs of the arts. Of all the national companies ENO would prove very vulnerable, as accessibility and adventurousness were central to its ethos.

ENO was responding with great dynamism to the challenge. The vibrant new image of the company was such, the Marketing Committee pointed out, that even bad reviews made the company sound interesting.[79] In none of its activities was this image more apparent than in its Verdi series, which revealed an affinity to the German school of conceptual and postmodernist production, particularly in the case of *Simon Boccanegra* on 2 April 1987, *La traviata* in 1988 and *A Masked Ball* in September 1989.

Mark Elder, for whom Verdi was a 'huge passion', described him as a composer who 'wanted bold subjects that would arouse, stimulate and probe the full range of human experience'. Although Elder recalled Colin Graham's 1968 *Force of Destiny* and the excitement of it being on the Coliseum scale, he was nonetheless fully behind strong reinterpretations, arguing that as nineteenth-century historical melodrama had vanished from the theatre, both director and audience had to get themselves into a different gear to understand such operas as *A Masked Ball* and *Don Carlos*.[80]

Elder, Pountney and Alden saw themselves as the pioneers in seeking a new, intense, dramatic aesthetic.[81] Elder said that he preferred working with directors like Herz, Pountney and Alden who were also musicians. 'The way I can relate to a director and his imaginative response to the piece', he explained, 'does inevitably depend on the director's musical knowledge and skill.' He could respond to their vision of the music and 'marinate' his conducting during the rehearsal period.[82] For Pountney, the influence of Kupfer and Herz had been as powerful as it had for Elder. From them he had learnt the technique of 'absolute control over every aspect of an operatic performance', whereby every element of a production was a possible tool for interpretation.[83]

The designer David Fielding was the fourth element in the equation. He, like Alden, had been much influenced as a young designer by German theatre. In particular Fielding admired designer and director Wilfred Minks in Hamburg, and especially Karl-Ernst Herrmann, who was working at Peter Stein's Berlin Schaubühne theatre. Herrmann's spare, clean, contained spaces, in which the choreographed performers themselves become part of the design, combined with starkly symbolic objects were a particular inspiration. Fielding and Alden, who had also spent time in Germany, felt liberated from what they saw as the more conservative and literal English approach to theatre and opera interpretation by the innovations they witnessed in Germany, to create what Fielding referred to as a more antagonistic, rough and ready theatre with an 'edge of brutality'. His designs were intended to provide the visual element for the conceptual framework and to aid the process of unlocking the hidden meanings of the piece, using powerful symbolic visual references. They were moving on, Fielding believed, from both the 'pure decoratism' of the Copley era as well as the 'abstract decoratism' of Fielding's teacher, Ralph Koltai, in order to 'create emotional turmoil'.* They also brought with them the visual references – skewed angles, sharp contrasts and menacing shadows – of the stylised, melodramatic expressionist film industry of the 1920s and 1930s.[84]

Alden and Fielding in a long interview with Milnes in *Opera* in

---

* Although Copley gave Lazaridis his first opportunities and worked closely with him, Fielding excluded him from accusations of 'decoratism' as he was himself on a 'journey'. Fielding wrote: 'He started out in this style following in the footsteps of his teacher Georgiadis, but later took up the new Coliseum conceptual style in conjunction with Pountney and Warner' (email to author, 4.1.08).

November 1986 explained that the directors whom they admired were essentially deconstructionalist.[85]* Alden was reacting against what he called the limited, American, naturalistic theatrical tradition of the Actor's Studio, as well as Hollywood and television, by moving closer to a European outlook. He and Fielding were following on a huge wave of similar productions in Europe, especially those of Ruth Berghaus.

The work of Berghaus stood in stark contrast to the psychological realism and social contextualisation of Felsenstein, Strehler and Peter Brook. The function of the postmodernist avant-garde was rather to express criticism of bourgeois institutions of art through parody or irony in order to create a disturbing experience. Alden told Milnes:

Half of you has to be extremely ironic and detached from the work, because of the implications of how the world has changed and because of the irony of doing a piece which is based on a musical harmony that was part of the world then and is absolutely, sadly and interestingly not part of the world now.

He was half involved and half 'casting a cold and critical eye on it'. It was, he believed, the tensions between those two points of view that made electricity.

In the book *Power House*, compiled by Nicholas John,

---

* Postmodernism has been described by Professor Christopher Butler as a 'kind of despair about the enlightenment', which manifests itself in the asking of questions and the addressing of issues rather than the search for answers. In a world where universal truth is impossible and relativism mankind's fate, a loss of textual authority becomes inevitable. Meanings become 'the property of the interpreter, who is free to play, deconstructively, with them'. By the mid-1960s characteristics of postmodernism in literature and the arts were recognised as 'less obviously masterful, more playful and anarchic' and 'more concerned with the process of understanding than the pleasures of the artistic finish or unity, less inclined to hold a narrative together, and certainly more resistant to a certain interpretation than much of the art that had preceded it'. Deconstructionist discourse tended to use very obscure, not to say obfuscating modes of speech or presentation, since clarity of expression was considered to be based on 'bourgeois' certainties concerning the world order. According to Butler, the thousands of echoes of the obscure writings of the French masters of postmodernism – Derrida and Foucault – made up 'the confused and often pretentious collective psyche of the postmodernist constituency' (Christopher Butler, *Postmodernism: A Very Short Introduction*, Oxford: Oxford University Press, 2002, pp. 8, 23).

Pountney wrote that ENO had its own distinct, less intellectual brand of postmodernism. *Rienzi, Mazeppa, Moses* and *Carmen* 'provided a rumbustious, iconoclastic production style quite different from the highly aesthetic and intellectual deconstruction techniques of contemporary European theatre', mainly because attention to detail was not quite so strong in the British temperament. The richly talented group of directors who worked at the Coliseum in the 1980s happily drove the Mercedes on the wrong side of the road, 'put a few dents in the bodywork and filled the boot with muddy Wellington boots (not to mention suitcases, trilbies, wonky bedsteads, dark glasses and other gnomic properties)'.[86]

While not being at the epicentre of mainstream European deconstruction, ENO's Verdi productions shared the self-involved, sceptical discourse as well as the obscure, sometimes obfuscating, language of postmodern literature and art. There was an element of relativism whereby meanings became the property of the interpreter and were intended to provoke and needle. 'One chooses a role to play,' Alden told Milnes, 'putting oneself in opposition to the establishment areas of society to which opera is tied.' For Alden and Fielding one of the joys of doing opera was 'the whole game that has to be played'. They saw their role as very much part of the avant-garde. 'Art is always confrontational when it's new and fresh,' Fielding explained. 'It's the shock of the new, basically.' The two men saw themselves as *enfants terribles*: 'There is something about us together that seems to be provocative and causes a certain amount of combustion. Even within the profession people talk about us in this way.' They shared what Elder described as a 'bold, challenging but almost offensive approach to the audience'.*

Elder recalled how Alden, in the last hours of rehearsals, 'proceeded to mystify his productions'. Just before the opening of *Simon Boccanegra*, he had placed some stuffed birds at the edge of the stage. Elder recalled:

---

* Milnes wrote in his review about hearing the press officer greeting critics at the opening night of *Simon Boccanegra* with a cheery laugh: 'Ambulances at 10.30.' He had also been 'wittily' seated by ENO management next to Fielding and had 'ended the evening in a state of silent near apoplectic rage' (*The Spectator*, 25.4.87).

On the first night the huge silk curtain came across and knocked one skew-whiff and the audience laughed. I said, 'Get rid of it, it's stopping us having a success.' It's not good, that sort of talking with the two Davids, Fielding and Alden. They're not interested in success, they are interested in creating the type of theatre that they want and they hope everybody will be impaled on it. They don't want to be told what to do . . . they don't want to give a palliative to the audience to have an easy success.

It was, Elder believed, 'the icing on the cake that was intended to say, "This is David Alden and David Fielding and don't you forget it!" That alienated people.' If the public could have seen it without the trappings, Elder believed, their work would have been more appreciated.[87]

Alden's method was to create tension on the stage by imposing a twentieth-century rhythm over and against Verdi, while at the same time using props and scenery to pre-empt the story from the music. The audience and critics inevitably focused on the deliberate dislocation and use of symbols. Milnes questioned them about the many restless visual stimuli thrown at the audience, especially the lighting plot, and about what he called 'design tics', such as the bare light bulbs, a lonely wooden chair, the mix and match of unrelated clothing styles, chain mail, great coats, Bisto Kids suits, medieval robes, overcoats, floppy hats, shawls and a Gothic seat on adjustable television-set legs. Loppert dubbed the visuals 'dislocated stage management' that broke up the scenes and prevented the piece moving at its natural pace, chopping them into alienated little sections.[88] When Milnes suggested that the deliberately provoked reactions of confusion, anger or mystification interfered with the listening process, Alden responded that he thought that homogeneous things on stage were boring and pasteurised and that he did not like realistic or musical lighting. When Milnes asked why, when Amelia sang about the waves shimmering, they showed a stormscape, Alden replied: 'You have Brecht to blame for that. It's an ironic gesture, yet not entirely ironic – the waters are dangerous around Genoa.'

Elder relished the 'dislocation' and symbolism, finding the visual images beautiful and powerful. Paolo burning something in a bucket to suggest duplicity and corruption was, he said, 'such an incredible counterpoint to the sound I was trying to make'. Boccanegra wrapping himself in the inscription and the little girl lurking in recesses were images of great power and pertinence, he believed. The story is so confused and the details so hard to follow, he thought, that in a straight performance you have to listen to every word. Audiences and critics were more uncertain. The great finger in the council chamber pointing to Boccanegra was intended to show how this one little man was to make one gesture of real moral authority. Like the stuffed birds, it induced mirth with its resonances of *Monty Python*. When Milnes asked if they were going to keep it, Alden responded that 'there were only a few titters'.

Many critics mourned the absence of humanity and dignity. John Higgins wrote that 'by focusing on poisoning and plotting – jackboots and metal spikes on trapdoors' Alden pushed aside the Verdi themes of paternal love and patriotism. The result was a *Boccanegra* 'without heart and humanity, the two essential ingredients of the work'. Alan Blyth was also disturbed by the fact that every image was imbued with threat and menace. David Cairns echoed Blyth: the new ENO *Boccanegra* was, he believed, a youthful work, the work of a bright adolescent – and Verdi, of all opera-creators, belongs to adults.[89]

Nevertheless, the musical standards of ENO's Verdi were uniformly high. Elder said that working with Alden had inspired his interpretation and, ironically, his musical preparation and his masterly grasp of the scores were as unanimously praised as the direction was criticised. Musically *Boccanegra* was considered one of the finest things that ENO had done. Peter Heyworth wrote that the recognition scene was incandescent.[90]

The cast also excelled, although they too were visually in conflict with the music. Arthur Davies, as Gabriele, sang with much feeling despite a costume that made him look like a *Monty Python* character, and Gwynne Howell's Fiesco, looking like a down-at-heel hobo, gave a performance of sweeping dignity, thought Blyth. Jonathan Summers was a strong and intelligent Simon, 'noble, broad and with genuine distinction of colour and line', according to Loppert, and Alan Opie tackled the role of Paolo 'glowingly well', thought Heyworth. He also thought that Janice Cairns was a powerful, accurate and musical Amelia, despite a lack of honeyed warmth, and that she had the measure of the music, a graded crescendo rising to top C and accurate musicianship.

John Higgins wrote about the Jekyll-and-Hyde nature of ENO:

one ENO was cherishable and admirable, casting with care, bringing on its singers and showing scrupulous musical preparation under Elder. The other was the unlikeable ENO: 'A haven for opera producers, out for self-indulgence, determined to twist the intentions of composers and librettists alike into the most brutal shapes.' It was, perhaps, 'Zeffirelli phobia'.[91]* It was the production that most divided followers of ENO. For Elder, *Simon Boccanegra* was the production he admired above all others, believing it to have been critical in defining what sort of house ENO was. Its aesthetic, he said, 'was startlingly unexpected and unusual while at the same time it had the virtue of scale'.[92]

*Boccanegra*'s ten performances at 64 per cent attendance did not bring it up to budget, while *Don Giovanni*'s full houses were making up for the disappointment. On 9 April the Opera Committee's chairman Leonard Hoffman expressed his irritation at some aspects of the production, but Jonas stood up for his policy: *Boccanegra* was part of an exclusive production style. Furthermore, the high turnover of shows meant that nearly all current productions would soon fit that style and that it was necessary to 'dead' older sets as there was a shortage of storage space. Miller's 1981 *Otello*, Graham's 1980 *Boris*, *Arabella*, *Parsifal*, *Valkyrie* and *Manon*, which some members of management wanted to keep, would all have to go as they 'no longer fitted the company style'. The 1974 *Don Carlos* was also to be 'deaded', even though Elder thought it should be kept for the Schiller festival.[93]

Pountney's *La traviata*, designed by Lazaridis, which opened on 14 September 1988, was also not lacking in symbolism. Central to their concept was a pun on the word 'consumption', Lazaridis told the *Independent*. Violetta was consumed as a sexual commodity with 'always this element of voyeurism'.[94] The scene opened in Lazaridis's handsome wine-red room with mirrored, heavy gilt doors, in which guests in nineteenth-century costumes were enjoying themselves in 'hard-hearted fashion'.[95] David Murray saw this as a brothel with mirrors in a tumescent red chamber. Top-hatted

---

* Mark Elder told the *Independent* that ENO Verdi was 'an antidote to Zeffirelli-ism, to the idea that the lyric theatre should be a treasure house of beauty first and foremost'. Kupfer had told him, he recalled, that if the stage were harsher the beauty of the music would well up and make itself seem more beautiful (Elder interview in the *Independent*, 12.9.92 and 16.9.92).

gentlemen observers and their doxies with servants as pimps, and guests leering up skirts, together with jerky strobe lighting, reduced *Traviata* to a 'sordid peep show'. In Act II Helen Field's Violetta was a blonde in underwear in a surrealistic cornfield, which burst through a table. 'Jaded guests tossed in some payment for their evening's entertainment' at the end of the Act I party scene. The corn symbolised Violetta's 'Rosebud' – a lost childhood of freedom and happiness, thought Higgins.[96]

Arthur Davies's Alfredo was made to look 'as though he was pushing middle age', and within the production Helen Field sang well but failed to arouse compassion. Elder was thought to lack warmth, in keeping with the spirit of the staging as a whole. He later said he did not think that in the end the emotional heart of the piece had been powerfully expressed.[97] At the first night the audience was muted. Peter Heyworth contrasted Pountney's *Traviata* with Peter Stein's new *Falstaff* at Welsh National Opera, writing of Stein that 'unlike so many of his *confrères* he does not find it necessary to rape a work in order to demonstrate his interpretative prowess'. He set out to liberate the score's dramatic powers – there was not a detail that went against the grain of the music: 'Stein found his way so deeply into the imaginative world of Shakespeare, Verdi and Boito', while Pountney's new production of *Traviata* seized attention with a 'plethora of peripheral detail that fails to disguise the hollow handling of the entire drama'.[98]

David Alden's production of *A Masked Ball* was the next Verdi production in house style. It was greeted by a cacophony of boos and bravos on 14 September 1989.* Fielding himself had reservations about the opera and Verdi's dramaturgy, and felt that Alden's concept of *A Masked Ball* as a 'dance of death' 'reinforced the hollowness of the sentiment' that the listener was meant to invest in Gustavus on Verdi's part.[99] He nonetheless worked with him to prepare a show full of striking visual symbols: a tilting gilt picture

---

* Mark Elder recalled an incident on the night of the broadcast, when, between the very loud chords that start the second scene, somebody in the dress circle shouted out in upper-class tones: 'This is a load of absolute rubbish.' Elder played the next very loud chord, after which somebody in the stalls shouted in an equally fruity accent: 'Will you be quiet, some of us down here are trying to enjoy ourselves.' He then played the third chord even louder (interview, 14.4.08).

frame in Act I; the love scene of Act II, scene i, dominated by a clock face with frantic hands; a ballroom dominated by a Horseman of the Apocalypse. The characters were similarly delivered: Arthur Davies's Gustavus in high-street casuals and disguises; Lesley Garrett a chain-smoking Oscar with a goatee beard, red wig, glasses and wings; Linda Finnie's Mlle Arvidson in a silver lamé ball gown.

Elder did not think the production was as successful as *Boccanegra*, although he found some elements, especially the lighting by Wolfgang Göbbel, inspiring. He also admired the strongly choreographed chorus, which he felt was allied to emotional awareness and was more effective than it would have been if given naturalistic freedom. At the opening of *A Masked Ball*, when the men's chorus advanced slowly in bowler hats and black suits, he found the scene 'really sinister and yet apparently benign'.[100]

There was a growing philosophical division in the directors' world. Miller, Moshinsky and Hytner were more concerned with the social and historical context of the works and to cast light on the relationships and narrative using music and text rather than symbolism and counterpoint. Moshinsky, worried that the humanitarian tradition of performer-centred direction would be lost, attacked the pervading language of irony in Verdi production. Verdi was a moral philosopher and realist of great perception who 'used the sometimes crude operatic conventions at his disposal to dramatise ethical and social questions' and who 'created dramatic milieus that allowed him to express the human condition'. Like the great novelists of the time, Verdi used 'long narrative, multi-plot structures, and verisimilitude of character to present the epic and humanistic point of view'. He often had to change his settings for reasons of censorship, which some directors, including Alden, used as an excuse to distance themselves from the works. Moshinsky wished to embrace Verdi's humanism directly and 'to give dramatic life to his great themes and characters without a protective layer of irony'.[101]

Pountney naturally defended Alden from his detractors, whom he accused of being 'marooned in the doldrums of naturalism'. Alden was not concerned with irony, he argued. Rather, his work shocked because it emphasised rather than papered over opera's 'violent tendency to dislocate from reality, juxtaposing high-octane performances with astonishing and forceful symbolic images'. His direction was an inspired reinvention of the theatrical language of romantic melodrama in which Verdi was writing. His 'visionary and highly visceral direction embodied the disturbing and shocking attributes of the composer'. On the other hand, he conceded that ENO's poverty meant that anything grandiose or glamorous had to be presented with a degree of irony.[102]

Nicholas Hytner, while he was welcomed to ENO, was nonetheless considered to be somewhat conservative by his colleagues. He too favoured a more humanistic approach, finding some German directors visually exciting but alien in thinking and sensibility. He was firmly on the side of the text, explaining that each production must find a world suitable for the opera it was representing and a way of behaving – a style of acting – consistent with that world and everyone in it. The world of the opera is in its music, but the contemporary world was based on cinematic realism, he wrote, and directors had to renegotiate the non-naturalistic works. He felt that their challenge must be to relish the difficulties and meet them head on.[103]

Miller later spoke more personally about the deconstructionists and their attitude to their audience:

They stand in the wings in a state of exalted excitement as the curtain goes up and the audience boos. It comes from the idea that deconstruction is an art, and from an illiterate memory of something they have not actually experienced – an audience booing at some great work of modernism such as the *Rite of Spring*. It makes them part of the heroically 'be-booed' community. They must 'épater le bourgeoisie'. German directors were committed to something that is part of German and French literary criticism, which is itself incomprehensible to anyone who is not part of the debate. Such obscurantism is unacceptable in all but the most complex scientific subjects such as neurotransmitters or nuclear physics. There is a straightforward language to talk about what we do.

While all direction is a form of reinterpretation and reconsideration, Miller continued, the English followers of the German notion of *Konzeptregie* and deconstruction tended to ignore the deeper meanings that are consistent across eras and the need to take into account the drama of people reacting to each other in a recognisable social world. While Miller was a devotee of abstraction and modernism in the visual arts, in drama, where people were involved, he believed that it was crucial to take into account the social background of the proponents to create credible relationships and motivations. It was necessary to have a literate understanding of horizontal and vertical relationships and social theories of kinship and hierarchy, and not to rely upon deconstructed relationships and questionable symbolism.[104]

The chairman of British Steel, whose company had sponsored *A Masked Ball*, disliked the production, championing John Schlesinger's Salzburg production, which Jonas described as 'boring, flatulent and overdone'. Jonas was unrepentant, telling Goodison that in government and Arts Council circles British Steel has come out 'smelling like roses' because ENO had been so innovative, adventurous and courageous.[105] Jonas, in his report of the year for the Arts Council, wrote that *A Masked Ball* was the production that made the triumvirate feel most proud to be part of ENO. Exciting, stimulating and really musical, it was also a staging that broke into a new aesthetic world for ENO, only just approached in *Simon Boccanegra* some two years before.

The local debate was part of a wider discussion in the operatic world about the merits of 'director's opera'. In Italy, Giorgio Strehler believed that the excessive emphasis placed on the director's role was not healthy for the theatre. The director had become too much of a star, like the great actors of the eighteenth and early nineteenth centuries. 'Our role is to love the theatre,' he said, 'in all its complexity and above all the text.' This involved an 'undeviating search for the truth of the text and the organic unity of meaning and feeling'.[106]

Richard Eyre in May 1989, after taking over as director of the National Theatre, expressed his concern for what he described as the 'rise of the new orthodoxy, the opera ethos – camp and self-referential', and 'a reluctance to engage with any feeling or humane detail or ambivalence'. He believed that expressionism was 'a fascist aesthetic'.[107] Looking back in 2007, Nicholas Hytner said that there had indeed been an element of 'Euro-bollocks that never has to be comprehensible to anybody but the people sitting there conceiving'. Although Hytner believed that the work of the Alden brothers, Christopher and David, was very influential in England and was more genuinely vibrant than that of their detractors, he felt that it did not evolve much over the next twenty years. He nonetheless believed that the achievement of the triumvirate had been to make ENO 'the most exciting theatre in London'.[108]

Some operas sat more comfortably within the house style than did late Verdi. When Shostakovich's *Lady Macbeth of Mtsensk* opened on 22 May 1987, critics were unanimous that Pountney's implacably busy inventiveness and penchant for expressionism, together with Lazaridis's overpowering set – a dark grey, incessantly revolving steel-laddered slaughterhouse hung with carcasses – were excitingly compatible with the work in hand. The team were also felt to have done full justice to the vast stylistic range of the complex score of 'tragi-satire', with their references to early cinema – Keaton, Chaplin and Fritz Lang – again evoked in the familiar mechanised chorus movement. Heyworth thought that Elder's orchestra responded with masterful flair and momentum and the chorus sang with thrilling power. Josephine Barstow's Katerina held the show together, 'singing with unfailing power and musical sympathy and brilliantly conveying every facet of a character that is at once hateful and tragic'. Her discipline of voice and body, as well as her command of stillness, her passion and courage, overwhelmed all the critics.[109]* Willard White's Boris was utterly convincing, and the scope of the piece matched the forces of the company and size of the stage to its full limits.

The audience response was ecstatic – they were screaming with enthusiasm on opening night – and the excellent reviews combined with a specially mounted pre-publicity campaign resulted in business that broke house attendance records. Within the house the big shows inspired and excited. Stage manager Philip Turner recalled that *Lady Macbeth* used the stage to its full limits – both physically and technically. 'In those days we took risks and presented great huge shows to the public, who came and loved it.' Working on them was exhausting and thrilling: 'We worked till it was done.' He remembered the spectacular first-night parties where tension was released and the shared effort celebrated.[110]

The production won the Laurence Olivier Award for outstanding

---

* Barstow, who had not understood the character, recalled how Pountney had advised her to be still and do very little, otherwise leaving her much to her own devices, and how she found the 'black centre' inside Katerina, 'an evil, mysterious, motiveless malignancy' which served to draw in the audience to answer their own questions about the character. This interaction, she pointed out, 'is what theatre is about'. She also remembered the occasion on which she walked out of a stormy *Lady Macbeth* rehearsal and Strowbridge had to follow her to Trafalgar Square to bring her back (interview, 26.2.08).

achievement in opera and played to 83 per cent houses.* After years of deficits the company ended the 1986/7 season with a small surplus of £20,363, due to increased box office of 7.6 per cent and donations.[111] Within two years Russell Willis Barnes had increased ENO's donations almost threefold, from £273,417 in 1985 to £729,757 in 1987.[112]

The Arts Council assessment of April 1987 acknowledged that ENO offered a better return on its grant, as measured by subsidy per seat, than any other UK opera company – the Royal Opera House, Opera North, Scottish Opera and Welsh National Opera received between £30 and £40 per seat, and ENO under £20 – and its artistic achievement was recognised by the public, the critics and its international peers.[113]

The board was concerned that the improvement in the financial situation might not continue. It was soon proved right. The new season began just before the Black Monday stock-market crash on 19 October 1987, which was to affect both the box office and donations. Furthermore, plans for the 1987/8 season had been built round Sondheim's *Pacific Overtures*, which management had hoped would be a box-office success similar to *The Mikado*. Some board members had expressed the opinion that the season was too dependent on one production. Focusing on *Pacific Overtures* proved to be a costly miscalculation by management.[114] Directed by Keith Warner, it opened on 10 September and, although it was a worthwhile achievement, did not have the 'bankable' success of ENO operettas or Gilbert and Sullivan.

* Amongst the Olivier Awards won by ENO since 1978 'for outstanding achievement in opera' were for 'enterprising repertoire' in 1978; for *Così fan tutte* in 1980; *Rigoletto* in 1982; Mark Elder for conducting *Duke Bluebeard's Castle, Macbeth, Pelleas and Melisande* and *Wozzeck* in 1991; the orchestra for *Inquest of Love* and *Lohengrin* in 1994; Paul Daniel for *From the House of the Dead* and for his contribution to ENO in 1998; for championing Handel in 2000; and to Mark-Anthony Turnage and Amanda Holden for *The Silver Tassie* in 2001. Best new production award went to *Khovanshchina* in 1995, *Tristan and Isolde* in 1997, *The Trojans* in 2004 and *Madam Butterfly* in 2006. Simon Keenlyside won an award for outstanding achievement in opera (Royal Opera's *1984* at the Royal Opera House and English National Opera's *Billy Budd* at the London Coliseum), as did Amanda Roocroft as *Jenůfa* in 2007. ENO won two Olivier awards for the 2008/9 season: *Partenope* for best production and Edward Gardner for outstanding achievement in opera.

Ralph Koltai and Marie-Jeanne Lecca designed a clean, spare set, with a very beautiful soft grey silk curtain across the front, and a brush-stroke line of hills and scarlet margin ruled above the white screens and boxes; the whole brilliantly lit by Nick Chelton. Musically, *Overtures* ranged in style from Kabuki to Broadway in telling its tale of the Westernisation of Japan in the 1850s. Milnes supported ENO doing the piece and thought it was cleverly written, revealing more at each hearing. He was impressed by Sondheim's 'elaborately constructed musical play with music' and its 'ambiguity, subtly disturbing resonances and wit'.[115] Kenyon, on the other hand, found the music thin, veering as it did between restrained pentatonicism for the Japanese and parody nationalism for the invading forces. It was an evening, he thought, dominated by 'tiny half melodies accompanied by bubbly ostinatos, with no real people to engage the attention'.[116] Cairns thought ENO, although it had expanded mightily from its Volksoper origins, remained a popular vernacular house and was right to include works like *Pacific Overtures*. It was, he thought, a thoroughly serious work that had been performed with assurance, skill and charm.[117]

*The Pearl Fishers* in the old Moody translation was definitely not in the house style. It opened on 21 September to a rapturous audience reception, mainly due to its fine cast and Mackerras's conducting. Valerie Masterson, so happy in French music, floated alluring lines and delicate nuances as Leila; Adrian Martin as Nadir was a fine stylist and Russian baritone Sergei Leiferkus commanded the stage with his still, excitingly appealing presence, a strong and lyrical Zurga.[118] There was unanimous praise for him despite his rather thick Russian accent.* So too was there for Mackerras, who, in Loppert's words, drew out 'all the score's exotic sensuousness (occasionally at perilously slow speeds) and pseudo-Oriental primitivism in a boldly executed reading'. Mackerras made out as good a case as possible for Bizet's haunting, though dramatically weak and musically uneven work, conducting with a wealth of 'appreciative affection and light fingered exactitude'.[119] Director Prowse's design was architectural, with peripatetic pagoda-like towers. The very

---

* Jonas had spotted the Russian baritone at Edinburgh in November 1986, and thought his fine lyric voice would solve the problem of casting *The Pearl Fishers*. Leiferkus was a frequent visitor to the West after appearing at Elaine Padmore's 1980 Wexford Festival and singing Don Giovanni at Scottish Opera.

English chorus – singing splendidly – looked a bit ridiculous in Hindu dress and masks, according to Griffiths.[120]

Leiferkus, not with tongue in cheek, told Hugh Canning that he was enjoying being at ENO 'because it is impossible to do such modern productions at the Kirov'. In Leningrad the operagoing public wanted to see the characters they know from the libretti and experience something that was 'different from their everyday lives'. This was not, however, how Jonas and Pountney saw the production. Pountney described it as 'lamentable',[121] and when the Opera Committee expressed their delight at Leiferkus on 29 September 1987, Jonas told them that he thought *The Pearl Fishers* had been presented in an 'undemanding and unconvincing' way and that they were lucky to have had a success with it. Whatever management felt about the production, *Pearl Fishers* and *Salome* made up for the poor results of *Pacific Overtures*, which had fallen £50,000 short of its projected budget. The Opera Committee wondered whether it had been wise, with the benefit of hindsight, to plan *Pacific Overtures* as the 'banker' with so many scheduled performances.[122]

Miller's last production for ENO for six years was *The Barber of Seville*, designed by Tanya McCallin, in November. The Opera Committee found the production visually flat, but Jonas reminded them that Miller had been given a restrictive brief to take up very little space so that it could be played in repertory with other shows.[123] Within senior management there was reluctance to use Miller and a certain hostility to him, although Jeremy Caulton defended him from unfair criticism. Although Caulton thought that the *Barber* was his least interesting production, he wrote: 'What he lacks in organisation of detail is more than compensated for by the strength of his basic ideas,' adding, 'The strengths of *Rigoletto*, *The Turn of the Screw* and *The Mikado* cannot be laid entirely at other people's doors!'[124]

Miller's *Barber* was still in the repertoire in the 2008/9 season and provided many well-attended revivals. At the opening the cast shone, with Alan Opie a marvellous Figaro and Della Jones a gloriously accomplished Rosina. John Higgins liked the 'exceptional clarity' of the production and praised the translation of Amanda and Anthony Holden. They were, he believed, the Edward J. Dent of the 1980s, sharing his delight in outrageous rhymes, 'the magpie instinct for the clichés of speech that stick in the mind and a blessed ability to write words that are easily singable'.[125]

Amanda Holden was to translate many operas for ENO over the next decades with great sensitivity and comprehensibility. Milnes believed that her work, together with that of another musician, the director, writer and composer Jeremy Sams, led to an increasingly high standard of translation at the turn of the century. Amongst Sams' most famous and long-lasting translations were *The Magic Flute* for Nicholas Hytner's production and *Figaro* for Graham Vick. Pountney preferred to prepare his own translations for his stagings. After Rodney Blumer had prepared two excellent translations for Pountney – *Rusalka* and *Osud* – he decided that he should control all aspects of his own productions, believing that translations could be slanted to fit the concept and were, like the productions themselves, ephemeral and discardable. He was the translator of the next great ENO hit, *Hansel and Gretel*, since he wanted to leave behind the 'playful nursery cutesiness' of the 1950s productions to provide something 'grungier'.[126*]

*Hansel and Gretel*, which opened on 16 December, was another great hit for ENO, and, like *Lady Macbeth* and *Rusalka*, aptly fitted the concept of Pountney and Lazaridis. It was also another big, ambitious show that revealed ENO at the height of its technical skill and expertise. Mark Elder, having been concerned that Pountney's concept might be too dark for the music and that it was very difficult to balance musically, had been more involved than usual during the production's gestation. It worked beautifully in Pountney's updated, post-war Crippsian England, set in a grassy park with municipal bench, chimneys smoking comfortably against a starry sky and a painstakingly realised 1950s suburban kitchen, complete with coin-fed gas meter. Cathryn Pope's Gretel in a flowery frock and Ethna Robinson's dreamy Hansel in Fair Isle sweater and knee-length shorts were part of a family which had fallen through the net of the fledgling welfare state. Norman Bailey's husband was drink-

---

* Amongst Pountney's other translations were *The Flying Dutchman* (1982), *The Gambler* (with Rita McAllister, 1983), *Christmas Eve* and *La traviata* (1988), *Der Freischütz* (1999), *Lady Macbeth of Mtsensk*, *Königskinder*, *The Adventures of Mr Brouček* and *Nabucco* (2000). His collaborations include *Orpheus* (with Snoo Wilson) and *Die Fledermaus* and *The Bartered Bride* (with Leonard Hancock).

ing away the money and Felicity Palmer's Mother/Witch gave a tour de force rendition of the wife's despair taken out on the children. The angels protecting the sleeping children were represented by all the familiar symbols of post-war security – postman, corner-shop grandma, Dixon of Dock Green, the milkman.

Critics thought it not only delightful but with something serious to say: the redemptive final scene was turned into an amnesty for all abused children, the music and story purged of saccharine. Loppert pointed out that *Hansel and Gretel*, like *Rusalka*, works very well on many levels.[127] The music was 'wonderful territory' for Elder.[128] The gala opening on 16 December was attended by the Princess Royal for the Save the Children Fund. The company was enthusiastic, and in general morale in the company was maintained as the administrative reorganisation continued. *Hansel and Gretel* was another direct hit for the ENO team, which was riding the crest of a wave of success and, on the whole, bringing its audience enthusiastically along with it.

# 1987–1993: 'Ruthlessly Pressing
for *Lebensraum*'

ENO's lively and provocative planning had made the Coliseum an exciting and stimulating venue and a place to contend with on the local and international arts scene. Despite Arts Council parsimony, its success had been sustained by energetic fundraising and increased ticket prices, and the 1986/7 season saw a surplus of £20,363 after several years of deficits. But the good times could not go on for ever, and after the collapse of the stock market in October 1987 the storm clouds started to gather. The underperformance of both *Pacific Overtures* and a restaging of the 1977 *Werther* had contributed to a box-office shortfall of £50,000, while production and technical costs were £241,000 overspent.[1]

Although the recession meant that it would be much more difficult to raise funds from private sources, the Arts Council maintained its pressure on the national companies to increase their self-generated income by initiating a variety of schemes rather than increase core funding. One was the 'incentive scheme'.

In March 1988 the secretary general, Luke Rittner, informed Harewood that the incentive scheme marked 'a radical change in the arts funding that we have known for so long'. Incentive funding was designed to 'encourage and pay for the development of business and marketing skills' and reward a sustained increase in earnings. The Arts Council would set clear targets that could be measured over time. ENO would have to raise enough private funds to meet those targets and would have to show at the worst an accumulated break-even by April 1991, on the basis of a probable 2 per cent increase in subsidy for 1989/90. If this were not achieved, the Arts Council would not be able to take a favourable view of incentive funding. Even if they fulfilled the criteria, ENO might not get it.[2]

Furthermore, the scheme would not recognise ENO's past achievements in fundraising, and would thus set the base from which to demonstrate improved fundraising performance at a high

level. Another new Arts Council scheme, 'enterprise funding', proposed that the Arts Council *might* provide up to £250,000 for specific projects if the company satisfied them that they could 'manage
change' and increase their income by twice the government's grant.
Another great worry was the proposed community charge or poll
tax, which would almost certainly diminish the willingness and
ability of the local authorities to support the arts and could result in
the loss of Westminster County Council's £1.5-million subsidy.

Board member Lord Carr had expressed his dismay at the Arts
Council's hypocritical attitude in November; in his view, their continued refusal to provide the necessary headroom for implementing
Price Waterhouse's recommendations for improvements made nonsense of the incentive-scheme criteria. Members of the board were
urged to use all their personal contacts with ministers to stress that
the Arts Council must improve core funding.[3] In December the Ken
Russell *Tannhäuser*, planned for May 1988, was cancelled and
replaced by a revival of *Fidelio*.

When the grant for 1989/90 was finally announced on 9
February 1988, it was £6,917,000 – an increase of 2.5 per cent,
although the increase in the Arts Council's own grant from the government was 8 per cent and inflation was 7.5 per cent. All the
national companies were on strict rations: the Royal Opera House
on 2 per cent, plus £500,000 for touring, the Royal Shakespeare
Company and the National Theatre on 2.5 per cent and 1.35 per
cent, respectively. Jonas decided to go public. His press statement
on 9 February expressed a sense of betrayal of ENO's efforts to
increase both its audiences and its income from box office and
sponsorship.[4] For years they had been told that there was no money
and, now there was money, the national companies were not a priority. He was starting to question the role of the Arts Council in
funding the national institutions.

Harewood informed Rittner that the elimination of the deficit
within three years was neither realistic nor appropriate, and asked
to meet him and Rees-Mogg.[5] At the time it was suggested to ENO's
finance director, David Elliott, by Anthony Blackstock, his opposite
number at the Arts Council and sympathetic to ENO, that a less
confrontational style by Peter Jonas might serve ENO's interests
better.[6] Meanwhile, Elliott was trying to work out a three-year programme that would not result in insolvency, hoping that the Arts

Council would accept a reduction of £458,000 in the deficit rather than its elimination.[7]

As with other institutions and non-profit-making bodies of the welfare state, the national performing-arts companies were receiving inadequate basic funding, were being set targets more suitable for profit-making businesses and were to be punished for any troubles they might fall into, regardless of their artistic performance. ENO was in severe danger of losing its main *raison d'être* – access to all at affordable prices. On 1 March it was pointed out by the board that ticket prices would have increased by 36 per cent in three years. On 12 April it was proposed that top seat prices should rise to £26. Altogether, during the Thatcher era seat prices rose sixfold, from £6.20 to £37.50 for top-price tickets and from 90p to £4 for the cheapest.

The erosion of the arm's-length principle was a threat to the independence of all the national arts institutions. Sir Roy Shaw – Arts Council secretary general from 1978 to 1983 – wrote an article in the *Independent* in December 1988 denouncing the fact that the incentive scheme had been dictated to the Arts Council by the government. He echoed Peter Hall's comment that whereas the role of the Arts Council had been historically to represent the needs of the arts, it was becoming an agency of government policy, a concern that had disturbed him increasingly since 1979, when the Council's vice-chairman, the sociologist and writer Richard Hoggart, had been dropped by the new Conservative administration because he was 'not one of us'.[8] Rees-Mogg was unashamedly open about his Tory allegiance, writing in the *Independent* before the 1987 general election that he hoped Thatcher would win another term.

Against this background the team continued to bring fresh talent to ENO. The thirty-five-year-old Tim Albery was personally invited by Pountney, who thought his *Mary Stuart* with Fiona Shaw in Greenwich 'really stupendous . . . blazingly original', to direct *Billy Budd* at ENO.[9] Albery was to find Pountney generous, consistently supportive and encouraging, and ENO a technically highly efficient and artistically creative environment.* Despite being freelance, Albery recalled, 'they gave you the feeling that

* Albery had directed his first opera, *The Turn of the Screw*, at the Batignano Festival, after which Graham Vick, who saw his work there and was at the time

you had joined a team'. The stage management and technical side under Technical Director Louise Jeffreys were, at every level, Albery recalled, with their depth of history and experience the best he ever worked with.

ENO's first *Billy Budd* in February proved an unqualified triumph, despite senior management's general lack of enthusiasm for the piece. They had doubts about the opera's 'clumsy' libretto and possible public indifference. They only decided to replace Reimann's *Lear* with *Billy Budd* when it was learnt that Thomas Allen felt that *Lear* was too big a role and too early in his career and that he had no time to study it.[10] As Budd, Allen was a huge hit, although management had considered him to be too mature for the part.[11]

*Billy Budd* was distinguished both by Albery's production and by the superb performances of three great singing actors at the peak of their powers: Philip Langridge's young, incisive, finely sung Vere, intensely enacting his abject betrayal of Billy; Richard Van Allan's dark, cold, ruthless Claggart; and Thomas Allen's moving Billy, whose 'Captain Vere, save me!' rang out through the Coliseum as a 'searing cry of pain'.[12] David Atherton's conducting allowed the orchestra and voices to expand wonderfully in the Coliseum's accommodating space.[13] Albery and his designers, Tom Cairns and Antony McDonald, focused on the society of the ship, setting *Billy Budd* on a huge, tilted deck, surface-edged in grey metal and backed by an abstract purple bruised skyscape. Belowdecks were claustrophobic, cramped spaces. Albery handled the choreography of the battle-stations scene superbly, as he did the chorus, especially the shuffling, mutinous mob after the execution.[14]

*Billy Budd* sold out completely. Milnes wrote in his review that the Arts Council's cuts were as abject a betrayal of ENO as was that of Billy by Captain Vere.[15]

Nicholas Hytner and designer Bob Crowley's *Magic Flute* on 30 March was not only extremely distinguished but continued to speak to audiences for over twenty years. Hytner compared *The Magic Flute* to *As You Like It* because of its faith in the development of romantic love and its confidence to contain a Touchstone character

---

director of productions at Scottish Opera, introduced him to Nicholas Payne at Opera North. Out of this emerged Albery's engagement on the ON/SO co-production of *Midsummer Marriage*.

to send it up. Despite the great seriousness of its theme of the spiritual quest for wisdom and enlightenment, Hytner sought to find a 'lightness of touch that can tolerate no pomposity' and convincingly to show a community searching for the answers.[16]

Hytner's love, understanding and respect for the work helped him to create an ingeniously self-contained world that absorbed both the comic and the sublime. He turned round with dexterity and intelligence the references to the lascivious Moor and rightly emphasised the elevation of Pamina over the misogyny of the brotherhood, and her leadership through the ordeals. Bob Crowley created a set of shimmering mirror-floors and white curved walls that cracked like an iceberg to reveal hieroglyphs, a horned moon for the Queen of Night, lush forest and finally a broad-brimmed, Quaker, enlightened New World utopia full of happy children.[17] According to *Opera*, Hytner 'gently clarified, straightened and corrected with a diplomatic, unexaggerated touch that should leave even the doughtiest anti-director fanatics unenraged'. The sharpness of humour in the witty translation of Jeremy Sams was never indulged at the expense of the simple dignity with which Hytner underpinned the humanitarian progress towards peace, love and wisdom embodied in the nobly sung Sarastro of Gwynne Howell. The fine singing of Thomas Randle as a personable, handsome, stripped-off Tamino and Lesley Garrett as a delightful Papagena, together with the conducting of Ivan Fischer, contributed to what Loppert described as a production not only discerning of the important issues but also often uproariously funny, 'delightful, wondrous in its moments of spectacle, charming and touching in its tender romance, secure in its sense of the work's poetic beauty'.[18]

Pountney was disappointed by Hytner's *Flute*, as well as his production of Schiller's *Don Carlos* at the Manchester Exchange, contrasting his 'shallow level of achievement' with that of Albery.[19] Pountney later said he thought Hytner's work with Fielding was more interesting than was his work with Bob Crowley.[20] Jonas argued that their work was not like the 'share option market' and that they should continue to invest in Hytner, even though he was not 'hitting the boundaries' at the time.[21] Hytner was fully aware that the delight was in the front of the house and not at the back, whence there came, he recalled, 'waves of disapproval – the fact that it delighted its audience was a badge of shame'. In 2007 Hytner reflected that there had been 'a sense that the connection to the public did not matter'. In the social set based on David Fielding's house, where Hytner spent much time in the 1980s, there was a sense that if you were not 'challenging, baffling and even infuriating the public you were letting the side down'.[22]

The delight certainly helped the box office, which by the end of the season had recovered sufficiently for there to be an overall surplus against the budgeted deficit of £160,000. Costs, especially of overtime, had also been rigorously contained. The accumulated deficit nonetheless remained a cause for concern at £407,000.[23] The board decided in September that it was reasonable to continue trading on the basis of Elliott's three-year business plan, in which the projected accumulated deficit would be slightly reduced by 1991.[24] With a prospective grant increase of 2 per cent per year, which was less than half the rate of inflation, Elliott's financial projections were based on an increase in ticket prices of 15 per cent each August and a higher target for development income. ENO's image was to be built up as a venue for 'stimulating, visually exciting and approachable music drama'.[25]

Pountney's *Traviata* was followed in November by Philip Glass's *The Making of the Representative for Planet 8*, with a libretto by Doris Lessing based on her novel. Encouraged by David Gockley of Houston Grand Opera, it was decided that ENO should be the co-commissioner and would put on the European premiere at a cost to ENO of £45,000. Jonas had been persuaded by Glass to use the Japanese design/direction team of D. Eiko Ishioka and Minoru Terada Domberger. Since they had little experience working in the UK, Pountney advised inviting Harry Silverstein as co-director. At the last moment, during the final rehearsals, after much discussion with the cast and staff directors, it was decided that Silverstein alone would coax the production through to opening night. Jonas informed a balcony regular, with whom he was in correspondence, that by the end he was 'shivering with the sweat of embarrassment and longing for Oswald Stoll's trap door to shoot him to the Victorian sewers below'.[26] It was a failure at the box office, although Jonas felt that ENO got off lightly with the press.

The English premiere of Reimann's *Lear* on 24 January 1989 was directed by Eike Gramss with a set by Eberhard Matthies. It was a second-hand production originally seen by Caulton in Krefeld. Paul Daniel, who was fully committed to the piece, conducted the ENO premiere – the eleventh that Reimann had attended since *Lear*'s premiere ten years earlier in Munich. Claus Henneberg, dramaturge at the Deutsche Oper Berlin, wrote the libretto after Joachim Eschernberg's eighteenth-century translation.

Critics were divided in their response. Barry Millington thought that *Lear* 'provided the kind of excitement that is characteristic of music theatre at its best', with serial techniques as well as quartertone aggregates and clusters, batteries of brass and percussion. Paul Griffiths wrote that Reimann used the 'surgery of German expressionist music drama' and an orchestra of 'knives, grinders and mailed fists'. Paul Daniel, he wrote, 'set off the detonations with perfect timing and brought out the intense colours in the score.' Max Loppert called it a 'drama of sterile cruelty virtually unrelieved' with a 'musical language suited to the theatre of cruelty'.[27] The committed cast included Monte Jaffe as Lear, Phyllis Cannan and Vivian Tierney as Goneril and Regan, counter-tenor Christopher Robson as Edgar and Rosa Mannion as Cordelia.

Despite a full and enthusiastic first-night audience, *Lear* fell far below its budget expectations, while *The Pearl Fishers* was sold out. The public, responding to good marketing and critical favour, were still prepared to pay more for tickets, the Arts Council assessed at the end of the year.[28]

The new year, however, saw the beginning of the change that was to threaten ENO's future as the recession began to bite. Corporate funding had hitherto helped to make up the gap in the Arts Council grant, but the recession started to affect not only the box office but the private sponsors themselves. There were also problems with the Musicians Union, which had threatened to strike the previous November. The dispute had gone before ACAS, the Advisory Conciliation and Arbitration Service. On 5 January ACAS, much to the alarm of the board, supported the orchestra's claim for parity with the Royal Opera House. A month later the arbitrator's two-year award was 12.6 per cent and 10 per cent to the orchestra, while ENO had offered 9 per cent and 7 per cent. The award upset ENO's three-year plan, failing completely to take into account the company's ability to pay the extra £82,000 the following year.[29]

With the Arts Council grant for 1989/90 increasing by only 2.5

per cent in response to ENO's request for 6.8 per cent, Elliott now predicted a budget deficit of above £500,000. He was also concerned about management's decision to increase ticket prices by an average of 23 per cent, as opposed to the three-year plan's assumption of 15 per cent per annum. One board member argued that there was no reason that seat prices should not be comparable to those of the Royal Opera House, while others pointed out that accessibility was 'one of the Company's key objectives'.[30]

An incentive award of £250,000 announced in March did not resolve ENO's long-term problems. The financial prospects for 1989/90 were deteriorating as inflation had increased by 6.25 per cent and the three-year plan had been assessed on the basis of a Treasury forecast of a 4 per cent increase.

In early 1989 the replacement of Rees-Mogg by Peter Palumbo, a property developer and art collector, as chairman of the Arts Council was welcomed by Jonas after a period destructive for both the Arts Council and its clients. The two men later became friends, as they shared a passion for architecture and design. Palumbo agreed to meet Jonas and Harewood within three days of his appointment. Shortly afterwards Jonas told the *Evening Standard* that he had been much cheered not to have been greeted like a ravenous, threatening wolf. He found Palumbo a curious and naive man who had a vision and believed in the arts.[31] At their April meeting Palumbo acknowledged the gap between the grant increase and the rate of inflation and promised to approach the prime minister to make funds available for ENO's proposed Russian tour, despite some grave doubts in the Arts Council boardroom after the American tour imbroglio. The 'nationals', Palumbo stated, 'must be properly funded', and the Arts Council would continue to lobby.[32]

Pountney was a generous facilitator and originator. In the summer of 1989 he set up the Contemporary Opera Studio, with Henrietta Bredin as its artistic administrator and David Parry its music director. It was intended to invent new ways of commissioning original work, by identifying librettists as well as composers and making it possible for potential creators to meet and share their ideas in a workshop environment. Working alongside ENO's new commissions programme, the Studio had an open membership base and a steering group drawn from composers, directors, designers, writers and publishers, together with ENO music and production staff.

The Studio got off to a flying start at a residential weekend in January 1989 at Dartington Hall, co-hosted and funded by Channel 4, where Bredin arranged for singers, players, writers, composers and directors to get together. As a result of this exhilarating meeting, the aims and ideals of the Studio were formulated and it was decided to open dress rehearsals to enable such encounters to continue. Out of these meetings grew such collaborations as that of Jonathan Dove and April De Angelis, who went on to write their highly successful Glyndebourne opera *Flight*, after their mini-opera *Pig*, which was written for the Studio. Specially commissioned for the Dartington weekend was a television opera by Orlando Gough, with a libretto by Anthony Minghella, called *The Mathematics of a Kiss*.

The Studio suffered from not being funded from ENO's core budget. It was also a concept with no home and no physical base, until Bredin, Parry and Pountney set up a lively relationship with the artistic directors of the Almeida Theatre, Ian McDiarmid and Jonathan Kent. This grew into the annual Almeida Opera Festival, which produced a steady output of new work.

One of the most successful pieces to emerge from the Almeida connection was Thomas Adès's *Powder Her Face*, to Philip Hensher's libretto – commissioned by the Studio and the Almeida. Although Bredin modestly recollected that there was no way anyone could have prevented Adès's opera being as clever as it was – 'the best stuff floats' – there is no doubt that such an atmosphere of informed encouragement and support facilitated the creative process.[33] Other Studio/Almeida Opera achievements included Nigel Osborne and Howard Barker's *Terrible Mouth*, a disturbing experimental piece about Goya, Julian Grant and Nick Dear's *A Family Affair* and Kevin Volans's *The Man with the Wind at His Heels*, based on an idea by Bruce Chatwin.

It was hoped that in the long term the work would become more closely tied to the commissioning for the main stage, but when the triumvirate left ENO, the Studio was put under a different management and the Almeida connection was severed, although Almeida Opera continued under the direction of Jonathan Reekie.

In the meantime the main stage commissions continued to be patchy. David Blake's *The Plumber's Gift* on 25 May 1989, directed by Richard Jones and designed by Nigel Lowery, was not part of the Studio's programme and suffered from a lack of workshopping with singers and players. It was as small scale as the composer's 1977 *Toussaint* had been large, and was sadly disappointing. It was melodic and sometimes lyrical with a set of abstract ideas but no narrative thrust gained from John Birtwhistle's libretto. It was, however, somewhat salvaged by Richard Jones and Lowery's designs, which included what were to become his signature effects: gaudily tacky 'clashing wallpapers, utility furniture, brainless ornaments'.[34] Malcolm Hayes wrote that any 'incipient pretentiousness' was subverted by one of 'the most brilliant displays of the producer's and the designer's art' that he had ever seen.[35] Its three contrasting couples emerged like a 'low key Alan Ayckbourn, a comedy of manners at the seaside', within which context Jones coaxed flawless performances from Peter Coleman-Wright as a sweet plumber, Sally Burgess as a sexy secretary and Ann Howard as the middleaged guest-house manager. Lionel Friend conducted 'with care and buoyancy'.[36]

Jonas and Caulton pondered the disappointments of many of the new commissions, wondering whether there were too many discussions and post-mortems and not enough time to peruse the scores and libretti in order to be stricter about enforcing cuts at final rehearsals. Richard Jones had done well, they considered, when not too confused by the high-flying intellectual ramblings. One thing was certain: Nigel Lowery's set had extracted more for the pound than anyone had seen at the Coliseum, on the very low budget of £65,000. Jonas reported at the end of the year that 'when Paul Griffiths in *The Times* wrote that it was the most important British work since . . . I am afraid that we at ENO kept a very low profile'.[37] New commissions continued, some with greater success.

As well as looking forward with the Contemporary Opera Studio, ENO management was aware that in order to have a future it was necessary to guard and preserve the past. Thus in 1990 the archivist Clare Colvin was asked by Richard Elder to set up the ENO archive, with a grant that she negotiated with the Pilgrim Trust. The archive includes the company's administration records, photographs, programmes, press cuttings and posters. Colvin, working on a shoestring budget, began to sort and list the collection, and in the mid-1990s she started a computerised database of all its productions. The archive rapidly trebled in size, and by 2007 also included wardrobe bibles and an extensive audio-visual collection. The archive's resources are available to the public but mainly used internally, and continue to be regarded as the guardian and historic cornerstone of the company.

In the summer Jonas was being courted to be the next artistic director of Salzburg from September 1991 but, according to Pountney, after 'much heart-searching' turned it down.[38] Salzburg must have been a tempting offer. The recession was beginning to bite. The budget gap in the plans was still £275,000 in August 1989 and costs were up 36 per cent on the previous year. As Elliott had feared, the increases in ticket prices of the previous two years were already beginning to create resistance.[39] The board was convinced it could not bridge the gap caused by inflation, which was being forecast at 5 per cent for 1991/2.

Despite this clear warning of dangerous waters ahead, the triumvirate continued to plan for a bold and very ambitious 1990/1 season that would be based entirely on twentieth-century works; to lighten the repertoire some Mozart would be added in recognition of the bicentenary of his death. Pountney had introduced his idea for a twentieth-century retrospective for the last decade of the century to the enthusiastic planners on 16 June 1986, when they immediately drew up a long list of potential operas.[40] The ideas had been refined and by the autumn of 1989 were well advanced. The season was to be called 20⁺. Jonas later admitted that in getting the plans finally accepted he had 'pulled the wool' over the eyes of the board, with a carefully judged degree of 'optimistic budgeting'.[41]

On 7 September Harewood expressed his disappointment at the 20⁺ season not including *Der Rosenkavalier* or *War and Peace*, and warned against Delius's *Fennimore and Gerda*, which he dismissed as rather a '*jejune* affair'.[42] Jonas was not to be persuaded, telling Harewood that he wanted *Lady Macbeth* and not *War and Peace*, and that *Der Rosenkavalier* would have to wait for Miller's new production.[43] Harewood later recalled that Copley's production 'stood for all the old-fashioned staging which they disapproved of'. They were, he believed, wrong not to have put it in the season.[44]*

On 12 October Pountney and Fielding presented Weill's *Street Scene*, which he had written in 1946 in the United States and subtitled 'An American Opera in Two Acts'. The production had originally opened at Scottish Opera on 23 May with John Mauceri conducting. It was set by Fielding in the high heat of summer in a crumbling tenement that swung back during the dance routine to reveal the illuminated Manhattan skyline. Milnes, who was a staunch advocate of Weill, described *Street Scene* as a work of fierce social protest and of music theatre 'that knows precisely what it wants to do and does it; the target is hit dead centre with a positively Puccinian certainty of aim, and content, form and achievement are indissoluble'. Its strength lay, like *Porgy and Bess*, in the creation of a community, the multiracial inhabitants of a tenement block in a New York slum. It ends with two young lives totally destroyed, and its 'sense of social protest throughout is all the stronger for not being overt, though ever present'. Milnes praised the cast: Richard Van Allan and Kristine Ciesinski as Frank and Anna, Janis Kelly and Bonaventura Bottone as the star-crossed couple and Philip Gould and Catherine Zeta-Jones – in an early stage role – for their delightful tap-dancing routine.[45]

In their review, Jonas and Caulton blamed the opera's structural weaknesses and problems of audibility in the auditorium for *Street Scene*'s lack of box-office success. It was a piece, they believed that was 'fascinating, haunting, but not really commercial'. They also realised that they had probably been guilty of scheduling too many performances.[46]

David Freeman directed Monteverdi's *Return of Ulysses*, which opened on 8 November, in what was described by *Opera* as an enthralling new production showing complete faith in the ability of Monteverdi to hold the undivided attention of modern audiences. Freeman was sensitive to the baroque medium, providing a seamless unity of the old and the new. It was designed by David Roger, with

* Jonas later recalled that his only serious row with Pountney, and the only time he had to assert his authority, was over the commissioning of Miller, with the support of Harewood, to direct *Der Rosenkavalier*. In the event it did not take place during his time at ENO (interview, 9.5.08).

classical columns that stood alongside a crumbling back wall in a vivid sequence of beautifully lit images. Loppert praised Freeman's 'intensely concentrated ensemble performance of eloquent simplicity and heart-lifting beauty'.[47] Each word was delivered with impeccable clarity by a fine cast including Anthony Rolfe Johnson, Sally Burgess and Jean Rigby, whose Penelope sat at her loom, visible throughout the opera. Paul Daniel scored the music for a restrained period ensemble of plucked and bowed strings, organ and harpsichord, lutes, double harps and recorders.[48] Kenyon wrote that Freeman had mustered the same magic as he had with his *Orfeo*, describing Ulysses as 'absorbing, powerful and moving'.[49] Although Jonas admitted that it had been a distinguished, highly successful and popular show, and that 'David Freeman's work was extraordinary', he felt that the design was a backward-looking 'neo-Peduzzi' step for ENO.[50*]

The last new production of 1989 was Prokofiev's *The Love for Three Oranges* on 6 December, originally directed for Opera North by Richard Jones, which skilfully combined Meyerhold's earthy comedy and Eisenstein's epic barbarism. It was designed by the Brothers Quay with sepia flats, Sue Blane's bizarre and dazzling costumes and Nick Chelton's lighting.[51] It was hugely enjoyed by Loppert, who wrote that it was a 'feast of hilarity, a joy and a delight, a production of unrepeatable originality and style, which strikes with deadly precision at the centre of Prokofiev's modernist comic fantasy'. The prep-school rude jokes in the wind-breaking tradition of Farfarello were combined with *commedia dell'arte* and graceful tributes to the Venetian sources of the libretto as well as to Russian revolutionary art.[52] The superb cast presented a fizzing pantomime for Christmas: Bottone's Truffaldino, Anne Collins's fruity Princess, Jane Eaglen's Fata Morgana, Donald Maxwell as the evil prime minister, Leander, Alan Woodrow the hypochondriac Prince, and Lesley Garrett's Princess Ninetta, with her warm lyrical singing.[53] Jonas thought it was 'splendidly done'.

As the recession worsened, and in line with the three-year plan, management focused on strengthening ENO's corporate identity and logo by using arresting and graphic images and publicity mate-

---

* French designer Richard Peduzzi was Patrice Chéreau's designer for the famous 1976 Bayreuth *Ring*.

rial to promote the company and its work. Jonas believed that the theatregoing experience began when first looking at the poster and that the ethos of the company should be reflected in every aspect of its activities, from the programme book to the ushers, the foyer and even the corporate typeface. The new logo in particular – a distinctive EN above a large O like a gaping mouth to symbolise a new young audience being sucked in – introduced at the beginning of the 1991/2 season, provided a long-lasting graphic image for the company.[54]

Keith Cooper, the new director of public relations, was restructuring the format of press releases so they were shorter and made a greater use of gimmicks.[55] His press publicity campaign kicked off with an advertisement in *The Times* on 29 September showing a sexy stagehand naked to the waist. In the October *Opera* editorial entitled 'Extremely Naff Opera', Milnes criticised the *Magic Flute* image of a sweaty male torso with a huge snake, which he thought 'looked a little too specialised in its appeal'. He also wondered why the billboards and press advertisement spaces on the Underground had dispensed with 'fuddy-duddy old style information, like titles of operas, casts and dates of performance'. Poor Lesley Garrett was seen 'in what Lorelei Lee would have called a flimsy negligay' miming nameless pleasures; David Freeman looked magnificently moody. Milnes winced at the prospect of 'nine more little snaps to complete this cringe-making series'. Such 'arch triviality', he thundered, 'was light years away from the high-minded principles of Lilian Baylis, hitherto loyally maintained and developed by successive managements'.[56]

Jonas wrote to an indignant Alan Blyth to explain that Cooper had received the full support of the board for the nine posters. Market research had shown that despite progress in extending the audience for opera, there were still 'vast numbers of people' who, rightly or wrongly, were put off by the 'stuffy institutionalised aura that opera surrounds itself with'. It was believed that there would be a good response to eye-catching, well-produced, stimulating 'generic' advertising. It had not been too costly, as ENO had developed their own strategy in house, using their own graphic designers. The board was fully behind the campaign. Unlike Milnes, Jonas thought the campaign was completely in tune with Baylis's efforts to extend the audience for British opera and theatre.[57] The public seemed to enjoy the campaign and it made the impact it was supposed to. Caulton believed that the poster campaign, like Miller's *Rigoletto*, had raised ENO's profile, especially amongst people who had a limited interest in opera.[58] On 15 October Pountney in the *Mail* observed: 'We have to cut through this red-and-gold image that says this place is only for toffs – everyone loves a good tune, it's the stuffy packaging that puts people off.' However appealing ENO's marketing, with top-price tickets at £37.50, affordability was becoming a problem, even though the cheapest seat prices were frozen until 1992/3.

Jonas's hopes that autumn were pinned on Palumbo as well as on ENO's striking new corporate image. The Arts Minister, Richard Luce, had managed to secure a 12 per cent increase of £19.5 million for the Arts Council and, unlike the previous year, had paid tribute to the work of the national companies.[59] In November the Arts Council increased ENO's grant for 1990/1 by 11 per cent (to £7,832,000). Jonas announced that since Palumbo had been chairman of the Arts Council the climate had changed and now the figures were beginning to change.[60] In the spring budget of 1990 the government announced the gift aid scheme, which allowed donations of between £600 and £5 million to qualify for tax relief.

Palumbo had also helped ENO with the Russian tour of June–July 1990. When he met Jonas, he offered to ask the foreign secretary about the political importance of ENO's proposed tour to Russia. He and the minister were very keen on the tour, but the Foreign Office was mainly interested in a possible visit to British week in Kiev.[61] Jonas later recalled the origins of the tour. The prime minister, at one of her meetings with President Gorbachev, had announced that she would send to Russia 'our English National Opera' – by mistake, Jonas believed, having meant to say 'our great national Royal Opera company'. In the ensuing furore ENO was determined to hold on to the initiative and, with the support of Palumbo, the British ambassador to Russia, Rodric Braithwaite and the prime minister's office, the great political and financial obstacles were overcome. Doors were opened in Russia, whereby state-controlled hotels and transport facilities were made available.[62] The British Council and the Midland Bank agreed to provide £55,000 each and the National Westminster Bank £5,000. Two board members contributed a further £15,000. With a funding gap of only

£21,000, on 19 December the board reversed its decision that the tour could not go ahead.[63]

By the end of the year, however, the box office was deteriorating and the extra advertising needed from August to October for *The Magic Flute*, *Katya Kabanova* and especially the *Masked Ball* revival, together with the disastrous *Street Scene*, meant that Cooper's advertising budget by 30 November had been exceeded by 24 per cent. The increase of 23 per cent in seat prices for the season had resulted in only 5 per cent extra cash being received at the box office and paid attendance was down to 76 per cent. The blame was laid at the door of the general economic situation but it was noted that Covent Garden, although it was expecting a £3-million deficit, was not doing badly at the box office.[64]

Finance Director David Elliott resigned in December 1989 on twelve months' notice. He later recalled that he had become increasingly worried at the financial implications of the repertory plans. The deficit for the next year was likely to exceed £500,000, and could be nearer £1 million, and the significant progress made in the previous three years in reducing the company's accumulated deficit and becoming free from the bank overdraft was in danger of being reversed. He also felt that the increase in ticket prices was reaching the limit of what ENO audiences were willing to pay for an increasingly challenging programme and that he was being asked to put his name to budgeted box-office figures he did not believe to be realistic. Planning for the Russian tour was, in his opinion, distracting management from these problems and absorbing energy that should have been focused on strategic issues. He believed that Jonas was not interested in compromise, however, remaining convinced that Palumbo and the Arts Council would bail ENO out.[65]

Jonas himself later reflected that Elliott, who was a man of the utmost propriety and decency, was indeed very concerned by the financial situation as a consequence of which there were difficulties between them. Jonas, looking towards the German model, was convinced that artistic leaders are judged and remembered only for the quality of the work on the stage and not by whether they made deficits or not. Maybe, he added, they were too harsh on Elliott, but they believed it was their duty to have the courage to stick to their aesthetic beliefs.[66]

Advance bookings even for *La traviata*, *Hansel and Gretel* and

*The Mikado* were slow by January 1990. By April, however, with extra marketing, *Mikado* had crept closer to its budget. Jonas thought the *Mikado* revival was the best ever, with 'Lesley in the best vocal form she has been in for the last five years and Richard Suart absolutely brilliant as Ko-Ko'.[67] Jonas praised staff director David Ritch, who had revived *Mikado* tremendously well and 'proved his value beyond measure'.[68]

Like Elliott, however, the board was increasingly concerned. On 23 January 1990 Lord Hoffman warned that hard decisions would have to be taken as not only was the 20⁺ budget for 1990/1 still £1 million in deficit but there was also a severe squeeze on corporate-sector cash flow. Lord Carr urged great confidentiality over the prospective deficit.[69] There was relief in February when the Arts Council agreed to make up the shortfall in the Westminster grant, but in the spring Jonas reported to Harewood that balancing the budget of the 20⁺ season was proving the most difficult task he had ever experienced. He was, he wrote, fighting like Custer to save a revival of *Street Scene*.[70] On 6 March Carr reiterated that it was not prudent to budget for another large deficit and urged the cancellation of *Street Scene*.[71] Two days later Jonas acknowledged that Custer's fight was lost and *Street Scene* was cancelled. On 20 March a budget with a deficit of £145,000 was accepted by the board, a decision taken in the light of worrying signs.[72] In the spring of 1990 financial information had been produced on the in-house computer for the first time. It showed that from April to August there was a major deterioration at the box office, as well as overruns on the sets and costumes for both *Macbeth* and Robin Holloway's *Clarissa*.

On 23 April Jonas announced the 20⁺ season at the same time as the delay of the new *Rosenkavalier* and the cancellation of the revival of *Street Scene*. Jonas took the opportunity to criticise Rees-Mogg, whom he believed had damaged the arts, and express his hopes for a better future under Palumbo.[73] Jonas was described by the *Guardian* as the notorious forty-two-year-old warrior, who was 'consciously modernist and gloriously uncompromising'. He was a charmer whose little vanities – like his ENO 1 car number plate – were legion.[74]

ENO's next Verdi production, *Macbeth*, on 5 April, directed by Pountney and designed by Lazaridis, marked the beginning of a questioning of the house style both inside and outside the building. Musically it was on a level with Elder's previous Verdi offerings. He was stirred by the metaphysical nature of *Macbeth*, which gave the music a 'headlong nervous quality'. Milnes found it a shattering musical experience:

The players were as one, the phrases in perfect unison, the fortissimo chords unbelievably unanimous and crisp (their degree of loudness carefully graded), the very special low-woodwind colouring that gives the work its unique tinta and overwhelming sense of foreboding well to the fore. Throughout the clarity of the accompanying figures was ideal, none of them treated as mere routine, none of them slipping imperceptibly into waltz time, always a danger in early Verdi . . . The opening of the banqueting scene established an atmosphere of barely concealed hysteria, with its little pauses, thrilling chattering woodwind, and headlong forward impetus painting the sound picture of a world gone mad, alienated from itself, helplessly adrift.

He also loved the production, while pointing to the by now 'familiar design tics': the wonky bedstead (here sticking out of a wall fifteen feet up), a baritone in vest and braces, slouch hats, suits, uniforms (some cannibalised from other productions) all spanning the centuries and set within walls that tilted vertiginously. For Milnes the setting perfectly represented 'a world out of kilter', possibly an East European tyranny with its samizdat typewriter and state heavies at public ceremonies. Of Duncan's green blood, Milnes asked: 'Why not, if the effect is so chilling?' He found the suburban housewives' witches coven in Miss Marple hats indulging in black magic to be an 'alarming ritual falling out of the everyday'.[75] Kenyon too found the production to be 'a contemporary extravaganza of moral decay' with a choreographic air and 'admirable tautness of gesture'. All were agreed that Elder made Verdi's score 'blaze and bounce'.[76]

There were, however, those who were beginning to be irritated by what seemed like a parody of ENO style: the slanted stage with surrealist dangling bed, Ciesinski singing her opening aria on a bedstead suspended on a tiny platform, then sleep-walking by crawling out from under the shower curtain in the neon-lit shower room, washing her hands at the kitchen sink. Michael John White said it was so self-regarding that it felt like parody. Higgins wrote how Pountney liked to tease, provoke and most especially to obfuscate.[77]

Within the board there was a growing concern that productions were becoming straitjacketed into one style. The Opera Committee thought that there was a danger of the perceived house style becoming repetitive and prone to cliché, even self-parody. The committee agreed there should be a constant examination of ENO's direction and warned of the danger of sticking to any style too rigidly.[78] In their report for the Arts Council, Jonas and Caulton wrote that despite the controversy, feelings in the company had been 'almost entirely positive'. While it was true that they had seen the raincoats before, the military uniforms and indeed the wonky bedstead, there seemed no doubt that this production succeeded in 'making the clichés work'. Most of the costumes had been 'cannibalised' and they loved the green elements – not just the blood.[79] Jonas later reflected: 'Raincoats are cheaper than doublets and hoses.'[80]

The next new production, on 18 May, was *Clarissa*, composed by Robin Holloway in 1976 and earlier turned down by Harewood. There was much pre-publicity, analysing Samuel Richardson's sprawling eighteenth-century novel on which it was based. Paul Driver described it thus: man wants girl; she resists; man rapes girl.[81] Nicholas Kenyon and other critics wrote about the 'sumptuous beauty' of the work's late Romantic and Britten/Tippett-inspired music, but even within this praise lay the uneasy feeling that whatever lyricism there was in the piece was being parodied. It was not a drama but rather a duologue, so Pountney took refuge in 'detached irony and cynical comment'. Clarissa became a jerkily moving doll-like figure, and both she and the rake Lovelace, with five other automaton clones, danced by the group Second Stride, created a complete stylisation. Porter wrote that at the end Pountney seemed to be mocking Holloway's tender, transfigured music. The rape was staged with 'fantastic insensitivity as a gang bang', despite the fact that his stage instructions requested 'obscurity' and the lament after the curtain.[82] The work was performed with commitment by Vivian Tierney and Graeme Matheson-Bruce, and conducted by Oliver Knussen.

Jonas and Caulton again reported 'another very impressive and, yes, successful Pountney production'. In this case it was a clarification of an extremely problematic work. The end, however, 'did seem a moment when David Pountney's tendency to over-invent

428

gave us some business which was rather at odds with the music and not particularly helpful from the dramatic point of view either'.[83]

Since the early spring, management's attention had been taken up by hugely complex planning for the Russian tour, which was part of the month-long Festival of British Days in the Soviet Union. The tour began in Kiev on 7 June. Russian critics and audiences alike were delighted by ENO's work. Used to heavy traditional set pieces, they responded to the lightness of touch in *Xerxes*, which was shown on 7 and 9 June at the beautifully maintained T. G. Shevchenko Opera House in Kiev. Prime Minister Thatcher attended the 9 June performance after a gruelling day, 'staggering with fatigue', in the words of Ambassador Braithwaite, who also recalled that she insisted on going backstage to talk to the company, despite the efforts of the KGB to prevent her as they had not reconnoitred the route.[84]

Board member Brian Unwin was impressed by the affection and hospitality shown to the company and coveted the spacious reception and ambulatory areas of the theatre and the good maintenance of its fabric.[85] Local stagehands were open-mouthed at the haircuts and earrings of the ENO stage crew, as well as their electric screwdrivers and the technology of the sets. There was also amazement that a woman, Louise Jeffreys, was in charge of the technicians. She was 'the unsung heroine of the tour'.[86]

*The Times* reported the tour's progress on 11 June. Critic Ludmilla Zhilina, seeing her first Handel opera, wrote: 'The orchestra sounds like the fluttering of a butterfly. The singing is like a spring in the forest, natural, without tension, the flow swift and clean.' The laughs were slow in coming, as opera was no laughing matter in Russia, but audiences were soon won over by the 'sheer sparkle and subtle integrity of the orchestra under Mackerras', and there was constant interruption for applause. *The Times* said it was the greatest ovation they had ever heard from the full house, with hundreds of flowers being hurled onto the stage. One musician was heard to say: 'We need this like we need air.' Five-rouble tickets were being sold on the black market for 150 roubles.

Unwin reported to David Elliott that *Xerxes* had been an enormous success. Soviet accompanying officials were 'completely won over and enthused for days, humming the stony-hearted duet as I was seen off at the airport to Leningrad'. Russian audiences were unfamiliar with but impressed by the counter-tenor Christopher Robson, as they were by the 'meticulous and inventive nature of the production'.[87] Between 7 and 24 June Miller's *Turn of the Screw*, *Xerxes* and *Macbeth* were performed in Kiev, Moscow and at the Kirov Opera House in Leningrad. Pountney's *Macbeth*, set in a recognisably East European tyranny, just a few months after the overthrow of Nicolae Ceauşescu in Romania and with the fear of bloodshed occurring in Russia, spoke directly to audiences. They were also excited by what Pountney described as the 'sheer freedom of associative interpretation' and the 'virtuoso execution by the chorus'.[88] The imagery, ideas and design of *Macbeth* haunted *Pravda* critic Dmitry Morosov 'long after the final curtain'.[89]

Elder was excited to hear the company performing in opera houses with the most excellent acoustics, which brought a truer perspective of the company's sound to performers and audience alike, as well as textual clarity. The tour was altogether a unifying experience for the company. Equally satisfying, it was not considered financially disastrous, with an overspend of £52,600, some of which was due to overtime necessitated by protracted applause.[90]

The 20+ season opened on 23 August 1990 with *Tosca*, which had been first performed in 1900. Elder commented to the *Guardian* that it was the opening season of the last decade of the century and 'it was about time we felt at home in it since we were about to leave it'.[91]

Bold though the 20+ season's concept was, advance bookings were well down, although *The Magic Flute* fortunately received excellent notices and its box office was improving. By May the projected year's deficit was £393,089, despite the 24 per cent increase in seat prices the previous August. An increasing number of tickets were being sold on standby at £9.50 and sets were being delivered late. Elliott in his annual report stated that there was resistance to the sharp increases in ticket prices: 'There were inherent limits on the ability of an opera company to continually expand their self-generated income at the rate necessary to make up for less than inflationary increases in grant income.' There had been a rapid shift in the balance between patronage and the public sector. Had ENO's public-sector grants over the past five years grown in line with the retail price index, they would have been able to eliminate the deficit with a healthy surplus.[92]

Amongst senior management there were signs of strain. An angry Cooper defended criticism of the subscription company he had employed by blaming the unpopular repertoire and the recession.[93] An equally serious problem was urgently noted at a planning meeting three weeks before the season opened: despite warnings from Elliott, a cardinal error had been committed by the planners in their failure to accumulate a collection of easily revivable, popular pieces to choose from when they hit a problem in the short-term planning of the season.[94]

The growing crisis prompted an urgent meeting between Elder, Jonas and Pountney and their senior management on 6 September 1990. The problem of a lack of communication between the planners and senior management during the planning process emerged during the discussion. Finance director David Elliott, three months before he left ENO, argued that the cancellations and compromises were the result of a lack of teamwork. Mark Elder wondered whether there had been a conscious decision that the planners should not meet as a group with their senior managers, to which Jonas responded that opera houses were by their very nature not democratic. He saw himself as the big pusher, 'ruthlessly pressing for *Lebensraum*' to achieve things artistically. Richard Elder, the director of administration, suggested that in taking key decisions it should still be possible to have a team that worked effectively.

At the meeting it also became clear that decisions had been made without regard for their marketing implications. Richard Elder pointed out that by the time senior management became involved in the planning process it was too late to be of influence. Elliott had no recollection of any discussion of the risks to marketing of the $20^+$ season, which was taking place in such a bad economic climate. Cooper said that the audience for twentieth-century music was limited to 20,000 people. Pountney and Caulton pointed out that when $20^+$ was planned, there was money about and it seemed that audiences could not get enough opera. Although the original idea had indeed been formulated in June 1986, by the autumn of 1989 ENO ticket sales were already in decline and the risks of putting such a programme before the ENO audience had become apparent. Pountney and Jonas, however, remained determined to push the boundaries, even if risks were involved. It was, Pountney said, enormously difficult to make the repertory suitable to the tastes of the public. When Elliott expressed surprise that *The Pearl Fishers* had been dropped from the live shows list, Jonas explained that although it might seem an odd financial decision, he could not bear the production and felt it was not right to do it again in this house. Elliott argued that more people than the Planning Committee should be involved in such decisions and pointed out that the Royal Opera House was getting better audiences while ENO's were diminishing. Mark Elder was disappointed that the 20⁺ slogan had acted like a shutter, but perhaps it could suddenly be a success. Pountney now accepted, as Harewood had urged, that *Der Rosenkavalier* could have been scheduled instead of the *Oedipus* and *Bluebeard* double bill, but although the music 'would have been much enjoyed, the Copley production was borderline'. Elliott would have liked to have been consulted. He felt there was a morale problem in the company and that middle management was showing signs of strain, working long hours, including Saturdays, and earning too little.

For the future, Elliott suggested that longer runs of fewer productions would save more in costs than would be lost in box-office income. Jonas felt that they were facing painful decisions, reiterating that they were in a 'Custer's Last Stand' situation. The question of working in a more popular style was also discussed. Mark Elder wondered if ENO to some extent was driving audiences towards other theatres. It was difficult, Jonas responded, for a designer to feel he must design something to be popular. The triumvirate acted upon informed hunches and it was not right to dictate to a producer. Cooper warned that there was a danger that the popular style might be forgotten. Pountney addressed the issue of what was becoming known even within the house as the Coliseum cliché, justifying it on the grounds that many items on the stage now derived from the low-budget (Norwest Holt) shows, i.e. bedsteads and trilbies. The *Macbeth* chorus were costumed as they were because there was no money for anything else. It was, he said, important to continue to have low-budget shows, but they should slip out of the stylistic trap they had got themselves into.

Jonas was unrepentant: 'You will never achieve satisfying everyone – nor should you try to,' he declared, adding, 'Avoid the tyranny of the reader.' Pountney thought it odd that this sort of discussion did not take place more often. Elliott appealed that in the search for new audiences the faithful followers should not be forgotten. The tight-knit management team over which Jonas had presided during his first five years was showing signs of unravelling.[95]

Cooper was worried that the new *Königskinder* and the *Masked Ball* revival would create marketing problems in the 1992/3 season, but Jonas viewed *Königskinder* as his 'luxury piece' at £110,000 – indeed, he later described it as a labour of love that at first nobody else wanted.[96]

The growing deficit was also creating tension between the triumvirate and the board, who discussed the crisis and the three-year plan on 25 September but had only received the papers on the same day as the meeting. Harewood told Jonas that it was essential for the board to receive lengthy communications earlier than they did at present. At the board meeting there was general gloom and consternation. In one way or another everyone expressed the view that it was impossible for ENO fully to discharge its artistic mission and live within its means, that it was no longer possible to make up for the decline in grants by increases in self-generated income and that there was no room for further economies. Jonas explained that the plan showed that with grant increases of only 2.5 per cent and 3 per cent for the next two seasons the accumulated deficit would rapidly escalate to a point that it would be impossible to sustain. Inspiration and the confidence to continue would be lost.[97]

Nicholas Hytner later reflected that the 'power house' team had come unstuck when adopting an unhealthy set of values that were brought over from the highly subsidised continental theatres and opera houses that worked for the approval of a self-elected elite and were able to delight only themselves. There had been a feeling at ENO, with which he had been uncomfortable, that 'the barrage of boos was what you were doing it for'. The management ignored the fact that English theatre had its roots in a golden age, which was then, as now, part subsidised and partly dependent on the box office and connected to a wider public. Down on the South Bank at the Globe they had needed the Lord Chamberlain and the King, but above all they needed the public to come and buy tickets. Our theatre, Hytner argued, had always been popular theatre, which had also required support from the state.[98]

The 20+ season was greeted by Michael Billington as a 'staggeringly audacious enterprise' shortly before its first new production, Berg's *Wozzeck* – a work first performed in Berlin in 1925. It opened on 13 September to a divided critical response. In Milnes's opinion, Pountney had delivered another 'standard essay in expressionism', with 'an awful lot of pulling of horrible faces, exaggeratedly jerky movements, and freaky make-up for the horror movie chorus', all of which undermined the complex text. *Wozzeck* was partly a study in paranoia and partly a deeply felt autobiographical statement. The tale of an 'inarticulate soldier driven to murder and suicide as much by the world around him as by his own disorder loses some of its power if he's as mad as a snake from the word go, if his chief tormentors the Doctor and the Captain are merely Grosz carica-tures, if the woman he loves is a slut unredeemed by the spiritual beauty that her music suggests'.[99]

Others thought it a good example of house style: 'austere, hard edged and tight'.[100] There was, however, unanimity about the qual-ity of the music. Porter wrote how Elder provided a thrilling, 'charged, vivid, precise performance with sharp-edged detail and passion in the handling of the colours, phrases and structures'. The singers too were praised for the intensity of their performances. Donald Maxwell was a moving, intelligent and self-aware Wozzeck and Kristine Ciesinski gave an admirably enacted Marie.[101] Equally impressive were Alan Woodrow as the Captain and Richard Angas as the Doctor, although John Treleaven's drum major was handi-capped by a Toy Town soldier's costume.[102] However controversial the stagings of the season, the music-making of orchestra and cho-rus under Elder proved to be of a consistently high standard and versatility.

The next 20+ production was *Greek*, composed by Mark-Anthony Turnage, which Henze had commissioned for the Munich Biennale in 1988, where it won prizes, reaching Edinburgh a few months later. It was based on Steven Berkoff's 1980 play the *East End Oedipus*, which had been updated with anger, Milnes wrote, to a London of urban decay and nihilistic despair. It received three per-formances from 27 September. All were agreed that Turnage, a protégé of Henze, was a rare talent with a truly personal voice. Kenyon thought it was a real opera, full of invention and in complete control of the music drama, the message deepened by the music. The Almeida Ensemble was conducted by Richard Bernas, with an energetic cast including Quentin Hayes and Fiona Kimm as Mum. Kenyon found the production of Jonathan Moore and David Blight refreshingly distant from the current ENO house style. It nearly achieved its budget of 66 per cent, and the third performance almost sold out. Jonas wrote in his report that he had been right to 'lie down in the road' for it.[103]

It was back to ENO style with a vengeance on 7 November with a reviled production by Julia Hollander and Ultz of Delius's *Fennimore and Gerda*, a dark expressionist tale adapted from the novel by the Danish writer J. P. Jacobson, and influenced by Strindberg and Nietzsche, which had been premiered on 21 October 1919. Paul Griffiths thought it 'dramatically slack and broken-backed'.[104] Milnes thought that Hollander had concentrated on symbolism at the expense of drawing performances out of Peter Coleman-Wright and Adrian Martin. Sally Burgess was in fine voice, with a 'Munch-like intensity', but nothing was gained, he felt, from the lovers rolling round on the floor smearing themselves with red paint and climbing into the piano for their final exit.[105] The piano, Harewood later reflected, was 'an idea, but not a good one'.[106] Although Harewood's warnings against the piece during the planning period had been ignored, Jonas and Caulton blamed the opera rather than the production for the failure.[107]

*Fennimore* was partnered by *Gianni Schicchi*, which had first been performed on 14 December 1918 at the Metropolitan Opera New York. Canning thought it a 'horrible miscalculation' by director Stephen Unwin and designer Ultz to play it as 'a ghastly vulgar romp'.[108] When it was suggested that it be revived with Alden's *Duke Bluebeard's Castle*, Harewood told Jonas that he much disliked ENO's farcical production, and thought that Alden would too, if he saw it.[109] Management agreed that it had not been a good double bill but *Fennimore*, it was explained, had been sponsored by the Delius Trust.

*Pelleas and Melisande*, first staged in 1902, was the next new production of the 20[+] season, on 30 November. It was directed by Pountney and designed by Marie-Jeanne Lecca, Kupfer's 1981 production having been damaged by water in store. According to Jonas and Caulton, there had been a simple disagreement with Pountney about what actually happened in the work. Pountney, having decided that the baby was Pelleas's and not Golaud's, delivered the piece with a sort of literalness rather than uncertainty and mystery.[110] In place of the turn-of-the-century doomed and inbred society 'so powerfully suggested in Maeterlink's text', Milnes found himself in a world of '*crime passionnel*', dangerously close to *Pagliacci*. Cathryn Pope's skimpily attired and knowing little Melisande was an angel of destruction for both the wimpish Pelleas of Thomas Randle and the upright, powerful Golaud of Willard White.[111] Sutcliffe hated the 'hideous' modern design of Lecca's hotel-cum-nursing-home, with its broken wall and a pile of debris strewn across the forestage. Pountney, he felt, neglected the 'emotional reality of the acting'. The new production did not work as the models had suggested, thought Jonas and Caulton, and the use of water, though beautiful, could not be seen in the stalls. Melisande's vast tresses evoked giggles – according to Sutcliffe – and were later shorn.[112] Elder, once more, found all the beauty, mystery, passion and colour of Debussy's score in contrast to the goings-on on stage.

The season continued with David Alden's *Duke Bluebeard* and *Oedipus Rex* on 23 January 1991. The budget had been severely reduced, with rehearsal and costume time especially hit, but the response to *Bluebeard* was favourable, especially for Elder's 'incandescent account of the score' and for the strong, risk-taking performances of Howell and Burgess.[113] The Opera Committee, however, were told on 18 March that Nigel Lowery and Alden had not been in harmony over the costumes and that Alden would tackle the piece with more understanding if asked to do it again. Alden had felt thrilled by the audience's reception of *Bluebeard*, but had been rather bewildered as he did not feel he had done enough with it.[114] His comic-strip, skewed set, low-budget *Oedipus Rex* impressed more for its economy than for its illumination of Stravinsky's ritualistic opera-oratorio about fate, a work so much part of ENO's illustrious production pre-history in the 1960 production of Michel St-Denis. Philip Langridge's portrayal of Oedipus and Rigby's of Jocasta, together with Elder's conducting, lent the piece musical distinction. The box-office returns were still depressing by the end of March.

The season also boasted some fine revivals of the twentieth-century repertoire, including *Rusalka* in February, with a moving Nancy Gustafson, and in May a joyous *Cunning Little Vixen*, conducted by Mackerras with Lesley Garrett as the Vixen. Billington described Garrett as 'teasing, energetic, sexy, playful, dangerous'.[115] *Lady Macbeth* returned – even more 'electrifying with a display of the rarest kind of ensemble artistry'. According to Loppert, Barstow was 'simply staggering', both to listen to and to watch, in one of the 'supreme operatic performances of the post-war period'.[116]

Tim Albery, with designer Hildegard Bechtler and lighting by Jean Calman, presented *Peter Grimes* on 17 April. Critics were overwhelmed by the power of Albery's expressionist production and Bechtler's set, an abstract, shallow acting space backed by a slab smeared ox-blood red. So were they by the orchestra's brilliance under David Atherton and by the cast, especially Langridge's revelatory Grimes, haunted, violent, angry and justifiably paranoid. Equally appreciated were Josephine Barstow's restrained Ellen and the sympathetic Balstrode of Jonathan Summers. The chorus, zombie-like and expressionless, presented a community brutalised by their harsh lives, monolithic and as frightening as Grimes's perception of them. The whole company – chorus, orchestra and principals – was seen at the height of its powers, turning out extraordinary work, despite the financial uncertainties. 'David Atherton's magnificently controlled conducting inspires the orchestra and chorus to their highest flights of corporate artistry,' wrote Loppert.[117] Jonas welcomed the 'refreshing' production, its European outlook and lack of cosiness.[118]

The world premiere on 17 May of *Timon of Athens* by Stephen Oliver, directed by Graham Vick and designed by Chris Dyer, was the last new production of the 20+season. The Opera Committee thought it skilfully written, although the orchestration obscured the text. On the whole they felt that it showed once again how difficult it was to write an opera for our time that was theatrically adroit and also musically accessible. Jonas admitted that yet again it had been presented late in the day, and the combination of over-scoring, a straight Shakespearean text and a lack of female voices contributed to the lack of audibility. It performed poorly at the box office.[119]

Despite the generally disappointing box-office results, within the house there were no doubts as to the season's value. Jonas and Caulton's report of August 1991 for the Arts Council underlined their belief that the 20⁺ season had been a 'stunning success', especially amongst the critical fraternity. The orchestra and chorus had excelled themselves. The disappointing box office might be shown to be more due to the recession than to the nature of the repertoire. The only shortcoming in any of the new productions was the treatment of the chorus in Act II, scene iv, of *Wozzeck*, which some had found over-busy. But that, in their view, was really just to search for something to criticise, as their document was beginning to read like an 'endless paean of praise' for themselves.[120]

The 20⁺ season had indeed been a bold and musically thrilling venture – Elder excelling in styles as diverse as Debussy, Bartók, Berg, Stravinsky and Shostakovich. Nonetheless, it could be argued that many of the productions became more a late-twentieth-century commentary on the works than a reflection upon the upheavals, vicissitudes and developments of the century through its operatic repertoire. Furthermore, as the season progressed, the disappointing box office and growing deficit were causing grave concern to the board. By November 1990 Elliott had been reporting that the accumulated deficit for the financial year could reach £1 million. The board was made aware that, under the provisions of the Insolvency Act passed in 1986, the directors of a company going into liquidation could be individually liable for its debts, as well as disqualified from the boards of other companies. It was clear that ENO needed an overdraft of £2 million during the first three months of 1991, but Coutts had agreed only to £1.5 million.

While ENO found itself facing a massive deficit somewhat in a state of denial, Prime Minister Thatcher was also in denial as to her own vulnerability. In a triumphalist mood since October 1989, when the Berlin Wall collapsed and with it the hegemonic power of communism, she blithely waded deeper into the poll-tax imbroglio, undermined her colleagues and, in ever-greater isolation, insulted her closest political ally, Geoffrey Howe. On 28 November 1990 she was forced to resign. Playwright Howard Brenton recalled how the day became known as 'Enlightenment Thursday' to arts folk. They felt that the curse had been lifted. Parties broke out and the telephone never stopped ringing. It was 'the talk of excited survivors who experienced the eighties as a philistine hurricane against the idea of culture itself'.[121]

The new prime minister, John Major, was one of an increasingly rare breed of senior politicians who showed some interest in the arts and was a regular attender of ENO. His wife was also an opera lover and had published a biography of Joan Sutherland in 1991. During a visit to the Coliseum in June 1989 when Major was at the Treasury, Jonas had reported to Harewood that they had done their best to make him aware of their problems.[122] Jonas was delighted when, as Chancellor of the Exchequer, Major re-introduced the word 'generosity' into the arts-funding debate in March 1990, after years of focusing on marketing jargon and catchphrases.[123] Major put his friend David Mellor into the Ministry of National Heritage as someone who would be a strong advocate for the arts, and it was Major who was responsible for the Act of Parliament introducing the National Lottery in October 1993.

In the autumn of 1990 there were several meetings between Jonas, the Arts Council and Mellor to discuss ENO's future. Although the early concern was about the deficit, in November the focus shifted to ENO's long-term future and its tenure of the Coliseum. There was also talk of a capital injection to cover the deficit, but not of increasing the core grant. Jonas warned that if they did not get what was required in terms of a core grant, the company's activities would have to be wound down, with redundancies and artistic cuts.[124]

While Jonas was trying to persuade the Arts Council to give ENO the kiss of life, Elliott made one last suggestion before he left in late November and his place was taken by Harriet Earle, with Ian Giddons as chief accountant. The most beneficial contingency plan for the next season, he suggested, was to replace *Königskinder* and *Pelleas* with *The Pearl Fishers* in order not to lose the new production of *Figaro*.[125] On 23 October it had been reported that it would be a big job to retain the corporate members the following year, as there was a 'worrying degree of muttering' from them about the 20+ programme and the cost of membership.[126]

On 27 November Carr told the board that the forecast deficit was almost entirely due to the poor box office. In turn they started to question ENO's house style more intently.[127] Two days later the

Opera Committee asked Jonas to discuss production styles at ENO, and whether the house style should be more diverse. In discussion, senior management stressed the importance of maintaining loyalty to certain interpreters so as to encourage long-term acceptance by the public. At the same time, Jonas said letters he was receiving revealed a disturbing trend: a dislike of adventurous work in relation to the recession. The public, he said, seemed to have a stronger desire for comfortable, more traditional productions when economic times were bleak. Pountney argued that ENO could be boxed into a house style by lack of funds, with costumes often adapted from other productions. At the same time, there was quite a spread of styles.[128]

There was indeed a great variety of directors working at ENO. In their book *Power House, The English National Opera Experience*, Pountney and Nicholas John mentioned several ENO talents of the era. These included Alden with five productions, Hytner two, Vick three, Albery three, Jones three, Freeman two and Hollander one. Jonathan Miller had directed four shows, plus one co-production with Scottish Opera, but only *Barber* after 1986/7. Pountney produced seventeen out of the era's total of forty-one new productions, and his aesthetic set the tone of the house style just as the work of Copley and Graham had in previous eras. At the Opera Committee meeting, the triumvirate were in total harmony. When Nicholas Goodison asked if management would invite a modern and surrealist image from the production team for another Verdi production or a more classic production style, Jonas replied that there was a rare uniformity of belief between him and his colleagues as to what production styles should achieve. He reiterated that opera 'should not be merely a decorative art in terms of the visual aesthetic of productions'.

The board was becoming more critical of some of the choices. Goodison expressed the opinion that it had not been fair to have asked such a young and inexperienced director as Julia Hollander to stage *Fennimore and Gerda*. Dr David Cohen declared it the worst production he had ever seen at the Coliseum. Jonas, however, defended the choice of Hollander, saying it was a brave production.[129]

By early December there was a grave cash crisis as well as a financial crisis, with the deficit for the year approaching £1 million. The box-office shortfall comprised around 60 per cent of the deficit. There were also production-cost overruns on *Wozzeck*, the *Dr Faust* revival and *Pelleas*.[130]

On 17 December the Arts Council offered £10,432,300 for 1991/2, including £600,000 from the 'enhancement fund', which was a 14 per cent uplift, conditional on the accumulated deficit being eliminated. The board was relieved at the good news, and agreed to respond positively to what it considered to be a vote of confidence from the Arts Council, even though severe cuts would still be necessary for 1991/2 in order to make progress in eliminating the deficit. On 18 December Jonas informed the board that it could reach £1.4 million by March 1991. On 22 January 1991 Keith Cooper decided to close the graphics department in the spring with the loss of three jobs and without consulting the Staff Association.[131] In future the work would be contracted out. This marked the end of Cooper's high-profile advertising campaign.

On 18 December the board held an informal meeting at which Jonas reassured the board that it was essential to respond to the grant increase by demonstrating to the Arts Council that progress was being made with regard to the deficit. By cancelling the new production of *Lulu* and revivals of *Beatrice and Benedict* and *Werther* and substituting them with *La bohème* and extra performances of *Don Giovanni*, it was hoped to lead to a surplus of £270,000 the following season. Not only did the board consider that such a saving was inadequate, it was also not sanguine that the proposed measures would be sufficient. It was felt that the January/February box office looked particularly weak with *Königskinder* and *Pelleas* or *Street Scene*, and there was concern about the proposed long runs of *The Mikado* and *Don Giovanni* in the spring. Harewood urged management to look for a surplus of £600,000 for 1991/2.[132]

Harewood later recalled that he had insisted to Jonas that it was essential to make a profit during the following season and that he must not put in loss-making repertory. He received Jonas's assurance, but he later felt that not enough effort had been made ('We lost, he did not try'). He believed that Jonas took the attitude that ENO had always lost money and that it would not be held against him.[133]

Jonas himself later said that although 'superhuman efforts' had been made to design a fiscally responsible programme, he did not believe that the accumulated deficit was that important – indeed, that it was 'important to carry a manageable deficit'. For him deficits were 'simply a record of where you had been'; cash flow was what mattered, and 'if this was healthy the bank would support overdraft facilities at year end if the Arts Council paid its grant instalments late, which it often did'. It was fatal and irresponsible, in his view, to build up reserves and eliminate the accumulated deficit at the expense of the work on stage, and of well-ordered and consensual employee relations.[134] Harewood later reflected: 'I am sure he did not believe deficits were important, the trouble is, I did and so did the Board.'[135]

Nicholas Hytner later recalled, when he was director of the National Theatre, that ENO had been very slow to realise that the days of unconditional bailing-out had gone for ever. They were 'operating in a way that you could in the 1970s', he commented, as Peter Hall had at the National. Hall, however, had stopped at the right time and 'did things like closing the Cottesloe Theatre for six months. She [Thatcher] hated Peter but he played it better. Peter in the end was more public-spirited and he left at the right time and Richard [Eyre] was intensely public spirited and read the runes much more cleverly. Richard just ran a theatre that balanced its budget – it was always possible to do that.'[136] Harewood also recalled that he had been 'dead against *Königskinder*', which proved to be a financial disaster. The triumvirate were, he said, 'very convinced of what they were doing, which they should have been, and nothing would stop them'.[137]

Problems were aired and exposed when the board and management met at the annual Harewood House Conference in February 1991. Pountney had prepared a paper on artistic policy for Harewood in which he claimed that, in essence, ENO policy had remained consistent with a very long-standing tradition, and represented a change of emphasis with a new generation rather than any radical change in direction. He accepted that the maintenance of an ensemble company may have been slightly watered down in the last decade by the increasing mobility of British singers, but it nonetheless remained in part an ensemble.[138]

There was, however, a growing realisation that the audience was being lost. Jonas and Caulton assembled some views on the theme, including those of Cooper, who thought that there was a danger of alienating the core audience, which could not be brought along as fast as ENO wanted it to be. He was concerned when a season had too many Pountney productions. Jonas had received a letter from a member of the public complaining of 'overbearing hauteur and dull pretensions'. ENO had taken the enjoyment out of opera, with a house style that was no more than some ageing form of 'street-cred'. Where was grace, beauty and poetry in design and direction?[139]

Some members of the board also felt that all was not perfect. Despite the many successes, an element of cerebral intensity had crept in and the house was a little short on 'poetry, beauty and even fun'. It was urged that some scope should be given to more traditional directors such as Jonathan Miller, perhaps in the direction of 'innovative conservatism'. More balance was necessary in the style of production if middle-of-the-road ENO audiences were not to be alienated.

The board sought to assert itself, with Lord Carr suggesting that the Opera Committee should be the vehicle for greater board involvement so they could better 'own and defend the repertoire' and keep an eye on the need to curb expenditure in the following year. Management was accused of sometimes being unnecessarily defensive when its view or conclusions were challenged, and it was necessary to improve the atmosphere between executives and non-executives. Sponsors were vulnerable to recession and were also uneasy about the current repertory. Jonas accepted that there was a need to vary the diet if the people who gave ENO £1.5 million a year were to continue to find ENO appetising. The threat of financial insolvency meant that accessibility was being seriously compromised.[140]

By 9 April the accumulated deficit for the end of the year was estimated at £1.5 million. There were rumours again of amalgamation with Covent Garden emanating from the Arts Council and the Office of Arts and Libraries, though not, Jonas recalled, from the chairman.[141] Jonas wrote to Palumbo urging that a merger of the two houses was not a good solution to the problems, pointing out that cities like Vienna, Berlin and Munich sustained more than one opera house.[142]

Management had been working on two scenarios for the revised three-year business plan, assuming grant increases of 3.5 and 2.5

per cent. Jonas told the board on 9 April that he thought that the consequences of the first scenario, which met the Arts Council's demand that the accumulated deficit be totally eliminated by the third year but meant cancelling all new productions from 1992/3 and many redundancies, would be very serious and incompatible with the aims and objectives of the company. The second scenario, which predicted 'somewhat higher grant increases' while involving tight financial controls and difficult decisions, would eliminate the deficit while maintaining the artistic mission. The 1992/3 increase should be 10.8 per cent and for 1993/4 just 4.4 per cent.[143] The budget for 1991/2 was intended to reduce the deficit by a third by improving the box office with more popular repertoire, increased ticket prices and more performances. There was also an ambitious development-income target. The new production of *Lulu* would be replaced by a revival of *Beatrice and Benedict* and a longer run of *La bohème*.[144] On 23 April the board approved the three-year plan.

Although the Arts Council appreciated the arguments in the plan, which would bolster their approach to the minister, Jonas was worried that Palumbo was not as confident as he had been the previous year that he could 'fire up' the minister into 'producing the goods'.[145]

On 7 June Jonas had to report to senior management that the manager of Coutts had warned him that the bank was not prepared to continue to grant ENO an overdraft facility. The accumulated deficit of £1.3 million was simply too high. If they could not meet their debts and liabilities when they fell due for payment, they would be technically insolvent. The legal repercussions on the directors and senior management were extremely serious and it was essential to reduce the deficit and to restore confidence. They were £175,000 behind the box-office targets.[146]

The final audited accounts for the year showed a deficit of £899,000, bringing the accumulated deficit up to £1,403,000.[147] The board pointed out that it was common knowledge that all the banks were going through a very difficult period and that Coutts, as significant bankers to arts organisations, were probably concerned at their exposure. They should be told that the facility was only sought from January to March, when the Arts Council grant would return the company to a 'positive cash flow'.[148] Jonas warned the deputy secretary general, Anthony Everitt, that Coutts were refusing overdraft facilities for the beginning of year, which threatened ENO's ability to continue trading.[149]

Mark Elder had been mulling the idea of leaving ENO since he had conducted *Figaro* at the Met in 1988. Jonas had been offered many posts, but, according to Elder, was waiting for Munich. It was the custom in Munich for Intendants to start planning their first season two years before they actually took over, so, when Jonas accepted the job, Elder agreed to stay for two years in order that they could leave at the same time, although neither Pountney nor Elder announced their future plans at the time. Harewood urged Jonas to stay until the future of the Coliseum was assured, but he said that not only would it take too long, but that he felt that it was time for Pountney and Elder to move on as well. Harewood did, however, convince Jonas that securing the Coliseum freehold should be his highest priority for the last two years of his tenure.[150]

Elder had hoped that Jonas would stay to settle in his own successor, as Harewood had, but Jonas had said they should all 'go out in a blaze of glory', Elder recalled. Jonas's appointment at Munich was made public on 5 April 1991, and the pending departure of Elder and Pountney was announced a week later. The Munich annual budget was reported to be £55 million, 65 per cent paid for by the state, with a repertoire of thirty-five opera productions and fifteen ballets. The simultaneous departure of the triumvirate contrasted with the carefully prepared and steady handover of Harewood to Elder, Pountney and Jonas.

While the triumvirate pondered the future of ENO without them, the market-research company Millward Brown was preparing a survey of 2,086 audience members, at four performances in six focus groups. In September 1991 the board received its findings. There was still a high degree of loyalty from the 'core' audience and they saw the house as accessible, friendly and not intimidating, but raised ticket prices were causing the solid supporters to take advantage of standby price and avoid advance booking. The most significant factor to emerge was that only 25 per cent wanted opera in English, as they could not hear the words in any case. Forty-three per cent of those questioned wanted surtitles, which had been introduced at Covent Garden and by 1988 were being used for all foreign-language operas. Millward Brown recommended that ENO should consider surtitles, and offer 'entertaining opera'.[151]*

The problem of the comprehensibility of the words was increasingly linked to the growing pressure for surtitles, which were being discussed by critics, practitioners and the operagoing public. Pountney was appalled by the suggestion of abandoning the English language and horrified at the prospect of surtitles. He wrote a powerful paper on 13 June, in which he argued that it was the text that justified music's place in the secular world of the theatre. It therefore had to be in the language of the audience, and any arguments against it were to do with incompetence in execution. Political and philosophical damage was done to ENO's case because of the poor acoustics for words at the Coliseum, since the use of the English language was one of the strongest arguments for maintaining two houses in London. The subsidised theatre was there to support artistic policies based on idealism rather than commercialism and should maintain the ideals of ensemble music theatre as developed by Felsenstein at the Komische Oper, whereby 'the sense arrives like a glowing hot coal from the mouth of the singer, and strikes instantly at the head and the heart of the listener'. The surtitle, he wrote, was a 'catastrophic gooseberry in this vital act of theatrical intercourse'.[152]†

The 1991/2 season opened on 17 August with a revival of *Don Giovanni*, and continued five days later with a revival of Keith Warner's sombre *Werther*, which did not do well. *La bohème* was, in management's words, a 'fairly sad affair' which had been 'cobbled together' from the remains of the last-minute cancellations of *Lulu* and *Beatrice and Benedict* – using in many cases singers contracted for those other operas. Despite its artistic failings, it attracted an average paid attendance of 85 per cent over seventeen performances. *The Mikado* on 28 September was much better but

---

* Harewood was not impressed, telling Jonas that as far as audience research was concerned he slightly shared the concerns of Leonard Hoffman in that the reports told them what they already knew. Some people, he wrote, 'believe in them strongly, but I don't think Lennie is of that number, nor I suspect am I! Particularly as they cost quite a lot of money' (3.2.91, Ad 166 Box 172).
† The question of audibility remained a serious one in the next decades. Harewood commented later, 'Nobody complained about inaudibility when I was there and when Edmund Tracey was there' (interview, 11.6.07).

did not sell well, despite Rosemary Joshua's much-praised first leading role.[153]

*Figaro's Wedding*, which opened on 30 October, was, in Jonas's view, the 'single critical and popular success of the season', Graham Vick and Richard Hudson bringing a 'welcome splash of primary colour into the repertoire' with costumes designed in varying hues of red. Jeremy Sams' translation was a 'huge and very funny success', and also, as the critics agreed, the words were easily audible. Caulton and Jonas commented that the phrase 'new realism' began to emerge around this production. The critics thought it 'stylish and intelligent'.[154] All were agreed that Bryn Terfel was a 'towering' Figaro. Management realised how very lucky they had been to have booked him as soon as he came to their notice, although he had now slipped beyond their reach.[155] Higgins also praised Anthony Michaels-Moore's reptilian Count, 'coiled up in self satisfaction', and the Countess of Joan Rodgers.[156] Paul Daniel conducted with great style. Harewood wrote to Jonas that he thought the show nothing short of a triumph, with musical preparation of the highest quality imaginable and everyone in the cast giving more than could be hoped for.[157] Jonas circulated his letter around the company. Budgeted at 78 per cent, it did 87 per cent. The November *Masked Ball* revival, however, budgeted at 65 per cent, did a poor 56 per cent.

The extremely high hopes pinned by management on the Richard Jones *Die Fledermaus* on 2 December 1991 were disappointed. It was peppered with ideas of brilliance, Jonas wrote, but did not add up to the sum of its parts and there were too many gags. Conductor Adam Fischer, however, was exemplary.[158] Budgeted at 78 per cent, it did 69 per cent. The longer runs were having a detrimental effect on the box office, with the worst nights of *La bohème* registering a record low 57 per cent. When *Die Fledermaus* was revived in December 1993, Milnes, who admired Jones's 'constructively anarchic work' and his success in putting 'the jokes back in *Rheingold*' at Covent Garden, was pleased that he had courageously edited many of the unfunny sight-gags that had upstaged both singers and music to produce a 'snappy Christmas show'. Rosemary Joshua stood out with a 'brilliantly sung and vivaciously acted' Adele.[159] In Richard Fairman's view, in the tightened-up production Jones's sense of the ridiculous produced plenty of off-centre zany fun. His

*Fledermaus*, he wrote, had 'never been nearer to Austria than the end of Brighton pier' and was splendidly brash and vulgar.[160]

On 3 October Coutts had at last agreed to extend the overdraft to the end of April 1992, and on 28 November ENO learnt that the Arts Council grant for 1992/3 would be £11,371,207 – a 9 per cent uplift – on condition that the company plan to eradicate its accumulated deficit. Although it was less than the three-year plan envisaged, thanks were to be offered to the Arts Council. The recession continued to be a major factor. The mailing list had peaked in 1988 at 21,000 but then declined by 50 per cent over the next three years, with the sharpest downturn in the 20+ season.[161]

In the new year Harriet Earle, the finance director, reported that the box office continued to be disappointing, and the next new production did not fare well.[162] It was Jonas's treat, Humperdinck's *Königskinder*, directed by Pountney and magically designed by Sue Blane. It opened on 30 January 1992 and most critics were pleased to have had a chance to assess Humperdinck's neglected second opera, enjoying its poetry, melancholy and its Wagnerian, Tristanesque echoes. It was not felt, however, that the production totally vindicated a work, with a thin narrative and underdeveloped characters. There were reservations about the level of singing provided in the extremely difficult roles of the Goosegirl and the Prince by Cathryn Pope and Joseph Evans. Nor was it felt that Pountney had scored as direct a hit as he had with his previous fairy-tale triumphs, *Rusalka* and *Hansel and Gretel*. Jonas considered it a 'brave stab' at a very tricky piece which presented a considerable challenge vocally, orchestrally and for the director, who had had to work to a tight budget. It had also been terribly difficult to cast, with only Sally Burgess's Witch and Alan Opie's Fiddler truly admirable.[163] Although the budget of £134,200 was not as tight as some, it had been exceeded by £3,000. The attendance was disastrous: budgeted at 70 per cent, it achieved 46 per cent.[164]

The last Pountney/Elder Verdi production, *Don Carlos* on 2 April, was another fine musical achievement. Milnes wrote of the 'fastidiousness of texture, phrase and musical outline' that Elder evinced. He felt that Edmund Barham as Don Carlos had been seriously undervalued by the critics, in what was a most demanding role. The Posa of Summers and Gwynne Howell's Philip were finely drawn, making every word of Porter's translation tell. Plowright, back on vocal form, was commanding in her grand impersonation of the Queen. In sum, he felt, Londoners were lucky to have had an endlessly demanding score so soundly and seriously sung.

Fielding designed a semi-abstract white box steeply tilted to the right, with *objets trouvés* decorating the stage and a steadily increasing number of coffins under a false stage-left, while the costumes were in handsome period style. Milnes thought that Pountney elicited too much eye-rolling and 'mad-acting', especially from Barham.[165] Some other critics felt that the blend of symbolism, naturalistic costumes and a melodramatic acting style was an uncomfortable one. Within the organisation it was considered musically one of the most distinguished Verdian achievements and, although the reviews were mixed, audiences had been ecstatic.[166] Budgeted at 78 per cent, it did 71 per cent.

John Buller's commission, *Bakxai* (*The Bacchae*), directed by Julia Hollander and designed by Bechtler, opened on 5 May after much debate, followed by final acquiescence from the Opera Committee to Buller's insistence on using Greek. Jonas reported that Buller had declared himself inspired by the rhythms and incantations of the language but had then gone on to compose a naturalistic and conversational opera, unlike *Oedipus Rex* and *Akhnaten*, whose sound evoked an understanding of the dramatic situation. Pountney said that Buller had resisted workshops.[167] Critics were divided by the use of Greek, some finding its incomprehensibility frustrating and suggesting that the work would be more suited to a concert hall. Loppert described its seventeen linked scenes as a 'frieze, expertly arrayed'.[168] Others suggested that it was the purest form of opera: the score as 'text-based as Monteverdi', wrote Milnes, 'the sense vividly conveyed through musical shapes'. Critics and management praised the uniformly strong cast: Tom Randle as Dionysus, convincing even in Ancient Greek, Graham Matheson-Bruce as Pentheus and Sarah Walker as Agave. Budgeted at 43 per cent, it achieved 32 per cent.

In July Earle reported a box-office shortfall of £240,000,[169] and the accumulated deficit remained daunting at £1,315,000.[170] In May the decision had been taken to rent the ENO shop to the Music Discount Centre, and the board accepted Keith Cooper's recommendation of a steep rise in balcony prices for 1992/3, while the rest of the house was to have frozen or reduced prices.[171]

After the season Lord Carr, who was about to leave the Finance Committee, expressed to Harriet Earle his increasing worries for the future in the light of the box-office figures, which continued to make 'abysmal reading'. He had somehow to go on believing that when the annual crunch came, ENO would continue to receive sympathetic consideration, as he did not think that the John Major government – recently re-elected on 9 April 1992 – would allow ENO and the other national companies to go under. Major had relieved some of the damage done to the arts during the Thatcher years, though the recession was still biting deeply. Until it lifted there was no way to increase self-generated income, let alone reduce the deficit. There might be some sympathy for their plight, Carr said, but even under Major there would be no understanding if expenditure were not controlled.[172] Cooper thought the word 'abysmal' an overstatement, pointing out that they were doing better than the West End, while Jonas noted that the economy as a whole was performing 'abysmally'.[173]

Carr's belief that the government was committed to ENO had been given substance in the spring, when Timothy Renton, the Secretary of State for National Heritage, announced the purchase of the Coliseum freehold from Stoll Moss for £10.8 million. On 10 March 1992 Jonas thanked him and announced that for ENO the resolution of the problem of their tenure seemed in artistic terms to be 'like the Berlin wall coming down'. As Jonas later reflected, for years the question of the Coliseum lease had been for ENO like an iceberg in front of the ship, as its gradual winding down affected the balance sheet and there was no guarantee that ENO would be able to continue to trade when the lease finally ran out.

The future of the Coliseum had been under debate since November 1986, when a property working party had been set up by the board to look into whether ENO should stay at the theatre, whose roof occasionally let in waterfalls, or to move when ENO's lease expired on 31 March 1996. In 1988, after a feasibility study, it was decided to purchase the Coliseum.[174] After the stock-market crash it seemed, even to the Arts Council, that acquiring the theatre for ENO would be better value than any other potential scheme.[175]

The negotiations had been long and arduous. At first the owner,

Robert Holmes à Court, said he was not prepared to sell the Coliseum freehold and would be putting the rent on a more economic basis, since large-scale musicals were becoming more popular. Jonas recalled how he sought the advice of his friend Daniel Barenboim, who knew Jim Wolfonsohn – head of the World Bank and a childhood friend of Holmes à Court. Wolfonsohn suggested that in view of the economic situation, a direct offer to Holmes à Court – made face to face – to purchase the theatre at its market price might be met with a positive response. The offer was on the table when Holmes à Court died in September 1990, at the age of fifty-three, from a heart attack. With the recession at its height, the possibility of a sale was far more likely.[176]

Jonas, Harewood and Palumbo went to the Office of Arts and Libraries to see if the government might help to acquire the freehold. On 2 November 1990 David Mellor had agreed that the government would support the company's future at the Coliseum and that Harewood and Jonas could meet the owner's widow, Janet Holmes à Court.[177] He also enabled Jonas and Robert Carr to talk to the Treasury officials to facilitate the vote in the House of Commons to approve the government grant of £10 million.[178] Mellor later recalled that he had had trouble persuading John Major to support the proposal, as it might be thought to be an election bribe.[179] By the end of November Mellor had been replaced by Timothy Renton, but the promise was upheld and in June 1992 the Office of Arts and Libraries secured funding to purchase the Coliseum for £12.8 million. The transaction was completed in March 1992 with £10.8 million from the ACGB and two Heritage grants of £1 million.[180*]

As Major had anticipated, the decision was seen, by the *Evening Standard* at least, as a 'burst of pre-election largesse'. Milnes in *Opera* magazine suggested that the combination of Stoll Moss needing the cash, a slump in property prices and the election had conspired to make the deal possible. He also pointed out the poisoned-chalice element, which was the commitment to refurbish the building for at least £17 million. Small-scale repertoire was

* Financially the purchase was more advantageous as rent saved rather than an asset acquired, since a condition of the grant was that the Arts Council could buy back the freehold for £1 in the event of ENO ceasing to perform there or wishing to sell.

either avoided or often got drowned in the expanses of the Coliseum stage. ENO was caught in a trap, he wrote, 'a tender trap but a trap nonetheless'.[181] The refurbishment fundraising campaign began in June 1992. In January 1993 the consultant architects Sheppard Robson were appointed to undertake an initial assessment for a sum of £380,000. The first meeting of the Redevelopment Steering Subcommittee was in October.

The purchase of the Coliseum was a momentous decision with long-term ramifications for the company. It seemed to offer security both financially and physically for ENO, and was a vote of confidence in the company by the government. The Coliseum's location, a few moments' walk from Charing Cross station and next door to Trafalgar Square, was near perfect for Londoners, as well as for people who lived outside London and visitors from abroad. ENO audiences were fiercely loyal to the building, as Richard Eyre discovered in 1998 when he was preparing his report for the Arts Council. On the other hand, its design as a music hall entailed many logistical problems and inefficiencies for a repertory opera house. Its rehearsal studios were still located in West Hampstead. It was also a house whose acoustics meant that without rigorous attention, words easily became indistinct. This, together with changes in styles of singing, was making the incomprehensibility of words an increasingly contentious issue. Furthermore, according to Mark Elder, the big sound, especially Wagner, flourished in the house's generous and spacious acoustic, which was not the case for fast music, such as Rossini, or for operetta. It was, he said, a wonderful forum for big-scale, large-throated company efforts, but not so good a 'Volksoper' theatre where communication with the audience in their own language was the *raison d'être*. The very size of the house dictated what sort of shows would work best. As Pountney later remarked, 'The theatre steers you towards too many areas in which Covent Garden is liable to be pre-eminent.'[182] A full house was exhilarating, Elder commented, but it was a hard house to fill and called for big bold events like *Lady Macbeth of Mtsensk*.[183*] Such events required a large-scale company, which was to prove

---

* There had been another breakthrough for ENO on 21 January 1992 when BECTU, after long and arduous negotiations, had reached agreement with management while maintaining the important principle of the five-hour minimum overtime call, after which the working atmosphere was much improved.

increasingly out of kilter with the free-market philosophy of the twenty-first century.

The economic climate remained grim into the autumn of 1992, as Jonas's last season began. ENO was faced by 'sponsorship fatigue' and the box-office budget was not being met. Jonas hoped that at best the year would break even; at worst there might be a doubling of the accumulated deficit. Cuts rather than increased income were the main focus, with the board accepting a restriction of recruitment. The Arts Council would have to be asked to write off the accumulated deficit, which had reached £1.3 million.[184] On 20 October Keith Cooper attended his last meeting before joining Covent Garden as director of public affairs and marketing.

Elder's last Verdi production as music director was *The Force of Destiny* on 16 September. It was directed by Hytner with his usual 'probing dramatic intelligence and astute direction of individual character' and a clear narrative. There was some suggestion that Hytner, fresh from his West End hit *Miss Saigon*, treated some of the chorus scenes like a musical. The action moved forward well but was conventional.[185] Richard Hudson brought some more colour back into the Coliseum with an abstract set and vaguely nineteenth-century costumes. The slightly noisy revolve allowed an epic sweep of open space and moving surfaces. Milnes described Barstow's amazing breath and dynamic control, which she combined with a fine Verdian line and dramatic intensity to present, according to Michael Kennedy, a 'Leonora in a thousand'.[186] Barham showed himself at his best as a brazen, trumpet-toned Don Alvaro who could also employ a properly melancholy dusky mezzoforte. Summers was a powerful if too dotty Don Carlo and John Connell an earthy Father Superior with an inky black tone.[187]

More production cuts were instituted in the autumn, starting with *Ariodante*, whose budget was cut to £120,000 from £170,000. Equity was warned on 6 November that recruitment was to be restricted, and both BECTU and the Musicians Union accepted the plans in December.[188] Management sought to reassure staff that they would try not to increase their workload, but they were soon feeling the pressure.

The success of the forthcoming *Princess Ida*, directed by Ken Russell, was crucial, but there was anxiety about its discouraging sales before it opened on 14 November. Nor was it anticipated that the notices would do much to boost the box office. Three days before it opened, Jonas urged senior managers to be 'particularly astute at leading loud applause, especially at the arrival of the sushi-burger'.[189] On the night, the *Evening Standard* reported that 'a delegation in drag from Gerlinsky's night club dressed outrageously enough to upstage even the peroxide wigs and Madonna-style basques created for the show by designer James Merrifield' had been planted in the audience.[190] Critics were appalled, Michael White writing: 'Not just bad, execrable.' Loppert called it 'Vulgar, boring and incompetent . . . A heedlessly energetic blending of the crass, the coarse and the witless.'[191] The talented young soprano Rosemary Joshua did her best in the title role, while Henderson complained of the indignities imposed on artists of the calibre of Anne Collins and Anne-Marie Owens. Loppert praised the conductor, Jane Glover, for managing to maintain the charm and elegance of the music despite the clunkings on stage. The box office for *Ida* was so bad that it was immediately clear that the seventeen performances scheduled for 1993/4 would have to be replaced. It was, Elder later recalled, 'a complete and utter disaster'.[192] *Hansel and Gretel* was also facing a surprisingly bad box office.[193]

The Pountney/Lazaridis *Brouček* in December disappointed those who loved the warmth and humanity of Janáček. The relentless high jinks of Pountney's fertile and extravagant imagination, the constant costume changes and tons of scenic clutter led to what Porter described as 'One production number after another . . . a self indulgent display of styles and techniques – without character, heartless.' No one, he noted, encountering the opera for the first time could guess what it was about. Janáček's Nannetta and Fenton, Malinka and Mazal, sung by Vivian Tierney and Bonaventura Bottone, were reduced to cartoon-strip characters.[194] Clark's Brouček, in Milnes's words, was restricted to 'grotesque movement and expression, farcical high jinks, with little to suggest the equivocal central character he is playing – and with precious few words'.[195] Canning thought that Pountney now seemed to be parodying himself with high-flying bedsteads, green paint and petticoats. He was unamused: 'So much of what is now seen on the stage at the Coliseum is designed for a coterie of opera people, professionals and committed fans who are "in the know",' he wrote.[196] Milnes agreed: 'There were in-jokes so arcane that they can have meant something only to half a dozen people.'[197] At the same time, critics found Lazaridis's visual invention spectacular, the fantasy exuberant and the cinematic sweep exhilarating. But, as was often the case at the 'power house', the heart and soul of the piece emanated from the pit. After a lively and fractious rehearsal period, Mackerras 'phrased nobly, warmly – with spirit, love, understanding and humour', Porter commented.[198]

On 18 December ENO learnt that the Arts Council grant for 1993/4 would be a 2.5 per cent uplift. Jonas sent his Christmas message with a warning of the 'toughest challenge to survive' and thanking the company for support so far received. In the new year Jonas told the Production Committee that the audience could no longer be relied upon to come even to the most popular pieces. Average financial capacity was 52 per cent. Managers in charge of budgets were told that, in their approach to cutting overheads, nothing was sacred and that they could consider measures that would have previously been dismissed out of hand. *Princess Ida* would not be revived in March 1994, and in its stead *The Pearl Fishers* was being considered.[199]

As the crisis deepened, the relationship between the triumvirate and the board became more strained. On 22 January 1993 Jonas complained to Harewood that the board were discussing functional, essentially management matters or artistic detail when they should be focused on the future of the building and capital campaign. Although it was tempting for laymen and women to discuss artistic matters, discussions rapidly descended into superficial waffle. Apart from Harewood, board members were in the same position as he, Jonas, would be if he tried to discuss 'the Quantum Fund, merchant bankers' responsibilities, the law of tort, pork belly futures, or auctioneering corruption at Christie's'. The board often complained about not having a clear role, and he would have thought that redevelopment was the ideal one. Board member Brian Unwin told Harewood that he thought Jonas's letter a 'little unfair', as every artistic decision was also a financial one, though he agreed that discussions about voices etc. were 'depressingly anecdotal and unconstructive'. It would create a sense of alienation if Jonas sought to head people off these areas too strongly.[200] It seemed light years since the time when Harewood, as director of ENO, considered his Opera Committee as providing support and wise counsel.

The board was not alone in creating ripples. Edmund Tracey, whose skills and knowledge had been undervalued since Harewood ceased to be general director but had nonetheless remained closely involved in casting with Caulton, wrote a highly critical paper on 31 January for the Harewood House Conference. There was a feeling, he sensed, that ENO was much less interesting and adventurous than it used to be.

We have become very dull over the last few years: untheatrical, too high-brow, too intellectual and university minded. We don't entertain people as they would like and as we should. In addition to all the other things, going to the opera should be fun. One of the reasons why our box office attendances have collapsed so wretchedly is because the Coliseum and ENO have got the reputation of being pretentious and non-fun.

He suggested fewer revivals at inflated prices, more new productions, a shorter season and musicals by 'really good composers, such as Kern, Porter or Rodgers (NOT Sondheim)'. Ian Judge had urged Jonas to do *Show Boat* and, when nothing happened, he had gone to Opera North and made a 'huge success of it'.

The work we present must be of a high artistic standard, but it does not have to be dependent on mountains of scenery and expensive costumes. Present a rep of smashing interest in itself – present operas and operettas that audiences are curious to see – but if financially necessary present them in blacks and tracksuits. I don't mean that the production team should take up attitudes – trench coats, suitcases, bedsteads, naked light bulbs – but they should go down to the bedrock of the work and present it purely. Adopt this purity as the standard and then put the meaning and truth of the work into the gesture, the intensity of the acting, the imagination of lighting and of course the high standard of the musical presentation and performance. When this attitude has been adopted in the past – provided the artists have talent and integrity – it has always succeeded.

Examine the new commissions, Tracey urged, and question the 'strange preference contemporary composers have for working with a musical language that 95 per cent of the audiences find incomprehensible' which meant that new operas emptied the house. Above all, he wrote, 'reduce the seat prices and ENCOUR-

AGE PEOPLE TO COME AND ENJOY OUR WORK'.[201]*

Tracey was also concerned that the roster of permanent singers was much too small. In 1970 ENO had been able to embark on a complete *Ring* cycle, with all parts cast from the company. It had been a stupendous achievement. Nothing like it was remotely possible in 1992. The ensemble at the end of the triumvirate's time was indeed much reduced in number. Rosemary Joshua was one of a few young singers still on contract whose careers were to be developed within the company. Senior management did not see the need or financial justification for retaining singers, as it was more cost effective to employ them only when required and it was a system that was to be repeated throughout the world of business and industry. In any case, it was increasingly difficult to secure even middle-ranking singers because of the fee differentials.[202]† Elder believed that flexibility of casting was advantageous and that company members were now defined as those like John Tomlinson who did not want to be on contract but would be glad to sing each year with the company as their careers expanded.[203]

There was increasing concern that in the popular imagination the house style had become a cliché at a time when the Royal Opera House was enjoying a rise in critical popularity with such productions as Harrison Birtwistle's new opera *Gawain*, Moshinsky's *Simon Boccanegra*, Vick's *Mitridate*, Graham's *Death in Venice* and Freeman's *The Fiery Angel*. Caulton prepared a paper in which he analysed the declining audience. Things had started to go wrong for ENO in the 1989/90 season at a time when the company was reaping the rewards of its own success.[204]

The concept of 'enjoyment' was making more and more of an appearance in discussions. At the Price Waterhouse strategy day on 12 March there was a general emphasis on the need for audiences

* Tracey himself had had a hard time during the 'power house' era, particularly at its beginning. Close friends later spoke of his silent suffering and stoicism in the face of demotion and humiliation, and his exclusion from policy-making until Jonas came to realise the value of his experience and knowledge.
† The board had not appreciated how out of line with European rates ENO was until, on 18 January 1992, Caulton pointed out that singers like Joan Rodgers, Ann Murray, John Tomlinson and Marie McLaughlin received 60 per cent more at Covent Garden. ENO's highest fee per performance was £2,500, Covent Garden's £4,000; in Germany, the top fee was £5,500, and in Italy £7,000 (Harewood House Conference, 18.1.92, B63 Box 119).

to find a visit to the Coliseum an entertaining and enjoyable experience, on accessibility and communication with the audience in its own language. The Coliseum was the home of popular entertainment, the largest theatre in the West End, with a tradition that saw opera as a 'glamorous and exciting experience in which the highest art form could prove truly popular'.[205]

At last, as the days of the 'power house' drew to a close, Harriet Earle reported to Jonas on 26 February that Lew Hodges of the Arts Council seemed to accept that the deficit in its entirety was impossible to clear in the medium term and that there was little point in pursuing its total elimination. On the basis of an accumulated deficit of £2.3 million he would accept the 1993/4 budgeted surplus of £350,000.[206]

Jonas was beginning to acknowledge that 'anecdotal evidence' suggested that there was sometimes unpredictable resistance to production style. Sensitivity, he wrote, to changing public and critical taste was critical when the company was standing at a 'particularly dangerous moment' and needed to maintain a competitive position in the light of a hostile critical and financial climate.[207] On 27 April the board discussed press criticism of ENO's production style and design. Management admitted that currently the press was over-critical of ENO and was praising Covent Garden, a reversal of the position of only a year or two earlier. Whether this was cyclical or whether it reflected a change in fashion with which ENO would have to come to terms was as yet unclear, Jonas reflected.[208]

In the autumn of 1991 it had been decided that Dennis Marks, head of music programmes at the BBC, would take over as general director in June 1993. Nicholas Payne had been Harewood's first choice and he tried to persuade him, but Payne had decided to go to Covent Garden as Jeremy Isaacs' opera director. Marks was a Cambridge English graduate who, like Isaacs at Covent Garden, had worked in television, but, unlike Isaacs, he had been mainly concerned with music and was the producer of such BBC arts series as *Omnibus* and *Arena*. Since 1985 he had formulated music policy at the BBC, and since 1987 had been in charge of BBC TV's serious music output and had commissioned new operas for the screen, including Mark-Anthony Turnage's *Greek*. He had also been responsible for bringing ENO's work back onto the screen.

The appointment came as a surprise to opera's inner circles, wrote Milnes.[209] According to ENO's *Friends Magazine*, Marks was as surprised as anyone at his appointment, having believed he had not had a good interview.[210] Twenty-nine-year-old Sîan Edwards was to be the new music director. She was also inexperienced and even more of a surprise appointment, but reports reaching ENO's management and board were excellent; another leading possible candidate, Paul Daniel, had only recently started at Opera North. In 1984 Edwards had spent a year at the Leningrad Conservatoire. She had conducted at Covent Garden, Scottish Opera and Glyndebourne, as well as ENO. She later admitted that she had hesitated before accepting the task, but Jonas had encouraged her to reconsider. ENO was a young people's company, he urged, and that ethos needed to be preserved. Reassured that she did not need to come with ready-made views and be the 'big boss', she accepted.[211]

Shortly before they took over, Marks and Edwards discussed with Caulton a new look for 1994/5 involving fewer revivals, shorter runs and more new productions. On 19 April Marks told the board that he would rather let the season unfurl before making any large-scale new pronouncements in the public arena. The time for reformulation would be when it was needed to make the greatest impact, at the launch of the new capital campaign.[212]

Productions in the last months of the old regime did not break away from the spirit of the era. On 19 February *Don Pasquale*, distinguished by Joshua's delightful first Norina, was, in Milnes's opinion, at the level of the humour of 1950s television light entertainment.[213] Then, on 17 March, Monteverdi's dramatic cantata, the *Duel of Tancredi and Clorinda*, beginning with five Monteverdi madrigals as though they were an integral part of the work, was paired with *Duke Bluebeard's Castle*. Both were directed by David Alden. The double bill was described thus by Porter: 'Two singers and a soprano, loutishly dressed, sing, sometimes bawl the madrigals in a succession of loutish poses.' It was, he wrote, 'an Alden not a Monteverdi or Bartók evening'.[214]

Alden's *Ariodante*, designed by Ian MacNeil, an exciting young designer working for the first time in opera, broke the disappointing pattern on 28 April. It was the first ENO/Welsh National Opera

Handel co-production, possessing powerful theatrical vitality which displayed Alden's recovery of form.[215] He translated Handel into an 'arresting modern physical language', wrote Canning.[216] With *Ariodante*'s good reviews and a favourable response to the press conference, on 18 May the board noted evidence of the box office picking up.

The world premiere of Jonathan Harvey's *Inquest of Love* on 5 June was the last new production of the regime. It was a co-production with La Monnaie which Pountney directed and Nigel Lowery designed. Harvey added three synthesisers, one effects unit, one ring-modulation unit, pre-recorded tape, mixer and amplification to conventional orchestra and voices in his quest to explore the spiritual dimension of life. Its theme, shared with *The Magic Flute*, which was in repertoire at the same time, was of healing and redemption.[217] Porter called it a 'stirring and beautiful musical adventure' which Elder conducted with 'passionate precision'.[218] Elder's control of an enormously complex score, Pountney's 'spectacular staging' and the use of a semi-chorus of young singers and Second Stride dancers provided an exit for the team in a 'blaze of glory'.[219]

On 25 June the triumvirate marked their final departure with a performance of *Macbeth*. Jonas, who had been desperately ill with near-fatal septicaemia and was brought by ambulance straight from Barts hospital to the final performance in a wheelchair and kilt, spoke from the stage. While Jonas returned to hospital, the company celebrated with a Scottish-themed party. 'One has a shelf life – it is time to go,' Jonas told the *Evening Standard*.

The post-mortems of the regime had begun before the final curtain. Pountney was a Jekyll-and-Hyde character, wrote Michael Kennedy in April: Jekyll in *Osud*, *Rusalka* and *Dr Faust*, but Hydeish in *Valkyrie* and *Carmen*. He coined the term 'Pountneyfiction' to define what he saw as the use of opera as a branch of sociology in order to educate the audience. 'To the accusation that he had been more intent on instant sensation and shocking the bourgeoisie than anything else,' wrote Kennedy, 'Pountney would probably reply with some justification that he had taken opera out of the museum.'[220] Christiansen added: 'It was opera *engagé*', with its 'extravagant expressionist excitement, fascist thuggery, blood-spattered white walls and boundless contempt for the suburban middle classes'. At its best – *Rusalka, Dr Faust, Osud, Lady Macbeth, Hansel and Gretel*, Hytner's *Xerxes* and Albery's *Budd* and *Grimes* – 'it swept opera off that mantelpiece out into the storm of life'.[221] On the whole, the somewhat despised suburban middle classes followed gratefully.

Pountney, whose own demeanour ranged from creative enthusiasm and youthful high spirits, through irony to sarcasm, wrote, together with Nicholas John, the triumvirate's own eulogy in the book *Power House*. ENO, they claimed, had been called 'provocative, challenging, irreverent, iconoclastic, cheeky, populist, vulgar, outrageous, wilful, radical', yet their book was, in fact, a salute to the tradition of Lilian Baylis, that the 'rest' deserved the best too. Opera was 'an easy target for the ideologues of the left, who decline to make a distinction between Rembrandt and rap, Keats and "Kilroy" and Bach or a busker. Opera requires a host of formidable skills to perform and create; it is Eurocentric – indeed is a pinnacle of Western European culture – and it is largely created by Dead White Males. It is costly to produce and to watch, politically – gloriously incorrect: in short, elitist. But Lilian Baylis wanted everyone to have their slice of the elitist cake.'

The right wanted to scythe down the whole notion of subsidised culture. But Baylis had believed that 'adventures of the heart and mind should necessarily and desirably be available and accessible to everyone'.[222]

Jonas, who was a charismatic leader and believed in the cult of personality, also laid claim to Baylis's aspiration to make opera a popular art form. Sadly, declining government funding did not permit the realisation of such a dream. As the financial squeeze had continued, ticket prices had gone up from between £3.50 and £15.50 in 1984/5 to between £10 and £42.50 in 1992/3, the year in which balcony prices more than doubled. As ticket prices increased, ENO's own artistic policy had become in its own way exclusive, and had failed to maintain its traditional supporters. Pountney's belief that opera productions should be of the moment had also resulted in a dearth of easily revivable popular pieces.

The triumvirate never slackened in its dedication to the company, maintaining meticulous standards and artistic excellence. Those involved, as Henrietta Bredin put it, 'felt part of an extraordinary, exciting artistic adventure'.[223] Above all, it was fine music-making that underpinned the success of the era. The dynamism and brazen self-assurance of the leadership, together with Elder's musical leadership, kept audiences visiting and revisiting until the recession caught the company in a straitjacket somewhat of its own making. As the recession bit deeper after 1988 they also developed an element of defensiveness and exclusivity in their determination to pursue their artistic goals in the face of economic realities, and, on the stage, a tendency to cynicism. It had nonetheless been a period of astonishing zest, drive and creativity, with 1985–7 marking its high point, with a succession of extraordinary and exciting productions that challenged traditional and complacent attitudes to opera as an art form, as well as making the Coliseum one of the most dynamic theatres in London.

The *Power House* polemic concluded that 'survival through this rather unpleasant decade was an exciting obstacle race – fun to win but dangerous to lose'.[224] At its conclusion a growing deficit, and the diminution of accessibility due to high ticket prices, together with the possible advent of surtitles, left ENO more vulnerable than ever in a world in which the Treasury and Arts Council were hesitating in their commitment to the long-established great national companies.

# 14

# 1993–1997: 'A Reduced Role for ENO'?

During the last decade of the century the major institutions of the post-war welfare state, after years of underinvestment, were under increasing pressure to reduce their overheads and their work-forces. ENO, as one of the last great ensemble arts companies, was in an exposed position. The gap between funding and activities had been growing rapidly since the mid-1980s and Marks inherited an accumulated deficit of £2,296,000, which quickly mounted.[1]*

Marks, however, was a positive thinker and an enthusiast, with some strong views of his own, and was determined to preserve what he regarded as one of the great artistic institutions.[2] He was guardedly hinting to the press at a desire to move away from the ideological, embattled and visually overloaded production style of the past, telling Hugh Canning that by the late 1980s opera directors, 'enthralled by the leading German directors of the day had fallen into repetition and *cliché*'.[3] He felt, he told Peter Conrad, that recent alternatives to naturalism, such as Ruth Berghaus's neo-expressionism, had not travelled well. They were specific to their countries of origin, and had been born of a post-war ideology that sought to distance itself from a Nazi past.[4]

Marks also embarked on a comprehensive administrative re-arrangement, telling Richard Morrison of *The Times* that Pountney's composite role as producer, translator and repertory planner was to be divided. The post of director of productions lapsed and in its stead Marks created two new departments, business and administration, and artistic administration and dramaturgy, which incorporated the managerial aspects of the old

* The deficit for the year ending March 1993 alone was £981,000. The box office had been 23 per cent (£1.6 million) below budget, with the largest short-falls on *Princess Ida* and *Brouček*.

Pountney and Caulton production department.\* In September 1993 Guus Mostart became director of artistic administration and dramaturgy after advertisement and interviews with other candidates. Mostart had been at Glyndebourne from 1977 to 1985, and since 1989 had been artistic director in Vancouver. Jeremy Caulton, who had been entrusted with casting by Harewood in 1976, and was subsequently appointed director of opera planning, left at the end of November 1993. John Berry became the casting director in May 1994. Edmund Tracey, who had reached retirement age, also left at this time after thirty years with the company.

Marks intended to increase ENO's revenue rather than trim its sails. In the months before he took over he decided that the marketing department needed more focus in order to rebuild the core audience, and in February 1993, on the advice of Peter Jonas, he had invited Maddie Morton to run it. John Nickson remained as head of development, with Morton responsible for communications, box office and the database. Jane Livingston – who had joined ENO's marketing team in October 1987 and who valiantly fulfilled her duties as press manager and, later, head of press for over twenty years – remained responsible for the press liaison. Just before Marks's arrival, Keith Cooper had gone to Covent Garden and it had been agreed between Marks and Jonas that a new approach to marketing would be beneficial. The newly computerised box office made it possible to do more direct marketing after the Cooper publicity, poster and corporate-image campaign had run its course. A strategy was developed whereby there would be shorter runs and less frequent returns of revivals. Advertisements were to focus on individual productions rather than pushing the 'corporate image'.

With the information from the box office, Morton was in a stronger position to devise a new ticket-pricing system that enabled ENO to increase the number of reasonably priced seats and maximise income without putting up prices.† The marketing department

---

\* The new enlarged department would be responsible for company style, the selection of repertoire, the choice of principal singers, directors, designers, choreographers, chorus, staff producers and house dramaturges (memorandum by Guus Mostart, 2.2.94, B133 Box 209).

† With average prices having risen by 75 per cent in the previous six years, the aim was to have half the tickets priced at £25 or less, and to ensure that the top

and the artistic planners, steered by Marks, came up with a 'rule of thumb' method to programme a theoretically perfect season combining new and revived productions. The result, based on previous experience and the expertise of the team, was 'pretty accurate', Morton recalled.[5] The prediction was that audiences would average 80 per cent – 2,000 per performance – though discounts for students and subscribers would reduce takings to 67 per cent of the maximum.

Marks's three-year business plan in 1994 reflected his policy of increasing revenue rather than cutting costs. He expressed the need to rebuild audiences by restoring the core repertory and by giving staple works in productions that had a chance of survival, especially the depleted stock of revivable Verdi. Marks's artistic ambitions were, however, easier to conceive than to achieve, and Mostart's programming saw the usual mixture of hits and misses.

The 1993/4 season was still largely the result of planning by the previous regime. The first new production was Steven Pimlott's *La bohème* on 15 September. Tobias Hoheisel designed a clear, abstract, composite set. Milnes pointed out that the cool response to Pimlott's production revealed that *La bohème* was one of the few operas that were still felt to require a traditional set. However, he believed that the production's determination to focus on 'deep personal guilt over youthful misdemeanours' revealed, as had John Cox's at Glyndebourne in 1978, the 'precious metal in the piece'.[6]

Tim Albery's pared-down, telling production of *Lohengrin* on 20 November struck gold, with Elder's masterful conducting and Amanda Holden's lucid, easily audible new translation. This was Elder's first appearance as a guest. Jonathan Miller returned to ENO on 2 February 1994 with *Der Rosenkavalier*. Miller conceived the piece in a pre-First World War setting, which was beautifully designed by Peter J. Davison and lit by Jean Kalman, with Sue

---

price would never be £10 more than that of a West End musical. At the time it was felt that the top price should be kept below £50, which was believed to be a psychological ceiling, and the median price comparable to a stalls price at the National Theatre. After analysing sales data and commissioning pricing research that explored levels of price elasticity, Morton and her team changed the allocation of seats within the price bands and, without increasing the top price, managed to generate an average of 10 per cent more income per performance.

Blane's costumes all in muted taupes and ivories splashed with discreet colour. Both Miller's lucid and unpretentious production and the fine performances of Anne Evans, Sally Burgess, Rosemary Joshua and John Tomlinson provided a distinguished and cogent account as well as much psychological insight.[7]

The first two productions of Marks's own planning were the Nicolette Molnar *Così fan tutte* on 5 May and Lucy Bailey's *Jenůfa* in June. Milnes loved the youthful impulsiveness and vitality of both the production and conducting of *Così*, as well as fine performances from Vivian Tierney, Christopher Booth-Jones, Susan Bickley and Neill Archer. On the whole, however, it was the poverty apparent in the sets and lack of rehearsal time that were most commented on. *Jenůfa* was less successful. Having failed to persuade Declan Donnellan, Marks assigned the commission to the twenty-nine-year-old Lucy Bailey. It was her first opera production in a major house and was described by Clements as 'loose and unfocused'. Technical problems on the first night meant the curtain had to be lowered.[8] It was designed by Simon Vincenzi, with a giant swivelling cinema screen with bright plain colours. The critics singled out the singers alone for praise, particularly Barstow as Kostelnička and Susan Bullock as Jenůfa, who acted with searing conviction and beauty of tone despite a lack of distinguishable words.

Lack of clear diction was becoming an increasingly vexed subject for both management and audience. Since Tracey's departure no one had had prime responsibility for ensuring the projection of the text.[9] On 4 May Marks wrote a paper in which he stressed that the question of diction needed to be addressed 'as a matter of great urgency' if ENO were to continue to justify the policy that underpinned everything it did. He was not as averse to surtitles as Pountney, believing them to be a technical and not an aesthetic problem.[10] He told the board that Rodney Milnes, in *Opera*, was leading a campaign against surtitles because he believed that singers would give up trying to articulate clearly and audiences would cease focusing on the stage. Board member Rodric Braithwaite suggested that if the principals could not sing more clearly, surtitles could be considered as an adjunct to and not as a substitute for remedial measures.[11]

There were some exciting new ventures. Thirty-nine-year-old

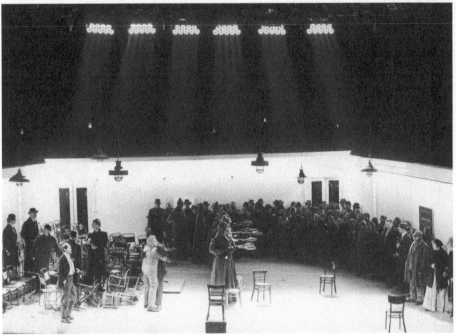

Three iconic productions of the late Harewood era:
25  Dvořák's *Rusalka*, March 1983. David Pountney's production with Cathryn Pope, Joan Rodgers and Linda McLeod as wood nymphs, Richard Van Allan as the Water Spirit, and Eilene Hannan on the swing as Rusalka.
26  Tchaikovsky's *Mazeppa*, December 1984. David Alden's controversial first production for ENO, designed by David Fielding.

27 *Xerxes*, 1985: Nicholas Hytner's first production for ENO and a landmark for Handel staging – still in the repertoire thirty years later.

28 Jonathan Miller's production of Gilbert and Sullivan's *Mikado*, September 1986, designed by Stefanos Lazaridis – a box office hit for over thirty years.

29 The triumvirate: David Pountney, Peter Jonas and Mark Elder, on the *Xerxes* deckchairs, with members of the company in Red Square, Moscow, on the June 1990 tour, with (left to right) Gillian Sullivan, Rodney Macaan, Eileen Hulse, Christopher Robson, Christine Bunning, Michael Lloyd, Malcolm Green, Kristine Ciesinski, Malcolm Donnelly, Lesley Garrett, Ethna Robinson, Yvonne Kenny, Ann Murray, Geoffrey Pogson, Menai Davies, Christopher Booth-Jones and John Connell.
30 High 'powerhouse' style: *Simon Boccanagra*, April 1987, directed by David Alden and designed by David Fielding.

31 *Lady Macbeth of Mtsensk*: ENO at the height of its ambition and technical strength in May 1987.

32 Philip Langridge as Oedipus in David Alden's production of *Oedipus Rex*, January 1991 – thirty years on from the production of Michel St-Denis.

33 Lesley Garrett in a fine revival of the David Pountney/Maria Bjørnson *Cunning Little Vixen*, May 1991.

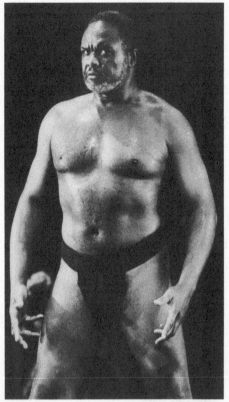

34  Dennis Marks, ENO's General Director from 1993 to 1997.
35  Willard White as Prince Andrey Khovansky in Francesca Zambello's production of Mussorgsky's *Khovanshchina*, November 1994.
36  Susan Gritton as Xenia, John Tomlinson as Boris, Timothy Webb as Fyodor in *Boris Godunov*, November 1998.

37 Nicholas Payne, General Director from 1998 to 2002, and Paul Daniel, Music Director from 1997 to 2005, study a model for the Italian season in the autumn of 2000.
38 A world premiere: *The Silver Tassie* by Mark-Anthony Turnage with a libretto by Amanda Holden; Gerald Finley as Harry Heegan, February 2000.
39 In May 2002 Richard Jones directed a bleakly humorous *Lulu*. Lisa Saffer as Lulu.

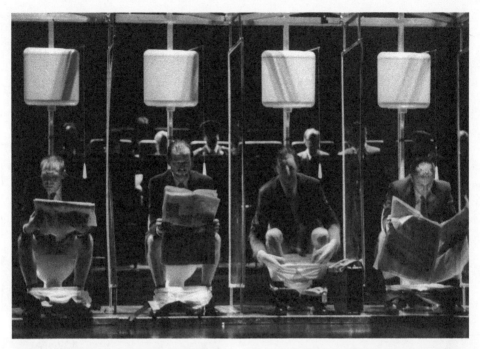

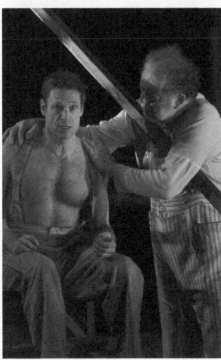

40  *A Masked Ball*, February 2002. Calixto Bieito made a stir with his latrines.
41  *Billy Budd*, December 2005, with Simon Keenlyside as Billy and Gwynne Howell, an
ENO stalwart since the 1960s, as Dansker.
42  November 2005, new management for ENO: Chief Executive Loretta Tomasi and
Artistic Director John Berry.

43 *Death in Venice*: Deborah Warner directed Ian Bostridge as Aschenbach in May 2007.
44 Edward Gardner, ENO's Music Director from 2007.
45 David Alden was back at ENO for a spooky *Lucia di Lammermoor* with Anna Christy as Lucia and Mark Stone as Enrico in 2008.

Judith Weir's ENO commission *Blond Eckbert*, drawn from Ludwig Tieck's 1797 folktale *Der blonde Eckbert* and featuring the folklore and supernatural elements of early-nineteenth-century German Romanticism, was premiered on 20 April 1994. It was ninety minutes long and employed just four singers. Staged by Tim Hopkins and designed by Nigel Lowery, the production's expressionist busyness undermined the beauty and narrative of a spare, direct and economical piece. Clements thought that the production was more inclined to send up the opera than to 'serve its deeper, darker purposes'.[12] The opera was nonetheless recognised as an accessible work of haunting originality and inventiveness.

Towards the end of his first season Marks felt that the uneven response of the press was understandable at a time of transition. As the season progressed he observed that certain descriptions were beginning to appear with regularity, such as the 'illuminating clarity' of *Der Rosenkavalier* and the 'subtlety and insight' of Julia Hollander's production of *Eugene Onegin*. It was, Marks felt, 'quite pleasing to note a preoccupation with clarity, directness and dramatic truth', despite criticism of the obvious austerity and impoverishment, especially of Hollander's deliberately low-budget *Onegin*.[13]

Jane Livingston had set up press lunches with the critics to facilitate a 'channel of communication' and to listen to what they had to say. They were, she reported, desperate to be supportive, but she felt that as this might not last, ENO should not let the moment pass.[14] By 10 May Marks was able to tell the board that the critics felt that they were being listened to and that there was a reservoir of goodwill.[15]

Marks's efforts were, however, overshadowed by the inherited deficit, which was mounting. With a grant of £11,655,000 from the Arts Council and £157,200 from Westminster City Council, it was estimated in March 1994 that the deficit would reach £3 million by the end of the season. While Marks was determined not to dismantle the ensemble, it was clear that there would have to be some rationalisation backstage. On 30 March Marks and Nicholas Goodison met the Arts Council's outgoing and incoming secretary generals, Anthony Everitt and Mary Allen, who accepted Marks's three-year strategy of renewing the repertoire while instituting cost-saving working practices.* The changes would themselves be costly, however, with projected redundancy payments of up to £1 million. This could bring the accumulated deficit to nearly £4 million, which would need a guarantee from the Arts Council in order to ensure that the bank would continue its overdraft facilities. Goodison reminded Allen and Everitt that this was the only hope for the future and that the Arts Council and government had a 'responsibility not to let the People's Opera House go under'. That same day, Lord Gowrie – the new chairman of the Arts Council – told Marks that he was willing to talk to the bank informally but that it was imperative that the declining audience trend be reversed.[16]

In April the board received legal advice on insolvency, after some members had expressed concern that they would be distrained by ENO's creditors if Coutts withdrew its overdraft facility.[17] They were reassured that the only question to be asked was whether the Arts Council – recently redesignated Arts Council England (ACE) – would continue to fund ENO and that proof of real dishonesty and not over-optimism on the part of the board was required in order to establish fraudulent trading. In May the board learnt that Gowrie was sympathetic to ENO's plight and that Mary Allen would provide a 'letter of comfort'.[18]

Meanwhile, there was a concerted effort to increase revenue. In March Marks had launched the New Stages appeal, whereby the audience was encouraged to contribute to new productions, hopefully increasing their number from six to eight. By the end of the year £230,000 had been raised from 1,800 individuals.

In the spring Nickson had reported that the box office was doing better. It was 5 per cent up on the end of the previous season, with *Rigoletto* well above budget and *Der Rosenkavalier* both a critical and financial success.[19] In April ENO won Olivier Awards for *Lohengrin* and for the orchestra in *Inquest of Love*. But the end of the season was disappointing, with the average financial capacity of the box office slipping back to 47 per cent in June. The biggest let-

---

* It was proposed that the technical department would alter its work practice from a three-day shift to small salaried teams plus a pool of contract labour for busy times. There would be up to forty redundancies and the restructured salary arrangements might mean reduced earnings. Everitt could not support measures that might result in a strike, but Allen asked Marks to prepare an analysis of the financial situation in case this occurred.

down was *Jenůfa*, which achieved 30 per cent against the budgeted 52 per cent. Marks also blamed an over-optimistically long run of *Peter Grimes*, planned by Jonas, which made 35 per cent against its budgeted 47 per cent.[20]

Despite the efforts to increase revenue, Mary Allen and the Arts Council's director of finances, Lew Hodges, told Marks on 30 June that they were concerned that their 'letter of comfort' had not been met with surpluses in the three-year plan. She said it was not long since ENO had negotiated for the long-term elimination of the deficit and now it had increased. It might be necessary, she warned, to suspend the operations of some of the Arts Council's clients.[21]

Marks, however, was insistent on maintaining the basic fabric of the company and, although cost-cutting exercises continued, in his discussions with the Arts Council he tenaciously hung on to recruitment restrictions rather than a programme of redundancies. If freelance workers were introduced in too many areas, he warned the board, 'the team spirit of the company would fragment'.[22] His determination seemed to have prevailed when Allen accepted the three-year plan on the basis of an increase in seat prices of 1 per cent above inflation and a reduction of costs in the technical department. On 8 August Coutts agreed to a £3,650,000 overdraft. To alleviate anxiety in the company, Marks wrote a letter to the staff in August to explain that all decisions were being taken in consultation with the unions.

The negotiations with the stage staff about redundancies and the removal of the remaining restrictive practices were very tense. On 29 October Marks proposed a 19 per cent basic pay increase coupled with disturbance pay to cushion the loss of overtime earnings. Gerry Morrissey of BECTU counter-proposed that the removal of restrictive practices, such as the maximum fifteen-hour call, could only be in conjunction with a 43 per cent increase in basic pay. Morrissey later pointed out that in the past, low basic pay had been supplemented by large amounts of overtime, which had resulted not only in much unproductive 'down time' but also in working hours that were very long and increasingly out of kilter with European health and safety regulations. Marks, he believed, coming as Morrissey himself did from a background in the BBC, was more aware of the need to enable staff to have a reasonable work/life balance. What the employers considered to be 'restrictive practices' the union regarded as penalties for management's poor performance and their imposition of a low-basic-pay culture.[23]

In early November there was nearly a strike but, after long and tough negotiations throughout November and with the involvement of ACAS, agreement was reached on 2 December whereby the majority of the three-year plan's proposals were accepted and the strike was called off.[24] Management was to schedule work on the basis of skill and the requirements of the workload, and there was to be basic pay for a forty-five-hour week. The three-day working week, in place since 1970, was replaced by a five-days-in-seven roster with alternate weekends off. Overtime payments for night work were also discontinued at this time.

Marks hoped that this agreement would save £1.3 million up to 1997/8. It would in the short term, however, cost the company about £920,000.* This helped to bring the accumulated deficit up to £3.98 million at the end of the 1994/5 financial year. The BECTU agreement went a long way towards solving the problems of lack of flexibility, although not all the changes were actually carried through, and negotiations in the late 1990s continued to improve both working practices and industrial relations.

At the beginning of Marks's second season the box office at last seemed to be improving. Morton's box-office changes were proving beneficial, with advance bookings up for the new season, which opened on 14 September 1994 with the new Keith Warner *Tosca*. The production, designed by John Conklin, was not an overwhelming success. Milnes wrote of Warner's inclusion of 'any number of glossy effects', and concluded that it was very depressing that so much time should have been spent on 'all this flummery, which detracted fatally from any concentration, at the expense of serious investigation or even basic characterisation'.[25] Canning thought that Rosalind Plowright's planned comeback after a career crisis and singing in Germany was not aided by Warner's production.[26]

The first real hit of the Marks era was provided by Ian Judge, together with designer John Gunter. Massenet's *Don Quixote* on 8 October was welcomed as an enjoyable night out and as resembling

---

* According to the annual report, the costs included £550,000 in redundancy payments for BECTU members and £370,000 for reorganisation in other departments.

a good, if cheaply contrived, West End musical. In his review Canning noted that ENO's resources were stretched almost to breaking point in its endeavour to keep hold of a recession-hit audience. Design budgets were pegged at a level that would be regarded as a joke anywhere else in western Europe. In Canning's opinion, ENO deserved a resounding popular success with Judge's vivacious staging of *Don Quixote*, which was the 'kind of old-fashioned theatre magic that the hair-shirted Powerhouse regime despised'. Alan Opie and Richard Van Allan were much praised.[27]

It was the 'grand opera' shows, as Marks was the first to say, that suited both the Coliseum and the company. Thus ENO's first-ever production of Mussorgsky's *Khovanshchina* on 24 November was both enthusiastically received and financially successful. Sîan Edwards conducted with authority and Francesca Zambello marshalled her large forces with skill, directing a strong cast that included Willard White, Gwynne Howell, Anne-Marie Owens, Kim Begley and Paul Whelan, making his debut. John Allison called it a 'triumph for the company as a whole', with Zambello and Edwards overcoming the notorious difficulties of both the opera's subject and structure, as well as the lack of a definitive edition. Allison considered Alison Chitty's 'succession of striking images' as 'nothing short of overwhelming'.[28] *Khovanshchina*, with its epic qualities, recalled ENO's glory days, winning the Olivier Award for best opera production.

That autumn and winter the box office seemed at last to be recovering, with an extremely successful first booking period that exceeded the budget by £300,000. Punters were still enjoying *Rigoletto* – this time with Rosa Mannion. Short runs of *Ariadne auf Naxos* with Eaglen and *The Mikado* combined with more realistic budgets were making the crucial difference, and Hytner's classic, well-revived *Magic Flute* also went very well, with an ambitiously scheduled seventeen performances in October. Marks was able to inform Allen that the November box office was 77 per cent and the financial capacity 67 per cent compared with 56 and 47 per cent in the first part of the financial year.[29]

The economy was picking up and ENO was taking full advantage of the change with realistic budgeting, investment in casting and improvements in targeted marketing.[30] The Arts Council agreed that ENO was performing above the average of arts organisations and that with the changes in working practices it should be possible to deliver surpluses of £300,000. There remained, however, the continuing problem of grants failing to rise in line with inflation. Marks warned that it would be demoralising to ask the chorus and orchestra to accept cuts in real terms more than once, and that with an increase that year of only 5 per cent the surplus achieved would be wiped out. He urged Allen to restore the loss. Everyone at ENO was labouring heroically to turn round the position with stringent economies, artistic endeavour, energetic and inventive marketing and bold repertory planning – all of which were making their contribution. It was so frustrating, he said, for members of the company to see their effort swallowed up by rising prices. All he was asking for was a 'level playing field against inflation'.[31]

The Arts Council informed ENO on 13 December that it was to receive an increase of £300,000, which was 2.57 per cent. Some organisations were getting no increase at all. But the failure of the Arts Council at this juncture to give ENO its 'level playing field' was to prove perilous for the company's continued healthy development. It was, Morton recalled, 'quite soul-destroying: everyone was doing their best and were just running hard to stand still'.[32]

That Christmas ENO let the Coliseum to the Birmingham Royal Ballet for a three-week season.

There was another problem confronting ENO, which was the need to restore the increasingly shabby Coliseum, as agreed when ENO acquired the freehold in 1992. On 3 September 1994 ENO had announced a bid to fund the restoration, for which the London architects Sheppard Robson – appointed by Jonas – were the consultants. The £40-million scheme was to be partially Lottery funded and partially funded through a capital campaign, and masterminded by Shaun Woodward, the former director of communications for the Conservative Party and a member of the ENO board from 1991 to 2002. The building was in such a serious condition that it would have to close for the interior to be redecorated to the original scheme of the Coliseum's architect, Frank Matcham, and for general improvements to be made to the front of the house, as well as to the backstage and storage facilities. National Lottery funding was sought and the theatre would be closed from mid-1998 to the end of 1999, with the company appearing at the Lyceum in the interim.

Although ENO was committed to restoring the Coliseum, through no fault of its own the timing proved detrimental to the company's interests and plans. In January 1995 the Royal Opera House applied for £78.5 million from the Lottery for its own restoration scheme, which was going to cost £198.5 million altogether. The demands on the Lottery of the Coliseum and the Royal Opera House, which was to close from 1997 to 2000, and the need to rebuild so much of the UK's seriously neglected arts infrastructure was becoming a concern to ACE and to the arts minister. Not only Covent Garden and the Coliseum but also Sadler's Wells and the South Bank Centre were in need of substantial renovation. The Arts Council had therefore commissioned Dennis Stevenson, an influential businessman, to prepare a report on the provision of opera and dance in London, which was presented in January 1995.*

It became apparent that the loss of audience during the latter years of the Jonas regime had had a detrimental effect politically as well as financially. The Stevenson report was the first of its kind to suggest that there was too much provision of opera for the existing audience. Hitherto, ever since Harewood's report for the Arts Council in 1966, the efforts of the Arts Council had been directed towards increasing both supply and demand for opera, in the hope and expectation that it might become as popular an art form in the UK as it was in Europe. ENO, with its emphasis on accessibility, had always played a central role in this great project, both providing affordable seats and nurturing English-speaking talent. ENO had also been instrumental in establishing one of the most successful regional opera houses – Opera North. After Stevenson's report, there was to be a shift in thinking, focused on reducing the number of seats available in London, to fit what was believed to be a constant audience, incapable of growth.

* Other members of the committee were Genista McIntosh and Stephen Phillips. Graham Devlin was the accounting officer to the report. Dennis Stevenson was a director of Pearson plc and chairman from 1997. He was chairman of the Trustees of the Tate Gallery from 1989 to 1999 and chairman of Aldeburgh Music from 2000. He was also a member of the Panel on Takeovers and Mergers from 1992 to 2000. From 2001 he was chairman of HBOS plc, from which he resigned in 2008.

The committee backed up its argument with detailed research, statistics and graphs showing that there had been a constant audience for opera of about 600,000 seats a year for twenty years. There were 4,150 seats available per night, which, it was claimed, would be increased by up to 10,000 if the various redevelopments went ahead.* At the same time, it reported a need for a greater provision of dance, as both attendance and availability were declining. There was, it suggested, a need for a network of different-sized theatres for dance. The rebuilt Sadler's Wells might supply up to 900 seats, and a larger venue could be supplied by making the Coliseum available to dance for longer periods.

The report did not suggest that ENO should be closed and its funding released to support other opera projects, although both Graham Devlin and Dennis Stevenson were aware of murmurings to that effect in the corridors of power.[33] Indeed, it argued that it would be difficult to defend the dismantling of the 'People's Opera', especially if some of the released funds were given to Covent Garden in order to reduce its prices. The loss of ENO would also squeeze the amount of time available to the Royal Ballet at Covent Garden yet further. It also pointed out that both ENO and Covent Garden received the lowest subsidies in Europe.[34]

Nonetheless, the report clearly suggested that grand opera was the domain of Covent Garden and that the role of ENO should be reassessed. It therefore recommended 'a reduced role for ENO' and that it should 'reassess its output'. Performances should be reduced to 185 a year, from a peak in the early 1990s of 215 and its present rate of about 200. This reduction should be accompanied by reassessing 'the infrastructural support' needed to sustain its revised output. A freelance orchestra could be considered and shorter seasons at the Coliseum, which would be made available for rental for dance. With its new reduced infrastructure and reduced overheads,

* ENO refuted this figure both in February 1995 and in June 1996 following a feasibility study. According to their estimate, the Royal Opera House and the Coliseum would have 2,100 and 2,350 seats, respectively, Sadler's Wells up to 1,700 and the Lyceum would return to the commercial sector. The smaller spaces of Covent Garden and the South Bank would replace existing inadequate venues that were returning to other performing arts. They put the figure nearer to 6,500 ('Feasibility Study, Summary Report and Key Conclusions', 7.6.96, ENO, p. 10).

it would be able to mount seasons of smaller-scale work at another London theatre.[35]

The Stevenson report marked the beginning of a process that took over a decade to complete. There were those who fought to maintain the great ensemble character of ENO, to regain its lost audience and maintain its traditional role as the accessible second great opera house, and on the other side of the debate were those who believed that a large company was an unsustainable model, and that its fixed costs and the high output of its work in the unwieldy Coliseum were not the modern way of doing things. Stevenson himself believed his report to have been 'very influential in government and Arts Council policy'.[36]* Harewood, representing the unreformed ENO, later recalled that the report was 'a bad, bad blow for ENO'.[37]

It was to prove a long and bitter battle. When Marks met members of the Arts Council including Mary Allen on 1 March, and Lord Gowrie eight days later, he stressed that the review had not taken into account the effect of the company's business plan in improving audiences. ENO was responding to the dance question in consultation with Sadler's Wells, and regular Christmas, spring and summer slots would be provided for UK and foreign dance companies. Gowrie and Allen had reassured him that they still supported ENO as a full-time, year-round operation presenting affordable opera as a complement to Covent Garden. They agreed that the report did not take into account ENO's business plan and improved box-office prospects. The Arts Council agreed to look into the possibility of an integrated plan for the provision of large-scale dance.[38]

The first skirmish was won by the 'defenders', and thoughts moved on to the redevelopment. A subcommittee was to prepare the Lottery appeal case, which would be pursued vigorously at a time convenient to ENO, regardless of Covent Garden.[39]

---

* Stevenson said in 2007 that he had believed his report had been necessary to prevent ENO embarking 'on a complete flight of fantasy' by building a new opera house for £250 million while 'Rome was burning and what was at stake was the survival of ENO'. The decision to prepare a feasibility study on a new theatre was made four months after the delivery of the Stevenson report, and the study itself was not delivered until 1997. The suggested cost of the new theatre in the feasibility study was £80–120 million.

By June 1995, however, the idea of building a new theatre had emerged during discussions about the cost of redeveloping the Coliseum. Revised costing showed the Coliseum restoration at approximately £46 million and the closure costs, including renting the Lyceum for two years, at £14–16 million.[40] Marks later recalled that both he and the capital campaign chairman, Shaun Woodward, agreed that not only was the development plan very expensive but that it would not reduce operating costs. They believed that it would be easier to raise money for a new purpose-built opera house. Both Woodward and Marks saw the landlocked nature of the area backstage and the consequent need to move scenery by hand as the decisive element in the need for the project.[41] It was decided to undertake a feasibility study to test both hypotheses.

On 20 July, the day that Covent Garden received a positive answer to its own Lottery application, Marks announced a Lottery grant of £1,384,000 for a feasibility study into the Coliseum as a home for the company and visiting dance companies and to look into the constraints of the Edwardian music hall.* Both grants were made against a background of growing press hostility to opera Lottery funding as elitist and London-centred, Rupert Murdoch's *Sun* leading the campaign against the 'Greedy Beggar's opera'.

During the following year ENO initiated a press campaign to draw attention to the Coliseum's condition. When Ted Murphy, the reinstated 'striker' of 1974 who was now the head of technical services, showed Richard Morrison round the Coliseum on 10 May 1996, he told Morrison, 'We have to call in a structural engineer to make sure that the roof can support the extra load on top as sets are suspended from a grid built in 1904.' The rehearsal rooms were non-existent, 'the air-conditioning Victorian, its plumbing Plantagenet, backstage cannot be expanded as it is landlocked – so scenery will always have to be moved by hand'. Morrison was not entirely convinced, pointing out that audiences and the company loved the theatre. 'Like some veteran chorus girl,' he wrote, 'it looks like a wreck by day, yet still puts on a hell of a show each night.'[42]

---

* ENO announced in October 1995 that a study, overseen by Laurence Newman of KPMG management consultants, would be undertaken jointly by architects Terry Farrell and Partners, theatre consultants Carr and Angier, market researchers Harris, cost consultants Bucknall Austin and accountants Binder Hamlyn.

Health and safety concerns were becoming more serious as the authorities were becoming tougher in the light of the delayed re-development.[*]

While it was yet to decide on the potential merits of a new thea-tre, ENO's board was becoming more focused on financial controls. On 22 March the board had decided that John Baker would suc-ceed Harewood as chairman. Baker was described in the press release as a 'tireless and effective leader of industry and a passion-ate supporter of excellence in the arts'. He was a good chairman, as Nicholas Payne later testified: 'around enough to keep his finger on the pulse but knowing when to stand back and trust the man he had appointed'.[43]

Baker later said that one of the reasons he had been brought in was 'to bury the management attitude that the Arts Council could not stand by and see the company go under', and to get some wider disciplines into the company in terms of financial controls. Baker recognised that, for good or ill, fundamental changes were taking place in the relationship between government and the performing-arts institutions, who were 'being required to conform more pre-cisely to public sector rules of governance, transparency and accountability, notwithstanding that state subvention was only part of their funding'.[†] Baker felt that the challenge to ENO would be to find ways of satisfying these requirements while maintaining the artistic independence of the company.[44] Symbolically, the great and much loved facilitator of less stringent financial days, Arnold Goodman, died in May.

Marks and Mostart's planning took advantage of Maddie Morton's redesign of the programme planning of the season. On 3 February ENO's first performance of Tippett's *King Priam* took place, in a production originally designed and directed by Tom Cairns for Opera North four years previously. It was well adapted to fit the Coliseum and, tightened up by Cairns, won high praise for its fine

[*] Harewood's successor John Baker later recalled several board discussions as to whether the theatre would have to be closed on health and safety grounds.
[†] Following various corporate concerns, corporate governance had been sub-ject to review during 1992 when the Cadbury report ('Financial Aspects of Corporate Governance') made a number of recommendations as to the struc-ture and governance of corporate boards and recommendations for financial reporting systems.

cast and a thrilling performance by Andrew Shore. Paul Daniel 'brought point and purpose to the score' and obtained superlative playing from the orchestra, according to Clements.[45] Equally successful that winter were revivals of *Figaro's Wedding* with Rosa Mannion and Rosemary Joshua, Susan Bullock's blazing *Butterfly*, and *Vixen* with Lesley Garrett. Marks reported that Davies, Rendall and Bottone were all doing sterling work, covering for each other during that winter's flu epidemic. By March the box office was 9 per cent above budget.

Unfortunately, the next new production of the season fared even worse than the previous year's *Tosca* had. *Don Giovanni*, directed by Guy Joosten and first seen in September 1994 in Antwerp, opened on 15 March to savage reviews. Canning described it as one of the 'most hopeless performances of a Mozart opera that he had ever heard from a professional company'.[46] Critics urged management to bring back Miller's production immediately.

The British premiere of Alfred Schnittke's *Life with an Idiot* on 1 April had mixed reviews both for the production and for the work itself. The loss of a day's stage rehearsal resulted in some serious technical hitches on press night. Milnes, who thought it an important work, was disappointed that the production was neither politically demanding nor technically proficient, and he described an air of blind panic from the stage staff at the delayed start and during the performance. Robert Carsen's production of Britten's *A Midsummer Night's Dream* was ENO's first on 17 May. Originally seen at Aix, it fared little better. Nor did *Mahagonny* on 8 June. While some liked the crass comedy of the *Dream*, Canning and Milnes wrote of 'designer chic', and Alexander Waugh pointed to the technical hitches of many shows and the poor amplification of stage and pit for *Mahagonny*. Of the latter, Milnes had asked what the 'carefree musical comedy staging' in cool elegant designs by Nick Ormerod had to do with Weill's angry elegy for a dying civilisation?

Despite this disappointing run, the 1994/5 season achieved 63 per cent financial capacity against the 59 per cent budget and the previous year's 49 per cent. Ticket-price rises had been kept below inflation. On 10 July Marks announced that the 1994/5 season had turned the corner for ENO, with attendances up by 25 per cent – the highest seat capacity since 1989. Even *King Priam* and *A Midsummer Night's Dream* were above expectations. The New Stages appeal had raised £250,000. Marks thanked the company for their great efforts and their commitment, talent and admirable restraint.[47]

The adverse criticism of the previous season, especially from the *Daily Telegraph* and *The Spectator*, was very worrying for Marks, who suggested that as ENO had the smallest press PR department of any of the major companies, they should employ somebody to run the press and PR functions of the company, reporting directly to the general director.[48] In October Maggie Sedwards returned to the company to fill the post as the new director of communications.

Jonathan Miller was also back in September for his new production of *Carmen*, which sported an excellent cast of Louise Winter as Carmen, Robert Brubaker as Don José, Robert Hayward as Escamillo and Janice Watson as Micaëla. Katarina Karnéus was Mercédès, and Mary Plazas, Frasquita. It gave the new season a start described variously by the critics as 'sizzling', 'piquant' and 'compelling', despite comments about a lack of sexual chemistry at the centre. Critics commented on Miller's exile during the 'power house' era and pointed to his latest productions of *Der Rosenkavalier*, *Così fan tutte* at Covent Garden and the new *Carmen* as reasons to welcome him back to the UK opera scene. Marks himself called it a strong, intelligent reading, focusing on human and social aspects, with its broad naturalism and a cleverly revealing time shift to the 1930s.[49]

*Carmen* achieved a paid attendance of 82 per cent on the first night and one matinee achieved 102 per cent seat capacity. The October revival of *Rusalka* was graced by Susan Chilcott in what Marks described as 'one of the most captivating performances of recent seasons'.[50] David Pountney's pantomime *Fairy Queen* the same month was enjoyed by Milnes as 'exhilarating, funny, romantic and sexy', although Clements found it a 'coarse parade of high camp'.[51]

On 6 November Sîan Edwards's resignation was announced to the press. She left on 31 December, her reasons for doing so subject to a confidentiality agreement. Two weeks later David Atherton conducted Christopher Alden's *Turandot* against a background of speculation that he was one of the contenders for music director, together with Paul Daniel. The event was mainly noted for its loudness, which abetted the general inaudibility of the singers and their words. The disappointing production had been rented from Welsh National Opera after it was discovered that David Hockney's San Francisco production did not fit the Coliseum stage. The situation was not improved when Jane Eaglen pulled out at the last moment, to be replaced by Austrian Sophia Larsen.[52] Milnes, angered by the lack of clearly articulated words, wrote that changes in the style of singing were putting ENO's future in the balance.[53]

*La Belle Vivette*, Michael Frayn's version of *La Belle Hélène*, should have been a great coup for Marks, whose personal perseverance had brought the sceptical Frayn to tackle the piece. But some critics felt that it lacked Offenbach's sharp satire, although there was lots of verbal wit to enjoy as well as James Holmes in the pit, bringing vivacious sparkle, and some visual amusement. The show was also adorned by Lesley Garrett's beautiful and sexy Vivette.[54] Milnes was sad to see her potential earthiness wasted, since Offenbach's royal nymphomaniac was replaced by Frayn's romantic lead. He also mourned the loss of smuttiness.[55]

The box office continued to improve. Corporate funding, which faced a shortfall of £360,000, was, however, a different matter. As a result of a further development in governance requirements – the Nolan Committee's 'Report on Standards in Public Life' – sponsorship was no longer in the gift of the chief executives of the great corporations, and was now handled by hard-headed managers of corporate public-affairs departments as part of their advertising and promotional activities.[56] Some individual 'white knights' would be needed for the capital campaign.[57] By mid-December the board chairman designate, John Baker, together with Nickson and other members of the board had reduced the shortfall from £360,000 to £200,000.*

Marks remained committed to ENO's mission. There were four new company artists by March 1995, whose number Marks hoped to increase to thirty – although he only managed to sign up twenty-three by the time he left. Milnes was full of praise for Marks's policy of rebuilding the company, and for the 'treasure trove' of people like David Ritch, the staff production team and the music staff who made up the company.[58]

* Nickson resigned in December 1994 to take up a senior post at the Royal Academy. Susan Davenport took over his work in February 1995.

After Sîan Edwards stepped down several interviews were held for the post of music director, with Marks supporting the candidature of Paul Daniel. At the end of the process the board agreed to offer Daniel the post.[59] His appointment was announced in January 1996. He was to take up his post in the summer of 1997, but would be involved in planning beforehand.

Marks also continued to support the work of the Contemporary Opera Studio and the Baylis Programme. In 1994 the Arts Council had made funds available for Mark-Anthony Turnage to be Composer in Association from 1995–8.* When Marks learnt that a decommissioned library in Hoxton had become available from Dalston City Partnership, the regeneration body in the East End of London, with rent subsidised by Hackney Borough Council, he decided to house the two organisations together. The building also had space for orchestra rehearsals and for the archive, which had the potential to become an easily accessible educational resource for the company.

In April 1995 Sarah Hickson had replaced Henrietta Bredin as artistic administrator of the Contemporary Opera Studio, which Bredin had co-founded. When the Baylis Programme moved out of the Coliseum, Rebecca Meitlis, who was still running it, felt that it was time to branch out and move on. Steve Moffitt and Alice King-Farlow were the new team chosen by Marks. Moffitt, an educationalist with experience in the theatre but not in opera, had both an excellent connection with children and an understanding of work with communities, as well as an inventive and imaginative concept of how the programme could be further developed. King-Farlow had great organisational skills and extensive experience of working within the Opera North and the City of Birmingham Touring Opera companies.

Like their predecessors, Moffitt and King-Farlow saw the Baylis

---

* Turnage was to compose a song cycle to poems by Jackie Kay, *Twice Through the Heart*, commissioned by Aldeburgh, and the short chamber opera *The Country of the Blind*, from a story by H. G. Wells. *Twice Through the Heart*, a monodrama for mezzo-soprano and sixteen players, was performed by the Contemporary Opera Studio at Aldeburgh in June 1997 and at the Coliseum in October 1997. Both works were performed at the Queen Elizabeth Hall, fully staged, with the ENO orchestra on 3 July 1997. Turnage would also continue working on his full-scale opera *The Silver Tassie*, commissioned by ENO with a libretto by Amanda Holden.

Programme as more than a way of creating a new audience. They were determined to give young people who would never have considered entering an opera house the opportunity for informed choice and the training to understand and articulate their feelings about the experience of opera. Aware of the responsibility resulting from the large public subsidy ENO received, they also understood that the Baylis Programme could and should use the great resources of ENO, thereby keeping alive its tradition of education and commitment to the community. By taking it out of the Coliseum, as Moffitt later explained, they were bringing the Baylis Programme back into the kind of environment envisaged by Baylis herself and giving it the opportunity to look at its work in a new way.[60] At the same time, Moffitt and King-Farlow succeeded in involving all areas of the company, from carpenters, props and costumes to the development department.

The large studio also provided a space in which young people could make work that did not have to be dismantled until the projects were completed. During the 1998 *Hansel and Gretel* project, primary-school children were able to enter specially created sets and perform with ENO singers. Over the next nine years the programme attracted hundreds of schools, with about 16,000 people a year participating, and culminating in an ambitious series of events for the millennium. Baylis ventures were not confined to children and there were regular projects for all ages, including pensioners, under the leadership of singer Mary King.

The Contemporary Opera Studio and the Baylis Programme opened their doors to the public in their new base at the old Hoxton library building in January 1996. Mark-Anthony Turnage told John Allison: 'Opera may be a dirty word at the moment but open day will enable visitors to see that we are pretty normal.' He believed that workshops would help young composers who were the victims of careless commissioning and too much pressure.[61] While in the building, ENO organised the Hoxton Singers, a group of local senior citizens who gave concerts there.

By the end of 1995 Marks felt sufficiently confident to declare that ENO's mission was once again on target. 'Accessibility through affordability and the English language, friendliness of atmosphere and the values of an ensemble company were as true as ever and in the process of becoming truer,' he said, and continued: 'We are a grand opera company and of course we produce grand opera. The reason we exist is to be able to do so for everyone regardless of their social circumstances, income or geographical location.'[62]

The second part of the 1995/6 season saw some substantial successes. Mark Elder, with 'returning hero status' at ENO, together with Elizabeth Connell, making magnificent music, stole the show in David Alden's spare and disciplined, if slightly deconstructed *Tristan and Isolde* on 10 February 1996. Graham Vick, Paul Brown and Richard Hickox presented *Fidelio*, translated by Pountney, as a tale of ordinary folk, two months later. Kathryn Harries was a vulnerable, moving Leonore, Anthony Rolfe Johnson a striving, near-heroic Florestan. *Salome* in May, directed by David Leveaux, in Hammond's translation, was compared unfavourably with Luc Bondy's Covent Garden production, although it scored points for Alan Woodrow's convincing Herod and Andrew Litton's conducting.

In June Nikolaus Lehnhoff's 1991 Munich production of Hans Werner Henze's 1960 opera *The Prince of Homburg* was a fine tribute to the composer on his seventieth birthday. The work, with its operatic know-how and lyrical communicativeness, was a repertoire piece in Europe, but had not been heard in Britain other than at Sadler's Wells in a touring version in 1962. It was conducted with ardour by Elgar Howarth, with Peter Coleman-Wright as a dashing prince and Susan Bullock as Princess Natalie. The new season started with another thoughtful Miller production, *La traviata*, with a captivating performance by Rosa Mannion but with a lack of drama from Steven Mercurio in the pit.[63]

Bernd Alois Zimmermann's *Die Soldaten* had its English premiere on 19 November, thirty years after its first performance in Germany. It was directed by David Freeman, designed by Sally Jacobs and conducted by Elgar Howarth. With its massive forces, orchestral and technical, including film and electronics, it was hailed as a heroic act of defiance in times of stringency, as well as a miracle of coherence technically and musically. Lisa Saffer as Marie made light of the technical difficulties as well as giving a musical, lyrical performance.[64]

Marks's bullishness about the company's traditional mission being on target was about to hit the reality of its frozen subsidy, which had fallen in real terms by £1 million since 1993. In addition, fundraising was nearly £400,000 short of its £1.7 million target and the box office was down 6 per cent. There was a serious possibility that the season's shortfall might be as much as £950,000. Budget cuts and reduced rehearsals would once again have to be imposed, as well as a freeze on the Studio and recruitment deferrals.[65]

ENO was not alone. The Arts Council reported that 80 per cent of its clients were in the same position.[66] The government, however, remained unmovable and on 26 November the Arts Council announced that it had received another standstill grant-in-aid of £186.1 million. It was better than the £3-million cut announced in the Budget, but nonetheless caused Gowrie to write: 'I pointed out that a number of arts bodies of all kinds remain at risk and we have been warned by some that they might cease trading.'[67] As a consequence, ENO's grant was yet again below inflation at £11.995 million.

Under this pressure, the Arts Council was about to enter a new era of rescuing beleaguered arts companies with a system studied by Mary Allen from the Ford Foundation in the United States. According to John Baker, 'stabilisation' was a strategy whereby foundations and trusts dealing with failing arts institutions could restructure their operations to what Baker described as a 'lower and sustainable cost base', and provide 'endowment' for their future running. In the UK the problem was that the endowment element was lacking and, as Baker explained, since at the end of the process the institutions were not put in a better than break-even position, they were as vulnerable as ever to the slightest downturn in their revenues.[68] As Nicholas Payne later said: 'It was a flawed concept that if you wiped the slate clean, then took some tough management decisions – which is a euphemism for sacking people and using the stabilisation money to pay for the redundancies – somehow you will have a fitter, leaner, more businesslike entity, which will in future be able to operate within available – i.e. no more – money.'[69]

Stabilisation seemed at the time to offer the only way forward for ENO. In September 1996 Marks reported that stabilisation funding was becoming crucial for ENO's survival and that he hoped that ENO would be the first of fifteen guinea pigs as it qualified under nineteen of the twenty listed requirements. Marks explained the increasingly desperate plight of the company to chairman John Baker on 5 December. He wrote that when he became general director in 1993, the company had been carrying an accumulated deficit of £2.25 million, and since that time the Arts Council grant had fallen in real terms by £1.25 million. The new BECTU working agreement cost £850,000 in redundancy payments. Added together, he wrote, 'these figures come to £4.35 million'. Although average paid attendance had gone up from 59 per cent to 73 per cent – with financial capacities up from 49 per cent to 63 per cent – development income had fallen short by £400,000 per annum, which meant that ENO could not cover the redundancy payments, let alone make inroads into the deficit. The Arts Council, he wrote, should indicate 'how they expect us to trade solvently when they continually erode our core income'. In order to increase private support, the formation of the Trust should help develop new relations with individuals and corporate givers.[70]

As minds became focused on stabilisation, ENO announced the results of the feasibility study into the options of restoring the Coliseum or building a new theatre. In its 300 pages, including twenty-eight appendices, on 3 January 1997, KPMG, the tax advisory service, discussed various possibilities. The cheapest scheme at £5–8 million would provide minimum health and safety requirements for the Coliseum plus some improvements for the audience and limited improvements for the staff, and the maintenance of Lilian Baylis House. Another option was a major refurbishment of £73 million to include a new staircase and air-conditioning, with some improvements backstage, including provision for lorries to unload off Bedfordbury, at the back of the Coliseum, some increased storage and slightly better circulation backstage. Due to the landlocked nature of the site, with a river below and strict planning laws preventing development above, the plan would still not solve the technical constraints of the theatre or reduce overnight and Sunday working, and consequently there would be no savings to operating costs. It was not considered 'particularly good value for money' by KPMG.[71] Instead, they advised that £70 million for redeveloping the Coliseum, including £20 million of relocation costs as well as some backstage improvements, did not constitute a 'responsible use of public funds' and concluded that the best solution would be an £80–120 million new purpose-built lyric theatre or a large and small theatre on a central London site. The larger auditorium would seat between 1,800 and 2,110, and the smaller one 800–900. The study recommended this would be the most cost-effective way of serving south-east England. Covent Garden, the redevelopment of which was costing £198.5 million, had 2,050 seats and the Coliseum 2,400.

The plan envisioned that the future of ENO as a major repertory house, performing technically challenging repertory throughout the year and a nursery of talent, would be assured into the twenty-first century. It would have side stages, a fly tower and lifts, none of which were possible in the landlocked Coliseum. Overnight set changes would be unnecessary – something that, in addition to being very expensive, was becoming more difficult with the increasingly stringent enforcement of noise-pollution laws – and overtime would be eliminated. The company would have all its technical resources on site – wardrobe, props, rehearsal space – as well as the Baylis Programme and Contemporary Opera Studio, which could use the small theatre for their workshops and performances. It was also envisaged that ENO would expand its work in the two houses, maybe even increasing the size of the company as it continued to perform up to sixteen productions a year in the big house and smaller, rare and more experimental work in the small venue. Young singers could be developed and inexperienced teams could try out their work in smaller and less formal surroundings. Above all, it was hoped that the problem of the audibility of words could be solved. The larger house could also be let to visiting companies and the smaller one host exciting collaborations with other companies and media. Stevenson had called for a venue for large-scale dance in London, and the proposed twin-audience complex would be shared by dance and opera.[72*]

Marks was convinced that the new building was ENO's only hope for a truly secure future as a repertory company. A working party had explored the potential sites, of which Paddington basin was the least liked. The King's Cross development was going to take at least ten years, and so Potter's Field in Southwark, directly

---

* La Scala seats 3,000 and has the Piccolo Scala, which seats 600. The Munich Staatsoper seats 2,100 and performs at the Residenztheater (523). The Bastille comprises the Grande Salle (2,700) and the Salle Modulable (600–1,500) and studio (240).

opposite the Tower of London, became the favoured option.* The working party had also explored the acquisition of a soon to be decommissioned dental school adjacent to the Potter's Field site, which would replace Lilian Baylis House and be co-located. It would mean that the Baylis Programme would remain in the heart of a local community. The Potter's Field option, Baker recalled, was broadly accepted by the board, although there were some who believed that there was a real risk of losing the 'walk-in' trade and that the decision to abandon the Coliseum would be received with hostility.

Despite these misgivings, the level of hostility to the proposal came as a surprise to both Marks and his board. In two in-depth pieces in *Opera* in February and March, Milnes described the location in 'darkest Southwark' as 'frankly dotty'.[73] David Mellor was furious, 'calling the proposal an outrageous breach of faith'. Brian McMaster, like Jonas, believed that the Coliseum was the best location in London. Dennis Stevenson was, and remained, appalled at the idea, as he believed it to be a distraction from ENO's real problems, which were backstage with the unions and fundamentally financial. How could ENO, he later said, deal with the unions while at the same time planning 'a great new shiny palace'?[74] Jonas told Tom Sutcliffe that he thought the idea was 'insane'.[75] Morrison at *The Times*, despite the inadequacies of the Coliseum, was not convinced that it was a good idea to take ENO out of the centre of town. Brian Unwin, who was between stints on the board and had facilitated the purchase of the Coliseum, wrote a long letter to Marks in which he expressed his strong opposition to the scheme – for both political and practical reasons, in particular his 'gloom' in terms of the attractiveness and convenience of the proposed locations as well as the difficulty of finding support for a brand-new theatre.[76]

Nonetheless, there were many who saw the long-term benefits of

---

* The West End at the time was considered by many to be shabby and unsafe; when he visited the Potter's Field site Marks was struck by the possibilities of what had been termed a 'string of pearls' from the South Bank and the eventually redeveloped Royal Festival Hall past the Oxo Tower to Tate Modern and the Globe. The Globe is about halfway between the proposed Tucker/Arlen theatre near the old County Hall and Potter's Field. In 1997 it was about to become more accessible with the new millennium extension to the Jubilee Line.

providing ENO with a purpose-built theatre, so many years after the company had had their dream of a South Bank opera house shattered. Within the ENO family Harewood recalled that he had been convinced by the idea,[77] and John Baker also thought it was the right long-term solution for ENO. He also foresaw the move as a contribution to a wide-ranging revitalisation of the South Bank from Westminster to Tower Bridge. He quickly realised, however, that there was no consensus for the move.[78] The originally sceptical head of technical services, Ted Murphy, had also come to believe that the new theatre – with a fly tower and modern handling facilities – was the right thing for the new century, when health and safety would become more of an issue and the Edwardian theatre would prove increasingly unsustainable.[79]

Nicholas Payne later called Marks 'visionary before his time', while acknowledging that the timing had been a 'political error of judgement'.[80] 'One of the terrible things', Pountney later reflected, was that the proposal was badly timed and that 'nobody (and that is a criticism of the media) even bothered to read what he was proposing despite the fact that it had been seriously researched'. A lack of serious thinking 'allowed a good idea to be swept away as idiotic, which it wasn't'.[81]

The money could have been found – the Millennium Dome cost the Lottery and taxpayers £700 million in 1999 – but at a time of popular journalistic hostility to opera, following so soon after Covent Garden's successful and extremely unpopular £78.5-million Lottery bid in July 1995, and with growing ambivalence about the need for a second house, the timing was disastrous. It was also, as Stevenson stressed, a concept that was swimming violently against the increasingly powerful tide of retrenchment, restructuring and outsourcing. ENO's traditional role was increasingly seen as financially indulgent by government, Baker recalled, and there had been lobbying from the Royal Opera House at the time to ensure its interests were put first in the allocation of subvention.[82] The new theatre was part of a vision for the 'People's Opera House' in the new century, but it came at a time when the concept of a permanent ensemble of home-grown artists performing high-quality work at affordable prices was becoming financially unacceptable to the government and Arts Council.

*

On 23 January 1997 ENO was accepted into the Stabilisation Pilot Programme on condition that it appoint independent consultants to produce and institute a programme of works, with continued monitoring, in order to ensure that there would be no more borrowings and a break-even budget within its existing grant of £11.5 million. If the company failed to meet these conditions it would lose the stabilisation grant and possibly even the core grant. Company and board representatives were to attend all-day meetings with the stabilisation director. The consultants were funded by the Arts Council.

That same day Baker reported that he had met the Arts Council and did not believe that it had a 'secret agenda' to merge the companies. He nonetheless warned that they had to be realistic in recognising that even with stabilisation funding, ENO's survival was not assured. Baker was aware that the process of the consultants' review would impose considerable strains, but that there was no alternative. Quentin Thompson, Kathryn McDowell, the ACE director of music, David Pratley, ex-ACE, and Caroline Felton were the consultants who were to provide the 'outside invigilation'.[83]

Whether or not ENO's application was accepted, the funds from stabilisation would not start to flow till September 1997, so Marks was advised by Baker to embark on immediate remedial measures and not wait for the consultants' report, in the hope that this would demonstrate that ENO was in charge of its own destiny. There was one chance and one chance only to get the deficit-reduction process right, whatever the 'short-term damage to the long-term position'.[84] McDowell said Allen had agreed with Baker to suspend the feasibility study in relation to the new theatre during the stabilisation process.[85]

Marks was beginning to see the writing on the wall. He later recalled that he believed that the Arts Council's stabilisation conditions, particularly the requirement to budget for three years' standstill grant funding, would lead to long-term decline as well as short-term decimation.[86] On 6 January Marks stated his position clearly to board member Charles Alexander. If he discovered in the next twelve months that there was no possibility of building a new lyric theatre for ENO, he would stay and fight for the company and the artistic ideals in which he believed, however tough the fight. But if he thought that the board of ENO regarded the Contemporary Opera Studio, the Baylis Programme and works that were not mainstream as dispensable, then they would not see him 'for dust'. It would remove the entire purpose for his doing the job.[87]

Marks wrote to Rodric Braithwaite in February, warning that it was not possible to make up the lost Arts Council grant from box-office income. The figures that were realistic were 67 per cent for financial capacity, as recommended by Price Waterhouse, and £1.7-million income from development. Matching artistic policy to financial reality, he said, had a glass ceiling above which there was 'the unfashionable thing known as political will'. He warned that two years after the completion of stabilisation ENO would 'cease to be viable on commercial grounds'.[88] Although Braithwaite agreed that the artistic 'envelope' had to be pushed, he warned that 'if you go bankrupt you cannot realise your artistic vision. In the end you do have to match artistic policy to financial reality.' During his forty years at the Foreign Office, he did not remember the 'political will' argument ever working. It was a mistake to plan on the assumption that the Arts Council was bluffing, and it was essential to plan for a break-even budget.[89]

Although stabilisation seemed, in Paul Daniel's words, 'like a great new dawn', Marks was canny enough to realise that it might be a false one, since there was no recognition of inflation.[90] For the next six months the drafts of the memorandum of understanding went back and forth, with Marks holding out for an inflation-proof grant. Baker recalled that the board took the 'pragmatic view' that without stabilisation money there would be no ENO within a matter of weeks or months and, whatever the contract might say, in practice the whole question would 'most likely be revisited in future years to meet the realities of whatever would be the situation at the time'. On the other hand, he said, Marks took a 'more absolute view' that without the right guarantee from the Arts Council for what he considered adequate core funding, no agreement should be entertained.[91] Daniel believed that Marks, in objecting to the lack of guarantee, appeared to be ungrateful, whereas he had, as it turned out, been 'very astute and on his own'.[92]

Immediate measures were once again needed to prevent insolvency. The Coutts overdraft facility was increased to £4.5 million, and on 4 April ENO received an advance on the 1997/8 grant of £3.5 million.[93] 'Candle end' savings of £100,000 had to be found. It was proposed that Gavin Bryars's *Dr Ox's Experiment* be postponed and replaced by *Don Pasquale*, *Ulysses* by *Mikado* and *The House of the Dead* by *Lady Macbeth*. Miller's *Don Giovanni* would be brought back instead of *The Elixir of Love*.[94]

The stabilisation process was revealing the nature of the problem. On 3 March ACE apologised for not sending a document entitled 'Pilot stabilisation programme "towards a set of stabilisation outcomes". Revised for Technical Assistance Manual version 3.0.' According to this document, ENO had been failing to provide 'self-generated resources or external funding to maintain and renew its physical assets as well as systematically to review its performance against internal targets and external benchmarks' and to examine 'the scope for outsourcing'.[95] 'Strategic Stock-Take Report, Draft Three' was written by Caroline Felton, Quentin Thompson and Michael Bishop, who were technical advisers to the pilot stabilisation scheme. ENO's mission, they wrote, was 'complex and requires interpretation to achieve a balance between potentially conflicting aims; it therefore needs to be supported by policies which clarify this balance for implementation'.

Before ENO could achieve stabilisation, certain key challenges had to be met. Morale in some areas was very low, Felton wrote, and it would be 'vital both to communicate positively and constructively about the stabilisation process and to involve staff, wherever possible, in the identification and planning of change'. The changes required for successful stabilisation, by definition, were likely to be radical and to challenge 'fundamentally some of the constraints on and some of the processes involved in planning and producing opera today'. Unless all members of senior management were willing to consider such changes, and to lead and participate in new thinking, the chances of success were limited.[96]

ENO's budget projection for 1998/9 took into account that the Arts Council grant was at a standstill, while inflation was forecast at 3 per cent. This meant an annual decrease of £750,000 in real terms. Plans assumed a successful stabilisation grant application, without which the company would not be solvent after March

1998. Hopes for additional fundraising of £205,000 were pinned on the new team.[97]

By mid-April the stabilisation consultants had been in the company for two months, during which period there had been four Stabilisation Information Forums. Marks not surprisingly reported to Braithwaite that one of the reasons for fluctuating morale within ENO was that they had become so 'hung up to the point of obsession with financial managerial issues'. He urged that the forthcoming weekend conference at Sarsden – Shaun Woodward's home near Chipping Norton in Oxfordshire – should begin by talking about ENO's artistic mission, with Harewood making the keynote speech.[98]

The last quarter of the season was again mixed. Gluck's *Orpheus and Eurydice* on 3 March was a co-production, designed by the highly successful and very busy American John Conklin. Allison was delighted by the clarity of diction but found the director Martha Clarke's dance redundant for Gluck's formal, emotionally precise music, and regretted the relegation of the chorus, who should have been providing a Greek-style commentary, to the pit. He praised Michael Chance's counter-tenor Orpheus and Lesley Garrett's passionate Eurydice.[99] Canning found Clarke's work 'beautiful and strangely moving'.[100]

David Alden directed Berlioz's *Damnation of Faust*, with Bonaventura Bottone and Louise Winter. It was, in Christiansen's words, 'A mess of tattered dreams and tawdry imaginings' in another 'childish attempt to shock', with transvestites, fascist police, nuns in naughty knickers and 'twitching straight-jacketed lunatics'. Alden, who seemed nonplussed by Berlioz's work, presented an incoherent and muddled account, while the audience was baffled and bored. Elder conducted with the style and shape lacking on the stage. It was, Christiansen said, just like old times, with Elder in the pit and Jonas at the bar.[101]

The public had more pleasure on 5 June from Handel's *L'Allegro il pensero ed il moderato* and the Mark Morris Dance Troupe. Morris's troupe kicked up their heels with the joy of nature, wrote Judith Mackrell in the *Guardian*, while Janice Watson, Susan Gritton and Ian Bostridge sang magnificently under Glover's baton.[102] A well-received but ill-attended revival of *Don Pasquale* ended the season on 25 June. For the year's work, ENO won Olivier Awards for *Die Soldaten* and *Tristan*.

On 2 May New Labour won the general election and Tony Blair became prime minister, appointing Chris Smith Secretary of State for National Heritage. There was no new dawn for ENO, however, as the new chancellor intended to keep a tight rein on public spending, and the next two crucial years for ENO were to see further reductions in real terms of core funding. Baker recalled that in July 1997 he had warned Marks that the incoming Labour administration would not mean that the heavens would open and all would be well.[103]

Hopes were pinned on the ability of Paul Daniel, whose appointment as music director was announced in May, to retrieve ENO's musical standards. He had enjoyed a successful period at Opera North with Nicholas Payne from 1990, where he had been delighted and inspired by the respect for the audience and the resulting trust in the company that Harewood had established in its early days. It was a wrench for him to leave but, urged by Marks, he accepted the challenge.

Daniel, like Marks, was determined to maintain the traditional ENO, but having become embroiled in stabilisation, the battle was just beginning. At the Sarsden Conference on 30–31 May 1997, the board considered the draft memorandum of understanding drawn up with Coopers for the Arts Council. Marks reported to the board that Coopers and Lybrand had been told unequivocally that the company's mission was 'not up for grabs', so they had left it off the 'Technical assistance brief'. Marks told the board that ENO must fight for a level of funding to support implementation of their mission, which would, he believed, be in the order of £13–13.5 million.* The current grant was £11.97 million. Quentin Thomas of Coopers Lybrand would bring the request before the ministry, as it was not within the Arts Council's power to assure such support for ENO. It was hoped that stabilisation funding would be flowing by September 1997.

Marks firmly restated the mission he was determined to fight for, stressing the communication of the English text and vigilance in

* This figure was not achieved until 2000/1.

493

articulation, together with the rebuilding of the ensemble and education. Affordability was being addressed, with the lowest prices in the next season at £2.50 for standby and £5 in the balcony, placing ENO alongside local cinemas. This too would require higher funding.

It was the first time Paul Daniel had addressed the board, and he intentionally focused on the artistic mission: ENO was the company best equipped in the UK to do large works requiring the full ensemble. He was also keen to increase the ensemble of young singers and establish close ties with a handful of established singers.

Marks told the board about the Studio and Baylis/ENO Works, which had made contact with 2,000 people in 1996. They were attractive in ways which had clear 'social added value' of the kind sought by corporate donors, for whom old-style sponsorship was now a thing of the past. There was collaboration between ENO and the Union Dance Company in 1998, when young dancers, musicians and singers gave a version of *Orpheus and Eurydice*. Twelve ENO orchestra members were joining in the *Carmen* project in local schools. The new Labour government claimed that education and youth were amongst its highest priorities, which made the ENO programmes more realisable. Nevertheless, Marks told the board, the management consultants were finding it 'a struggle to tie the ENO Works into the business plan'. Although Baylis and the Contemporary Opera Studio provided a public service and were integral, it was part of the brief that non-income-generating activity had to be cut.

Despite the hostile reception to the feasibility study, Marks had been given the green light to continue with the new theatre development project by Mary Allen and David Pratley, although there was to be no final decision until after stabilisation. The board decided that the company should continue to plan for the Potter's Field site at Tower Bridge, which was available immediately, as Covent Garden had decided not to build a temporary theatre during their redevelopment and Southwark Council were keen.[104]

Mostart therefore presented his five-year plan by outlining the repertoire for the closing years at the Coliseum and before ENO moved into its new purpose-built, two-auditoria theatre. The 'power house' staples were now out of date and a new Graham Vick *Ring* cycle for 1999/2000 was being planned, with some of the new company singers such as Rita Cullis, Anne-Marie Owens and Willard White, and young singers such as Susan Parry. The millennium season would include *The Silver Tassie* and *On the Town*.[105] They were exciting plans – but they were based on the premise that increased funding would be forthcoming.

Then, in the middle of the stabilisation process, the operatic world entered a period of great instability when, in May 1997, Genista McIntosh, the chief executive of Covent Garden, left in controversial circumstances after just four months. The Covent Garden chairman, Lord Chadlington, hurriedly appointed Mary Allen to take her place. The new Secretary of State for National Heritage, Chris Smith, just days into his new job, did not prevent the appointment, although he was concerned about the lack of due process. Allen immediately left the Arts Council so there could be a decent gap before she took up her appointment at Covent Garden – one of the Council's major clients. These events later played a part in the crises of governance at Covent Garden and also at ENO. The House of Commons Select Committee on Culture, Media and Sport decided to look into the appointment, a process that lasted from July to November, as Covent Garden lurched from management crisis to crisis, with Chadlington threatening bankruptcy in late October.[106]

At the Arts Council Graham Devlin took over from Mary Allen as acting secretary general until Peter Hewitt took up the position in 1998. Kathryn McDowell was the music director. Hitherto, Marks had dealt with Mary Allen. It was to prove a difficult period for ENO, which, John Baker later reflected, found itself 'in the tail wind' of Covent Garden's financial crises.[107]

As the season drew to a close, the accumulated deficit was causing great anxiety amongst the board. According to the 1996/7 annual report, it was £3.5 million, which included an operating deficit of £859,000 and further exceptional charges of £804,000 for the year. Baker recalled that they were calling in the auditors at regular intervals to check that they were a going concern. The board met in June, at which time it became clear that without stabilisation or an extension of bank credit the company was not viable. Tensions were growing. In July Braithwaite wrote to Marks to say how much he appreciated what he had done for the company and to sympathise with the burden placed upon him by the bureaucratic requirements of the stabilisation process. There also clearly needed to be a greater focus on development, for which the board as well as management were responsible.[108]

Marks himself was endeavouring to rectify the lapse in development income, telling Braithwaite that the recently appointed director of development, John Ward from the West Yorkshire Playhouse, was creating a new structure with fourteen people under him. He would work out a strategic plan with board members from whom committed leadership was needed. Marks had become 'desperately concerned that ACE has developed such a Byzantine bureaucracy that they have driven all the inspiration and joy out of the business of managing the arts in this country'.[109]

On 17 July the Finance and General Purposes Committee, chaired by Bob Boas in the absence of John Baker and Charles Alexander, learnt that Coutts had agreed to extend the bank facility in the sum of £4 million, even though the Arts Council had not been willing to offer a letter of understanding. They also discussed the fact that the Arts Council had delivered a final and clear message, through Kathryn McDowell, that the stabilisation strategy was to be based on a cash standstill with no indexation over the four years of its implementation. ENO was also required to remain at the Coliseum, although it was not clear to Marks or the board whether there was a ban on all activity relating to a move to a new opera house or not. The board agreed that both paragraphs were 'highly unsatisfactory', and Marks was invited to 'explore their implications further with the Arts Council'.[110] It was decided that a full board meeting should be called one week later.

The refusal to countenance an increase in the core grant in line with inflation had been a bitter blow and had marked the beginning of the end of the battle for Marks. John Baker later recalled that the Arts Council grant went a very long way, but that if ENO had received a further £3 or £4 million it would have prevented further problems quite shortly thereafter.[111]

Paul Daniel's first performance as music director was a new production of *The Flying Dutchman* on 15 September 1997. The *Daily Telegraph* pointed to his informal collarless shirt and jacket, as well as his sharing his first curtain calls with a member of the chorus and the leader of the orchestra, as signs of a resurgence of the People's Opera. *Dutchman* started off the season with a bang. Andrew Porter wrote of the evening's 'enthusiasm, energy, accomplishment and full-blooded singing', despite Norwegian Stein Winge's feeble direction. Willard White was firmly, even grandly voiced, with beauty of tone and a wide range of dynamics. Rita Cullis sang with great generosity and freedom. Porter was in nostalgic mood, feeling that Cullis needed Reggie Goodall to say, 'Don't scream, dear.' Because Winge had made her quite a frumpy Senta – he suggested '(would it be impertinent?) that John Copley show her how to move with dignity'. He harked back to the 1958 Arundell/O'Brien production, 'that season after season used to take our breath away as the phantom ship whirled into view, that made us hold our breath when Senta and the Dutchman locked eyes, motionless'.[112]

Within twenty-four hours of *Dutchman*'s premiere Marks had left ENO. He had returned from his summer holidays and, after further discussion with the board, decided to resign. Harewood believed that Marks had been left 'with no ground to stand on'. The Arts Council was querying what was going on, he later said, and the board had decided not to stand up for him. Harewood added that Marks had had 'very good ideas', but lacked the experience of running an opera company.[113] Braithwaite wrote to Marks in appreciation of his having poured out 'his heart's blood' for ENO. His dedication, determination, artistic ambitions, flair and amazing range of contacts had transformed the company from the low point of 1992/3, 'when it had run out of artistic ideas, reduced the critics to irritated boredom and begun to lose the audience'. It was now 'right back on form', and the audiences had responded accordingly. Nonetheless, even if they managed to 'cobble together a short-term solution', the long term remained murky.[114]

The exact reasons for Marks's departure remain unknown, since Marks and the company entered into a confidentiality agreement. It is perhaps reasonable to speculate that at the heart of Marks's decision to resign was a difference of view between him and the board as to how to secure the company's immediate and longer-term future. Whatever the truth of the situation, the pressures on Marks were clearly extreme and highly stressful, as they were for the board, with the constant threat of insolvency hanging over them.

The Arts Council had not been supportive of Marks, but his

departure did not help ENO as much as it might have. According to Baker, Marks's departure 'loosened the Arts Council's purse strings', but not as much as he had hoped and thought he had been promised. Baker believed that when he reviewed the state of the company with Lord Gowrie at the time of Marks's resignation, he was given a clear indication that an 'enhanced stabilisation award' would be made, and reported this to the board. But this expectation was not in the end realised, as the award finally made was not considered by ENO to be sufficient to secure the company's medium- to long-term financial equilibrium, although it lived to fight another day.[115] The Stevenson debate as to the nature of ENO and its function therefore progressed into another era, under different but ultimately equally vulnerable leadership.

Christiansen in the *Daily Telegraph* reflected that although many people disliked Marks's brusque managerial style, he had a lot of right on his side, there were some good shows in the pipeline and he was 'beginning to find his feet'.[116] Milnes too thought that with his top priorities of winning back audiences and rebuilding company artists, Marks had at least given the impression that two important ENO principles had been reborn. 'The sad thing for Dennis,' Nicholas Payne later said, was that 'the really good things came to fruition in my time'.[117]

John Baker later recalled that throughout the publicly funded period of the history of Sadler's Wells/ENO there had been 'intense and unresolved dilemmas around the conflict of artistic mission versus financial stringency', as well as those of 'artistic independence versus public accountability in return for access to taxpayer monies'. There would always remain, he said, 'irresolvable dilemmas since there is no formula that works for all time. It is a matter of a series of temporal accommodations that will depend on the mood of the times, as well as issues of personal chemistry.'[118]

Marks was unfortunate to find himself fighting his battles on the cusp of the new era. He later reflected that he had been a 'bit player in the last act of a drama at the end of the half century between the Depression and the Big Bang, when the cultural values of the Arts Council under Kenneth Robinson and Arnold Goodman breathed their last'.[119]

# 15

# 1997–2002: Not Entirely Stabilised

After Marks's departure, the Arts Council stabilisation funding was urgently needed to prevent insolvency, since Coutts had extended ENO's overdraft facility only until 30 September.[1] Finance director Michael Woolley had noted in July that ENO could meet its obligations until 31 October, but after that the continued support of the bank could not be taken for granted. The Arts Council had refused to grant a 'letter of understanding', so Coutts were waiting for the outcome of the stabilisation process.[2]

Russell Willis Taylor, who had been ENO's director of development from 1985 to 1989, was the person charged with presenting the new stabilisation application, as acting interim managing director. She immediately set about preparing an interim revised stabilisation strategy, which was to be submitted in two parts. The first, in October 1997, two months after Dennis Marks's departure, was to enable enough funds to be released to maintain the overdraft facilities.

Willis Taylor's report was based on maintaining the ensemble company, the Contemporary Opera Studio and a full-time orchestra of 'symphonic size', for which it was estimated that £8,627,000 would be needed. Of that sum, it was hoped that £5,100,000 would be released immediately to pay off the debt and the remaining amount would be paid during the following eighteen months, as ENO fulfilled certain agreed commitments such as IT development. When the completed strategy was finally submitted, it would include additional funds to 'pump prime' the new artistic programmes. The plan included a more effective development department, to deliver an increase in income of 60 per cent over the next five years.[3]

The stabilisation money was not to be so easily extracted from the Arts Council. After studying her report it paid, in October, not the £5.1 million requested, but £2.5 million, which was an 'exceptional grant towards debt mitigation'.[4] The report stated that in the coming months ENO should translate its vision into a 'coherent artistic strategy and plan'. In the meantime it would take immediate action to implement those '"enabling" elements that would provide short-term financial viability to meet the challenges of their artistic vision'.

Marks had planned a wide range of new shows and revivals for the season. On 20 October Milnes saw Janáček's *From the House of the Dead*, with its twenty named roles, as a tribute to Marks's unfinished work of rebuilding the core ensemble of ENO. The combination of company members and closely associated guests made it an evening of searing intensity, he wrote. A cast that included David Kempster, Robert Brubaker, John Daszak and Andrew Shore all conspired 'to reproduce that sense of spiritual uplift at the heart of the work'. Daniel's direction lovingly recreated Janáček's 'weird sound world, at once so jagged and so intensely lyrical'. Tim Albery replaced Pountney's expressionist WNO production with a cooler but no less harrowing vision. Milnes applauded Daniel's coupling of the Janáček with Mark-Anthony Turnage's *Twice Through the Heart*, a monologue of a wife imprisoned for killing her violent husband. It was, he wrote, like *House of the Dead*, a work of compassion and anger.[5] The evening was an ENO special, in terms of 'its company spirit, its collective energy and force'.[6] Fiona Maddocks urged the public to support the powerful and brave venture so as not to frighten the board into year-round *Toscas*.[7]

*Falstaff*, directed by Matthew Warchus in November, had originated at Opera North in 1996. It was conducted by Oliver von Dohnányi, and was, according to Allison, a true ENO show blazing with Verdian humanity and wit on stage and in the pit. A packed audience hung onto every word of Amanda Holden's translation, which was articulated by a well-integrated cast. Alan Opie's lovable rogue Falstaff led the cast, Rita Cullis was a 'wickedly funny Alice', Sarah Connolly a 'wry, dotty Meg', Catherine Wyn-Rogers an attractive Quickly, Keith Latham a focused Ford, Mary Plazas and Charles Workman Nannetta and Fenton. It was a show that made it quite clear, Allison wrote, what ENO stood for and also showed how far Marks had succeeded in revitalising the ensemble.[8] The 1997/8 season succeeded in achieving a paid attendance of 75 per cent and a surplus of £150,000.

*

In September the Department of National Heritage was renamed the Department of Culture, Media and Sport. The new department had some plans for ENO, which, just a few weeks after Marks's departure, found itself facing yet another proposition of amalgamation with Covent Garden. It was announced by Chris Smith that Richard Eyre, until recently director of the National Theatre, should chair an enquiry into the feasibility of Covent Garden becoming a 'hosting house' for large-scale performance for the opera and ballet companies of Covent Garden and ENO 'as equal partners', as well as the Royal Ballet. Eyre was also to explore how access could be improved by touring and education, which was slightly ironic, given the history and ambitious plans for the Baylis Programme at this time. Eyre's brief included consideration of the future of the rebuilt Sadler's Wells theatre using £36 million of Lottery money. The announcement was made on 3 November, and Eyre would report by May 1998.

There was surprise and anger at the government intervening so directly in Arts Council business, and, it seemed, posing the question in a way that permitted only a limited selection of answers. It rapidly became clear to the Royal Opera House management, once they started considering the practical ramifications, that 'shared housing' would effectively mean the amalgamation of Covent Garden and ENO.* The need to sort out the problems of the opera houses had been under discussion for some time. In July, during the height of the Covent Garden crisis, when Richard Eyre had met Mark Fisher, the Minister for the Arts, he was told that there was a 'need to start again from scratch – abolishing ENO and getting Peter Jonas and Jenny McIntosh to run Covent Garden . . . of the need for hard decisions and the need to be unpopular'.[9]

Having spoken to the chairman of Covent Garden, Lord Chadlington, and John Baker, who received the news of Smith's proposal by telephone, Chris Smith informed Daniel of his plan late on 3 November. 'I left him politely, but in shock,' Daniel later said.

---

* Mary Allen, the Covent Garden chief executive, noted in her diary the impossibility of the component parts of the two companies functioning under one roof, not least because it would reveal the weakness of English-language performance (Mary Allen, *A House Divided*, London: Simon and Schuster, 1998, p. 116).

The pressure on Daniel was intense. He went back to ENO and told Maggie Sedwards the news. Nobody, he recalled, had had any idea what was about to hit them. He was summoned to talk on Radio 4's *Today* programme the following morning, before he had a chance to tell the company.[10]

The Covent Garden chairman responded that it was an interesting proposal. Daniel, however, was up in arms, and immediately found himself leading the campaign against it. Baker and he agreed that it would be better if their concerns were represented by the artistic rather than the 'suited' community. Daniel, Baker later said, did brilliantly.[11] It was indeed his finest hour. Encouraged by the company, he was in fighting mode, rallying the audience to write to their MPs after the evening performance of *From the House of the Dead*. 'It was his Falklands,' Nicholas Payne recalled. 'It dredged out of him reserves I suspect he did not know he had.' The *Guardian* later reported that the DCMS had telephoned him at home to tell him to calm down.[12]

David Dyer, a member of the chorus since 1992, also spoke to the audience, telling them that he was proud to be a member of the ENO family, with its inheritance from Lilian Baylis. That very evening there were, he recalled, a number of children from the Baylis Programme in the house.[13] Making nightly speeches from the stage, Daniel and other members of the company galvanised the public, who responded by sending thousands of letters to Westminster. Mark Elder offered encouragement, recalling his and Harewood's own successful battle against amalgamation in 1979.[14]

ENO soon had powerful allies as opposition to the merger proposal gathered momentum. Some members of the Royal Opera House's board, who were energetically fundraising for Covent Garden's development, were outraged. On 4 November a Conservative MP demanded to know how Chris Smith dared to set up a review with the questions already answered. Smith defended himself by saying it was less a plan than a proposal.[15] There were many articles in the press the following day, including one by an angry Rodney Milnes. It was hogwash, he wrote, to suggest that London could not afford two houses when Paris had four, Berlin three, and Munich two. There had been, he wrote, too much gleeful talk of redundancies, of 'throwing in the bin hundreds of highly skilled craftsmen who over the past 50 years have led to London being recognised as one of the leading operatic centres in the world – and they started from virtually nothing'.[16] If the merger were put into effect, Milnes warned, 'there would be disturbances in St Martin's Lane on the scale of the poll tax riots'.[17]

The news stirred ENO's supporters, who were flocking to the Coliseum in higher numbers. Daniel had many conversations with Eyre. He also recalled making a curtain speech at a packed performance of *Falstaff* in November, when he said that with both Covent Garden and ENO playing to capacity, the public would be the real losers if there was just one house to be shared between the four companies – especially ENO's famous balcony. A few weeks later Daniel invited Chris Smith to ENO to watch a performance with him from his box, where he observed the minister enjoying the huge success the campaign had engendered, with a full house, as well as a fine performance. From that moment he felt that Smith was on the side of ENO.[18] That Christmas Daniel wrote the company a letter in which he mentioned Smith's growing encouragement for ENO and its work, as well as a deluge of support from colleagues all over the world, the media, politicians and especially from audiences, with houses achieving between 95 and 100 per cent capacity.[19]

On 8 February 1998 the appointment of the fifty-three-year-old Nicholas Payne as ENO general director was announced. Baker recalled that the board had set up an interview panel with Daniel as adviser, and interviewed several strong candidates before taking a recommendation to the full board. The Arts Council was kept informed of progress, including the decision to offer the job to Payne.[20]

As requested by the board, Payne had made a presentation for his interview in which he set out the targets for 2000. These included 50/50 grant/self-generated income, the improvement of cash capacity from 65 to 75 per cent and an increase in the average ticket price from £23.50 to £27.50. There should be a 60 per cent increase in private-sector contributions as demanded by the stabilisation agreement. On the artistic side, he intended to employ the best British singers and perform the epic operas that showed ENO at its best, as well as 'stimulating productions of popular classics'. There should be between 160 and 170 performances of sixteen operas, with an average attendance of 2,000 people per performance (i.e. 85 per cent of seats sold).*

Payne had responded positively to his second offer to work at ENO, despite his sadness at leaving Covent Garden, where he had been opera director. The renewed ENO offer was welcome now that Paul Daniel was *in situ* and John Baker was proving to be a good chairman. Payne later said that he believed in opera in the language of the audience and loved the feeling of 'native singers communicating in their native language'. Once he crossed the threshold his commitment to ENO was total. He was to work out his contract with Covent Garden to the following summer but would be privy to ENO's facts and figures and involved in the stabilisation process. Both ENO and the Arts Council were keen to make sure the agreement was something he believed in and to which he had contributed.[21] Payne persuaded Russell Willis Taylor, who loved the Coliseum, to stay on as executive director when he took over.

The press was supportive of the new appointment. Canning pointed out that Opera North had produced shows that were 'intellectually stimulating and entertaining', a good recipe for ENO approaching the millennium. He urged Payne to learn from the box office's delighted response to eminently sensible shows like *The Magic Flute* and *Onegin*, which were achieving between 96 and 101 per cent capacity and 'for which you do not need a degree in the history of modern art and psycho-analysis and/or to be a close friend of the director to understand them'.[22]

Immediately facing Payne was the suggestion being addressed by Eyre that ENO should perform at Sadler's Wells. When he attended his first planning meeting on 13 March 1998, he said that it was essential that any submissions to the Eyre review should stress that ENO's viability depended on being in a theatre that sold on average 2,000 tickets per night. A season at a smaller theatre such as Sadler's Wells would be very expensive for the company. Sedwards pointed out that Sadler's Wells was a notoriously difficult house to fill and that ENO rarely played to less than 1,500 a night. An early exercise undertaken by Payne had shown clearly that a month-long season at Sadler's Wells would entail a loss of about £400,000.[23]

* By the 1999/2000 season there were 181 performances of nineteen operas, and average prices had reached £27.20.

The only basis on which performances at Sadler's Wells would be feasible, Payne later pointed out, would be if a smaller company were employed. It was not cost-effective to employ an orchestra of eighty and a chorus of sixty if the company was putting on a chamber opera such as *Punch and Judy*.[24*] Neither Payne nor Daniel was working on such a model, nor as yet was the board. Their united front was crucial in maintaining the existing model.

In robust manner, Payne was planning a strong 1999/2000 season, when Covent Garden was to reopen after its redevelopment. His idea was to survey four centuries of opera, from Monteverdi to Turnage. There must be a roster of first-class directors, more new productions and a 'statement about the significance of opera in the twenty-first century'.[25] In April Daniel announced the setting up of a young singers programme. Thanks to Marks's initiative, there were now twenty-one company principals on salary, including Christine Rice, Christopher Maltman, Sarah Connolly and Toby Spence. The revitalised ensemble, he said, would drive the repertory.[26]

The programme continued to be interesting. In May David McVicar and Tanya McCallin set *Manon* in a segment of a bullring grandstand. Milnes, an admirer of Massenet, was delighted by the 'vindication' of *Manon*, which revealed 'the old wizard's sheer theatrical know-how'. It was possible almost to see the fleas and smell the soiled underwear in the set and costumes, which restored a Hogarthian element to the piece. Rosa Mannion was on sparkling form and Paul Daniel displayed an 'easy precision and control of dynamics'.[27]

In June Gavin Bryars's delayed *Doctor Ox's Experiment*, from the Jules Verne novel, was slow-moving and, for many critics, dull. Porter called it 'earnest, lugubrious and slow', while Canning thought it a triumph.[28] Although Marks had been forced during the stabilisation process to delay it, the opera came in 10 per cent above budget. *Carmen* also exceeded its high budget. The box office was

---

* Mary Allen in her diary recorded a conversation on 12 March with Cameron Mackintosh, impresario and owner of seven West End theatres, during which he said that ENO should return to Sadler's Wells and that the Royal Opera House should not only house the Royal Opera Company but also host orchestral, operatic and solo concerts. All three companies would have a single management and a single board (Allen, *A House Divided*, p. 269).

doing better than in the previous season, which was not surprising, given that Covent Garden had been closed for restoration since July 1997.

Eyre's report was published on 30 June. The night before, he was invited to No. 10 Downing Street, where he told Prime Minister Blair that the arts needed an extra £60 million. His report focused on the worth, need and effect of government subsidy and urged that the 'attritional effect of a number of years of standstill funding be reversed'. To achieve a stable ecology in the performing arts, he stressed, adequate funds for revenue support must be secured.

As far as ENO and Covent Garden were concerned, Eyre totally rejected the one-house solution. Access would be reduced as there were not enough alternative venues, touring was too expensive and, above all, ENO and the Royal Opera would lose their identities. The closure of Covent Garden and the ENO audience's fierce loyalty to the Coliseum, revealed during his investigation, showed that both companies needed their own homes. By closing one of the venues, he wrote, 'we would acknowledge that we have lost the fight to ensure that opera and ballet are not just for the middle-class, middle-aged man from the Home Counties; we would confirm that it's not worth the effort trying to change that'.[29] Contrary to the findings of the Stevenson report, Eyre believed that it was still worth trying to widen opera's appeal, that it was possible to grow audiences by growing the work, as had been demonstrated by Birmingham Royal Ballet and Opera North.

Eyre's advocacy of the Baylis heritage was uncompromising. Access to the arts was the rationale for subsidy, he declared, adding:

It is the enduring belief in the civilising benefits that the arts bestow on a nation that has nourished the fertile landscape that we enjoy today, and which has allowed this country to thrive as a cultural force. The arts enrich our lives, and it is the birthright of all this country's citizens to be able to fulfil their creative potential as participants and spectators.[30]

Eyre also pointed out that the British taxpayer was getting good value for money. The Royal Opera House subsidy for 1998/9 was £14.4 million, ENO's a fraction under £12 million, while La Scala's was £34 million, the Berlin Staatsoper's £30.7 million and the Hamburg Staatsoper's £28.6 million.

Although Eyre should have laid to rest once and for all the suggestion of one house for the companies, or a reduced role for ENO, it was such a long-standing and recurring theme that it was unlikely to go away. Paul Daniel later said, 'We had won the battle, but the war went inexorably on.' The idea had only been put 'to sleep for a while', John Baker later commented.[31]

After more work by Payne, Maggie Sedwards and Guus Mostart, with Caroline Felton providing some 'methodology' or jargon, part two of the stabilisation report was submitted in June 1998, shortly before Payne officially took up his post. As a result of its acceptance, a £9.2-million stabilisation grant was confirmed in September 1998. It was to be paid in two instalments, £4.5 million immediately in October 1998 and £4.7 million the following year, subject to certain milestones having been reached.

After much deliberation with Willis Taylor and searching questions from the Arts Council's Stabilisation Committee, Payne repeated Marks's stricture that the stabilisation process had demonstrated conclusively that the level of grant had to be re-examined and adjusted to ensure that ENO did not re-enter financial crisis. He did not, however, make this a condition and it was agreed that the issue would be addressed after the approval of stabilisation.[32] The trouble with five-year plans, Payne later reflected, was that it was impossible to predict what would happen that far ahead. Although it should be possible to predict what would happen within eighteen months, he did not think that financial planning was worth the paper it was written on beyond three years – a point with which the board agreed.[33]

Payne officially started work at ENO at the end of the 1997/8 season. His first task was to welcome Eyre's report at the end of June 1998, when he took the opportunity to reiterate that he was comfortable with ENO staying at the Coliseum. In an interview with Rupert Christiansen he talked about access, education, dance, limited touring and value for money. Above all, he saw his challenge as to entertain and stimulate, to educate and delight. He reported on the rich 1998/9 season that he had inherited from Marks, when ENO would be the main provider of opera in London while Covent Garden was closed. Indeed, by 10 September the Royal Opera House was in crisis, with the threat of total suspension of all its work during the redevelopment, as well as the dismissal of its orchestra and chorus.

Payne gave a feeling that an enthusiastic and confident hand was on the artistic rudder. It also seemed to be a time of greater optimism financially. With the debt about to be finally cleared by the stabilisation grant, and with the box office improving, it was possible to look and plan forward.[34] He told Andrew Clements that he believed that it was necessary to shake and 'tease the audience while responding to their needs'. Although productions should have 'attitude', he thought that some of the 'power house' productions had been 'tyrannised by design'. He stressed that the Coliseum was a matchless site, and that it was a precondition of ENO's financial viability that its theatre should be the size of the Coliseum. Its 2,358 seats meant it was a large house, but it was friendly and welcoming. He also recalled the glory days – 'the ability to do epic rep'.[35]

Payne's buoyant public optimism hid his doubts about the long-term efficacy of the Coliseum. He remained unconvinced that it was an opera house in the way that Covent Garden and the Grand Theatre Leeds were. While he thought that Matcham's 'fantastic sight lines' made the Coliseum a great dance theatre, it was too wide, its pit too broad and open for opera. In the centre stalls it was often difficult to hear the words. This, he believed, was going to be his biggest challenge. Opera in English, which was their 'unique selling point', would be under pressure, because ENO's singers were finding it difficult to be intelligible. The pressure for surtitles was 'an inexorable historical wave' which he would do his utmost to resist.[36]

The start of the Payne/Daniel era was greeted by John Allison with appreciation for an excellent *Rusalka* revival on 8 September.[37] There were more fine revivals originally planned by Marks and Mostart, including Pountney's 1987 *Hansel and Gretel* in October, and in November Miller's 1987 *Barber of Seville*, which did very well with the attraction of Lesley Garrett. Payne thanked the box office for their hard work: although the targets had not quite been reached, they had been set very high.[38]

The new productions of the autumn and winter season had also been planned by Marks and Mostart, including, on 11 September, a controversial staging of *Otello* directed by David Freeman. It was set in a Famagusta military encampment with surveillance towers and radar antennae, on the Green Line between Greek- and Turkish-controlled Cyprus. According to Milnes, the translation and designs of the artist and composer Tom Phillips were carefully thought out, and a strong cast was aided with consideration by Paul Daniel. Susan Bullock was a beautifully sung Desdemona, David Rendall an Otello with a trumpety top and a 'steady stream of hon-eyed tone'.[39] Robert Hayward was a convincingly sinister Iago in a green beret.

In November Francesca Zambello's *Boris Godunov*, conducted by Daniel, showcased the ensemble strength of the company as well as the essential atmosphere of the work, if not quite capturing the heroic scale of ENO's classic shows. It was designed by Hildegard Bechtler and Nicky Gillibrand with fast-flowing stage pictures. Its fine cast included John Tomlinson's doomed Boris, John Connell's eloquent Pimen, Robert Tear's smirking Shuisky and John Daszak's moving Grigory. Every member of the chorus added to what was a stirring company show.[40]

In February 1999 Milnes thought that Nikolaus Lehnhoff's pro-duction of *Parsifal*, together with the poetic lighting of Wolfgang Göbbel, redeemed the work by playing down the elements of Christian symbolism and racial purity, focusing instead on Wagner's intimations of Buddhism. Lehnhoff created a wasteland world, with Kim Begley's vibrantly sung Parsifal a dreadlocked noble savage and Kathryn Harries's Kundry an unsettlingly erotic figure. In keep-ing with the production, Elder approached the work as drama and not as ritual, carefully balancing orchestra and an augmented cho-rus in superb form.[41] Gwynne Howell was a masterly Gurnemanz. Christiansen missed the spiritual journey to redemption, while Canning considered it politically sanitised.[42]

The future was looking positive for ENO. As the year ended, Payne's plans for a season celebrating 400 years of Italian opera in the autumn of 2000 were progressing. At a Production Committee meeting Payne reported that he had encountered a surprising amount of enthusiasm for the idea. There would be eight or nine new productions, with Lazaridis the designer-in-chief. Changeovers would be limited to one and a half hours and each production would have its own director, costumes and lighting.[43]

\*

Meanwhile, the wider arts community was increasingly disappointed by New Labour, a feeling articulated by Doris Lessing in a letter to *The Times* on 11 November 1998. The money being poured into the white elephant of the Millennium Dome, she wrote, could transform the arts. The theatre was dying and literary figures were furious that the Dome was to be a book-free zone.

There was, however, a positive shift in government policy that winter. The minister of the DCMS, Chris Smith, after the stringent spending controls of Labour's first year in office, managed to prise a 17 per cent increase in arts funding out of the Treasury. On 17 December the government announced an increase in the Arts Council's grant-in-aid from £189.6 million to £218.9 million for 2000/1 and to £243.7 million for 2001/2. The Royal Shakespeare Company gained most with £12.7 million – a 25 per cent increase. There would also be substantial increases for the National Theatre, whose subsidy would be £15.7 million with an increase of 7.6 per cent the following year. Orchestras and galleries were beneficiaries as were the regional theatres, whose existence had been threatened by the erosion of their grants. When music director Bernard Haitink resigned in protest to save his orchestra at the Royal Opera House after it had been threatened with disbandment to cut costs, Chris Smith had agreed that Covent Garden would receive three-year funding as part of its 'recovery' programme on reopening. It was granted a 24 per cent increase of £5 million a year.

ENO was in a special position: while still receiving the stabilisation money, the uplift in its core grant for 1999/2000 would be just 3 per cent, to just over £12.5 million, with a one-off extra amount of £300,000 for programming. Management felt that it could not make a fuss about its inequitable treatment in relation to the other national companies – especially the Royal Opera House, which had now been put on a sounder long-term financial footing – because it would have seemed ungrateful in the light of the stabilisation grant.

With Covent Garden still closed, ENO's box office was doing well. At a production meeting on 11 March 1999, Payne said that attendance was the best for eleven years, with Miller's 1987 *Barber* 24 per cent above budget. The development director, John Ward, said that the development income targets had also been exceeded, because ENO's work was outstanding and individuals, trusts and companies wanted to support the company. He hoped they would stay with ENO when Covent Garden reopened in its 'fantastic new building'.[44]

The next new show – Boito's *Mephistopheles*, planned by Guus Mostart and directed by Ian Judge – was described by Clements as a worthless opera and a waste of money in what was a seemingly extravagant production.[45] 'Kitsch and camp,' said Maddocks. 'Twaddle,' said Milnes.[46] Robert Carsen's production of the Handel/Congreve *Semele* from Aix 1996 was staged as a bawdy erotic comedy – with references to contemporary royalty – and a luscious Rosemary Joshua more secure than ever and singing with terrific charm and abandonment. John Mark Ainsley was also excellent.[47]

Phyllida Lloyd's *The Carmelites*, again planned by Marks, was an exemplary and riveting staging built around five remarkable singers: Josephine Barstow as Mother Marie, Joan Rodgers as Blanche, Rita Cullis as Mme Lidoine, Elizabeth Vaughan as Mme de Croissy and Susan Gritton as the young novice. Daniel conducted with 'evangelical passion'. Michael Kennedy described the sixty-four-year-old Vaughan's harrowing portrayal of the dying de Croissy as one of the most moving and powerful ENO performances for a long time.[48]

The 1998/9 season made a surplus on continuing operations of £379,000, according to the annual report, with paid attendance at 82 per cent capacity. The box office had risen by 5 per cent to £7.4 million, sponsorship and donations were up to £1,881,000, while costs of production and performance had risen by 9 per cent to £14.1 million. Payne hoped to continue Marks's work of strengthening the ENO family, signing up Rodgers, Bostridge, Rolfe Johnson, Amanda Roocroft and John Mark Ainsley as guests for the following year. Singers were thinking of three-year commitments in order to lead less peripatetic lives.

Guus Mostart left ENO in April 1999, after which the post of director of artistic administration and planning lapsed. John Berry remained as casting director. The first new production of Payne's first fully planned season was Weber's 1821 *Der Freischütz*, last performed by the company in Byam Shaw's 1966 production. It opened on 10 September. Musically it was a triumph for Elder, with John Daszak as Max and Alwyn Mellor as Agathe. 'If only it were possible to pass over Pountney's production in silence,' wrote

Milnes. Fiona Maddocks, too, felt constrained, writing that so dismal, chaotic and overburdened with notions was the production that it pre-empted the principal aim of criticism, which was not to pour scorn.[49]

In November Payne brought David McVicar, to whom he had given his first job at Opera North in 1993, to direct ENO's first production of Handel's *Alcina*. McVicar's style, Clements wrote, was 'visually rich, flamboyant', occasionally flippant, but at the same time emotionally vulnerable. It was 'more about people than ideas' and was never less than intelligent and was 'a refreshing change from the concept-ridden world of the 1980s and 1990s'.[50] Thirty-two-year-old McVicar described the first act of *Alcina* as a world of 'amoral chaos, with lots of cross-dressing'. In the second 'everyone starts to examine themselves'. His production was enchanting and true to life, with Michael Vane's inventive sets and Sue Blane's dazzling high Georgian costumes. Amanda Holden's crisp and witty new translation added speed and sparkle.[51] With Mackerras conjuring up a 'big yet authentic Handelian sound', it was described as a serious ENO event.[52] The excellent results of ENO's recent nurturing of company principals were recognised. Sarah Connolly's Ruggiero confirmed her as a star of the baroque firmament. Joan Rodgers in a series of fabulous wigs and dresses sang with pure and liquid tone in the title role.[53]

In January 2000 ENO learnt that the anticipated rebasing of the grant – requested as part of stabilisation – would not materialise for 2000/1. Payne made great efforts to reduce the cost of the season, including the removal of Jonathan Miller's *Cavalleria rusticana* and *Pagliacci*. Despite his endeavours, there was still an anticipated deficit of £400,000, which the board and the Arts Council agreed to allow and which would be paid off by ENO in future seasons.[54]

At the beginning of the year Payne wrote an upbeat but serious letter to the company, thanking them for their contribution to the successes of the last century. While trying to be non-confrontational, he was honest about the sacrifices that would be needed in the new millennium. Warning of difficulties ahead, he urged that it was more important than ever to show quiet confidence in ENO's values and standards and not become defensive or appear stubborn. Although the slight uplift in the grant was disappointing in relation to the quantum increase for Covent Garden, he pointed out the extra

£300,000 ENO had received for 2000/1 in 'recognition of the particular needs of a highly innovative programme over the coming
year'. It was no longer possible to gamble with deficits, he
warned. The new house agreements would have to recognise the
need for other media and achieve greater flexibility without
exploitation.

Competition resumed when Covent Garden reopened on 2
December, but ENO was more than a match for it. The long-
awaited world premiere of *The Silver Tassie* was on 16 February
2000. Turnage's first full-length, large-scale opera was an auspicious start to the new millennium for ENO. Canning wrote in
*Opera* that the great enthusiasm of *Tassie*'s first-night audience
called to mind the rapture and enthusiasm that had greeted *Peter
Grimes* forty-five years earlier. Turnage's and Holden's transformation of Sean O'Casey's 1928 anti-war play had Brittenesque resonances for Canning, with its 'sense of dramatic pacing', its
'symphonic' use of the orchestra and its lyrical, singable vocal style.
Gerald Finley gave a deeply moving and gloriously sung portrayal
of Harry Heegan, the 'vigorous, handsome, swaggering, confident
football hero' transformed into the tortured, wheelchair-bound ex-
soldier.

Canning welcomed Turnage's and Holden's great achievement,
applauding its clarity and audibility. In Bill Bryden's respectful and
clear production, the opera and its participants spoke with great
immediacy to the wildly appreciative audience. He praised Sarah
Connolly, who sang the unsympathetic Susie 'with sumptuous
tone'.[55] The theatre critic Michael Billington wrote in the
*Guardian* that Turnage's richly diverse score and Holden's 'won-
drously taut libretto' had given O'Casey's play a tragic unity that
spoke urgently to the heart.[56] Payne gave credit to Marks on the
opening night.

On 23 March Richard Jones's unsparing production of *Pelleas
and Melisande* was described by Milnes as 'one of the great opera
productions of our time'. Melisande was sung by Joan Rodgers
with 'heart-stopping beauty'. Daniel's conducting also seemed to
Milnes 'just right, with a keen sense of compassion for suffering
humanity and the wounds it will persist in inflicting on itself'.[57]
Clements loved the production's 'emotional truth and dramatic
concision', in which the tragedy unfolded remorselessly.[58] Payne

himself later described this *Pelleas* as 'as near perfect as you can get in this imperfect world'.[59]

John Adams's *Nixon in China*, premiered in Houston in 1987, ended the season with a bang on 7 June. Harewood had spotted its potential for ENO five years earlier, writing to Dennis Marks on 19 March 1992 to say that it was 'highly representative of an operatic development and was highly enjoyable – which of course is not necessarily to say either long lasting or the highest art'. It was, he wrote, 'very well composed dramatically, full of contrast and very easy to listen to and to see . . . both satirical and highly serious'.[60] Allison found John Adams's music, Daniel's conducting and Peter Sellars's production a stunning combination, describing the opera and Mark Morris's choreography of the ballet of the *Red Detachment of Women* as 'grand opera meets Broadway'.[61] There were strong dramatic performances from Robert Brubaker as Mao, David Kempster as Chou En-lai, Judith Howarth as Mme Mao and Janis Kelly as Mrs Nixon. James Maddalena repeated his 'unnervingly faithful' Nixon from Houston, singing expressively with moving dignity.[62] All critics felt that the thirteen-year wait had been worthwhile and that the work had lost nothing of its potency during the interim. It had been 'thrilling', Payne later recalled, to have had to delay the start of both *Nixon* and *Silver Tassie* because there were people queuing round the block.[63]

The 1999/2000 financial year left ENO with a healthy surplus of £352,000 on continuing operations, partially as a result of the slight uplift in the Arts Council's core grant and despite a slight decline in the box office of 2 per cent – £181,000. Audiences had averaged 74 per cent.

The new editor of *Opera*, John Allison, who had taken over from Milnes in January, celebrated the return to form of ENO, which was 'once again offering work like nowhere else – original and exciting'. In particular he pointed to the throngs of people attending the last night of *The Silver Tassie* as a sign of revival and warned the Treasury to take note of where the 'really deserving work' was taking place.[64]

With the plan for stabilisation agreed, the board had reverted to the question of the future location of the company. According to Baker, it had been implicit in the Arts Council's approach to stabilisation that ENO should remain in St Martin's Lane at a restored Coliseum.[65] Payne and the board had decided to proceed with the restoration as soon as possible after Covent Garden reopened. As Payne later commented, 'had the restoration project been planned earlier in the life of the Lottery, ENO might have expected an ACE Lottery grant in the region of £30 million',* but in fact only £12 million was offered, which meant that ENO had to lower its sights to a much-curtailed scheme.[66] The board reviewed their options against this background and in June 2000 the restoration plans were announced.

The plan now had to settle for phase one of what had been envisaged as a two-part programme; this would include front-of-house improvements for the public and cover health and safety demands but no backstage work. The cost would be £41.2 million, financed by £9.2 million Heritage funding for the restoration of the façade, the £12-million Lottery grant and the balance from private funding. Having decided to do one part well, it was sad for Payne that resources were not sufficient to improve the backstage set-up: 'To embark on phase two, the backstage improvements, would have needed the acquisition of some adjacent properties and a budget of virtually the same again, making a total for the two phases not so very far short of the £85 million projected for Dennis Marks's new opera house scheme earlier in the 1990s.' It was a defining moment for ENO, as the Coliseum would remain a theatre in which it was impossible to run a repertory company with cost-efficient change-overs. It also meant that much energy, especially that of the board, became focused on the building rather than the company, with serious consequences.

Architects Renton Howard Wood and Levin's specialist division, The Arts Team, were experts in the restoration of Matcham buildings. They were to add 40 per cent more public space, new stairs to the basement, a bigger Dutch Bar, and new lavatories. Board member and chartered surveyor Christopher Jonas was to oversee the redevelopment project, representing the company with the consultants and the contractors with great skill and success. Morrison at *The Times* greeted the announcement with pleasure – down to the details of the restoration of Matcham's purple drapes.

* Covent Garden had already received a £78.5-million grant, and the National Theatre over £30 million for its makeover.

At the start of the 2000/1 season Payne wrote an article in *Opera* which exuded confidence and a sense of direction and purpose. His sense of personal enjoyment and enthusiasm lit up the piece as he highlighted the previous year's achievements: *The Silver Tassie*, *Pelleas*, Alan Opie and Peter Rose in *Ernani*, Orla Boylan and Anthony Michaels-Moore in *Onegin*, *Nixon in China*, ENO's orchestra and chorus 'raising the roof' with *Peter Grimes* at the Snape Maltings for the first time, Mark Morris's dancers and Sarah Connolly sublime in *Dido and Aeneas*. The next season promised more excitement with the Italian season in the autumn celebrating the development of Italian opera since the seventeenth century and exploring how the legacy was interpreted for the present day. Lazaridis's single basic set would be a metaphor for destruction and renewal.

'We remain predominantly an ensemble company,' Payne declared, where no individual was more important than another. The number of singers had now reached thirty, including seven who were part of the Jerwood Young Singers Programme.* The Coliseum invited epics and they were to build a new *Ring* for the new decade, replacing the Porter translation with a new one by Jeremy Sams. Handel, Purcell and Britten would take their rightful place at the centre of ENO planning.

The three-month Italian opera season opened on 18 September with ENO's first production of Puccini's *Manon Lescaut*. Payne – supported by the board – was keen to show 'clear blue water' between ENO and Covent Garden in its first full season after its redevelopment. With eight new productions it was an expensive project, but one to which the Arts Council had given its blessing. Payne was making the statement that Covent Garden was 'swish and plush' and that ENO was presenting 'rough theatre' intended to take audiences on a journey. The production budget was £800,000, to which Payne had added a secret contingency, knowing that Lazaridis, who had argued for £1 million, might go above budget.[67] The main structure of the set, with its scaffolding walk-way around the front of the dress circle, proved to be expensive and technically very demanding, as well as limiting for some of the directors who were presented with the ready-made framework.[68]

* A programme of development and support for young singers at ENO designed by the casting director John Berry in 1999.

Ted Murphy also recalled that the technical production managers were not given the opportunity to express their misgivings about the technical problems in time to prevent overspends.[69]

Artistically the season was a mixed endeavour, with some productions proving more successful than others. Keith Warner's *Manon Lescaut* was one of the less successful, despite a fine cast that included Nina Stemme as Manon, singing with good diction and beautiful tone, and Martin Thompson as Des Grieux, hurling out notes with confidence and ease. The next night brought the season to life with Steven Pimlott's *Coronation of Poppea*. He used Lazaridis's rampway with restraint, placing the orchestra behind the action so that every word of Christopher Cowell's racy new translation was audible. Audacious direction of David Walker's Nero was carried off admirably. It was, according to Michael Tanner, an exhilarating, 'imaginative, colourful, funny, upsetting production'.[70] Alice Coote as Poppea, with her 'voluptuous voice, gamine profile and strong stage temperament', revealed her enormous talent, wrote Andrew Clark. Tim Albery's production of Leoncavallo's *La bohème*, which opened in November, presented an interesting rarity.

Clark complained that there was no opera by a living composer, such as Berio's *La vera storia*.[71] Payne, however, had preferred to create a triple bill consisting of Dallapiccola's *The Prisoner* partnered by Berio's *Folk Songs* and Nino Rota's score of the 1954 Fellini film *La Strada*, involving thirty children from Westminster schools who were participating in the Baylis Programme. It opened on 17 November. Neil Armfield directed with an indeterminate setting. Susan Bullock and Peter Coleman-Wright sang and acted superbly in the Dallapiccola, conducted by Richard Hickox.[72] Edward Seckerson saw the disparate works of the triple bill as a powerful and moving tale of two worlds, childhood and adulthood, and thought it an overwhelming drama in three acts.[73]

Pountney's *Nabucco* and *The Turk in Italy*, however, disappointed. Lesley Garrett had pulled out of the latter show, which affected sales, although Judith Howarth sang very well. Lazaridis's protruding platform 'disenfranchised a chunk of the audience', Payne recalled, which resulted in lots of complaints.[74]

The Italian season ended on 9 December with the Verdi *Requiem*. Andrew Clark described the season as an honourable failure, arguing that it lacked a theme, dramaturgical ideas and intellectual backbone. The only link between the random choice of operas, he felt, would have been Italian, which was lost in translation, while the other possible unifying feature, Lazaridis's 'environment', was artificial. Only *The Coronation of Poppea* was worthy of further airings, but because of Lazaridis's set it could not be revived.[75]

Payne later pointed out that his intention had not been to make a dramaturgical point but to show the variety of Italian opera and to 'shake the box'. He had chosen Lazaridis not for his intellect but because he was a man 'of theatrical instincts'. Lazaridis's plans for a huge, off-white canvas curtain to be raised to the ceiling, as if turning the pages of a book, had been abandoned when a large chunk of ceiling fell into the empty orchestra pit when it was raised.[76]

After the Italian season Payne nonetheless held a post-mortem, which revealed a general feeling that there had been huge effort and not all that had come from it was worthwhile. 'Andrew's criticism, though harsh, was not unfair,' he admitted, but it had 'had its excitement and many had enjoyed the journey'.[77] Even Clark had recognised that the public were enthused and the principals stimulated.

The season had also made an unusual and inspiring contribution to the Baylis legacy in the work of the Baylis education programme. Payne, who recognised that ENO was an educational charity, fully supported the team Marks had brought in to run the programme and encouraged its head, Steve Moffitt, to use the company's resources. This coincided with the Charity Commissioners tightening up on the charitable status of organisations such as ENO, and 'educational spending' became vital for maintaining charitable status.

Building on Marks's structure, and with the support of an enthusiastic board, Payne ensured that the programme would receive £513,000 whether its fundraising activities were successful or not. It was hoped that this would go up to £750,000 over the next few years. As well as continuing to run many excellent programmes in schools based on the repertoire at the Coliseum, three major projects were developed for the millennium year, including two related to the Italian season. One was the *La Strada* involvement, with the schoolchildren taking part in six weeks of rehearsal under the supervision of the Baylis team as well as the director, Neil Armfield. The lively children, most of whom were unused to being in a theatre, were selected for their talent rather than any previous training. They were gradually integrated into the show as well as the house. The second project connected with the Italian season, in collaboration with the Children's Music Workshop, resulted in two performances of the Verdi *Requiem* by 270 nine- to eleven-year-olds at the Coliseum, with seventeen players from the orchestra and Paul Daniel conducting. Some music written by the children was integrated into the score.

The most ambitious project of all was the community opera *The Palace in the Sky*, three performances of which were staged at the Hackney Empire in early November 2000. In 1996 composer Jonathan Dove had proposed writing a community opera to reflect cultural diversity in Hackney, which was taken up by Christina Coker of the Hackney Music Trust as a millennium project, and Sarah Hickson. Together with the ENO Studio – the renamed Contemporary Opera Studio – Steve Moffitt and Alice King-Farlow took over the staging of the project, shortly after they had moved to Shoreditch. With librettist Nick Dear, Dove wrote an opera for a cast of 350 professional and amateur singers, Turkish saz players, a brass band, African drums, Hackney youth steel and jazz orchestras, and Hackney's Centre for Young Musicians and the ENO orchestra.*

Dove, with the involvement of the principal singers, including the tenor Robert Tear, developed his ideas in local schools and with community music groups. In the summer of 2000 young people and their families from schools across the borough took part in workshops. The production, directed by Jo Davies and conducted by Stuart Stratford, used every corner of the theatre and its boxes, with different groups performing in each area – the main action taking place on the stage. The result was uplifting, vibrant and energetic and had a very positive effect for music and community spirit in Hackney and for ENO.

Steve Moffitt, originally an educator from the theatre, said that he learnt from his time at ENO that – as Baylis had known – 'people connect to the human voice, kids, adults, whoever'. Beyond the narrative, music had an intangible, extra power to communicate, and by making use of every component of the company – technical,

* Funding for development was provided by Anderson Consulting, through Vernon Ellis, and business advice was provided by Jim Peers at the Baring Foundation, which also funded the commission.

orchestra, chorus and administration – he was once again connecting the company with the community. The Baylis Programme continued to be, in Moffitt's words, a 'health check' by which ENO could revisit its moral values.[78]

Restoring the core repertory was proving elusive. In November 2000 ENO had announced that Payne and Daniel were to direct *Il trovatore* for the Verdi centenary in 2001, having failed to engage three directors who had been approached. It was an unfortunate decision. Payne's previous experience consisted of two productions in the mid-1970s at the Oxford Playhouse and *The Pearl Fishers* for Reading University. It opened on 9 April 2001. Milnes passed briskly over the production to speak warmly of Daniel's musical preparation and his mastery of the relentless rhythm of the score, despite Julian Gavin deploying a 'can belto' style rather than a more lyrical one. Sally Burgess, he wrote, 'would grace any opera house in the world'.[79] Some critics were harsher, suggesting that the lack of definition of characters, the ragged ends of scenes and the histrionic poses suggested 'unpractised hands'.[80]

Despite the severe criticism of the production, *Il trovatore* fared well at the box office.[81] It had, however, been an ill-judged venture. Baker later recalled the consternation of both singers and ENO technical staff during rehearsals. It was, in his view, the first false step Payne had taken – a 'dip' in what had otherwise been a sustained period of excellence and energetic optimism within the company.[82]

After *Il trovatore* came David Sawer's *From Morning to Midnight*, which was received with enthusiasm on 27 April. It was, wrote Milnes, an astounding new opera coming so soon after *The Silver Tassie*. Sawer's work revealed his love for Debussy and Ravel and had some good Prokofiev-style 'grotesquerie'.[83] Based on the German expressionist play by Georg Kaiser, the opera had a large canvas and cast but, Clements thought, a slender story chock-full of incident, whose characters lacked inner life.[84] Richard Jones provided another brilliant and very funny production. On 15 June the *Lady Macbeth* revival was every bit as impressive as ten years earlier, with Mark Wigglesworth's galvanising conducting.

Payne's next choice – the production of *Don Giovanni* by the Catalan director Calixto Bieito – proved to be the most controversial of his time at ENO. It reached, according to Michael Kennedy, 'a new nadir in vulgar abuse of a masterpiece'.[85] The soft-spoken Bieito had grown up in Franco's Spain and was educated in a severely repressive Jesuit school in Barcelona, where he had received a rigorous cultural education as well as severe physical punishment. Central to his language was sex and violence, and he set *Don Giovanni* in club culture with lashings of drug-filled sex and violence, with Giovanni ritually knifed to death at the end by those whom he has wronged. He believed that he had placed the opera in a world reflecting 'the melancholy and the illness' in current society – 'the nihilism of the modern world'.[86] Black humour was in the tradition of his country, he explained, making reference to Buñuel and Dalí, Picasso and Velásquez.[87]

The first-night audience on 31 May did not appreciate the references and booed heartily. The critics mourned Mozart and da Ponte. Milnes called it 'yawn-inducingly tedious' and was not amused by Donna Anna and Ottavio simulating copulation while she tried to sing 'Non mi dir', or the load of beer-swilling, coke-sniffing yobs and slappers, horrible misogyny and brutal cuts. Everyone 'scuttled out after the booing as fast as possible in a state of embarrassment at anything so crass and irrelevant to ENO's function hitting the stage'.[88]

Payne was unrepentant. He considered *Don Giovanni* one of the best things ENO had done, later describing it as 'a violent Spanish drug-fuelled night in downtown Barcelona'.[89] Paul Daniel was equally positive. Bieito came, he said, from a chaotic theatrical tradition and was in some ways 'more in tune with the improvisatory drama that Mozart himself envisaged'.[90] In his annual review Payne admitted that the production had 'suffered from excess energy and its fiercely contemporary vision had upset some of the traditional audience'.[91]

With the next production – David McVicar's *Rape of Lucretia* on 21 June – Payne and Daniel revived ENO's connection to Britten and created a relationship with the Aldeburgh Festival's Jonathan Reekie which was designed to facilitate productions of Britten operas for both organisations.* Critics were unanimous that Christopher Maltman was a 'ferocious, magnetic' Tarqinius, and

---

* The Britten Estate supported the production, which would be seen both at Aldeburgh and in London.

Sarah Connolly a restrained, moving and beautifully sung Lucretia.[92] John Mark Ainsley sang with searing intensity and beauty of tone, Orla Boylan with generous voice. Paul Daniel conducted the twelve instrumentalists with audacious extremes of tempo, relishing Britten's 'rich and resourceful orchestration'.[93] It was designed by Yannis Thavoris, whose set was dominated by a letterbox-shaped aperture like a machine-gun emplacement. This, together with timeless costumes, reflected the view of Britten's opera as very much a work about the aftermath of war. Hugh Canning was still bemused by Ronald Duncan's 'arty farty' libretto, and disturbed by the inherent misogyny in the piece, but congratulated McVicar in tackling both elements 'unflinchingly' by making the male and female choruses sing to each other and not the audience, as 'antagonists in a contemporary sex war', the female chorus incredulous at the male chorus's Christian 'platitudes of redemption'. He praised McVicar's directorial restraint and the physicality of the acting.[94] Michael Kennedy was delighted that ENO had ended a distinctly patchy season with 'all guns blazing'.[95]

The 2000/1 season won ENO several awards, including an Olivier Award for outstanding achievement in opera for Turnage and Holden's work on *The Silver Tassie*, and best new opera productions for *Pelleas* and *The Coronation of Poppea*. At the same time the annual report showed a deficit on continuing operations of £311,000 for the financial year.

Payne attributed the shortfall in ticket sales to over-scheduling of revivals of popular favourites and the adverse reaction to the new *Giovanni*. The seventh revival of Miller's *Barber of Seville* in March was nonetheless well reviewed, with its excellent cast that included Christopher Maltman, Christine Rice and Toby Spence. Lesley Garrett sang in the June performances, which did less well at the box office.[96] In March, however, *Carmen*, which replaced the new Miller *Cavalleria rusticana* and *Pagliacci*, enabled Canning to write of a very happy full house, enjoying the 'utterly bewitching' Carmen of Sally Burgess.[97] The creation of revivable core repertoire was proving elusive for Payne. While he had little respect for the old store of productions such as *Carmen*, ENO's crown jewels remained the old classics of long-past eras, such as Hytner's *The Magic Flute* and *Xerxes* and Miller's *Mikado* and *Rigoletto*.

\*

Payne's and Daniel's contracts were renewed at the beginning of the year. Payne recalled that in March 2001 a meeting took place at the Arts Council with ENO chairman John Baker, in the presence of the Arts Council chairman Gerry Robinson, the chief executive Peter Hewitt and the new Arts Council music officer Hilary Boulding, at which it was at last agreed that the core grant was to be raised to a realistic sum. Payne was to plan for future operations in the restored Coliseum on the basis of a £16-million grant. He later said that he had asked for £16.5 million but accepted the lower figure, as he believed that ENO could raise £5 million from private contributions and £10 million from the box office, reaching an annual turnover exceeding £30 million.[98] Baker later recalled with pleasure that this deal, which he and Payne together had brokered with ACE, heralded at last the prospect of real financial stability for ENO, making it a good moment for him to hand over to a successor who could concentrate on the restoration of the Coliseum.[99]

Thus it was that shortly after, on 1 April, investment banker Martin Smith took over as chairman from Baker, with whom Payne had got on very well. Smith's appointment was the direct result of the need to raise nearly £20 million in private funds for the forthcoming restoration. Baker, Payne and Willis Taylor had identified Smith as the man to lead the campaign to raise the required sum. John Baker later said that the reason Smith was made chairman straight away rather than being asked to chair the Development Committee was that 'he made it quite clear that if he were going to lead the effort it would have to be from the chair'.[100] The board accepted him, and the Arts Council thought he would be a good chairman. At the same time, Vernon Ellis, chairman of the international consultancy firm Accenture, joined the board.

Martin Smith's company, New Star Asset Management, was about to be floated on the stock exchange, which it was thought would increase his formidable personal fortune. Charlotte Higgins at the *Guardian* wrote: 'Individualistic and competitive, with employees dismissed if performance wobbles, New Star is perhaps the antithesis to ENO, with its tradition of ensemble, a company ethos.' Smith was, she wrote, 'a dapper figure with a taste for bow ties and suede shoes, and an undulation of white hair atop a face that tends to be rubicund'.[101] He had been at McKinsey Management Consultants before his city career. One of Smith's first decisions was to delay the start of the restoration project for one year, as the private funding had not yet been secured.[102]

The Department of Culture, Media and Sport was also undergoing a change of leadership. On 14 June Richard Morrison in *The Times* bade farewell to Chris Smith, who was, he felt, a decent chap who had displayed a love for the arts rare in culture ministers, had prised a surprising amount from the Treasury and had wanted to break down barriers. It was his misfortune to have been unfairly clobbered with the odium of the Dome. His successor, Tessa Jowell, had revealed little interest in the arts.

Daniel's determination to display the epic operas in which ENO excelled resulted in another fine production of *War and Peace*, which opened on 1 November. Tim Albery, who was always adept at handling the big choruses, proved to be the right director for such an undertaking. The production was 'grown up' and musically fine, wrote Milnes, with Simon Keenlyside a near ideal Andrei, Willard White a magnificent Kutuzov, Sandra Zeltzer a gorgeous Natasha and John Daszak a fervently sung Pierre. Once again it was 'a marvellous company show . . . massively educated and aware' and a complete success. Since the 1972 Colin Graham production, much had become known about the pressure exerted on Prokofiev from the Stalinist regime to be propagandistic. As a consequence of this knowledge, Albery 'deftly but not didactically' intertwined 1941 and 1812 throughout the production.[103] People dressed in the style of 1941 shifted Hildegard Bechtler's timeless sets, while Ana Jebens's elegant empire costumes placed the protagonists firmly in the period of the tale. In collaboration with Daniel, some of the long heroic choruses were made somewhat 'sleeker'.[104] Daniel conducted with brilliance, according to Allison, 'capturing the work's distinctive ebb and flow and inspiring alert playing from the orchestra'.[105]

Payne decided to schedule a new production of *The Marriage of Figaro* between the two big productions of *War and Peace* and *The Rake's Progress*, which filled the theatre with scenery. With Vick unable to return to revive his *Figaro's Wedding*, and with a fine young cast, Payne decided to give £15,000, the cost of a revival, to a staff producer for what he called a 'paper-handkerchief *Figaro* – not one for the storeroom'. His intention was to create something new with a decent rehearsal period.[106] Steven Stead's production opened on 8 November. It was described by Payne as 'the equivalent of a Tracey Emin painting, let's throw all the jumble into the tent ... grunge theatre'. Most critics were appalled. Clements said the junk-room *Marriage of Figaro* was a strong candidate for the worst production at the Coliseum 'in the last two decades'.[107]

The production, Payne conceded in his annual review, 'inhabited a pop culture judged insufficiently serious for this masterpiece'.[108] Looking back some years later, he could see that it might have seemed that, six months after *Don Giovanni*, 'having dug up Mozart's body we were despoiling it'. Actually, he said, the production came out of love, as had Bieito's *Don Giovanni*.[109]

The 29 November *Rake's Progress* directed by Complicité's Annabel Arden was set in the 1950s in Mother Goose's bordello, with a mystifying plug hole, a good cast and lots of choreography. David Murray found it creative and beautiful and appreciated the monstrous Nick Shadow of Gidon Saks with his baritone of 'molten tar'. The fine young Russian conductor Vladimir Jurowski – later to be music director at Glyndebourne – elicited remarkable orchestral clarity.[110]

A concert performance of *Valkyrie* in January was a dry run for the later staging to be directed by Phyllida Lloyd. It was considered a work in progress, 'in the best sense', by a supportive Milnes, but was far less generously treated by the other critics.[111] It had been a distinctly erratic season.

The board held its annual conference at Sarsden on 30 November 2001, at which Payne's business plan for 2002/3 to 2004/5 was discussed. Payne recalled that his plan was based on the new core grant figure of £16 million, which ENO had been promised at the Arts Council meeting in March, and a total income of £30.5 million. It was designed to set ENO straight again by taking £1 million out of the budget in 2002/3 and £1 million in 2003/4. The deficit had to be eliminated completely by March 2004, and the 2002/3 season must not increase it.

Payne's long-term business model retained a full-time ensemble of singers, orchestra, chorus and technicians, with an extended season of opera in three- or four-week repertory playing an average of five performances a week, except during the summer. There would continue to be a growth in education activities, the ENO Studio, the

young artists programme, fundraising and IT. The five-year repertory plan included the first full two seasons in the reopened
Coliseum. There would be 150 opera performances of eighteen
operas, with eight new productions, as well as twelve weeks of
dance.

ENO was now facing serious problems from many angles, with
the capital fundraising campaign for the restoration having a detrimental effect on raising revenue for running costs. Budgets had to
be revised downwards and expenditure reduced. Costs had to be
cut by a combination of unfilled vacancies, reduced salary budgets
and more flexible scheduling to avoid overtime. Payne realised that
it would be necessary to be more proactive on job losses and that he
would have to take short-term measures to cut expenditure. He was
nonetheless determined that ENO would remain a company in
which people wanted to work, and steady support would be necessary over the next two years if the cutbacks and disruptions were
not to lead to the demoralisation of the company and its audiences.

At Sarsden the relationship between the board and the general
director became strained, as Payne was taking time to find consensus within the company for the business plan. Martin Smith later
said that there was an 'increasing degree of discomfort' within the
board about management's business plan, as they felt that it did not
take account adequately of the effect of the restoration on the economics of the company.[112] After a discussion in January, however,
the slightly revised business plan was accepted by both the board
and the Arts Council.

Management was keenly feeling the loss of its executive director,
Russell Willis Taylor, who had had to return to America in
December 2000. According to John Ward, ENO's development
director, Willis Taylor's 'more extrovert style' complemented that of
the 'inspirational but sometimes enigmatic Payne'. She had been
Payne's 'formidable ally in dealings with the board and Arts
Council', and if this partnership had been able to continue, Ward
believed that it might have left a powerful mark on the history of
British arts institutions. Furthermore, she was to have taken personal responsibility at executive level for overseeing the building
and fundraising elements of the Coliseum restoration project. It
proved very hard to replace her.[113]

Payne nonetheless continued with his planning. On 17 February he had dinner with the film director Anthony Minghella, when he agreed to direct *Madam Butterfly* for ENO. During the month there were also discussions about surtitles, about which Payne was not enthusiastic, but for which he was examining the technology.

Bieito's second production for ENO, *A Masked Ball*, premiered on 21 February 2002 to a newspaper chorus of disapproval at the opening image of Gustavus's courtiers in what Roger Parker described as 'ritual convocation' on the lavatories of the executive washroom. Parker, Professor of Music at Cambridge and a Verdi scholar, endeavoured to decode some of the visual images and to distinguish between Bieito's insights and his penchant for being *méchant*. The drab workshop set, the bare light bulbs, grim scaffolding, even a wheelchair, were almost nostalgic of 'power house' days, while the 'dropped trouser as an uncoordinated leitmotif', gross sexual assault, male rape and copulation in the chorus were less so.[114] Milnes thought the production very tame in comparison to TV 'after the watershed'. The nasty bits were discreetly lit and he was sorry to see the loos go up into the flies as nothing interesting took their place and they were nicely lit. It had nothing to do with Verdi, since Bieito was not interested in text, a cardinal sin for Milnes. 'Oh dear,' Milnes sighed, 'I do wish Bieito would go away and leave opera alone.' He felt that Andrew Litton's conducting together with the fine performances of Claire Rutter as Amelia, John Daszak as Gustav and David Kempster as Anckarstroem were wasted in the production.[115]

Bieito, Payne and Daniel remained unrepentant. Payne told John Allison that Bieito was a fine director with a background in European theatre and cinema, which some of ENO's more traditional audience found disturbing. 'What do people want?' he asked. 'That we should never take risks? That's pathetic.'[116] In his annual review, Payne wrote: 'On mainland Europe, or at the Coliseum in the 1980s, most of these ventures would have been regarded at least as brave risks and in some cases as groundbreaking. Today's climate in the UK is more cautious and more responsive to fundraising perceptions in the American manner.'[117] Harewood later commented quietly: 'Well, I wouldn't have engaged Mr Bieito for two seasons running before one sees how it is going . . . I think that was the wrong kind of risk.'[118] Martin Smith later said that 'many people had had real difficulties with *A Masked Ball*' and that it had been a 'difficult time'.[119]

In March 2002 the Arts Council informed ENO that it was holding back £500,000 of the promised grant. Payne recalled that this late reduction unbalanced his three-year business plan, which would have to be revised. Under normal circumstances it should have been possible to make adjustments, but the imminent closure added a tension that was harder to manage.[120]

On 20 March Payne met Hilary Boulding, Henry Little and the finance director Jan Clarke at ACE to brief them about the business plan and budgets prior to a board meeting later that day. In April Charlotte Higgins in the *Guardian* reported that *A Masked Ball* had played to 65 per cent houses and that Payne was about to institute a business plan that would try to make savings of £700,000 for the closure, without redundancies. He was, she reported, 'fire-fighting to save the next year's budget'. Richard Jones, fearing that Payne's position was threatened, leapt to his defence, pointing out that ENO had a personality and was not a corporate anodyne opera shop. It was not a Starbucks opera house, but one with a definite personality, and it was 'one of the last skittles standing' because of his vision.[121]

The chairman and board were keeping a close eye on developments. On 17 April Payne discussed audience development and the repertory plan with the board. The next day there was a meeting with Martin Smith and vice-chairman Charles Alexander, at which Daniel and Payne were quizzed about their plans.

The season continued in April with a variety of hits and misses. Max Loppert defended Francesca Zambello's production of Spontini's *La Vestale* from its dismal notices, having returned after opening night to find the cast, and especially Jane Eaglen, in radiant and ample voice, in an opera he described as 'an elevated example of Napoleonic Classicism eminently worthy of presentation on the Coliseum stage'. It shared, he wrote, a 'Gallic largeness of aim warmed by an Italian emotional vitality'.[122] Payne later commented that it had nonetheless failed to excite the public's interest.[123]

John Allison called *Lulu*, on 1 May, a 'redemptive' production for ENO. Richard Jones emphasised the black humour of the work rather than its expressionism, and provided a series of queasily eye-catching scenes.[124] As a co-production it was not, Milnes wrote, one of ENO's poverty-stricken evenings. It was 'properly grotesque and shocking in its violence, but also extremely funny and rather sexy'.[125] Allison appreciated Daniel's hauntingly natural and beautiful interpretation of the score and Lisa Saffer's 'remarkable assumption' of the title role. Saffer's Lulu was, he wrote, quoting Wedekind, 'a creature of infinite colours'.

Matthew Warchus's production of *Così fan tutte* at the end of the month was welcomed by Andrew Clark as restoring a core repertory piece with ENO's values: inspiring musicianship, coherent ensemble and communication of the text.[126] It was, according to Christiansen, 'a thoughtful, humane and sensitive staging'.[127] Mary Plazas was a sexy soprano Dorabella, and Susan Gritton a bright Fiordiligi.[128] Toby Spence and Christopher Maltman were convincingly cocksure young bloods and Andrew Shore a commanding Don Alfonso. The witty translation of Jeremy Sams was clearly audible.

The season ended on 6 July and, whatever the success or failure of individual productions, the ENO ensemble was in strong and vibrant form. The season had seen some excellent revivals, including Sarah Connolly triumphant in *Ariodante* in March, a well-conducted, well-sung *Elixir of Love* in April, *Falstaff* in May, *Lady Macbeth* in June and a revival of *The Silver Tassie* in July. With twenty productions and 174 performances, it had also been very productive.

The box office, however, was £930,000 below its budget of just under £8.2 million. In his annual review Payne reported that there had been too many performances of two revivals. There had been fourteen *La traviatas* in September–October and more in January–February. Although Milnes wrote that the 1996 Miller production still looked good and Sandra Ford was excellent, it was a large number to sustain. Then, sixteen routine performances of *La bohème* between September and November with the inexperienced pair of Rhys Merion and Linda Richardson and the unexciting conducting of Michael Lloyd constituted even more optimistic programming. Together they accounted for 52 per cent of the shortfall, and a further 32 per cent resulted from the two Bieito productions.

The final box-office disappointment had been Gluck's *Orpheus*, which had coincided with the 11 September terrorist attack on New York's World Trade Center. There was also what Payne described as a general West End 'malaise' that had been exacerbated for ENO by a public perception that the scaffolding-clad Coliseum was already closed. Fundraising revenue was also down, with individual support competing with the capital campaign. The fact that the company had valiantly and successfully striven to control expenditure was obliterated by the box-office disappointment. 'The crucial 67 per cent [cash] houses were not coming through,' Payne later reflected, and 'if you slip down the sixties – which happened after Covent Garden reopened and we were closing and the building got tackier and tackier and we did not programme intelligently enough – that's when you are on the skids.'[129] The deficit for the year on unrestricted funds was £1,317,000.[130]

The future was even more worrying. During the 2002/3 season the Coliseum would be closed for refurbishment for three months, so there would only be 125 performances, and in 2003/4 for six months, when there would be only ninety performances. In the light of the box-office failures of the previous season Payne had had to readjust the business plan for the closure by marking down estimated box-office revenue. Consequently, the £1.25-million deficit of the previous season would be increased in the next season to £1.85 million. He was making plans to eliminate it and make up to £1 million in the course of 2003/4 by culling any loss-making projects from the season at the Barbican during the restoration and adjusting the Coliseum spring season. Payne, ever the fighter and optimist, set to work to reduce the deficit, eliminating projects that could be reintroduced when times were easier.[131]*

Martin Smith later recalled that he believed that there could be a deficit of a 'few million pounds' by the end of the period of restoration. There was, he said, a gap between what the board believed was likely to happen and what Payne believed, and there was a 'degree of disbelief' that the 'leadership was going to be able to get us through the difficult period'.[132] New board member John Nelson later recalled looking at the accounts shortly after joining and telling Smith that unless there was significant change the company would go over the edge of a financial precipice and there was a danger of being forced to stop trading. He felt the Arts Council would not support the company 'without real management change'.[133]

* One helpful development was that for the first time ENO was making its own CDs. The first was *The Silver Tassie*.

Notwithstanding this growing disquiet, Payne continued to plan and work for the future. Having been asked to do some research about surtitles, despite his own lack of enthusiasm for them, he submitted a paper to the board in which he 'tried to be terribly judicious'.[134] He showed willingness to consider the options, hedged his bets and suggested that it would be wise not to waste precious resources on a technology that might become outdated very soon. During the early summer he also successfully negotiated new, non-inflationary, three-year agreements with Equity and BECTU, which traded increased flexibility and productivity for job security. The unions had also agreed that 2002/3 and 2003/4 would be two lean years in order to get through the closure. He was also in the process of negotiating a verbal agreement with the chorus, orchestra and technicians, who agreed to take unpaid leave during the closed period provided they were reinstated after closure.[135]

On 19 June Payne attended what turned out to be his last board meeting, at which the 2002/3 budget and plans for the Baylis Programme were discussed. He continued to put forward plans that would fit the budget for the closure and beyond. Both Judith Weir's *Blond Eckbert* and a revival of *Street Scene*, as well as Rachel Portman's children's opera *The Little Prince*, were cut.[136]

Plans for the Baylis Programme during the closure, and for its closer integration into life at the reopened Coliseum, had been progressing with Steve Moffitt and Alice King-Farlow. The outreach team had grown to eight by 2002 and it was hoped at the reopening to reach out beyond schools and to commission a work based on *The Ring*, as well as three children's operas. They had also been collaborating with Channel Four for a four-part series, *Operatunity*, charting the progress of would-be opera singers from diverse backgrounds, to be broadcast in 2003. On 5 July Payne attended a performance of the *Operatunity* finalists in the RCM's Britten Theatre with Steve Moffitt, who was moving on from ENO after six years to work for Creative Partnerships, a new government initiative designed to develop the skills of young people across England. That afternoon Payne had production planning meetings for *The Handmaid's Tale* and *King Arthur*. The season ended the next day.

Relations between Payne and his chairman had broken down. Smith recalled that 'it was recognised' by himself and his board that as the 'economics were not working' and if a 'vitally needed further injection' of some £10 million in stabilisation money were to be requested from the Arts Council to get through the restoration, a new economic model was required for the company. The closure 'needed to be used not only as an opportunity to restore the Coliseum to its former magnificence but also to enhance the box office and revenues by bringing new artistic freshness and a new artistic leadership'. At the same time it was necessary 'to reduce the company's overheads by lowering the headcount'.[137]

This was not the way forward for Payne, who had hoped to maintain the company at full strength after the redevelopment. Furthermore, he did not believe it was necessary to go back into stabilisation, as it should be possible to run the company full time on £16 million, even if it involved some programme modifications. He later said that he had not been aware of any board discussions about cuts to the company, and that such moves would not have taken place under his stewardship.[138]

Martin Smith twice consulted John Baker, who stated unequivocally that he believed Payne was a 'positive force for good'. Baker also believed that Payne could have rectified the situation. He always knew that his job was to manage the whole business and not just the stage. 'My advice to Martin was, "Stick with him, he knows what he is doing,"' he recalled. Smith complained to Baker that Payne played his cards 'close to his chest'; Baker responded that this had not been a problem in his time.[139] Payne later recalled that as well as the Sarsden away weekend there were regular monthly board meetings, Finance and General Policy Committee meetings and discussions in between, for all of which detailed plans of performances and financial projections were prepared. 'It would have been difficult', he wrote, 'to be more transparent.'[140]

On 9 July Payne was summoned to Smith's offices in Knightsbridge. On 12 July a press statement announced that ENO was 'reallocating the responsibilities of the General Director recognising the increased burden being borne by this position as a consequence of the planned transition of the company to its newly restored home the London Coliseum'. Payne 'announced his decision to stand down from his full-time role with the company', but would continue to act as a consultant. Caroline Felton was to assume the role of Acting Managing Director, 'responsible for the overall management of the company as a business'.

Smith had reported developments to ENO's president Lord Harewood shortly before the meeting. Harewood recalled that he had told Smith, although he thought it was probably too late to influence him, that he believed Payne could claw back the deficit. He also suggested that Smith should have given Payne the opportunity to put forward his plan to undo the damage, which had admittedly been done – the incurring of a big deficit – and argue his case before the full board. As far as Harewood was concerned, both Payne and Smith were at fault for failing to get on with each other.[141]

Smith recalled that Caroline Felton's appointment had been suggested to him by the Arts Council.[142] She was ready to take over, but Payne requested that she did not start until he left at the end of the month. She had been released from Welsh National Opera, where she had been engaged in their stabilisation process.[143]

The Arts Council officers Kim Evans and Hilary Boulding had been working closely with Martin Smith and were supportive of his plans, according to Christiansen, who later reported in the *Daily Telegraph* that the Arts Council had 'goaded' the board to appoint Felton as executive director. The current breed of arts apparatchiks, he wrote, did not like the concept of 'General Director'; they wanted accountant managers to call the shots and to 'discipline the artistic executive'.[144] Tom Sutcliffe wrote in *The Spectator* that 'Hilary Boulding's iconoclastic and demotic instinct is to question the insatiable appetite of opera for subsidy'. He believed that Smith's 'wielding of artistic power' was 'agreeable to Boulding and Kim Evans'.[145] The Arts Council announced that they were delighted that Felton was stepping in.[146] She was due to start work on 1 August.

Payne was of the school of executive directors who were highly knowledgeable and led the company from an artistic perspective. In the next five years the two London opera houses were to adopt a new model whereby the executive was led by a business manager and an accountant, with the artistic director answerable to them. By dispensing with the old style, experienced, highly knowledgeable producer, the balance of authority between the board and executive at ENO was altered and the balance between artistic leadership and financial control was to be weighted in favour of the latter. The 'old model' directors – Tucker, Arlen, Harewood and Jonas – had relentlessly pursued artistic excellence, with cost a secondary consideration, since it had been understood that the Arts Council would cover deficits. They had made a great company and great work, but with below-inflation funding the deficits had grown and had become increasingly less tolerable for the Arts Council.

In his annual review Payne referred to fundamental changes in relations between management and the board since Smith became chairman and other individuals had joined the board in April 2001. The board had become more interventionist and sceptical and the presence of company managers at board meetings had been discouraged. He believed there had been direct consultation between board members and Arts Council officers. Payne ended his report by saying that the agreed business plan of March had stated that the company would require steady support over the next two years if the cutbacks were not to demoralise both the company and the audience. He had felt destabilised by the withdrawal of support by the board and officers of the Arts Council at a most difficult time. He stressed that the dedicated and courageous company deserved better. At the end of his review Payne stated that ENO's core values needed to be reasserted more than ever.

Milnes, who had kept a watchful eye on the governance of both national companies as editor of *Opera* and was about to retire from journalism, wrote an enraged piece for *The Times*. The Arts Council had already closed down Phoenix Opera, Kent Opera and the English Music Theatre Company, and now ENO was threatened: 'Brutally and without any public consultation, it has been decided by a faceless handful to cut down to size a great public institution and put hundreds of people out of work.' The most depressing aspect of plans for the radical restructuring of ENO, he wrote, was the cynicism with which the first stage – the ousting of Nicholas Payne – was achieved. The company and the audience were about to go on holiday, so there was no focus for protest or for a public appeal. 'For heaven's sake,' he wrote, 'putting on opera has never been a business and never will be. It's a question of finding the money. If the Board can't grasp this simple fact, and its only response to persistent underfunding is to demand cuts rather than fight for a reasonable subsidy, then we may as well pack up and go home.' Could opera get any cheaper, he asked, more pared down than it already was in St Martin's Lane? 'ENO as we know and love it, as Lilian Baylis conceived it nearly a century ago is in desperate peril.'[147]

The arts and opera worlds were incensed. In a letter to *The Times* on 18 July, Jonas, Elder and Pountney called the ousting of Payne 'dangerous for the future of opera' and 'shabby' in its execution. Boards used to be tolerant and brave, but of the current board they wrote: 'fundraising effectiveness is leading it to believe that it can lead the company. Such attitudes should be questioned by all those who value artistic integrity and artistic freedom.' That same day six directors – Tim Albery, Richard Jones, Jude Kelly, Phyllida Lloyd, Deborah Warner and Francesca Zambello – wrote to the same newspaper, saying that Payne's departure was a 'catastrophic torpedoing of British operatic theatre'. They urged the Arts Council to review the board's decision. The board had become too involved as a result of the development campaign. Charlotte Higgins reported that the previous year ENO had raised £7.5 million from the board alone, with Vernon Ellis giving £5 million. Deborah Warner told Higgins that ENO had lost the one person who was capable of fulfilling the role of general director – who was both an artistic visionary and a scrupulous financial manager.[148]

For the press, ENO was a news story again and there were more post-mortems. On 17 July the *Guardian*'s Martin Kettle suggested that Payne might have missed the fact that 'the market for *épater les bourgeois* productions has reached saturation point'. On 17 July Christiansen used the word 'truculent' to describe Payne's behaviour 'as he doggedly defended the high ground and lost his cool with those advising him to trim his sails'. Higgins wrote that Payne could be tricky to work with, but he was honest, without airs and graces and was supportive of artists.[149]

Paul Daniel was reported to be very upset. There were those who said that he should have resigned at the same time, but he believed that if he did not stay there would be no one left to fight to maintain crucial elements of the company. If he did not stand in the doorway, he later said, 'it could have gone overnight'.[150]

Payne looked back in sadness rather than in anger. 'You are the one who takes the rap – I don't argue in any way with the principle that the board is there to hire and fire the chief executive.' But he was disappointed: 'For four years you are pushing a stone uphill and eventually you gain enough credibility and know-how to get it to the top and then you can do something.'[151] But Payne had lost his chance, and, with his encyclopaedic knowledge of the opera world, he would prove difficult to replace.

# 16

# 2002–2009: A New Model

What would the company look like after the restoration? Rumours were rife in late July and August 2002, when Martin Smith, who was answering for the board, was away. On 25 July there were reports in *The Stage* and the *Observer* that he was intending to close the company down for sixteen months, lay off large numbers of its staff and reopen as a part-time company, performing six months a year, possibly employing outside orchestras.

If the rumours emanated from the Arts Council, it would not have been the first time that it had been the source of the concept of reducing ENO's role. An Arts Council insider later said that in the minds of the Arts Council there was indeed a plan to close down the company completely during the restoration and disband most of the staff. ENO's official response was that there were 'several contingency plans' and the disbandment of the orchestra was never confirmed by the board. Vernon Ellis later said that the board believed that if they disbanded the staff, the company might never be able to rise again.[1]

Daniel, perceiving the threat, decided to stay and fight for the orchestra, confronting the board and telling them that it was impossible to employ freelance players of quality in an opera company because 'each show is a long commitment, not like a concert'.[2] Shortly after Payne's departure, Daniel was invited to address the board and put forward his overall vision for the company and its outreach programmes.[3]* Daniel realised that the chances to stand up for the full ensemble would be few, and that he must convey to

---

* After Steve Moffitt's departure, Alice King-Farlow was left with the task of running the Baylis Programme during this tempestuous period. Its expansion as envisaged by Payne was now out of the question, but, despite losing five of her team, she succeeded in keeping it afloat, bringing in Catherine Sutton to assist her and commissioning three children's operas which were performed after she left in 2003.

the board his urgent belief in its survival. He was surprised that instead of meeting with opposition, his 'rather outspoken appeal' became 'an embarrassing success' – the board applauding his statement. The confrontation meant that the more radical proposals for reduction would not be acceptable to the board.[4]

On 26 July Daniel wrote to reassure the staff that although there would be changes during the eighteen-month restoration, the integrity and crucial components of the company – the orchestra, chorus and music staff, the Baylis Programme and the producing and administrative teams – would be maintained.[5] Daniel had received verbal assurances from the chairman that he was not seeking a reduced role for the orchestra or looking to use other orchestras in its place and quoted this assurance in his letter.[6] The Musicians Union representative, Horace Trubridge, later recalled that the union had also believed the threat to bring in an outside orchestra to be false, stirred up by the press.[7]

On 24 August Peter Hewitt, chief executive of ACE, responded to Tom Sutcliffe's article in *The Spectator* of 10 August, stressing that ACE had no intention of 'redrawing' the UK's operatic map to reduce pressure on its music budget. Nor were there plans for ENO to go part-time or to hire another orchestra. ACE's priority was to ensure that ENO would return to the restored Coliseum in the 'best possible artistic and financial health'.[8]

Although the orchestra was secure, restructuring the company was inevitable as far as the board was concerned. 'We either had to go bankrupt or be bailed out,' Vernon Ellis recalled. 'The stabilisation grant had to be accompanied by a plan for the future.'[9] Caroline Felton of Coopers Lybrand was the person employed to initiate the plan and the restructuring.

Part-time or full-time, there were many who thought that the old-model ENO was doomed. Political journalist Adrian Hamilton believed that developments indicated the death knell of ENO's ensemble company, which, like that of the Royal Shakespeare Company, had contributed so much to the British arts. They had been repertory theatres based on a permanent acting and production staff with shared values and vision. Gerry Robinson at ACE, he wrote, was interested in good housekeeping rather than artistic excellence and thus promoted like-minded businessmen to boards: Smith at ENO and Lord Alexander at the RSC. Both were compa-

nies that had had good and bad patches but overall they had contributed hugely to the cultural life of post-war Britain, with exciting
and distinguished work, complementing the classical work of
Covent Garden and the National Theatre.[10]

Restoration work at the Coliseum continued from July to October
2002, with concerts of *The Rhinegold* and *Valkyrie*, as planned by
Payne, taking place at the Barbican. Critical opinion on the musical
preparation of ENO's *Ring* improved with these performances.
Daniel was thought by the critics to have grasped the measure of the
music with a forceful *Valkyrie* full of light and shade and shattering
climaxes.[11] Canning also praised Daniel and the orchestra for a
well-played and well-paced account of *The Rhinegold*.[12]

The Coliseum season opened on 1 November with a revival of
*The Barber of Seville*, followed by a revival of *Xerxes* and, on 21
November, a new *Tosca*. Fiona Maddocks found the occasion
dispiriting at 'a time of rudderless chaos off-stage, consultants in
charge, jobs being reallocated . . . the absence of Daniel in the pit
made for an un-reassuring lacklustre musical evening'. The orchestra sounded 'uncharacteristically out of sorts'.[13] A concert performance of *Siegfried* at the Barbican in December showed the orchestra
and Daniel back on form, with the musical preparation of *The Ring*
receiving growing critical appreciation and support. Michael
Kennedy thought the orchestra played 'magnificently'.[14]

Meanwhile, it was proving difficult for the Search Committee –
consisting of Smith, Ellis, John Tusa, Richard Eyre and Michael
Berkeley – to come up with a replacement for Payne. Pierre Audi,
who had founded the Almeida Festival in the 1980s and had been at
the Netherlands Opera for ten high-profile years, was the main con-
tender but was reported as wavering. It was pointed out in the press
that the Netherlands Opera did not have a permanent orchestra and
received a far higher proportion of its income from the state than
did ENO.[15]

Other candidates were Graham Vick, Richard Jones and
Francesca Zambello. Jones suggested working in tandem with
Louise Jeffreys, the excellent technical director of the Jonas era.
This idea was dismissed by one member of the board, despite the
excellent reputation of Jeffreys in both the financial and technical
areas. Zambello was said to be extremely interested and was liked

by the company, but with her very busy schedule it was believed that she could only do nine months a year *in situ*. She was therefore passed over.

Felton's 'Strategy for Change' was presented to ACE in December. As a result, on 22 January 2003, just five years after the last stabilisation grant of £9.2 million had been awarded, it was announced that ENO would be admitted into its second stabilisation programme. The final plans had yet to be agreed, but in order to qualify an initial schedule of redundancies had already been accepted. On 18 January ENO had announced that no firm plans had yet been made: 'What has come out now is a series of discussions not a series of outcomes. We are not rethinking the company, but we're looking at areas of the company and at strategy for the long term. Key roles and objectives of the company will not change.'[16] A summary of the strategy itself was published on 7 March.

The 'rethink' was already in motion. Amongst those who were made redundant at this time were the three staff conductors: Michael Lloyd, Alex Ingram and Noel Davies. The most senior of the three, Davies, who had been with the company since 1975, was greatly appreciated by singers and by Charles Mackerras for his exceptional talent as a coach and conductor. Anne Evans said that ENO was 'his whole life' and being made redundant 'broke his heart'.[17] Davies died on 13 March 2008. In his *Guardian* obituary he was described as a true company man, respected and held in affection by all those who knew him for over thirty years.[18]

The initial plan for the chorus was a reduction from sixty-eight to forty, and the process had already begun. The chorus learnt of the redundancies on 17 January, as they were rehearsing *Khovanshchina*. Felton was disregarding Payne's negotiation with the choristers of the previous January, whereby there would be at least sixty choristers (down from sixty-eight) during the closure. Payne's reduction was to have been made through departures and early retirements, with the possibility of a further reduction in the future. Payne had not committed to an immediate return to sixty-eight after the reopening, but had undertaken that there would be a full chorus repertory.

In protest, and with Equity's support, the choristers refused to sing out in full voice during the dress rehearsal of *Khovanshchina*, with the sole exception of the prayer, during which they were almost tearful with emotion. The conductor, Oleg Caetani, far from feeling let down as they had feared, was full of support and praise for them. To the choristers' surprise, the audience stood up and cheered and whistled after the performance.

Although their contracts prohibited members of the company from speaking to the press without permission, they felt free to speak out during the industrial action, when they were in any case in breach of contract. One chorister, after thirty-five years devoted to the company, told the *Guardian* that there had been a complete betrayal of the chorus and the company. Another told the *Telegraph*: 'I'm in my mid-fifties, I've never missed a performance, and I've given more than twenty-five years of my life to ENO. If I am one of the ones sacked, I'd be lucky to get £30,000 redundancy. Not much of a reward for a career ended by their incompetence.'[19]

On 21 January the chorus went down to ACE and sang the 'Chorus of Hebrew Slaves' from *Nabucco* outside Gerry Robinson's office, and then 'Defend Our Homes and Children' from *Khovanshchina*. According to the *Telegraph*, Robinson came down to tell them it was 'the most beautiful protest' he had ever heard.[20]

Although management did not know what would happen on the opening night of *Khovanshchina* on 23 January, back at the Coliseum after five months in exile, the chorus did in fact sing out. As one chorister recalled, they had never intended to let down their audience by not singing out at the actual performance. Both the chorus and the orchestra were vociferously and justly acclaimed by critics and audience alike.[21] The choristers sang as if their lives depended on it, Tim Ashley wrote, with the work proving to be a powerful protest under Oleg Caetani's baton.[22]

*Khovanshchina* was followed four days later by the first part of Richard Jones's production of *The Trojans*, *The Capture of Troy*. Set in a modern Los Angeles, a 'post-apocalyptic landscape', Andrew Clark found the production to be of 'blistering contemporary allusiveness', a 'drama of our time'. He praised the chorus once again for a 'radiant performance'.[23]

On 28 January 2003 Smith held a press briefing accompanied by Felton and Daniel. In the press release Smith announced that ENO would have gone into receivership the previous week had ACE not intervened – an echo of the Royal Opera House chairman's similar claim to the House of Commons Select Committee in November

1997 during the enquiry into Covent Garden's management. ENO was chronically sick financially, Smith said, with an underlying deficit that had been on average £1–2 million per year for nearly ten years. The projected deficit would be £4.2 million by March 2004. The 1997 stabilisation injection of £9.2 million had unfortunately not resulted in the company achieving all the necessary reforms to enable it to break out of its 'boom-and-bust' cycle. Consequently, Smith declared, 'my board and I felt passionately that we had to use the restoration project as a unique, once-in-a-lifetime opportunity to address ENO's financial problems'. The economic models, he explained, kept going wrong because ENO's fixed costs were too high and some employment contracts no longer reflected best market practice. There would be the same number of players in the pit and on the stage but they would be paid differently.

John Baker, Smith's predecessor as chairman, found it necessary to answer Smith's statement about the average yearly deficit. He wrote to *The Times* on 3 February pointing out that in the seven years to 2000/1 ENO had achieved a modest surplus in five years and deficits in two. He hoped that the Arts Council's gift would not prove to be a Trojan horse, destroying the ENO from within. Maggie Sedwards, who had left the company in December 2000, added her voice in a letter to the *Telegraph* the next day: from 1994/5 to 1997/8 there had been box-office surpluses, with attendance sometimes reaching 90 per cent and averaging 75 per cent, even though there had been deficits more recently. Smith's implication that the company had been mismanaged for ten years was 'an insult to previous regimes' who had kept ENO 'alive, intact and flourishing'.[24]

On 18 March an ENO spokesman responded that Smith had been 'misunderstood', adding that he had been talking about 'under-investment' and an 'underlying deficit'.[25] Smith defended himself eleven days later, writing to *The Times* that although there had been a cumulative surplus of £820,000 for the period 1991/2–2001/2, it included £5 million of stabilisation money from the Arts Council from 1997–9. The forecast debt for 2002/3 and 2003/4 was £3.8 million, which, he calculated, would make a cumulative underlying debt for ten years of £12.2 million, or £1.2 million per annum. The Arts Council would only support ENO if it did not get into the same problems – so there had to be cuts. In March the editor of *Opera*, John Allison, expressed surprise at hearing Smith talk of Daniel running the 'music side of the business' at the press conference – a shocking moment for those involved with the company. Allison urged that Smith should go and Payne be reinstated.

A reading of the published annual financial reports makes it difficult to find support for the suggestion of an underlying £1 million a year deficit. Furthermore, some of the deficits were as yet only estimated and Payne had been in the process of preparing business plans that would eliminate them, without asking for stabilisation money, which entailed becoming embroiled in the restructuring agreed to by the board and the Arts Council officers. At the centre of the company's problems lay the inevitable loss of revenue resulting from the closure for the restoration of the theatre, as well as the loss of passing trade from those who were put off by the scaffolding outside the theatre even when it was open. The company was paying the price for restoring a building of national importance.

ENO's 'fixed costs' that Smith had referred to were the company of 500 employees, which, as Tom Sutcliffe had pointed out, compared very modestly with Deutsche Oper am Rhein's 1,400.[26] Reports were emerging of fewer long-term contracts and that members of the company would no longer make up the total numbers demanded by whatever repertory would appear on the stage. It was also becoming clear that performances at the Coliseum would be reduced. Smith did not deny the figure of 110 redundancies alleged by David Lister on 25 January 2003 in the *Independent on Sunday*. It was also reported that the orchestra was to be paid an extra £500,000 to perform outside the Coliseum at the Barbican during the exile, a sum they had agreed to relinquish as part of the wage negotiation with Payne.[27]

It had been six months since Payne's departure and still no one had replaced him. There were reports in the *Guardian* that Audi had been asked to reconsider, after having turned down the offer, but had again declined.[28] Smith later said that the day Audi pulled out had been a 'very bad' one.[29] The delay in finding a successor to Payne made his removal seem even less wise.

On 21 January news surfaced of a fresh candidate to be ENO's director. Seán Doran, an Irishman with a Music and Fine Art degree and a MMus in Ethnomusicology, had been identified by the headhunter who had introduced general director Tony Hall to the Royal Opera House in 2001. Doran's CV consisted mainly of the directorship of festivals, including Belfast and Perth, while he had no experience with a major full-time arts company. Smith later said that during his interview, it emerged that Doran had a 'very interesting track record' and connections. Smith also recalled that he had been advised that the director of the company should be an artistic person, but that in retrospect, after Audi withdrew, he probably should have gone for an executive head of the company, not an artistic one, as had happened at Covent Garden.[30]

Harewood was not consulted, but recalled that he was familiar with all but two of the names on the list of candidates shown to him by Tusa as they were people involved in opera. Doran's was not one of them. Doran was good in many ways at running a festival, Harewood said, but it was not necessary to 'know about opera to run a festival'. Harewood presumed that he had been very good at the interview but believed that interview alone was a 'false method'.[31] Ellis later agreed that 'interviewing does not give you a crystal ball', but it was felt that Doran 'had done exciting things in festivals and would be able to introduce new things'.[32]

Doran's appointment was announced on 7 February 2003. Smith thought that he was the right man to rescue a 'chronically sick' opera company.[33] There were some sceptical press responses. That day John Allison pointed out that although Doran was 'an amiable chap', he had never run a theatre. Doran was unfazed by the adverse publicity: 'I prefer people having low expectations because it gives you more space to get on with things,' he said, and added, 'How long ago would a Northern Irish Catholic, as it were, come into running something in the Establishment? This is not a testament to me but to the people who appointed me.'[34]

The next industrial action by the chorus was their failure to appear in a scheduled performance of *The Trojans* on 18 February, instead of which they gave a free concert of the Verdi *Requiem* at St Paul's church in Covent Garden. There was massive publicity, with the BBC covering the concert on both its morning *Today* radio programme and its 6 o'clock evening news broadcast. Amongst the soloists was Susan Bickley, who was to sing Cassandra in *The Trojans*, and David Rendall. Three members of management attended, as did Paul Daniel, despite being told that to do so would be looked upon very unfavourably.[35]

Barry Millington reported that at the packed church meeting the Equity general secretary, Ian McGarry, made a speech before the performance in which he asserted, to loud cheers, that if Smith, who had refused to consult about numbers, could not 'understand the difference between an ensemble of forty and sixty choristers he should go back to banking where he belongs'. Nicholas Payne and John Ward were also there to hear a terrifying rendition of the *Dies Irae*.[36] By the end of the performance the audience were stamping and cheering their support.

On 18 February Smith announced a ninety-day period of consultation with all three unions and staff, who were asking whether, after the £41-million refit, the Coliseum would reopen with nothing inside. Equity had said that when they called for emergency talks, all management said was 'Please don't go on strike', and that they had not been consulted at any stage. They accused Smith of exaggerating the company's financial problems and argued that savings could be made elsewhere, especially since managers dominated ENO staff numbers.[37]

Smith gave an interview to the *Sunday Telegraph* on 23 February in which he focused on the company's contracts as the main source of ENO's problems. He was quoted as saying that he had to ensure that ENO operated according to 'current market practice'. Numbers on stage would be the same but some of them would be freelance. ENO's chorus was facing twenty losses, said Smith, whereas the banking world had lost 50,000 jobs in the downturn. In the article Boulding at the Arts Council was quoted as defending Smith.

At the revival of *Der Rosenkavalier* shortly after Smith's announcement, the gallant company continued to give of its best, with David Ritch in charge. It looked and sounded better than ever, with Diana Montague as Octavian, Janice Watson as the Marschallin, Susan Gritton as Sophie and John Tomlinson as Ochs. Fiona Maddocks wrote: 'Hearing cheers in the Coliseum brought back memories of those long lost days – is it months or maybe years ago? – when ENO had a clear artistic policy, a generally happy audience and a chorus not obliged to strike for its life.'[38]

Allison at *Opera* magazine received a communication from the chorus that the decision to strike had been a hard one, since the chorus, though committed to assisting in ENO's future, had not been consulted and felt betrayed. They had already adopted a more flexible work pattern, including job sharing and Sunday working. They believed that reducing their numbers would be very detrimental to ENO's efficiency and purpose as the chorus had 'a vast memory bank of shows' and worked as a team. The board seemed to want to reduce the repertory and the scale of their work, thereby changing the essence of ENO.[39]

The Musicians Union had also been angered by the interview given by Smith to the *Sunday Telegraph* on 23 February – picked up by Magnus Linklater in *The Times* – in which he asserted that the orchestra worked under an outdated system that Covent Garden had dispensed with years ago, describing it as the 'last residue of old-fashioned union power'. On 7 March the *Independent* reported the MU's indignant response to what seemed to be a suggestion that the unions were responsible for ENO's problems.* The Musicians Union considered that the orchestra was already flexible, with Sunday working, tours, agreements on recordings of CDs and a challenging repertory of long operas. For two years there had been no pay increase, and they were upset by the policy of leaving vacancies unfilled, which had reduced the orchestra from ninety-one to seventy-one.

The 'strategy for change' was announced officially in a press release that same day. It was intended to reduce the annual costs by £3 million by the end of 2005/6. A more 'flexible approach to artistic planning' entailed reducing the company by 100 from 500, and the 'outsourcing' of various functions. There would be perform-

---

* They also objected to his reference to 'generous extra payments' whenever the company performed outside the Coliseum, when they had negotiated an arrangement with Payne for the closure period at the Barbican, whereby management could have organised all outside work within the existing contract and also a pay freeze for the two years. On 9 October, disregarding his arrangement, Felton told them she was looking for a three-month breathing space and would make the extra payments rather than continue negotiating at that stage. 'It was explicitly discussed and agreed at this meeting', they wrote, 'that this would not be held against us or raised in the press against us.' On 15 October she had said that she wanted to roll forward existing agreements but would make extra payments at the Barbican. The Musicians Union had been 'bewildered' that she would prefer to pay extra fees rather than continue the negotiations. The orchestra had proposed a reduced number of contracted sessions and extra times to be paid only if worked (Orchestra Committee to ACE, 7.3.03).

ances in alternative venues. The company's mission of making the highest quality opera available to the greatest number of people at affordable prices could best be achieved, it was stated, by reducing the number of performances even further to 150 (from 174 in 2001/2) and the number of productions from eighteen to fifteen. There would be six new productions and nine revivals, plus occasional straight runs of a single opera and more visiting companies. 'No change', it was stated in the strategy, was not an option, as ACE support depended on ENO not falling back into deficit. The strategy was subject to the same variables as its predecessors, and the magic formula of a show that could be put on over a long period in a straight run, in order to avoid expensive changeovers, remained as elusive as ever.

A brief respite from the pain arrived when *Operatunity* was broadcast on Channel Four in early 2003. It had been organised by Payne, who had agreed to let Michael Waldman make the programme despite his 1996 BBC2 fly-on-the-wall series *The House*, which, though attracting a large audience, had presented a controversial image of the Royal Opera House.[40] *Operatunity* followed the fortunes of aspiring amateur singers, from the hundred first auditioners to the fourteen selected for intensive training down to the choice of six finalists. The winner was to take part in a performance at the Coliseum. Mary King, one of the panel of judges, delighted audiences of nearly 8 million during the series with her enthusiastic encouragement, lively movement and changing hair colour. The winners, thirty-one-year-old Denise Leigh, blind from birth, and Jane Gilchrist, a thirty-six-year-old Tesco check-out operator, were announced on 26 February. Each shared the role of Gilda in a performance of *Rigoletto* conducted by Paul Daniel on 1 March. Richard Morrison, who greatly surprised himself by enjoying the programme, found the timing of the show disturbing as ENO's staff were being sacked and suggested a sequel, '*Shoperatunity*', to follow a group of ENO chorus members retraining as Tesco check-out clerks.[41]

Anthony Legge, the head of ENO's music staff, was headhunted after fourteen years with the company to become head of opera at the Royal Academy of Music on 17 March. At the same time ballot papers were going out to the stage technicians, props and costume staff about the proposed 'outsourcing', and the chorus was planning a second walk-out on 3 April.[42]

As a result of the chorus's campaign, a compromise settlement was reached and announced on 20 March. It entailed twelve permanent chorus members taking voluntary redundancy, instead of twenty involuntary redundancies as intended by Felton, leaving a chorus of fifty. There would be a salary increase of 4 per cent from 1 July 2003, but a reduction for the six months from 1 May 2003 to 1 January 2004 during the closure period. The suggestion of the reduced salary was made by Equity to help resolve the situation. There was to be a special media agreement. First call would be given to ex-chorus members for employment as extra choristers for the next three years. The voluntary nature of the redundancies was a relief to the choristers, but resulted in an imbalance of voices in the sections. The imbalance had not been fully corrected by the start of the 2008/9 season.

The process of restructuring was far from complete. On 21 March the Arts Council announced that it had earmarked a specific sum for ENO's stabilisation budget and that discussions over final plans were ongoing. ACE Chairman Gerry Robinson welcomed the agreement but warned: 'ENO is worth saving, but not at any cost.' It had to deliver value for money and break its pattern of recurring financial crises.[43]

Caroline Felton left ENO in April. Ellis later commented that 'with the benefit of hindsight', the negotiations had been 'clumsily handled', resulting in the concert given by the chorus when they were on strike, and 'all the sympathy' that went with it. There were 'attacks on Martin and the board for being cutters and financiers who do not love opera . . . combined with the residual press sympathy for Nicholas Payne' which had put them 'further on the back foot'. Ellis confirmed that the first stage of the restructuring had been less successful than envisaged.[44]

At the time Felton left, Loretta Tomasi was appointed interim finance director and shortly after interim executive director, reporting to Doran. Tomasi was an Australian-born accountant who had trained with Coopers Lybrand and had worked for twelve years with Andrew Lloyd Webber's West End commercial company, The Really Useful Theatre Group – formerly Stoll Moss.

While the final restructuring was being decided on, Dennis

Marks made a last appeal for the old-model ENO in the *Independent*. 'Where in Europe', he asked, 'can one find 200 singers and orchestral players with the musical, dramatic, technical, and administrative staff to support them performing the full range of the operatic repertoire throughout the year at prices almost everyone can afford? What can substitute for one of the largest scale operatic ensembles left in Europe?' He believed that the ensemble, with its 'shared values, collective experience, training, exploring and changing together', was endangered. Collective creation, mutual trusts and shared sensibilities had made companies from the Royal Shakespeare Company to the Berliner Ensemble great. Marks had grown up inspired by the team players of the 1960s who later became stars – from Colin Davis, Norman Bailey, John Tomlinson, Anne Evans and Graham Clark to Ian Holm and David Warner.[45]*

The performers continued – as always – to give of their best. On 6 March Poul Ruders's *The Handmaid's Tale* – based on the novel by Margaret Atwood – received its British premiere, directed by Phyllida Lloyd. Canning thought that the score 'combined technical mastery with a rich palette of orchestral colour', while Paul Bentley's libretto reflected Atwood's own lack of depth in the subsidiary characters. He found it a 'powerful evening of music-theatre', well structured and fast moving. The orchestra under Elgar Howarth could not be faulted.[46] *The Trojans at Carthage* lacked the sharp focus of *The Capture of Troy* in May. There were also revivals of *Tosca* and McVicar's lively *Alcina* in March and April.

According to the 2002/3 annual report, there had been an operating deficit in unrestricted funds of £3,052,000, which had been covered by the first instalment of the Arts Council stabilisation grant. The deficit was partially due to the reduced number of performances resulting from the long summer closure for restoration

* In May 2004 Tessa Jowell gave a speech entitled 'Government and the Value of Culture', in which she cited the Kroll Opera and Klemperer, and Simon Rattle and the Berlin Philharmonic's education programme as 'showing that access and excellence could co-exist'. While virtually quoting Lilian Baylis in her remarks about 'bringing people the possibility for experiencing the best in opera and music by giving them access to resources and possibilities that were hitherto the preserve of the middle and upper classes', she made no mention of ENO or its Baylis Programme.

and low box-office revenue, with average paid attendance at 63 per cent. There had been 133 performances, including six at the Barbican. *The Trojans* won the 2003 Olivier Award for best new opera production.

Negotiations with the Arts Council had continued. Tomasi later said that the numbers had needed 'more back up and refinement so that the figures of the three-year strategy were deliverable'.⁴⁷ After submitting a revised plan, it was agreed in November that ENO would be awarded a £10-million stabilisation grant. Smith recalled that 'we persuaded the Arts Council to come up with £10 million by developing a new economic model for ENO'. As a result of the plan a series of redundancies were 'actioned' at the time of the closure of the Coliseum for restoration, which continued from June 2003 to February 2004.

Board member Christopher Jonas liaised with the architects and engineers on behalf of the board for the Coliseum restoration. Smith was proud of the achievement: 'I gave four and a half years of my life to the restoration,' he said, adding, 'It nearly killed me.'⁴⁸ The restoration of the Coliseum was completed at a cost of £41 million, of which £18 million was private funding, £10 million was from the Heritage Lottery Fund and £13 million was from the Arts Council Lottery Fund.

In October ENO announced the Sky Artsworld's £3-million sponsorship for ENO, which Smith later said he had personally negotiated with Tony Ball, Chief Executive of Sky. Board member John Nelson had made the introduction. The press release announced that the major sponsorship underpinned ENO's reputation as the People's Opera and would enable it to reach a wider audience than ever before with its 'unique blend of stimulating and adventurous opera and music theatre'.

The early part of the 2003/4 season took place at the Barbican, starting on 20 September with *Così*, and continuing with concert performances of *Thaïs* three days later, *I Capuleti e I Montecchi* in October and *Twilight of the Gods* in November. A revival of *The Rape of Lucretia* also took place at the Barbican. Average paid attendance was 85 per cent, according to the press release.

On 4 December, shortly before the Coliseum reopened, Daniel announced that he would be leaving at the end of his contract eighteen months later, in July 2005. He believed that he had held a line and had prevented many of the originally intended cuts. He had also achieved his goal of ending the freeze on orchestra recruitment. Over the previous two years, 26 per cent of the orchestra's positions had been frozen, at a time in which it had performed some of its largest-scale repertory, including *The Ring* and *The Trojans*. Daniel felt that he had spent too much time being a 'politician and manager', and that his music-making had been compromised. Mark Elder had pointed out to him that in his own time he had been protected from management burdens by both Harewood and Jonas. Daniel felt that it was time to go. 'Seán was in place and he knew what I felt the company should be.' Shortly after he left ENO, the freeze was put back on orchestral appointments.[49]

In mid-January 2004 it was announced that there would be a two-week delay in the opening of *Nixon in China* as the building work was not completed. Then, a fortnight later, that all its performances were cancelled; the building would reopen instead with a special event on 21 February. Andrew Clark wrote of Doran's 'gift for the blarney', as he announced his plans and said that he was committed to an ensemble of singers.[50] Doran intended to combine a focus on the English repertoire, including Purcell's *King Arthur* and *Sir John in Love*, with more unusual events such as a Steven Spielberg *Moses and Aaron* and *Billy Budd* in Trafalgar Square.[51] He also intended to bring singers from the world of jazz, rock, pop and folk in for an end-of-season 'festival of the voice'.[52]

At its reopening on 21 February, the restored Coliseum looked magnificent, the Renton Howard Wood and Levin Arts Team having supervised a detailed and loving restoration of the Matcham design and the Dutch Bar. A new staircase to the improved basement ladies and gentlemen's lavatories was incorporated, as well as additional seating and a new air-cooling system. The interior was fully restored in deep Roman purples and reds, with its marble columns and gold-leaf decoration, its myriad friezes, chariots, cherubs, slaves, lions, musical instruments, mosaics and, literally above all, the great ceiling rose, previously a black hole, revealed as a glittering stained-glass dome. In the newly named Sky Bar the glass ceiling was restored and the famous Coliseum globe rotated for the first time in 100 years. The terracotta façade had been scrupulously cleaned and restored with the Heritage grant. There had been some minor improvements to the backstage area, including the stage door, new stage lighting and some changing rooms. The problems of the backstage facilities and loading areas had not been resolved, nor had the conditions for members of the company been improved. The smell from the drains continued to cause intermittent problems.

Once the run of *Nixon in China* was cancelled, it was decided to open with a one-act version.[53] Despite a fine cast, in costume, including Gerald Finley as Chou En-lai, the performance seemed tame without Peter Sellars's staging and in the context of such an important event for ENO. The *Guardian*'s arts correspondent Charlotte Higgins later spoke of the embarrassing scene of James Naughtie on stage interviewing a 'jocular' Smith, quite oblivious to the chorus, which, to a man, was looking on in 'stony-faced near mutiny'. The champagne launch party in the new Sky Bar, she felt, also seemed inappropriate to ENO.[54]

The first new production was *Rhinegold*, which opened on 27 February. Three weeks of rehearsal time in the new theatre had been lost, so Doran delayed the press night by three days to the second scheduled performance. Translated by Jeremy Sams, *Rhinegold* was directed by Phyllida Lloyd, who focused on the banality and shallowness of contemporary culture. Richard Hudson's Valhalla was an unfurnished apartment with en suite bathroom, interpreted as either Ikea style or Belgravia. Wotan's family was seen as a cross between the Blair and Bush first families. The Rhinemaidens were leggy pole dancers, the giants hard-hatted Bob the Builders.[55] It was to be a *Ring* without myth, wrote Clements, 'dealing more in stereotypes than archetypes'.[56] Robert Hayward's portrayal of a property developer Wotan fitted Lloyd's concept. Andrew Shore's pugnacious Alberich and Tom Randle's Loge stole the honours.

A month later Clements judged Phyllida Lloyd's *Valkyrie* to be an assembly of muddled ideas, which added little to Wagner's drama except puzzlement.[57] Musically it was disappointing, although Erica Jeal thought that Daniel's control of the ebb and flow of the music was growing as the cycle progressed.[58] Kathleen Broderick's Brünnhilde was strained, although sympathetic in character, and Hayward's Wotan continued to be too blustery.

Given the circumstances, it was something of a miracle that it took place at all.

At the end of the season on 28 June the company brought its Baylis commission, *The Early Earth Operas*, onto the main stage. The trilogy, by composer John Browne with a text by Jane Buckler, had been developed by Moffitt and King-Farlow over three years, and was directed by Moffitt and two other directors. It was a three-part work, inspired by children's responses to the Book of Genesis, and included 600 children from four London boroughs.

The Baylis Programme, retitled ENO Baylis, had been brought back to the Coliseum after the restoration with its own modest but flexible space, the Clore Education Room. Catherine Sutton took over from King-Farlow as its head in November 2003. The focus of ENO Baylis's work returned to bringing people of all ages into the Coliseum, as well as continuing to work with schools in Lambeth and Southwark and community projects in Westminster. In 2006/7 over 11,000 people took part in ENO projects, which had been separated into three categories. One was Baylis Live, which was designed to reach audiences of all ages and included events for families, seniors and community groups as well as schools. Baylis Live's 'Enjoy Opera' programme provided fifty seats at £7 for certain performances. The second category was Baylis Training, which included courses for pre-professional singers and young people between the ages of four and eighteen. The third area was Baylis Interactive, which was intended to create an 'opera community' website and give audiences behind-the-scenes access to ENO's work. Sutton's budget of £248,000 from ENO was augmented by £52,000 from Westminster Council for specific projects and £100,000 from foundations. During the season ENO Baylis worked with up to 300 artists, who were sourced from auditions conducted by Teresa Deacon. These included company artists, company covers and ENO chorus and orchestra members.

It was not only ENO Baylis that was endeavouring to reach out to new audiences. Doran had arranged that a version of Act III of *Valkyrie* would take place at the Glastonbury Festival in July, where it was conducted by Daniel before a vast and enthusiastic crowd and broadcast live on television. An open-air performance of *La bohème* in Trafalgar Square on 20 July was washed out by a torrential downpour and transferred to the Coliseum. In a reflection on the season, Charlotte Higgins reported scepticism in the opera world towards the programming. It was felt that ENO was being run as a festival with spectacular events rather than by 'looking at why people go to ENO day in, day out'. A work to be written by the Asian Dub Foundation about Libya's Colonel Gaddafi had been announced and introduced by Alex Poots, briefly ENO's director of contemporary art. Asian Dub Foundation described themselves on MySpace as a 'combination of hard ragga-jungle rhythms, indo-dub basslines, searing sitar-inspired guitars and traditional sounds gleaned from their parents' record collections, shot through with fast-chat conscious lyrics'.[59] Anthony Minghella's production of *Butterfly*, planned by Payne, was also announced.[60]

Higgins also reported that Doran had spoken of a surplus at the end of the 2003/4 season of £800,000. According to the annual report, there had been an operating deficit in unrestricted funds of £2,861,000 for the year. This was mainly due to the closure for restoration, which had resulted in only eighty-three performances – sixty-one of which had been in the Coliseum. This deficit had been covered by the stabilisation grant of £10 million, which was both to cover the shortfall and for 'restructuring'. Doran publicly stated that the 'tough' new executive finance director, Loretta Tomasi, was implementing improved controls.[61] The annual report put average paid attendance at 62 per cent.

There was uncertainty hanging over the still unresolved question of who would become the new music director, with several potential candidates, including Mark Wigglesworth, apparently unwilling to take up the role. Andrew Litton, the capable young Anglophile American whose ENO *Falstaff*, *Salome* and *Masked Ball* had all been very well received, was reported to be ready to pack his bags, but was passed over.[62]

At the opening of the new season an article by Damian Whitworth reported rumours of unease in the company and poor box office, especially for the twelve scheduled performances of Bieito's *Don Giovanni*. Only *Pirates of Penzance* was selling well. An unnamed former senior employee was reported as telling Whitworth that Doran was 'indecisive' and that working with him was 'very challenging indeed'.[63] In October it was reported that plans for a complete *Ring* cycle had been abandoned. Gerald Barry's *The Bitter Tears of Petra von Kant* was to open the 2005/6 season.

Four new board members joined ENO in December 2004: Nicholas Kenyon, director of the Proms; Peter Bazalgette, chairman of Endemol, the UK's biggest production company and creator of *Big Brother*, *Changing Rooms* and *Fame Academy*; Francis Mackay, chairman of Compass Group plc, provider of food and hospitality services for industry and health care; and Janis Susskind, the publishing director of Boosey and Hawkes.

The 2004/5 season had opened with both parts of *The Trojans* on 24 September. The next instalment of *The Ring*, *Siegfried*, in November, lifted the project out of its doldrums. It was centred upon Richard Berkeley-Steele's strongly sung and convincing bolshie teenage Siegfried, who shared a dingy bedsit with John Graham Hall's Mime, described by Erica Jeal as 'a riveting portrait of Gollum-like festering misery'. Jeal also found Daniel and his orchestra more assured and taking on a 'real glow'.[64]

*The Pirates of Penzance*, borrowed from Chicago, was not appreciated by the critics but was averaging 90 per cent box office before Christmas and revealing the ENO audience's traditional enthusiasm for Gilbert and Sullivan. On 17 December ENO announced an average paid attendance of 67 per cent, with *Rhinegold* and *The Magic Flute* reaching 89 per cent and all other shows other than *Falstaff* reaching no less than 68 per cent. The twelve *Don Giovannis* were well below 67 per cent.[65]

In January Doran looked forward with a positive announcement of a 'new vision', which put English music from Purcell onwards at the heart of the programme and claimed Britten as the 'house composer'. A Britten opera was to be produced every year, starting with *Billy Budd* and followed by *Death in Venice*, for which Ian Bostridge was already lined up to sing Aschenbach.[66] Deborah Warner was to direct. Canning pointed out that the Minghella *Butterfly* and *On the Town*, also announced by Doran, had been planned by Payne.

At this point Smith announced that he intended to remain chairman of the board beyond his controversial first four years. The appointment of Oleg Caetani as music director was finally announced on 18 February. He would be doing the job part-time in conjunction with his contract with the Melbourne Symphony Orchestra.

Tippett's oratorio *A Child of Our Time*, in January, did not translate well to the stage. Clements thought that Jonathan Kent, in endeavouring to universalise the work as a parable of oppression, failed to be more than sincere, sometimes verging on sanctimonious. The chorus and cast headed by Susan Gritton were, however, in fine voice.[67]

Some comfort was provided by ENO's first staging of Mozart's *Clemenza di Tito* on 5 February, directed by McVicar and elegantly translated by Amanda Holden. It was heralded as a cause for celebration, hopefully marking a revival in ENO's fortunes. Christiansen found Emma Bell's Vitellia fearless and thrilling, while Sarah Connolly's glorious Sesto made the confrontations crackle. Together with Paul Nilon's Tito they invested the production with a depth of psychological motivation and visceral immediacy.[68] Sally Matthews was an enchanting Servilia. With ravishing stage pictures provided by Yannis Thavoris's set and Paule Constable's lighting, ENO had at last hit the jackpot, wrote Canning in the *Sunday Times*.[69] *On the Town* in March was ENO's first Bernstein musical. It was directed with zest by Jude Kelly and choreographed by Stephen Mear, and delighted audiences and critics alike with its exuberance.

*Twilight of the Gods* completed Lloyd's anti-mythic *Ring* in April. Erica Jeal was impressed by the growing focus of the interpretation musically and in terms of its direction. She praised the strong individual performances of Richard Berkeley-Steele's Siegfried, Iain Patterson's Gunther and Gidon Saks's Hagen. Kathleen Broderick's Brünnhilde had grown in stature with each instalment and there was a growing consensus that the complete cycle should be staged. Lloyd's ending, however, proved more controversial. Boos were reported after Brünnhilde was portrayed as a suicide bomber detonating herself in the immolation scene, while Lloyd explained that Brünnhilde 'destroys everything that is poisonous', and that she was just trying to 'express the terrible violence, not draw a parallel with fundamentalist acts of terror'.[70] ENO's new *Ring*, which was not to have a chance to develop into a complete cycle, underlined the difference between the ENO of 1970 and 2004, both in terms of attitudes to production and in the ability of the company to put on such demanding work in its new model.

*

Shortly before his last performances, Paul Daniel gave a long interview to Higgins, which was published in the *Guardian* on 22 April
2005. In it, he talked about his time at ENO, the repertoire, the
achievements, and his strategy of bringing back the big signature
operas into the company, and the connection with Aldeburgh. At
the end of their conversation he told Higgins of his concerns for the
future of ENO. Doran, he said, 'needed very strong people within
the company to actually help run the whole business'. He was worried about the reduced number of performances and the shift in
focus away from repertoire based on ENO's ensemble of chorus and
orchestra to such events as the Asian Dub Foundation's *Gaddafi*,
and a new Monteverdi opera cycle that would not use the ENO
orchestra. The ensemble 'was not something that you drag behind
you but something you push out in front of the audience'. Of the
new music director, Oleg Caetani, Daniel said that he was steeped
in opera. Nonetheless, Daniel was concerned about the time pressure he would encounter while continuing with his annual three-
month commitment in Australia. Of Smith, Daniel said that
although he had collected an awful lot of money for ENO, 'the
company was not with him'.

There was another major development for the new-model ENO
on 8 June, when Doran announced that surtitles would be used. He
quoted the Baylis legacy as the basis for his decision, as well as the
failure of singers to make their words comprehensible. Harewood,
as president of ENO, had warned strongly against the introduction
of surtitles, which he believed might obviate the main reason for the
company's existence – opera in English. Politicians, he warned, in
times of stress and financial squeezing which were always lurking
would hold it against them. Harewood did not accept the argument
that the Coliseum acoustics made audibility impossible. It was, he
said, a technical problem that could be overcome by 'believing it
was important' to make the words audible.[71]

The 2005/6 season opened on 16 September as planned with
Barry's *The Bitter Tears of Petra von Kant*. It was a setting of the
1972 Rainer Werner Fassbinder play and film about lesbian love,
obsession, jealousy and passion. It was directed by Richard Jones
with faithfulness to the piece, 'veering from high camp to devastating tragedy', and designed by Ultz, with what was described by

Tom Service as a 'nightmarish vision of 70s kitsch'.[72] The critics were divided. Service found it full of 'visceral emotional power', with its remorseless high-octane music, while Christiansen found it a 'repellent opera, stuffed with cheap contempt, arty pretensions and hideous music'.[73] It was a disappointment at the box office.

There were, however, packed houses for the scenic glories of film director Anthony Minghella's *Madam Butterfly* in November. Minghella's production, together with his wife Carolyn Choa's choreography and Hang Feng's riotously colourful costumes, was a visual feast. With its Japanese lanterns and an entire orchard of pink cherry blossom, beneath a great mirrored roof, Michael Levine's set provided a fabulous framework for the fragile Butterfly of Mary Plazas and the ardent, if stout, Pinkerton of Gwyn Hughes Jones. Responses to the puppet portraying Butterfly's child were mixed. Morrison thought that Italian emotions and Japanese puppets did not really work.[74] *Butterfly* was a co-production with the Metropolitan Opera, a relationship that was to be further developed.

The season also provided a very well-received *Carmelites* revival conducted by Daniel on his first return to the company.[*] There was a life-enhancing revival of Hytner's *Xerxes,* now twenty years old, which was described by Martin Kettle as 'one of the key operatic shows of the modern era'. Katarina Karnéus sang and acted Xerxes with 'command, wit and sexiness'.[75] Shortly before the opening one of seven large wooden tassels above the stage fell into the empty orchestra pit. The other six were removed and were still not replaced by the start of the 2008/9 season.

On 29 November it was announced that Doran was 'leaving the organisation', less than three years after he had arrived. Tomasi was to take over as Chief Executive, with John Berry as artistic director. No explanation for Doran's departure was given; instead, Smith, in the press announcement, spoke of ENO enjoying a renaissance, with a very successful season that was breaking box-office records. There were rumours in the press that middle management had lost confidence in Doran's leadership and that after their threatened resignations, Vernon Ellis had been inside the building for three weeks

---

* Like *Lulu* and *Falstaff* before, *Carmelites* was recorded on the Chandos label.

observing the day-to-day running of the company, following concern expressed at a board meeting.[76]

Ellis later spoke of his close involvement in the daily organisation in the latter days of Doran, in order to ensure that there was a schedule for the following year and to see at first hand 'how the process of collaborative planning was working, or not'. Although he was aware that such involvement was not a job for a board member, his fellow members had requested it of him. The decision to appoint Berry and Tomasi resulted from his observation at this time that 'they got on and respected each other'. Ellis described Tomasi as 'a solid rock' who had been growing from 'just finance into much broader management' during the previous eighteen months.[77] Board member John Nelson later described her as 'firm, clear and when necessary tough', someone who would make it clear to everyone what their job was and 'get the company pointing in the same direction'.[78]

The 'forty-four-year-old, willowy, bearded Berry', as Higgins described him, had been director of opera programming at ENO since 2003, having been casting director from 1995. He had, he later said, learnt 'everything about production teams and directors' from having observed Payne at close quarters and he had built up many connections during the Payne era. When asked about Payne's departure, he said that even though he liked him enormously, 'if the box office doesn't add up, life moves on; it's a really hard tough business'. The old working model had to be changed.[79] Ellis believed Berry to be 'artistically creative, imaginative and original', capable of bringing together an artistic team with a sense of adventure in the 'modern way'.[80]

The appointments, however, were made without advertisement, causing much controversy. The same day as the announcement, 29 November, the Arts Council discussed the events with its officers Hilary Boulding, Kim Evans and Henry Little also present, after which the Council registered its 'strong disapproval' of the selection process.* The officers reported that they had clearly informed ENO

---

* Attending were Sir Christopher Frayling, Diran Adebayo, Janet Barnes, Sue Woodford Hollick, Kentaké Chinyelu-Hope, Professor Alan Livingston, Sir Brian McMaster, François Matarasso, Elsie Owusu, William Sieghart, Professor Stuart Timperley, Dorothy Wilson, Peter Hewitt, Carol Bewick, Kim Evans, Keith Harrison and Helen Flach. Also present for the ENO discussion were Hilary Boulding and Henry Little.

that recruitment without advertisement was contrary to best practice. Smith had replied that the board took the view that, given the challenges ENO was facing and the urgent need to produce a long-term solution for the company, an interim appointment and a longer recruitment process would not have been in the best interests of ENO. Members of the Council asked Frayling to write on their behalf to Smith, advising him of their views 'in the strongest possible terms'.[81]

In a letter to *The Times* on 5 December Martin Smith explained that 'at a time when the company was doing very well', the board had decided not to 'enter into an extended period of uncertainty and speculation', but rather to confirm the appointment of 'two individuals with proven artistic and managerial records'. They had the full confidence of the board. Smith claimed that ENO was in rude health, with *Butterfly* and *Budd* sold out and *On the Town* achieving 87 per cent. The Sky sponsorship had been renewed to 2009.[82]

Christopher Frayling and Peter Hewitt responded in a letter to *The Times* on 8 December in which they stated that ACE expected all arts organisations to 'follow best practice in their recruitment processes'. Although public advertisement was not a legal requirement, ACE believed that 'transparency and openness' were ways of building trust in public institutions receiving public funding.[83]

According to Smith, the appointments had been discussed with the Arts Council's officers. Then and later he argued that the reason for making the appointments immediate was because 'there were two excellent in-house candidates' and 'the company was taking a battering from the press'.[84]

Smith wrote later that the two appointments had been made 'subject to confirmation after a six-month probationary period'.[85] The *Guardian* reported that on 7 December ENO staff had written to ACE to say that they would have expected the appointments of internal senior management to be interim measures while a suitable artistic director and chief executive of 'international standing and visionary strength was recruited'.[86]

The Tomasi and Berry appointments put in place the structure of management that Smith later said he might have preferred at the time of the appointment of Doran. General directors were no longer, according to Ellis, 'one man bands' but teams like Nicholas

Hytner and Nick Starr at the National, and Tony Hall and Antonio Pappano at the Royal Opera House.[87]

In the *Guardian*, Higgins questioned the changing face of the boards of artistic institutions. There is a certain type of board member, she wrote, who 'seems depressingly prevalent at the moment. He (usually he) has made a fortune in the City. He genuinely loves the arts. But he regards arts administrators as a bit amateurish and thinks that the fact that he has run a bank qualifies him to "know best" how to run a theatre . . . He may harbour frustrated artistic ambitions. He likes the idea of being invited to interesting parties, or getting a knighthood.' But being on a board was about 'trusting artists and helping them to fulfil a vision'. There needed to be greater accountability.[88]

News of Doran's departure had reached the company while it was rehearsing *Billy Budd* – Neil Armfield's production borrowed from Welsh National Opera – which opened on 3 December. Allison wrote of *Billy Budd* that 'the multi-layered success shows that ENO is still a company to be saved . . . one of those rare operatic experiences where everything comes together'. A 'galvanising' Andrew Litton was 'alert to the unique tone colour of the all-male cast' and shaped the picturesque flurries, building them into the bigger canvas. The heroic company responded with shattering impact. Simon Keenlyside sang with virile tone and great poetry while swinging around the ladders and girders, interacting intensely with John Tomlinson's Claggart, Timothy Robinson's Vere and Gwynne Howell's Dansker.[89] Canning said that the company sounded close to its form in the Elder era, which was no mean feat on Litton's part, given the 'evidently poisonous atmosphere in the building'.[90] Both Canning and Allison asked why he had not been chosen to be music director.

The company itself was reported to be disturbed by the events. Higgins wrote on 8 December that the ENO staff were mutinous and that BECTU was threatening to strike as a response to the 2.77 per cent pay rise, which they considered utterly inadequate.[91] Tomasi and Berry had told employees that they were available to discuss any problems, but what people wanted to know was whether they would have a job the following year, Andrew Stewart reported.[92]

Smith was now himself in the firing line. Rupert Christiansen described Doran as a 'pleasant and well-intentioned man', but suggested that he should never have been appointed in the first place. He pointed the finger at Smith, declaring that 'the time has come for Martin Smith, who bears responsibility for appointing Doran, to resign'.[93] Peter Jonas in the *Evening Standard* said that Smith should fall on his sword.[94] Pountney added his voice on 16 December, calling for Smith's resignation in an open letter also signed by Philip Langridge, Jonathan Dove and novelist Jeanette Winterson, which was to be handed to the board before Prince Charles attended a gala performance of *Madam Butterfly*. The letter stated that the opera world felt 'despair and bafflement' at the fate of the company and the failure of the board to oust Smith. Pountney was reported as saying, 'I think the ACE is a very enfeebled body.'[95] In a letter to *The Times*, Pountney added that the task of a non-executive board 'should be to give support to the professional executive and, where appropriate, discreet guidance' as part of a relationship based on mutual 'tact and a certain grace'. This had been the case at the time of Harewood and Arnold Goodman, when the company had prospered.[96] On 17 December the Commons Culture Select Committee urged an enquiry.

Smith stepped down on 21 December and Ellis assumed the role of acting chairman. Smith's letter to the board of 20 December stated that since the board had announced the latest management changes, 'the intensity, inaccuracy and personal nature of the attacks' on him had escalated substantially. The media had obsessively focused on management issues, 'with persistent hostility towards the board and in particular me'. He felt that his ability to continue helping ENO had been damaged by the campaign against him.[97]

John Allison in *Opera* was highly critical both of Smith's chairmanship and of his resignation letter. Board member Brian Unwin later spoke of the 'artistic mafia' ganging up on Smith and the distress this had caused.[98] Smith received retrospective appreciation later in the year from board member and Barbican director John Tusa, in an article on 7 May 2006 in the *Evening Standard*, where he wrote of the need for bankers to support the arts and the ingratitude shown to Smith, who had given £1 million, had never been thanked and had been 'shockingly treated'. There was concern that his resignation might deter the City high-fliers, whom he was encouraging to get involved in the arts.[99]

Vernon Ellis and John Baker thought that Smith had been unduly vilified by the press, but Baker nonetheless pointed out that unlike Smith, he had been careful to keep a low profile during his tenure, ensuring that the public face of the company was represented by the artistic leadership.[100] Ellis was very supportive of Smith. Losing two directors put 'huge pressure on the chairman', he said, and Smith 'did a very honourable thing by resigning'. Ellis had great sympathy for Smith in what had been 'a very, very difficult decision'.[101]

Smith's resignation further widened the spectrum of opinions and differences in the perception of events. Nicholas Hytner later commented that it was unfortunate when Martin Smith decided that he could 'run ENO better than the people who were running it'. Whenever the board of any performing-arts company has moved in and taken over, it was because that same board had allowed the company to get into financial trouble. The problem was that the people who were really suffering at ENO were the people who had been there for decades.[102]

Smith himself later wrote of his 'pride' in the achievements 'on his watch as chairman', when the board 'saved the company from bankruptcy, sorted out the company's economic model, secured its principal sponsor' and appointed virtually all of the board and management team, who still at ENO at the time of writing.[103] His accession to the chairmanship of the ENO had indeed been a turning point for the company. The need to restore the Coliseum had precipitated the crisis that saw the end of the era when chairmen facilitated and fought for the plans and work of an artistically led executive and a large, full-time ensemble company, and the beginning of the implementation of the new working model. Furthermore, the dividing line between the people who create the work and the governors became less distinct than had been the case historically.

ENO was coming out of stabilisation in March 2006 and had to submit the 2006/7 budget and a report on its proposals for long-term stability.[104] According to Tomasi, they had to provide a three-year business plan to prove that ENO could 'survive post-stabilisation'.

The plan involved further 'restructuring' and was completed in consultation with ACE,[105] who reported that different 'options and models were being developed and their associated risks evaluated'. ACE needed to be convinced that ENO had a strong vision driving the company, and senior managers and a board capable of implementing a programme of radical change.[106] ENO received a welcome £2-million gift for new productions from Lord Laidlaw in March.

The Arts Council discussed ENO's future with its officers on 31 January 2006. The new management team at ENO was said to be 'taking a considered and rigorous approach to artistic and business planning'. The paper for the March meeting would include the proposals from ENO for 2007/8 onwards and confirmation that the proposals would work within 'the existing financial envelope'. Vernon Ellis was acting chairman and ACE officers were in close contact over the process for the appointment of the new chair. The results of the deliberations would be made known in early 2007.[107]

When Doran had left ENO, his choice for music director, Oleg Caetani, was also reconsidered, and Nicholas Kenyon was designated to head the Search Committee. On 8 March the appointment was announced of Edward Gardner, the thirty-two-year-old protégé of Mark Elder, who was to take over in May 2007. Gardner, as with so many successful conductors, had been on the Glyndebourne music staff and had been music director of Glyndebourne Touring Opera. He had sung at Cambridge, studied at the Royal Academy, where he had spent time accompanying singers, and had spent three summers at Salzburg working as a répétiteur. He had also been Elder's assistant at the Hallé. His love of opera had been developed as a teenager at the ENO in the later years of the Pountney/Elder era at such shows as *Lady Macbeth* and at the Covent Garden promenade *Ring* cycle in the 1990s.

It was an appointment welcomed by everyone who held ENO dear, and especially within the company. Tomasi said that Gardner was 'steely' in his determination to make a success and that management was fully behind him.[108] In November 2006 John McMurray, an experienced former agent with a good knowledge of vocal talent, was appointed casting director.

Meanwhile, Doran's plans were reaching the stage. In March

2006 Vaughan Williams's *Sir John in Love*, an opera that had not been heard since the New Opera Company production at Sadler's Wells in 1958, was directed by Ian Judge and designed by John Gunter. It contained some beautiful lyrical music as well as folk music and, conducted by Caetani, was sung by a cast that called to mind the great days of the ENO company. The tender young lovers of Sarah Fox and Andrew Kennedy were surrounded by Jean Rigby's Mistress Ford, Sally Burgess's Mistress Quickly and Marie McLaughlin's Mistress Page. Judge set the piece at the turn of the twentieth century. Andrew Shore's Sir John was, for Clements, a 'true man of the shires'.[109]

The Laurent Pelly/Chantal Thomas production of the 2001 Paris Châtelet *Belle Hélène* still contained some of the 'cheeky wit and brisk pace' originally noted by Milnes when it crossed the Channel on 3 April. It was also graced with the sophisticated naughtiness, elegant phrasing and clarity of diction of Felicity Lott as Hélène, as well as the appealing Paris of Toby Spence.[110]

In April Chen Shi-Zheng's production of Monteverdi's *Orfeo*, planned by Doran, was praised by Canning for a cast that included Elizabeth Watts, Wendy Dawn Thompson, Brindley Sherratt and Tom Randle, with John Mark Ainsley's brilliantly sung Orpheus at its heart.[111] The ENO orchestra was only augmented and had not been replaced by members of the Orchestra of the Age of Enlightenment, as had been rumoured earlier.

Mackerras celebrated his eightieth birthday with a new production by Christopher Alden of *The Makropoulos Case* in May with Cheryl Barker. It contained the familiar expressionist, fluorescent-lit Alden imagery, set in a steel and glass deco foyer, a shivering mechanistic world with caricature figures floating around an alluring Barker. Mackerras brought out from the pit all the passion and feeling lacking on stage with electrifying clarity and vitality. Mark Morris's *King Arthur* at the end of the season on 26 June was a flop.[112]

The annual report for the year ending 31 March 2006 showed a deficit in unrestricted funds of £2,063,000, which was partially covered by the continuing Arts Council stabilisation grant of £1,688,000, leaving a deficit of £375,000. Neither the box office nor fundraising had reached their targets, with the season achieving average audiences of only 65 per cent in 139 performances. The grant had been increased by 3 per cent to £16,556,000.

The headhunting for a new chairman resulted in the appointment on 26 June of Vernon Ellis, who had been acting chairman since Smith's resignation. John Baker thought him an excellent and popular choice – 'hugely generous, knowledgeable about music' and a 'friendly, unassuming personality'.[113] Christiansen, however, questioned the wisdom of appointing someone who had been so closely involved in the period of ENO's worst 'discomfiture' and warned against further redundancies that would dismantle 'what little company spirit remains at ENO after all its recent tribulations'.[114]

The manner of Berry's appointment and the effect of years of management and board controversy overshadowed his work and choices in the early period of his office. He later pointed out that he had had to put the 2006/7 season together at the last moment in difficult circumstances.[115] Some good shows emerged out of what could have been a disaster.

Berry decided that Seán Doran's *Gaddafi* would not be removed from the schedule. It opened on 27 August. The work was the brainchild of Alex Poots, who had since moved on to the Manchester International Festival, together with Steve Savale of Asian Dub Foundation and playwright Shan Khan. Khan was looking forward to the 'prospect of a scrap with operagoers' and believed that he and his colleagues would be 'storming the barricades of the cultural establishment'.[116] In the event it was left to the skilled hands of David Freeman and James Morgan to get the work onto the stage. Savale's score was based on bass guitar, drums, sampled sound effects, electric violin and oud, and some harmonious minor-scale interjections from the ENO orchestra. Few operagoers turned up to be stormed at the barricades, even on the 'heavily papered' first night.[117] Critics wrote of its ineptitude, offensiveness, and its 'agit prop' cynicism.

Berry's achievement in putting the season together at the last moment was not taken into account by the critics, who presented every weak production as a failure of management. Hugh Canning was particularly outspoken. In October 2006, after *Traviata*, he launched a fierce attack on Berry for a failure of artistic leadership in permitting the director Conall Morrison from the Abbey Theatre to set the opera in Dublin. The phoney Catholic–Protestant antagonism, said Canning, was a 'feeble' idea that should not have been allowed past the preliminary discussion stage. Jonathan Darlington was a non-dynamic conductor and it was not a first-rate first cast, Rhys Meirion, a Berry protégé, having pulled out at the last moment.[118]

Berry had also popped into the season at the last moment the Gilbert and Sullivan *Gondoliers* as a miniature Venice cartoon 1950s update, with what Christiansen described as garish Smartie colours.[119] The responsibility for its overanxious jollity lay as much with Gilbert as with director Martin Duncan. Surtitles, it was pointed out, were shamefully necessary. The young soprano Sarah Tynan – one of the three remaining company principals who were not members of the ENO young singers programme – was the brightest light for the future.[120]

The production of *Jenůfa*, directed by David Alden and shared with Houston, was a project first mooted by Payne but not taken up by Doran. One of the first things Berry did was to revive the plan. By chance, Amanda Roocroft was free.[121] Set in a grim, mid-twentieth-century urban landscape, in familiarly angled sets and stark lighting, *Jenůfa* was distinguished by Roocroft's commanding performance. ENO received three Olivier nominations for best opera production: for *Jenůfa*, *Makropoulos* and *Orfeo*. *Jenůfa* won.

In November, as part of the effort to restore the core repertory, *The Marriage of Figaro* was entrusted to Olivia Fuchs, who had worked at Holland Park Opera and Opera North. Some critics found the production slightly lacking in focus. David McVicar was a more experienced Coliseum hand. His camp and dirty *Agrippina*, borrowed from La Monnaie in Brussels (2000), opened on 6 February 2007. It delighted – not least with a fine cast that included Sarah Connolly in killer heels 'singing with total stylistic and technical assurance, as well as playing the queen bitch with terrific relish'.[122] Christine Rice was a coke-snorting punk brat of a Nerone. Lucy Crowe, standing in at the last moment for Rebecca Evans as Poppea, was a revelation for the critics. Amanda Holden's witty translation kept the long evening lively.

In February a shadow was cast over the revival of *La bohème* when director Steven Pimlott died just before the opening. Nicholas Hytner spoke of his grace and courage in the face of illness.[123]

The restructuring of the company continued during the winter of 2007. Tomasi told the staff on 23 February that one in ten members of the company, forty-five in all, were to be laid off. Gerry Morrissey, general secretary of BECTU, was reported as saying that it looked as if management were trying to 'casualise its work-force'.[124] He believed that too great a reduction was a retrogressive step for ENO as the best would go elsewhere and the company needed a permanent staff.[125]

The 'actioning' of the redundancies began in March. Tomasi later described the process: 'The implementation of the plan to make the company more flexible involved an overhaul of contractual arrangements and some job losses across various areas of the com-pany, reducing it to circa 400 staff. This would allow the company to operate with a solid level of core staffing supplemented when needed.'[126] The Musicians Union's London organiser, Dave Webster, was told that the Arts Council was no longer prepared to bail out ENO and there were to be nine redundancies and vacancies unfilled, leaving a core orchestra of sixty-two.[127]

ENO confirmed that the redundancies were 'in line with the process and timescale agreed with ACE twelve months ago'. The chairman of the Arts Council, Christopher Frayling, said on 29 March that ENO had a year in which to prove itself. ENO 'exited ACE's stabilisation process in March 2006 and as with any organ-isation in this situation, the ACE would continue to monitor ENO's progress as it continued to develop and implement its plans'.[128]

The redundancies entailed the loss of many individuals, some of whom had been there for over thirty years and whose accumulated experience had been the invaluable resources of a previous era. There was a gradual erosion of both talent and technical experi-ence, of people who had been – in Henrietta Bredin's words – pre-pared to go 'the extra mile' as part of a team; to create 'work that thrilled'.[129]

In May 2007, after another threat of industrial action, the Musicians Union and Tomasi negotiated the final size of the orches-tra, which would be sixty-nine instead of the suggested sixty-two, with no compulsory redundancies. The new music director, Edward Gardner, was involved in the discussions. Long and arduous negoti-ations continued between July and December, when a two-year con-tract was agreed, with a pay increase in return for longer hours, together with limited Sunday working and media work. Dave

Webster later recalled that the negotiations were difficult at times but ultimately constructive. Both Webster and Gerry Morrissey found Tomasi a tough but fair and straight-speaking negotiator.[130]

Agreement with the stage and flying departments was not reached until March 2008 and not until after another strike threat, after the failure to achieve the loss of eleven positions voluntarily was met with a management warning of compulsory redundancies. On 12 March management accepted the offer of eight volunteers, two compromise agreements and one position to be lost through 'natural wastage'. ENO agreed to a one-off payment of £150 per person to buy out the current restrictions under the BECTU agreement regarding broadcasting and recordings and worldwide distribution and all media. By the start of the 2008/9 season there was a permanent crew of fourteen grade-one staff and four senior flys technicians. Extra staff, many of whom were old ENO hands, were to be contracted as required, depending on the demands of the production.[131]

At the height of the redundancies in April 2007, the heroic staff and chorus put on a miraculous performance of Philip Glass's Gandhi opera, *Satyagraha*. With its endlessly repeated patternings, it was extremely demanding for the chorus to sing as well as to learn, since it was written in Sanskrit. The opera was thought to be 'a masterwork of theatrical intensity'. A co-production with the Met, it did not stint on fabulous design and was a stirring success. Phelim McDermott directed, assisted by set designer Julian Crouch and his theatre group Improbable. Image after image was etched indelibly on the memory in its masterly fusion of the aural and visual, wrote Hilary Finch in *The Times*.[132]

The season's last new production was Deborah Warner's *Death in Venice*, planned by Seán Doran. Gardner's convincing first performance since taking up his post gave heart to the critics. Allison described how the score's vivid evocations, from the throb of the steam ship to the bells of St Mark's, emerged in fascinating detail, thanks to his 'muscular conducting'. Warner, who refused to allow surtitles on the first night, created a production which, in Tom Pye's magical sets, was utterly convincing in its evocation of Venice conjured by bells, images of gondoliers swallowed up in the mist and great wafting drapes, while Kalman's 'hazy, choleraic' lighting provided suggestions of sickness. Ian Bostridge was a young if world-weary Aschenbach – more neurotic than afraid of old age and the loss of inspiration. Allison saw *Death in Venice* as a 'strong artistic statement from a beleaguered company'.[133]

Gardner also made a compelling contribution to the last operatic offering of ENO's short season with a dynamic yet sensitive rendering of *Clemenza di Tito*, a revival of McVicar's February 2005 production. Alice Coote was a lustrous Sesto and Emma Bell a fine Vitellia.

The last run of excellent shows was followed by two long runs of musicals. A revival of *On the Town* was rumoured to have lost £100,000. It was followed by the 1953 Broadway hit *Kismet*, a musical described by Richard Morrison as 'the blue Stilton of Broadway', a tacky production that Sir Cameron Mackintosh would not have touched with a 'sterilised bargepole'.[134] In Allison's view, ENO management showed an alarming lack of judgement in putting on such 'offensive rubbish'.[135] The timing was inappropriate for a jaunty musical set in Baghdad at a time when terrible violence in the city was being reported daily on the news. Celebrity guest Michael Ball was accompanied by Alfie Boe, Sarah Tynan and Donald Maxwell. Even though Berry's last-minute planning had salvaged some distinction for the season, *Kismet* left a bad impression.

According to the annual report for 2006/7, the season had resulted in an operating deficit of £896,000. The annual report also showed that box-office attendance had reached 65 per cent of capacity as against a target of 74 per cent. Fundraising was lower than budget, while the grant had been £17,011,000, an increase of 2.75 per cent over 2005/6. The accounts showed an overall surplus of £5,487,000 after accounting for a profit on the sale of the freehold property at Dalgleish Street, Stepney, of £6,997,000.

The sale of the Stepney property meant that urgent repairs and the repainting of sets could no longer be done in-house and had to be sent out to commercial firms, causing inconvenience. There was also less space for storage. As with so many institutions of the post-war welfare state, assets were being sold both to raise revenue and to reduce overheads.

Shortly after Gordon Brown became prime minister on 28 June

2007, James Purnell took over from Tessa Jowell at the DCMS. He immediately called for an end to the tyranny of targets and appointed Brian McMaster to advise on how best to 'create the trellis' on which the artistic flower could thrive. On 12 October the arts community heaved a sigh of relief that they would not have to face the threatened cut in arts spending when Purnell promised a further £50 million by 2010/11 (£467 million in all by that year). Even so, ENO's grant for 2008/9, at a shade under £17.5 million, failed to take inflation into account and its announcement was accompanied by a warning that ENO must be on its best financial behaviour.

The policy of the 2007/8 season was to create many productions new to London. As Berry's first full season progressed, he was full of confidence and determination. The ten new productions would 'introduce new work with a wide contingency of creative teams from across the arts, directors, stage and video designers, dancers – a huge mix'. It was, he said, echoing the thoughts of both Ellis and Tomasi, a 'new way of working'. London was a 'huge melting pot of the arts' and he wanted ENO to be at the heart of it. Such an ambitious programme would partially be paid for by co-productions with the Met, the Mariinsky, La Scala and Houston. ENO, Berry said, was also 'leading the way' with online interactive programming. He was 'pushing all the buttons' that he wanted to push.[136]

Before the start of the season, ENO Baylis's interactive website Inside Out, which had shown work behind the scenes on *La bohème* in 2006/7, now focused on the first new production of the season, *Carmen*. The site was designed in collaboration with film director Sally Potter's company, Adventure Pictures, in the summer of 2007, and presented video clips about the process of the production as well as blogs and interviews with the cast. One hundred and seventy people took up the opportunity to write reviews. The next project, on *Aida*, was a dressing-up doll on which visitors to the site could mix and match the costumes of a collection of Zandra Rhodes designs. Catherine Sutton, Head of ENO Baylis and later a Senior Producer in ENO Baylis, described ENO's interactive website as a 'portal for a big conversation about opera' and a way for the audience to become involved with the company.[137] Although it was impossible to quantify the impact of the website,

with 50,000 hits a month it was unquestionably attracting interest.*

Carmen, directed by Sally Potter, and The Coronation of Poppea,
conducted by Laurence Cummings and directed by Chen Shi-
Zheng, opened the 2007/8 season. They were both severely censured by the critics. The Coronation of Poppea was described by
Canning as a 'fatuous and chichi non-production' of a work that
required direction of Shakespearean psychological insight, rather
than 'beautiful if empty stage pictures'. The participation of the
Orange Blossom Dance Company he found a 'distracting impertinence'.[138] The critics were almost unanimous in their condemnation
of Sally Potter's expunging of all dialogue in Carmen. Meilhac and
Halévy were, according to Milnes, amongst the best librettists in
nineteenth-century Europe and the dialogue was part of the work's
dramatic structure. Carmen without dialogue was, in the words of
Milnes, 'sheer nonsense'.[139] Canning was making no allowances
and was still on the warpath as he pointed not only to the failings
of concept, execution, translation and the expunged dialogue but
also to the ENO Carmen website and Potter blog. In it, Potter had
suggested that she was fulfilling her dream of bringing opera, 'so
often steeped in history and nostalgia, crackling into the present',
and of expunging Carmen of its 'Spanish clichés'.[140] What the critics perceived as a combination of arrogance, ignorance and ineptitude made the production and producer vulnerable to criticism.

It was risky to bring first-time directors to ENO without an experienced director of productions to oversee the work, who could give
support, advice on lighting and keep an eye on the punctuation of
the show. Tim Albery regretted that although there continued to be
music directors, few houses in the US and none in the UK had maintained an in-house director of productions.[141] Ellis, however, was
strongly behind what he called the 'modern', adventurous, risk-
taking way of planning opera, and defended the engagement of
Sally Potter, who had had no previous experience of directing
opera. He rebuffed the critics who said, 'that's what you get when
you use a film director'; he believed that Minghella's Butterfly had
been an unqualified success and, although Carmen 'did not appeal

---

* ENO also posts content on social networking sites such as Facebook and
MySpace, as well as providing YouTube broadcasts, audio podcasts, blogs and
online photo albums.

to everyone', it had had 'some interesting ideas, sold well and provoked a lot of intelligent debate in the audience – a real buzz of discussion at every performance'.[142]

*Aida* was a co-production with Norwegian National Opera, San
Francisco Opera and the Grand Opera in Houston, where it had
premiered in 2006. It was directed by Jo Davies in an old-fashioned
way, which was camouflaged by the much-heralded, garishly
colourful, occasionally beautiful designs of Zandra Rhodes. The
critics, in part reacting to the hype emanating from the marketing
department, which focused on the costumes and scenery, condemned *Aida* without giving weight to the fact that it was well sung
and showed the remaining company heroically tackling one of the
most challenging pieces in the repertoire, despite the stress and
strain. Milnes thought that Claire Rutter sang Aida with a security
and beauty of sound astonishing in one so young. Equally satisfactory were Iain Patterson's Amonasro, despite his unacceptably fuzzy
wig, and Hudson's physically stolid but vocally impressive
Radames. The principals, together with Gardner's youthful yet
thoughtful and intense reading and the brave chorus, placed hope
for the future of ENO decisively on the music.[143]

The experienced opera director David McVicar was back for *The
Turn of the Screw* on 26 November. The cast was strong: Rebecca
Evans as the Governess, Cheryl Barker as Miss Jessel, Ann Murray's
Mrs Grose, George Longworth as Miles and Nazan Fickret as Flora
all contributed to a spine-chilling and disturbing production of
what George Hall described as Britten's 'masterpiece of ambiguity'.[144] Hired from the Mariinsky Theatre, the production of
Britten's chamber opera was universally welcomed as professionally
competent and the first worthy production of the season. Insiders
were as aware as the critics of the weaknesses of the first three productions and yet the full houses showed clearly that not only did the
audience exist for grand opera, but that with the reduced ration of
performances they were hungry. *The Turn of the Screw* made well
above budget. The policy of putting on many new productions and
giving audiences a rare opportunity to see *Aida* also contributed to
the box-office improvement.

As the season neared the end of its first quarter, Berry was excited
by packed houses every night of between 88 and 100 per cent.
ENO, he said, was causing a debate, splitting opinion, creating a

dialogue and 'opening up how to engage with the audience'. ENO was beginning to set up a 'social networking base' where issues were being discussed with the audience, and was 'causing a conversation and causing people to write and causing debate'. As a result he believed that ENO now had, both locally and internationally, a 'huge profile'. Instead of ENO being perceived as 'London's second opera house', it was quite possibly 'the house with the bigger profile'.[145]

The new model meant that there were long periods when the Coliseum was let to the ballet. The autumn 2007 season went from 29 September (with one performance in September) to 8 December and the spring season from 31 January 2008 to 8 March. There was to be a season at the Young Vic from 4 to 27 April and the summer season would run from 24 April to 12 July.

After the winter break *The Mikado* enjoyed a 'spick and span' revival in February.[146] David Alden returned to direct a gripping *Lucia*, in a new edition by Roger Parker and Gabrielle Dotto, which re-established an extensive part for glass-harmonica that added, in Morrison's words, 'a Hammer-horror spookiness to Act III, perfectly complementing the heroine's disintegration and the hallucinatory, almost stream of consciousness music'. Alden's expressionist production placed the piece in a derelict Scottish castle with rusty radiators and swinging electric lights, with a macabre chorus leering at the unfolding tragedy. Anna Christy's abused Lucia, 'tossed and trussed' in the macho stand-off between lover and brother, convincingly conveyed her vulnerability with plangent and incisive coloratura. Mark Stone's 'tremendously sung, repulsively characterised' Enrico, Barry Banks's disgruntled Edgardo in dominating and ringing tenor, together with Paul Daniel's impassioned conducting, contributed to the show's 'torrid energy and whirlwind momentum'.[147]

The new model was proving financially sound. ENO announced a surplus of £1 million in April. The choice of repertory also reflected the new way of working. The spring saw the first ENO season in the Young Vic – a venture that had its roots in the Stevenson report's suggestion of seasons in smaller venues for a reduced ENO. For Olga Neuwirth's *Lost Highway*, based on David Lynch's cult film of 'parallel lives, swapped personalities and morbid sexual fantasies', the director Diane Paulus and designer Riccardo Hernandez made brilliant use of the space with a fibreglass room suspended above a highway-like central acting area, according to Canning.[148] In April Birtwistle's *Punch and Judy*, directed by Daniel Kramer and conducted by Gardner, gave credence to the policy of ENO performing in a chamber space. Morrison praised Kramer for placing Punch firmly in his seaside origins, while 'boldly opening up the terrifying psychological hinterlands' and 'violently ritualistic puppet play aspects of the story'. At the same time Gardner provided the necessary light and shade – a 'lacerating blitz of sound or sardonic, frenzied dance', when required.[149]

Gardner was increasingly seen as the focus for ENO's future. A member of the chorus, David Dyer, spoke of his 'inspiring and galvanising leadership'; he was 'personable yet still the boss, demanding in his standards, and keen for the company to succeed'.[150] A good company person, full of talent and infectious enthusiasm, like his mentor Mark Elder he had the crucial gift of connecting with the stage. Described by Hugh Canning as 'handsome, slightly built and a natty dresser', he was also both charming and an easy communicator.[151] While learning the nitty-gritty of being a music director, he had the right spirit and was holding onto the core values of ENO. He was closely involved in planning and, since there were no longer any company principals, hoped to identify and develop the loyalty of a group of British singers who could tackle the great Verdi and Wagner pieces that so suited the Coliseum and ENO's traditions. Aware of his inexperience, he was in no rush to do the big pieces, and was planning to bring in other conductors. At the same time he loved Strauss, Verdi and Wagner and was keen to do such works as *Simon Boccanegra* and *Don Carlos*. He also recognised how important it was to work with experienced directors like Warner, McVicar and Jones. In the new model the amount of each year's work would be decided year by year. 'I would hate our mantra' to be that 'we do things in a new way', Gardner said. What ENO had to do was to provide 'the highest quality opera in English' at accessible prices.[152]

The company needed inspiring artistic leadership after its recent travails and as it adjusted to the latest ENO 'model'. The size of the company had been greatly reduced over the previous thirty years. Company principals had been on weekly contracts in the days of Sadler's Wells and the early ENO. From the mid-1960s to the 1970s, when there were still two tours going round the country, there were between forty-five and fifty-five company principals. After the days of touring and as singers and management became less willing to commit to such terms of employment, numbers declined. In the mid-1980s there were slightly over thirty on weekly contracts, while there was always a pool of regular visitors, some of them ex-company members. These numbers had declined to twenty by the end of the Jonas era – largely due to financial constraints. In the early 1990s Marks increased their number to about twenty-five. By 1998 there were twenty-two, which increased to twenty-eight with the addition of the Jerwood Young Singers. By 2007/8 there were just six company principals, of whom four were members of the young singers programme.

The chorus had also seen a steady diminution. In Harewood's time there had been eighty choristers, in Jonas's seventy-six, then seventy-two. Felton, who had wanted a reduction to forty, had got their numbers down to fifty. By 2007/8, however, there were the equivalent of one part-time and forty-four full-time choristers. There had been thirteen people in stage management in 1978 and there were four in 2007. There had been ninety-one musicians in the orchestra in 1985, eighty-one in 2002 and there were seventy in 2007/8, going down to sixty-eight after further retirements.[153] The music staff had been reduced from thirteen in the 1974/5 season to three by the 2008/9 season.

With the decline in staff numbers had come a reduction in the number of performances. In 1973/4 there had been 165 at the Coliseum and 100 on tour. In 1983/4 there had been 170 in London and touring had been reduced to twenty-four, in the United States. The greatest number of performances in a single year was in 1991/2, when there were 219.* In 1994/5 there had been 178 performances and in 1995/6 192. In 2005/6 there were 150 performances, in 2006/7 there were 145 and in 2007/8 119 were announced, but in the event there were 121, of which eleven were at the Young Vic. There were 108 visiting company performances of ballet at the Coliseum.

The new model involved features common to all such restruc-

---

* The Stevenson report on the lyric theatre produced a detailed table of performances at both Covent Garden and ENO between 1971/2 and 1993/4. The lowest number of performances in a year at the Coliseum was 164 of twenty-six operas in 1973/4 (six of which were new) and the highest 219 of nineteen operas in 1991/2 (five of which were new). The average was 186.

tured institutions: more work being done by fewer people, 'out-sourcing' and the casualisation of labour. It was a system justifiable from an accounting perspective but one that caused difficulties and strains in practical, human and artistic terms. For the chorus there was no recovery time if anyone fell ill. For large-scale work such as *Aida*, extra chorus and extra staff had to be brought in on short-term contracts. Extra choristers had cost £85.53 per session in 2006/7 and £90.15 in the 2007/8 season. They also had to learn the old productions afresh, whereas the old chorus had a memory bank of productions and long experience of working as an ensemble.

The diminution of numbers meant there were no longer depart-ments in which people could be trained and brought on. Those charged with making sure that there were sufficient numbers to cope with a repertoire of large and demanding operas were con-stantly juggling to ensure that the short-term freelancers were avail-able and suitable. The work of the wardrobe technicians was now done by freelancers, who had professional commitment to each show rather than to the company and many of whom were not familiar with the singers and their needs, physical and emotional. The loss of ten stage staff and the employment of freelancers and different crews within a run also meant that there were greater dif-ficulties in maintaining the technical continuity of the shows. As a result of the new way of working, stress levels within the company were high and the pressures unrelieved. At the end of the 2007/8 season one insider said that while ENO had not felt overstaffed for a long time, it now felt distinctly understaffed and that getting the shows on stage depended on the professional pride of the staff, who had a relentless workload and were feeling the strain.

In a world of strict financial accountability and of funds that would not stretch to the employment of a large permanent staff, 'restructuring' had become inevitable. Management and board believed that without the cuts ENO would not have survived at all. When asked about the morale of the company, Berry replied that the cuts meant it had a future and that the alternative would have been to shut down altogether or become part-time.[154]

The 2008/9 season began in the midst of cataclysmic events in the financial world – just five days after Lehman Brothers in New York filed for bankruptcy on 15 September and three days after the

American Insurance Group, which provided insurance and financial services in more than 130 countries, was saved and in effect nationalised by an $85-billion loan from the US government. Stock markets reeled and the financial and economic outlook was more precarious than at any time since the 1930s.

Despite the background of uncertainty, after a season that had seen a healthy surplus and box-office figures of 80 per cent for paid tickets (financial capacity 70 per cent and total attendance 85 per cent), ENO's chairman Vernon Ellis was 'feeling good about the future'. There were reserves in the bank from the sale of Stepney and he was optimistic about ENO's ability to withstand whatever lay in store and to continue to pursue an adventurous artistic policy. In order to meet the constant challenge of maintaining an oversight of artistic planning while not encouraging the board to start micromanaging the artistic programme, he had initiated a system whereby a management subcommittee would look at artistic planning twice a year. This would enable the board to be involved in the process before plans were a 'done deed'. The board would 'comment, probe and look ahead', taking care to keep the plans in line with ENO 'brand values of creativity, adventure and engagement', while ensuring that they were likely to result in balanced budget. To help to achieve this latter objective ENO had recently recruited a new finance director from Welsh National Opera, Andrew Gambrell, who, according to Ellis, was reputed to be 'one of the shrewdest financial operators in British opera'.

In the 'good old days', Ellis explained, the general director had said, 'This is what I want . . . producer-push mentality'; now the team worked together to get the right balance. One of the things that gave Ellis confidence was that Tomasi, Berry and Gardner respected each other and worked well together. They were also very committed to supporting ENO; for example, Gardner regularly participated in dinners for patrons despite a very busy schedule.[155]

Berry gave the board an appraisal of the previous and the forthcoming 2008/9 season on 17 September. As in the previous season, there would be fewer revivals (five) and more new productions (ten). Ellis commented that houses everywhere were finding revivals harder to sell than in the past, when there had been more interest in particular singers. These days, 'interest was restricted to big international stars, who were more likely to alight on a short rehearsal revival at the Royal Opera House'. He was very enthusiastic about the programme, which would see ENO regulars such as Richard Jones and David Alden and also the return of Tim Albery – for a new production of *Boris Godunov*, with Gardner conducting – and Jonathan Miller directing a new production of *La bohème*. At the same time, Ellis reiterated the company's commitment to directors new to opera, including Fiona Shaw for Vaughan Williams's *Riders to the Sea*, Penny Woolcock for *Dr Atomic*, Iranian film director Abbas Kiarostami for *Così fan tutte*, Katie Mitchell for *After Dido* at the Young Vic and the performance director and choreographer Daniele Finzi Pasca for Finnish composer Kaija Saariaho's *L'Amour de loin* at the end of the season. There was heavy emphasis on international collaboration, and further plans for co-productions with the Met, Bregenz and Salzburg were nearing completion.

Responding to a comment by Hugh Canning in an interview with Gardner that ENO was doing fewer performances in 2008/9 than at any time since the company moved into the Coliseum, both Gardner and Ellis explained that health and safety legislation did not permit as many performances as before and that new productions, of which there were several, required more preparation.[156*]

Ticket prices ranged from the lows of day seats at £10 and balcony at £16, up to £87 top price, with a great variety of pricing depending upon the opera and the day of the week. Middle-range tickets in the upper circle on a weekday were between £28 and £55. Ellis spoke of initiatives aimed at bringing students and the under-thirties into the house with the 'Access All Arias' scheme, which offered discounts to its members, of whom there were over 9,000 by the end of the season – 'the largest such scheme in Europe', Ellis commented.

The season was starting with what Ellis described as Richard Jones's 'brand new conception' of *Cavalleria rusticana* and *Pagliacci*.[157] *Pagliacci* was well received as a 'black-humoured Ortonesque romp wittily updated in Lee Hall's adaptation – Michael Frayn's *Noises Off* reinterpreted by Quentin Tarantino', wrote Morrison. He liked Jane Dutton's imposing Santuzza and *Pagliacci*'s

* Health and safety had been one of the main reasons that the Feasibility Study in 1997 had considered a change of venue.

cast of Geraint Dodd's heartbroken Kenny (Canio), Christopher Purves's slimy Tony, Mary Plazas's pert, two-timing Nelly and Mark Stone's Woody, her 'brawny bit of rough'. Clements praised the chorus in both works and considered the double bill 'high class company work'. Milnes thought that the singers were 'people who in the good old days would all have been under contract'.[158]

Lord Harewood, ENO's president, wrote in September 2008: 'ENO seems at present to be sailing on a fair wind, with interesting and appropriately youthful casting and with some enterprising choices of repertory. That is the way I hope it goes on, always searching for the new, while not forgetting the needs of its traditional public.'[159]

In the new, reduced model, ENO indeed seems secure at last, after a long period of upheaval and crisis, supported by the Arts Council and doing convincing work under strong leadership. It is also a relief that the word 'embattled' has at last disappeared from the media vocabulary when referring to ENO. Nonetheless, with a smaller company and both backstage and front-of-house freelance staff brought in when needed at great expense, and with a higher proportion of new productions than in recent years, which demand more rehearsal time, only a reduced number of performances can be sustained, which inevitably limits the possibility of developing the sort of inclusivity for which Baylis and the postwar enthusiasts had fought.

Inclusiveness has been central to the company's philosophy from its birth. Baylis believed that her local community deserved a respite from the ugliness and difficulties of their surroundings and enabled them to experience the beauty of opera and drama. Dennis Marks expressed it well in a 1996 lecture at the Atheneum entitled 'The Future of Opera in English': 'She believed that the deserving poor of these two boroughs deserved more than music halls and cheap cinemas and she believed with equal fervour that Shakespeare and Verdi spoke to people in a language that only required conviction and clarity to engage anyone and everyone. Whether the language was iambic pentameters or strophic Italian song it belonged to all and should be available to all.'

After the war Sadler's Wells played a central part in the subsidised cultural firmament and in the effort to make opera a more popular art form, an aspiration articulated by the Arts Council in

1969, when it pointed out that to a large extent, supply creates demand, 'particularly if the supply is regular and of high quality'.[160] Yet the role of the Arts Council itself has undergone substantial changes since its conception, when it thought of itself as the nurturer of the new Covent Garden company and, despite some ambivalence, the supporter of Sadler's Wells' expansion. While there were always those in the Arts Council pressing for audience expansion and greater inclusiveness, there were also those who believed that the subsidy for opera took up too great a proportion of the grant-in-aid and who questioned the need for two large companies. The latter attitude took root after the decision that the company should move to the Coliseum instead of the South Bank in 1968, when the Arts Council failed to grasp the nettle of funding two major opera companies doing different things but on an equally grand scale. In response to the increasing funding demands of opera, the amalgamation of Sadler's Wells/ENO and Covent Garden was a recurring theme that raised its head every five to fifteen years with varying degrees of seriousness. Since 1932 there have been seven suggestions that Sadler's Wells/ENO and Covent Garden be amalgamated.

It was under the chairmanship of William Rees-Mogg that the arm's-length tradition was weakened and the financial thumbscrews were put on the national arts institutions. In the management struggles of the new century, there was a lack of accountability in the actions and behaviour of Arts Council officials which affected ENO's destiny. How far decisions were based on personal relationships and how far on the need to protect taxpayers' money is unclear. What is clear is that ever since ENO's move to the Coliseum, the question of sufficient funding for the kind of work required in such a large house has never been squarely addressed.

Furthermore, however demanding opera was on the resources of the Treasury, the amounts of money involved were an insignificant fraction of government spending. Brian Unwin recalled that during his time controlling public expenditure at the Treasury, 'the provision for the arts was rarely considered by very senior officials as it was too small to merit attention at that level'.[161] The *Guardian* in September 2008 published a chart of public expenditure, which showed that the arts received £0.428 billion – slightly less than the £0.5 billion it cost to subsidise TV licences for those over seventy-five. Within the context of overall departmental spending of £586.35 billion, the sums involved for the arts are insignificant. It is clear that ENO could have been funded to maintain its historical role in the Coliseum, especially since increases in core funding historically often came just too late to prevent the build-up of deficits.

Low prices were crucial in maintaining the steady growth of audiences, but the Arts Council did not remain committed to them. In the 1980s the monetarist economic policies of Thatcher and the stewardship of Rees-Mogg at the Arts Council reversed the progress. A report by the Arts Council opera study group in July 1985 pointed out that growth was inexorably linked to ticket prices, and that in London, where prices had gone up 16 per cent in real terms in five years, audiences were declining.[162] At ENO there has been since the 1980s a substantial steady real increase in prices, as well as a decline in the number of performances.* With the supply of performances greatly reduced in quantity, neither the inclusive nature of ENO's tradition nor the ambitions of the Arts Council's 1969 report could be entirely realised.

Nor could the great ENO ensemble company of the Harewood and 'power house' eras be sustained towards the end of the century. In Harewood's time there had been different solutions to the challenge posed by the lack of international star singers such as Covent Garden could muster to bring new life to tired productions. Not only did Arlen and Harewood develop ENO's own 'stars' whose careers the public followed, but the singers worked as a long-term unit, with the intimacy and trust that builds as a result. As Harewood told the company in 1979, seeking to bolster morale and contrast ENO with Covent Garden: 'We have an ensemble, we are a team, we can at our best prove a sharper weapon than they do.' They all had a stake in the company, he told them, and it was theirs at least as much as it was management's. Its successful running depended 'on the subordinating of personal and individual wishes for the overall good'.[163]

The combined subsidy and development income proved insufficient to cover the amount of work being performed and the numbers employed. Deficits had consistently been incurred both as a

---

* By 2007/8 top-price tickets were £83, middle prices between £49 and £53, and the balcony between £16 and £21. There were between thirty-four and forty day seats selling at £10 and £15.

result of inefficiency and in the cause of pushing artistic boundaries. The system had depended on Arts Council bail-outs, and by 2000 those increasingly burdensome deficits were no longer acceptable to the Arts Council. Neither was the free-market era concerned with the 'overall good' or the ideology of ensemble. The management crises of the early 2000s can be seen as a battle between those who defended the traditional large-ensemble ENO and those who saw modernisation and flexibility of the workforce as the only way of saving the brand. At the time of the restoration closure the board and the Arts Council decided to opt for the 'reduced role' model, and what emerged was neither the Sadler's Wells Volksoper nor the second grand – yet open and popular – People's Opera House. It was a smaller ENO, much of whose traditional work was 'out-sourced' and whose reduced workforce could fit more 'flexibly' into whatever financial circumstances ENO found itself, augmented when necessary and when funds permitted.

Over the 138 years of the company's existence it has overcome countless difficulties – including two world wars. It has adapted to many different social and political circumstances since its origins in the social idealism of the days of the Christian Socialist humanists of the late nineteenth and early twentieth centuries. From the earliest primitive days of the Vic to the great English *Ring* of the early 1970s, Sadler's Wells/ENO endeavoured to widen the audience for the great and inspiring works of the operatic canon. It has consistently brought art, music, creativity and sustenance to the most excluded and vulnerable in the wider society: from the woman sitting with her children on the stairs of Lilian Baylis's Vic, to the bombed-out victims of the Blitz, to the young prisoners at Feltham Young Offenders Institute in 1991. It has also been the nursery of countless talents and skills both behind and in front of the curtain. Its workforce has given of its best no matter what the circumstances. It has pushed the boundaries of opera and been uncompromising in its striving for excellence.

The company's collective historical memory creates a fierce loyalty. Jane Livingston, ENO's tirelessly loyal and deeply respected head of press, who retired in August 2008 after more than twenty years with ENO, declared at the time of her departure: 'My pride in the company, whether on stage or backstage, is absolute.'[164] This collective memory resides in its remaining members. The chorus at

ENO is in many ways the bastion of the Baylis tradition – proud that its history is handed on from generation to generation, and that at each performance it reaches out to and maintains the relationship with the audience. David Dyer recalled that when he joined ENO he knew people whose colleagues had sung with Carl Rosa and the first Sadler's Wells chorus. Whenever the chorus sing *Peter Grimes*, he said, they feel a proprietorial connection to the 1945 production and the Britten legacy.[165] At the start of the 2008/9 season Dyer expressed the pleasure of the chorus in the planning of several large chorus shows during the year – *Cav* and *Pag*, *Boris*, *Aida*, and especially *Grimes* – to which they felt they could contribute in a strong way. 'When ENO is bold dramatically, brilliantly prepared, singing directly to their audience in their own language and allied to Ed Gardner's musicality,' he said, the company still has something unique and direct to say and can continue 'to make the case for opera as a living, dramatic, relevant art form'.[166]

This case was indeed made as the season progressed and the critics began to recognise the revival of ENO's artistic mission. Gardner told Richard Morrison of *The Times*, on 3 April 2009, that 'the chorus and orchestra have a massive hunger to be great', and together they were seen to be fulfilling their refound ambition. In *Boris* and *Grimes* the augmented chorus was praised for singing its heart out to thrilling effect, while the orchestra under Gardner's baton was repeatedly praised for opening hearts and ears to music both familiar and unfamiliar.

At the same time, although an ensemble of singers is a thing of the past, the building up of close relationships with artists results in performances that have the ring of true company work, as well as producing some fine individual performances, including Amanda Roocroft, compelling as both Jenůfa and Ellen Orford. There was also Garry Magee's charming Figaro and Andrew Shore's immaculate and subtle Bartolo in a revival of Miller's 1987 *Barber of Seville*; Roderick Williams's vivid and nobly sung Papageno in a revival of another classic ENO production, Hytner's *Magic Flute*; Clare Rutter's thrilling Aida; Patricia Bardon's moving Maurya in *Riders to the Sea* – a show overshadowed by the tragic death of conductor Richard Hickox at the age of just sixty. Gerald Finley gave remarkable portrayals of Robert Oppenheimer in *Doctor Atomic* and a deeply flawed Balstrode in *Peter Grimes* in May 2009. It was this latter show that finally proved that the company was once again capable of great work. It was justifiably seen as a superb company achievement, and one that underscored ENO's historical connection to the work.

Charles Kraus, the chorus manager, is one of the longest-serving members of the company. At the start of the 2008/9 season he confirmed that despite all the difficulties it had faced, the spirit of ENO is indeed still alive and that as well as professional pride in each show, there was still a sense of loyalty to the company and an undiminished belief in performing opera in the language of the audience. 'I don't know why,' he added with a smile. 'Maybe it's the ghost of Lilian Baylis.'[167]

# Appendix 1: The Critics

Critics play a significant part in this history of Sadler's Wells/ENO – not least because their reviews are often the only record of the actual performances. Apart from a few recordings and broadcasts, their comments are the sole evidence of the ethos, style and effectiveness of what is by its nature an ephemeral art form. At their best their work is not only wise and rooted in historical perspective, but demonstrates an enduring belief in, and a point of view about, the value of opera. The best critics share a deep knowledge of both words and music, and in the debate about the sanctity of the text their judgement is a guide to both audience and practitioners. They can be sharp and, if they care, given to expansive language, sometimes even to anger and indignation, but the best are never cruel and avoid passing destructive judgement on artists. Above all, they have a passion and love of their subject. A sense of humour also helps, as does an insatiable appetite – or at least stomach – for viewing countless performances at every level, from the sublime to the dire.

Companies and individuals can be defensive about critics, dismissing them as conservative and lacking vision. What is surprising is that there is such a variety of responses amongst them. Only at the extreme ends of the scale – from excellent to turkey – does there tend to be unanimity. At the excellent end their responses are usually shared by the audience. Occasionally management takes a masochistic delight in bad reviews – courting controversy and pitching itself against what it regards as an uncomprehending, lazy or reactionary press and public.

As with every profession it is clear that critics, like the practitioners themselves, have varying degrees of skill, experience, knowledge and self-awareness, as well as their own preferences. Discerning readers know how to distinguish between them and learn which ones share their own views. As Nicholas Hytner remarked, the English punter has a keen critical sense. 'The best of British art thrives because it communicates,' he wrote, adding that the public's 'bullshit detector was more alert than the elite's'.[1] The same is true for the serious and experienced critic, and the more confident and self-aware practitioners know that they can learn from them, just as the open-minded critic can learn from the practitioner. After reading hundreds of reviews the voices of wisdom start to stand out. No one is infallible and sometimes even the critic admits he or she has got it wrong or has underestimated the worth of a changing style of production.

How much the reviews influence the public is debatable – not least because the runs of shows are often not very long. In audience surveys of the 1980s, word of mouth seemed to be the most significant factor. In the 1950s Desmond Shawe-Taylor ceaselessly championed the work of Janáček, but it took many years before the Czech composer's work filled the house, and even then not reliably. What critics can do, over a period of time, is act as a gauge and keep a watchful eye over the general quality of work being put on, which in turn reflects on the attitude of the arts community and Arts Council.

The company, from the Old Vic and Sadler's Wells to ENO at the Coliseum, has on the whole enjoyed support from the critics who have recognised and endorsed its role in making opera both accessible and popular. Before the First World War critics had begun to take note of the company, focusing on the positive, on the building of an ensemble with such singers as Joan Cross growing in stature and the slow but steady improvements in production. The tradition of encouragement – even positive discrimination – of Sadler's Wells continued into the Coliseum years, with Andrew Porter pointing out shortly after the move that it would not be long before the company would and should be judged purely on its merits. It was on this basis that standards improved and the critics became more demanding.

Before the Second World War it had been customary for critics to write anonymously – for example, P. A. Hatton was known only as 'Figaro' in *Musical Opinion* from 1910 until his death in 1938. He was one of the earliest critics to cover the Wells and point out the qualities of their singers. Even after the war *The Times* maintained this tradition with Frank Howes and later William Mann, who still wrote anonymously until the mid-1960s.

Pre-war critics included Neville Cardus in the *Guardian*, Richard Capell at the *Daily Telegraph* and 'Ernest Newman' (William Roberts), who wrote for the *Sunday Times* from 1920 to 1958. The son of a tailor, Newman was self-taught in music, studying piano and developing a knowledge of opera, especially Wagner, about whom he published several books. He started writing regularly about music in 1894, becoming the *Guardian* music critic in 1905, and from 1906–19 was at the *Birmingham Post*. His method was to combine dialectic skill and scepticism with accuracy, and he acted on the Shavian principle of 'deciding what you think with the utmost seriousness and then saying it with the utmost levity'.[2] His preference for the Teutonic flavoured his negative response to some of the work Norman Tucker championed in the 1950s, not least Verdi. He castigated the 'absurdities of the romantic world in which Verdi's dramatic models lived'. It was, he wrote, 'a muddled fantastic world in which parents and nurses were careless with their babies to an extent of which no welfare worker would approve'. He preferred Wagner's 'narration of antecedent' to Verdi's 'point by point story-telling'.[3]

After the Second World War a generation of professional opera critics grew up, one of whom was the well-liked William Mann – an expert on Strauss and Mozart. In the late 1940s and early 1950s John Higgins was arts editor at the *Financial Times*, where the proprietor, Lord Drogheda, later Covent Garden's chairman, was behind the inclusion of a substantial arts page in the newspaper. Higgins was responsible for employing Andrew Porter and David Cairns, two highly respected critics for over fifty years. Cairns wrote a two-volume biography of Berlioz, and Porter went on to write for *The New Yorker* and the *Times Literary Supplement*. Michael Kennedy was another survivor from the 1950s, maintaining his critical pen and still writing in the new millennium at the *Sunday Telegraph*.

Other critics of the 1950s were Eric Blom, later the editor of the *Grove Dictionary*, who wrote for the *Observer*, and Philip Hope-Wallace, the highly professional critic of *Time and Tide* and the *Guardian*. Hope-Wallace was a kind and encouraging mentor to the next generation as well as very often being right. He was famous for being able to emerge from a show and immediately dictate 400 words down the phone – a skill that once resulted in his apparently having attended a performance of *Doris Godunov*. Desmond Shawe-Taylor was also much respected, writing for the *New Statesman and Nation* and, for many years, the *Sunday Times*. At the *Observer*, Peter Heyworth, the biographer of Otto Klemperer, was a good balance to Shawe-Taylor in the 1960s.

In their turn, these critics were the mentors for the generation that followed – one of whom was Alan Blyth, who started writing for *The Times* and *The Listener* and, along with so many of his colleagues, contributed to *Opera* magazine until his death in 2007. *Opera*, founded by Lord Harewood and his friend Richard Buckle as *Opera and Ballet* in 1950, and retitled *Opera* from 1951, was edited first by Harewood, then Harold Rosenthal from 1953, Rodney Milnes from 1986 and John Allison from 2000. With its combination of erudite articles, spiky and concerned editorials and an eminent list of critical contributors in the UK and abroad, it became highly respected and influential in the international world of opera.

As the century drew to a close the importance of *Opera* grew – not least because the generation of critics who followed in the 1990s and 2000s had to contend with a new phenomenon: the erosion of the space devoted to opera and classical music in the national press's arts pages by material on pop, jazz, world music and other interests. In the 1950s it was not uncommon for an opera criticism to be 2,000 words, whereas today rare indeed would be one longer than 500, other than in the pages of *Opera*. This development reflects the general retreat that has followed the great advances of opera in the postwar years – itself so much a part of the ENO story.

# Appendix 2: Chronological List of First Nights of the Resident Company Productions of Sadler's Wells and ENO Operas from 1931

Before 1931 there were very few new productions at the Old Vic – that is, 'new' in terms of design and direction as we would understand the term today. From 1923 Frederick Hudson was credited with the title 'producer' but was really just a stage manager. It was Clive Carey who, together with Edward J. Dent, developed the concept of interpreting the work and rehearsing the operas with the performers in a dramatic and individualistic way. Carey's new productions before 1931 included:

1920 *The Marriage of Figaro*
December 1920 *The Magic Flute*
November 1921 *Don Giovanni*

Other new productions prior to Sadler's Wells were:

1926 *Madam Butterfly*
1928 *La bohème*
1929 *Tosca*
1929 *The Force of Destiny*

SADLER'S WELLS

*1931*
20 January *Carmen* first SW
21 January *Faust* first SW
23 January *The Magic Flute* first SW
28 January *Il trovatore* first SW
 5 February *Lohengrin* first SW
18 February *Tosca* first SW
20 February *Cavalleria rusticana* and *Pagliacci* both first SW
25 February *Maritana* first SW
17 March *The Lily of Killarney* first SW
18 March *Madam Butterfly* first SW
20 March *Aida* first SW
14 April *The Marriage of Figaro* first SW
15 April *Tannhäuser* first SW
16 April *La bohème* first SW
17 April *Othello* first SW
12 May *The Bohemian Girl* first SW

*1931/2*
29 September *Samson and Delilah* first SW

29 October *La traviata* first SW
 6 November *Dido and Aeneas* first SW
24 November *The Tales of Hoffmann* first SW
22 December *The Daughter of the Regiment* first SW
23 December *Hansel and Gretel* first SW
27 January *A Masked Ball* first SW
25 February *Mignon* first SW
 8 April *Don Giovanni* first SW

*1932/3*
19 November *Così fan tutte* first SW
 8 December *The Devil Take Her* first SW
25 January *Othello*
10 February *The Force of Destiny* first SW
12 April *The Snow Maiden* British premiere

*1933/4*
11 October *Tsar Saltan* British premiere
29 November *Orpheus and Eurydice* first SW
14 February *The Bosun's Mate* first SW
12 April *Macbeth* (Collingwood) first public performance

*1934/5*
24 October *The Marriage of Figaro*
17 November *Die Fledermaus* first SW
12 December *Eugene Onegin* first SW
20 February *Fra Diavolo* first SW
 3 April *The Travelling Companion* first SW

*1935/6*
30 September *Boris Godunov* British premiere of the original version
23 October *Savitri* first SW, *Il tabarro* first performance in English
21 November *The Bartered Bride* first SW
11 March *Falstaff* first SW

*1936/7*
24 September *Carmen*
21 October *Aida*
11 November *Madam Butterfly*
 2 December *The Mastersingers*
24 February *Rigoletto*
31 March *The Magic Flute*
21 April *Hugh the Drover* first SW

*1937/8*
 2 October *La bohème*
 3 November *Fidelio* first SW
17 November *Pagliacci*
 8 December *The Valkyrie* first SW
22 December *Hansel and Gretel*
 5 February *Faust*

9 February *Don Giovanni*
23 February *Cavalleria rusticana*
23 March *Greysteel* world premiere, *The Impresario* first SW

*1938/9*
2 November *Tannhäuser* Paris version
6 December *Don Carlos* first performance in English
25 January *Il trovatore*
8 March *Der Rosenkavalier* first SW
19 April *The Wreckers* first SW

*1939/40*
7 December *Othello*
21 December *Die Fledermaus*
28 February *The Barber of Seville*
13 March *La traviata*

*1940 Summer Season*
28 August *Tosca* new production on tour
29 October *La traviata* (Victoria Theatre Burnley)

*1940/1*
28 October *The Marriage of Figaro* (Victoria Theatre Burnley)
23 December *Die Fledermaus* (Coliseum Oldham)
16 January *The Beggar's Opera* (Victoria Theatre Burnley)
1 July *Dido and Aeneas, Thomas and Sally* (New Theatre London)

*1941/2*
5 January *Madam Butterfly* (Victoria Theatre Burnley)
12 January *Rigoletto* (Victoria Theatre Burnley )
13 January *La traviata* (Victoria Theatre Burnley)
10 March *The Magic Flute* (Arts Theatre Cambridge)

*1942/3*
17 September *La bohème* (New Theatre London)
27 November *The Marriage of Figaro* (Arts Theatre Cambridge)

*1943/4*
20 October *Hansel and Gretel* (New Theatre London)
10 November *The Bartered Bride* (New Theatre London)

*1944/5*
29 August *Così fan tutte* (Prince's Theatre London)
26 October *Gianni Schicchi, Il tabarro* (Theatre Royal Newcastle)

*1945/6*
7 June *Peter Grimes* world premiere
11 June *Madam Butterfly*
23 January *La bohème*
4 April *Sir John in Love* first SW
2 May *Il tabarro*
7 June *School for Fathers* British premiere

*1946/7*
14 October *The Snow Maiden*
18 December *Tosca*
22 January *Cavalleria rusticana*
18 February *Shepherds of the Delectable Mountains* first SW
16 April *Pagliacci*

*1947/8*
14 October *Faust*
17 December *Die Fledermaus*
18 February *Il trovatore*
17 March *Lady Rohesia* world premiere

*1948/9*
27 October *Simon Boccanegra* British premiere
15 December *Schwanda the Bagpiper* first SW
22 February *Carmen*
 5 April *Gianni Schicchi*

*1949/50*
25 October *Don Giovanni*
13 December *Falstaff*
22 December *Hansel and Gretel*
21 February *La traviata*
 9 May *Hugh the Drover*

*1950/1*
28 November *The Barber of Seville*
16 January *Don Carlos* new version
10 April *Katya Kabanova* British premiere

*1951: Festival of Britain Season*
22 May *Dido and Aeneas*

*1951/2*
23 October *The Marriage of Figaro*
 5 February *Werther* first SW
22 May *Eugene Onegin*

*1952/3*
 2 October *The Seraglio* first SW
23 October *Cavalleria rusticana*
20 November *Samson and Delilah*

*1953 Coronation Season*
28 May *The Immortal Hour* first SW
11 June *Riders to the Sea* first SW

*1953/4*
 1 October *Luisa Miller* first SW
26 November *Don Pasquale* first SW
23 December *Hansel and Gretel*

17 March *The Pearl Fishers* first SW

*1954/5*
22 September *Nelson* world premiere
11 November *The Consul* first SW
24 February *The Magic Flute*

*1955/6*
21 September *Rigoletto*
24 January *Pagliacci*
 3 February *The Consul*
18 April *The Marriage of Figaro*

*1956/7*
13 September *Martha* first SW
14 November *Fidelio*
30 January *Suor Angelica* first SW
 1 May *Il trovatore* (first night 25 March 1957, Theatre Royal Newcastle)
24 May *The Moon and Sixpence* world premiere

*1957/8*
26 October *Samson and Delilah* reproduction of earlier production
29 October *The Telephone, Duke Bluebeard's Castle* first SW
20 January *The Merry Widow*
 4 March *Falstaff* reproduction of earlier production

*1958/9*
29 October *The Flying Dutchman*
18 February *Rusalka* first professional British production
15 April *Die Fledermaus* production for Coliseum (first night 7 April, New
 Theatre Oxford)
 9 July *Land of Smiles* production for Coliseum

*1959/60*
13 October *Andrea Chenier* first SW
29 October *Cinderella* first SW
 9 December *Tannhäuser*
17 December *The Merry Widow*
15 January *Oedipus Rex* first British stage production
 2 April *Tosca*
16 May *Orpheus in the Underworld* first SW (first night 18 April, Brighton
 Hippodrome)
10 August *Merrie England* first SW (first night 27 June, New Theatre Oxford)

*1960/1*
 5 October *La traviata* (first night 5 September, Manchester Opera House)
25 October *The Nightingale* New Opera Company production; first SW
 7 December *The Barber of Seville*
26 December *Orpheus in the Underworld* first SW (first night 18 April,
 Brighton Hippodrome)
25 January *Ariadne on Naxos* first SW

22 March *The Cunning Little Vixen* first SW

24 May *La Vie Parisienne* (first night 9 May, Manchester Opera House)

*1961/2*

27 September *Carmen* (first night 11 September, Coventry Theatre)

23 January *La traviata*

24 January *Iolanthe* first production after expiry of D'Oyly Carte copyright (first night 1 January, Theatre Royal Stratford-upon-Avon)

25 January *La bohème* (first night 2 October, Theatre Royal Norwich)

 2 February *The Rake's Progress* first SW

21 March *The Bartered Bride*

10 April *The Village Romeo and Juliet* (first night 3 April, Alhambra Theatre Bradford) first SW

29 May *The Mikado* first SW

 3 July *Murder in the Cathedral* London premiere

*1962/3*

11 October *Idomeneo* first SW

12 October *The Turn of the Screw* (first night 20 September, Manchester Opera House) first SW

 5 December *The Girl of the Golden West* first SW

16 January *The Rise and Fall of the City of Mahagonny* British premiere

20 February *Count Ory* first SW

 7 March *Boulevard Solitude* New Opera Company production; first SW

24 April *The Love for Three Oranges* in association with the New Opera Company

31 May *La Belle Hélène*

*1963/4*

12 September *Der Freischutz* first SW (first night 19 August, New Theatre Oxford)

16 October *Peter Grimes* (first night 23 April, New Theatre Oxford)

26 November *Attila* first SW

19 December *Hansel and Gretel*

12 February *The Makropoulos Case* British premiere

 3 April *The Seraglio*

16 April *Volpone* New Opera Company production; first SW

 9 June *The Gipsy Baron* first SW (first night 26 May, Leeds Grand Theatre and Opera House)

26 June *Our Man in Havana* in association with Rostrum Opera Company; first SW

*1964/5*

16 September *Faust* (first night 8 September, Manchester Opera House)

13 November *Madam Butterfly*

27 January *A Masked Ball*

24 February *The Mines of Sulphur* world premiere commissioned by SW opera

18 March *L'Enfant et les sortilèges* first SW

18 March *L'Heure Espagnole* New Opera Company production; first SW

 9 April *The Marriage of Figaro*

*1965/6*

16 September *Fidelio* (first night 7 September, Alhambra Theatre Bradford)

5 October *Orfeo* (first night 6 July, Cambridge Arts Theatre; sung in Italian)

28 October *From the House of the Dead* London premiere

27 January *The Thieving Magpie*

2 March *La bohème*

29 March *Die Fledermaus*

18 May *Bluebeard and his Six Wives*

*1966/7*

14 September *The Queen of Spades* first SW

15 September *The Barber of Seville*

21 October *Gloriana* first SW

29 November *The Violins of St Jacques* world premiere commissioned in association with the Calouste Gulbenkian Foundation

28 February *Ernani* (first night 19 January, Royal Shakespeare Theatre Stratford-upon-Avon) first SW

31 May *Don Pasquale* (first night 29 March, Leeds Grand Theatre and Opera House)

*1967/8*

9 August *The Magic Flute*

4 October *Orpheus and Eurydice* (first night 25 May, New Theatre Oxford)

21 December *Rigoletto* (first night 13 December, Manchester Opera House)

31 January *The Mastersingers*

Sadler's Wells Opera Company moves to the London Coliseum Theatre. For the first season at the Coliseum the list includes old and new productions.

*1968/9*

21 August *Don Giovanni* inaugural production at the London Coliseum

22 August *Orpheus in the Underworld*

24 August *The Mastersingers*

2 September *Rigoletto*

24 September *La Belle Hélène*

15 October *The Italian Girl in Algiers* first SW

6 November *La bohème*

12 November *The Marriage of Figaro*

15 November *Samson and Delilah*

27 November *The Violins of St Jacques*

18 December *The Force of Destiny*

26 December *Hansel and Gretel*

8 January *La traviata*

29 January *The Flying Dutchman*

5 February *Madam Butterfly* major revival

19 February *Gloriana*

5 March *Die Fledermaus*

20 March *Orfeo*

25 March *The Barber of Seville*

2 April *Iolanthe*
16 April *La Vie Parisienne*
23 April *The Magic Flute*
15 May *The Thieving Magpie*

*1969/70*
13 August *The Damnation of Faust* first SW
 9 October *Patience* first SW
18 December *Lucky Peter's Journey* world premiere commissioned by SW
29 January *The Valkyrie*
18 March *Leonora* first SW
 6 May *Carmen*

*1970/1*
20 August *The Tales of Hoffmann*
21 October *Semele* first SW
27 November *Fidelio* based on the production of *Leonora*
24 December *Kiss Me, Kate!* first SW
29 January *Twilight of the Gods* first SW
13 March *The Seraglio* (gala performance 16 March)

*1971/2*
12 August *Lohengrin*
29 September *Cavalleria rusticana* and *Pagliacci*
24 November *The Coronation of Poppea* first SW (gala performance 1
 December)
 1 March *The Rhinegold* first SW
17 March *Duke Bluebeard's Castle*

*1972/3*
23 August *Il trovatore*
11 October *War and Peace* British stage premiere
25 October *Cavalleria rusticana*
 7 December *The Merry Widow*
 8 February *Siegfried* first SW
14 March *La traviata*

*1973/4*
12 September *Katya Kabanova*
 1 November *The Devils of Loudon* British premiere
14 November *The Coronation of Poppea*
13 December *Mary Stuart* first SW
28 February *Madam Butterfly*
13 March *The Story of Vasco* world premiere commissioned in association
 with the Calouste Gulbenkian Foundation

ENGLISH NATIONAL OPERA

*1974/5*
21 August *Don Carlos*
10 October *The Bassarids* British premiere

16 January *The Magic Flute*
29 January *Der Rosenkavalier*

*1975/6*
4 September *La Belle Hélène*
11 December *Salome* first ENO
4 February *Tosca*
16 March *King Roger* New Opera Company production

*1976/7*
26 August *Don Giovanni*
3 November *Bomarzo* New Opera Company production; British premiere
8 December *A Night in Venice* first ENO
2 February *The Royal Hunt of the Sun* world premiere
16 March *Werther* (Silver Jubilee gala performance)

*1977/8*
30 August *La Vie Parisienne* adapted from production purchased from
   Phoenix Opera (first night 12 April, Theatre Royal Bath)
9 September *La bohème*
28 September *Toussaint* world premiere commissioned by ENO
2 November *Euryanthe* first ENO
8 February *Gianni Schicchi*
5 April *Julietta* in association with New Opera Company; British stage
   premiere
4 May *The Two Foscari* first ENO

*1978/9*
12 August *The Consul* first ENO
22 August *The Seven Deadly Sins* first ENO
20 September *The Seraglio* (first night 11 May, Theatre Royal Norwich)
22 November *The Marriage of Figaro*
28 December *The Adventures of Mr Brouček* British stage premiere
13 February *Dido and Aeneas*, *Les Mamelles de Tiresias* ENO North
   productions
12 April *Manon*
2 May *The Nose* New Opera Company production

*1979/80*
16 August *Die Fledermaus*
6 September *Cinderella* adapted from production purchased from English
   Music Theatre
26 September *Aida*
6 November *The Turn of the Screw*
5 December *Julius Caesar* first ENO
23 January *The Merry Widow*
16 April *The Barber of Seville* (first night 3 May, Kings Theatre Southsea)
10 May *Fidelio* (originally scheduled for 11 March)

*1980/1*
24 September *Così fan tutte*

16 October *Arabella* first ENO
26 November *Boris Godunov*
14 January *Romeo and Juliet* first ENO
7 April Bartók Triple Bill (*Duke Bluebeard's Castle* and the ballets *The Wooden Prince* and *The Miraculous Mandarin*)
23 April *Ariadne on Naxos* (first night 25 March, Theatre Royal Nottingham)
7 May *Anna Karenina* world premiere commissioned by English National Opera

*1981/2*
8 August *Tristan and Isolde*
20 August *Orfeo* (first night 11 March, Theatre Royal Nottingham)
24 September *Othello*
25–27 September Music Marathon
28 October *Louise* first ENO
25 November *Pelleas and Melisande* first ENO
10 February *The Flying Dutchman*

*1982/3*
11 August *The Makropoulos Case*
22 September *Rigoletto*
2 December *Le Grand Macabre* first ENO
20 January *The Queen of Spades*
16 March *Rusalka*
28 April *The Gambler* first ENO

*1983/4*
15 September *Ariadne on Naxos*
29 September *Rienzi* first ENO
22 October *The Valkyrie*
16 November *The Rape of Lucretia* first ENO
1 December *Mireille* co-production with Geneva Opera; first ENO
4 February *The Mastersingers*
19 April *The Sicilian Vespers* borrowed from Paris Opera

*1984/5*
8 September *Osud* British stage premiere
8 September *Mahagonny Songs* first ENO
27 September *Madam Butterfly*
20 December *Mazeppa* first ENO
26 January *Tristan and Isolde*
23 February *Xerxes* first ENO
4 April *The Bartered Bride*
15 May *The Midsummer Marriage* first ENO
17 June *Akhnaten* British premiere

*1985/6*
5 September *Orpheus in the Underworld* (gala performance 2 December; production originally scheduled October 1984)
24 October *Faust*

4 December *Don Giovanni*
16 January *Moses* first ENO
31 January *The Magic Flute*
15 March *Parsifal* first ENO
25 April *Doctor Faust* British stage premiere
21 May *The Mask of Orpheus* world premiere

*1986/7*
27 September *The Mikado* (previews from September 18; performance 8
    April 1987 in aid of the Royal College of Surgeons)
29 October *Cavalleria rusticana* and *Pagliacci*
27 November *Carmen*
19 December *The Diary of One Who Disappeared* first ENO
28 January *Tosca*
 2 April *Simon Boccanegra*
23 April *The Stone Guest* British stage premiere
22 May *Lady Macbeth of Mtsenk* first British production of the original score

*1987/8*
10 September *Pacific Overtures* London premiere
21 September *The Pearl Fishers*
 7 October *Werther* (restaging of the 1977 production)
17 November *The Barber of Seville*
16 December *Hansel and Gretel* (gala performance)
24 February *Billy Budd* first ENO
30 March *The Magic Flute* (gala performance 12 May)
 9 June *The Cunning Little Vixen*

*1988/9*
14 September *La traviata*
 9 November *The Making of the Representative for Planet 8* European
    premiere
14 December *Christmas Eve* first ENO
24 January *Lear* British premiere
22 February *Falstaff*
12 April *Eugene Onegin*
25 May *The Plumber's Gift* world premiere commissioned by ENO

*1989/90*
14 September *A Masked Ball* (gala performance 24 October)
12 October *Street Scene* first ENO
 8 November *The Return of Ulysses* first ENO
18 November *Madam Butterfly* (gala performance 8 December)
 6 December *The Love for Three Oranges*
25 January *Beatrice and Benedict* first ENO
 5 April *Macbeth* first ENO, but not first SW
18 May *Clarissa* world premiere

*1990/1*
13 September *Wozzeck* first ENO

27 September *Greek* first ENO
7 November *Fennimore and Gerda* first ENO, *Gianni Schicchi*
30 November *Pelleas and Melisande*
23 January *Duke Bluebeard's Castle*
23 January *Oedipus Rex*
17 April *Peter Grimes*
17 May *Timon of Athens* world premiere

*1991/2*
30 October *The Marriage of Figaro*
2 December *Die Fledermaus* (gala premiere in aid of the Royal Academy of
  Arts and ENO)
30 January *Köningskinder, or The Prince and the Goose-Girl* first ENO
2 April *Don Carlos*
5 May *Bakxai (The Bacchae)* world premiere commissioned by ENO

*1992/3*
16 September *The Force of Destiny*
14 November *Princess Ida* first ENO
18 December *The Adventures of Mr Brouček*
19 February *Don Pasquale* co-production with Welsh National Opera
17 March *The Duel of Tancredi and Clorinda* first ENO
28 April *Ariodante* first ENO; co-production with Welsh National Opera
5 June *Inquest of Love* world premiere of an ENO commission

*1993/4*
15 September *La bohème* (royal gala performance)
20 December *The Two Widows* first ENO; co-production with Welsh
  National Opera
2 February *Der Rosenkavalier*
31 March *Eugene Onegin*
20 April *Blond Eckbert* world premiere of ENO commission
5 May *Così fan tutte*
8 June *Jenůfa* first ENO

*1994/5*
14 September *Tosca*
8 October *Don Quixote* first ENO
24 November *Khovanshchina* first ENO
3 February *King Priam* first ENO
15 March *Don Giovanni*
1 April *Life with an Idiot* British premiere of ENO co-commission
17 May *A Midsummer Night's Dream* first ENO
10 June *The Rise and Fall of the City of Mahagonny*

*1995/6*
13 September *Carmen*
19 October *The Fairy Queen* first ENO
11 December *La Belle Vivette*
10 February *Tristan and Isolde*

24 April *Fidelio*
25 May *Salome*
22 June *The Prince of Homburg* first ENO

1996/7
12 September *La traviata*
19 November *Die Soldaten* first ENO
18 January *The Italian Girl in Algiers*
 3 March *Orpheus and Eurydice*
 7 April *The Damnation of Faust*
 5 June *L'Allegro, il Penseroso ed il Moderato*

1997/8
15 September *The Flying Dutchman*
20 October *From the House of the Dead, Twice through the Heart* (the latter
  commissioned by the John S. Cohen Foundation)
15 November *Falstaff*
26 January *L'Elisir d'amore*
24 February *The Tales of Hoffmann*
 8 April *Suor Angelica*
15 June *Doctor Ox's Experiment* world premiere sponsored by ENO and the
  BBC, supported by the ACGB, the Idlewild Trust and the Leche Trust,
  developed in association with Botton and Quinn Ltd

1998/9
 5 October *Mary Stuart*
11 November *Boris Godunov*
13 February *Parsifal*
18 March *Mephistopheles* first ENO
19 April *Semele*
20 May *Dialogues of the Carmelites* first ENO

1999/2000
10 September *Der Freischütz*
29 November *Alcina* first ENO
16 February *The Silver Tassie* world premiere
23 March *Pelleas and Melisande*
 5 April *St John Passion* first ENO
11 May *Ernani*
28 June *Four Saints in Three Acts, Dido and Aeneas*

2000/1 *(September–December: Italian opera season)*
18 September *Manon Lescaut* first ENO
19 September *The Coronation of Poppea*
23 September *La Gioconda* (concert performance)
11 October *The Turk in Italy* first ENO
 2 November Leoncavallo's *La bohème* first ENO
17 November *The Prisoner/Folk Songs/La Strada* first ENO
30 November *Nabucco* first ENO
 9 December Verdi's *Requiem*

9 April *Il trovatore*
27 April *From Morning to Midnight* world premiere commissioned by ENO, supported by the Britten-Pears Foundation
31 May *Don Giovanni*
21 June *The Rape of Lucretia*
4 July *A Better Place* world premiere commissioned by the ENO Contemporary Opera Studio

*2001/2*
1 November *War and Peace*
8 November *The Marriage of Figaro*
29 November *The Rake's Progress*
3 April *La Vestale* first ENO
1 May *Lulu* first ENO
29 May *Così fan tutte*

*2002/3 concerts, new and old productions during restoration*
18 October (Barbican) *The Rhinegold* (concert version)
30 October (Barbican) *The Valkyrie* (concert version)
1 November (Coliseum) *The Barber of Seville*
7 November (Coliseum) *Xerxes*
21 November (Coliseum) *Tosca*
10 December (Barbican) *Siegfried* (concert version)
23 January (Coliseum) *Khovanshchina*
27 January (Coliseum) *The Trojans* (Part I: *The Capture of Troy*) first ENO
7 February (Coliseum) *Rigoletto*
28 February (Coliseum) *Der Rosenkavalier*
6 March (Coliseum) *The Handmaid's Tale* British premiere
10 March (Coliseum) *Tosca*
16 April (Coliseum) *Alcina*
8 May (Coliseum) *The Trojans* (Part II: *The Trojans at Carthage*) first ENO
24 May (Coliseum) *Tristan and Isolde*

*2003/4 concerts, new and old productions during restoration*
20 September (Barbican) *Così fan tutte*
23 September (Barbican) *Thaïs* (concert)
8 October (Barbican) *I Capuleti e i Montecchi* (concert)
7 November (Barbican) *The Rape of Lucretia*
24 November (Barbican) *Twilight of the Gods* (concert)
27 February (Coliseum) *The Rhinegold*
8 May (Coliseum) *The Valkyrie*
28 June (Coliseum) *The Early Earth Operas* world premiere of ENO Baylis Programme commission

*2004/5*
24 September *The Trojans* (Parts I and II) first ENO
6 November *Siegfried*
4 December *The Pirates of Penzance* first ENO
21 January *A Child of Our Time* first ENO
5 February *La clemenza di Tito* first ENO

5 March *On the Town* first ENO
2 April *Twilight of the Gods*
12 May *Jephtha* first ENO

2005/6
16 September *The Bitter Tears of Petra von Kant* world premiere co-commissioned by RTÉ and ENO
19 October *Salome*
5 November *Madam Butterfly*
3 December *Billy Budd*
2 March *Sir John in Love*
3 April *La Belle Hélène*
18 May *The Makropoulos Case*
26 June *King Arthur* first ENO

2006/7
7 September *Gaddafi: A Living Myth* world premiere of ENO commission
27 September *La traviata*
2 November *The Marriage of Figaro*
18 November *The Gondoliers*
5 February *Agrippina* first ENO
5 April *Satyagraha* British premiere
24 May *Death in Venice* first ENO
25 June *Kismet* first ENO

2007/8
29 September *Carmen*
18 October *The Coronation of Poppea*
8 November *Aida*
26 November *The Turn of the Screw*
16 February *Lucia di Lammermoor* first ENO
4 April (Young Vic) *Lost Highway* first ENO, British premiere
19 April (Young Vic) *Punch and Judy* first ENO
24 April *The Merry Widow*
22 May *Der Rosenkavalier*
23 June *Candide* first ENO

2008/9
20 September *Cavalleria rusticana* and *Pagliacci*
9 October *Partenope* first ENO
10 November *Boris Godunov*
27 November *Riders to the Sea*
2 February *La bohème*
25 February *Dr Atomic* British premiere
15 April *After Dido*
9 May *Peter Grimes*
29 May *Così fan tutte*
3 July *L'Amour de loin* first ENO

# Notes

For a list of archive locations and abbreviations, see pp. 661–2.

CHAPTER I 1869–1912: BEGINNINGS AT THE OLD VIC

1. Richard Findlater, *Lilian Baylis, the Lady of the Old Vic* (London: Allen Lane, 1975), p. 31.
2. The model dwellings are described in the *Country Magazine* and the *County Council Magazine*, April 1989: Findlater, *Lilian Baylis*, p. 40. Findlater documents many of Cons' other activities in his biography of Baylis, in which he also writes about Toynbee Hall and the new model music halls (p. 41).
3. Henry Mayhew, *London Labour and the London Poor*, ed. and intro. Victor Neuberg (London: Penguin, 1985), pp. 41, 37, 40.
4. Edward Norman, *Victorian Christian Socialists* (Cambridge: Cambridge University Press, 1987), p. 110.
5. Sybil and Russell Thorndike, *Lilian Baylis* (London: Chapman & Hall, 1938), p. 16.
6. Morley College magazine, October 1894, OVSB/00031 6, RVHF.
7. This and other quotes about the Royal Victoria are taken from George Rowell, *The Old Vic Theatre: A History* (Cambridge: Cambridge University Press, 1993), p. 6.
8. Findlater, *Lilian Baylis*, p. 45.
9. Elizabeth Schafer, *Lilian Baylis: A Biography* (University of Hertfordshire Press/The Society for Theatre Research, 2006), p. 62.
10. Rowell, *Old Vic Theatre*, p. 61.
11. E. Harcourt Williams (ed.), *Vic-Wells: The Work of Lilian Baylis* (London: Shenval Press, 1938), p. 4.
12. Findlater, *Lilian Baylis*, pp. 52–3.
13. Sadler's Wells annals, October 1956, ILHC.
14. E. J. Dent, *A Theatre for Everybody: The Story of the Old Vic and Sadler's Wells* (London: T. V. Boardman and Co., 1945), p. 29.
15. Joan Cross, unpublished memoir, Britten-Pears Foundation, Aldeburgh, p. 18.
16. G. R. Searle, *A New England? Peace and War 1886–1918* (Oxford: Oxford University Press, 2004); Barnett quoted at p. 539.
17. Morley College magazine, October 1894, OVSB/00031 6, RVHF.
18. The Baylis–Cons correspondence quoted in this chapter is from OVLB/000047, RVHF.

19. ECM, 9.3.06, RVHF. The City Parochial Foundation was an independent charitable foundation established in 1891, which brought together under one body the assets from 1,400 individual charitable gifts, some 400 years old, which were to be used for the churches or the poor of 112 parishes in the City of London and the Metropolitan Police District of London. Their charter remained that of empowering the poor of London to tackle poverty by ensuring that the funds reached those most in need and by supporting schemes not financed by local or central government. Education for the working man was an early priority, hence their support for the Vic, the Chelsea Physic Garden and the Whitechapel Art Gallery.
20. These and other figures in this chapter are taken from ECM, 1906–22, RVHF.
21. ECM, 12.1.1912 and 14.1.12, RVHF.
22. Beatrice Webb, *My Apprenticeship* (London: Longmans 1926), quoted in Findlater, *Lilian Baylis*, p. 23.
23. Findlater, *Lilian Baylis*, p. 32.

CHAPTER 2 1912–1931: 'THE PEOPLE'S OPERA HOUSE'

1. OVLB/000003/18, RVHF.
2. Baylis to Smithson, 2.3.18, quoted in Elizabeth Schafer, *Lilian Baylis: A Biography* (University of Hertfordshire Press/Society for Theatre Research, 2006), p. 93.
3. Old Vic annual report, 1911/12. This and other Old Vic annual reports are in OV/F/000004, 1911–54, RVHF.
4. Sybil and Russell Thorndike, *Lilian Baylis* (London: Chapman & Hall, 1938), p. 114.
5. Quoted in Richard Findlater, *Lilian Baylis, the Lady of the Old Vic* (London: Allen Lane, 1975), p. 108.
6. Ibid., p. 98.
7. E. Harcourt Williams (ed.), *Vic-Wells: The Work of Lilian Baylis* (London: Shenval Press, 1938), p. 8.
8. George Rowell, *The Old Vic Theatre: A History* (Cambridge: Cambridge University Press, 1993), p. 98.
9. Thorndike and Thorndike, *Lilian Baylis*, pp. 28–9, 119.
10. Findlater, *Lilian Baylis*, p. 255.
11. These and other financial details are from OVECM/000002, 1906–22, RVHF.
12. Dent quoted in Findlater, *Lilian Baylis*, p. 149.
13. Quoted in Schafer, *Lilian Baylis*, p. 178.
14. Edward J. Dent, *A Theatre for Everybody: The Story of the Old Vic and Sadler's Wells* (London: T. V. Boardman and Co., 1945), p. 37.
15. Quoted in Findlater, *Lilian Baylis*, p. 163.
16. *Time and Tide*, 15.7.21, p. 673, quoted in Schafer, *Lilian Baylis*, p. 121.
17. *Old Vic Magazine*, vol. 2, no. 4, January 1921, OVM/000002/4, RVHF.
18. Playbill for *The Streets of London*, OVSB/000381, RVHF.

19. Dent, *A Theatre for Everybody*, p. 69.
20. Cross quoted in Findlater, *Lilian Baylis*, p. 151.
21. OVSB/000452, RVHF.
22. E. Harcourt Williams, *Four Years at the Old Vic* (London: Putnam, 1935) and Williams, *Vic-Wells*, p. 51, for a description of working conditions by Irene Beeston.
23. E. J. Dent, obituary of Muriel Gough in *The Times*, 14.7.52.
24. Carey to Dent, 23.5.43, EJD 4-073-71.
25. Dent to Carey, 9.8.19, FCSC 1-1-8-223-1.
26. Dent to Carey, 1.12.19, FCSC 1-1-8.
27. Dent, *A Theatre for Everybody*, p. 87.
28. Dent to Carey, 18.2.20, FCSC 1-1-8.
29. Williams, *Vic-Wells*, p. 77.
30. Dent, *A Theatre for Everybody*, p. 91.
31. Sadler's Wells minute book, ILHC.
32. OVECM, 9.10.22. These and other financial minute-book data from OVECM/000002, RVHF.
33. Findlater, *Lilian Baylis*, p. 164.
34. Schaffer, *Lilian Baylis*, p. 186.
35. Joan Cross, unpublished memoir, Britten-Pears Foundation, Aldeburgh, p. 23.
36. Quoted in Rowell, *The Old Vic Theatre*, p. 109.
37. Cross, unpublished memoir, p. 16.
38. Findlater, *Lilian Baylis*, p. 190.
39. Dent, *A Theatre for Everybody*, p. 89.
40. Dent, obituary of Muriel Gough.
41. Cross unpublished memoir, pp. 1, 3.
42. Dent, *A Theatre for Everybody*, p. 70.
43. Ibid., p. 94.
44. Cross, unpublished memoir, pp. 19, 29.
45. *The Times*, 13.11.28.
46. Cross, unpublished memoir, pp. 30, 32.
47. Ibid., p. 79.
48. *The Times*, January 1928.
49. *Daily Telegraph*, 16.4.29.
50. Findlater, *Lilian Baylis*, p. 201.
51. Ibid., p. 207.
52. Sadler's Wells Trust minute book, ENO Box 84, and Dent to Carey, 24.10.30, FCSC 1-1-9.
53. This and what follows taken from Sadler's Wells minute books, ILHC.
54. Fundraising, Old Vic, 1925–9, ILHC.

CHAPTER 3 1931–1937: 'A WORLD OF AWE AND WONDER' – LILIAN BAYLIS AT SADLER'S WELLS

1. *Old Vic and Sadler's Wells Magazine*, vol. 2, no. 5, September–October 1932, OVM/000012, RVHF.
2. Quoted by Arthur Jacobs in *Opera*, September 1974, p. 830.

3. Joan Cross, unpublished memoir, Britten-Pears Foundation, Aldeburgh, p. 88.
4. These details and those in the next paragraphs appear in the Sadler's Wells minute books, 28.5.31, 25.6.31 and 22.9.31, ILHC.
5. Cross, unpublished memoir, pp. 88–9.
6. Management Committee, Sadler's Wells minute book, 13.10.31, ILHC.
7. Williams, E. Harcourt, *Four Years at the Old Vic* (London: Putnam, 1935), p. 122.
8. *Music Lover*, ENO Box 114.
9. Sadler's Wells minute book, 9.3.32, ILHC.
10. Bruce Worsley cited in E. Harcourt Williams (ed.), *Vic-Wells: The Work of Lilian Baylis* (London: Shenval Press, 1938), p. 38.
11. Sadler's Wells minute book, 13.11.31, ILHC.
12. Dent to Carey, 16.11.30, FCSC 1-1-9.
13. Cross, unpublished memoir, p. 93.
14. Cited in Williams, *Vic-Wells*, p. 4.
15. *The Times*, 15.9.31.
16. Cross, unpublished memoir, p. 100.
17. Ibid., p. 95, and reviews, p. 96.
18. Meeting of the governing body, Sadler's Wells minute book, 11.7.32, ILHC.
19. Ibid., 19.9.32.
20. Ibid., 11.6.32.
21. Dent to Carey, 10.9.32, FCSC 1-1-9.
22. Dent to Carey, 7.10.32, ibid.
23. Meeting of the governing body, Sadler's Wells minute book, 19.10.32, ILHC.
24. Both papers on 17.12.32.
25. *Old Vic and Sadler's Wells Magazine*, vol. 2, no. 5, September–October 1932, OVM/000013/5, RVHF.
26. Dent to Carey, 28.2.33, FCSC 1-1-9 and 12.5.33, FCSC 1-1-9-287.
27. *Old Vic and Sadler's Wells Magazine*, vol. 2, no. 5, September–October 1932, OVM/000013/5, RVHF.
28. Sadler's Wells minute book, 9.5.33, ILHC.
29. Dent to Carey, 20.4.33 and 12.5.33, FCSC 1-1-9-287 and FCSC 1-1-9.
30. Dent to Carey, 29.8.33, FCSC 1-1-9-295; 12.5.33, FCSC 1-1-9-287; 22.8.33, FCSC 1-1-9-293.
31. Quoted in *Opera*, June 1981, p. 571.
32. *Yorkshire Post*, 20.9.33.
33. Cross, unpublished memoir, pp. 101, 103.
34. Dent to Carey, 22.6.34. FCSC 1-1-9-302-6.
35. Dent to Carey in Hugh Carey, *Duet for Two Voices: An Informal Biography of Edward Dent Compiled from His Letters to Clive Carey* (Cambridge: Cambridge University Press, 1979), p. 148.
36. Herbert Hughes in the *Saturday Review*, 20.10.34.
37. Sybil and Russell Thorndike, *Lilian Baylis* (London: Chapman & Hall, 1938), p. 103.
38. Williams, *Four Years*, p. 217.

39. Tyrone Guthrie, *A Life in the Theatre* (London: Readers Union/Hamish Hamilton, 1961), pp. 107–8.
40. George Rowell, *The Old Vic Theatre: A History* (Cambridge: Cambridge University Press, 1993), p. 122.
41. Cited in Williams, *Vic-Wells*, p. 68.
42. Richard Findlater, *Lilian Baylis, the Lady of the Old Vic* (London: Allen Lane, 1975), pp. 265–9.
43. Guthrie, *A Life in the Theatre*, p. 117.
44. *Guardian*, 2.10.35.
45. *The Times*, 12.3.36.
46. Sadler's Wells minute book, 8.5.36, ILHC.
47. Cross, unpublished memoir, p. 97.
48. Guthrie, *A Life in the Theatre*, p. 157. Hugh ('Binkie') Beaumont was, in the opinion of Guthrie and many others, 'the most powerful West End manager of the interwar years' (p. 142). He founded the Tennent Beaumont Partnership with Henry Tennent in 1936 and remained the dominant force in the West End theatre into the early 1960s. Beaumont and H. M. Tennent Ltd were described by Richard Eyre as the 'byword for star-studded, impeccably mounted, middlebrow theatre' and their power as 'absolute' (*Changing Stages*, London: Bloomsbury, 2001, p. 120). Beaumont died in 1973.
49. Sadler's Wells minute book, 11.12.36, ILHC.
50. Dent to Carey, 25.8.36, in Carey, *Duet for Two Voices*, p. 146.
51. EJD 4-073-62.
52. Baylis to Cross, 29.7.37, Joan Cross archive, Britten-Pears Foundation, Aldeburgh.
53. Reported in Reginald Rowe's review of Cobden-Sanderson and the Thorndikes' books about Baylis in *The Listener*, 18.5.38.
54. Carey to Dent, 6.3.42, EJD 4-073-70-1.
55. Dent to Carey, 27.10.38, FCSC 1-1-10.
56. Thorndike and Thorndike, *Lilian Baylis*, pp. 7, 80.
57. Quoted in the *New Statesman and Nation*, 24.10.36.
58. Undated memo (?autumn 1945) by Dent and Guthrie, EJD 2/7/3.
59. Cicely Hamilton and Lilian Baylis, *The Old Vic* (London: Jonathan Cape, 1926), pp. 188–9.
60. Cross, unpublished memoir, p. 121.

CHAPTER 4 1937–1945: A HEROIC STRUGGLE – JOAN CROSS AND THE WAR

1. Hugh Walpole cited in E. Harcourt Williams (ed.), *Vic-Wells: The Work of Lilian Baylis* (London: Shenval Press, 1938), p. 6.
2. Dent to Carey, 26.2.38, FCSC 1-1-10-340-2.
3. Dent to Carey, 14.3.38, FCSC 1-1-10-342-1-4.
4. Dent to Carey, 7.3.38, FCSC 1-1-10-341-2.
5. Dent to Carey, 1.2.38, FCSC 1-1-10-337-2.
6. Dent to Carey, 26.2.38, FCSC 1-1-10-340-2.
7. Dent to Carey, 8.11.38, FCSC 1-1-10-346-2.
8. Executive Committee, Sadler's Wells minute books, 14.10.38 and

10.2.39, ILHC. References to the governors' meetings and decisions are from the Finsbury archive unless otherwise referenced.

9. Carey to Dent, 5.11.38, EJD 4-073-63-1 and 4.

10. Dent to Carey, 27.10.38, FCSC 1-1-10-345; EJD 4-073-63.

11. Dent to Carey, 8.11.38, FCSC 1-1-10-346-3.

12. Executive Committee, Sadler's Wells minute book, 10.2.39, ILHC.

13. Dent to Carey, 25.11.38, FCSC 1-1-10-347, and 26.2.38, FCSC 1-1-10-340-4.

14. Special meeting of governors, Sadler's Wells minute book, 24.2.39, ILHC.

15. Dent to Carey, 22.8.41, FCSC 1-1-9-353-3.

16. *The Bystander*, 11.10.39.

17. Carey to Dent, 17.2.40, EJD 4-073-65.

18. Carey to Dent, 24.7.40, ibid.

19. Dent to Carey, 5.3.40, FCSC 1-1-10-349.

20. Dent to Carey, 15.9.40, FCSC 1-1-10-350-3.

21. Tyrone Guthrie in Eric Crozier (ed.), *Opera in English*, Sadler's Wells Opera Books No. 1 (London: John Lane/The Bodley Head for the Sadler's Wells Foundation, 1945), p. 8.

22. Sadler's Wells minute book, 14.6.40, ILHC.

23. Dent to Carey, 25.9.44, FCSC 1-1-10-368-1.

24. Sadler's Wells minute book, 12.7.40, ILHC.

25. Guthrie, 5.6.45; undated newspaper clipping, ENO archive.

26. Joan Cross, diary ms, Britten-Pears Foundation, Aldeburgh. This diary is the source for Cross's chronicle of events throughout the war, although she kept it less regularly after 1943.

27. Guthrie to Cross, 10.9.40, Joan Cross archive, Britten-Pears Foundation, Aldeburgh.

28. Sadler's Wells minute book, 13.9.40, ILHC.

29. Cross, undated note (1940), Joan Cross archive, Britten-Pears Foundation, Aldeburgh.

30. Margaret Harris in Cathy Courtney (ed.), *Jocelyn Herbert: A Theatre Workbook* (London: Art Book International, 1993), p. 211.

31. Guthrie to Dent, 30.9.40, EJD 4-176.

32. Sadler's Wells minute book, 11.10.40, ILHC.

33. From Cross, diary ms, as are following quotes unless otherwise referenced.

34. Sadler's Wells minute book, 8.11.40, ILHC.

35. ACGB, 1/1038.

36. Dent to Carey, 22.8.41, FCSC 1-1-9-353-2.

37. Dennis Arundell, obituary of Valetta Iacopi in *Opera*, February 1978, p. 139.

38. Cross, diary ms, 31.3.41.

39. These events were reported by Dent to Carey, 7.4.41, FCSC 1-1-10-352-1 and 2.

40. Dent to Carey, 7 and 8.4.41, FCSC 1-1-10-352-1-4. Dent's biographer, Karen Arrandale, does not believe that Dent was anti-Semitic, not least because of his active role in rescuing many Jewish musician friends

throughout the 1930s, including Otto Deutsch, Egon Wellesz and Paul Hirsch and his music library, which became the backbone of the music collection in the British Library. Dent insisted that a letter from Johannes Wolff about what was really happening to Jewish music and musicians, sent in 1936 from Jerusalem, be read out at the Barcelona International Society for Contemporary Music conference.

41. Sadler's Wells minute book, 4.4.41, ILHC.
42. Ibid.
43. Cross, diary ms, 12.5.41.
44. Dent to Carey, 22.8.41, FCSC 1-1-9.
45. Sadler's Wells minute book, 10.10.41, ILHC.
46. Dent to Carey, 22.8.41, FCSC 1-1-9-353-2.
47. Dent to Carey, 22.8.41, FCSC 1-1-9-353-1.
48. Dent to Carey, 22.8.41, FCSC 1-1-9-353-4.
49. Cross, diary ms, 8.9.41.
50. Dent to Carey, 22.8.41, FCSC 1-1-9-353-3.
51. Ibid., also Dent's reply in the same file.
52. Cross, diary ms, 13.10.41 and 10.11.41.
53. Cross to Johnson, 8.11.41, Johnson 1945–6, 0-2 Metropolitan Archive.
54. Dent to Carey, 18.2.42, FCSC 1-1-10-355-1.
55. Sadler's Wells minute books, 30.1.42 and 8.5.42, ILHC.
56. Ibid., 8.5.42.
57. Joan Cross in Crozier (ed.), *Opera in English*, p. 21.
58. Tyrone Guthrie, *A Life in the Theatre* (London: Readers Union/Hamish Hamilton, 1961), p. 224.
59. *Cambridge Evening News*, 10.3.42.
60. Dent to Carey, 30.3.42, FCSC 1-1-10-356-2.
61. Cross, diary ms, p. 24.
62. Dent to Carey, 30.3.42, FCSC 1-1-10-356-3.
63. Dent to Carey, 18.2.42, FCSC 1-1-10-355-1-4.
64. James Cox (Ambassadors Scenic Studios Ltd) to George Chamberlain, 9.2.42, Sadler's Wells admin, ILHC.
65. Cox to Chamberlain, 9.2.42, and Higgins to Guthrie, 12.2.42, Sadler's Wells admin, ILHC.
66. *The Times*, 14.3.42.
67. Dent to Carey, 30.3.42, FCSC 1-1-10-355-3.
68. Dent to Carey, 30.3.42, FCSC 1-1-10-356-1.
69. Dent to Carey, 16.5.42, FCSC 1-1-10-357-4.
70. Cross, diary ms, 24.8.42.
71. Ibid., 26.10.42 and November 1942.
72. Reported in *The Stage*, 13.8.42.
73. Memorandum, TNA T161 1433.
74. Dent to Carey, 25.7.43, FCSC 1-1-10-360-1.
75. *The Times*, 30.4.43.
76. Referred to during name-change debate on 19.7.72, ENO Ad 146 Box 129.
77. Hans Keller in *Opera*, May 1951, p. 291.
78. *The Times*, 30.6.43.

79. Donald Mitchell and Philip Reed (eds.), *Letters from a Life: Selected Letters and Diaries of Benjamin Britten*, vol. II, *1939–45* (London: Faber and Faber, 1991), p. 1,152.

80. Cross, diary ms, 8.8.43.

81. Dent to Carey, 18.11.43, FCSC 1-1-10-362-1.

82. Ibid.

83. Dent to Carey, 16.1.44, FCSC 1-1-10-363-3.

84. Edwin Evans, Sadler's Wells Opera, in Crozier (ed.), *Opera in English*, p. 14.

85. Dent to Carey, 18.11.43, FCSC 1-1-10-362-1.

86. Cross, diary ms, 4–27.10.43; Cross in Old Vic annual report 1943/4, OV/F/000004, 1911–54, RVHF.

87. Cross in Crozier (ed.), *Opera in English*, p. 22.

88. Carey to Dent, 13.2.44, EJD 4-073-73A-1.

89. Dent to Carey, 16.1.44, FCSC 1-1-10-363-2.

90. Dent to Carey, 25.5.44, FCSC 1-1-10-365-1.

91. Carey to Dent, 13.2.44, EJD 4-073-73A-2.

92. Mitchell and Reed (eds.), *Letters from a Life*, p. 1,198.

93. Cross, diary ms, June 1944.

94. Dent to Carey, 25.5.44, FCSC 1-1-10-365-5.

95. Dent to Carey, 25.9.44, FCSC 1-1-10-368-2.

96. Keller in *Opera*, May 1951, p. 291.

97. Dent to Carey, 16.1.44, FCSC 1-1-10-363-2.

98. Robert Skidelsky, *John Maynard Keynes, 1883–1946: Economist, Philosopher, Statesman* (London: Macmillan, 2003), p. 729.

99. Dent to Carey, 25.5.44, FCSC 1-1-10-365-6.

100. Cross, diary ms, 31.7–11.9.44.

101. Dent to Doris Carey, 14.7.44, FCSC 1-1-10-366-3.

102. Dent to Carey, 17.8.44, FCSC 1-1-10-367-1.

103. Dent to Carey, 25.9.44, FCSC 1-1-10-367-3.

104. Ibid.

105. Dent to Carey, 25.9.44, FCSC 1-1-10-368-2.

106. Memorandum, 25.9.44, FCSC-1-1-10-368-1.

107. Undated memorandum, EJD 2-7-3.

108. Dent to Carey, 15.10.44, FCSC 1-1-10-369. In 1932 the second Earl of Lytton had been sent by the League of Nations to Manchuria. His report on the Japanese conquest of Manchuria in 1931 led to Japan's withdrawal from the League of Nations.

109. Dent to Carey, 25.9.44, FCSC 1-1-10-368-1.

110. Ibid.

111. Dent to Carey, 5.1.45, FCSC 1-1-10-371-2.

112. Ibid.

113. 12.1.45, in George Rowell, *The Old Vic Theatre: A History* (Cambridge: Cambridge University Press, 1993), p. 135.

114. Dent to Carey, 27.3.45, FCSC 1-1-10-373-2.

115. Document in the Royal Opera House archive headed 'Notes on a Programme for Covent Garden', dated April 1945. See John Lucas, *Reggie: The Life of Reginald Goodall* (London: Julia MacRae, 1993), p.

89. Reginald Goodall was the forty-four-year-old conductor who had joined Sadler's Wells in September 1944.

116. Dent to Carey, 25.4.45, FCSC 1-1-10-374-2. The *New Statesman* (founded by the Webbs in 1913) and the *Nation* (chairman of the board, J. M. Keynes) were amalgamated on 6 January 1934 and then moved markedly to the left. In 1938 they refused to publish Orwell's Barcelona dispatch critical of the Communists in Spain.

117. Carey to Dent, 18.8.45, EJD 4-073-78-1.

118. Richard M. Titmuss, *Problems of Social Policy* (HMSO/Longmans, Green, 1950), p. 506, quoted in Peter Hennessy *Never Again: Britain 1945–51* (Jonathan Cape, London 1992), pp. 38, 69, 71.

119. Guthrie in Crozier (ed.), *Opera in English*, p. 9.

CHAPTER 5 1945–1959: NORMAN TUCKER, 'THE CUCKOO IN THE ARTS COUNCIL NEST'

1. Joan Cross, unpublished memoir, Britten-Pears Foundation, Aldeburgh, p. 127.

2. Eric Crozier in *Opera*, June 1965, p. 412.

3. There is an excellent account on the background to the rehearsals and fall-out from *Peter Grimes* in John Lucas's biography of Reginald Goodall, *Reggie: The Life of Reginald Goodall* (London: Julia MacRae, 1993), pp. 85–6.

4. Crozier in *Opera*, June 1965, pp. 412–13, 414–16.

5. Cross, unpublished memoir, p. 128.

6. For an account of the rehearsals of *Peter Grimes* see Lucas, *Reggie*, pp. 86–7.

7. Ibid.

8. Ibid., p. 129.

9. Ibid., p. 88.

10. Michael Kennedy *Britten* (London: J. M. Dent, 1983), p. 41.

11. Cross, unpublished memoir, pp. 131, 130.

12. Guthrie to Dent, 25.5.45, EJD 2/7/3.

13. Lucas, *Reggie*, p. 92.

14. Undated press clipping, ENO archive.

15. *News Chronicle*, 8.6.45.

16. Joan Cross, letter to *The Times*, quoted in Donald Mitchell and Philip Reed (eds.), *Letters from a Life: Selected Letters and Diaries of Benjamin Britten*, vol. II, 1939–45 (London: Faber and Faber, 1991), p. 1,263.

17. Frank Howes in *The Times*, 15.6.45.

18. William Glock in the *Observer*, 10.6.45.

19. Britten to Mrs Wright, mother of Basil Wright the film director, quoted in Mitchell and Reed (eds.), *Letters from a Life*, pp. 1,252–9.

20. Ernest Newman in the *Sunday Times*, 24.6.45.

21. *The Stage*, 19.7.45.

22. Cross, unpublished memoir, pp. 140–3.

23. Tyrone Guthrie, *A Life in the Theatre* (London: Readers' Union/Hamish Hamilton, 1961), p. 311.

24. Lucas, *Reggie*, p. 96.
25. RVH minute book, April 1945–July 1946, OVRVH/000002, RVHF.
26. Mitchell and Reed (eds.), *Letters from a Life*, p. 1,275.
27. Lucas, *Reggie*, pp. 97–8; Dyson's warning to Chamberlain quoted ibid., p. 99.
28. Dyson to Chamberlain, 21.8.45, Sadler's Wells archive, ILHC, quoted in Lucas, *Reggie*, p. 99.
29. Cross, unpublished memoir, p. 141.
30. RVH minute book, April 1945–July 1946, OVRVH/000002, RVHF.
31. Lucas, *Reggie*, p. 99.
32. Lord Harewood, *The Tongs and the Bones: The Memoirs of Lord Harewood* (London: Weidenfeld and Nicolson, 1981), p. 30.
33. Patricia Hollis, *Jennie Lee: A Life* (Oxford: Oxford University Press, 1997), p. 248.
34. Arts Council, *Report of Opera and Ballet Companies*, third draft, 3 May 1967, ENO Ad 62 Box 11.
35. Mitchell and Reed (eds.), *Letters from a Life*, p. 1,279.
36. Bruce Worsley, BOAR report, autumn 1945, EJD 2/7/3.
37. Warwick Braithwaite, unpublished autobiography, Braithwaite papers, pp. 179–80.
38. Violet Bonham-Carter to Dent, 23.1.46, EJD 2/7/3.
39. Dent to Carey, 28.10.45, FCSC 1-1-10-376-1.
40. Dent to Carey, 10.12.45, FCSC 1-1-10-382-2.
41. Undated, unsigned memorandum (?winter 1945/6 by board member Barbara Ward), EJD 2/7/3.
42. Violet Bonham-Carter to Dent, 23.1.46, EJD 2/7/3.
43. Dyson to Dent, 29.1.46, EJD 2/7/3.
44. Desmond Shawe-Taylor in *The Spectator*, 25.1.46.
45. *Evening Standard*, undated clipping, ENO archive.
46. Dyneley Hussey in *The Spectator*, 2.1.46.
47. Philip Hope-Wallace in *Time and Tide*, 2.2.46.
48. *Evening Standard*, 11.2.46.
49. Shawe-Taylor in *The Spectator*, 15.2.46.
50. Jennie Lee in *The Tribune*, 29.3.46.
51. RVH minute book, April 1945–July 1946, OVRVH/000002, RVHF.
52. Interview with Charles Mackerras, 7.4.06.
53. *Observer*, 7.4.46.
54. Dent to Carey, 9.1.46, FCSC 1-1-10-383-2.
55. Dennis Arundell, *The Story of Sadler's Wells, 1683–1977* (London: David and Charles, 1978), p. 220.
56. *The Times*, 10.6.46.
57. *New Statesman*, 16.6.46.
58. ACGB 1/1308.
59. Arundell, *Story of Sadler's Wells*, p. 220.
60. Shawe-Taylor in *New Statesman and Nation*, 26.7.47.
61. Arundell *Story of Sadler's Wells*, p. 222; John Amis in the *Financial Times*, 12.10.53, commenting on a revival.
62. Norman Tucker, *Musician: An Autobiography before and after Two*

*Decades at Sadler's Wells*, ed. J. Audrey Ellison (London: Lewis Reprints, 1978), pp. 59–60.

63. Arundell, *Story of Sadler's Wells*, pp. 222–3.
64. Ibid., p. 54.
65. Arnold Goodman, *Tell Them I'm on My Way* (London: Chapmans, 1993), p. 337.
66. Michael Mudie, memorandum on Sadler's Wells policy, December 1947, EJD 1/7/3.
67. Mackerras interview, 7.4.06.
68. *The Times*, 18.12.47; *Observer*, 21.12.47.
69. Mackerras interview, 7.4.06.
70. *The Times*, 19.2.48.
71. Nancy Phelan, *Charles Mackerras: A Musician's Musician* (London: Victor Gollancz, 1987), pp. 81, 84.
72. Ibid., p. 86.
73. Mackerras interview, 4.4.06.
74. Tucker, *Musician*, pp. 58–9.
75. Fundraising, Old Vic, ILHC.
76. Tucker, *Musician*, p. 61.
77. Andrew Porter in the *Financial Times*, 2.12.55.
78. Guthrie, *A Life in the Theatre*, p. 224.
79. *The Times*, 22.2.49.
80. Mackerras interview, 7.4.06.
81. Dent to Harewood, 9.3.49, EJD.
82. Mackerras interview, 7.4.06.
83. Quoted in Phelan, *Charles Mackerras*, p. 86.
84. Mackerras interview, 4.4.06.
85. Harold Rosenthal in *Opera*, April 1950, p. 48.
86. Guthrie, *A Life in the Theatre*, p. 225.
87. *The Times*, 21.9.50.
88. Mackerras interview, 4.4.06.
89. Lord Harewood in *Opera*, April 1950, p. 54.
90. Fourth Meeting of the Opera and Ballet Subcommittee of the Arts Council of Great Britain, 12.4.50, ENO Ad 82 Box 59.
91. Editorial, *Opera*, August 1951.
92. ENO/FGPC, 7 and 24.11.50, B8 Box 65.
93. Arundell, *Story of Sadler's Wells*, pp. 225–6.
94. Guthrie, *A Life in the Theatre*, p. 225.
95. Arundell, *Story of Sadler's Wells*, p. 227.
96. Lord Esher in the *Manchester Guardian*, 29.1.46.
97. Tucker, *Musician*, p. 68.
98. George Devine, interview in *The Stage*, 15.5.52.
99. Lord Harewood in *Opera*, March 1951, pp. 205–10.
100. *The Times*, 16.1.51.
101. Felix Aprahamian in the *Sunday Times*, 21.2.51.
102. Mackerras interview, 7.4.06.
103. Tucker, *Musician*, p. 68 and Irving Wardle, *The Theatres of George Devine* (London: Jonathan Cape, 1978), p. 145.

104. Quoted in Phelan, *Charles Mackerras*, p. 93.
105. Mackerras interview, 7.4.06.
106. Ibid. and letter to author, 13.8.08.
107. Shawe-Taylor in *New Statesman and Nation*, 14.4.51.
108. Lord Harewood in *Opera*, June 1951, p. 369.
109. Mackerras interview, 7.4.06.
110. Mackerras to author, 13.8.08.
111. Edward Greenfield in the *Guardian*, 21.8.68.
112. Tucker, *Musician*, pp. 65–6.
113. Lord Harewood in *Opera*, December 1951, pp. 718–19.
114. ACGB 1/1037.
115. *The Times*, 6.2.52.
116. Rosenthal in *Opera*, April 1952, p. 33.
117. *Times Educational Supplement*, 10.9.52.
118. Shawe-Taylor in the *Observer*, 23.11.52.
119. Interview with Ralph Koltai, 29.10.07.
120. Lord Harewood, *Opera*, March 1952, p. 180.
121. *The Times*, 12.6.53.
122. *Observer*, 4.10.53.
123. Rosenthal in *Opera*, November 1953, p. 694.
124. Porter in *Financial Times*, 31.12.53.
125. Porter in *Opera*, November 1954, p. 690.
126. Vilem Tausky, *Vilem Tausky Tells His Story* (London: Stainer and Bell, 1979), p. 132.
127. ENO/FGPC B8 Box 65.
128. ACGB 1/1037.
129. Paper of 4.2.54 concerning using up of reserves and how deficits have been dealt with since 1951, ENO Ad 54 Box 10.
130. Memorandum, 19.10.55, ACGB 1/1037.
131. Sadler's Wells annual report, 1953/4, p. 7. This and other Sadler's Wells annual reports may be found in the ENO archive.
132. *The Times*, 4.2.54.
133. Tucker, *Musician*, pp. 78, 123.
134. ENO/Trust, 17.5.55, B1 Box 62.
135. Eric Walter White to Douglas Lund, 29.4.55, ACGB 1/8601.
136. ENO/Trust, 8.12.55, B2 Box 62.
137. Joint meeting ENO/OSC and ENO/FGPC, 31.1.56, B14 Box 66 and B3 Box 62.
138. ENO/Trust, 1.2.56, B2 Box 62.
139. ENO/Trust, 9.3.56, B2 Box 62.
140. Ibid.
141. ENO/Trust, 20.7.56, 15.6.56, and Smith to Clark, 21.9.56, B3 Box 62.
142. Williams to Johnston, 23.1.57, TNA T227 512.
143. Williams to Johnston, 20.2.57, ibid.
144. Joint Meeting of Governors Executive Committee and Finance Committee, 24.2.57, B3 Box 62.
145. ENO/FGPC, 8.3.57, B14 Box 66.
146. Clark to Johnston, 12.2.57, TNA T227 512.

147. Notes of 9.4.57, ibid.
148. Ibid.
149. Notes of 9.5.57, ibid.
150. Internal memorandum, Johnston to Sir Roger Makins, 10.5.57, ibid.
151. *Opera*, June 1957, p. 391.
152. Tucker, *Musician*, p. 88.
153. Andrew Porter in the *Financial Times*, 21.11.57.
154. Johnston minute, 21.5.57, TNA T227 512.
155. Johnston minute, 28.5.57, ibid.
156. Arts Council, *Opera in London*, ibid.
157. Williams to Johnston, 12.6.57, ibid.
158. Press statement, 17.6.57, B3 Box 62.
159. Johnston to Makins, 19.6.57, TNA T227 512.
160. Johnston to Williams, 20.6.57, ibid.
161. Notes by Kenneth Couzens, Assistant Secretary to the Treasury, 25.7.57, ibid.
162. Meeting at Arts Council, ENO/Trust, 8.8.57, B3 Box 62.
163. ENO/Trust, 19.8.57, ibid.
164. Berlin to Moore, draft version, 30.9.57, MS Berlin 388, f. 66, and final version, 7.10.57, in Covent Garden archive.
165. Moore to Berlin, 7.10.57, Covent Garden archive.
166. TNA T227 512.
167. ENO/Trust, 14.10.57, B3 Box 62.
168. Tucker's memorandum of 6.11.57, ENO/Trust, ibid.
169. Arundell, *Story of Sadler's Wells*, pp. 241–3.
170. Box-office returns, appendix to memorandum for LCC, March 1958, ENO Ad 90 Box 84.
171. Lionel Dunlop in *Opera*, January 1958, p. 64.
172. Tucker, *Musician*, pp. 92 and 96.
173. Arundell, *Story of Sadler's Wells*, p. 244.
174. Reported ENO/Trust, 24.1.58, B3 Box 62.
175. Minutes of meeting with Arts Council at 4 St James's Square, 7.2.58, ENO Ad 50 Box 10.
176. Tucker, *Musician*, p. 79.
177. Arts Council: résumé of crisis, 18.3.58, TNA T227 512.
178. Minutes of special meeting, 10.2.58, ENO Ad 50 Box 10.
179. Johnston to Makins, 24.2.68, TNA T227 512.
180. Tucker, *Musician*, p. 79.
181. Tucker to Smith, 25.2.58, ENO Ad 50 Box 10.
182. Tucker, *Musician*, p. 80 and ENO/Trust, 14.3.58, B3 Box 62.
183. Sir Thomas Padmore to Johnston, 5.3.58, TNA T227 512.
184. Note by K. E. Couzens, 6.3.58, ibid.
185. Johnston to Mr Wyatt, 5.3.58, ibid.
186. Padmore minute, 7.3.58, ibid.
187. ENO/Trust, 14.3.58, B3 Box 62.
188. On 18.3.58, TNA T227 512.
189. Denison to SW, 24.3.58; Williams to Smith, 28.3.58, ACGB 1/8603.
190. Denison to Williams, ibid.

191. Arlen proposal, 6.6.58, ibid.
192. LCC decision on 15.7.58 and other details in ENO Ad 50 Box 10.
193. ENO/Trust, 8.12.58, B3 Box 62.
194. Richard Eyre, *Changing Stages* (London: Bloomsbury, 2001), p. 51.
195. Interview with Timothy O'Brien, 12.1.06.
196. Interview with Rodney Milnes, 11.10.05.
197. Tucker, *Musician*, p. 60.
198. O'Brien Interview, 12.1.06.
199. William Glock in the *New Statesman*, 6.12.58.

CHAPTER 6 1959–1966: A HOME ON THE SOUTH BANK?

1. Norman Tucker, *Musician: An Autobiography before and after Two Decades at Sadler's Wells*, ed. J. Audrey Ellison (London: Lewis Reprints, 1978), pp. 113–15.
2. ENO/Trust, 11.5.49, 14.5.59 and 9.7.59, B4 Box 63.
3. ENO/OSC, 30.4.59, B14 Box 66.
4. Harold Rosenthal in *Opera*, December 1959, p. 819.
5. Interview with Colin Davis, 18.9.06.
6. Philip Hope-Wallace in the *Guardian*, 11.12.59.
7. Andrew Porter in the *Financial Times*, 12.1.61.
8. Porter in the *Financial Times*, 30.10.59.
9. Porter in the *Financial Times*, 18.9.64.
10. Desmond Shawe-Taylor in *Opera*, December 1959, p. 826.
11. Tucker, *Musician*, p. 75.
12. Shawe-Taylor in the *Sunday Times*, 17.1.60.
13. Peter Heyworth in the *Observer*, 17.1.60.
14. David Cairns in *The Spectator*, 22.1.60.
15. David Cairns, 'Old Wells and New', *New Statesman*, 1968, reprinted in Cairns, *Responses: Musical Essays and Reviews* (London: Secker and Warburg, 1973), p. 256.
16. ENO/Trust, 18.1.60, B4 Box 63.
17. Meeting between Sadler's Wells and Arts Council, ENO/Trust, 28.1.60, ibid.
18. ENO /Trust, 16.11.59, ibid.
19. Paper of 16.11.59, ENO/FC, ibid.
20. ENO/OSC, 18.2.60, ibid.
21. *The Times*, 20.10.60.
22. Interview with John Tooley, 1.12.05.
23. Sackville-West to Berlin, 25.5.60, MS Berlin 389, f. 113.
24. Porter in the *Financial Times*, 18.5.60.
25. Rosenthal in *Opera*, June 1981, p. 650.
26. Edmund Tracey in the *Observer*, 14.8.60.
27. William Mann in *Opera*, September 1960, p. 645.
28. *Times Educational Supplement*, 19.8.60.
29. ENO/Trust, 19.9.60, B4 Box 63.
30. Davis interview, 18.9.06.
31. ENO/Trust, 13.9.60, B14 Box 66.

32. Shawe-Taylor in *Opera*, March 1961, p. 199.
33. Porter in the *Financial Times*, 22.8.79.
34. Shawe-Taylor in *Opera*, May 1961, p. 338.
35. ENO/Trust, 17.4.61, B4 Box 63.
36. Report of an Independent Committee of Enquiry on Sadler's Wells to Advise the London County Council, 9.3.59, ENO Ad 90 Box 84. Two of its five members were Sir Adrian Boult and Philip Hope-Wallace.
37. Rosenthal in *Opera*, December 1959, p. 817.
38. ENO/Trust, 21.11.60 and 19.12.60, B4 Box 63.
39. ENO/FGPC, 14.2.61, B14 Box 66.
40. Special Trust meeting, ENO/Trust, 10.3.61, B4 Box 63.
41. For the story of the contenders for the role of National Theatre management see Terry Coleman, *Olivier* (London: Bloomsbury, 2005), p. 338.
42. Memorandum by Selwyn Lloyd, December 1960, quoted in George Rowell, *The Old Vic Theatre: A History* (Cambridge: Cambridge University Press, 1993), pp. 148–51.
43. 'The Next Steps', April 1961, TNA T227 2132.
44. Parliamentary debates (Hansard), vol. 230, no. 68, p. 695.
45. Smith to Berlin, 15.6..61, MS Berlin 390, f. 98.
46. Copy of Cabinet Conclusion: Minutes and Papers: CAB 128/35 Treasury file TNA T227 2133.
47. Lloyd to Hayward, 23.6.61, TNA T227 2133.
48. Griffiths minute, 10.7.61, ibid.
49. Berlin to Pavitt, 24.3.61, MS Berlin 390, f. 50.
50. Drogheda to Lloyd, 13.7.61, TNA T227 2133.
51. Drogheda to Lloyd, 9.8.61, ibid.
52. Tucker, press statement, ENO/Trust, 18.7.61, B4 Box 63.
53. Tucker, *Musician*, p. 126.
54. Smith to Chandos, 13.7.61, ENO Ad 88 Box 61.
55. ENO/Trust B4 Box 63.
56. Note on possible opponents to the scheme, ENO Ad 88 Box 61.
57. Barger to Arlen, 22.8.61, and Arlen to Barger, 25.8.61, ENO Ad 88 Box 61.
58. Rubinstein Nash to Arlen, 30.8.61, all references to the new theatre are in ENO Ad 88 Box 61.
59. ENO/FGPC, 8.9.61, B14 Box 66.
60. Joint Council Minutes, 20 and 25.9.61, quoted in Stephen Fay, *Power Play: The Life and Times of Peter Hall* (London: Hodder and Stoughton, 1995), p. 176.
61. Arnold Goodman, *Tell Them I'm on My Way* (London: Chapmans, 1993), p. 338.
62. Treasury minute, 13.10.61, TNA T227 2134.
63. Treasury note of a telephone conversation with the Chairman of the Arts Council, Lord Cottesloe, who had talked to Clark and Chandos, 11.10.61, ibid.
64. Interview with Colin Davis, 18.9.06.
65. Tucker, *Musician*, p. 89.
66. Arlen to Rae, 11.61, ENO Ad 58 Box 11.

67. Note by Mary Loughnane, 28.12.61, TNA T227 2134.
68. Quoted in Fay, *Power Play*, p. 180.
69. Tucker, *Musician*, p. 127.
70. ENO/Trust, 15.1.62, B4 Box 63.
71. Porter in the *Financial Times*, 4.2.62.
72. Davis interview, 18.9.06.
73. *The Times*, 26.1.63; *Daily Telegraph*, 3.2.63.
74. Interview with Rupert Rhymes, 1.6.06.
75. ENO/Trust, 19.2.62, B4 Box 63.
76. Tucker: 'Sadler's Wells New appointments', 7.3.62, ENO Ad 57 Box 10.
77. ENO Ad 57 Box 10.
78. Porter in the *Financial Times*, 28.9.61.
79. Davis interview, 18.9.06.
80. Porter in the *Financial Times*, 28.9.61.
81. Interview with Charles Mackerras, 7.4.06.
82. ENO/OSC, 6.6.61, B14 Box 66.
83. *The Spectator*, 5.1.62.
84. Cairns, 'Old Wells and New', p. 256.
85. Porter in the *Financial Times*, 25.1.62.
86. Davis interview, 18.9.06.
87. Plans for South Bank Opera House, 29.11.61, in Lasdun papers 167 (LaD/166/2) and ENO Ad 58 Box 11.
88. Jenkins to Arlen, 21.3.62, ENO Ad 58 Box 11.
89. Minute of 13.4.61, ENO Ad 53 Box 10.
90. Arts Council response, 25.4.62, TNA T227 2135.
91. Memorandum on National Theatre scheme, 17.4.62, ENO Ad 58 Box 11.
92. Brooke to Treasury, 5.5.62, TNA T227 2135.
93. Treasury memorandum, 14.5.62, ibid.
94. Report of a meeting at the LCC called by Sir William Hart, ENO Ad 71 Box 56.
95. Edward Renton note to Byam Shaw and Davis, on 15.8.62, ibid.
96. Agenda item for South Bank Theatre and Opera House Board meeting, 12.9.62: 'How to formulate a policy on Sadler's Wells building to allay opposition', ENO Ad 88 Box 61.
97. B5 Box 63.
98. Interview with Iris Arlen, 20.19.05.
99. *The Times*, 13.10.62.
100. Rosenthal in *Opera*, November 1962, p. 825.
101. Stanley Sadie in *Time and Tide*, 18.10.67.
102. Interview with Timothy O'Brien, 12.1.06.
103. Heyworth in the *Observer*, 9.12.62.
104. Koltai interview in *The Times*, 9.1.63.
105. Koltai interview, 29.10.07.
106. Arthur Jacobs in *Opera*, March 1963, p. 198.
107. The *Sunday Times*, 24.2.63 and *The Times*, 21.2.63.
108. Cairns in the *Financial Times*, 23.4.65.
109. Shawe-Taylor in the *Sunday Times*, 20.1.63.
110. ENO Ad 71 Box 56.

111. 12.7.64, ENO Ad 88 Box 61.
112. Heyworth in the *Observer*, 22.9.63.
113. *New Statesman*, 21.2.64.
114. Shawe-Taylor in the *Sunday Times*, 16.2.64.
115. Treasury note, 22.11.63, TNA T221 2138.
116. The scheme and the process of planning is described in William J. Curtis, *Denys Lasdun: Architecture, City Landscape* (London: Phaidon, 1994), p. 120.
117. Note of 11.10.63 and Cozens, 14.10.63, TNA T221 2138.
118. Cottesloe to Boyd-Carpenter, 24.1.64, ibid.
119. 'Notes on Requirements of New Opera House', Sadler's Wells' paper, October 1962, ENO Ad 88 Box 61, and 'Brief for Lasdun', 11.2.64, Lasdun papers 167A (LaD/166/5).
120. Tucker to Lasdun, 17.6.64, Lasdun papers 167 (LaD/166/2).
121. ENO/Trust, 20.7.64, B5 Box 63.
122. Ibid.
123. Ibid.
124. Tucker, *Musician*, p. 89.
125. ENO/Trust, 21.9.64, B5 Box 63.
126. Tucker, *Musician*, p. 89; Davis interview, 18.8.06.
127. Memorandum, 16.10.64, Lasdun papers 167A (LaD/166/2).
128. Arlen to Lasdun, 23.10.64, Lasdun papers 146 (LaD/164/5–165/3).
129. K. E. Couzens, note, 12.11.64, TNA T227 2139.
130. David Cairns, obituary of Edmund Tracey in the *Guardian*, 25.4.07.
131. Porter in the *Financial Times*, 31.12.65.
132. *Times Literary Supplement*, 30.4.65.
133. Nancy Phelan, *Charles Mackerras: A Musician's Musician* (London: Victor Gollancz, 1987), p. 145.
134. Charles Mackerras, 'What Mozart Really Meant', *Opera*, April 1965, pp. 241, 243.
135. Phelan, *Charles Mackerras*, p. 147.
136. Shawe-Taylor in the *Sunday Times*, 18.4.65.
137. *Times Literary Supplement*, 30.4.65.
138. Cairns in the *Financial Times*, 10.4.65.
139. *The Times*, 29.10.65.
140. Memorandum of 28.8.78, B106 Box 194.
141. R. A. H. Duke to Arts Council, 6.1.67, ENO Ad 61 Box 11.
142. Tucker, *Musician*, p. 89.
143. Memorandum on meeting held with Lord Chandos, Laurence Olivier, Kenneth Rae and Denys Lasdun at the National Theatre offices on 24.2.65, Lasdun papers 146 (LaD/164/5–165/3).
144. White paper, February 1965, Parliamentary papers, TNA.
145. Lasdun note, 23.3.66, Lasdun papers 167A (LaD/166/5).
146. I. R. M. Thom to Mr Summers, 20.10.65, TNA Ed221 7.
147. ENO/Trust, 18.10.65, B5 Box 63.
148. N. Summers to Maxwell-Hyslop (DES), 15.10.65, TNA Ed221 7.
149. According to Patricia Hollis in *Jennie Lee: A Life* (Oxford: Oxford University Press, 1997), p. 259.

150. Notes of Meeting at Arts Council on 22.10.65, TNA Ed221 7 and ENO/Trust, 18.2.65, B5 Box 63.
151. Lasdun to Lynex (South Bank Theatre and Opera board), 1.12.65, Lasdun papers.
152. See *Opera*, March 1966, for Alderman Sir Maurice Pariser, who advised Sadler's Wells on the provinces.
153. Lasdun note, 18.1.66, Lasdun papers 146.
154. Arlen to Lasdun, 27.1.66, Lasdun Papers 167 (LaD/166/2).
155. 'Manchester and the South Bank', 28.1.66, ENO Ad 88 Box 61.
156. Arts Council meeting, 26.1.66, TNA Ed221 5.
157. Arlen to Lord Harewood and brief notes of a meeting at County Hall, 31.1.66 and 2.2.66, and Arlen to Abernethy, ENO Ad 88 Box 61.
158. Memorandum: Meeting at County Hall, 16.2.66, Lasdun papers 146 (LaD/164/5–165/3).
159. Brief Notes of a Meeting held at County Hall on 16.2.66, Lasdun papers 167A (LaD/166/5).
160. Arts Council press statement, 25.2.66, Lasdun papers 146 (LaD/164/5–165/3).
161. South Bank board to Lasdun, 28.3.66, ibid.
162. Lasdun memorandum, 5.8.66, Lasdun papers 167A (LaD/166/5).
163. Tucker, *Musician*, p. 127.
164. Ibid., p. 129.

CHAPTER 7 1966–1972: 'ARLORIUM'

1. Edmund Tracey, obituary of Stephen Arlen, *Opera*, March 1972, p. 221.
2. Report of Arts Council Committee of Enquiry, 20.2.75, p. 45, ENO Ad 112 Box 121.
3. ENO/Trust, 18.4.66, B5 Box 63.
4. ENO/Trust, 16.5.66, ibid.
5. The Arts Council of Great Britain Opera and Ballet Enquiry, Opera Subcommittee, fourth meeting, ENO Ad 60 Box 11.
6. Arlen to Goodman, 6.9.66, ibid.
7. Memorandum of 8.9.66, ibid.
8. Arlen to Harewood, 26.10.66, ibid.
9. Arlen to Lasdun, 28.10.66, ENO Ad 53 Box 10 and Lasdun papers 167 (LaD/166/2).
10. Harewood to Arlen, 15.11.66, ENO Ad 61 Box 11.
11. ENO/Trust, 23.11.66, B5 Box 63.
12. Harewood to Arlen, 6.12.66; Arlen to Harewood, 12.12.66, ENO Ad 61 Box 11.
13. Harewood to Arlen, 29.12.66, ibid.
14. Arthur Jacobs in *Opera*, May 1966, p. 411.
15. *The Times*, 19.5.66.
16. *The Times*, 15.9.66.
17. Andrew Porter in the *Financial Times*, 30.11.66.
18. Tracey to Arlen, 9.8.66, ENO Ad 65 Box 55.

19. ENO/Trust, 22.8.66, B5 Box 63.
20. Littler to Arlen, 20.2.67, ENO Ad 61 Box 11.
21. Memorandum of 20.2.67, Lasdun papers 167A (LaD/166/5).
22. In file relating to the Arts Council Committee of Enquiry into Opera and Ballet, 20.3.67, ENO Ad 60–3 Box 1.
23. ENO/Trust, 20.3.67, B5 Box 63.
24. Arlen, 'After One Year', ENO Ad 66 Box 55.
25. ENO/Trust, 16.1.67, B5 Box 63.
26. Interview with Charles Mackerras, 27.4.06.
27. Tracey to Arlen, 2.5.67, ENO Ad 65 Box 55.
28. Tracey, unpublished interview with John Lucas, 1991.
29. 1.5.67, ENO Ad 65 Box 55.
30. Goodman to Arlen, 21.6.67, ENO Ad 62 Box 11.
31. Arts Council Enquiry, 7.11.67, ibid.
32. Harold Rosenthal in *Opera*, November 1967, p. 862.
33. Arlen to Tracey, 19.8.67, ENO Ad 66 Box 55.
34. Memorandum on future policy, 13.11.67, ibid.
35. Memorandum, October 1967, ENO Ad 66 Box 56.
36. Graham to Arlen, 20.10.67, ENO Ad 65 Box 55.
37. ENO/Trust, 30.11.67, ENO Ad 66 Box 56.
38. ENO/Trust, 18.12.67, B5 Box 63.
39. Desmond Shawe-Taylor in the *Sunday Times*, 4.2.68.
40. David Cairns in the *New Statesman*, 23.2.68.
41. Lord Harewood, *The Tongs and the Bones: The Memoirs of Lord Harewood* (London: Weidenfeld and Nicolson, 1981), p. 156.
42. ENO/Trust, 9.1.68, B6 Box 64.
43. Note, ACGB 1/1353.
44. Arlen, memorandum, 6.2.68, ENO Ad 47 Box 10.
45. The detailed discussions about the estimates of Sadler's Wells' costs and income after the move are in TNA Ed221 7.
46. Cruft, memorandum, 20.2.68, ACGB 1/1353.
47. ENO/Trust, 5.3.68, B6 Box 64.
48. ENO/Trust, 18.3.68, ibid.
49. Notes and minutes in January to May 1968 in TNA Ed221 7.
50. 28.3.68, ENO Ad 43 Box 9.
51. ENO/Trust, 22.4.68, B5 Box 64.
52. Edward Greenfield in the *Guardian*, 21.8.68.
53. Arnold Goodman, *Tell Them I'm on My Way* (London: Chapmans, 1993), pp. 302–3.
54. CG/SW 1, ENO Ad 69 Box 232.
55. Arlen to Donaldson, 2.5.68, ENO Ad 69 Box 5.
56. ENO/Trust, 19.8.68, B6 Box 64.
57. Quoted in Jonathan Croall, *Gielgud: A Theatrical Life* (London: Methuen, 2000), p. 437 and vividly remembered by Ann Howard.
58. Shawe-Taylor in the *Sunday Times*, 25.8.68.
59. Rodney Milnes in *Queen*, September 1968.
60. Shawe-Taylor in the *Sunday Times*, 25.8.68.
61. William Mann in *The Times*, 22.8.68.

62. Porter in the *Financial Times*, 22.9.68.
63. CG/SW 1, ENO Ad 69 Box 232.
64. ENO/Trust, 21.10.68, B6 Box 64.
65. *Opera*, June 2007, p 671.
66. Covent Garden and Sadler's Wells Repertory Planning, note of a meeting held at 44 Floral Street on 22.10.68, ENO Ad 43 Box 9.
67. CG/SW 1, ENO Ad 69 Box 232.
68. Arts Council of Great Britain, *A Report on Opera and Ballet in the United Kingdom, 1966–69* (London: n.p., 1969), pp. 7, 24, 48–53.
69. Martin Cooper in the *Telegraph*, 16.10.68 and Mann in *The Times*, 16.9.68.
70. Porter in the *Financial Times*, 6.10.68.
71. Rosenthal in *Opera*, February 1969, p. 164.
72. ENO/Trust, 20.3.67, B5 Box 63.
73. Cruft to Thom, 8.11.67, ACGB 1/1660.
74. Correspondence of 15, 18 and 20.11 and 2.12.68, ACGB 1/1660.
75. Rosenthal in *Opera*, February 1969, p. 256.
76. Anthony Field, 22.2.69, ACGB 1/160.
77. Richard Law in *Opera*, February 1969, p. 262.
78. John Higgins, interview with Arlen, *The Times Saturday Review*, 12.12.70.
79. John Higgins interview with Byam Shaw and Lord Harewood, *The Times*, 20.7.78.
80. Jacobs in *Opera*, January 1969, p. 74.
81. Interview with Anne Evans, 3.5.07.
82. ENO/Trust, 20.1.69, B6 Box 64.
83. Tracey to Porter, 6.2.69, ENO Ad 84 Box 55.
84. Mackerras memorandum, 6.9.69, ENO CA1 Box 129.
85. Obituary in *The Times*, 1.5.01.
86. Rodney Milnes, interview with Rita Hunter, *Harper's & Queen*, August 1972.
87. Porter to Colin Graham, 27.5.74, in discussions about the *Don Carlos* translation, ENO P61 Box 15.
88. Evans interview, 3.5.07.
89. ENO/Trust, 25.10.69, B6 Box 64.
90. Tracey to Porter, 18.11.69, ENO Ad 84 Box 55.
91. Mackerras memorandum, 18.2.69, ENO CA1 Box 129.
92. CG/SW 1, ENO Ad 69 Box 232.
93. *Daily Telegraph*, 23.8.69.
94. Alan Blyth in *Opera*, October 1969, p. 899.
95. Stanley Sadie in *The Times*, 23.8.69.
96. Porter in the *Financial Times*, 10.10.69.
97. ENO/Trust, 15.9.69, B6 Box 64.
98. Mackerras interview, 29.4.06.
99. By Richard Fisher, 11.9.69, ENO Ad 47 Box 10.
100. Evans interview, 3.5.07.
101. Shawe-Taylor in the *Sunday Times* and Ronald Crichton in the *Financial Times*, 31.1.70.
102. Shawe-Taylor in the *Sunday Times*, 1.2.70; Mann in *The Times*, 30.1.70.

103. Mann in *The Times*, 30.1.70.
104. Crichton in the *Financial Times*, 31.1.70.
105. Tracey to Porter, 3.2.70, ENO Ad 84 Box 55.
106. CG/SW, 18.3.70, ENO Ad 69 Box 55.
107. ENO/OSC, 8.1.70, B14 Box 66.
108. ENO/Trust, 16.1.70, B6 Box 64.
109. ENO/FGPC, 16.2.70, B16 Box 67.
110. Mackerras to Arlen and Tracey, 14.2.70, ENO CA1 Box 129.
111. ENO/OSC, 10.2.70, B16 Box 67; ENO/OSC, 4.12.69, B15 Box 66.
112. Mackerras interview, 29.4.06, and phone conversation; and Nancy Phelan, *Charles Mackerras: A Musician's Musician* (London: Victor Gollancz, 1987), p. 181.
113. ENO/OSC, 10.2.70, B16 Box 67.
114. ENO/Trust, 16.2.70, B6 Box 64.
115. ENO/Trust, 4.6.70, B16 Box 67.
116. Interview with Stefanos Lazaridis, *Guardian* (Arts section), 19.8.72.
117. Cairns in the *New Statesman*, 29.5.70, and Blyth in *The Times*, 5.8.72.
118. Interview with John Copley, 15.10.07.
119. Interview with Ann Howard, 1.11.07.
120. Shawe-Taylor in the *Sunday Times*, 23.8.70.
121. John Higgins in *The Spectator*, 16.5.70.
122. Interview with David Ritch, 21.8.06.
123. Goodman, *Tell Them I'm on My Way*, p. 280.
124. ENO/OSC, 5.8.70, B16 Box 67.
125. Urwick, Orr & Partners (management consultancy), 'Report: Sadler's Wells at London Coliseum', 28.9.72, ENO Ad 95 Box 84; Gerard Wood, Minutes of Proceedings of Arts Council Committee of Enquiry, 13.2.75, p. 7, ENO Ad 112 Box 121.
126. Gerard Wood, Minutes of Proceedings of Arts Council Committee of Enquiry, 20.2.75, p. 43, ENO Ad 112 Box 121.
127. Urwick, Orr, 'Report', ENO Ad 95 Box 84.
128. ENO/Trust, 17.8.70, B6 Box 64.
129. ENO/FC, 16.9.70, B16 Box 67.
130. Handwritten notes between the meetings of 1 September and 16 September 1970, ACGB 1/2053.
131. ENO/FC, 13.10.70, B16 Box 67.
132. ENO/Trust, 19.10.70, ibid.
133. Arts Council of Great Britain, *Report*, pp. 10, 57, ENO Ad 112 Box 121.
134. Ibid., pp. 11–12.
135. Interview with Gerry Morrissey, 12.9.08.
136. Ibid.
137. Minutes of Proceedings of Arts Council Committee of Enquiry, 13.2.75, p. 24, ENO Ad 112 Box 121.
138. Snape to Wood, 28.1.75, B71 Box 32.
139. ENO/FC, 13.10.70, B16 Box 67.
140. Nicholas Payne to author, 12.11.07.
141. Arlen to Goodman, 10.10.70, ACGB 1/2051.

142. Minute, 9.11.70, ACGB 13/229.
143. Preliminary meeting of Arts Council subcommittee set up to investigate the financial situation at Sadler's Wells, 29.10.70, ACGB 1/2556.
144. Minutes in ACGB 1/2556 and notes in ACGB 1/2051.
145. ENO/FC, 10.11.70, B16 Box 67.
146. Willatt to DES, 11.11.70, ACGB 1/2051.
147. ENO/Trust, 16.11.70, B6 Box 64.
148. Report of 23.11.70, ACGB 13/229.
149. ENO/Trust, 22.12.70, B6 Box 64.
150. Peter Heyworth in the *Observer*, 1.11.70.
151. The technical director, John Harrison, had been authorised to order four hydraulic rams at a total cost of £1,000 on 24 November, since two hydraulic rams would be impractical for touring. The scenery and props were now estimated at £19,000. John Wykham to Edward Renton, 17.12.70, ENO Ad 51 Box 126.
152. Mackerras interview, 27.4.06.
153. Mackerras memorandum, 30.12.69, ENO CA1 Box 129.
154. ENO/OSC, 1.12.70, B16 Box 67.
155. *Observer*, 3.1.71.
156. Shawe-Taylor in the *Sunday Times*, 31.1.71.
157. Porter in the *Financial Times*, 15.3.71.
158. ENO/FC, 14.1.71, B16 Box 67 and ENO/OSC, 5.1.71, ibid.
159. ENO/Trust, 18.1.71, B6 Box 64.
160. ENO/OSC, 2.2.71, B16 Box 67.
161. ENO/FC, 10.3.71, ibid.
162. ENO/Trust, 15.3.71, B6 Box 64.
163. Mann in *The Times*, 30.9.71.
164. Mackerras to Blatchley, 31.5.72, ENO P52 Box 15.
165. Shawe-Taylor in the *Sunday Times*, 8.11.71.
166. Porter in the *Financial Times*, 26.11.71.
167. Shawe-Taylor in the *Sunday Times*, 8.11.71.
168. Sadie in *Opera*, January 1973, pp. 85–6.
169. ENO/MC, 10.1.78, B26 Box 70.
170. Porter in the *Financial Times*, 10.12.71.
171. It was accepted by the ENO/OSC, 17.1.72, B16 Box 67.
172. Milnes in *Opera*, January 1972, p. 180.
173. Tracey to Hammond, 14.12.71, ENO P52 Box 15.
174. Note of meeting at the ACGB, 6.12.71, ENO Ad 162 Box 172.
175. Field to Arlen, 8.12.71, ACGB 1/2553.
176. John Higgins interviews with Byam Shaw and Lord Harewood in *The Times*, 20.7.78.
177. Mackerras interview, 27.4.06.
178. Interview with Lord Harewood, 14.6.04.
179. Peter Heyworth in the *Observer*, 5.3.72.
180. Willatt to McKenna, 29.2.72, ENO Ad 163 Box 172.
181. Blyth in *Opera*, March 1972, pp. 275–6.
182. Report in the *Evening Standard*, 2.3.72.
183. Tribute to Arlen in *Opera*, March 1972, pp. 219–21.

CHAPTER 8 1972–1975: ENGLISH NATIONAL OPERA, 'A GENUINE MUSIC THEATRE'

1. Lord Harewood, *The Tongs and the Bones: The Memoirs of Lord Harewood* (London: Weidenfeld and Nicolson, 1981), pp. 29, 32, 61.
2. Harewood's introduction to the 1976–8 biennial report.
3. Interviews with Lord Harewood, 27.3.06 and 1.10.07.
4. Lord Harewood, John Tooley and Harold Rosenthal, 'Our Current Operatic Problems', *Opera*, July 1973, p. 576.
5. Interview with Jeremy Caulton, 27.2.07.
6. Henze to Harewood, 25.5.07, ENO P162 Box 161.
7. ENO/OSC, 21.2.72, B16 Box 67.
8. ENO/OSC, 15.5.72, ibid.
9. Interview with Charles Mackerras, 27.4.06.
10. Harewood interview, 27.3.06.
11. ENO/OSC, 15.5.72, B17 Box 67.
12. Harewood interview, 27.3.06.
13. Ibid.
14. ENO/OSC, 24.7.72, B17 Box 67.
15. Mackerras interview, 27.4.06.
16. Nancy Phelan, *Charles Mackerras: A Musician's Musician* (London: Victor Gollancz, 1987), p. 181.
17. Mackerras interview, 27.4.06.
18. Andrew Porter in the *Financial Times*, 24.8.72.
19. Harewood interview, 27.3.06.
20. William Mann in *The Times*, 24.8.72.
21. Porter in the *Financial Times*, 24.8.72.
22. Interview with Colin Davis, 18.9.06.
23. Mackerras interview, 29.4.06.
24. *Guardian* (Arts section), 19.8.72.
25. John Higgins, interview with John Copley, *The Times*, 22.8.72.
26. ENO/Trust, 11.9.72, B7 Box 64.
27. John Snape memorandum, 28.1.75, ENO RM342 Box 342.
28. ENO/Trust, 5.6.72, B7 Box 64.
29. Mackerras interview, 29.4.06.
30. ENO/FSC, 22.6.72, B16 Box 67.
31. According to the NATTKE officer Tom Lever on 28.9.72: Urwick, Orr & Partners (management consultancy), 'Report: Sadler's Wells at London Coliseum', 28.9.72, ENO Ad 95 Box 84.
32. Meeting of Arts Council Committee of Enquiry, 13.2.75, ENO Ad 112 Box 121.
33. Caulton interview, 27.2.07.
34. ENO/Trust, 11.9.72, B7 Box 64.
35. ENO/Trust, 2.10.72, ibid.
36. Interview with Anne Evans, 3.5.07.
37. *Opera*, November 1972, p. 102.
38. ENO/OSC, 16.10.72, B17 Box 67.
39. ENO/OSC, 20.11.72, ibid.

40. ENO/OSC, 26.2.73, ibid.
41. Arthur Jacobs in *Opera*, February 1973, p. 180.
42. Mackerras interview, 29.4.06.
43. ENO/OC, 17.6.75, B78 Box 166.
44. Alberto Remedios in the *Contemporary Review*, July 1973.
45. Bryan Magee in *Music and Musicians*, May 1973.
46. Porter to Tracey and Tracey to Porter, January 1971, ENO P61 Box 15.
47. ENO/FGPC, 26.10.72, B17 Box 67.
48. Internal memorandum, ENO Ad 52 Box 126.
49. Stanley Sadie in *The Times*, 15.3.73.
50. Stephen Walsh in the *Observer*, 18.3.73.
51. Interview with Josephine Barstow, 26.2.08.
52. Interview with John Copley, 15.10.07.
53. Mann in *The Times*, 1.8.73 and 7.8.73.
54. Philip Hope-Wallace in the *Guardian*, 6.8.73.
55. Rodney Milnes in *Opera*, October 1973, p. 934.
56. David Fingleton, interview with John Blatchley, *Contemporary Review*, July 1973.
57. Mann and Porter in *The Times*, 13.9.73, and the *Financial Times*, 14.9.73.
58. Article by Christopher Ford in the *Guardian* (Arts section), 31.10.73.
59. Mann in *The Times*, 2.11.73.
60. Porter in the *Financial Times*, 6.11.73.
61. ENO/Trust, 24.7.72, B7 Box 64.
62. Hope-Wallace in the *Guardian*, 14.12.73.
63. Mann in *The Times*, 14.12.73.
64. Ronald Crichton in the *Financial Times*, 1.3.74; William Mann in *The Times*, 1.3.74.
65. Artists contracts, 13.5.74, ENO A486 Box 156.
66. Harewood interview, 27.3.06.
67. Rosenthal in *Opera*, May 1974, p. 382.
68. ENO/OSC, 12.3.74, B78 Box 166.
69. Alan Blyth in *Opera*, May 1974, p. 452.
70. Mackerras interview, 29.4.06.
71. Hope-Wallace in the *Guardian*, 3.9.73.
72. Rosenthal in *Opera*, January 1974, p. 160.
73. Milnes in *Opera*, May 1975, p. 492.
74. ENO/OSC, 14.5.73, B7 Box 64.
75. Barstow interview, 26.2.08.
76. ENO/OSC, 19.6.74, B26 Box 70.
77. ENO/Trust, 2.7.74, B23 Box 68.
78. ENO/MC, 13.3.74, B26 Box 70.
79. Snape to Field, 22.3.74, ENO Ad 163 Box 172.
80. Field to Snape, 30.5.74, ibid.
81. Payne–Diamand correspondence, B85 Box 175 and Ad 36 Box 9.
82. ENO/Trust, 19.4.71, B6 Box 64.
83. ENO/OSC, 17.5.71, B17 Box 67.
84. John Cruft, the Arts Council assessor, in May, ACGB 1/2553.

85. Arts Council Finance Committee, 13.7.71, ACGB 1/2557.

86. ENO/Trust, 15.11.71, B6 Box 64.

87. ENO/OSC, 20.9.71, B16 Box 67.

88. Arts Council to McKenna, ACGB 1/2553.

89. Tracey to Rhymes, 13.9.72, ENO Ad 146 Box 129.

90. ENO/Trust, 11.9.72, B7 Box 64.

91. J. H. Macphall (Insurance and Companies Department, Department of Trade and Industry) to Snape, 29.12.72, ENO Ad 146 Box 129 and Insurance and Companies Department of the Department of Trade and Industry to Arts Council, ACGB 1/2553.

92. Walker to Robinson, 5.2.73, ENO Ad 146 Box 129.

93. ENO/FGPC, 20.8.73, B17 Box 67.

94. Arts Council note, 3.9.73, ACGB 1/3079. It had even been suggested that the title be changed to include the word Rosebery.

95. Meeting of 11.9.73, discussed in ENO/FGPC, 17.9.73, B17 Box 67.

96. Harewood interview, 11.6.07.

97. Howe to Robinson, 2.11.73, ENO Ad 146 Box 129.

98. ENO/Trust, 7.11.73, B7 Box 64.

99. Both letters in ENO Ad 13 Box 7.

100. ENO/Trust, 4.12.72, ENO Ad 13 Box 7.

101. Quoted in Report of the Arts Council of Great Britain on the State of Industrial Relations at the Coliseum Theatre (1975), p. 13, ENO RM342.

102. Ibid., p. 15.

103. ENO/FGPC, 14.8.74, B25 Box 69.

104. ENO/Board, 1.10.73, B7 Box 64.

105. Harewood to all departments, Committee for Liaison between Artists and Management (later, Staff Association), 1970–76, B44 Box 82.

106. Porter in *Opera*, August 1974, pp. 665–73.

107. Peter Heyworth in the *Observer*, 25.8.74.

108. Tracey to Harewood, 5.9.74, ENO P61 Box 15.

109. Graham to Tracey, 27.8.74, ibid.

110. Rosenthal in *Opera*, October 1974, pp. 921–2.

111. Heyworth in the *Observer*, 13.10.74.

112. Hans Werner Henze in *Opera*, February 1975, pp. 130–1.

113. Interview with Ted Murphy, 17.12.07, and telephone conversation, 6.2.08.

114. ACGB, Minutes of Proceedings of Committee of Enquiry, 20.2.75, p. 37, and 26.2.75, pp. 13, 16, ENO Ad 113 Box 121.

115. Ibid., 13.2.75, pp. 23–4.

116. Peter Bentley-Stephens's diary of events of 1.11.74, ENO RM342.

117. ACGB, Minutes of Proceedings of Committee of Enquiry, 20.2.75, p. 57, ENO Ad 113 Box 121, and Arts Council Report, p. 25, ENO RM342.

118. Arts Council Report (1975), p. 57, ibid.

119. ACGB, Minutes of Proceedings of Committee of Enquiry, 20.2.75, p. 45, ENO Ad 113 Box 121.

120. Mackerras, letter to the author, 16.5.06.

121. Arts Council Report (1975), p. 30, ENO RM342.

122. ENO/Board, 4.11.74, B23 Box 68.
123. Arts Council Report (1975), pp. 37–8, ENO RM342.
124. Murphy interview, 17.12.07.
125. Harewood to ENO, 8.11.74, ENO RM341.
126. Cruft memorandum, 19.11.74, ACGB 1/2819.
127. Arts Council Report (1975), p. 3, ENO RM342.
128. ENO/Board, 2.12.74, B30 Box 70.
129. ENO/Board, 11.12.74, ibid.
130. ENO/FGPC, 22.10. 74, B78 Box 166.
131. ENO/FGPC, 19.11.74, ibid.
132. Mackerras interviews, 27.4.06 and 29.4.06.
133. Crichton in the *Financial Times*, 31.1.75.
134. Milnes in *The Spectator*, 8.2.75.
135. Shawe-Taylor in the *Sunday Times*, 23.2.75.
136. Crichton in the *Financial Times*, 1.1.75.
137. Heyworth in the *Observer*, 19.1.75.
138. ENO/Board, 6.1.75, B30 Box 70. The committee included Sir Roy
     Wilson QC, president of the Industrial Arbitration Board, and Lord
     Feather, general secretary of the Trades Union Congress from 1969 to
     1973.
139. Cruft, note, 4.2.75, ACGB 1/2819.
140. Fontaine's memorandum on personnel arrangements, 4.3.75, B30 Box
     70.
141. This and next pp.: Mackerras interview, 29.4.06.
142. Mackerras to ENO directorate, 22.3.75, ENO C8 Box 342.
143. ACGB, Minutes of Proceedings of Committee of Enquiry, 13.2.75, p. 45,
     ENO Ad 112 Box 121.
144. ENO/Trust, 7.4.75 and 5.5.75, B30 Box 70.
145. ENO/Board, 7.4.75, ibid.
146. Ibid.
147. Arts Council Report (1975), pp. 53, 31, 34, 59, 38, ENO RM342.
148. ENO comment on Arts Council Report (1975), 23.7.75, ENO Ad 5 Box
     7.
149. ENO/Board, 4.8.75, B30 Box 70.
150. Arts Council Report (1975), pp. 17, 18, ENO RM342.
151. Caulton interview, 27.2.07.
152. Mackerras interview, 29.4.06.

CHAPTER 9  1975–1978: 'SURE OF ITS MISSION' – THE LAST MACKERRAS
YEARS

1. Harewood to McKenna, 15.8.72, ENO Ad 34 Box 9.
2. Harewood–Robinson correspondence, ENO Ad 5 Box 7.
3. ENO/MC, 19.2.75, B30 Box 70.
4. Interview with Lord Harewood, 27.3.06.
5. ACGB to ENO, 25.4.75 and 30.5.75, ENO Ad 163 Box 172.
6. Ibid., 18.4.75.
7. ENO/Appeals, 2.2.76, 6.9.76, B31 Box 71.

8. Reported in *Opera*, June 1977, p. 535.
9. Goodison to Rhymes, 14.6.77, B33 Box 71.
10. Angus Stirling (Arts Council) to Harewood, ENO Ad 163 Box 172.
11. Harewood to Arts Council, 19.6.74, ACGB 1/3079.
12. Notes in Arts Council file between Cruft and Willatt, Nicholas Payne and Anthony Field, November 1974, ACGB 1/2819.
13. ENO/Board, 7.4.75, B30 Box 70.
14. Payne to McMaster, 20.11.74, ENON 2 Box 204.
15. Harewood Memorandum, 17.12.75, ibid.
16. Ernest Bradbury in the *Yorkshire Post*, 19.12.74, ibid.
17. Rhymes to Harewood, 30.1.76, ibid.
18. Rhymes/Jarman memorandum, 1.3.76, ENON 1 Box 204.
19. Undated letter, ENON 2 Box 204.
20. Rhymes to Harewood, 8.3.75, ibid.
21. Rhymes to Harewood, 21.4.75, 24.5.75, B31 Box 71.
22. Yorkshire Arts Association proposal to budget money to create back-up unit for ENO in Leeds, 6.4.76, ENON 2 Box 204.
23. Peter Heyworth in the *Observer*, 7.9.75.
24. Ronald Crichton in the *Financial Times*, 8.9.75.
25. Alan Blyth in *Opera*, March 1976, p. 290.
26. Memorandum, 9.19.75, ACGB 1/3352. Payne pointed out that the Royal Opera House Finance Committee had financial expertise that included Claus Moser, Professor Robbins and John Sainsbury.
27. ENO/OSC, 15.4.75, B30 Box 70.
28. William Mann in *The Times*, 12.12.75.
29. Crichton in the *Financial Times*, 12.12.75.
30. Milnes in *The Spectator*, 20.12.75.
31. Heyworth in the *Observer*, 14.12.75.
32. Interview with Josephine Barstow, 26.2.08.
33. Harold Rosenthal in *Opera*, January 1976, pp. 171–3.
34. Harewood interview, 27.3.06.
35. ENO/OSC, 21.10.75, 11.12.75, B31 Box 71.
36. Heyworth in the *Observer*, 14.12.75.
37. Stanley Sadie in *The Times*, 17.9.76.
38. Harewood to Robinson, ENO Ad 5 Box 7.
39. Interview with Lord Harewood, 27.3. 06.
40. Interview with Mark Elder, 9.4.07.
41. Max Loppert, interview with Mark Elder, *Financial Times*, 12.6.93.
42. Elder interview, 2.3.07.
43. Blyth in *The Times*, 6.2.76.
44. Rosenthal in *Opera*, April 1976, p. 375.
45. ENO/MC, 15.12.76, B26 Box 70.
46. Basil Horsfield (Artists International) to Harewood, 18.12.75, ENO P92 Box 55.
47. ENO/OSC, 21.10.75, B85 Box 175.
48. ENO/OSC, 10.2.76, B31 Box 71.
49. Harewood to Robinson, 5.1.76, ENO Ad 5 Box 7.
50. ENO/OSC, 9.3.76, B31 Box 71.

51. Roy Shaw (secretary general, Arts Council) to Robinson, August 1976, ibid.
52. FGPC, 19.7.76, ENO/OC, 13.7.76, ibid.
53. Harewood to Robinson, 9.9.76, ENON 2 Box 204.
54. Mann in *The Times*, 30.9.76.
55. Andrew Porter in *Opera*, November 1976, pp. 1056–8.
56. Rodney Milnes in *The Spectator*, 31.12.76.
57. Porter in *Opera*, November 1976.
58. ENO/MC, 15.2.78, B26 Box 70.
59. ENO/FGPC, 20.12.76, B33 Box 71.
60. Interview with Charles Mackerras, 29.4.06.
61. Lazaridis to Tracey, 7.1.77, B33 Box 71.
62. ENO/FGPC, 21.2.77, ibid.
63. ENO/Board, 10.1.77, ibid.
64. ENO/Board, 7.3.77, ibid.
65. Ibid.
66. ENO/OSC, 11.12.75 and other references in B85 Box 175.
67. Noël Goodwin in *Opera*, February 1977, pp. 149, 152.
68. Crichton in the *Financial Times*, 4.2.77.
69. Rosenthal in *Opera*, April 1977, pp. 383–6.
70. Shawe-Taylor in the *Sunday Times*, 6.2.77.
71. Edmund Tracey's memo for the Harewood conference of 12.3.93, B92 Box 185.
72. 1976–8 review.
73. Rosenthal in *Opera*, December 1977, p. 189.
74. ENO/OC, 11.10.77, B85 Box 175.
75. 1976–8 review.
76. Mann in *The Times*, 17.3.77.
77. John Higgins in *The Times*, 4.4.77.
78. ENO/MC, 15.12.77, B26 Box 70.
79. Cruft minute, ACGB 1/3925.
80. ENO to Cruft, 4.7.77, B33 Box 71.
81. ENO/Board, 7.11.77, B23 Box 68.
82. ENO/Board, 21.11.77, ibid.
83. Harewood in *The Times*, 20.7.78.
84. Milnes in *The Spectator*, 12.11.77.
85. ENO/OC, 13.12.77, B105 Box 194.
86. Rosenthal in *Opera*, February 1978, p. 206.
87. Interview with Brian McMaster, 27.9.07.

CHAPTER 10  1978–1982: 'THE MOST CRITICAL BATTLE TO SURVIVE'

1. Goodison to Harewood, 12.1.78, B105 Box 194.
2. Cruft and Phipps to Shaw, 15.3.78, ACGB 1/3935.
3. ENO/FGPC, 17.4.78, B105 Box 194.
4. ENO/MC, 10.1.78, ibid.
5. ENO/Board, 5.6.78, B106 Box 194. Harewood thought Rita Hunter's withdrawal from *Tristan* might mean that if Gwyneth Jones replaced

her, an original-language production would be possible.

6. Tracey's paper for the Management Committee, 23.8.78, B105 Box 194.
7. ENO/Board, 4.9.78, B106 Box 194.
8. ENO/OC, 12.9.78, ibid.
9. ENO/Board, 2.10.78, ibid.
10. David Cairns in the *Sunday Times*, 19.3.78.
11. Max Loppert in *Opera*, July 1978, p. 728.
12. ENO/Board, 8.5.78, B105 Box 194.
13. ENO/FGPC, 24.7.78, B106 Box 194.
14. ENO/FGPC, 6.9.78, ibid.
15. ENO/FGPC, 6.11.78, ibid.
16. Arthur Jacobs in *Opera*, March 1977, p. 292.
17. Graham/Elder statement, 17.1.78, ENO Press 20 Box 53; Harold Rosenthal in *Opera*, April 1978, p. 416.
18. Interview with Lord Harewood, 27.3.06.
19. Ibid. and interview with Jonathan Miller, 19.8.06.
20. Bayan Northcott in the *Sunday Telegraph*, 26.11.78.
21. Miller in *The Times*, 22.11.78.
22. Cairns in the *Sunday Times*, 26.11.78, and Bayan Northcott in the *Sunday Telegraph*, 26.11.78.
23. Harewood interview, 11.6.07.
24. ENO/OSC, 27.3.79, B53 Box 83.
25. Desmond Shawe-Taylor in the *Sunday Times*, 28.12.78.
26. 20.8.80 and 21.8.80, ENO AC486 Box 156.
27. 'In Memoriam N.W.G.T', volume of tributes edited by J. Audrey Ellison (privately printed), p. 27.
28. Harewood interview, 15.6.04.
29. Phipps to Covent Garden/Sadler's Wells, 24.1.77, ENO CG/SW9 Box 194.
30. Phipps to Angus Sterling (ACGB), 11.2.77, ACGB 1/3352.
31. Harewood to Sterling, 10.6.77, ACGB 1/3295.
32. ENO/Board, 2.5.77, B33 Box 71.
33. ENO/Board, 13.6.77, ibid.
34. ENO/MC, 14.8.77, B26 Box 70.
35. Phipps minute, ACGB 1/3925.
36. ENO Opera North Box 204 and ENO/Board, 7.11.77, B23 Box 68.
37. ENO Opera North, 7.2.78, B28 Box 70.
38. ENO/Board, 6.3.78, 10.3.78, and 5.6.78, B106 Box 194, B28 Box 70; ENON, 9.8.78, ENON 4 Box 20.
39. Alan Blyth in *Opera*, January 1979, p. 80.
40. Rodney Milnes, ibid., p. 82.
41. Rosenthal, interview with David Lloyd-Jones, *Opera*, November 1978, p. 1052.
42. ENO/Board, 2.10.78, B106 Box 194.
43. Field to Finance Director, 5.12.78, and ENO/Board, 2.10.78, ibid.
44. Staunton to Lazaridis, 6.11.78, ENO P92 Box 55.
45. ENO/OC, 15.8.78, P106 Box 194.
46. Harewood to Tracey, 28.1.79, P117 Box 135.

47. Memorandum by Amanda Stein, 31.12.79, ENO Prod 8 Box 204.
48. ENO/OC, 22.2.80, B54 Box 83. Only by asking the stage staff to work hard on Easter Monday, which was 'triple time', could the schedule be made to work. This was fraught with difficulties, as if the staff earned £200 in overtime per person over Easter they might then refuse to work the following Sundays on *Tosca* or *Barber*, or on rehearsals for Herz's forthcoming *Fidelio* (ENO Prod 8 Box 204).
49. ENO/Board, 3.3.79, B53 Box 83.
50. Nicholas de Jongh in the *Guardian*, 25.7.79, ENO Ad 21 Box 8.
51. Company Talk, 11.7.79, ibid.
52. Milnes in *Opera*, October 1979, p. 1004.
53. Blyth in *Opera*, June 1979, pp. 608–10.
54. Interviews with Rodney Milnes, 15.6.06, and Mark Elder, 2.3.07.
55. Milnes in *The Spectator*, 6.10.79.
56. Peter Heyworth in the *Observer*, 30.9.79.
57. Robert Henderson in the *Daily Telegraph*, 28.9.79.
58. Milnes in *The Spectator*, 6.10.79.
59. Harewood interview, 27.3.06.
60. Loppert in the *Financial Times*, 8.11.79.
61. Stephen Walsh in the *Observer*, 11.11.79.
62. Harewood interview, 27.3.06.
63. Rosenthal, interview with Mark Elder, *Opera*, October 1980, pp. 976–7, 979.
64. Gillian Widdicombe in the *Observer*, 16.11.79.
65. Elder interview, 9.4.07.
66. Geoffrey Wheatcroft in *The Times*, 10.1.85.
67. Widdicombe in the *Observer*, 16.12.79.
68. Profile of Pountney in *Scottish Opera News*, December 1976.
69. Elder interview, 9.4.07.
70. Elder interview, 14.4.08.
71. Elder interview, 9.4.07.
72. Interview with Jeremy Caulton, 9.6.07.
73. Pountney to Harewood, 30.7.79, ENO Ad 696 Box 183.
74. Pountney to Harewood, 19.10.79, AC440 Box 133.
75. David Murray in the *Financial Times*, 7.1.80.
76. Rosenthal in *Opera*, March 1980, p. 302.
77. Elder interview, 9.4.07.
78. John Higgins, interview with Janet Baker, *The Times*, 5.12.79.
79. Loppert in the *Financial Times*, 27.12.79.
80. William Mann in *The Times*, 6.11.79.
81. Milnes in *The Spectator*, 29.12.79.
82. Blyth in *Opera*, February 1980, p. 191.
83. ENO/OC, 22.2.80, B54 Box 83.
84. Interview with John Copley, 15.10.07.
85. Joachim Herz interviewed in *The Times*, 9.5.80.
86. Heyworth in the *Observer*, 18.5.80.
87. Rosenthal in *Opera*, July 1980, pp. 721–4.
88. Elder interview, 2.3.07.

89. Milnes, email to author, 5.3.07.
90. Milnes in *The Spectator*, 25.10.80.
91. John Higgins, interview with Jonathan Miller, *The Times*, 16.10.80.
92. Peter Stadlen in the *Daily Telegraph*, 18.10.80; Milnes in *The Spectator*, 25.10.80; Ronald Crichton in the *Financial Times*, 18.10.80.
93. Patrick Carnegy in the *Times Literary Supplement*, 5.12.80.
94. Record of meeting, 18.2.80, ACGB 1/4515.
95. Caulton interview, 26.2.07.
96. Elder interview with Clare Colvin, 7.12. 93, ENO Auc 84 Box 141.
97. ENO/FGPC, 3.12.79, B54 Box 83 and 3.4.80, ENO Ad 21 Box 8.
98. Minute of 20.3.80, ACGB 1/4515.
99. Peat Marwick report, ENO Ad 121 Box 121, p. 4.
100. David Fletcher to Harewood, 12.11.80, B46 Box 82.
101. Field to Harewood, 13.10.80, ibid.
102. ENO/Board, 31.3.80, B54 Box 83.
103. ENO/FGPC, 3.12.79, ibid., and 3.4.80, ENO Ad 21 Box 8. On 2 June 1980 Elder asked for contracts that would buy 'greater loyalty from the players', in order to improve the standard of the orchestra. There would be special contracts over minimum rates, for eight to twelve members (ENO/Board, 2.6.80, Box 82 B46).
104. ENO/FGPC, 23.10.79, B54 Box 83.
105. Tracey to Harewood, 10.11.80, B46 Box 82.
106. ENO/Board, 29.1.81, B55 Box 83.
107. Harewood to St John Stevas, 14.11.80, ENO Ad 9 Box 7.
108. John Tooley in *Opera*, February 1981, p. 116.
109. Tom Sutcliffe in the *Guardian* (Arts section), 23.1.81.
110. ENO/OC, 22.1.81, B69 Box 136.
111. Guy memorandum, 26.3.81, ENO Ad 14 Box 7.
112. J. Walter Thompson, 'The English National Opera', ENO Ad 124 Box 121, pp. 23, 25, 52.
113. Fred Silvester (J. Walter Thompson), 23.7.81, ENO Ad 136 Box 126.
114. Guy to Harewood, 23.12.82, ENO Ad 97 Box 85. The group was chaired by Sir Jack Rampton with Alan Hare and Sir Ronald Swayne.
115. Interview with Philip Turner, 12.12.07.
116. Minutes of Evidence taken before the Education, Science and Arts Committee of the House of Commons, 29.6.81 (Hansard), p. 368.
117. Discussion of J. Walter Thompson Report, 28.4.82, B56 Box 83.
118. ENO/Board, 12.7.81, B56 Box 83. On 20 May 1982 it was decided that an education unit should be started up, with workshops, study packs, schools visiting and receiving visits from ENO, audio-visual aids. The scheme would require sponsorship (Ad 22 Box 8).
119. ENO/Board, 27.1.82, B47 Box 82.
120. ENO/Board, 7.10.82, B56 Box 83.
121. Colin Graham to Harewood, April 1981, B69 Box 136.
122. Henderson in the *Daily Telegraph*, 10.8.87.
123. Shawe-Taylor in the *Sunday Times*, 16.8.81.
124. Milnes in *What's On*, 20.8.81.
125. Rosenthal in *Opera*, October 1981, p. 1078.

126. Higgins in *The Times*, 1.10.81.
127. ENO/Board, 17.11.81, 30.11.81, B56 Box 83.
128. Elder interview, 29.8.08.
129. Mann in *The Times*, 27.11.81.
130. Milnes in *The Spectator*, 5.12.81.
131. John Rosselli in the *Guardian*, 27.11.81.
132. Andrew Porter in *Opera*, February 1982, p. 198.
133. Elder interviewed in the *Independent*, 16.9.92.
134. Porter in *Opera*, February 1982, pp. 196–201.
135. Tom Sutcliffe in the *Guardian*, 23.11.81.
136. Milnes in *The Spectator*, 20.2.82.
137. Heyworth in the *Observer*, 14.2.82.
138. Milnes in *The Spectator*, 20.2.82; Rosenthal in *Opera*, October 1982, p. 420.
139. ENO/OC, 3.6.82, B69 Box 136.
140. Miller interview, 19.8.06, and telephone conversation, 18.12.07.
141. Andrew Clements in the *Financial Times*, 19.8.83; Peter Stadlen in the *Daily Telegraph*, 24.10.82; Loppert in the *Financial Times*, 24.9.82.
142. Loppert in the *Financial Times*, 24.9.82.
143. *Opera*, November 1982, p. 1197.
144. ENO annual report, 1982/3, ENO archive.
145. Hugh Canning in *Opera*, January 1988, pp. 106–7.
146. Miller interview, 19.8.06.
147. Caulton to directorate, 29.7.83, B162 Box 234.
148. William Mann in *Opera*, February 1983, pp. 207–10.
149. Milnes in ENO annual report, 1982/3.
150. ENO/OC, 13.1.85, B69 Box 136.
151. Janet Baker, *Full Circle: An Autobiographical Journal* (London: Julia MacRae, 1982), pp. 119, 137.

CHAPTER II 1982–1985: 'A "EUROPEAN" VIEW OF PRODUCTION'

1. Rodney Milnes, interview with David Pountney, *Harper's and Queen*, March 1983.
2. Interview with David Pountney, 28.12.07.
3. Interview with Mark Elder, 9.4.07.
4. Telephone conversation with Jeremy Caulton, 10.4.07.
5. Elder interview, 9.4.07.
6. Elder interview with Clare Colvin, 6.5.93, ENO Auc 84 Box 141.
7. *Daily Telegraph*, 17.11.84.
8. David Pountney, 'What the Programme Is For', 22.3.91, ENO P170 Box 185.
9. Pountney interview, 22.6.07.
10. Interview with Lord Harewood, 14.6.04.
11. Elder interview, 2.3.07.
12. ENO/CC, 10.8.82 and 18.8.82, B161 Box 233.
13. Caulton interview, 27.2.07.
14. ENO/OC, 24.9.82, B34 Box 71.

15. ENO/CC, 10.8.82 and 21.7.82, B161 Box 233 and Harewood's notes for ENO/OC, 24.9.82, B56 Box 83. Hytner was suggested to Caulton by Tracey. Caulton thought this a splendid idea and put it to Harewood, who proceeded to approach Elder and Hytner (Caulton, email to author, 5.3.08).
16. Rodney Milnes in *The Times*, 5.4.93.
17. Max Loppert in the *Financial Times*, 22.1.83.
18. ENO/OC, 25.9.1980, and ENO/CC, 7.10.80, B160 Box 233.
19. Pountney, interview with Clare Colvin, 6.5.93, ENO Auc 81 Box 141.
20. Robert Henderson in *Opera*, July 1983, p. 791.
21. ENO/OC, 4.10.83, B34 Box 71.
22. Michael Billington in the *Guardian*, 29.9.83.
23. Michael Tanner in the *Times Literary Supplement*, 14.10.83.
24. David Murray in the *Financial Times*, 3.10.83.
25. ENO/OC, 10.10.83, B34 Box 71.
26. Rhymes's calendar of events leading up to cancellation, 3.11.83, ibid. The history of the *Valkyrie* overspend is also described by R. J. Mantle in Paper 3 for the Oxford conference of December 1984, dated 3.1.84, B50 Box 83.
27. Elder interview, 9.4.07.
28. Calendar of Events, 3.11.83, B34 Box 71.
29. Gillian Widdicombe in the *Observer*, 16.10.83.
30. Tom Sutcliffe in the *Guardian* (Arts section), 24.10.83.
31. David Cairns in the *Sunday Times*, 30.10.83.
32. Loppert in the *Financial Times*, 24.10.83.
33. Milnes in *The Spectator*, 29.10.83.
34. Paul Griffiths in *The Times*, 24.10.83; Peter Heyworth in the *Observer*, 23.10.83.
35. ENO/Board, 7.11.83, B36 Box 72.
36. Fletcher to Harewood, 23.11.83, ENO T40 Box 22.
37. Oxford board conference, 11–12.11.83, B35 Box 72 and B36 Box 72; interview with Jeremy Caulton, 27.2.07.
38. ENO/FGPC, 5.12.83, B36 Box 72. The history of the *Valkyrie* overspend was described in Mantle's paper (see n. 26), which broke down the expenditure into individual items, amongst which was the timberwork – £55,000 of which had been allocated to common *Ring* elements and £25,000 to *Valkyrie*, figures which, in fact, should have been reversed. Overtime labour costs of £22,000 had been incurred following the late arrival of the designs and a switch in rehearsal priorities due to the illness of a singer. There was also an overspend of £10,000 on the complicated Act I tree.
39. ENO/CC, 10.11.83, B162 Box 234.
40. ENO/Board, 9.1.84, B36 Box 72.
41. Correspondence with Bjørnson, February–May 1984, ENO AC1031 Box 259.
42. ENO/Board, 5.11.84, B37 Box 72.
43. Harewood to Directorate,7.11.83, B162 Box 234.
44. Caulton interview, 27.2.07.

45. Harewood interviewed in the *Sunday Times*, 8.9.85.
46. In the *Independent*, 20.4.88.
47. ENO/Board, 11.11.83, B36 Box 72.
48. Arts Council to Harewood, 21.12.83, ibid.
49. Harewood interview, 11.6.07.
50. Response to the Arts Council's Arts Development Strategy, 21.12.83, B36 Box 72. The board also responded to what might be achieved with the tantalising fantasy of a 25 per cent increase: pension schemes, a proper contingency, publicity and education, a capital programme, increases in orchestral and other salaries that could begin to match other comparable jobs, affordable seat prices.
51. Interviews with Zeb Lalljee, 15.11.07, and Josephine Barstow, 26.2.08.
52. The decline was not confined to ENO. All music-lovers were suffering from the increases in ticket prices. Most classical-music audiences were hovering around 60 to 65 per cent, with a slowly declining middle- and upper-class audience. The Royal Opera House was experiencing similar problems, with only *Otello* sold out. The National Theatre was also struggling, except for the Cottesloe, which had a flat price of £4 (Maggie Sedwards and SWETM, 'Box Office Trends', ENO Ad 18 Box 7).
53. Sedwards and SWETM, 'Box Office Trends'; ENO/FGPC, 13.12.83, B36 Box 72.
54. Sedwards and SWETM, 'Box Office Trends'; ENO/FGPC, 14.12.83, ibid.
55. Extraordinary meeting of FGPC, 18.1.84, and ENO/FGPC, 13.2.84, ibid.
56. City University survey, ENO Ad 18 Box 7.
57. ENO/FGPC, 9.1.84, B36 Box 72.
58. Goodman to Gowrie, 4.1.84, ibid.
59. ENO/FGPC, 22.2.84, ibid.
60. ENO/FGPC, 6.2.84, ibid.
61. *Opera*, July 1985, p. 738.
62. ENO AC530 Box 156.
63. Harewood interview, 27.3.06.
64. Cairns in the *Sunday Times*, 12.2.84.
65. Paul Griffiths in *The Times*, 6.2.84.
66. Bayan Northcott in the *Sunday Telegraph*, 26.2.84.
67. Sutcliffe in the *Guardian*, 6.2.84.
68. Heyworth in the *Observer*, 12.2.84; Northcott in the *Sunday Telegraph*, 26.2.84.
69. Nicholas Kenyon interviews with Pountney, Elder and Harewood, *Sunday Times*, 11.3.84.
70. ENO/OC, 29.3.84, B69 Box 136.
71. Planning matters discussed at meeting of directorate, 11.4.84, ENO AC1031 Box 259.
72. ENO/FGPC, 2.4.84, recommended the 1984/5 budget, which was accepted by the board on 14.5.84, B36 Box 72.
73. *Sunday Telegraph*, 8.4.84.
74. ENO/Board, 6.11.82, draft report to board, B47 Box 82.

75. ENO/CC, 23.11.82, B161 Box 233. On 9 December Obolensky and Associates sent a report detailing fundraising events such as that to be held in Houston in January, where Mrs Van Remoortel's committee were arranging a Barry Manilow charity concert, with dinner, at the popular new Boccaccio club aimed at raising $5,000. It was stressed how important it was to have members of the royal family involved in the events. Fees for fundraising were 20 per cent of net profit (Box 82 B47).

76. ENO/Board, 10.1.83, B34 Box 71.

77. ENO/Board, 16.1.84, B36 Box 72.

78. ENO/Board, 2.2.84, ibid.

79. White to Harewood, 24.2.83, ibid.

80. Minutes of US Tour Subcommittee, 9.4.84 and 11.4.84, B36 Box 72.

81. ENO/Board, 14.5.84, ibid.

82. Reported in *The Times*, 31.5.84.

83. Minutes of US Tour Subcommittee, 25, 30.7.84 and 8.8.84, B36 Box 72.

84. ENO/Board, 25.7.84, ibid.

85. Williams to Goodman, 13.9.84, ibid.

86. ENO/CC, 20.9.84, B163 Box 234.

87. Elder interview, 9.4.07.

88. ENO/CC, 20.9.84, B163 Box 234.

89. Milnes in *The Spectator*, 22.9.84.

90. Cairns in the *Sunday Times*, 11.9.84.

91. Griffiths in *The Times*, 10.9.84.

92. Milnes in *The Spectator*, 22.9.84.

93. Loppert in the *Financial Times*, 29.8.84.

94. Milnes in the *Observer*, 30.9 84.

95. ENO/Board, 9.7.84, B36 Box 72 and email from Jonas to author, 5.8.08.

96. Stephen Fay in the *Sunday Times*, 8.9.85.

97. Sir Roy Shaw in the *Independent*, 2.12.88.

98. Rees-Mogg speech to IBM reproduced in *The Economist*, 11.3.85.

99. ENO/FGPC, 6.8.84, B36 Box 72.

100. Nicholas Kenyon in the *Observer*, 14.4.85, and interview with Peter Jonas, 9.5.08.

101. Quoted in Patrick Cosgrave, *The Strange Death of Socialist Britain: Postwar British Politics* (London: Constable, 1992), p. 193.

102. Kenyon in the *Sunday Times*, 14.4.85.

103. ENO/FGPC, 3.12.84, B37 Box 72.

104. Oxford board conference, 30.11.84, ibid.

105. Ibid.

106. ENO/OC, 16.12.84, B69 Box 136.

107. Interview in the *Guardian* (Arts section), 20.12.84.

108. Geoffrey Norris in the *Times Literary Supplement*, 4.1.85.

109. Milnes in *The Spectator*, 5.1.85.

110. Loppert in the *Financial Times*, 22.12 84.

111. Norris in the *Times Literary Supplement*, 4.1.85.

112. This file contains many letters including Dr J. A. Ramsden to Harewood, 23.12.84, ENO Ad 16 Box 7.

113. Harewood to Douce Barrett, 15.2.85, ENO Ad 16 Box 4.
114. Pountney letter, 26.2.85, P19 Box 13.
115. Pountney interview, 22.6.07. *Mazeppa* had been budgeted at £62,000 and had cost £69,400.
116. Harewood to Elder, Pountney and Jonas, 27.1.85, B163 Box 234.
117. ENO/CC meeting, 8.2.85, B163 and B164 Box 234.
118. Michael Tanner in the *Times Literary Supplement*, 15.2.85.
119. Milnes in *The Spectator*, 2.2.85.
120. Stephen Walsh in the *New Statesman*, 1.3.85.
121. Tom Sutcliffe in the *Guardian*, 25.2.85.
122. Hilary Finch in *The Times*, 25.2.85.
123. Kenyon in *Opera*, April 1988, pp. 419–23.
124. Milnes in *The Spectator*, 16.3.85.
125. Kenyon in the *Sunday Times*, 3.2.85.
126. David Murray in the *Financial Times*, 9.4.85, and Sutcliffe in the *Guardian*, 8.4.85.
127. Harewood to Elder, Tracey and Pountney, 18.7.82, B161 Box 233.
128. Review of season, 1.10.85, B68 Box 136.
129. Harewood interview, 11.6.07.
130. ENO/OC, 11.2.85, B37 Box 72.
131. ENO/FGPC, 4.3.85, B136 Box 68.
132. ENO/OC, 11.4.85, B37 Box 72.
133. Harewood to Caulton, 23.3.85, B164 Box 234.

CHAPTER 12 1985–1987: 'THE SHOCK OF THE NEW'

1. Jonas to Harewood, 7.6.91, ENO Ad 166 Box 172.
2. Interview with Mark Elder, 9.4.07.
3. Interview with Peter Jonas, 9.5.08.
4. Jonas to Harewood, 20.11.91, ENO Ad 166 Box 172.
5. Jonas to Rittner, 1.9.85, ENO Ad 171 Box 173.
6. Jonas to Rittner, 7.7.85, ibid.
7. ENO/FGPC, 3.9.85, B37 Box 72.
8. Interview with David Elliott, 11.6.08, and email to author, 18.6.08.
9. ENO/FGPC, 3.9.85, and ENO/Board, 16.9.85, B72 Box 37.
10. ENO/FGPC, 8.10.85, ibid.
11. David Murray in the *Financial Times*, 12.9.85.
12. Rodney Milnes in *The Spectator*, 26.10.85.
13. Paul Griffiths in *The Times*, 16.11.85.
14. Andrew Clements in the *New Statesman*, 13.12.85.
15. Max Loppert in the *Financial Times*, 6.12.85.
16. David Elliott to Jonas and Caulton, 29.1.86, P6 Box 196.
17. Jonas to Rittner, 14.1.86, B38 Box 72.
18. Rittner to Jonas, 6.1.86, ibid.
19. Jonas to Rittner, 14.1.86, ibid.
20. Willis Barnes memorandum, 7.3.86, B41 Box 73.
21. Elliott to Jonas, 22.10.87, ENO Ad 173 Box 173.
22. Interview with Russell Barnes in *Classical Music*, 15.11.86.

23. Interview with Richard Elder, 29.4.08.
24. Interview with David Elliott, 11.6.08, and email to author, 18.6.08.
25. ENO/Plannng, 8.10.85, B165 Box 234.
26. ENO/Board, 24.2.86, B38 Box 72.
27. Milnes in *The Spectator*, 29.3.86.
28. Clements in the *Financial Times*, 14.4.86.
29. ENO/OC, 5.6.86, B38 Box 72.
30. Box-office report, 25.3.86, B41 Box 73. David Elliott reported that although *Parsifal*'s set was not very heavy, the need to focus the light before each performance had been time-consuming and had resulted in increased technical labour costs. In general in March overtime in the technical departments cost £160,000, compared with the original budget of £67,600. Elliott was working with the technical departments to produce a predictive model that would anticipate and avoid such a 'heavy concentration of overtime' (David Elliott assessment, 27.3.86, B41 Box 73).
31. Milnes on *Kaleidoscope*, BBC Radio 4, 29.4.06.
32. Barry Millington in *The Times*, 22.10.90.
33. Fiona Maddocks, interview with Harrison Birtwistle, *The Times*, 16.5.86.
34. Dominic Gill in the *Financial Times*, 23.5.86.
35. Milnes in *The Spectator*, 31.5.86.
36. 'D.A.K.' [Don Keller], box-office report, 1.7.86, B41 Box 73.
37. ENO/FGPC, 10.6.86, ibid.
38. ENO/Planning, 10.6.86, B166 Box 234; ENO/FGPC, 5.2.87, B41 Box 73.
39. ENO/Board, 21.4.86, B38 Box 72.
40. ENO/FGPC, 10.6.86, B41 Box 73, 8.7.86, B43 Box 82; ENO/Board, 21.9.86, B41 Box 73.
41. Alan Blyth, interview with Peter Jonas, *Daily Telegraph*, 22.5.86.
42. ENO/Board, 8.10.85, B37 Box 72, and 18.11.85, B38 Box 72.
43. ENO/Planning, 24.10.85, B165 Box 234, and *Sunday Telegraph* magazine, 7.9.86.
44. Miller interview, *Sunday Telegraph* magazine, August 1986.
45. David Murray in the *Financial Times*, 29.9.86.
46. ENO/Board, 20.10.86, B38 Box 72.
47. ENO/OC, 4.12.86, B69 Box 136.
48. Interview with Lord Harewood, 11.6.07.
49. ENO/Board, 20.10.86 and 4.11.86, B38 Box 72.
50. Jonas interview, 9.5.08.
51. ENO/Board, 24.2.87, B39 Box 73.
52. Richard Elder to Jonas, 5.10.90, ENO Ad 173 Box 173, B84 Box 169.
53. Louise Jeffreys memo, 4.11.92, ibid.
54. Interview with Ted Murphy, 17.12.07.
55. Memorandum, 6.11.86, and ENO/Board, 17.1.86, B38 Box 72.
56. According to Jonas's report of 25.10.88, ENO Ad 173 Box 173.
57. Draft note of a meeting at 105 Piccadilly, 7.11.86 (ENO and Arts Council), ENO Ad 172 Box 173 and ENO/FGPC, 9.12.86, B42 Box 82.

58. Arts Council press release, 27.11.86, B41 Box 73; Barnes memorandum, 4.12.86, ENO Ad 171 Box 173; *The Times*, 15.12.86.
59. Jonas letter, 21.11.86, ENO P114 Box 165.
60. Loppert in the *Financial Times*, 20.10.86; Griffiths in *The Times*, 30.10.86.
61. ENO/Board, 17.11.86, B38 Box 72.
62. David Pountney interview, *Classical Music*, January 1987.
63. Milnes in *Opera*, January 1987, p. 100.
64. Nicholas Kenyon in the *Financial Times*, 30.11.86.
65. Mark Elder interview, 9.4.07.
66. John Higgins, interview with Jonas, *The Times*, 15.12.86.
67. ENO/OC, 13.8.86, B38 Box 72. The visual reference was Roberto Rossellini's 1945 film, *Roma, città aperta*.
68. Edward Greenfield in the *Evening Standard*, 30.1.87, and Milnes in *Opera*, March 1987, pp. 337–8.
69. ENO/Board, 24.2.87, B39 Box 73.
70. Tom Sutcliffe in the *Guardian*, 30.8.88.
71. Hugh Canning in the *Sunday Times*, 4.4.87.
72. ENO/Board, 18.6.87, B39 Box 73.
73. ENO/FGPC, 13.1.87, B42 Box 82.
74. ENO/FGPC, 10.3.87, ibid; Harewood House Conference 13–14.2.87, B52 Box 83.
75. ENO/FGPC, 7.4.87, B39 Box 73 and 28.4.87, B86 Box 175.
76. ENO/Board, 30.6.87, B39 Box 73.
77. ENO/FGPC, 12.5.87, ibid.
78. Shaw quoted in the *Independent*, 2.12.88 and 20.4.88.
79. ENO/MC, 13–14.2.87, B86 Box 175.
80. 'Elder's Ten Years', *Coliseum*, spring 1990; Ed Vulliamy in the *Guardian*, 11.4.92 and the *Independent*, 16.9.92; interview with Michael Billington, *Guardian*, 11.9.90.
81. Mark Elder interview, 9.4.07.
82. Elder interview with Clare Colvin, 6.5.93, ENO Auc 84 Box 141.
83. Pountney to Harewood, 20.1.91, ENO P170 Box 185.
84. Interview with David Fielding, 22.12.07.
85. Alden and Fielding's opinions expressed in the following passages are from *Opera*, November 1986, pp. 1,290–301, unless otherwise stated.
86. Nicholas John, Peter Jonas, Mark Elder and David Pountney, *Power House, The English National Opera Experience* (London: Lime Tree, 1992), p. 15.
87. Mark Elder interview, 9.4.07.
88. Loppert in the *Financial Times*, 4.4.87.
89. Higgins in *The Times*, 4.4.87; Blyth in the *Daily Telegraph*, 4.4.87; David Cairns in the *Sunday Times*, 5.4.87.
90. Peter Heyworth in the *Observer*, 5.4.87.
91. Higgins in *The Times*, 4.4.87.
92. Elder interview, 9.4.07.
93. ENO/OC, 9.4.87, B39 Box 73; ENO/FGPC, 12.5.87, B39 Box 73.
94. Lazaridis quoted in the *Independent*, 25.8.88.

95. Robert Henderson in the *Daily Telegraph*, 16.9.88.
96. Higgins in *The Times*, 16.9.88.
97. Mark Elder interview, 9.4.07.
98. Heyworth in the *Observer*, 18.9.88.
99. Fielding interview, 22.12.07, and email, 4.1.08.
100. Mark Elder interview, 9.4.07.
101. Elijah Moshinsky in *Opera*, October 1992, pp. 1,164–8.
102. Pountney quoted in the *Sunday Times*, 24.11.91, *Opera*, December 1992, and in interview with Clare Colvin, 6.5.93, ENO.
103. John Davison interviewed in the *Sunday Times*, 27.3.88, and *Opera*, April 1988, pp. 419–23.
104. Telephone conversation with Jonathan Miller, 27.12.07.
105. Jonas to Goodison, 25.10.89, B96 Box 185.
106. Giorgio Strehler in Mario M. Delgado and Paul Heritage (eds.), *In Contact with the Gods? Directors Talk Theatre* (Manchester and New York: Manchester University Press, 1996), p. 264. Strehler's 1971 La Scala *Boccanegra* had been a product of a more humane political tradition of theatre direction. The Piccolo Teatro had established his main concerns for theatre as a public service and for reaching a new audience through working in depth on the text. 'He combined an aesthetic sense of beauty with an efficient and critical examination of society, and endeavoured to bring the spectator the joy of theatre as a matter for serious reflection about human nature and the world . . . it represented the humanitarian, humanist strain in the European enlightenment and culture' (Michael Coveney quoted ibid.). Strehler was not part of the local London debate, but his *Boccanegra* had become a gold standard for Verdi production, though not for Alden and Fielding. They accused his gesture of taking away the wall at the end of the opera to show a giant ship as being sentimental. 'It was kind of beautiful,' Alden said, but he 'didn't really buy it'.
107. Richard Eyre, *National Service: Diary of a Decade at the National Theatre* (London: Bloomsbury, 2003), p. 75.
108. Interviews with Nicholas Hytner, 14.6.07 and 9.1.08.
109. Heyworth in the *Observer*, 24.5.87.
110. Interview with Philip Turner, 12.12.07.
111. Arts Council evaluation November 1987, ENO Ad 173 Box 173.
112. ENO annual reports, 1984/5 and 1986/7, ENO archive.
113. Arts Council evaluation, 2.4.87, B42 Box 82.
114. ENO/OC, 13.8.86, B38 Box 72, ENO/OC, 4.12.86, B69 Box 136.
115. Milnes in *The Spectator*, 26.9.87.
116. Kenyon in the *Observer*, 13.9.87.
117. Cairns in the *Sunday Times*, 13.9.87.
118. Robert Maycock in the *Independent*, 23.9.87, and Blyth in the *Daily Telegraph*, 23.9.87.
119. Loppert in the *Financial Times*, 23.9.87.
120. Griffiths in *The Times*, 22.9.87.
121. Pountney to Planning Committee, 14.7.88, P107 Box 134.
122. ENO/OC, 1.10.87, B39 Box 73.

123. ENO/OC, 3.12.87, ibid.

124. Caulton memorandum, 24.8.88, ENO Ad 173 Box 173.

125. Higgins in *The Times*, 20.11.87, and Loppert in the *Financial Times*, 20.1.87.

126. Telephone conversation with Pountney, 27.12.07.

127. Loppert in the *Financial Times*, 18.12.87.

128. Sutcliffe in the *Guardian*, 18.12.87.

CHAPTER 13  1987–1993: 'RUTHLESSLY PRESSING FOR *LEBENSRAUM*'

1. ENO/Board, 10.10.87, B39 Box 73 The box office had increased from £3,702,463 to £3,965,070 and development income was also up, by 33 per cent to £730,000 (Anthony Blackstock, Arts Council assessment, 15.10.87, ENO Ad 173 Box 173).

2. This and previous paragraph: Rittner to Harewood, 14.3.88, B40 Box 73.

3. ENO/Board, 17.11.87, B39 Box 73, and ENO/Board, 26.1.88, B40 Box 73.

4. Press release, ENO Ad 172 Box 173; ENO/FGPC, 9.2.98, B40 Box 73.

5. Harewood to Rittner, 5.4.88, B50 Box 73.

6. David Elliott, email to author, 7.8.08.

7. Elliott budget papers, 5.4.88, 6.4.88 and Harewood House Conference, 15–16.4.88, B60 and B40 Box 73.

8. Sir Roy Shaw in the *Independent*, 2.12.88.

9. Designers and Producers Fees and Budgets, 1979–88, 17.6.88, ENO Prod 6 Box 196.

10. ENO/CC, 31.1.86, 2.5.88 and 22.5.88, B166 Box 234.

11. ENO/CC, 17.10.85, ibid.

12. Max Loppert in the *Financial Times*, 26.2.88.

13. Andrew Clements in the *New Statesman*, 4.3.88.

14. Peter Heyworth in the *Observer*, 28.2.88.

15. Rodney Milnes in *The Spectator*, 5.3.88.

16. John Davison, interview with Nicholas Hytner, *Sunday Times*, 27.3.88, and Hilary Finch in *The Times*, 26.3.88.

17. Martin Hoyle in *Opera*, May 1988, pp. 617–8; Robert Henderson in the *Daily Telegraph*, 1.4.88; Bayan Northcott in the *Independent*, 1.4.88.

18. Loppert in the *Financial Times*, 2.4.88.

19. ENO/Production, 17.6.88, Prod 6 Box 196.

20. David Pountney, email to author, 10.8.08.

21. ENO/Production, 17.6.88, Prod 6 Box 196.

22. Interview with Nicholas Hytner, 14.6.07.

23. Elliott, Financial Overview, 1987–8, 29.6.88, B87 Box 184.

24. ENO/Board, 27.9.88, B40 Box 73. The accumulated deficit would be reduced to £355,000. The plan allowed for the computerisation of the box office, which would help the marketing and development offices.

25. ENO Three-Year Business Plan (draft), signed by Elliott, ENO/Board, 27.9.88, B40 Box 73.

26. Jonas letter, 15.11.88, ENO Ad 170 Box 172.

27. Barry Millington in the *Times Educational Supplement*, 3.2.89; Paul Griffiths in *The Times*, 26.1.89; Loppert in the *Financial Times*, 26.1.89.
28. Graham Marchant and Anthony Blackstock, ENO 1986/7 season Assessment Notes, 2.12.88, B40 Box 73.
29. ENO/FGPC, 7.2.89, B98 Box 192. ENO management was offering £218.50 per week, rising to £231.50 from 31 July 1989. The orchestra cost £1.4 million – nearly 10 per cent of total costs.
30. Ibid.
31. *Evening Standard*, 27.4.89 and 2.10.89, ENO Ad 170 Box 172.
32. ENO/Board, 25.4.89, B98 Box 192, and notes of meeting in ENO Ad 171 Box 173.
33. Interview with Henrietta Bredin, 7.11.07.
34. Tom Sutcliffe in the *Guardian*, 27.5.89.
35. Malcolm Hayes in the *Sunday Telegraph*, 28.5.89.
36. Michael John White in the *Independent*, 27.5.89; Hayes in the *Sunday Telegraph*, 28.5.89; Sutcliffe in the *Guardian*, 27.5.89.
37. October 1990 report for Arts Council, B62 Box 119.
38. Pountney to Unwin, 1.8.89, B95 Box 185.
39. New draft three-year plan, 12.9.89, B88 Box 184.
40. ENO/Planning, 16.6.86, B166 Box 234.
41. Interview with Peter Jonas, 9.5.08.
42. Harewood to Jonas, 7.9.89, ENO Ad 141 Box 131.
43. Jonas to Harewood, 12.9.89, ibid.
44. Interview with Lord Harewood, 11.6.07.
45. Milnes in *Opera*, July 1989, p. 868.
46. October 1990 review paper, B62 Box 119.
47. Loppert in the *Financial Times*, 10.11.89.
48. *Opera*, January 1990, pp. 12–13.
49. Nicholas Kenyon in the *Observer*, 12.11.89.
50. Jonas/Caulton annual review, October 1990, B62 Box 119.
51. Griffiths in *The Times*, 9.9.89.
52. Loppert in the *Financial Times*, 8.12.89.
53. John Higgins in *The Times*, 7.12.89.
54. Jonas interview, 14.5.08, and email to author, 13.6.08. Jonas recalled that the graphic designers CDT (Carroll Dempsey and Thirkell) were inspired by the auditorium floor plan of the Coliseum, which is circular, and also felt that it signified accessibility (Jonas email, 6.3.09).
55. Senior management meeting, 5.7.89, B104 Box 194.
56. Milnes in *Opera*, October 1989, p. 1,165.
57. Jonas to Alan Blyth, 9.10.89, ENO Ad 170 Box 172.
58. Telephone conversation with Jeremy Caulton, 17.6.08.
59. ENO Staff Association meeting, 13.11.89, B128 Box 208.
60. ENO press release and Arts Council press release, 21.11.89, B98 Box 192.
61. ENO/FGPC, 21.11.89, 5.12.89, B99 Box 192.
62. Jonas interview, 9.5.08.
63. ENO/Board, 19.12.89, B99 Box 192.
64. Elliott, Marketing Expenditure, 30.11.89, B88 Box 184; ENO/FGPC, 9.1.90, B99 Box 192.

65. Elliott, annual review, draft of 2.10.90, ENO Ad 173 Box 173; interview with David Elliott, 11.6.08.
66. Jonas interview, 9.5.08.
67. Jonas to Harewood, 2.2.90, ENO Ad 141 Box 131.
68. Jonas to Harewood, 10.4.90, ibid.
69. ENO/FGPC, 23.1.90, B99 Box 192.
70. Jonas to Harewood, 2.3.90, ENO Ad 141 Box 131.
71. ENO/FGPC, 6.3.90, B99 Box 192.
72. ENO/FGPC, 20.3.90, ibid.
73. The *Independent*, 25.4.90.
74. The *Guardian*, 23.4.90.
75. Milnes in *Opera*, June 1990, pp. 645–6.
76. Kenyon in the *Observer*, 8.4.90.
77. White in the *Independent on Sunday*, 8.4.90; Higgins in *The Times*, 7.4.90.
78. ENO/OC, 27.6.90, B99 Box 192.
79. Report for Arts Council, 18.8.91, B100 Box 193.
80. Jonas interview, 9.5.08.
81. Paul Driver in the *Sunday Times*, 20.5.90.
82. Andrew Porter in the *Financial Times*, 19.5.90.
83. Report for Arts Council, 18.8.91, B100 Box 193.
84. Braithwaite, Moscow Diary 1988–92, entry for 9.6.08, Braithwaite papers.
85. Unwin to Elliott, 11.6.90, B97 Box 185.
86. Martin Kettle in the *Guardian*, 21.6.90.
87. Ibid.
88. Pountney email, 10.8.08.
89. Dmitry Morosov in *Pravda*, 24.6.90.
90. ENO/OC, 27.6.90 and ENO/FGPC, 13.11.90, B99 Box 192.
91. Michael Billington, interview with Mark Elder, *Guardian*, 11.9.90.
92. Elliott, annual review, draft of 2.10.90, October 1990, ENO Ad 173 Box 173, and signed with Jonas October 1990, for Harewood Conference 1–2.2.91, p. 78, B62 Box 119.
93. Cooper to Elliott, 25.9.90, B99 Box 192. Jonas wrote to Harewood on 20.11.92 to report that subscriptions had fallen from a peak in 1989/90 of £1,039,941 – about 18 per cent of sales – down to £755,408 (10 per cent) in 1991/2, ENO Ad 166 Box 172.
94. ENO/Planning, 2.8.90, B76 Box 162 and Elliott interview, 9.5.08.
95. Rough notes of a meeting held between Planning and Senior Management Committees, 6.9.90, B72 Box 162.
96. Ibid. and, for 'labour of love', Jonas interview, 9.5.08.
97. Harewood to Jonas, 26.9.90, ENO Ad 141 Box 131; ENO/Board, 25.9.90, B99 Box 192.
98. Hytner interview, 14.6.07.
99. Milnes in the *Evening Standard*, 14.9.90.
100. White in the *Sunday Independent*, 16.9.90.
101. Porter in the *Financial Times*, 15.9.90.
102. Malcolm Hayes in the *Sunday Telegraph*, 16.9.90.

103. Jonas/Caulton artistic review, 18.8.91, B100 193.

104. Griffiths in *The Times*, 8.1.90.

105. Milnes in the *Evening Standard*, 8.11.90.

106. Harewood interview, 11.9.07.

107. Jonas/Caulton artistic review, 18.8.91, B100 Box 193.

108. Hugh Canning in the *Sunday Times*, 11.11.90.

109. Harewood to Jonas, 19.4.91, ENO Ad 166 Box 172.

110. Jonas/Caulton artistic review, 18.8.91, B100 193.

111. Milnes in the *Evening Standard*, 3.12.90.

112. Sutcliffe in the *Guardian*, 21.2.90.

113. David Murray in the *Financial Times*, 25.1.91.

114. ENO/OC, 18.3.91, B85 Box 175.

115. Billington in *Opera*, July 1991, p. 834.

116. Loppert in the *Financial Times*, 8.6.91.

117. Loppert in the *Financial Times*, 19.4.91.

118. Jonas/Caulton artistic review, 18.8.91, B100 193.

119. ENO/OC, 13.6.91, B85 Box 175.

120. Jonas/Caulton artistic review, 18.8 91, B100 Box 193.

121. *Guardian* (Review section), 29.11.90.

122. Jonas to Harewood, 3.7.90, B95 Box 185.

123. *The Times*, 27.3.90.

124. Senior management meeting, 2.11.90, B77 Box 162.

125. Elliott to Jonas and senior management, 13.11.90, A69 Box 204.

126. Nickson to Tracey, 23.10.90, ibid.

127. ENO/Board, 27.11.90, B99 Box 192. A record sum of £1,451,000 had been raised for sponsorship for 1990/1 and £200,000 savings had been made by the end of the year due to 'star chamber' meetings with each budget holder.

128. ENO/OC, 29.11.90, B85 Box 175.

129. Ibid.

130. Jonas to senior management, 5.12.90, ENO Ad 69 Box 204.

131. ENO/FGPC, 22.1.91, B83 Box 169, and 13.2.91, B128 Box 208.

132. Notes of an ad hoc meeting of ENO directors, 18.12.90, B99 Box 192.

133. Harewood interview, 11.6.07.

134. Jonas interview, 9.5.08, and emails, 13.6.08 and 19.3.09.

135. Harewood email, 10.6.08.

136. Hytner interview, 14.6.07.

137. Harewood interview, 11.6.07.

138. Pountney, paper for Harewood House Conference, 30.1.91, P170 Box 185.

139. Harewood House Conference, 1–2.2.91, B62 Box 119.

140. Harewood House Conference, ibid., and B100 Box 193.

141. Jonas emails, 18 and 19.6.08.

142. Jonas to Palumbo, 15.4.91, ENO Ad 175 Box 174.

143. Jonas to Anthony Everitt, 22.11.91, ENO Ad 175 Box 174.

144. ENO/FGPC, 9.4.91, B100 Box 193; Three-Year Financial Plan, 1991/2–1993/4, April 1991, B83 Box 169.

145. Jonas to Unwin, 3.6.91, B96 Box 185.

146. Jonas to senior management, 7.6.91, B77 Box 162.
147. ENO annual report 1990/1, ENO archive.
148. ENO/Board, 18.6.91, B100 Box 193.
149. Jonas to Everitt, 12.6.91 and 22.5.91, ENO Ad 175 Box 174.
150. Jonas interview, 8.5.08, and email, 13.6.08.
151. ENO Audience Research Report, December 1991, ENO Ad 193 Box 198 (draft October 1991) and B63 Box 119.
152. Pountney paper, 13.6.91, B100 Box 193.
153. Jonas/Caulton artistic review, 21.8.92, B80 Box 166.
154. Clements in the *Financial Times*, 1.11.91.
155. Jonas/Caulton artistic review, 21.8.92, B80 Box 166.
156. Higgins in *The Times*, 1.11.91.
157. Harewood to Jonas, 13.12.91, ENO Ad 166 Box 172.
158. Jonas/Caulton artistic review, 21.8.92, B80 Box 166.
159. Milnes in *The Times*, 6.12.93.
160. Richard Fairman in the *Financial Times*, 6.12.93.
161. Financial figures are in ENO Ad 175 Box 174, ENO/Board, January 1992–April 1993 B80 166, and ENO/Board, August–December 1992, B102 Box 193.
162. Earle's monthly financial reports are in B84 Box 169.
163. Jonas/Caulton artistic review, 21.8.92, B80 Box 166.
164. Management accounts to January 1992, B84 Box 169.
165. Milnes in *Opera*, June 1992, p. 723.
166. Jonas/Caulton artistic review, 21.8.92, B80 Box 166.
167. Ibid.
168. Loppert in the *Financial Times*, 7.5.92.
169. Management accounts the period to July 1992, B84 Box 169.
170. ENO annual report, 1991/2, B80 Box 166.
171. Application to Messrs Coutts & Co., 9.6.92, B101 Box 193. The projected overdraft requirement at 31.3.93 was £1.434 million.
172. Carr to Earle, 24.7.92, B94 Box 185.
173. Cooper to Earle and Jonas note, 28.7.92, B94 Box 185. Fresh wealth and expertise were brought on to the board in April in the form of Lord Wolfson and Rodric Braithwaite, the foreign-policy adviser to the prime minister and brother of the conductor Nicholas Braithwaite.
174. ENO/FGPC, 14.6.88, B40 Box 73.
175. Correspondence in ENO RM346. The working party was to consist of Harewood, Lord Carr, the managing finance and development directors, and the company surveyor.
176. Jonas interview, 9.5.08.
177. ENO/FGPC, 2.11.90, B99 Box 192.
178. Jonas interview, 9.5.08.
179. *Daily Telegraph*, 19.11.95.
180. ENO annual report, 1991/2, B80 Box 166.
181. Milnes in *Opera*, May 1992, p. 509.
182. Interview with David Pountney, 22.6.07.
183. Interview with Mark Elder, 9.4.07.
184. ENO/FGPC, 13.10.92, B84 Box 169.

185. Canning in the *Sunday Times*, 20.9.92; Henderson in the *Daily Telegraph*, 18.9.92; Milnes in *The Times*, 18.9.92.
186. Michael Kennedy in the *Sunday Telegraph*, 20.9.92.
187. Milnes in *The Times*, 18.9.92.
188. Jonas to John Robinson, 8.12.92, B102 Box 193.
189. Jonas memorandum, 11.11.92, B77 Box 162.
190. *Evening Standard*, 16.11.92.
191. Loppert in the *Financial Times*, 16.11.92. White in the *Observer*, 22.11.92.
192. Elder interview, 9.4.07.
193. Management accounts for period to November 1992, 11.1.93, B84 Box 169.
194. Porter in the *Observer*, 20.12.92, and *Opera*, February 1993, pp. 232–4.
195. Milnes in *The Times*, 18.12.92.
196. Canning in the *Sunday Times*, 20.12.92.
197. Milnes in *The Times*, 18.12.92.
198. Porter in the *Observer*, 20.12.92.
199. ENO/Planning, 5.1.93, B76 Box 162.
200. Unwin to Harewood, 29.1.93, B92 Box 185.
201. Draft report by Tracey, 13.1.93, ibid. Tracey, however, was concerned about the loss of ensemble. In the 1992/3 season the company consisted of four sopranos, Garrett, Mannion, Cairns and Pope, four mezzo-sopranos, including Sally Burgess, three tenors, three baritones, including Opie and Shilling, two bass baritones and five basses, including Van Allan – twenty-one in all (B102 Box 193). British singers were more in demand abroad than they were in the past. Tracey partly blamed the singers themselves. 'They let us down', he wrote, 'after agreeing to sing with us in order to go abroad.' They earned more money abroad and were not required to rehearse. They accepted smaller roles at Covent Garden which they would not agree to at ENO, 'because Covent Garden is great and grand and we are not . . . we sing in English and are not regarded as being truly in the mainstream of opera work'.
202. ENO/Board, 3.12.91, considers report from Opera Committee, B101 Box 193.
203. Elder interview, 9.4.07.
204. Caulton, draft paper, 15.2.93, and memo, March 1993, B92 Box 185.
205. Board Strategy Day, 12.3.93, B91 Box 184.
206. Earle to Jonas, 26.2.93, B92 Box 185.
207. Jonas to Earle, March 1993, ibid.
208. ENO/Board, 27.4.93, B91 Box 184.
209. Milnes in the *Evening Standard*, 26.9.91.
210. *Friends Magazine*, Summer 1992, pp. 26–7.
211. Martin Kettle, interview with Sîan Edwards, *Guardian*, 6.4.93.
212. Marks to Harewood, 19.4.93, B91 Box 124.
213. Milnes in *The Times*, 22.2.93.
214. Porter in the *Observer*, 21.3.93.
215. Loppert in the *Financial Times*, 30.4.93.
216. Canning in the *Sunday Times*, 2.5.93.

217. Hilary Finch in *The Times*, 2.6.93.
218. Porter in the *Observer*, 13.6.93.
219. Milnes in *The Times*, 7.6.93.
220. Kennedy in the *Sunday Telegraph*, 14.4.93.
221. Rupert Christiansen in the *Daily Telegraph*, 14.2.93.
222. Nicholas John, Peter Jonas, Mark Elder and David Pountney, *Power House, The English National Opera Experience* (London: Lime Tree, 1992), pp. 10–11.
223. Bredin interview, 7.11.07.
224. John et al., *Power House*, pp. 10–11.

CHAPTER 14  1993–1997: 'A REDUCED ROLE FOR ENO'?

1. ENO annual report 1992/3, ENO archive.
2. Marks quoted in *The Times*, 18.2.91.
3. Hugh Canning, interview with Dennis Marks, *Sunday Times*, 2.5.93.
4. Peter Conrad, interview with Dennis Marks, *Observer*, 13.6.93.
5. Interview with Maddie Morton, 18.6.07.
6. Rodney Milnes in *Opera*, November 1993, p. 1347.
7. Rupert Christiansen in *The Spectator*, 10.2.94; Milnes in *The Times*, 4.2.94.
8. ENO/Planning, 6.10.92, B76 Box 162.
9. Interview with Vernon Ellis, 9.10.07.
10. 1993–94 Season to Date: Press Comment and Analysis, 4.5.93, B131 Box 209.
11. ENO/APSC, 10.5.94, B133 Box 209.
12. Andrew Clements in the *Guardian*, 22.4.94.
13. 1993–94 Season to Date: Press Comment and Analysis, 4.5.94, B131 Box 209.
14. Unlabelled press cutting, ENO.
15. ENO/APSC, 10.5.94, B133 Box 209.
16. Summary of meeting with Anthony Everitt and Mary Allen and Lord Gowrie, 30.3.94, B139 Box 228.
17. Board discussions of 11 and 12.4.94, B112 Box 205; meeting with ACE, 13.4.94, B56 Box 233; P. J. M. Fiddler to Earle, 19.4.94, B115 Box 206.
18. ENO/Board, 17.5.94, B156 Box 233; Gowrie to Harewood, 24.5.94, B140 Box 228.
19. ENO/Board, 2.2.94 and 29.3.94, B111 Box 205.
20. ENO/Board, 20.7.94, B113 Box 205.
21. Allen and Hodges to Marks, 30.6.94, B140 Box 228.
22. ENO/Board, 31.8.94, B126 Box 208.
23. Interview with Gerry Morrissey, 16.9.08.
24. BECTU negotiations in B123, B126 Box 208.
25. Milnes in *The Times*, 16.9.94.
26. Canning in the *Sunday Times*, 11.9.94.
27. Canning in the *Sunday Times*, 16.10.95.
28. John Allison in *Opera*, January 1995, p. 10.

29. ENO/FGPC, 8.11.94, B118 Box 206.
30. Corporate Affairs Committee minutes, 29.11.94, B131 Box 209.
31. Marks to Allen, 9.11.94, press cuttings, ENO.
32. Morton interview, 18.6.07, and email to author, 11.9.08.
33. Interviews with Graham Devlin, 1.10.07, and Lord Stevenson, 7.11.07.
34. 'Survey into the provision of Lyric Theatre (Dance and Opera) in London' (Stevenson report), p. 10, draft of 22.12.94 and various interviews.
35. Stevenson report, draft of 22.12.94 and shorter version of January 1995, p. 9.
36. Stevenson interview, 7.11.07.
37. Interview with Lord Harewood, 11.6.07.
38. Notes on meeting with ACE, 22.3.95, B113 Box 206.
39. ENO/FGPC, 21.3.95, B138 Box 28.
40. ENO/Board, 6.6.95, B117 Box 206.
41. Dennis Marks, email comment on text, 25.4.08.
42. Richard Morrison in *The Times*, 10.5.96.
43. Interview with Nicholas Payne, 31.8.07.
44. Interview with John Baker, 5.8.08.
45. Clements in *Opera*, April 1995, p. 478.
46. Canning in the *Sunday Times*, 19.3.95.
47. Unlabelled press cuttings, ENO.
48. Memo, 14.9.95, B151 Box 230.
49. Marks report, 7.12.95, B117 Box 206.
50. Ibid.
51. Milnes in *The Times*, 21.10.95; Clements in the *Guardian*, 21.10.96.
52. Marks report, 7.12.95, B117 Box 206.
53. Milnes in *The Times*, 24.12.95.
54. Michael Billington in the *Guardian*, 13.12.95.
55. Milnes in *The Times*, 13.12.95.
56. Unlabelled press cuttings, ENO.
57. ENO/Board, 18.9.95, B117 Box 206.
58. Press cutting, 27.9.94, ENO.
59. Baker interview, 5.8.08.
60. Interview with Steve Moffitt, 30.10.07.
61. Allison, interview with Mark-Anthony Turnage, *The Times*, 18.1.96.
62. Marks report, 6.12.95, B139 Box 228.
63. Milnes in *The Times*, 14.9.96.
64. Canning in the *Sunday Times*, 17.11.96; Clements in the *Guardian*, 20.11.96.
65. Press cutting, 28.10.96, ENO.
66. ACE to ENO, ENO/FGPC, 12.11.96, B158 Box 233.
67. Statement from Lord Gowrie following the announcement of the grant-in-aid for 1997/8, 26.11.96, B153 Box 231.
68. Baker interview, 5.8.08.
69. Payne interview, 21.8.07.
70. Marks to Baker, 5.12.96, B134 Box 228.
71. Reports of Sarsden Conference, 30–31 May 1997, press cuttings, ENO.

72. 'Feasibility Study, Summary Report and Key Conclusions', 7.6.96, ENO.
73. Milnes in *Opera*, February 1997, p. 137.
74. Stevenson interview, 7.11.07.
75. Tom Sutcliffe in the *Evening Standard*, 6.1.97.
76. Unwin to Marks, 15.1.97, Unwin, private collection.
77. Harewood interview, 11.6.07.
78. Baker interviews, 8.10.07 and 5.8.08.
79. Interview with Ted Murphy, 17.12.07.
80. Payne interview, 2.8.07.
81. Interview with David Pountney, 22.6.07.
82. Baker interview, 5.8.08.
83. ENO/FGPC, 23.1.97, B158 Box 233; Baker interview, 8.10.07.
84. Baker interview, 8.10.07.
85. Notes of a meeting at the Coliseum, 4.2.97, B158 Box 233.
86. Interview with Dennis Marks, 3.7.07.
87. Marks to Alexander, 6.1.97, B135 Box 210.
88. Marks to Braithwaite, 7.2.97, ibid.
89. Braithwaite to Marks, 10.2.97, Braithwaite papers.
90. Interview with Paul Daniel, 29.8.07.
91. Baker interview, 5.8.08.
92. Daniel interview, 29.8.07.
93. M. J. Woolley note for FGPC meeting of 22.4.97, B158 Box 233.
94. David Stott (ENO production accountant) to Mostart and Marks, 25 1.97, B153 Box 231.
95. ACE to ENO, 3.3.97, ibid.
96. 'Strategic Stock-Take Report, Draft Three', undated, ibid.
97. Budget projection, 16.4.97, B158 Box 233.
98. Marks to Braithwaite, 20.4.97, B150 Box 230.
99. Allison in *The Times*, 5.3.97.
100. Canning in the *Sunday Times*, 9.3.97.
101. Christiansen in the *Daily Telegraph*, 10.4.97.
102. Judith Mackrell in the *Guardian*, 7.6.97.
103. Baker interview, 8.10.07.
104. Sarsden Conference, 31.5.97, B150 Box 320.
105. Ibid.
106. Susie Gilbert and Jay Shir, *A Tale of Four Houses, Opera at Covent Garden, Vienna, La Scala and the Met since 1945* (London: HarperCollins, 2003), pp. 840–2.
107. Baker interview, 8.10.07.
108. Braithwaite to Marks, 5.7.97, B135 Box 210.
109. Marks to Braithwaite, 8.7.97, ibid.
110. ENO/FGPC, 17.7.97, B158 Box 233.
111. Baker interview, 8.10.07.
112. Andrew Porter in *Opera*, November 1997, p. 1,278.
113. Harewood interview, 1.10.07.
114. Undated letter, Braithwaite collection.
115. Baker, email to author, 27.11.07.
116. Christiansen in the *Daily Telegraph*, 23.9.97.

117. Payne interview, 21.8.07.
118. Baker, email to author, 14.9.08.
119. Marks, email to author, 13.1.08.

CHAPTER 15  1997–2002: NOT ENTIRELY STABILISED

1. Stabilisation Strategy, Second Interim Report, October 1997, p. 18 ENO Ad 246 Box 226.
2. ENO/FGPC, 17.7.97, B158 Box 233.
3. Stabilisation Strategy Second Interim Report, October 1997, pp. 3, 4, ENO Ad 246 Box 226.
4. ENO Annual Report and Financial Statements for the year ended 31 March 1998, Companies House.
5. Rodney Milnes in *The Times*, 22.10.97.
6. Edward Seckerson in the *Independent*, 22.10.97.
7. Fiona Maddocks in the *Observer*, 20.10.97.
8. John Allison in *Opera*, January 1998, p. 112.
9. Richard Eyre, *National Service: Diary of a Decade at the National Theatre* (London: Bloomsbury, 2003), p. 411.
10. Interview with Paul Daniel, 29.8.07.
11. Interview with John Baker, 8.10.07.
12. The *Guardian*, 22.4.05.
13. Interview with David Dyer, 12.12.07.
14. Daniel interview, 29.8.07.
15. *Yesterday in Parliament*, Radio 4, 5.11.97.
16. Rodney Milnes in *The Times*, 5.11.07.
17. Milnes in *Opera*, May 1998, p. 507.
18. Daniel interview, 29.8.07, and email to the author, 16.12.07.
19. Unlabelled press cuttings, ENO.
20. John Baker, email to the author, 19.6.08.
21. Interview with Nicholas Payne, 21.8.07.
22. Hugh Canning in the *Sunday Times*, 8.2.98.
23. ENO/Planning, 13.3.98, B151 Box 231.
24. Payne interview, 21.8.07.
25. ENO/Planning, 13.3.98, B151 Box 231.
26. Daniel quoted in *Opera*, May 1998, p. 507.
27. Milnes in *The Times*, 15.5.98.
28. Andrew Porter in the *Financial Times*, 25.6.98; Canning in the *Sunday Times*, 21.6.98.
29. *The Eyre Review: Return to an Address of the Honourable the House of Commons Dated 30 June 1998 for the Report on the Future of Lyric Theatre in London* (London: The Stationery Office, 1998), p. 54.
30. Ibid., p. 52.
31. Daniel interview, 29.8.07; Baker interview, 19.8.07.
32. Payne, comment on the text, 27.9.07, and Stabilisation Strategy, Third Interim Report, June 1998, ENO Ad 247 Box 227.
33. Payne comment, 29.7.07; Baker interview, 5.8.08.
34. Rupert Christiansen in the *Daily Telegraph*, 10.9.98.

35. Andrew Clements interview with Nicholas Payne, *Guardian*, 11.9.98.
36. Payne interview, 21.8.07.
37. John Allison in *The Times*, 6.9 98.
38. ENO/Production, 2.12.98, B157 Box 233.
39. Milnes in *The Times*, 14.9.98.
40. Allison in *Opera*, January 1999, pp. 109–10.
41. Milnes in *The Times*, 15.2.99.
42. Clements in the *Guardian*, 15.2.99; Christiansen in the *Daily Telegraph*, 15.2.99; Canning in the *Sunday Times*, 21.2.99.
43. ENO/Production, 2.12.98, B157 Box 233.
44. ENO/Production, 11.3.99, ibid.
45. Clements in the *Guardian*, 20.3.99.
46. Maddocks in the *Observer*, 19.4.99; Milnes in *The Times*, 23.3.99.
47. Seckerson in the *Independent*, 21.4.99; John Higgins in *The Times*, 21.2.99.
48. Michael Kennedy in the *Sunday Telegraph*, 23.5.99.
49. Milnes in *The Times*, 13.9.99; Maddocks in the *Observer*, 19.9.99.
50. Clements in the *Guardian*, 29.11.99.
51. Edward Greenfield in the *Guardian*, 1.12.99.
52. Milnes in *The Times*, 1.12.99; Kennedy in the *Sunday Telegraph*, 5.12.99.
53. Andrew Clark in the *Financial Times*, 29.11.99.
54. Payne interview, 21.8.07; 'The Current Position' (Payne's business plan 2002/3 to 2004/5), March 2002, p. 2.
55. Canning in *Opera*, April 2000, p. 405.
56. Michael Billington in the *Guardian*, 17.2.00.
57. Milnes in *The Times*, 27.3.00.
58. Clements in the *Guardian*, 27.3.00.
59. Charlotte Higgins, interview with Payne, *Guardian*, 22.4.05.
60. Harewood to Marks, 19.2.92, ENO Ad 166 Box 172.
61. Allison in *Opera*, August 2000, p. 992.
62. Maddocks in the *Observer*, 11.6.00.
63. Payne interview, 21.8.07.
64. Allison in *Opera*, May 2000, p. 507.
65. Baker interview, 5.8.08.
66. Payne interview, 21.8.07.
67. Ibid.
68. Interview with Tim Albery, 12.12.07.
69. Interview with Ted Murphy, 17.12.07.
70. Michael Tanner in *The Spectator*, 30.9.00.
71. Andrew Clark in *Opera*, February 2001, p. 166.
72. Kennedy in the *Sunday Telegraph*, 26.11.00.
73. Seckerson in the *Independent*, 22.11.00.
74. Payne interview, 31.8.07.
75. Clark in *Opera*, February 2001, pp. 167–9.
76. Payne interview, 31.8.07.
77. Ibid.
78. Interview with Steve Moffitt, 30.10.07.

79. Milnes in *The Times*, 11.4.01.
80. Clements in the *Guardian*, 11.4.01.
81. Payne, annual review, July 2002, author's collection.
82. Baker interview, 5.8.08.
83. Milnes in *The Times*, 30.4.01.
84. Clements in the *Guardian*, 24.4.01.
85. Kennedy in the *Sunday Telegraph*, 3.6.01.
86. Billington, interview with Calixto Bieito, *Opera*, October 2002, p. 1,182.
87. Allison, interview with Calixto Bieito, *The Times*, 19.2.02.
88. Milnes in *The Times*, 2.6.01.
89. Payne interview, 31.8.07.
90. Michael Church, interview with Paul Daniel, *Independent*, 26.10.01.
91. Payne, annual review, July 2002.
92. Milnes in *The Times*, 11.6.01.
93. Tom Sutcliffe in the *Evening Standard*, 22.6.01.
94. Canning in the *Sunday Times*, 17.6.01.
95. Kennedy in the *Sunday Telegraph*, 24.6.07.
96. Payne, email to author, 17.12.07.
97. Canning in the *Sunday Times*, 4.3.01.
98. Payne interview, 31.8.07; Payne was supported in this supposition by his chairman John Baker (Baker interview, 8.10.07).
99. Baker interview, 5.8.08.
100. Baker interview, 8.10.07.
101. Charlotte Higgins in the *Guardian*, 16.12.05.
102. Interview with Martin Smith, 16.10.07.
103. Milnes in *The Times*, 29.12.01.
104. Hilary Finch in *The Times*, 23.10.01.
105. Allison in *Opera*, January 2002, p. 110.
106. Payne interview, 31.8.07.
107. Clements in the *Guardian*, 10.11.01.
108. Payne, annual review, July 2002.
109. Payne interview, 31.8.07.
110. David Murray in the *Financial Times*, 3.12.01.
111. Milnes in *The Times*, 26.1.02.
112. Smith interview, 16.10.07.
113. Interview with John Ward, 21.8.08.
114. Roger Parker in *Opera*, April 2002, p. 476.
115. Milnes in *The Times*, 22.2.02.
116. Allison, interview with Payne, *The Times*, 19.2.01.
117. Payne, annual review, July 2002.
118. Interview with Lord Harewood, 14.6.04.
119. Smith interview, 16.10.07.
120. Baker interview, 8.10.07; Payne interview, 31.8.07; Payne, email to author, 31.7.08.
121. Charlotte Higgins in the *Guardian*, 11.4.02, and Richard Jones, note to the author, 27.1.08.
122. Max Loppert in *Opera*, June 2002, p. 735.

123. Payne, annual review, July 2002.
124. Allison in *Opera*, July 2002, p. 811.
125. Milnes in *The Times*, 3.5.02.
126. Clark in the *Financial Times*, 31.5.02.
127. Christiansen in the *Daily Telegraph*, 30.5.02.
128. Porter in *Opera*, August 2002, pp. 982–3.
129. Payne interview, 21.8.07.
130. Payne, annual review, July 2002, p. 2.
131. Payne interview, 31.8.07.
132. Smith interview, 16.10.07.
133. Interview with John Nelson, 24.9.08.
134. Payne interview, 31.8.07.
135. Payne, email to author, 17.12.07.
136. Payne interview, 31.8.07.
137. Smith interview, 16.10.07.
138. Payne interview, 31.8.07, and email to author, 17.12.07.
139. Baker interview, 8.10.07.
140. Payne, email to author, 17.12.07.
141. Harewood interview, 1.10.07.
142. Smith interview, 16.10.07.
143. Payne interview, 31.8.07.
144. Christiansen in the *Daily Telegraph*, 17.7.02.
145. Sutcliffe in *The Spectator*, 10.8.02.
146. Quoted by Charlotte Higgins in the *Guardian*, 2.8.02.
147. Milnes in *The Times*, 18.7.02.
148. Charlotte Higgins in the *Guardian*, 2.8.02.
149. Ibid.
150. Daniel interview, 29.8.07.
151. Payne interview, 21.9.07.

CHAPTER 16  2002–2009: A NEW MODEL

1. Vernon Ellis, email to author, 25.7.08.
2. Interview with Paul Daniel, 29.8.07.
3. Richard Morrison, interview with Daniel, *The Times*, 21.1.03.
4. Interview with Paul Daniel, 15.5.08, and email to author, 30.8.07.
5. Reported in the *Guardian*, 22.4.05.
6. Daniel interview, 5.5.08.
7. Interview with Horace Trubridge, 24.9.08.
8. Letters page, *The Spectator*, 24.8.02.
9. Interview with Vernon Ellis, 9.10.07.
10. Adrian Hamilton in the *Independent*, 28.8.02.
11. Rodney Milnes in *The Times*, 31.10.02; Tim Ashley in the *Guardian*, 1.11.02.
12. Hugh Canning in *Opera*, December 2002, p. 1,513.
13. Fiona Maddocks in the *Evening Standard*, 22.11.02.
14. Michael Kennedy in the *Sunday Telegraph*, 15.12.02.
15. Andrew Clark in the *Financial Times*, 10.1.03.

16. Fiachra Gibbons in the *Guardian*, 18.1.03.
17. Interview with Anne Evans, 29.7.08.
18. Barry Millington in the *Guardian*, 17.4.08.
19. Fiachra Gibbons in the *Guardian*, 18.1.03.
20. *Daily Telegraph*, 22.1.03.
21. Andrew Porter in *Opera*, April 2003, p. 464.
22. Tim Ashley in the *Guardian*, 24.1.03.
23. Andrew Clark in the *Financial Times*, 24.1.03.
24. Letters to *The Times*, 3.2.03 and the *Daily Telegraph*, 4.2.03.
25. *Guardian*, 19.3.03.
26. Tom Sutcliffe in *The Spectator*, 10.8.02.
27. *Guardian*, 18.1.03.
28. *Guardian*, 19.1.03.
29. Interview with Martin Smith, 16.10.07 and email, Smith to author, 22.7.08.
30. Smith interview, 16.10.07.
31. Interview with Lord Harewood, 1.10.07.
32. Ellis interview, 9.10.07.
33. *The Times*, 8.2.03.
34. *Irish Post*, 15.11.03.
35. Daniel interview, 29.8.07.
36. Barry Millington in the *Evening Standard*, 19.2.03.
37. *The Times*, 19.2.03.
38. Maddocks in the *Evening Standard*, 3.3.03.
39. Orchestra Committee to the ACE, 7 March 2003, with a copy to *Opera* magazine.
40. *Sunday Times*, 9.2.03.
41. Morrison in *The Times*, 7.2.03.
42. *The Times* and the *Guardian*, 17.3.03.
43. ACE press release, 21.3.03.
44. Ellis interview, 9.10.07, and email, 25.7.08.
45. *Independent*, 7.3.03.
46. Canning in *Opera*, June 2003, p. 686.
47. Interview with Loretta Tomasi, 7.11.07.
48. This quote and previous paragraph: Smith interview, 16.10.07, and email, 22.7.08.
49. Daniel interviews, 29.8.07 and 14.5.08.
50. Clark in the *Financial Times*, 29.1.04.
51. *The Australian*, 30.3.04.
52. *Financial Times*, 29.1.04.
53. Daniel interview, 15.5.08.
54. Higgins in the *Guardian*, 20.7.04, and telephone interview with Charlotte Higgins, 10.1.08.
55. Anthony Holden in the *Observer*, 7.3.05; Roderick Dunnett in the *Independent*, 9.3.05.
56. Andrew Clements in the *Guardian*, 5.3.04.
57. Clements in the *Guardian*, 10.5.04.
58. *Opera*, July 2004, p. 861.

59. ENO Press file.
60. Higgins in the *Guardian*, 20.7.04.
61. Ibid.
62. Ibid. and Morrison in *The Times*, 2.12.05.
63. Damian Whitworth in *The Times*, 30.9.04.
64. Erica Jeal in *Opera*, January 2005, p. 83.
65. ENO press release, 17.12.04.
66. *Independent*, 14.1.05, *The Times*, 14.1.05.
67. Clements in the *Guardian*, 24.1.05.
68. Rupert Christiansen in the *Daily Telegraph*, 8.2.05.
69. Canning in the *Sunday Times*, 13.2.05.
70. Lloyd quoted in the *Observer*, 3.4.05.
71. Harewood interview, 11.6.07.
72. Tom Service in the *Guardian*, 17.9.05.
73. Christiansen in the *Daily Telegraph*, 19.9.05.
74. Morrison in *The Times*, 7.11.05.
75. *Guardian*, 26.11.05.
76. Nigel Reynolds in the *Daily Telegraph*, Mark Honigsbaum in the *Guardian* and Louise Jury in the *Independent*, 30.11.05.
77. Ellis interview, 9.10.07, and email, 25.7.08.
78. Interview with John Nelson, 24.9.08.
79. Interview with John Berry, 21.11.07.
80. Ellis, interview, 9.10.07.
81. ACE minutes, 29.11.05. These and other ACE minutes sourced at www.artscouncil.org.uk and available on written request from ACE, 14 Great Peter Street, London SW1P 3NQ.
82. Smith, letter to *The Times*, and press release posted on ENO website, 5.12.05.
83. Frayling and Hewitt, letter to *The Times*, 8.12.05.
84. Smith interview, 16.10.07, and email, 22.7.08.
85. Smith email, 22.7.08.
86. The letter was obtained under the Freedom of Information Act by Higgins and reported by her on 10.3.06 in the *Guardian*.
87. Ellis interview, 9.10.07.
88. Higgins in the *Guardian*, 14.12.05.
89. John Allison in the *Sunday Telegraph*, 11.12.05.
90. Canning in the *Sunday Times*, 11.12.05.
91. Higgins in the *Guardian*, 8.12.05.
92. Andrew Stewart in *Classical Music*, 17.12.05.
93. Christiansen in the *Daily Telegraph*, 1.12.05.
94. Peter Jonas quoted in the *Evening Standard*, 2.12.05.
95. Pountney quoted in the *Independent*, 16.12 05.
96. Pountney, letter to *The Times*, 16.12.05.
97. ENO press release quoted in the *Guardian*, 22.12.05.
98. Unwin interview, 17.9.08.
99. John Tusa in the *Evening Standard*, 7.5.03, and Higgins in the *Guardian*, 22.12.05.
100. Interview with John Baker, 8.10.07.

101. Ellis interview, 8.10.07.
102. Interview with Nicholas Hytner, 14.6.07.
103. Smith email, 24.7.08.
104. ACE minutes, 29.11.05.
105. Tomasi interview, 7.11.07.
106. ACE minutes, 29.11.05.
107. ACE minutes, 31.1.06.
108. Morrison, interview with Loretta Tomasi, *The Times*, 17.3.06.
109. Clements in *Opera*, May 2005, pp. 592–4.
110. Milnes in *Opera*, January 2001, p. 93; Michael Kennedy in *Opera*, June 2006, pp. 716–17.
111. Canning in the *Sunday Times*, 23.4.06.
112. Geoff Brown in in *The Times*, 22.5.06.
113. Baker, email to author, 14.8.08.
114. Christiansen in the *Daily Telegraph*, 6.9.06.
115. Berry interview, 21.11.07.
116. Khan quoted in the *Daily Telegraph*, 4.9.06.
117. Anna Picard in the *Independent on Sunday*, 22.10.06.
118. Canning in the *Sunday Times*, 8.10.06.
119. Christiansen in the *Daily Telegraph*, 21.11.06.
120. Canning in the *Sunday Times*, 17.3.06.
121. Berry interview, 21.11.07.
122. Anna Picard in the *Independent on Sunday*, 11.2.07.
123. Hytner quoted in the *Guardian*, 24.2.07.
124. Higgins in the *Guardian* (Tomasi) and Louise Jury in the *Independent* (Morrissey), 24.2.07.
125. Interview with Gerry Morrissey, 17.9.08.
126. Tomasi, email to author, 25.7.08.
127. Interview with Dave Webster, 24.9.08.
128. ACE minutes, 29.3.07.
129. Interview with Henrietta Bredin, 7.11.07.
130. Webster interviews 24 and 25.9.08; Morrissey interview, 16.9.08.
131. BECTU report on ENO, 2008, by Tony Norton, communicated to the author by email on 30.9.08, and email from Norton to author, 2.10.08.
132. Hilary Finch in *The Times*, 7.4.07.
133. Allison in the *Sunday Telegraph*, 3.6.07.
134. Morrison in *The Times*, 28.6.07.
135. Allison in the *Sunday Telegraph*, 8.7.07.
136. Berry interview, 21.11.07.
137. Interview with Catherine Sutton, 24.10.07.
138. Canning in the *Sunday Times*, 28.10.07.
139. Milnes, email to author, 5.12.07.
140. Canning in the *Sunday Times*, 7.10.07.
141. Interview with Tim Albery, 12.12.07.
142. Ellis interview, 9.10.07, and email, 25.7.08.
143. Milnes, email to author, 9.12.07.
144. George Hall in the *Guardian*, 28.11.07.
145. Berry interview, 21.11.07.

146. Hall in the *Guardian*, 5.2.08.
147. Morrison in *The Times*, 18.2.08.
148. Canning in the *Sunday Times*, 23.3.08.
149. Morrison in *The Times*, 21.4.08.
150. David Dyer, email to author, 28.9.08.
151. Canning in the *Sunday Times*, 14.9.08.
152. Interview with Edward Gardner, 4.12.07.
153. According to an email from Gardner's assistant on 20.8.08.
154. Berry interview, 21.11.07.
155. Ellis interview, 9.10.07.
156. Canning, interview with Gardner, *Sunday Times*, 14.9.08.
157. Ellis interview, 18.9.08.
158. Morrison in *The Times*, 22.9.08; Clements in the *Guardian*, 22.9.08; Milnes to author, 22.9.08.
159. Harewood, email to author, 26.9.08.
160. Arts Council of Great Britain, *A Report on Opera and Ballet in the United Kingdom, 1966–69* (London: n.p., 1969), esp. pp. 7, 24, 48–53.
161. Unwin interview, 17.9.08.
162. Jonas to Rittner, 1.9.85, ENO Ad 172 Box 173.
163. Harewood, speech to company, 2.8.79, ENO Ad 21 Box 8.
164. Interview in *Classical Music*, 16.8.08.
165. Dyer interview, 12.12.07.
166. Dyer email, 28.9.08.
167. Interview with Charles Kraus, 24.9.08.

APPENDIX I: THE CRITICS

1. Nicholas Hytner in the *Observer*, 12.1.03.
2. *Oxford Dictionary of National Biography*.
3. *Sunday Times*, 7.11.1948.

# Sources

ARCHIVE SOURCES

The following archive sources were consulted and are abbreviated in the Notes as indicated:

*Britten-Pears Foundation, Aldeburgh, Suffolk*
Joan Cross papers

*ENO Archive (ENO), Lilian Baylis House, London*
Minutes of meetings:
   Sadler's Wells Foundation
   Sadler's Wells Trust Ltd
   The Directors of Sadler's Wells Trust Ltd (Trust)
   English National Opera Ltd Board of Directors after August 1974 (Board)
   Appeals Committee (Appeals)
   Artistic Policy Subcommittee (APSC)
   Casting Committee (CC)
   Covent Garden/Sadler's Wells Co-ordinating Committee (CG/SW)
   ENO Staff Association
   Finance Committee (FC)
   Finance and General Purpose Committee (FGPC)
   Finance Subcommittee of Sadler's Wells Trust Ltd (FSC)
   Marketing Committee (MC)
   Opera Committee (OC)
   Opera Subcommittee (OSC)
   Planning Committee (Planning)
   Production Committee (Production)
   Sadler's Wells Trust Ltd subcommittees for Artistic Policy, Finance, Public
     Affairs and US Tour
ENO Artists' Contracts (AC)
English National Opera North (ENON)

*Companies House, London*
ENO Annual Reports and Financial Statements, 1995–2007

*Islington Local History Centre, Finsbury Library, 245 John Street, London*
*EC1V 4NB (ILHC)*
Sadler's Wells minute books and other material from the ILHC Sadler's Wells
   archive

*King's College Cambridge*
E. J. Dent archive (EJD, FCSC)

*Metropolitan Opera archive, New York*
Edward Johnson papers

*The National Archives, Kew (TNA)*
Treasury papers (T)
Department of Education papers (Ed)

*Old Vic Bristol*
(Courtesy of the Royal Victoria Hall Foundation (RVHF), University of
Bristol Theatre Collection)
Old Vic Scrap Books (OVSB)
Old Vic Executive Committee Minutes (OVECM)
Old Vic Lilian Baylis (OVLB)
*Old Vic Magazine/Old Vic and Sadler's Wells Magazine* (OVM)
RVH minute books (OVRVH)

*Oxford, Bodleian Library*
Isaiah Berlin manuscripts (MS Berlin)

*Victoria and Albert Museum Theatre Collections*
Arts Council of Great Britain (ACGB)/Arts Council England (ACE) archive

*Private Collections*
Braithwaite papers, courtesy of Roderic Braithwaite
Lasdun papers, courtesy of Lady Lasdun. The Denys Lasdun archive has since
   been moved to and recatalogued by the British Architectural Library,
   Drawings & Archives Collections at the Victoria and Albert Museum in
   London, on long-term loan from Lady Lasdun; the new archive references
   are given in brackets in the endnotes
Unwin papers, courtesy of Sir Brian Unwin

NEWSPAPERS AND PERIODICALS

| | |
|---|---|
| *The Age* | *Financial Times* |
| *The Australian* | *Friends Magazine* |
| *Birmingham Post* | *Gramophone* |
| *Burnley Express and News* | *Guardian* |
| *The Bystander* | *Harper's and Queen* |
| *Cambridge Daily News* | *Illustrated London News* |
| *Classical Music* | *Irish Post* |
| *Coliseum* | *John O'London's Weekly* |
| *Contemporary Review* | *The Listener* |
| *Coventry Evening Telegraph* | *Manchester Guardian* |
| *Daily Telegraph* | *Music Lover* |
| *Eastern Evening News* | *Music and Musicians* |
| *EK's Weekly* | *Musical Opinion* |
| *Era* | *New Statesman* |
| *Evening Standard* | *New Statesman and Nation* |

News Chronicle
Observer
Opera
Opera News
Pravda
Radio Times
Saturday Review
Scottish Opera News
The Spectator
The Stage
Sunday Observer

Sunday Pictorial
Sunday Telegraph
Sunday Times
Time and Tide
The Times
Times Educational Supplement
Times Literary Supplement
The Tribune
What's On
Wigan Examiner
Yorkshire Post

BOOKS AND ARTICLES

Allen, Mary, *A House Divided*, London: Simon and Schuster, 1998
Arts Council of Great Britain, *A Report on Opera and Ballet in the United Kingdom, 1966–69*, London: n.p., 1969
Arundell, Dennis, *The Story of Sadler's Wells, 1683–1977*, London: David and Charles, 1978
Baker, Janet, *Full Circle: An Autobiographical Journal*, London: Julia MacRae, 1982
Butler, Christopher, *Postmodernism: A Very Short Introduction*, Oxford: Oxford University Press, 2002
Cairns, David, *Responses: Musical Essays and Reviews*, London: Secker and Warburg, 1973
Carey, Hugh, *Duet for Two Voices: An Informal Biography of Edward Dent Compiled from His Letters to Clive Carey*, Cambridge: Cambridge University Press, 1979
Coleman, Terry, *Olivier*, London: Bloomsbury, 2005
Cosgrave, Patrick, *The Strange Death of Socialist Britain: Postwar British Politics*, London: Constable, 1992
Courtney, Cathy (ed.), *Jocelyn Herbert, A Theatre Workbook*, London: Art Book International, 1993
Croall, Jonathan, *Gielgud: A Theatrical Life*, London: Methuen, 2000
Crozier, Eric (ed.), with contributions from Tyrone Guthrie, Edwin Evans, Joan Cross, Edward J. Dent and Ninette De Valois, *Opera in English*, Sadler's Wells Opera Books No. 1, London: John Lane/The Bodley Head for the Sadler's Wells Foundation, 1945
Curtis, William J., *Denys Lasdun: Architecture, City Landscape*, London: Phaidon, 1994
Delgado, Mario M. and Paul Heritage (eds.), *In Contact with the Gods? Directors Talk Theatre*, Manchester and New York: Manchester University Press, 1996
Dent, Edward, *A Theatre for Everybody: The Story of the Old Vic and Sadler's Wells*, London: T. V. Boardman and Co., 1945
Eyre, Richard, *The Eyre Review: Return to an Address of the Honourable the House of Commons Dated 30 June 1998 for the Report on the Future of Lyric Theatre in London*, London: The Stationery Office, 1998

—, *Changing Stages*, London: Bloomsbury, 2001

—, *National Service: Diary of a Decade at the National Theatre*, London: Bloomsbury, 2003

Fay, Stephen, *Power Play: The Life and Times of Peter Hall*, London: Hodder and Stoughton, 1995

Findlater, Richard, *Lilian Baylis, the Lady of the Old Vic*, London: Allen Lane, 1975

Forsyth, James, *Tyrone Guthrie*, London: Hamish Hamilton, 1976

Gilbert, Susie and Jay Shir, *A Tale of Four Houses, Opera at Covent Garden, Vienna, La Scala and the Met since 1945*, London: HarperCollins, 2003

Goodman, Arnold, *Tell Them I'm on My Way*, London: Chapmans, 1993

Guthrie, Tyrone, *A Life in the Theatre*, London: Readers' Union/Hamish Hamilton, 1961

Hamilton, Cicely and Lilian Baylis, *The Old Vic*, London: Jonathan Cape, 1926

Harewood, Lord, *The Tongs and the Bones: The Memoirs of Lord Harewood*, London: Weidenfeld and Nicolson, 1981

Hennessy, Peter, *Never Again: Britain 1945–51*, Jonathan Cape, London, 1992

Holden, Amanda (ed.), *The Penguin Concise Opera Guide*, London: Penguin, 2005

Hollis, Patricia, *Jennie Lee: A Life*, Oxford: Oxford University Press, 1997

John, Nicholas, Peter Jonas, Mark Elder and David Pountney, *Power House, The English National Opera Experience*, London: Lime Tree, 1992

Jones, Peter d'A., *The Christian Socialist Revival*, Princeton: Princeton University Press, 1968

Kennedy, Michael, *Britten*, London: J. M. Dent, 1983

Lucas, John, *Reggie: The Life of Reginald Goodall*, London: Julia MacRae, 1993

Marshall, Norman, *The Other Theatre*, London: John Lehman, 1947

Mayhew, Henry, *London Labour and the London Poor*, ed. and intro. Victor Neuberg, London: Penguin, 1985

Mitchell, Donald and Philip Reed (eds.), *Letters from a Life: Selected Letters and Diaries of Benjamin Britten*, vol. II, *1939–45*, London: Faber and Faber, 1991

Napier, John, *Ralph Koltai: Designer for the Stage*, London: Nick Hern, 2003

Norman, Edward, *Victorian Christian Socialists*, Cambridge: Cambridge University Press, 1987

Phelan, Nancy, *Charles Mackerras: A Musician's Musician*, London: Victor Gollancz, 1987

Porter, Andrew (trans. and intro.), *Ring of the Nibelung*, London: Faber and Faber, 1976

Roberts, Philip, *The Royal Court and the Modern Stage*, Cambridge: Cambridge University Press, 1999

Rowell, George, *The Old Vic Theatre: A History*, Cambridge: Cambridge University Press, 1993

Salter, Lionel, *Going to the Opera*, London: Puffin, 1955

Schafer, Elizabeth, *Lilian Baylis: A Biography*, Hatfield: University of Hertfordshire Press/The Society for Theatre Research, 2006

Searle, G. R., *A New England? Peace and War, 1886–1918*, Oxford: Oxford University Press, 2004

Skidelsky, Robert, *John Maynard Keynes, 1883–1946: Economist, Philosopher, Statesman*, London: Macmillan, 2003

Tausky, Vilem, *Vilem Tausky Tells His Story*, London: Stainer and Bell, 1979

Thorndike, Sybil and Russell Thorndike, *Lilian Baylis*, London: Chapman & Hall, 1938

Tucker, Norman, *Musician: An Autobiography before and after Two Decades at Sadler's Wells*, ed. J. Audrey Ellison, London: Lewis Reprints, 1978

Wardle, Irving, *The Theatres of George Devine*, London: Cape, 1978

White, Eric Walter, *A History of English Opera*, London: Faber and Faber, 1983

Williams, E. Harcourt, *Four Years at the Old Vic*, London: Putnam, 1935

Williams, E. Harcourt (ed.), *Vic-Wells: The Work of Lilian Baylis*, London: Shenval Press, 1938

# Index